Hong Kong Legal Principles

To my family, my parents and my brother

Hong Kong Legal Principles

Important Topics for Students and Professionals

Second Edition

Stephen D. Mau

Funding for this book has been sponsored by
the Hong Kong Institute of Surveyors

THE HONG KONG INSTITUTE OF
SURVEYORS
香港測量師學會

香港大學出版社
Hong Kong University Press

Hong Kong University Press
The University of Hong Kong
Pokfulam Road
Hong Kong
www.hkupress.org

First edition 2006
Second edition 2013

ISBN 978-988-8139-74-3 (*Paperback*)

British Library Cataloguing-in-Publication Data
A catalogue record for this book is available from the British Library.

10 9 8 7 6 5 4 3 2 1

Printed and bound by Caritas Printing Training Centre; Hong Kong, China

Contents

Foreword

The Hong Kong Institute of Surveyors strives to serve the surveying profession in Hong Kong since its establishment in 1984. In 2010, the Institute began sponsoring publication of reference books that are more relevant to local surveying practice and needs. The Institute is delighted that the first title funded by the scheme, *Hong Kong Legal Principles: Important Topics for Students and Professionals, Second Edition*, written by Stephen D. Mau, is not only written for the surveying industry and students, but is also a useful reference for non-legal professionals and the general public in Hong Kong.

The landscape of the real estate and construction industry has changed in recent years; these changes are reflected in the booming development of the construction industry, the adjustment of property pricing, and the growing concern over rights protection for employees and consumers. In response to these recent changes, this revised edition of *Hong Kong Legal Principles* includes a wide range of examples and cases to illustrate the legal principles to non-legal students and professionals. It is written in accessible language and the notes and references have also been expanded extensively.

This book comprises four chapters, namely, Contract, Tort, Employment and Property, which are relevant to both professionals and lay readers. It is also an excellent reference for undergraduate and postgraduate students who are studying courses related to the field.

Sr Serena Lau
President, 2011–12
The Hong Kong Institute of Surveyors

Foreword

I am delighted to be able to write the foreword for the second edition of this book. I have known Stephen Mau for a number of years as a friend and a few years ago as a colleague collaborating in a major construction arbitration held in London and Hong Kong.

I started off my career as a civil engineer with a firm of consulting engineers. As with many other professionals I became involved in issues which required knowledge of legal principles. Dealing with claims for payment or extensions of time needed an understanding of contract terms. Questions of ownership of plant and materials when a contactor becomes insolvent raised more complex legal issues which can only be understood from the perspective of wider legal principles. My interest in these principles led me to an interest in the law and later a career as a barrister. This book may lead others along that path. It provides an excellent introduction to the general legal principles of contract and tort, as well as dealing with aspects of employment and property law. Whilst the book is written from the perspective of Hong Kong law, the fundamental common law principles are generally applicable to all those jurisdictions where that common law system applies.

Each of the chapters sets out the issues in a manner which is easy to understand and which gradually builds up the knowledge of the reader on each subject. For instance, the chapter on contract law starts by defining what is meant by a contract and reviews the various ways in which contract may be formed. It then continues with an analysis of how contracts are created before looking at breach, termination and remedies in damages. Usefully it illustrates the principles by referring to particular Hong Kong decisions where the principles have been set out or applied.

The chapter concerned with the law of tort concentrates on the main torts governed by the common law but also refers to particular statutory torts in Hong Kong. By analysing, in detail, the law of negligence, Stephen has provided an excellent introduction to the approach of the courts in deciding when liability in tort will be imposed. This is a difficult area and the views of judges in different jurisdictions have not always coincided. In addition, the existence of a duty of care is fact sensitive.

The chapters on employment and property law provide a practical analysis of Hong Kong law in these areas. Once it has been established that a person is an employee many of the responsibilities and liabilities are contained in particular ordinances and subsidiary regulations. In relation to property law both personal and real property are dealt with, with a section which analyses issues relating to land. There is also reference to the new land registration system being developed in Hong Kong.

Stephen has brought out practical aspects to the principles by presenting a number of scenarios which, from the time I have spent in Hong Kong over the years, is appropriately based on restaurants. They pose a number of problems which can be resolved by applying the principles in the book. Fortunately, my experience of eating in restaurants in Hong Kong has not raised the problems encountered at the hotpot restaurant.

This book therefore provides a comprehensive and easily understandable introduction to the law. Stephen is to be commended for having produced such a popular book. I am certain that the popularity will continue. Knowledge of general principles is now an essential part of education and training. The book should therefore form part of the necessary reading for students and professionals qualifying in a wide range of subjects.

Sir Vivian Ramsey
Judge of The Technology and Construction Court
The Rolls Building, Royal Courts of Justice, London
August 2012

Foreword

Law has become inexorable in its progress. An inevitable feature of our existence is that, however we might wish it to be otherwise, the law is very much with us late and soon.

Consequently, it is hardly surprising that there are many students in Hong Kong who need to acquire a basic knowledge of the civil law to obtain a particular qualification or certificate. There are others who wish to study the law to know more about their rights and obligations in day-to-day commercial transactions.

The present situation poses a challenge. How does one communicate what the civil law is about to the many different classes of persons in search of guidance? Only a minority of the population (those wishing to be barristers, solicitors or law professors) will need to know the law in all its depth and subtlety. For most of us, what we ideally yearn for is a short one-volume summary of the basics.

But this last ideal is easier said than done. A book should not be so brief and simplified in its account of legal principle as to be misleading. In that case, too little knowledge could do more harm than no knowledge at all. On the other hand, overly pedantic detail would hinder a lay person from obtaining a sound grasp of key principle. One would not see the proverbial forest because there are just too many trees.

Stephen D. Mau's *Hong Kong Legal Principles: Important Topics for Students and Professionals* strikes the delicate balance between too much and too little, in a robust and practical manner. It does this by sub-dividing the essentials of civil law into 4 principal subjects: contract, tort, employment law and property.

The importance of contract and tort are self-evident. Contract tells us what constitutes a valid agreement; when an agreement may be refused enforcement; and what remedies may be granted when an agreement is breached. Tort, on the other hand, stipulates when a person may owe duties or be liable to another despite the absence of an agreement.

Employment law is, to a great extent, a specific illustration of how the laws of contract and tort operate, in conjunction with statute, to regulate one of the most important social relationships of our everyday life: the relationship of employer and employee.

Finally, property reflects a concern of most individuals in Hong Kong and elsewhere. It tells us how we acquire rights or incur obligations in respect of personal things and in respect of land. Property is an important example of how contract law interacts with equitable principle to create a body of rules which impact on our daily lives.

The first edition of Stephen D. Mau's book has proved to be much in demand. This second edition is likely to share the same fate.

Stephen D. Mau is thus to be commended for producing a book which is neither too much, nor too little. Instead, this book attempts to steer the reader, step by step, into a greater and deeper understanding of the law that governs our dealings with each another.

A. T. Reyes
Retired, Former High Court Judge in Charge of the Construction and Arbitration List
Hong Kong
1 September 2012

Preface to the Second Edition

In 2006, I perceived a need for a general text on Hong Kong law for students and professionals in different commercial fields. In many professions, legal knowledge is essential or required for someone wishing to obtain a qualification. Legal principles are also vital in the daily operations of various business and commercial entities. However, understanding the law is usually not a simple subject for someone who is not a legal practitioner. The idea of creating a concise and useful tool for students and non-legal professionals to become familiar with the law resulted in the publication of the first edition of this work. After several years, that need seems to remain while our law, both the common law and the statutory law, continues to evolve with Hong Kong's dynamic society. I believe that now is the time to update this book so as to ensure that this tool remains as a helpful guide to the changing legal environment. Like the first edition, this second edition has the same goals and aspirations. These goals and aspirations include presenting a publication which provides coverage of the most commonly encountered legal areas to be used as resource which is sufficiently detailed for general, "everyday" use without being too general or so detailed that each legal topic requires several volumes to cover. It is hoped that this purpose has been achieved.

The areas covered in this book include contract, tort, employment and property. While the law of contract governs the creation and operation of the legally binding agreements and it is fundamental in commercial transactions, the law of tort relates to the liabilities arising without an agreement, for instance, an action in negligence. On the other hand, employment law set out the principles that regulate the relationship between employers and employees. Employment law also demonstrates the often overlapping areas of law in that employment frequently involves matters of contract law and tort law. The last topic, property law, concerns the rights and duties relating to land and personal items and brings this publication full circle in the sense that much of property conveyancing involves agreements and contract principles.

Although expanded and with some re-organization within each chapter, the overall organization of the second edition remains the same as the original publication. The more common law oriented subjects are presented first, transitioning to the more statutory law oriented topics. A summary of the principal legal concepts are presented in the main text with a more detailed discourse or explanation set out in the footnotes with citations to sources where additional and more comprehensive information may be found.

The law in Hong Kong has changed since the first edition. The second edition aims to include and to explain these changes through referral to court cases interpreting and applying the law and to the actual legislation. I have endeavored to state the law as of December 2010.

Acknowledgements

It is with gratitude that the author acknowledges the funding provided by the Hong Kong Institute of Surveyors which made possible the research and writing of this second edition.

The author also wishes to acknowledge with thanks the contributions made to the second edition of this title by the following individuals:

Mr. John Tsz-ho CHAN

Mr. Sebastian Yat-fung KO, solicitor (Hong Kong); attorney-at-law (New York)

Ms. Krystal Yeuk-ying LEE

Mr. Chris Wing-hong WONG

Ms. Ashlee Peng YU

Mr. Jack S. YU

Table of Cases

Table of Legislation

Introduction

After three reprints of the first edition, this second edition is updated, rewritten and reorganized where necessary to be more user friendly. For example, the chapter on contract has been thoroughly revised, particularly the sections on misrepresentation and mistake. The tort and employment chapters have been updated and expanded to reflect changes in the law, both statutory and case law. The property and conveyancing chapters in the first edition have now been consolidated and the redundancy removed. Furthermore, the new property chapter is also a product of changes in the statutory law and discusses new cases decided by the courts. Each one of these chapters is discussed in more detail below.

This second edition continues to seek to balance the theoretical principles and the practical application of legal topics most commonly encountered in Hong Kong in order to provide an understanding to those unfamiliar with the territory's laws. As with the previous edition, the main text in this edition presents an introductory overview containing the essential materials, while the footnotes provide further elaborations for those who seek additional detail and information. The aim of this organization is to introduce and explain the general principles of Hong Kong law to those with an interest or a need to be familiar with the territory's legal principles.

This book leads with the topic of contract law as this legal field appears to be the one that affects the most people most frequently — even when taking public transportation, ordering from a restaurant, or shopping in a mall. One ought to know the rights and/or obligations that might arise in an agreement, for example between a customer and a shop in relation to a purchase of goods and/or services. Equally important, one ought to know which agreements are enforceable in court as not all agreements are contracts. Many legal principles concerning the topic of contract arise from the decision on cases decided by the court; this is known as the "common law" and "equity". Other legal principles are derived from legislation passed into law; this is known as "statutory law".

The next chapter reviews tort. Like the topic of contract, the law of tort affects or could potentially affect a large number of people. Also like the law of contract, tort principles are premised upon the common law as well as statutory law. This topic is the second chapter in this book for several reasons. By grouping these two topics at the beginning of the book, one is able to contrast clearly the difference between these legal fields of study and yet be able to emphasize the manner in which they overlap. Tort, especially negligence, is a fast-growing field in other jurisdictions. Tort law might be involved in circumstances as diverse as concrete falling from a building, loss arising from an accident or an intentional act, noisy neighbours, or a public statement. Hong Kong, in its aspiration to become a world-class legal jurisdiction, should be prepared to remedy potential instances of tortious behaviour as the city lags behind in this area.

Employment is presented as the third chapter. This legal topic clearly demonstrates the overlapping nature of law. Employment frequently coincides with the legal fields of contract and tort. Employment matters often involve contractual relationships between employers and employees, or between employers and independent contractors. Additionally, employment might result in tortious liabilities arising within or outside of the workplace. For example, consider the situation where one worker drives another worker and, during this journey, both are injured in a traffic accident involving a third party. In terms of the basis for employment law in Hong Kong, the overlap between the common law and statutory law can also be observed. Further, the shift towards a field of law premised more upon statutory law rather than common law can be discerned in the employment chapter.

The final chapter introduces property. In this chapter, a summary overview of the various types of property interests is presented. This includes the various classifications or types of property and property rights. Included in this chapter is a section devoted to conveyancing oriented towards individuals engaged in real estate transactions, such as agents, buyers, sellers, landlords and tenants. The application of both the common law and statutory law can be seen here, for example, in the creation and termination of leases. The topic of intellectual property, such as copyright, is not included in this chapter as this topic is considered by many to be a separate and specialized field of law for study.

To assist the reader in understanding some of the legal principles and their applications, this book contains a self-help guide in the form of a scenario at the conclusion of this Introduction. The scenario was devised by the author and is intended to be a mechanism for the readers of this work to measure their understanding and mastery of the legal subjects presented herein. Hopefully, through the use of the scenario, the learning or understanding of "the law" can be made more interesting and practical, and less boring and intimidating. This scenario consists of a factual situation along with a series of questions designed to require critical thinking utilizing legal concepts. Thus, in order to analyse the scenario successfully, one must be able to understand the application of these legal concepts.

This scenario is intended to assist and encourage readers in undertaking a self-test to gauge their comprehension and understanding of the materials presented. While the scenario can be satisfactorily utilized by a reader individually, the full potential of the scenario comes into being in a group discussion where differing analyzes and reasoning can engender debate over the interpretation and application of a legal principle. With this process should also come the appreciation of the analysis and reasoning that is required in undertaking to answer a legal question, for law is not memorizing legal terms and reaching "black and white" conclusions. Law is more than the simple recalling and mechanical application of rules. One needs to appreciate the interplay of the legal principles, and the exceptions thereto, when applied to a particular set of factual circumstances. As is frequently the situation, the law or the rules are clear; their interpretation and application to a particular legal action is not. The scenario is intended to emphasize this proposition.

SCENARIO

The following is a set of facts which will be used to amplify some of the legal principles presented in this edition. A reader may, when reading this book, consider the application of certain legal principles to these facts. For example, this scenario may be used to analyse the formation or the creation of a contract or to review the application of the principles pertaining to negligence.

1. Albert sees his solicitor and friend Beth walking down the street after she had a "three Martini" lunch.* During their conversation, he states that they should have a meal together one day. Beth agrees, provided that she is in Hong Kong and that she has the time.
    a. Is there a contract between Albert and Beth?

---

* This is a lunch where more alcoholic beverages than food are consumed.

b. What factors argue for finding a contract?
c. What factors militate against finding a contract?
d. If there were a contract, what type or types of contract would this be?
e. If there were a contract, can either Albert or Beth avoid this agreement? If so, on what basis or bases?

2. Albert and Beth go to a Western-style restaurant where a hostess takes them to their table. Filled water goblets are immediately set before the two as they sit down at their table. Albert and Beth do not drink the water. Albert and Beth decide that the menu offered is not to their liking. They leave the restaurant.
   a. Is there a contract between Albert and Beth, and the restaurant?
   b. What acts constitute the offer and acceptance?
   c. When was the offer made and by whom?
   d. When was the acceptance made and by whom?
   e. If there were a contract, can Albert and Beth terminate the contract because they do not like the food on offer by the restaurant?

3. Albert and Beth then go to a Shanghainese restaurant where a hostess directs them to their table. The chilli sauce and peanuts are brought to the table after they sit down. They order a pot of jasmine tea. Before the tea arrives, Albert and Beth decide that the menu offerings are not to their liking. They leave the restaurant.
   a. Is there a contract between Albert and Beth, and the restaurant?
   b. What act constitutes the offer? When was the offer made and by whom?
   c. What act constitutes the acceptance? When was the acceptance made and by whom?
   d. If there were a contract, can Albert and Beth terminate the agreement because they do not like the food on offer by the restaurant?

4. Albert and Beth finally decide upon a hotpot restaurant famed for certain dishes. They sit and before they order, they notice a sign which states: "This establishment is not liable for any loss or injury whatsoever." They order the three dishes for which the restaurant is most renowned in addition to the hotpot. Several minutes later, Albert and Beth, realizing they ordered too much, try to cancel one of the three dishes. Cherry, the server, says that the chef has already started cooking the dish. Moments later, Cherry returns to inform these two diners that another of the three ordered dishes is unavailable. The food eventually

arrives. Beth is shocked to discover a partially eaten cockroach in the food and completely loses her appetite as a result.

a. Is there a contract between Albert and Beth, and the restaurant?
b. What act constitutes the offer? When was the offer made and by whom?
c. What act constitutes the acceptance? When was the acceptance made and by whom?
d. What are the terms of the contract?
e. Does the restaurant have a claim against Albert and Beth for cancelling a dish? If so, on what basis? Further, if there were to be a valid claim, what would be the remedy or damages to be paid?
f. Do Albert and Beth have any claims against the restaurant for advertising an unavailable dish on the menu? If so, what would be the basis for the claim? Further, if Albert and Beth have a valid claim, what would be the remedy or damages? Does the restaurant have any defences against such a claim?
g. Assuming a contract exists, does the cockroach entitle Albert and Beth to terminate the contract with the restaurant? Termination of the contract would be based on which legal principle? What type of damages might be recoverable by Albert and Beth? Why?
h. Does Beth have a claim against the restaurant for the cockroach in her food? If so, what would be the basis or bases or her claim? Further, if there were to be a claim or claims by Beth, what would be her remedies and/or damages? Does the restaurant have any defences against such a claim?
i. Would the analysis of the questions for paragraphs 2, 3 and 4 of this scenario differ if the eating establishment were:
   - a cafeteria-style or canteen-style of service; or
   - a fast-food-style of service, such as McDonald's?

5. Cherry, the server, brings the hotpot to the table. The lighter which Cherry uses to light the flame is provided by the restaurant but is to be kept and maintained by the server according to the restaurant's rules. As Cherry attempts to light the flame for the hotpot, the lighter explodes. Both Albert's and Beth's faces and hair are singed by the explosion. Cathy's clothes catches fire. Running away, Cherry knocks over Dan, delivering supplies to the restaurant, who twists his knee as he falls onto Ellen, a diner. Ellen stabs her tongue when Dan falls on her. Cherry, still on fire and still running, sets fire to the clean table cloths stacked by the kitchen door. The restaurant's sprinkler system fails to

activate and extinguish the fires as the system has not been maintained by the building's management company.

a. Do Albert and Beth have any claims against Cherry? Why or why not?
b. Do Albert and Beth have any claims against the restaurant? What would be the basis or bases of such claims?
c. Do Albert and Beth have any claims against the manufacturer of the lighter?
d. Do Albert and Beth have any claims against the building's management company or the building's owner? What would be the basis or bases for such claims?
e. Does Cherry have any claims against the restaurant? If so, would the claims be premised upon contract law, tort law or employment law? What would be the justification for such claims?
f. Does Cherry have any claims against the manufacturer of the lighter?
g. Does Dan have any claims against any of the parties? If so, what would be the legal principles involved in his claims?
h. Does Ellen have any claims against any of the parties? If so, what would be the legal principles involved in her claims?
i. Would any of the parties' potential claims be different or be affected if the restaurant is actually a small *cha chaan tang* where the servers wear no uniform and where the servers' only instructions from the owner/manager are to serve the patrons and to maintain the lighter? Cherry receives, and the *cha chaan tang* provides, no training.
j. Would any of the parties' potential claims be affected if Cherry were both the 17 year-old daughter of the *cha chaan tang* owner and only working in the *cha chaan tang* to help during the busy times?
k. Are any other claims possible against the building's management company or the building's owner?
l. Do any of the parties have any defences to the claims being made against them?

6. Frankie, a beggar, is scavenging for food scraps at the back of the restaurant. He observes the whole event through the restaurant's window. Since he is prone to anxiety and excitability, he suffers a heart attack. Gwen, an off-duty Fire Services ambulance attendant, administers CPR

to Frankie. In the process of attempting to save his life, Gwen breaks several of Frankie's ribs, one of which punctures his lung.

a. Does Frankie have any claims against the restaurant? Why or why not?
b. Does the restaurant have any claims against Frankie for trespassing on its property or taking its food? Why or why not?
c. Does Frankie have any claims against the building's management company or the building's owner? Why or why not?
d. Does Frankie have any claims against Cherry? Why or why not?
e. Does Frankie have any claims against Gwen? Why or why not?
f. Does Frankie have any claims against the Hong Kong government? Why or why not?
g. Are there any defences available to the potential defendants?

7. Henry is the owner of the restaurant. Before this incident occurred, he was negotiating the sale of the restaurant business to Irene while keeping the commercial space. As a result of this incident, Irene wishes to withdraw from this transaction, especially as no contract has yet been signed, although a "Preliminary Purchase and Sale Agreement" has been signed. Jay, the building's owner, wishes to increase Henry's rent should Irene take over the restaurant business. Jay wishes to increase the rent to reflect better the lost income from the interior space occupied by the restaurant's exhaust and ventilation ducts which rise from the interior of the restaurant through the first and second floors of the building. The exterior space of the building is already occupied by advertising, so the ducts must be situated in the interior of the building. Additionally, building regulations require the ducts to be at such height in order to prevent nuisance to pedestrians.

a. What types of property can be included in the sale of the restaurant by Henry to Irene?
b. What type of lease would be involved should the sale of the restaurant be successful? What would be the tenancy relationships between Henry, Irene and Jay?
c. Does the situation with the exhaust and ventilation ducts involve a licence or an easement?
d. If Irene decides to purchase the commercial space in addition to the restaurant business, describe the type of financing options available to her and how these options affect her title.

Chapter One
Contract

This chapter is concerned with the law that governs an agreement between parties. In particular, this chapter intends to review the common law principles relating to contracts. Consequently, less emphasis is placed on contracts regulated by legislation as to form or as to content. Likewise, little emphasis is placed on contracts which are highly specialized, such as an agreement which involves matters concerning employment which are generally categorized as employment law.

The Contract chapter is organized into three general sections. The first section provides the definition of the term "contract" in general and reviews the different types of contract. The next section presents an analysis concerning the creation of a contract and its legal application to the parties. The third and final section assesses the manners in which a contract may be terminated.

I. DEFINITION

A contract is a legally binding agreement between the parties to that agreement. The term "contract" has been described as referring to one or more of the following situations:

- a series of promises or acts that constitute a legally binding agreement, *e.g.*, a promise or a set of promises which the law will enforce;
- the legal relationship that results from a series of promises or acts; or,
- the document which embodies that series of promises or acts or the performance of that series of promises or acts.[1]

---

1. 7(2) Halsbury's Laws of Hong Kong para. 115.002 (2007) (citations omitted) [hereinafter 7(2) Halsbury's].

Contract law is concerned with the validity and enforceability of that agreement.[2] The law of contract consists of case law which serves as precedent and which applies generally to all types of contracts. Unlike tort law, one's liability under contract law depends on promises the parties have made to each other. Through their agreement, the parties make legally binding arrangements which will govern their relationship. Enforcement of a contract is effected through the law and the courts.

The basis of contract law can also be seen as reliance: to rely on receiving some future benefits as part of an agreed exchange and to reduce uncertainties associated with the exchange. One purpose of contract law is to provide a structure within which parties can organize their relationships, particularly commercial ones, with a high degree of certainty.[3] Thus, a contract can be seen as an allocation of risk between the parties, that is, an agreement determining which party will bear the risk of any loss in the transaction.[4] For example, the parties may agree that a seller in Hong Kong will bear the risk of loss of a shipment of goods until it is delivered to the buyer's warehouse in the United States.

II. TYPES

As mentioned above, a contract is a legally binding agreement. Some of the reasons for creating a contract have been discussed. In this section, some of the various types of legally binding agreements are presented, although some of these agreements may fall into more than one category.[5]

---

2. For an exhaustive discussion of the dichotomy of these two definitions of the term "contract", *see*, *e.g.*, 1 CHITTY ON CONTRACTS para. 1–001 (H.G. BEALE, *et al.* eds., 30th ed. 2008) [hereinafter CHITTY].
   The Hong Kong government's Bilingual Laws Information System's *The English-Chinese Glossary of Legal Terms* [hereinafter *BLIS Glossary*] translates "legal contracts" as 合法合同 and "legally binding" as 具法律約束力. See the *BLIS Glossary* website at: *http://www.legislation.gov.hk/eng/glossary/homeglos.htm* (last visited 1 Feb. 2011).
3. CAROLE CHUI & DEREK ROEBUCK, HONG KONG CONTRACTS para. 1.3 (2nd ed. 1991) [herein after CHUI & ROEBUCK].
   See also STEPHEN HALL, LAW OF CONTRACT IN HONG KONG: CASES AND COMMENTARY 2–7 (revised 2nd ed. 2009) [hereinafter HALL].
4. CHUI & ROEBUCK, *supra* note 3, at paras. 1.3; 2.1.
5. *See* 7(2) HALSBURY'S, *supra* note 1, at paras. 115.011–115.012. The Property chapter of this work will discuss contracts which must be in writing or which must be evidenced by writing.

A. Generally

A legally binding agreement may have many different forms and may have several classifications.[6] Thus, a contract may be a completely oral agreement; a completely written agreement; or, a partly oral and partly written agreement. As their classifications imply, oral contracts are legally binding verbal agreements; written contracts are legally binding agreements in writing.

Another classification places agreements which are enforceable legally into three different categories: contracts of record; simple contracts; and, contracts made by deed.[7] "Contracts of record" are not contracts in the sense in which that term is usually used but are judgments and recognizances[8] enrolled in the record of a court and in law imply an obligation arising from the entry on the record and not from any agreement between the parties.[9]

"Simple contracts" are contracts without a seal and thus require consideration. Simple contracts are all contracts other than contracts of record or contracts under seal.

> Simple contracts may be express or implied, or partly express and partly implied. Contracts are express to the extent that their terms are set out distinctly either by word of mouth or in writing. They are implied to the extent, if any, to which their terms are a necessary inference from the words or conduct of the parties.[10]

Another form of contract is known as a "contract under seal", sometimes referred to as a "contract made by deed", a "deed", or a "specialty contract".[11]

---

6. CHITTY, *supra* note 2, at para. 1–067 notes that contracts:

> may be classified in a variety of ways: according to their subject-matter; according to their parties; according to their form (whether contained in deeds or in writing, whether express or implied) or according to their effect (whether bilateral or unilateral, whether valid, void, voidable or unenforceable). (citations omitted)

This work is not intended to examine these categories in such depth; only the more common types or categories of contract will be introduced. For a detailed discussion of the myriad of contract types, *see, e.g., id.* at paras. 1–068 to 1–084.

7. 7(2) HALSBURY'S, *supra* note 1, at para. 115.010.
The *BLIS Glossary*, *supra* note 2, translates "deed" as 契據.
8. The *BLIS Glossary*, *supra* note 2, translates "recognizance" as 擔保.
9. 7(2) HALSBURY'S, *supra* note 1, at para. 115.010.
10. *Id.* at para. 115.013 (citations omitted).
11. *See* the discussion of this topic in sections II.C and III.C and the accompanying footnotes. *See also* 7(2) HALSBURY'S, *supra* note 1, at para. 115.011.

A specialty contract must be signed, sealed, and delivered.[12] A specialty contract requires no consideration and has the seal of the signer attached. A contract under seal must be in writing and is conclusive between the parties when signed, sealed and delivered. Delivery is made either by actually presenting the document to the other party or by stating an intention that the deed be operative even though the deed is retained in the possession of the party that signed the deed.[13] In Hong Kong, contracts under seal are found mainly in real property transactions, government construction contracts and certain insurance contracts. One purpose of a deed is set out as follows:

> The basis of the common law of contract is bargain. A party who wants to enforce a contract must show that he or she has given consideration. If A says to B "On your twenty-first birthday, I will give you $100,000 to set you up in life" and B says "Thank you. ...", there is certainly an agreement between them. But there is no contract ... because B has not given anything in return for A's promise. Each party to a contract must

---

The *BLIS Glossary*, *supra* note 2, translates "specialty" as 蓋印文據.
"A deed is a document which takes its effect from its formal nature." CHUI & ROEBUCK, *supra* note 3, at para. 11.1.

> At common law, contracts under seal, or specialties, were an important example of deeds and at common law a deed was an instrument which was not merely in writing, but which was sealed by the party bound thereby, and delivered by him to or for the benefit of the person to whom the liability was incurred. In no other way than by the use of this form could validity be given ... At common law, all deeds were documents under seal, but not all documents under seal were and are deeds. A deed must either:
>
> (a) effect the transference of an interest, right or property;
> (b) create an obligation binding on some person or persons;
> (c) confirm some act whereby an interest, right or property has already passed.

CHITTY, *supra* note 2, at para. 1–085.

12. BLACK'S LAW DICTIONARY 1350 (7th ed. 1999) [hereinafter BLACK'S LAW DICTIONARY] defines "seal" to be an "impression or sign that has legal consequence when applied to an instrument".
13. One authority expounds upon this requirement of delivery:

> "Where a contract is to be by deed, there must be a delivery to perfect it." "Delivered", however, in this connection does not mean "handed over" to the other party. It means delivered in the old legal sense, namely, an act done so as to evince an intention to be bound. Any act of the party which shows that he intended to deliver the deed as an instrument binding on him is enough. He must make it his deed and recognise it as presently binding on him. Delivery is effective even though the grantor retains the deed in his own possession. There need be no actual transfer of possession to the other party ...

CHITTY, *supra* note 2, at para. 1–093 (citations omitted).
See also BETTY M. HO, HONG KONG CONTRACT LAW 77–79 (2nd ed. 1994) (citation omitted) [hereinafter HO].

> give something (which may be a promise) to the other in exchange for what he or she gets. It is not a contract if one party takes rights without incurring corresponding duties. But consideration is not necessary if the contract is by deed.
>
> ...
>
> Moreover, it is possible to make a gift ... which will be binding without consideration. It is the promise which is not binding without consideration, not the transfer of property. ... if the subject matter is of such a nature that delivery is not possible, such as a promise, then a deed must be used.[14]

Contracts under seal will be discussed further in section II.C.

Another form of contract is referred to as a "unilateral contract". This is a contract where one party makes a promise or several promises in return for an act, as opposed to a promise, of another party. For example, where a person makes an offer of a reward for the return of a lost item, the person making the offer (known as the "offeror") will be the only one bound by the offer. No one is obligated to conduct a search for the lost item. However, if upon learning of the offer, someone recovers and returns the lost item, that individual is entitled to the reward.[15] In this type of contract, the offeror makes a promise while the person receiving the offer (known as the "offeree") is expected to perform an act rather than to make one promise in return. Therefore, this is a:

> contract under which only one party undertakes an obligation. ... It is to be noted, though, that the unilateral nature of the contract does not ... mean that there is only one party, nor that there is no need for an acceptance or the provision of consideration by the other party. An example of a unilateral contract may be found in the case of an offer for a reward for the return of lost property: here, a contract is formed (at the latest) on the return of the property, this constituting the offeree's acceptance of the offer and the furnishing of consideration for the creation of the contract. Bilateral contracts comprise the exchange of a promise for a promise, *e.g.* if you promise to pay me £1,000, I promise to sell you my car.[16]

14. CHUI & ROEBUCK, *supra* note 3, at para. 2.2.
15. 7(2) HALSBURY'S, *supra* note 1, at para. 115.048 explains that the mode of acceptance in a unilateral contract is the performance of his side of the contract by the offeree. The real distinction between bilateral and unilateral contracts lies not in the nature of the act of acceptance, but in whether there is a contract before performance of that act. In a bilateral contract there will be an executory promise by the offeree; in a unilateral contract the promise will be executed the moment it is made.
16. CHITTY, *supra* note 2, at para. 1–079.

One commonly cited example of a unilateral contract is the case of *Carlill v Carbolic Smoke Ball Co*, which is discussed in section III.B.ii.c.

Another type of legally binding agreement is referred to as a "collateral contract".[17] This type of contract may arise in the course of negotiation of a main contract. A collateral contract is a subsidiary agreement which stands alongside the main contract, in which a party is promised something as an inducement to enter into the main contract.[18] Thus, a collateral contract arises out of, or from, another legally binding agreement, the main contract, and is related to that contract.[19]

A collateral contract takes the form of a unilateral contract, under which one party offers that if the second party enters into the main contract, the first party will promise something else to the second party. The consideration for the promise is the making of the main contract.[20] In *City & Westminster Properties v Mudd* [1958] 2 All ER 733, the tenant had been sleeping in the shop which he rented. During lease renewal negotiations, the landlord attempted to include a clause stating that the premises should not be used for lodging, dwelling or sleeping. The tenant objected, but was verbally informed that if he signed the lease, he could continue living in the basement. The landlord then attempted to rely on the contract clause to terminate the lease, claiming that the tenant breached the lease agreement by sleeping in the premises.[21] The court held that the tenant established that the oral promise made to him was part of a collateral contract. Because of the oral promise and in reliance upon it, the tenant had signed the main contract with the landlord.

---

17. "The word collateral in this context simply indicates a contract which exists alongside a main contract. For instance, a contract of guarantee cannot exist without something to guarantee." CHUI & ROEBUCK, *supra* note 3, at para. 4.8.
See also MICHAEL J. FISHER & DESMOND G. GREENWOOD, CONTRACT LAW IN HONG KONG 166–167 (2nd ed. 2011) [hereinafter FISHER & GREENWOOD].
18. CHUI & ROEBUCK, *supra* note 3, at para. 9.2.6.
19. *See* 7(2) HALSBURY'S, *supra* note 1, at para. 115.133 which explains a collateral contract thus:

> A contract between A and B may be accompanied by a collateral contract between B and C, whereby C makes a promise to B in return for B entering into the contract with A or doing some other act for the benefit of C. Before B can succeed in an action against C for breach of C's promise, B must prove the following: (1) that C made a promise to B *animo contrahendi* [with the intent of a contracting party]; (2) in reliance on that promise, B entered into the contract with A or did the other requested act. (citations omitted)

20. RICHARD STONE, THE MODERN LAW OF CONTRACT 206–207 (8th ed. 2009) [hereinafter STONE].
21. *Id.* at 251.

B. Third Party Contracts and Privity

As discussed below in the section on Consideration, the benefit or the obligation of a contract may be directed to a third party, that is, someone not a party to the contract. A situation such as this might raise enforcement difficulties due to the principle of privity of contract. "Privity" refers to being a party to a contract.

> The common law doctrine of privity of contract means that a contract cannot (as a general rule) confer rights or impose obligations arising under it on any person except the parties to it.[22]

Thus, the general rule is that no one can sue or be sued on a contract to which that person is not a party. In other words, the provisions of a contract are only applicable to the parties to that contract.

As privity of contract dictates that only a party to a contract can sue or be sued on that contract, this doctrine will not allow a third party, *i.e.*, in other words, a party not involved in the legally binding contractual relationship, to sue either party to the contract. A commonly used example to demonstrate this doctrine assumes that Alan owes a debt to Bob. Alan enters into a valid contract with Calvin to pay Bob. Calvin fails to pay Bob. Under the principle of privity of contract, Bob cannot sue Calvin. Rather, Bob would need to sue Alan who would then sue Calvin.[23]

Much has been written about the purpose and application of this principle along with the recourse available to parties such as Bob. Conceptually, the privity doctrine has engendered some debate amongst legal writers.[24] This theoretical debate has carried over to the courts which have created ways to circumvent this doctrine, such as the notion of an agent, a trust, and, the application of certain land covenants. Legislation has also been

---

22. CHITTY, *supra* note 2, at para. 18–003. *Id.* at para. 18–021 states further:

> The common law doctrine of privity means … that a person cannot acquire rights, or be subjected to liabilities, *arising under* a contract to which he is not a party. For example, it means that, if A promises B to pay a sum of money to C, then C cannot sue A for that sum. Similarly, if a contract between A and B contains a term purporting to exempt C from tortious liability to A, the doctrine of privity may prevent C from relying on that term in an action in tort brought against him by A. [emphasis in original]

23. FISHER & GREENWOOD, *supra* note 17, at 432–433, 446.
For a full discussion of this topic, *see, e.g.*, *id.* at Chapter 16 ("Privity of Contract"); CHITTY, *supra* note 2, at Chapter 18 ("Third Parties").

24. FISHER & GREENWOOD, *supra* note 17, at 431–433.

enacted in order to limit the application of the privity doctrine. For example, in the United Kingdom there is the *Contracts (Rights of Third Parties) Act* 1999. In Hong Kong there is the *Married Persons Status Ordinance* (Cap 182). Additionally, in Hong Kong, the Law Reform Commission has issued a Consultation Paper[25] in 2004 and a Report on Privity of Contract[26] in 2005 suggesting that Hong Kong consider similar legislation to that found in the UK although to date no action has been taken by the legislature.

C. Formalities/Contracts Required to be in Writing

The most common forms or types of contracts have been discussed above. However, there are other types which, although perhaps not as common as the types of legally binding agreements above, should be mentioned. For these contracts, certain formalities need to be followed as to form or content, a requirement to be in writing or in the execution.

One type of contract requiring particular formalities has been introduced earlier: a contract under seal, also known as a contract made by deed, deed or specialty contract.[27] This type of legally binding agreement takes effect through its solemn form rather than through general contract principles. Therefore, a specialty contract must be signed, sealed, and delivered.[28] One reason for requiring this form is that a contract made by deed requires no consideration and has the seal of the signer attached. A contract under seal must be in writing and is conclusive between the parties when signed, sealed and delivered. Delivery is made either by actually handing the document to the other party or by stating an intention that the deed be operative even though the deed is kept in the possession of the party signing this document.

---

25. The Consultation Paper may be found at the following two web sites: *http://www.hkreform.gov.hk* (last visited 1 Feb. 2011) or *http://www.hklii.hk/eng/hk/other/hklrc/cp/2004/2.html* (last visited 1 Feb. 2011). *See* Fisher & Greenwood, *supra* note 17, at 444–449 for a review of the Consultation Paper.
26. The Report may be found at the following two web sites: *http://www.hkreform.gov.hk* (last visited 1 Feb. 2011) or *http://www.hklii.hk/eng/hk/other/hklrc/reports/2005/3.html* (last visited 1 Feb. 2011).
27. *See* the discussion of this topic on "Consideration" in section III.C and the accompanying footnotes. *See also* 7(2) Halsbury's, *supra* note 1, at para. 115.011.
28. "Delivered" is defined in Chitty, *supra* note 2, at para. 1–093. *See supra* note 13; Hall, *supra* note 3, at 21. For example, the *Conveyancing and Property Ordinance* (Cap 219) sections 19 and 20, respectively, provide the legal requirements for executing a deed by an individual or by a corporation.

Earlier, a deed was explained as being a legally enforceable agreement without consideration. A contract under seal may also be used where there is consideration.

> This has traditionally been done in relation to complex contracts in the engineering and construction industries. This is probably because, by virtue [of the law], the period within which an action for breach of an obligation contained in a deed is 12 years, whereas for a "simple" contract it is only six years. The longer period is clearly an advantage in a contract where problems may not become apparent for a number of years.[29]

Another category pertains to contracts which must observe some kind of formality (usually that the agreement be written or be written in a particular way) in order to be valid. Thus, for the purposes of this section, these are referred to as "contracts required to be in writing". These are contracts which are required by law either to be in writing or to be evidenced in writing, *i.e.*, something in writing which proves the existence of the agreement. One of the most common contracts required to be in writing is a legally binding agreement that affects land, *e.g.*, purchase and sale agreements, certain leases, easements and mortgages.[30]

Examples of contracts which require both a particular formality and a particular content can be found in situations involving a power of attorney (a document which gives one person the right to act on another individual's behalf) or the employment of an apprentice. The *Powers of Attorney Ordinance* (Cap 31) requires that, under certain circumstances, a written document, such as the form set out in the Schedule, be signed and sealed in the presence of two attesting witnesses.[31] The *Apprenticeship Ordinance* (Cap 47) requires a contract of apprenticeship to be in writing and in a particular form.[32]

Other Hong Kong ordinances which require a legally binding agreement to be in writing or evidenced in writing include the following examples:

- *Arbitration Ordinance* (Cap 609);
- *Bills of Exchange Ordinance* (Cap 19);
- *Companies Ordinance* (Cap 32);
- *Contracts for Employment Outside Hong Kong Ordinance* (Cap 78);

29. Stone, *supra* note 20, at 109. This subject is discussed in terms of the *Limitation Ordinance* (Cap 347) in section VIII.D.
30. *Conveyancing and Property Ordinance*, *supra* note 28, at section 4(2).
31. *Powers of Attorney Ordinance*, at section 2(2).
32. *Apprenticeship Ordinance* (Cap 47) section 8.

- *Marine Insurance Ordinance* (Cap 329); and,
- *Money Lenders Ordinance* (Cap 163).

III. ELEMENTS

In order to have a legally binding agreement, certain requirements must be fulfilled. Those requirements are that:

- the parties must have the intention to create a legal relationship;
- the parties must be in agreement;
- the parties' agreement must be supported by consideration or be made under seal;
- the agreement's terms must be sufficiently certain to enable enforcement; and,
- the parties must have the capacity to enter into a contract.[33]

The first three requirements are presented below. The last two requirements of a contract, *i.e.*, certainty of terms and capacity, are discussed in sections IV and V respectively.

A. Intent

For an agreement to be an enforceable contract, the parties must have the intention to create a legally binding relationship. In other words, the parties to the agreement intend it to be enforceable in court. Intention is determined objectively from the circumstances, including the nature of the words used or the conduct of the party making the offer.

In business transactions, there is a presumption that the agreement is intended to be legally binding.

> Indeed, the presumption in favour of intention in commercial agreements is so strong that it is rarely challenged. The presumption will be rebutted, however where the commercial agreement clearly states that it does not create legally binding obligations.[34]

In social or domestic situations, unless the parties state otherwise, the law presumes that such agreements are not intended to be legally binding. *Wu Chiu Kuen v Chu Shui Ching* (1992) HCA 4081/1991, [1992] HKCU 29

33. *See, e.g.*, CHARLES WILD & STUART WEINSTEIN, SMITH AND KEENAN'S ENGLISH LAW: TEXT AND CASES 288 (16th ed. 2010) [hereinafter SMITH AND KEENAN].
34. HALL, *supra* note 3, at 310.

is an example of a social situation where the plaintiff successfully asserted the existence of an intent to create a legal relationship. The case revolved around a *mah jong* parlour patron who purportedly agreed to share any Mark Six lottery winnings with the *mah jong* parlour employee sent to purchase the tickets. The employee contributed one-half the purchase price of the tickets. The court held that the plaintiff rebutted the presumption that this was a social arrangement and found in favour of the plaintiff.[35]

In the case of *Balfour v Balfour* [1919] 2 KB 571, the court found an agreement for the payment of maintenance between spouses to be unenforceable as it was a domestic agreement. The court presumed that the parties did not intend to create any legal relationship. In the case of *Jones v Padavatton* [1969] 1 WLR 328, the court held that family agreements were dependent upon the good faith of the parties in keeping the promises made and that the parties did not intend to make binding agreements. The case of *Sun Er Jo v Lo Ching* [1996] 1 HKC 1 involved the mother suing her children, particularly one claim for the expenses incurred in raising the youngest child. The court held in relation to the plaintiff's claim for rearing expenses that:

> it was right and proper that parents bring up their children and this did not form a basis for a compensation claim. Family arrangements made between parents and children, husband and wife, or brothers and sisters were generally not legally binding, unless it was shown that they have clearly intended to enter into legal relations.[36]

B. Agreement

There must be an agreement between the parties to a contract before one party can enforce another party's promise.

> Agreement is usually reached by the process of offer and acceptance … the law requires that there be an offer on ascertainable terms which receives an unqualified acceptance from the person to whom it is made.[37]

Thus, at times, courts will use the offer-and-acceptance approach to determine the existence and also the terms of a contract. Some courts are willing to be flexible where the words and conduct are unclear. These courts would

35. *See id.* at 306–309 for a discussion of this case.
36. [1996] 1 HKC at 3. (Headnotes)
See discussion in HALL, *supra* note 3, at 296–304.
37. 7(2) HALSBURY'S, *supra* note 1, at para. 115.026 (citations omitted).

look at all the circumstances at the time of the agreement to determine whether a contract was formed. However, for certain particular agreements, such as contracts under seal, the identification of offer and acceptance is not necessary.[38]

Consequently, this chapter uses this offer-and-acceptance approach. The following section concentrates on an offer-and-acceptance analysis. As contracts under seal are, comparatively, less commonly encountered, this type of legally binding agreement is presented in a later section.

i. *Offer*

An "offer" is a promise to do, or to refrain from doing, something in the future. An offer is also a display of willingness to enter into a contract on specified terms, made in such a way that a reasonable person would understand that an acceptance will result in a legally binding agreement.[39] Consequently, once an offer is accepted, a contract exists between the parties.

The party making an offer is the "offeror", also referred to as the "promisor". The party to whom this offer is made is the "offeree", also referred to as the "promisee". An offer may be made expressly, *i.e.*, by spoken or written words. An offer may also be made impliedly, *i.e.*, by conduct of the parties or by law.

An example of an implied contract by conduct is provided in the following example. A bus arrives at one of its designated stops along its route. A person gets on the bus and pays the specified bus fare. By conduct, the individual and the bus company have entered into a legally binding agreement (exceptions to creating a legally enforceable agreement are discussed later). The agreement in this example is that the person will pay the specified fare and the bus company will convey the person to one of the designated bus stops near the person's destination.[40] No words need to be spoken or written in this example.

---

38. If the contract is a formal written agreement, such as an agreement under seal, it would then be unnecessary to identify the offer and the acceptance. Contracts under seal are comparatively less frequently used and will be discussed later. Also note that the offer-and-acceptance examination by the courts sometimes remain important in determining the terms, rather than the existence, of a written contract.
    See CHITTY, *supra* note 2, at para. 2–110 for a discussion of the difficulty in applying an offer-and-acceptance analysis.
39. BLACK'S LAW DICTIONARY, *supra* note 12, at 1111.
40. CHITTY, *supra* note 2, at para. 1–076.

An implied contract by law would involve contract terms imposed by statute rather than negotiated by the parties. Such terms may involve matters such as employment (anti-discrimination), consumer protection, etc.

An offer must be made with the intention that upon acceptance, the offer and acceptance shall become binding in law.

> When determining whether an offer had been made, one should identify "an expression of willingness to contract on certain terms made with the intention that it shall become binding as soon as it is accepted by the person to whom it is addressed". The person effecting such expression is the offeror even though he may not have initiated the contact.
>
> It is difficult at times to determine which statements or which acts constitute an offer. It is particularly difficult where the parties are indiscriminate with the use of words. The test of an offer is the intention of an expression and not the words used.[41]

Thus, a statement will not be an offer if it is merely intended to supply information. Merely fixing a price does not imply an offer to buy or sell.

In the case of *Harvey v Facey* [1893] AC 552, Harvey sought specific performance[42] of an agreement for the sale of a property named *Bumper*

---

41. Ho, *supra* note 13, at 6.
42. "Specific performance" is defined as an equitable remedy whereby a court orders a party to a contract to specifically perform its obligations under the contract. This type of remedy for breach of contract is discussed later in this chapter.
BLACK'S LAW DICTIONARY, *supra* note 12, at 1297 defines "equitable remedy" as "a non-monetary remedy, such as an injunction or specific performance, obtained when monetary damages cannot adequately redress the injury".
Id. at 560 defines "equity" as:
    (1) Fairness; impartiality; evenhanded dealing.
    (2) The body of principles constituting what is fair and right; natural law.
    (3) The recourse to principles of justice to correct or supplement the law as applied to particular circumstances.
    (4) The system of law or body of principles originating in the English Court of Chancery and superseding the common and statute law when the two conflict.
As explained by FISHER & GREENWOOD, *supra* note 17, at 13:
> The maxims of equity still direct the courts in the exercise of their discretion whether or not to grant equitable relief. The principle that "he who comes to equity must come with clean hands" means that equitable remedies or "relief", will only be granted to those who have acted fairly in respect of the contract. The principle that "he who seeks equity must do equity" means that equitable relief will be granted only where the claimant is prepared to comply with the requirements of the court to do justice to the other party.

The *BLIS Glossary*, *supra* note 2, translates "equity" as 衡平法, "equitable relief" as 衡平法濟助. "Equitable remedy" is translated as 衡平法補救.

Hall Pen. The issue in this case involved the question of whether a legally binding sale and purchase agreement existed. The events transpired in the following sequence:

- Harvey telegraphs Facey, asking, "Will you sell Bumper Hall Pen? Telegraph lowest price for Bumper Hall Pen."
- Facey answers, "Lowest price for Bumper Hall Pen [would be] £900."
- Harvey responds by agreeing to buy the property for Facey's asking price of £900.

All these telegrams are duly received by Harvey and Facey so that there are no difficulties with communications.

Harvey argued that the telegraph correspondence was an implied acceptance of the first question in the first telegram. The court, however, decided that any contract must be determined from the telegrams, that Facey's response was a statement of the lowest price at which he would sell, and that the telegrams contained no implied contract to sell to the person making the inquiry.

The court held that there was no contract between these parties for the following reasons:

- The first telegram asked two questions. The first question concerned the willingness of Facey to sell the property to Harvey. The second question asked the lowest price. The word "telegraph" was addressed to only the second question.
- Facey replied to the second question only. By stating that £900 was the lowest price, Facey gave a precise answer to a precise question—the selling price.

Harvey's next telegram treated Facey's statement of a £900 sale price as an unconditional offer to sell to Harvey at that stated price.

The court found that Facey's telegram was only binding on him as to the £900 sale price and that the telegram was merely an offer to sell the property at a price of £900 because all the other terms of purchase were yet to be negotiated. Harvey's reply telegram could only be treated as an acceptance of Facey's offer to sell the property at a price of £900. Harvey's telegram was an offer to purchase the property for £900 to be accepted by Facey. Thus, the contract could only be completed if Facey had accepted Harvey's last telegram.

a. Bilateral and Unilateral Contract

An offer can be made to a particular person, a particular group of persons or to the public at large. Where it is made to a particular person or a particular group of persons, a contract is formed when the offeree accepts the offer. Such a contract is known as a "bilateral contract". Bilateral contracts thus are generally formed after negotiations have taken place resulting in a promise in exchange for another party's promise. Both parties make binding promises, and one promise is consideration for the other promise. As succinctly and simply summarized by one author:

> A bilateral contract consists of an exchange of promises. A "bilateral" offer, therefore, seeks a *promise* in return, eg Offer–"I [promise that I] will sell you my car for £500." Acceptance–"I [promise that I] will pay £500 for your car."[43]

As presented earlier, a unilateral contract involves a promise by the offeror followed by performance by the offeree, rather than an exchange of promises. Unilateral contracts may arise in advertisements of rewards, or agreements for contingency fees, *e.g.*, estate broker's contract. Where an offer is made to the public at large, a contract is formed when anyone performs the act requested in the offer. A contract thus formed is known as a unilateral contract. An offer arising from an advertisement may be an example of a unilateral contract where the offeror may be unaware of acceptance, until an offeree has performed according to the terms of the offer contained in the advertisement. In a unilateral contract only one party makes a promise; the offer is accepted by performing the requested act specified in the offer. The offeree does not make any promise(s). Compare this to a bilateral contract, where negotiations have taken place resulting in a promise in exchange for another's promise.[44]

---

43. Marnah Suff, Essential Contract Law 2 (2nd ed. 1997) [hereinafter Suff].

44. *Id.*

See section III.B.*ii.c*, "Invitation to Treat", and the discussion of *Carlill v Carbolic Smoke Ball Co* [1893] 1 QB 256.

As presented in Ho, *supra* note 13, at 45:

> A unilateral contract is a contract whereby one party promises certain consideration to another where such other makes no counter promise and has no obligations but would be entitled to the consideration promised by the offeror if he satisfied the terms of the promise. The common example is the promise of a reward for the return of lost articles or provision of information.

Traditional theory was that the offeror may revoke the offer at any time prior to complete performance, even after the offeree has commenced performance. Today, the commonly accepted view is that the offeror cannot withdraw the offer once the offeree has started to perform the required act.[45] Further, the offeree is not required to notify the offeror of performance, unless the offeror is located at a distance and would be unaware of the performance. This notice prevents the offeror from entering a contract with another person for the same purpose.

In bilateral, or even multilateral, contract situations, an offer must be communicated to an offeree and an acceptance must be communicated to the offeror. Generally, one cannot accept an offer unless one has knowledge of the offer.[46] The offer must be directed to a party entitled to accept; others who learn of the offer are not entitled to accept.

b. Termination of Offer

An offer is terminated by:

- rejection by the offeree;
- revocation by the offeror;
- lapse of time;
- death or other incapacity of one of the parties; or,
- where the offer is conditional, failure of the condition to materialize.

The offeror can revoke or withdraw the offer at any time before acceptance is made by the offeree. If the offeror decides to revoke the offer, the notice of revocation must be communicated to the offeree before acceptance.[47] The offeror, as part of the offer, may dictate the manner through which the offeree must make acceptance.[48] The general rule is that an acceptance of an offer must be communicated to the offeror before revocation of the offer or before the offer terminates through the lapse of time or

---

45. Fisher & Greenwood, *supra* note 17, at 71–73.
    See Cheshire, Fifoot & Furmston's Law of Contract 75–78 (M. P. Furmston, ed., 15th ed. 2007) [hereinafter Furmston].
46. This acceptance must be made with the knowledge of the existence of the offer. The offer must be the reason for the acceptance, and there must be a "meeting of the minds" prior to performance. For example, identical offers, one to buy and one to sell, that "cross" in the mail do not create a contract if neither offer was accepted with the knowledge of its existence. Chitty, *supra* note 2, at para. 2–027.
47. For further discussion, *see*, *e.g.*, 7(2) Halsbury's, *supra* note 1, at para. 115.039; Chitty, *supra* note 2, at paras. 2–087 to 2–091.
48. For a detailed discussion, *see*, *e.g.*, 7(2) Halsbury's, *supra* note 1, at para. 115.054; Chitty, *supra* note 2, at paras. 2–027 to 2–086.

otherwise. (An exception to this general rule is where there is an offer of reward.) Revocation is effective if it is communicated in a manner equal to or greater than the way the offer was publicized, even though the offeree has no knowledge of the revocation.

If an offer has been rejected by the offeree, the offer cannot be later accepted. *Lee Siu Fong Mary v Ngai Yee Chai* [2006] 1 HKC 157 is a recent case upholding this principle. In this case, Lee made loans to Ngai which were only partially repaid. Ngai offered to repay the outstanding amount over six years. Lee rejected the offer. Seven years later, Lee brought a court action to recover the outstanding amount of the loans. Ngai's defence was that Lee waited too long to take court action so that the plaintiff is now time-barred from suing. Lee's counter-argument was that Ngai's offer to repay the loans prevented the defendant from claiming this defence. The court held:

> The truth of the matter is that having rejected this offer ... on 21 May 1995 there was no further offer ... from the defendant for the plaintiff to accept later on. There was no evidence that the defendant had intended to leave the offer open so that it may be accepted by the plaintiff at some later time. There was also no evidence that the parties had discussed the time of repayment again after the offer was rejected by the plaintiff.
>
> An offer ... is simply an expression of willingness to contract made with the intention that it is to become binding on the person making it as soon as it is accepted by the person to whom it is addressed ... If the offer was rejected by the plaintiff, she could not unilaterally revive it by saying that she had later accepted it. ...
>
> ... the fundamental point is that there must be an offer or representation made by one party for the other party to accept or relied [*sic*] upon. The so-called representation by the defendant in this case was exactly the same offer he had made and rejected by the plaintiff. Once this was rejected then there was nothing for the plaintiff to rely upon ...[49]

c. Options

An "option" is where an offeror promises to keep the offer open for a specified time and the offeree pays for this promise. This is a separate contract, known as a "collateral contract", between the promisor and the promisee

49. [2006] 1 HKC at 161.

that the offer would be kept open for that stated period of time.[50] The mere promise by an offeror to keep the offer open is not legally binding, as the offeror's promise requires consideration unless the promise is made by deed.

ii. Acceptance

"Acceptance" is the unqualified agreement to the terms made in the offer.[51] Acceptance may be communicated to the offeror orally, in writing, by conduct, or a combination of these. If the offer prescribes a certain method of acceptance, acceptance must be made in the required manner. However, an offeror cannot impose silence as the prescribed method of acceptance. Acceptance of an offer by the offeree must be by genuine consent, *i.e.*, given voluntarily and freely. Acceptance must be unequivocal and unqualified. Any form of conditional acceptance is not acceptance according to the terms of the offer and consequently is not acceptance but is either a rejection of the offer or a counter-offer.[52]

a. Postal Rule

An exception to the rules of acceptance is the Postal Rule (also known as the Mailbox Rule),[53] by which acceptance of an offer by post is deemed

---

50. The topic of "collateral contract" is discussed in section II.A.
BLACK'S LAW DICTIONARY, *supra* note 12, at 319 defines this term as: "A side agreement that relates to a contract ... an agreement made before or at the same time as, but separately from, another contract."

51. CHITTY, *supra* note 2, at para. 2–027 (citations omitted).

52. One source notes:

> An offer cannot be accepted conditionally; the offeree has power to accept only on the terms stated in the offer and nobody else has any power of acceptance whatsoever. Thus, an attempted acceptance cannot operate as such where it is made subject to some condition, or includes some new or different term; or where the offer is only meant to be accepted by offerees jointly, and is not accepted by all of them. In each of these cases, however, the purported acceptance may amount to a counter-offer, though it will not necessarily do so.
>
> The rule that an acceptance must be unconditional does not necessarily require that there must be a precise verbal correspondence between offer and acceptance. But an acceptance must not introduce any new or different terms; nor leave any material term yet to be agreed; nor may it be made in any manner other than that prescribed in the offer.

7(2) HALSBURY'S, *supra* note 1, at para. 115.056 (citations omitted).
See also HO, *supra* note 13, at 14–16.

53. Although simple in concept, the application of the Postal Rule can become complicated when the time of an offer's acceptance or revocation is at issue, particularly where the letter is mis-directed, delayed or lost. *See* 7(2) HALSBURY'S, *supra* note 1, at paras. 115.071 to 115.081; CHITTY, *supra* note 2, at paras. 2–048 to 2–050.

to be communicated at the moment the letter containing the acceptance is posted, *i.e.*, placed in the control of the postal service.[54] This rule also applies to the use of telegrams.[55] Should the message never arrive, an agreement is nevertheless concluded provided there is no fault on the part of the promisee. An acceptance posted after a rejection (*i.e.*, the offeree had a change of mind) is not effective, until it is actually received by the offeror.

The application of the Postal Rule can become complicated when the time of acceptance or revocation of an offer is in dispute, particularly where the letter is incorrectly addressed, delayed or lost.[56]

However, the Postal Rule does not apply to an acceptance made by methods of instantaneous communication, *e.g.*, e-mail, telephone, telex or facsimile. The rationale for this distinction is that an acceptance of an offer made by such instantaneous or near instantaneous communication methods are usually acknowledged by the recipient.[57] Further, another authority posits the rationale to be that the offeree would know that the attempt to make acceptance was unsuccessful.[58] By comparison, a person who makes acceptance by post may never be aware of any loss or delay, and

---

54. 7(2) HALSBURY'S, *supra* note 1, at para. 115.075 notes:

> Ordinarily, a letter is not "posted" until it is put in a Post Office letter box. Thus, the delivery of a letter to a postman outside the course of his ordinary duties is not a posting of the letter, nor will such a letter be assumed to be in the lawful custody of the Post Office as soon as the postman enters the post office. (citations omitted)

Thus, for the purposes of this rule, the acceptance of an offer must be placed in the "control of the Post Office or of one of its employees authorized to *receive* letters. Handing letters to a postman authorised to *deliver* letters is not posting." CHITTY, *supra* note 2, at para. 2–048 (emphasis in original) (citation omitted).

55. For discussion of telegrams, *see* 7(2) HALSBURY'S, *supra* note 1, at para. 115.080; CHITTY, *supra* note 2, at paras. 2–049, 2–051.

56. *See, e.g.*, FISHER & GREENWOOD, *supra* note 17, at 65–67; STONE, *supra* note 20, at 72–84; CHITTY, *supra* note 2, at paras. 2–058 to 2–064.

57. 7(2) HALSBURY'S, *supra* note 1, at para. 115.072 (citations omitted).
FISHER & GREENWOOD, *supra* note 17, at 65 states:

> Email may be thought of as being an instantaneous communication. However, this is not strictly the case, as a message will have to pass through at least one server to reach its target destination. The sender knows that the recipient will only check his mail inbox from time to time. This means there will usually be a delay before it is read. Similarly, with telephone answering machines, the sender knows that the message has not been instantaneously received by the offeror. … given that the courts have shown a reluctance to extend the postal rule to other areas, it is far more likely that emails and similar will be viewed as subject to the normal rules; acceptance taking effect when and where notice of acceptance is received.

58. CHITTY, *supra* note 2, at para. 2–050.

may not have the opportunity to correct the problem in time. Therefore, instantaneous communications are normally governed by the general rule that an acceptance must be actually communicated to and received by the offeror.[59]

An application of these principles is found in *Susanto-Wing Sun v Yung Chi Hardware* [1989] 2 HKC 504. This case involved two contracts for the sale of goods and machinery by the defendant to the plaintiff. The defendant in Taiwan faxed each of the two agreements to the plaintiff in Hong Kong. Immediately upon receipt of each agreement, the plaintiff accepted the agreement by signing and faxing it back to the defendant.

---

59. In relation to acceptance made by e-mails, *see* Hong Kong's *Electronic Transactions Ordinance* (Cap 553) which provides that acceptance by e-mail will be effective only when received, unless the parties have agreed otherwise. In particular, section 19 of this Ordinance states in full:

> (1) Unless otherwise agreed between the originator and the addressee of an electronic record, an electronic record is sent when it is accepted by an information system outside the control of the originator or of the person who sent the electronic record on behalf of the originator.
>
> (2) Unless otherwise agreed between the originator and the addressee of an electronic record, the time of receipt of an electronic record is determined as follows—
>
> (a) if the addressee has designated an information system for the purpose of receiving electronic records, receipt occurs-
>
> (i) at the time when the electronic record is accepted by the designated information system; or
>
> (ii) if the electronic record is sent to an information system of the addressee that is not the designated information system, at the time when the electronic record comes to the knowledge of the addressee;
>
> (b) if the addressee has not designated an information system, receipt occurs when the electronic record comes to the knowledge of the addressee.
>
> (3) Subsections (1) and (2) apply notwithstanding that the place where the information system is located is different from the place where the electronic record is taken to have been sent or received under subsection (4).
>
> (4) Unless otherwise agreed between the originator and the addressee, an electronic record is taken to have been—
>
> (a) sent at the place of business of the originator; and
>
> (b) received at the place of business of the addressee.
>
> (5) For the purposes of subsection (4)—
>
> (a) if the originator or the addressee has more than one place of business, the place of business is that which has the closest relationship to the underlying transaction, or where there is no underlying transaction, the principal place of business of the originator or the addressee, as the case may be;
>
> (b) if the originator or the addressee does not have a place of business, the place of business is the place where the originator or the addressee ordinarily resides.

The court held that:

> It appears however, that the contracts were concluded in Taiwan and not in Hong Kong; because it was in Taiwan that the communication of the plaintiff's acceptance of the offer was received by the defendant. The rule relating to communications by telex is now well settled and the same rule must ... apply to communications by facsimile. The general rule is that as between ... [the parties] the contract, if any, is made when and where the acceptance is received ... the rule to which I have referred applies to instantaneous communication between principals.[60]

The Postal Rule can be excluded by the offeror expressly or impliedly.

> (6) Where the originator and the addressee are in different time zones, time refers to Universal Standard Time.

CHITTY, *supra* note 2, at paras. 2–050 to 2–051 states:

> The posting rule does not apply to acceptances made by some "instantaneous" mode of communication, *e.g.* by telephone or by telex. The reason ... is that the acceptor will often know at once that his attempt to communicate was unsuccessful, so that he has the opportunity of making a proper communication. A person who accepts by a letter which goes astray, on the other hand, may not know of the loss or delay until it is too late to make another communication. Such instantaneous communications are therefore governed by the general rule that an acceptance must be actually communicated, subject to the other exceptions to that rule stated in para. 2–047 above.
>
> It is now uncommon for acceptances to be made by telegram or telemessage dictated over the telephone and there is no authority on the question whether such an acceptance takes effect when the message is dictated by the sender or when it is communicated to the addressee. It is submitted that such an acceptance should, in accordance with the above reasoning, take effect as soon as it is dictated; for if it later goes astray, the acceptor is unlikely to have any means of knowing this fact until it is too late to make a further communication. Fax messages seem to occupy an intermediate position between postal and instantaneous communications. The sender will know at once if his message has not been received at all, or if it has been received only in part, and in such situations the mere sending of the message should not amount to an effective acceptance. It is also possible for the entire message to have been received, but in such a form as to be wholly or partly illegible. Since the sender is unlikely to know, or to have means of knowing, this at once, it is suggested that an acceptance sent by fax might well be effective in such circumstances. The same reasoning should apply to messages sent by electronic means, *e.g.* by e-mail or in the course of website trading: here again the effects of unsuccessful attempts to communicate should depend on whether the sender of the message knows (or has the means of knowing) at once of any failure in communication. (citations omitted)

See also HALL, *supra* note 3, at 35–36.

60. [1989] 2 HKC at 506.

b. Counter-offer

A "counter-offer" usually operates as a rejection of the original offer and the making of a new offer by the offeree. Withdrawal of the counter-offer does not revive the original offer such as to enable the offeree to accept the same. However, a request for information by the offeree is not a counter-offer. As the court explained in *Stevenson, Jaques & Co v McLean* (1880) 5 QB 346, the solicitation of information is "a mere inquiry which should have been answered and not treated as a rejection of the offer."[61] In this case, the defendant offered to sell 3,000 tonnes of iron at forty shillings per tonne. The offer remained valid until Monday. The plaintiff sent its first telegram early Monday requesting, "Please wire whether you would accept forty [shillings per tonne] for delivery over two months, or if not what is the longest limit you would accept." Receiving no reply, the plaintiff later that day sent a second telegram indicating acceptance at forty shillings cash. In the interim, the defendant had sold the goods elsewhere without informing the plaintiff until after the plaintiff had sent the second telegram. The court found that a contract existed between the plaintiff and the defendant.

c. Invitation to Treat

An "invitation to treat" is a request for an offer, *i.e.*, an invitation to make an offer.[62] An invitation to treat is a negotiating statement which does not show an offeror's intent to give an offeree the power to create a contract. For example, customers are invited to offer to buy, and traders keep to themselves the power to choose whether to accept that offer. Merely fixing a

---

61. (1880) 5 QB at 350.
62. One source explains:

> An invitation to treat is a mere declaration of willingness to enter into negotiations; it is not an offer, and cannot be accepted so as to form a binding contract.
>
> In practice, the formation of a contract is frequently preceded by preliminary negotiations. Some of the exchanges in these negotiations contain no declaration at all, as where one party simply asks for information. Others may amount to invitations to the recipient to make an offer, these being invitations to treat.
>
> Thus, a distinction must be drawn between those declarations which amount to offers, and those which only amount to invitations to treat. Sometimes, a particular type of declaration is, at least prima facie, put into one or the other category by statute or by common law; but in all other cases it is a question of intention. An express statement that a declaration is not an offer is effective to prevent it being an offer ...

7(2) HALSBURY'S, *supra* note 1, at para. 115.028 (citations omitted).

price does not imply an offer to buy or to sell. Consequently, the display of goods by a merchant, price-lists, circulars and advertisements for goods and services are normally construed as invitations to treat.[63]

The *BLIS Glossary*, *supra* note 2, translates "common law" as 普通法 and "rules of the common law" as 普通法規則.

Similarly, CHITTY, *supra* note 2, at paras. 2–008 to 2–010 states:

> A communication by which a party is invited to make an offer is commonly called an invitation to treat. It is distinguishable from an offer primarily on the ground that it is not made with the intention that it is to become binding as soon as the person to whom it is addressed simply communicates his assent to its terms. A statement is clearly not an offer if it expressly provides that the person who makes it is *not* to be bound merely by the other party's notification of assent but only when he himself has signed the document in which the statement is contained.
>
> Apart from cases of the kind just described, the wording of a statement does not conclusively determine the distinction between an offer and an invitation to treat. Thus a statement may be an invitation to treat although it contains the word "offer"; while a statement may *be* an offer although it is expressed as an "acceptance," or although it requests the person to whom it is addressed to make an "offer." …
>
> … the distinction between offer and invitation to treat is often hard to draw, as it depends … on the intention of the person making the statement in question. (emphasis in original)

63. In the case of *Fisher v Bell* [1961] 1 QB 394 the court held that the display of a knife in the shop's window was an invitation to treat. If the display were an offer, the shopkeeper would have been in violation of the *Restriction of Offensive Weapons Act*.

A similar situation arose in the earlier case of *Pharmaceutical Society of Great Britain v Boots Cash Chemists (Southern) Ltd* [1953] 2 WLR 427. The facts of this case involved customers selecting goods from the shelves and going to the cashier to make payment. By the check-out was a registered pharmacist who could prevent the removal of certain drugs from the store. Boots Cash Chemists was charged under an English statute requiring a registered pharmacist to "supervise sale". The issue in this case was whether the display of goods on the shelves of this self-service store was an offer or an invitation to treat. If the display were an offer, then a customer's act of removing the goods from the shelf and placing them in the shopping basket would constitute acceptance. The sale would, therefore, take place without the requisite supervision so an offence would be committed under the statute. The court held that the display amounted only to an invitation to treat. The court reasoned that if the display of goods were an offer, a customer, upon placing the goods in the basket, could not then have a change of mind and substitute the goods for other goods without being liable to pay for the goods originally chosen. This would not be viable commercially for self-service stores as customers would be too afraid to patronize them. Moreover, in theory, the shopkeeper should be able to refuse to sell the goods when presented to the cashier since shops were places to bargain over prices. However, this view was overruled in the case of *Debenhams Retail Plc v Commissioners of Customs and Excise* [2005] EWCA Civ 892. FISHER & GREENWOOD, *supra* note 17, at 46–49. *See* HALL, *supra* note 3, at 53–55 for discussion of two similar cases in Hong Kong: *HKSAR v Wan Hon Sik* [2001] 3 HKLRD 283; and, *HKSAR v Yu Wai Chuen* [2002] 2 HKLRD 347. Further examples may be found in 7(2) HALSBURY'S, *supra* note 1, at para. 115.029; HO, *supra* note 13, at 7; FURMSTON, *supra* note 45, at 39–47; CHITTY, *supra* note 2, at paras. 2–011 to 2–024.

The distinction between an offer and an invitation to treat lies in the intention or absence of intention to be bound as soon as the addressee accepts the terms stated. The distinction is that the offeror in making an offer shows an intention to be bound. An individual issuing an invitation to treat is making an invitation to the addressee to negotiate rather than an invitation to communicate an acceptance.[64]

At times it may be difficult to distinguish an offer from an invitation to treat. In *Carlill v Carbolic Smoke Ball Co* [1893] 1 QB 256 a manufacturer published an advertisement during an influenza epidemic, proclaiming the virtues of its product for curing ailments. The manufacturer further stated that anyone who bought one of its smoke balls, used it as directed, and then caught influenza, would be paid £100. Mrs. Carlill bought and used a smoke ball, but nevertheless caught influenza. She claimed £100 from the company. The defendant argued that the advertisement should not be considered to be an offer which would create a contract upon acceptance. The court, however, considered that since the advertisement stated the company had deposited £1,000 in its bank in order to show its sincerity, reasonable people could consider this as indicating the promise to pay £100 was serious, and that this act created a binding obligation.

Thus, whether an advertisement constitutes an offer will depend upon its wording and its natural meaning. If an advertisement is very specific and clear, it may amount to an offer, which may be accepted without qualification. An offer in this manner may be accepted by anyone, unless there is some restricted class of persons to whom the advertisement is directed. Even then, any member of that class may accept.

However, one source notes:

> Some recent developments have had the effect of altering traditional rules, as for example as has occurred in the case of a tender. Generally, the tender process is treated as three distinct parts: the invitation to treat by the party inviting tenders, the offers from those interested and the acceptance by the invitor of one of those offers. Acceptance results in a binding contract on the terms set out in the invitation to treat. In several cases, various courts have re-categorised the invitation to treat as an offer. This means there are two possible contracts. The first is the traditional contract which arises under the tender. The second is a collateral contract under which the invitor acts as an offeror because he expressly or by implication agreed to consider all offers. Failure to do

---

64. Ho, *supra* note 13, at 7.

> so gives rise to action for damages for loss of chance. As a corollary, the party submitting the tender may not be able to withdraw.[65]

Similarly, in auctions, the auctioneer invites bids. Each potential buyer makes an offer by making a bid, which the auctioneer must accept when the auctioneer's hammer falls. A buyer may withdraw the offer at any time before the hammer falls.[66] If the bid is withdrawn, it does not revive an earlier bid by another buyer. Thus, the bidding must restart. At an auction, the auctioneer's invitation for bids is impliedly made "with reserve" allowing the auctioneer to remove the item for auction if a sufficient price is not bid. If, however, an auction is expressly made "without reserve", the auctioneer cannot withdraw the item unless no bid was made.[67]

A recent case demonstrates these principles as well as offering a preview of the principles reviewed in the following sections of this chapter and the Property chapter. *Hoie Sook Fong v Ismail Halima* [2009] 1 HKC 326 involved the sale of land by an auctioneer whose authority to sell the property had been revoked for advertising the property below the owner's stated minimum price, also known as the "reserve" price. The plaintiff was the successful bidder of that flat being sold by the auctioneer on behalf of the owner. The plaintiff's successful bid was HK$1.88 million while the owner had set a reserve price of HK$1.98 million. The plaintiff sought to

---

65. 16 HALSBURY'S LAWS OF HONG KONG para. 230.147 (2010) (citing *Lobley Co Ltd v Tsang Yuk Kiu* [1997] 2 HKC 442; *Blackpool and Fylde Aero Club v Blackpool Borough Council* [1990] 1 WLR 1195; *City Polytechnic of Hong Kong v Blue Cross (Asia-Pacific) Insurance Ltd* [1994] 3 HKC 423; *City University of Hong Kong v Blue Cross (Asia-Pacific) Insurance Ltd* [2001] 1 HKC 463).
66. *Payne v Cave* (1789) 3 TR 148. In Hong Kong, auctions are regulated by two ordinances: *Sale of Goods Ordinance* (Cap 26) and *Sale of Land by Auction Ordinance* (Cap 27). Section 60 of the *Sale of Goods Ordinance* provides:

    > In the case of a sale by auction—
    > (a) where goods are put up for sale by auction in lots, each lot is prima facie deemed to be the subject of a separate contract of sale;
    > (b) a sale by auction is complete when the auctioneer announces its completion by the fall of the hammer, or in other customary manner. Until such announcement is made any bidder may retract his bid;
    > (c) where a sale by auction is not notified to be subject to a right to bid on behalf of the seller, it shall not be lawful for the seller to bid himself or to employ any person to bid at such sale, or for the auctioneer knowingly to take any bid from the seller or any such person. Any sale contravening this rule may be treated as fraudulent by the buyer;
    > (d) a sale by auction may be notified to be subject to a reserve or upset price, and a right to bid may also be reserved expressly [by] ... seller.

67. For further discussion, *see, e.g.*, HALL, *supra* note 3, at 63–67.

enforce the purported purchase and sale agreement signed with the auctioneer at the conclusion of the bidding.

In deciding this case, the court relied upon these legal principles:

1. An agent, including an auctioneer, who sells property without or in excess of authority will be liable to the purchaser in damages for breach of the implied warranty that he possesses the authority exercised.
2. It is trite that if the authority of the auctioneer to sell a property has in fact been revoked by the vendor before the auction, the auctioneer can give the highest bidder no right to the property, even though the bidder is unaware of the revocation.
3. Where a reserve price has been fixed by the seller and the sale is subject to a reserve, the auctioneer has no authority to sell below that reserve price. If the auctioneer does so, no contract is concluded as all bids amount to conditional offers and any acceptance is similarly conditional on the reserve price being reached or exceeded.[68]

The court held that the owner revoked the auctioneer's authority to sell the property; therefore, the auctioneer did not have the capacity to enter into a purchase and sale contract with the plaintiff on the owner's behalf. The judge also found the auctioneer liable to the plaintiff in damages for the breach of warranty of authority to sell the flat. Finally, this case demonstrates that a dispute can involve overlapping fields of law, in this instance: contract, agency and conveyancing.

C. Consideration

The case of *Currie v Misa* (1875) LR 10 Ex 153 defined "consideration" as some right, interest, profit or benefit accruing to one party; or, some forbearance, detriment, loss or responsibility given, incurred or undertaken by the opposite party.[69] In other words, consideration may be a party's promise to perform some act or to refrain from performing some act. The case of *Dunlop Pneumatic Tyre Co v Selfridge & Co* [1915] AC 847 also defined "consideration" as:

---

68. [2009] 1 HKC at 330 (citations omitted).
69. (1875) LR 10 Ex at 162.
For examples of benefits to the promisor or detriments to the promisee, *see* 7(2) HALSBURY'S, *supra* note 1, at paras. 115.112–115.113 respectively.
The *BLIS Glossary*, *supra* note 2, translates "consideration" as 代價.

> an act or forbearance of one party, or the promise thereof, is the price for which the promise of the other is bought, and the promise thus given for value is enforceable.[70]

Consideration is that which is actually given or accepted in return for a promise. Thus, consideration may be something other than money, such as a promise. In other words, consideration is a bargained for action (or the promise not to take action) or a return promise to pay.[71] Consideration is that which is actually given or accepted in return for a promise, and that which has real value. Consideration can be analysed as being either a benefit to the promisor or a detriment to the promisee. Consideration may be something other than money, *e.g.*, a promise.

> In other words, if one receives something to which he is not entitled he has received a benefit even though that thing may in fact not be beneficial to him. And, if one does something he is obligated to do or refrains from doing something he is entitled to do, he suffers a legal detriment even though the act or omission may in fact be beneficial to him.[72]

Note, however, that an illusory promise, a promise that is not actually binding upon the promisor, does not constitute valid consideration. For example, one party might reserve the right to alter or revoke the contract at any time.

Consideration must move from the promisee/offeree. Unless the promisee has provided consideration for the offeror's promise, the contract cannot be enforced by the offeree. It is unnecessary that the promisor should benefit

70. [1915] AC at 855.
71. Consideration can be categorized as "executed" and "executory". As explained in Fisher & Greenwood, *supra* note 17, at 89:

> It is generally the case that "executory" consideration is just as valuable as "executed" consideration: i.e. the promise of an act is as effective as the act itself. For example, if a seller of goods fails to deliver them on time, the buyer has a right to sue even though the goods have not yet been paid for. Executory consideration exists in the buyer's promise to pay for the goods when required to do so. Provided that the buyer has not indicated that he is no longer willing or able to proceed he is entitled to sue the seller for the latter's non-delivery. In cases of "unilateral" contracts, where only one party has undertaken obligations, the promisee's consideration can only exist in an act rather than a promise, since he gives no promise. Mrs. Carlill, for example, did not make any promises to the Carbolic Smoke Ball Co. Her consideration existed in the *act* of using the ball as directed; it was, in other words, executed rather than executory.

For further discussion, *see, e.g.*, 7(2) Halsbury's, *supra* note 1, at paras. 115.110, 115.114.

72. *Thomas v Thomas* (1842) 2 QB 851, 859.

by the consideration. It is sufficient if the promisee does some act from which a third party or person benefits.[73] Thus, the consideration needs not go to the promisor. Consideration may move to wherever the parties' agreement stipulates, such as to a third party.

> While consideration must move from the promisee, it need not move to the promisor. It follows that the requirement of consideration may be satisfied where the promisee suffers some detriment at the promisor's request, but confers no corresponding benefit on the promisor. Thus the promisee may provide consideration by giving up a job or the tenancy of a flat, even though no direct benefit results to the promisor from these acts. It also follows that the promisee may provide consideration by conferring a benefit on a third party at the promisor's request: *e.g.* by entering into a contract with the third party. …
>
> … the rule that consideration need not move to the promisor equally applies where the consideration consists simply in a benefit conferred by the promisee without loss to himself. Here the requirement of consideration is satisfied if a benefit is conferred either on the promisor or on a third person at his request.[74]

There is an exception to the requirement for consideration. This exception concerns a particular type of contract discussed earlier: a deed or a contract under seal. In situations involving this type of contract, a seal replaces the need for consideration. A seal thus takes the place of consideration.[75] A contract under seal is a document to which the maker's seal is attached and which is delivered as the maker's deed. Contracts under seal is discussed again at the end of this section.

i. *Adequacy and Sufficiency of Consideration*

Consideration need not be adequate, although it must be sufficient at law.[76]

> The rule is that "Consideration must be 'sufficient' (of some value) but need not be 'adequate' (of equal value to the other party's consideration).["] There is nothing wrong, in consideration terms, with an agreement to buy a valuable painting for $10 …

---

73. 7(2) HALSBURY'S, *supra* note 1, at para. 115.110. Consideration for a promise may consist in either some benefit for the promisor, or some disadvantage incurred by the promisee, or both. *Id.*
74. CHITTY, *supra* note 2, at paras. 3–039 to 3–040.
75. "The only contracts which are required by the rules of common law to be made by deed are contracts made without valuable consideration." 7(2) HALSBURY'S, *supra* note 1, at para. 115.016 (citations omitted).
76. As explained in CHITTY, *supra* note 2, at para. 3–014:

> Consideration is, essentially, a token of a party's intention to make a legally binding contract as opposed, for example, to a non-binding social arrangement. That token takes the form of the giving of something valuable in the eyes of the law. Consideration may not prove that a bargain is fair or equal but it *is* evidence of a legally enforceable contract, as opposed to a mere friendly arrangement never intended to be contractual. (emphasis in original)[77]

Therefore, £1.00 was held to be sufficient in law, although this may not be adequate in terms of money, as consideration for the possession of a house, even though the house is more valuable in monetary terms.[78]

> Under the doctrine of consideration, a promise has no contractual force unless *some* value has been given for it. But as a general rule the courts do not concern themselves with the question whether "adequate" value has been given, or whether the agreement is harsh or one-sided. The fact that a person pays "too much" or "too little" for a thing may be evidence of fraud or mistake ... [b]ut it does not of itself affect the validity of the contract ...
>
> The present rule is subject to a number of exceptions ... These indicate that the courts are (even where the legislature has not intervened) by no means insensitive to the problems raised by unequal or unfair bargains; but in none of them is a promise held invalid merely because adequate value for it has not been given. ... [T]he general rule applies that the courts will enforce a promise so long as *some* value for it has been given (emphasis in original) ...

In a similar vein, another authority propounds:

> At both common law and equity, the courts do not generally concern themselves with the adequacy of the consideration; that is, they make no attempt to audit the bargain made by the parties to see if it is a fair one. ...
>
> Whilst the courts are not substantively interested in the adequacy of the consideration, the fact that a contracting party pays too much or too little may be relevant for some other purposes. At common law, it may be evidence of duress or mistake; or it may induce the court to imply a warranty. In equity, it may give grounds for setting aside a bargain on the basis of fraud, undue influence or that it is unconscionable; or it may lead to a refusal to grant specific performance. ...

7(2) HALSBURY'S, *supra* note 1, at para. 115.117 (citations omitted).

The *BLIS Glossary*, *supra* note 2, translates "valuable consideration" as 有值代價.

77. FISHER & GREENWOOD, *supra* note 17, at 83.

7(2) HALSBURY'S, *supra* note 1, at para. 115.119 states that although:

> consideration need not be adequate it must be of some value. It has been settled that the following are no consideration: past consideration; a promise to do an act which is obviously impossible, or which has no legal effect; a promise which does not involve any legal obligation; or, possibly, a promise which is illegal or void. (citations omitted)

For a further discussion on this topic of sufficiency of consideration, *see*, *e.g.*, FURMSTON, *supra* note 45, at 104–141.

78. *Thomas v Thomas* (1842) 2 QB 851.

Love and affection is not considered valid consideration. The rationale is that although:

> consideration need not be adequate, it must be "of some value in the eye of the law", that is, it must be capable of estimation in terms of economic or monetary value, even though there may be no very precise way of quantifying that value. This is one reason why there is no consideration for a promise made "in consideration of natural love and affection", and why in *Thomas v Thomas* the testator's desire that his widow should live in his house was not part of the consideration for the executors' promise that she might do so.[79]

ii. Past Consideration

Consideration must not be past. If one party has wholly performed before obtaining a promise from the other party, there is no consideration for that promise as performance was already completed or "past" before the promise was obtained. In other words, if the consideration is something that has already been provided at the time the promise was made, and was independent of the promise, the benefit or detriment is considered to be past consideration and will not be recognized as valid consideration. With past consideration, the bargaining element between the parties is missing.[80]

Fulfilling an existing contractual obligation to a third party constitutes new consideration as the promisor gives the third party the right to sue in the event of non-performance by the promisor, a right the third party did not originally possess until the promise was made.

> While consideration may be executory or executed, it must not be "past". Past consideration exists when the apparent act, or promise, of consideration occurred *before* the promisor's promise. A simple illustration would be provided by the case of a drowning man, D, who cries for help. X generously rescues D who promises X a reward in gratitude. Since X's act of rescue occurred *before* D's promise, it is past consideration and the rule is that "past consideration is no consideration". The concept of past consideration is easy to understand if one bears in mind

---

79. Chitty, *supra* note 2, at para. 3–022 (citations omitted). *See Ian Hung Wai v Cheung Sau Kuen* [2011] 3 HKLRD 458, CA where the Court of Appeal held that the plaintiff's gifts made to the girlfriend during their courtship were absolute gifts given out of love rather than gifts made upon contemplation of, and conditional upon, marriage which would be returned should these parties not marry.
80. For a further discussion on past consideration, *see* Fisher & Greenwood, *supra* note 17, at 89–90; 7(2) Halsbury's, *supra* note 1, at para. 115.120; Ho, *supra* note 13, at 60–61.

> the requirement that consideration must be the "price" of the other party's promise: the act of rescue may well be a detriment to the rescuer but it cannot be the price of the rescued person's promise since that promise has not yet been made. (emphasis in original)[81]

Consequently, a promise supported only by past consideration is generally unenforceable because the benefit given or detriment incurred is not the result of the present promise. If one party has fully performed before obtaining a promise from the other party, there is no bargain or consideration for that promise. However, there are exceptions to this rule.

For example, one exception is the fulfilment of an existing contractual obligation to a third party. Assume that there is a contractual relationship between Alan, as the promisor, and Bob, as the promisee. Calvin, as the third party, can enter into a contract with Alan to pay him in order to ensure that Alan performs his contract with Bob. There is fresh consideration in this scenario because the promisor gives the third party a right to sue in the event of non-performance.

Another exception is where:

- The act or promise must have been done at the promisor's request;
- The parties must have understood that the act required payment, *i.e.*, cash or some other benefit; and
- The payment must have been legally enforceable had it been promised in advance.[82]

A final exception to the general rule that consideration cannot be past may arise from statute. For example, section 27 of the *Bills of Exchange Ordinance* (Cap 19) provides that valuable consideration may be constituted by an antecedent debt or liability. In other words, a debt or obligation that precedes the making of a bill of exchange can be good consideration under this law. A cheque is an example of a bill of exchange.

Related to the rule that consideration cannot be past is the rule that consideration must be real.[83] The consideration for a contract may not be something legally due or a legal detriment that the promisor is already legally bound to do. Consideration must be something more than the performance of an existing duty. A party bound by contract to perform certain obligations does not provide any consideration for another contract by promising

81. Fisher & Greenwood, *supra* note 17, at 89.
82. *Pao On v Lau Yiu Long* [1980] AC 614, 629, PC.
For a discussion of this case, *see*, *e.g.*, Stone, *supra* note 20, at 127.
83. *See* Chitty, *supra* note 2, at para. 3–022.

to fulfil those pre-existing obligations. Since one party is already legally entitled to the promises contained in the contract, to receive those promises is of no additional legal benefit. Similarly, since one party is already legally bound to provide those promised items or services, to do so is no additional legal detriment. Such existing contractual obligations provide no additional burden which can amount to consideration for a new contract.[84] This rule that consideration must be real is discussed in the next section.

iii. Performing an Outstanding Obligation

Performing or promising to perform an obligation already owed to the same party under a prior contract cannot be consideration for a new promise.[85] In the case of *Stilk v Myrick* (1809) 2 Camp 317, a ship's captain, unable to find substitutes for two sailors who deserted the ship, promised to divide the deserters' wages among the remaining crew if they would sail the ship home. The court held that the promise was unenforceable because of the absence of consideration. The court's rationale is that in sailing the ship home, the crew had done that which they were already required to do. The crew's original contract required them to meet the normal emergencies of the voyage, which included minor desertions.

If there were something new in the second promise which was not required under the previous contract, this new undertaking may be sufficient to constitute new consideration, *e.g.*, faster or better performance, a different form of performance or performing under unusually difficult circumstances. In the case of *Hartley v Ponsonby* (1857) 7 E&B 872, the facts were similar to the *Stilk* case: seventeen men out of a crew of 36 deserted the ship. The remaining men sailed the ship home on the promise that they would receive greater remuneration. The court held that the voyage was dangerous, as the number of deserters rendered the ship unseaworthy. The sailors could have refused to undertake the journey, as it went beyond the normal circumstances of a sea voyage. Therefore, the promise was binding as the plaintiff had gone beyond his duty, agreeing to sail an unseaworthy and severely undermanned ship.

Similarly, the payment of a smaller sum will not discharge a debt for a larger amount as the debtor does not provide consideration for a new agreement which arranges for settlement at the smaller sum. The reason

---

84. Satisfying an existing contractual obligation to a third party is new consideration because the promisor gives the third party a right to sue in the event of non-performance.
85. *See, e.g.*, Chui & Roebuck, *supra* note 3, at para. 3.7.6.3.

is that the existing duty remains to pay the debt in full. To provide consideration for settlement, the debtor must undertake some new burden, such as making payment at a different time than originally agreed, or, making payment at a different location than originally agreed.[86]

In the case of *Foakes v Beer* (1884) 9 App Cas 605, Mrs. Beer obtained a judgment against Dr. Foakes for a debt of more than £2,000 and court costs. Dr. Foakes agreed to settle this judgment by paying £500 immediately and £150 every six months until the whole amount was paid, and Mrs. Beer agreed not to take further action on the judgment. Dr. Foakes duly paid the amount of the judgment plus the court costs. However, judgment debts carry interest according to the law. Thus, while Dr. Foakes had been paying off the debt, interest amounting to £360 had been accruing on the outstanding balance. In this action, Mrs. Beer claimed the £360. The court held she could do so. Her promise not to take further action on the judgment was not supported by any consideration from Dr. Foakes.

The rule that performance of an existing duty is insufficient consideration is qualified in the case of *Williams v Roffey Bros* [1991] 1 QB 1. In this case, the defendant building contractor subcontracted carpentry works to the plaintiff for a certain amount. The plaintiff's sum was too low and the plaintiff began to experience financial difficulties. The defendant feared that there might be a delay to the works which would render the defendant liable for damages under the main contract. Therefore the defendant promised, but failed, to make extra payments to the plaintiff. The plaintiff sued for the extra payments. The Court of Appeal held that the benefits which the defendant received, *e.g.*, actual performance of the earlier contract or avoidance of the penalty for delay and of the inconvenience of engaging a substitute contractor, to be sufficient consideration for the promise of extra payments. The court stated:

- if A has entered into a contract with B to do work for, or to supply goods or services to, B in return for payment by B; and,
- at some stage before A has completely performed his obligations under the contract B has reason to doubt whether A will, or will be able to, complete his side of the bargain; and,
- B thereupon promises A an additional payment in return for A's promise to perform his contractual obligations on time; and,
- as a result of giving his promise, B obtains in practice a benefit, or obviates a disbenefit; and,

86. *See* the following discussion in this section and in section III.D on the subject of "accord and satisfaction".

- B's promise is not given as a result of economic duress[87] or fraud on the part of A; then,
- the benefit to B is capable of being consideration for B's promise so that the promise will be legally enforceable.[88]

This case appears at odds with *Stilk v Myrick* and both cases appear to be controversial.[89] It has been suggested that if a party improperly refuses to perform its contractual obligations unless for extra payments, the refusal would amount to economic duress and the promise for extra payments would not be enforceable. However there is no suggestion of duress in *Williams*. In such a circumstance there is nothing objectionable in enforcing the promise, since this also accords with commercial reality. *Williams v Roffey Bros* has been applied in Hong Kong in the case of *UBC (Construction) Ltd v Sung Foo Kee Ltd* [1993] 2 HKC 458.[90] On the other hand, its application is limited. In *Re Selectmove* [1995] 2 All ER 531, the English Court of Appeal refused to extend the principle in *Williams* to the context of *Foakes v Beer*, namely part payment of a debt.

D. Accord and Satisfaction

The term "accord" denotes agreement; "satisfaction" refers to consideration. Thus, accord and satisfaction is an agreement, with consideration, for

87. Economic duress is discussed in section V.B.*iii*. For present purposes, consider the term "economic duress" to refer to unfair business pressure.
88. [1991] 1 QB at 15–16.
89. For a discussion, *see* FISHER & GREENWOOD, *supra* note 17, at 99–105; 7(2) HALSBURY'S, *supra* note 1, at para. 115.128; HO, *supra* note 13, at 54; STONE, *supra* note 20, at 128–134; FURMSTON, *supra* note 45, at 117–119; CHITTY, *supra* note 2, at paras. 3–065 to 3–071.
90. In this case the contractor claimed it owed no additional monies to the plastering subcontractor for variation orders at the Wah Ming Estate because the disputed work was required under the contract rather than work which varied from the original requirements. Accordingly, the disputed work thus fell within the contracted sum. There would be no consideration for agreeing to pay the subcontractor a higher sum than the contract sum. The court stated at 468 [quoting KEATING ON BUILDING CONTRACTS (5th ed.) at 90–91]:

    An agreement to pay an additional sum for no extra work may not always fail for [lack of] consideration. When a sub-contract carpenter was in financial difficulties and the agreed price for his work was too low, it was held that there was consideration for the main contractor's promise to pay an additional amount for the same work in that the main contractor thereby secured benefits or obviated disbenefits from the continuing relationship with the sub-contractor. The benefits were:

    (1) seeking to ensure that the sub-contractor did not stop work in breach of contract;
    (2) avoiding the penalty for delay; and
    (3) avoiding the trouble and expense of engaging others to complete the work. (citation omitted)

the payment of a debt, in instances where the amount of the debt is not readily ascertainable, is not agreed between the parties or is disputed in good faith. Accord and satisfaction is the purchase of a release from an obligation by means of any valuable consideration, other than the performance of the obligation itself. The accord is the agreement by which the original obligation is paid, or by which the original debt is substituted with a new amount. The accord does not discharge the debt but merely suspends it until the accord is fully performed. If the debtor fails to perform the agreed accord, the other party can elect to enforce the terms of original contract, or to sue under terms of the accord. In short, the accord is the agreement by which the obligation is discharged; satisfaction is the consideration which makes the agreement operative.[91]

In an accord and satisfaction situation, a creditor, known as the "promisor", is promising to forgo the strict legal right to be paid in full in return for some additional benefit, to be provided by the debtor, known as the "promisee", or some additional burden or detriment, to be incurred by the debtor. For this reason, where there is no additional benefit or burden, there can be no consideration and the creditor can enforce the original contract. Consequently, a debtor who paid a lesser sum, claiming payment to be in full settlement of the debt, may be legally obliged to pay the balance if the creditor sues and proves that there was no consideration for the settlement, even though the creditor may have agreed initially with the compromise.

For there to be accord and satisfaction upon payment of a debt for less than the full amount of an existing indebtedness, a debtor must provide a creditor with something of additional value or suffer some additional detriment.

> There can be no satisfaction unless the accord is supported by consideration or made by deed. …
>
> As a general rule, payment or promise of payment of part of a debt does not amount to satisfaction in respect of the rest of the debt.[92]

Examples of consideration in an accord and satisfaction situation include:

- where the debtor makes early payment upon the creditor's request;
- where the debtor makes payment at a different place at the creditor's request;

91. *British Russian Gazette and Trade Outlook Ltd v Associated Newspapers Ltd* [1933] 2 KB 616, 643–644.
    Both 7(2) HALSBURY'S, *supra* note 1, at para. 115.396 and CHITTY, *supra* note 2, at para. 22–012 use this definition for the term "accord and satisfaction".
92. 7(2) HALSBURY'S, *supra* note 1, at para. 115.398 (citations omitted). Exceptions to this general rule are set out in *id.*

- where the mode of payment is changed; or,
- where the debtor gives some chattel of value together with a reduced cash payment.[93]

There is no accord if a creditor is forced to accept a sum smaller than the amount of indebtedness, as was the situation in *D & C Builders Ltd v Rees* [1966] 2 QB 617. The plaintiff, D & C Builders, performed work for Mr. Rees for which payment was outstanding. Initially, no dispute arose as to the quality of the workmanship but Mr. Rees failed to pay. In August and October 1964, the plaintiff received no reply to their requests for payment. In November 1964, Mr. Rees became ill and his wife contacted the plaintiff complaining about the quality of the work. She offered £300 in satisfaction. D & C Builders, facing bankruptcy without full payment, offered to accept the £300 and allow payment of the balance within a year. Mrs. Rees rejected this proposition, indicating that £300 was better than no payment. The plaintiff considered that it had no choice but to accept. Mrs. Rees paid by cheque and insisted on a receipt "in completion of the account". The plaintiff, concerned over its financial situation, sued the Rees for the unpaid amount. The Rees argued that there was a legally binding settlement between the parties. The court held that the payment of a smaller sum could not be settlement of a larger sum.

Generally, therefore, where a creditor accepts part payment of the debt as full satisfaction of the amount owed, this partial payment does not discharge the whole debt. An exception is where a third party pays a smaller sum which is accepted by the creditor to discharge the debtor's larger debt. The creditor cannot subsequently sue the debtor for the balance because otherwise it would be a fraud on the third party who paid to discharge the full debt.

There is another important exception to this general rule which is in relation to compositions with creditors. Where a debtor reaches a compromise[94] agreement with a number of creditors at the same time, no single creditor is entitled to return to its strict legal rights.[95] A composition may arise where there are several creditors. The debtor reaches an agreement

93. Chitty, *supra* note 2, at paras. 22–016 to 22–017.
Id. at para. 22–016 explains in relation to the partial payment of a debt:

> Where there is a claim … the liability for which is not in dispute, the acceptance of a smaller sum in satisfaction does not relieve the debtor for there is no consideration for the creditor's abandonment of the balance. This rule, which is generally known as the rule in *Pinnel's Case*, is nevertheless subject to a number of qualifications …

94. The *BLIS Glossary*, *supra* note 2, translates "compromise" as 妥協.

with some or all of the creditors whereby the creditors agree with the debtor, and with each other, to accept the debtor's partial payment of the amounts due to be full satisfaction of the whole of their claims. Such an agreement is binding on all parties, and, if the debtor complies with its obligations thereunder, will discharge the original debts.[96]

> Where two or more creditors enter into an agreement with a debtor whereby they agree to accept payment of a sum less than the debts in full satisfaction of their claims … the agreement will be supported by consideration. In Hong Kong, the special rule for composition agreements can also extend to situations where the agreement commits the creditors to receive deferred payment of their full entitlement.[97]

If a settlement agreement were to be made under seal, there would be no requirement for consideration. Recall the general rule that a contract must be supported by consideration unless it was made under seal. Recall, too, that a seal replaces or is substituted for consideration. A "contract under seal" is a document that has the maker's seal attached and that is delivered. However, a contract under seal, *i.e.*, without consideration, may not take advantage of equitable remedies, such as specific performance or injunction, in the event of a breach.[98] This is due to the principle that equity will not assist a volunteer.[99]

---

95. *See generally Bankruptcy Ordinance* (Cap 6) on voluntary arrangement.
Section 2 of this Ordinance states in part: "'voluntary arrangement' (自願安排) means a composition in satisfaction of a debtor's debts or a scheme of arrangement of a debtor's affairs."
See also Ho, *supra* note 13, at 386.
96. 7(2) Halsbury's, *supra* note 1, at para. 115.401.
97. Hall, *supra* note 3, at 200, citing to the case of *Chiu Wing Hang v BG Lighting Co Ltd* HCLA 67/1999.
98. Concerning contracts contained in a deed, the rule is that:

> equity never favoured voluntary transactions even if they were contained in a deed, and refused to grant its special remedies in cases where these were without consideration. So it has been laid down that specific performance will not be decreed of a contract contained in a deed which is entirely without consideration.

Chitty, *supra* note 2, at para. 1–108 (citations omitted).
See also id. at paras. 3–021, 27–030.
See section VIII.C on the subject of "specific performance".
The *BLIS Glossary*, *supra* note 1, translates "injunction" as 禁制令 or 強制令.
99. *See* Chitty, *supra* note 2, at paras. 3–021, 27–034.
For one perspective of the impact of the *Stilk*; *Williams*; *UBC*; and, *D & C Builders* cases along with the more recent Hong Kong case of *Tam Moon Tong v Lucky Dragon Restaurant Ltd* (2001) DCCJ 1706/2001, [2001] HKEC 968, *see* Hall, *supra* note 3, at 166–179.

E. Equitable Estoppel

Equitable estoppel[100] is a legal doctrine which permits a defendant to plead equity as a defence in order to prevent the plaintiff from enforcing its strict legal rights under an existing contract.[101] The basis for this defence is that equity will not allow a plaintiff to enforce legal rights where the plaintiff caused [102] the defendant to suppose that the plaintiff did not intend

---

100. Some sources refer to this doctrine as "promissory estoppel".

7(2) HALSBURY'S, *supra* note 1, at para. 115.386 describes this doctrine:

> Similar to waiver is the doctrine of promissory or equitable estoppel, whereby a party who has represented that he will not insist upon his strict rights under the contract will not be allowed to resile from that position, or will be allowed to do so only upon giving reasonable notice. This principle differs from estoppel properly so called in that (1) it applies to promises, not representations of fact; (2) it is generally only suspensory in operation; and (3) it is not clear to what extent the representee need have changed his position to his detriment in reliance on the representation. (citations omitted)

Another authority states:

> Estoppel at law arises where one person makes to another a clear and unequivocal representation of existing fact with knowledge of its falsehood and with the intention that it should be acted upon. In some circumstances, failure to speak or act may amount to a representation, if there is a duty to speak or act owed to the other person. If, in these circumstances, the person to whom the representation is made acts upon it to his detriment, the person making it may not thereafter assert in any proceedings which may arise that the facts were otherwise than as he represented them to be.
>
> Equitable estoppel is more flexible, both in its initial requirements and also in its consequences, than estoppel at law. Equitable estoppel takes two forms: proprietary estoppel … and promissory estoppel. … it has been suggested that there is one simple synthesis of both forms to the effect that it would be unconscionable for a party to be permitted to deny that which, knowingly or unknowingly, he has allowed another to assume to his detriment.

22 HALSBURY'S LAWS OF HONG KONG para. 340.111 (2008) [hereinafter 22 HALSBURY'S].

See HALL, *supra* note 3, at Chapter 6 ("Estoppel").

The *BLIS Glossary*, *supra* note 2, translates "law of estoppel" as 不容反悔法.

101. "Equity" is defined in *supra* note 42.

102. This involves a representation of some type or kind.

> The basis of promissory estoppel is that one party has been led by the conduct of the other to believe that that other's strict rights under the contract will not be enforced. … a promissory estoppel can only be founded upon a clear and unambiguous promise of future action. Thus, where the party being offered a concession in respect of the terms of the contract reasonably understands the concession in one way and the party granting the concession reasonably understands it in another way there is no foundation for a promissory estoppel.

7(2) HALSBURY'S, *supra* note 1, at para. 115.388 (citations omitted). *See also supra* note 100.

to enforce those rights, and the defendant has changed its position to its detriment.[103]

In the case of *Central London Property Trust Ltd v High Trees House Ltd* [1947] KB 130, the plaintiff in 1937 granted the defendant a ninety-nine year lease for a new block of flats at a rent of £2,500 per annum. During World War II, the flats were not fully let as people left London to avoid being bombed by the Nazis. The defendant realized that the rent to the plaintiff could not be met from the profits then being made on the flats. Consequently, in 1940 the parties entered into an agreement which reduced the rent to £1,250 per annum. This agreement was in writing but not sealed. The defendant continued to pay the reduced rent from 1941 to the beginning of 1945, by which time the flats were fully let. The defendant continued to pay the reduced rent thereafter. In September 1945, the plaintiff asked for arrears of £7,916, suggesting that the liability created by the lease still existed, and that the 1940 agreement was not supported by any consideration or any seal. The court held that as the agreement for the reduction of rent had been acted upon by the defendant, the plaintiff was estopped in equity from claiming the full rent from 1941 until early 1945 when the flats were fully let. After that time, the plaintiff was entitled to do so because the second agreement was only operative during the continuance of the conditions which gave rise to it, *i.e.*, World War II. To this extent, the claim succeeded. If the plaintiff had sued for the balance of rent from 1941, the case would have failed.

In sum, in order to raise the defence of equitable estoppel:

- there must be an original agreement between the parties by which the defendant owed an obligation to the plaintiff;

---

103. For equitable estoppel to apply, there must be a representation by one party to the contract which is relied upon by the other party to the contract to its harm or disadvantage. *Id.* at para. 115.389.

See also Fisher & Greenwood, *supra* note 17, at 112–120.

In the case of *Dixie Engineering Company Ltd v Vernaltex Company Ltd (t/a Wing Wo Engineering Company)*, (2003) CACV 344/2002, the court stated:

> 81. Broken down into its component parts, the doctrine of equitable or promissory estoppel, insofar as it applies in contractual situations, consists of:
>
> (1) A clear and unequivocal representation by A to B that he will not rely on his strict contractual rights. The representation may be by words or by conduct.
>
> (2) The representation by A must be made with the intention by him "or at least the knowledge" that B will act on it.
>
> (3) B must in fact have acted in reliance on the representation.

- the plaintiff, by words or conduct, must have waived its rights under the original agreement;
- the defendant has given no consideration for the plaintiff's promises;
- the defendant has altered its position in reliance on the plaintiff's promises; and,
- it would be inequitable to allow the plaintiff to insist on the terms of the original agreement.

A recent case from the United Kingdom demonstrates the application of promissory estoppel to a situation apparently involving accord and satisfaction. *Collier v P & M J Wright (Holdings) Ltd* [2007] EWCA 1329, [2008] 1 WLR 643 seems to be at odds with the court decision in *Foakes v Beer*. Contrary to the holding in *Foakes*, the *Collier* court appears to extend the application of promissory estoppel by finding that reliance upon a creditor's promise not to sue for the whole debt renders inequitable the creditor's failure to observe that promise. *Collier* involved three business partners jointly liable to Wright. Following the partners' bankruptcy, Wright attempted to collect the total partnership debt solely from Collier. Collier argued that as Wright had promised not to pursue Collier for the full amount of the partnership debt, Collier should be able to rely upon this promise. The court decided that unlike the decision in *Foakes*, partial payment of a debt will discharge the whole debt amount if the partial payment was made in response to the creditor's agreement or promise that the partial payment would satisfy the whole outstanding amount. The court in *Collier* concluded that:

1. If a debtor offers to pay only a portion of the amount owed;
2. The creditor accepts that offer;
3. In reliance upon the creditor's acceptance, the debtor pays that agreed portion of the amount owed;
4. The creditor, by the application of promissory estoppel, will be prevented from pursuing the debtor for the outstanding balance of the debt.[104]

This court decision applies only to the UK and it is yet unknown whether Hong Kong courts would follow this precedent. Nonetheless, the *Collier* case may be considered as an example of the ever-evolving common law.

104. [2008] 1 WLR at 659.

IV. INTERPRETATION

This section is concerned with the contents or provisions of a contract. In other words, this section will review the obligations and responsibilities of the parties based upon the provisions of their legally binding relationship.

A. Certainty of Terms

The parties to a contract undertake obligations and obtain certain rights as defined in the provisions of their contract. These provisions may be expressed or implied. These terms, however, must not be so vague, uncertain or ambiguous that a court cannot give clear expression to them; otherwise the contract is void for uncertainty. The general rule is that the courts will interpret a contract and the nature of its provisions in light of the parties' intentions at the time the contract was entered into.[105]

The case of *Professional Associates v Polytek Engineering Co Ltd* [1986] HKLR 20 involved the issue of the existence of a contract between an architectural firm and several companies proposing a hotel construction project in the People's Republic of China. The joint venture company responsible for the actual construction project had yet to be created and the approval of mainland officials had yet to be obtained. The Hong Kong High Court, in finding the existence of a contract, discussed the element of certainty by referring to the case of *Scammell and Nephew Ltd v HC and JG Ouston* [1941] AC 251. The Hong Kong court stated that:

> in order for a contract to be binding the terms must be so definite that no further agreement is necessary between the parties to render them

---

105. 7(2) HALSBURY'S, *supra* note 1, at para. 115.066 on the requirement of certainty in a contract:

> The general rule is that, if the terms of an agreement are so vague or indefinite that it cannot be ascertained with reasonable certainty what is the intention of the parties, there is no contract enforceable at law. This may happen in two ways: a clause may be devoid of any meaning or have such a wide variety of meanings that it is impossible to say which of them is intended.
>
> ...
>
> The courts, however, do not expect commercial documents to be drafted with strict precision; the court will look at the document as a whole ... in construing an agreement, a court should not hold a provision to be void for uncertainty unless it cannot resolve the ambiguity ... Finally, it should be remembered that the degree of uncertainty in an agreement is a factor which may go to the question of whether or not the parties intend to create legal relations. (citations omitted)

> certain ... As a matter of law the contract price must be certain. But certainty may be achieved by more than one route. The common and simple alternative is for an express fixed contract sum to be stipulated. However, the contract price is equally certain if instead of an express fixed sum, a formula is agreed upon under which the contract price may be ascertained, without further agreement by the parties.[106]

In *New World Development Co Ltd v Sun Hung Kai Securities Ltd* [2006] 3 HKLRD 345, CFA the court explained that these principles are applicable in Hong Kong:

> The principle for deciding when an agreement is incomplete in a manner which prevents it from being a legally binding contract ...
>
> > To be a good contract there must be a concluded bargain, and a concluded contract is one which settles everything that is necessary to be settled and leaves nothing to be settled by agreement between the parties. Of course it may leave something which still has to be determined which does not depend upon the agreement between the parties.[107]
>
> It is therefore important to note that an agreement is not incomplete in this fatal sense merely because it "leaves something which still has to be determined". It is often possible for the court to discern in the parties' agreement the intended principles, criteria or machinery, express or implied, for determining specific contractual rights and liabilities without requiring the parties to arrive at further agreement. Where this is possible, the agreement is not "incomplete". ...[108]
>
> ...
>
> Similarly, an agreement may be held to fail for uncertainty. This is where the parties have expressed themselves in language that is too uncertain, vague or unintelligible to make their agreement legally enforceable. ...[109]
>
> ...

---

106. [1986] HKLR at 34.
107. [2006] 3 HKLRD at 356 citing to *May & Butcher Ltd v R* [1934] 2 KB 17, 21.
108. [2006] 3 HKLRD at 357.
109. *Id.*

    Here, the court cited to *G Scammell & Nephew Ltd v JG Ouston* [1941] AC 251, 268 for the proposition that where:

    > the language used was so obscure and so incapable of any definite or precise meaning that the court is unable to attribute to the parties any particular contractual intention. The object of the court is to do justice between the parties, and the court will do its best, if satisfied that there was an ascertainable and determinate intention to contract, to give effect to that intention ... It will not

> The courts will endeavour to find practical meaning in commercial agreements and are reluctant to strike down as too vague and uncertain agreements which businessmen have made and acted upon. ...[110]

B. Contractual Provisions

i. *Generally*

The provisions of a contract define the obligations and the rights of the parties to that contract:

> Assuming that a contract has been validly created, it is necessary to consider the extent of the obligations imposed on the parties by the contract. In order to do this, the exact terms of the contract must be determined and their comparative importance evaluated.[111]

Thus, as discussed in the preceding section, the provisions or terms of a contract must be sufficiently certain or definite so as to be enforceable in court. Moreover, a contract's provisions or terms may be placed into several categories. Parties frequently dispute the interpretation or application of the provisions of a contract. If the interpretation of a particular provision is not in dispute, the category of the provision or term might determine the type and amount of recovery an injured party may receive in the dispute or

---

> be deterred by mere difficulties of interpretation. Difficulty is not synonymous with ambiguity so long as any definite meaning can be extracted. But the test of intention is to be found in the words used.

110. [2006] 3 HKLRD at 358.
The court follows on by quoting from *Hillas & Co Ltd v Arcos Ltd* (1932) 43 Ll L Rep 359, 367 which stated:

> Business men often record the most important agreements in crude and summary fashion; modes of expression sufficient and clear to them in the course of their business may appear to those unfamiliar with the business far from complete or precise. It is accordingly the duty of the Court to construe such documents fairly and broadly, without being too astute or subtle in finding defects ... however, [this] does not means that the Court is to make a contract for the parties, or to go outside the words they have used, except in so far as there are appropriate implications of law, as, for instance, the implication of what is just and reasonable to be ascertained by the Court as a matter of machinery where the contractual intention is clear but the contract is silent on some detail.

For further discussion of this topic, *see*, *e.g*, HALL, *supra* note 3, at 123–144 and the Hong Kong cases cited therein.

111. CHITTY, *supra* note 2, at para. 12–001 (citations omitted).

the consequences a party may face for failing to comply with its contract obligations.

ii. Express Term and Implied Term

Terms may be expressed or implied. An "express term" is an expressed promise which forms an integral part of the contract.[112] Express terms usually are found in signed documents.

> When a document containing contractual terms is signed … in the absence of fraud, or … misrepresentation, the party signing it is bound, and it is wholly immaterial whether he has read the document or not.[113]

In the case of *Bank of China (Hong Kong) Ltd v Fung Chin Kan* (2002) 5 HKCFAR 515, the court stated that:

> the fundamental principle … [is] when a person signs a legal document, he or she is bound by the act of signature. As a matter of general law, it is no defence to say that he or she did not understand the contents of a legal document; that person takes the chance of being bound by its terms, as he or she can take the simple precaution of not signing until its contents have been fully explained and understood.[114]

In situations concerning unsigned documents, the situation depends on whether a party had knowledge of the unsigned writing. Generally, these situations arise where a purported term of the agreement is printed on the reverse side of a ticket or receipt. Two cases provide examples. In the case of *Ho Sang v The Hong Kong & Kowloon European Style Tailors Union* [1953–1955] HKDCLR 121, the landlord provided to the tenant with a rent receipt with a clause forbidding gambling in the premises. The District Court held

---

112. Even such a simple concept can give rise to difficulties on application as noted by 7(2) HALSBURY'S, *supra* note 1, at para. 115.147 in that:

> where there is such a contractual document, it by no means follows that that document will contain all the terms agreed between the parties. Leaving aside the possibility of implied terms, there may be (1) express oral terms, for most contracts may be made wholly or partly by word of mouth; or (2) a collateral contract.Where there is a contractual document, the question whether the agreement between the parties contains additional, or even contradictory, oral terms is one of fact, to be decided by extrinsic evidence. Once all the express terms of a contract have been ascertained, their meaning is a matter of construction. (citations omitted)

113. *L'Estrange v F Graucob Ltd* [1934] 2 KB 394, 403.
114. (2002) 5 HKCFAR at 515.

that as the rent receipt was given to the tenant only after the tenancy agreement had been concluded, the anti-gambling clause was not incorporated into the tenancy agreement.[115] On the other hand, in the case of *Li Mun Chung v East Asia Steam Laundry Co* [1961] HKDCLR 28, there was a clause limiting the dry cleaner's liability printed on the back of the receipt. The District Court found the clause to be effective and valid as the plaintiff was aware that the dry cleaner's receipt contained conditions pertaining to their legally binding agreement.[116] Further discussion of whether unsigned terms are incorporated into a written document is found in section IV.B.*iv* ("Innominate Term") and section IV.D ("Exclusion Clauses").

An "implied term" is one which the parties intended and which they would have included expressly if they had addressed their minds to the question of the term's inclusion at the time of contracting. In order for a Hong Kong court to imply a term or terms into a contract, the term(s) should be:

- reasonable and equitable;
- necessary to give effect to the contract [known as "business efficacy"[117]];
- so obvious that it "goes without saying";
- capable of clear expression; and,
- consistent with, and not contradict, any express term of the contract.[118]

Parties may insert a "merger clause" into the agreement to indicate to the courts that the written terms are the complete agreement. In other words,

---

115. Hall, *supra* note 3, at 338.

116. *Id.*

117. *Id.* at 387 explains that:

> Where a contract is silent about a matter which becomes important for the agreement to work as intended by the parties, a clause will be implied where it is necessary to give the contract business efficacy.

118. Fisher & Greenwood, *supra* note 17, at 170–171 citing to *Attorney General v Melhado Investments Ltd* [1983] HKLR 327, 329; *Shun Shing Hing Investment Co Ltd v Attorney General* [1983] HKLR 432, 440; *On Park Parking Ltd v Secretary of Justice* [2004] 3 HKC 476.
See also BP Refinery (Westernport) Pty Ltd v President, Councillors and Ratepayers of the Shire of Hastings (1977) 180 CLR 266, 16 ALR 363, PC.
See Chris Turner, Unlocking Contract Law 154 (2nd ed. 2007) for a table listing examples of contract terms implied by fact (*e.g*, previous conduct of the parties, common usage, trade custom); terms implied by law (*e.g*, consumer protection ordinances such as *Sale of Goods Ordinance*, *supra* note 66; *Supply of Services (Implied Terms) Ordinance* (Cap 457)); and, terms implied by the common law (*e.g*, *Twinkle Step Investment Ltd v Smart International Industrial Ltd* [1999] 4 HKC 441, CFA; *The Moorcock* (1889) 14 PD 64; *Liverpool City Council v Irwin* [1977] AC 239, HL).

all the provisions of the legally binding agreement have been "merged" into the written contract. A merger clause is intended to prevent one party from attempting to later supplement the contract with terms that were not originally included in the contract.

iii. Condition Term and Warranty Term

Provisions of a contract may also be classified under the heading of "condition"[119] or under the heading of "warranty".[120] In the case of *The Moorcock* (1889) 14 PD 64, the court held that the expression "conditions" refers to

---

119. For the avoidance of confusion, the definition provided by CHITTY, *supra* note 2, at para. 12–025 is adopted:

> The word "condition" is sometimes used ... to mean simply "a stipulation, a provision" and not to connote a condition in the technical sense of that word. ... The most commonly used sense of the word "condition" is that of an essential stipulation of the contract which one party guarantees is true or promises will be fulfilled. Any breach of such a stipulation entitles the innocent party, if he so chooses, to treat himself as discharged from further performance of the contract, and notwithstanding that he has suffered no prejudice by the breach. He can also claim damages for any loss suffered. (citations omitted)

It is further noted in *id.* at para. 12–027:

> A condition in the sense mentioned above may conveniently be termed a "promissory" condition, being a promise or assurance for the non-performance of which a right of action accrues to the innocent party. This sense must be carefully distinguished from that of a "contingent" condition, *i.e.* a provision that on the happening of some uncertain event an obligation shall come into force, or that an obligation shall not come into force until such an event happens. (citations omitted)

Finally, note that there are two uses of the word "condition" in contract law. A condition of the type discussed above can be regarded as a promise, the breach of which allows the innocent party to sue. This meaning is different from that of a "contingent condition". If a contract requires an event to occur, but no party promises that the event will occur, then it is a contingent condition to the party's performance under the contract. The contingent condition is a provision that on the happening of some event an obligation or the contract shall come into force. This contingent condition is termed a "condition precedent". For example, a building contract can be agreed by the parties but is made contingent upon the government's issuance of permits. The issuance of the government permits is the condition precedent. Once the permits are issued, the condition is met and a legally binding agreement comes into effect. *See, e.g.*, *id.* at paras. 12–026 to 12–029; *Ian Hung Wai v Cheung Sau Kuen*, *supra* note 79.

A related concept is a "condition subsequent". A provision may provide that an obligation or the contract is ended, without any fault of either party, if a condition does not continue to be satisfied. Thus, if the specified condition subsequent occurs, the contract is ended. A party may waive this condition if it is inserted solely for the party's own benefit. This is demonstrated in the case of:

the significant provisions of a contract. A condition is a term which goes to the basis of the contract, to the whole of the consideration. "Warranties" refer to lesser provisions of a contract. A warranty is only part of the consideration.

> The predominant modern approach is to consider the nature of the terms of the contract in order to decide whether those terms are conditions or warranties. ... a breach of condition entitles the innocent party to rescind the contract and claim damages for any loss he may have suffered, whereas a breach of warranty only entitles him to damages.[121]

Failure to perform by an agreed deadline is usually not a material or substantial breach of the contract. However, if the date fixed in the contract is expressly made "time of the essence" by the parties, the failure to comply with this stipulation is a material breach. If the contract does not contain a deadline, the time for performance is whatever will be reasonable under the circumstances. An unreasonable delay in performance can constitute a material breach. In determining the reasonableness of the time of performance, the court will examine:

- the parties' intent;
- whether the parties have acted in good faith; and,
- any hardship to the aggrieved party caused by the failure to fulfil the contract in time.

> *Head v Tattersall* where A bought a horse from B which B warranted to have been hunted with the Bicester hounds. If it did not answer its description, A was to have the right to return it by a certain day. The horse did not answer its description and A accordingly returned it before the day. In the meantime, however, the horse had been injured without A's fault. It was held that the injury did not cause A to lose his right to return the horse and he could recover the purchase price paid. (citations omitted)

Id. at para. 12–030.

The *BLIS Glossary*, *supra* note 2, translates "condition precedent" as 先決條件; "concurrent conditions" as 同時履行的條件; "condition subsequent" as 後決條件; and, "contingent" as 或有的.

120. CHITTY, *supra* note 2, at para. 12–031 states that in:

> its most technical sense, however, it is to be understood as meaning a term of the contract, the breach of which may give rise to a claim for damages but not a right to treat the contract as repudiated. The use of the word "warranty" in this sense is reserved for the less important terms of a contract, or those which are collateral to the main purpose of the contract, the breach of which by one party does not entitle the other to treat his obligations as discharged. (citations omitted)

121. 7(2) HALSBURY'S, *supra* note 1, at para. 115.352 (citations omitted).

iv. *Innominate Term*

As will be further detailed below in section IV.C, the contemporary approach to these two traditional categories of terms of a contract includes another category of contract provisions. This head is known as an "intermediate" term or "innominate" term. "Innominate" means without a name.[122] A term is likely to be classified as "intermediate" if it is capable of being broken either: in a manner that is trivial and capable of remedy by an award of damages; or, in a manner that is so fundamental as to undermine the whole contract.[123] Depending upon the type and the consequences of a breach, the innocent party may or may not be discharged from the contract.[124]

A "representation" is the title given to a statement made to tempt or to persuade a party into making a contract.[125] As such, representations do not form part of the contract and the legal consequences are different.

---

122. CHUI & ROEBUCK, *supra* note 3, at para. 4.9.2.
Another authority explains that the consequences:

> depend not upon any prior classification of the undertaking as a condition or warranty but upon the effect of the breach. If the breach deprives the innocent party of substantially the whole benefit of the contract, or, in other words, if it goes so much to the root of the contract that it makes further commercial performance of the contract impossible, in addition to any remedy in damages the innocent party will be entitled to be discharged from further obligation; but if the event does not have that effect its consequences can be remedied only by an award of damages. However, though such 'innominate' terms occupy a large category of contractual undertakings, they have not replaced the traditional classification into conditions and warranties in those areas where such a division has been made by statue or judicial decision; that classification has the merit of predictability, which is important in relation to contractual clauses in common use.

7(2) HALSBURY'S, *supra* note 1, at para. 115.354 (citations omitted).

123. CHITTY, *supra* note 2, at para. 12–035.
See also FURMSTON, *supra* note 45, at 196–202.

124. CHITTY, *supra* note 2, at para. 12–020.

125. As explained by 7(2) HALSBURY'S, *supra* note 1, at para. 115.144:

> During the course of the formation of a contract, one of the persons who are to become parties to the contract may make representations to another such person. A representation is a statement made by one party (the representor) to another party (the representee) which relates, by way of affirmation, denial, description or otherwise, to a matter of fact or present intention.
>
> A representation of fact may or may not be intended to have contractual force; if it is so intended, it will amount to a contractual term; if it is not so intended, it is termed a mere representation.

The *BLIS Glossary*, *supra* note 2, translates "representation" as 陳述.

Accordingly, determining the difference between a statement which is a condition and one which is a representation becomes necessary.

> Basically, the problem is one of determining the intention of the parties as evidenced by their words and conduct, so that no general principal of interpretation can be universally true. Because, however, the intention of the parties seldom clearly appears, the courts have had regard to any one or more of a number of factors for attributing an intention.[126]

"Puff" refers to statements which neither party takes seriously. Puff may be considered to be the equivalent of the sales pitch made by a sales clerk to entice a customer to purchase an item.[127] Puff does not have any legal force.

A notable example in Hong Kong relates to estate agents' advertising where it is generally accepted that descriptions should not be taken literally. Attempts to sell new properties on the Pokfulam coast may feature photographs of apartments on the Mediterranean with the justification that what is being indicated is a "concept". Such behaviour is so widespread that it is fair to say that few Hong Kong people would take the images seriously. This view was given judicial support in *Chan Yeuk Yu & Another v Church Body of the Hong Kong Sheng Kung Hui & Another* where Burrell J, dealing with the words "regal surroundings for the select few" stated:

> ... taken in its context, namely on page 4 of a 27-page glossy and colourful sales brochure, I find it difficult to conclude that it is any more than "mere puff" or "sales pitch["].[128]

Whether a statement is a term (either a condition or a warranty); representation; or, puff depends upon the parties' intentions—whether the parties intended a statement to be a term, representation or puff under the circumstances in which the contract was made. Some guidelines are available to assist in classifying these statements:[129]

---

126. 7(2) Halsbury's, *supra* note 1, at para. 115.145 (citations omitted). An example of the factors for attributing an intention is set out in *id*.

127. Chui & Roebuck, *supra* note 3, at para. 4.3 notes:

> We have to allow for what is known as "trader"s puff'. ...
>
> One rule of thumb is that when the remark concerns facts which can be checked, it is more likely to be a representation. So if a car salesman says "this car has only had one owner", this cannot possibly be a mere puff, for a statement of fact is being made. If he says "this is a delightful little car", that sounds more like a puff.

128. Fisher & Greenwood, *supra* note 17, at 221.

129. *See* 7(2) Halsbury's, *supra* note 1, at para. 115.145; Chitty, *supra* note 2, at para. 12–003.

- Time: If a statement was made at the beginning of long negotiations and not repeated, it is likely to be a representation. If a statement was made repeatedly or emphasized near the conclusion of negotiations, it is likely to be a term.
- Importance: Occasionally this criterion overlaps with the time guideline. If a statement is made at the beginning of negotiations and not mentioned again, it is likely to be a representation. However, a statement may set the parameters of negotiations, in which case, it may be a term. For example, if great stress was placed upon a particular aspect of the negotiations, that matter may become a term.[130]
- Expertise of parties: A statement made by a person with special knowledge is more likely to be a term.
- Writing: With a written contract, the document is presumed to contain all the terms; any omitted statements are presumed to be representations.

The significance of how the statements are classified is found in the difference in remedies available to the injured party in the event of a breach:

- Breach of a contractual term may result in damages or specific performance. A breach of condition results in the innocent party having the right to terminate the agreement as well as the right to sue for damages. Should the innocent party terminate the contract, it does not need to fulfil its own duties under the agreement and may retain any benefit, so long as the agreement was terminated and notice given of the termination within reasonable time. In addition, the innocent party may sue for damages for the loss suffered. Alternatively, the innocent party may affirm the contract rather than terminate the contract. In such a case, the innocent party may also sue for damages, treating the breach of condition as a breach of warranty. A breach of a warranty results in the innocent party having the right to damages. The innocent party has no right to terminate the contract.
- Misrepresentation may result in rescission under the common law or in damages under statutory law.
- Puff which is untrue does not allow recovery.

130. In *Bannerman v White* (1861) 9 WR 784, the defendant intended to purchase grain from the plaintiff. During the negotiations, the defendant stated that he would not purchase any grain grown using sulphur. The plaintiff stated that no sulphur had been used in the cultivation, although, in fact, sulphur was used in growing the grain. The parties then entered into the contract for the sale and purchase of the grain. The court held that the plaintiff's assurance amounted to a term of the contract.

131. CHUI & ROEBUCK, *supra* note 3, at para. 4.7.

C. Judicial Interpretation and Application of Contract Terms

The general rule is that courts will interpret a contract according to the parties' intentions at the time the contract was made. "The contract is to be construed so as to find and give effect to the intentions of the parties to it."[131] Intention is to be found from the contract itself upon a proper construction of its terms as a whole, according to the decision in *Suisse Atlantique Société d'Armement Maritime SA v NV Rotterdamsche Kolen Centrale* [1967] AC 361. As one authority has noted:

> The cardinal presumption is that the parties have intended what they have in fact said, so that their words must be construed as they stand. ... the meaning of the document or of a particular part of it is to be sought *in the document itself*: "One must consider the meaning of the words used, not what one may guess to be the intention of the parties". However, this is not to say that the meaning of the words in a written document must be ascertained by reference to the words of the document alone. ... the courts will ... look at all the circumstances surrounding the making of the contract which would assist in determining how the language of the document would have been understood by a reasonable man.
>
> Further it has long been accepted that the courts will not approach the task of construction with too nice a concentration upon individual words.[132]

In matters concerning the interpretation of a contract, one should note the *contra proferentem* rule which states that courts will interpret any ambiguous contract provisions against the party who drafted the agreement.[133]

---

132. CHITTY, *supra* note 2, at paras. 12–043 to 12–044 (emphasis in original) (citations omitted).
As for the general rules of construction or interpretation used by the courts, *see id.* at paras. 12–045 to 12–094.

133. As explained by one source:

> *Contra* means against, and *proferentem* is a neat way of referring to the person relying on the document—that is, the drafter of it, the *proferens*. Any ambiguities are construed against the *proferens*. That is, the drafter never gets the benefit of any doubt.

CHUI & ROEBUCK, *supra* note 3, at para. 4.7.

KRISHNAN ARJUNAN & ABDUL MAJID BIN NABI BAKSH, BUSINESS LAW IN HONG KONG (2nd ed. 2009) [hereinafter ARJUNAN & NABI BAKSH] translates "*contra proferentem*" as 不利於提出合約的一方.

See, e.g., *Link Folk Ltd v Glorious Motors Ltd* [2011] HKEC 1237, DC.

The purpose in a judicial interpretation of contract provisions is to determine the importance which the parties to the contract had attached to these terms. This classification then assists in determining the consequences of a breach of those contract provisions. The type of breach determines the remedies available to the injured party.[134]

The seriousness of the consequences of a breach should serve as the determining factor in whether the breach was fundamental or minor.[135] If the breach is determined to be fundamental, the innocent party may treat its obligations under that contract as discharged and may also sue for damages. If the breach is considered to be minor, neither party may consider their obligations under that contract to be discharged until performance is completed. A court will then award damages upon proof of the breach.

The case of *Hong Kong Fir Shipping Co v Kawasaki Kisen Kaisha* [1962] 2 QB 26 sets out the current approach towards applying the intermediate or innominate term approach to interpret the provisions of a contract. Rather

---

134. *See*, *e.g*, 7(2) HALSBURY'S, *supra* note 1, at para. 115.145.

135. *Id.* at para. 115.355 explains:

> The terminology of "fundamental breach" and "breach of a fundamental term", which was originally adopted to deal with problems created by wide exclusion clauses, has also been brought into service to determine whether a breach of contract is sufficiently serious to justify the innocent party in treating himself as discharged from further obligations under the contract.
>
> There will be a fundamental breach … entitling the innocent party to be discharged, if the breach has produced a situation fundamentally different from anything which the parties could, as reasonable men, have contemplated when the contract was made. … a fundamental term is no more than a condition, that is a term which the parties have agreed either expressly or impliedly which goes to the root of the contract, so that any breach of that term … will allow the innocent party to treat himself as discharged. (citations omitted)

CHITTY, *supra* note 2, at para. 12–021 states:

> The fundamental term has been described as part of the "core" of the contract, the non-performance of which destroys the very substance of the agreement.
>
> …
>
> …
>
> Examples usually cited are those where a seller delivers goods wholly different from the agreed contract goods or delivers goods which are so seriously defective as to render them in substance not the goods contracted for: *e.g* the delivery of beans instead of peas, of pinewood logs instead of mahogany logs, or of a vehicle which is incapable or barely capable of self-propulsion instead of a motor car. In each case, so it is said, there is a breach of the fundamental term, that is to say, of the "core" obligation to deliver the essential goods which are the subject-matter of the contract of sale. (citations omitted)

than automatically classifying the breach as one of condition or of warranty, use of the innominate term seeks to be more flexible by recognising that the remedy for the breach will depend on the effect of the breach. This test considers all factors, including the circumstances involved in the contract's breach, in determining whether the innocent party has been deprived of the contract's benefits. If the answer is in the affirmative, the breach is treated as a breach of condition. If the answer is in the negative, the breach is treated as a breach of warranty.[136] Thus, the legal ramifications depend on the consequences flowing from the breach and do not follow automatically from a prior classification of the undertaking as a condition or as a warranty.

In *Hong Kong Fir Shipping*, the owners of a ship chartered the vessel to the defendants for 24 months from February 1957 under an agreement which provided: "She [the ship] being in every way fitted for ordinary cargo service." The owners also agreed to maintain the ship "in a thoroughly efficient state." At the time of delivery, the ship's engine room was undermanned and the staff incompetent. Upon the ship's arrival at one destination in May 1957, the defendants discovered that repairs to make the ship seaworthy would take 15 weeks. The charterers wrote to the ship owners in June 1957 repudiating the agreement because of the owners' breaches of contract, alleging the failure to provide a seaworthy ship and the negligent failure to maintain the ship in a proper state. The ship became seaworthy in September 1957. The Court of Appeal held that the breaches did not entitle the charterers to repudiate the contract since neither the unseaworthiness nor the delay entitled them to do so. The unseaworthiness and failure to maintain were not breaches of conditions and had not in this case caused damage which went to the root of the contract. Furthermore, the delay had not frustrated the venture's commercial purpose.

One reason for this decision seems to be that courts are generally reluctant to allow a party to repudiate a contract as a means of evading a bad bargain. It appears that the charterer in *Hong Kong Fir Shipping* was motivated to repudiate the contract because freight rates had fallen since the commencement of the charterparty[137] and the charterer could have thus chartered other ships more inexpensively. Moreover, the evidence did not show that the charterer had suffered any loss because the contract provided that the charterer did not have to pay hire for the ship while it was

---

136. Chui & Roebuck, *supra* note 3, at para. 4.9.2.
137. The *BLIS Glossary*, *supra* note 2, translates "charterparty" as 租船合約.

undergoing repairs. Furthermore, during the repair period, the charterer could have sent the goods at lower freight rates.[138]

In the case of *Cehave NV v Bremer Handelsgesellschaft mbH (The Hansa Nord)* [1976] 1 QB 44 the defendants sold citrus pulp pellets to the plaintiffs. A contract provision stated "shipment to be made in good condition". The goods were delivered in several consignments, and when a particular consignment arrived at Rotterdam the market price of the goods had fallen. Of the total consignment of 3,293 tonnes, there were 1,260 tonnes which suffered damaged. The plaintiffs rejected the whole cargo on the basis that the shipment was not made in good condition and claimed for recovery of the sale price of £100,000. A middleman purchased the goods for £33,720 and resold them to the plaintiffs at that price. The plaintiffs used the pellets to make cattle food, as originally intended. This transaction resulted in the plaintiffs receiving goods for which they had agreed to pay £100,000 at the reduced price of £33,720. The Court of Appeal decided in favour of the sellers. The court held that the contractual term "shipment to be made in good condition" was not a condition, but rather was an intermediate term. As the court said:

> If a small portion of the whole cargo was not in good condition and arrived a little unsound, it should be met by a price allowance. The buyer should not have the right to reject the whole lot unless the divergence was serious or substantial.[139]

D. Exclusion Clauses

Because of the liability involved in a breach of contract, parties have attempted to limit or eliminate their liability through the use of contractual provisions commonly known as "limitation", "exclusion" or "exemption" clauses.[140] Exclusion clauses exempt a party from certain liability which

---

138. *See, e.g.*, SMITH AND KEENAN, *supra* note 33, at 350 for further discussion of the different categories of contract provisions. The *Hong Kong Fir Shipping* case is discussed in SMITH AND KEENAN's 6th ed. (1989) at 650.

139. [1976] 1 QB at 61.

140. Contractual clauses which attempt to limit liability are referred to under various names.

> Though "exemption clause" is perhaps the most popular, clauses attempting to restrict liability have many names. "Limitation clause" is the term usually used to indicate that remedies have been cut down, not out completely. Typically, such a clause will say that claims will be restricted in type or amount. ... A laundry may accept your clothes only on terms that they will be liable for $100 or the full amount of the loss—whichever is the less. ...

may arise from a contract. The parties may include a provision which excludes liability for a specified breach or which otherwise limits liability in some way. Under the common law, such clauses must be strictly proved. If an exclusion clause can be invalidated or limited in its application, a court will often do so on the grounds of public policy.[141] The reason for this attitude is because these clauses deny the availability of legal remedies to the injured party. The *contra proferentem* rule of interpretation allows the courts to construe any ambiguity of an exemption clause against the party who inserted the clause and who later seeks to rely on this provision. Thus, under public policy, one party may not contract away liability for conduct that is a reckless disregard for the rights of others, or for intentional torts or gross negligence.

Where an exemption clause is contained in an unsigned document and/or notice, the following considerations are important in determining the clause's applicability:

- Did the document or notice form part of the contract? It is important to determine how and when the contract was made; the offer and acceptance approach may assist in making this determination. For example, a ticket which comes as a receipt, after the contract is made, cannot be part of that contract and cannot impose contractual terms. In another example, a notice on the inside of a hotel room door cannot exclude the hotel from its liability for negligence as the guest's registration takes place at the front desk, well before a guest enters the hotel room.
- Where the document or notice form's part of the contract terms, there nevertheless may be an issue over the adequacy of the notice to the other party. Unless clear notice of the exclusion clause existed at the time the contract was concluded, and assuming no previous course of dealing between these parties or assuming no basis for deeming

---

An "exclusion clause" suggests that no claim will be entertained. For example, the words "No responsibility is taken for any loss, damage or injury howsoever caused" may be found on a notice at the entrance to a car park. They clearly envisage that you will have no claim at all.

"Exception clause" is sometimes used instead of "exemption", but does not seem to have any different meaning. You can normally use exemption or exception clause to mean a limitation or exclusion clause.

CHUI AND ROEBUCK, *supra* note 3, at para. 8.4.

LEXISNEXIS, HONG KONG ENGLISH-CHINESE LEGAL DICTIONARY 718, 1123 (2005) [hereinafter LEXISNEXIS] translates "exemption clause" as 免責條款and "limitation clause" as 限制條款 respectively.

See, e.g., *Link Folk Ltd v Glorious Motors Ltd*, *supra* note 133.

141. The *BLIS Glossary*, *supra* note 2, translates "public policy" as 公共政策.

knowledge in the circumstances, a court will usually find the exclusion clause to be invalid. Whether a clause constitutes sufficient notice is a question of fact, but the more unusual the terms of an exclusion clause, the more explicit the warning must be.

- Where there has been a previous course of dealing between the parties, it may be that the exclusion clause will be deemed to be part of the contract and be valid, even where notice would be too late or inadequate in the usual case. The reason is that notice is only relevant where there is a lack of knowledge of the contract terms. A prior course of dealing implies knowledge of the contract provisions.[142]

---

142. 7(2) HALSBURY'S, *supra* note 1, at para. 115.166 provides in detail:

> For an exclusion clause to be incorporated into a contract, the party against whom it is to operate must be given reasonable notice of its existence. Whether such notice has been given is determined according to the following principles:
>
> (1) If the party against whom the clause operates has actual knowledge of the clause at the time when the contract is concluded he is inevitably bound by it.
>
> (2) When there is no actual knowledge, the party against whom the clause operates will not be bound if he has no reason to believe that the document containing the clause contained contractual terms.
>
> (3) If the party against whom the clause operates has reason to believe that a document given to him contains contractual terms he may be bound by those terms, including any exclusion clause, even though he does not choose to read the document; if the document contains what is reasonably necessary to bring the terms to the attention of a reader, the recipient will be bound, but he will not be bound if it does not do so.
>
> (4) If the party putting forward the exclusion clause in his favour (the proferens) has done that which is normally sufficient to give reasonable notice of the clause, it may bind the other party even though, due to some personal disability, he is unable to understand the clause. It may be, however, that if such disability is known to the party seeking to impose the exclusion clause he must take such further steps as are reasonable to bring the clause to the notice of the person under the disability.
>
> (5) It may be that the more onerous the consequences of the exclusion clause for the party on whom it is imposed, the more forceful must be the notice which he is given of it.
>
> (6) In the absence of fraud or misrepresentation a party will be bound by an exclusion clause in a document which he has signed, provided at least that the document appeared to be of a contractual nature and that the term was capable of exclusion.
>
> (7) If the effect of an exclusion clause is misrepresented by the party seeking to impose it, or by his agent, he will be held to the meaning of the clause as represented; and a similar principle applies where that party or his agent gives a collateral assurance that varies or extinguishes the effect of the exclusion clause. (citations omitted)

The case of *Thornton v Shoe Lane Parking Ltd* [1971] 2 QB 163 demonstrates the application of some of these rules. The plaintiff paid a fee and then received a ticket upon entering the car park. On the reverse side of the ticket was a clause excluding liability for personal injuries to customers. The plaintiff was injured and sued the defendant who relied upon the exclusion clause. The court determined that this exclusion clause came too late to be part of the contract. As the court stated:

> The customer pays his money and gets a ticket. He cannot refuse it. He cannot get his money back. He may protest to the machine, even swear at it. But it will remain unmoved. He is committed beyond recall. He was committed at the very moment when he put his money into the machine. The contract was concluded at that time. It can be translated into offer and acceptance in this way: the offer is made when the proprietor of the machine holds it out as being ready to receive the money. The acceptance takes place when the customer puts his money into the slot. The terms of the offer are contained in the notice placed on or near the machine stating what is offered for the money. The customer is bound by those terms as long as they are sufficiently brought to his notice before hand but not otherwise. He is not bound by the terms printed on the ticket if they differ from the notice, because the ticket comes too late.[143]

Exemption clauses contained in signed documents are treated differently. The general rule is that a party who signs a document is bound by its signature. A party is presumed to know the contents of a document that the party has signed.[144] An example of an effective exemption clause may be found in the case of *Ying Wei (Hop Yick) Cargo Service v Nanyang Credit Card Co Ltd* [1993] 1 HKC 56. The defendant contracted to hoist the plaintiff's computer equipment up to its fifth floor offices. In the course of being hoisted, the computer equipment fell to the fourth floor, damaging the equipment. The contract between the parties provided that "price not included [*sic*] insurance charges"; that insurance against damage should be covered by Nanyang Credit Card Co Ltd; and, that "not [*sic*] damage claim to our company for this hoisting operation."

The credit card company sued for breach of contract, tort and bailment. The defendant relied on the exemption clause. The credit card company argued that:

143. [1971] 2 QB at 169.
144. *Id.*

- the contract phrase "hoisting operation" was unclear and should only cover proper hoisting, *i.e.*, without negligence;
- the contract phrase "not damage claim" was not clear and should cover only pure consequential or economic loss as opposed to physical damage to the equipment itself; and,
- the clause in the contract was unclear because it was not grammatical and not even a sentence.

The court rejected these arguments, holding that the exemption clause was clear enough to exempt any damage claim against the defendant in respect of the hoisting operation even if the clause were construed *contra proferentem* against the defendant. Although the clause did not expressly exclude liability based on negligence, "it is difficult to see that the parties could not have had in mind primarily claims for negligence."[145] This view is reinforced by the fact that the contract required the plaintiff to procure insurance.

Legislation may place certain restrictions upon the effect of exemption clauses. Other jurisdictions have enacted laws to restrict the application of exclusion clauses, particularly in consumer contracts. In Hong Kong, statutory control of such clauses is minimal. The principal statute controlling exclusion clauses is contained in the *Control of Exemption Clauses Ordinance* (Cap 71) which states its purpose as:

> To limit the extent to which civil liability for breach of contract, or for negligence or other breach of duty, can be avoided by means of contract terms and otherwise ...[146]

This law generally applies to business liability. According to section 2(1) of the Ordinance:

> "business" (業務) includes a profession and the activities of a public body, a public authority, or a board, commission, committee or other body appointed by the Chief Executive or Government.

Section 2(2) provides:

> In the case of both contract and tort, sections 7 to 12 apply ... only to business liability, that is liability for breach of obligations or duties arising-

145. [1993] 1 HKC at 59.

146. For a summary of the provisions in this ordinance, *see* BUTTERWORTHS HONG KONG CONTRACT LAW HANDBOOK 248–249 (2nd ed. 2006).

> (a) from things done or omitted to be done by a person in the course of a business (whether his own business or another's); or
> (b) from the occupation of premises used for business purposes of the occupier,
>
> and references to liability are to be read accordingly; but liability of an occupier of premises for breach of an obligation or duty towards a person obtaining access to the premises for recreational or educational purposes, being liability for loss or damage suffered by reason of the dangerous state of the premises, is not a business liability of the occupier unless granting that person such access for the purposes concerned falls within the business purposes of the occupier.

The provisions of this Ordinance generally apply where one of the parties enters into a contract as a consumer or uses the other party's standard printed form.[147] However, for the sake of completeness, note the application of the *Control of Exemption Clauses Ordinance* does not apply to contracts such as:

- insurance;
- those affecting the disposition of land;
- those concerning intellectual property;
- those affecting the creation or dissolution of companies; or,
- those pertaining to the creation or transfer of securities.[148]

Where the *Control of Exemption Clauses Ordinance* does apply, the statute imposes two major restrictions upon the use of exclusion provisions. The first limitation is the prohibition against the use of exemption clauses to avoid liability for injury or death. Section 7(1) of this ordinance provides:

---

147. 7(2) HALSBURY'S, *supra* note 1, at para. 115.186.
See section 8 of the *Control of Exemption Clauses Ordinance* (Cap 71), which provides:

> (1) This section applies as between contracting parties where one of them deals as consumer or on the other's written standard terms of business.
> (2) As against that party, the other cannot by reference to any contract term-
> (a) when himself in breach of contract, exclude or restrict any liability of his in respect of the breach; or
> (b) claim to be entitled—
> (i) to render a contractual performance substantially different from that which was reasonably expected of him;
> (ii) or in respect of the whole or any part of his contractual obligation, to render no performance at all,
>
> except in so far as (in any of the cases mentioned above in this subsection) the contract term satisfies the requirement of reasonableness.

148. *Control of Exemption Clauses Ordinance*, *supra* note 147, at Schedule 1.

> A person cannot by reference to any contract term or to a notice given to persons generally or to particular persons exclude or restrict his liability for death or personal injury resulting from negligence.

The other major restriction upon the use of exemption clauses pertains to the reasonableness of the exclusion.[149] In other words, in order for an exemption clause to be valid, the clause must be reasonable. The guidelines

---

149. *See, e.g., id.* at section 3 which provides in relevant part:

(1) … the requirement of reasonableness for the purposes of this Ordinance and section 4 of the Misrepresentation Ordinance (Cap 284) is satisfied only if the court … determines that the term was a fair and reasonable one … having regard to the circumstances … when the contract was made.

(2) In determining … whether a contract term satisfies the requirement of reasonableness, the court … shall have regard in particular to the matters specified in Schedule 2; but this subsection does not prevent the court … from holding, in accordance with any rule of law, that a term which purports to exclude or restrict any relevant liability is not a term of the contract.

(3) In relation to a notice (not being a notice having contractual effect), the requirement of reasonableness under this Ordinance is satisfied only if the court … determines that it would be fair and reasonable to allow reliance on it, having regard to all the circumstances …

(4) In determining (under this Ordinance or the Misrepresentation Ordinance (Cap 284)) whether a contract term or notice satisfies the requirement of reasonableness, the court … shall have regard in particular … to whether … the language in which the term or notice is expressed is a language understood by the person as against whom another person seeks to rely upon the term or notice.

(5) Where by reference to a contract term or notice a person seeks to restrict liability to a specified sum of money, and the question arises (under this Ordinance or the Misrepresentation Ordinance (Cap 284)) whether the term or notice satisfies the requirement of reasonableness, the court … shall have regard in particular (but without prejudice to subsection (2) or (4)) to-

(a) the resources which he could expect to be available to him for the purpose of meeting the liability should it arise; and

(b) how far it was open to him to cover himself by insurance.

See id. at Schedule 2 which provides additional guidelines for determining "reasonableness":

(a) the strength of the bargaining positions of the parties relative to each other, taking into account (among other things) alternative means by which the customer's requirements could have been met;

(b) whether the customer received an inducement to agree to the term, or in accepting it had an opportunity of entering into a similar contract with other persons, but without having to accept a similar term;

(c) whether the customer knew or ought reasonably to have known of the existence and extent of the term (having regard, among other things, to any custom of the trade and any previous course of dealing between the parties);

for reasonableness are set out in section 3 and in Schedule 2 of the statute. This test of reasonableness is flexible and will depend upon the facts of each case.

Further, this Ordinance also prevents:

- making the liability or its enforcement subject to restrictive or onerous conditions;
- excluding or restricting any right or remedy in respect of the liability, or subjecting a person to any prejudice in consequence of his pursuing any such right or remedy; and,
- excluding or restricting rules of evidence or procedure.[150]

Other examples of statutory control of exemption clauses may be found in the:

- *Sale of Goods Ordinance* (Cap 26) section 57;[151]
- *Misrepresentation Ordinance* (Cap 284) section 4;[152] and,
- *Supply of Services (Implied Terms) Ordinance* (Cap 457) section 8.[153]

(d) where the term excludes or restricts any relevant liability if some condition is not complied with, whether it was reasonable at the time of the contract to expect that compliance with that condition would be practicable;

(e) whether the goods were manufactured, processed or adapted to the special order of the customer.

150. 7(2) HALSBURY'S, *supra* note 1, at para. 115.196.

151. The ordinance states in part:

(1) Where any right, duty or liability would arise under a contract of sale of goods by implication of law, it may (subject to the Control of Exemption Clauses Ordinance (Cap 71)) be negatived or varied by express agreement, or by the course of dealing between the parties, or by usage if the usage is such as to bind both parties to the contract.

(2) An express condition or warranty does not negative a condition or warranty implied by this Ordinance unless inconsistent therewith.

Sale of Goods Ordinance, *supra* note 66, at section 57.

152. This section is entitled "Avoidance of provision excluding liability for misrepresentation" and sets out the following:

If a contract contains a term which would exclude or restrict-

(a) any liability to which a party to a contract may be subject by reason of any misrepresentation made by him before the contract was made; or

(b) any remedy available to another party to the contract by reason of such a misrepresentation,

that term shall be of no effect except in so far as it satisfies the requirement of reasonableness as stated in section 3(1) of the Control of Exemption Clauses Ordinance (Cap 71); and it is for the person claiming that the term satisfies that requirement to show that it does.

Misrepresentation Ordinance (Cap 284) section 4.

153. The relevant provision provides:

E. Void for Uncertainty

A contract is void for uncertainty in instances where the contract terms are so vague, uncertain or ambiguous that a court cannot give clear expression to the terms. Courts will generally do their utmost to give expression to a contract, as there is a presumption that the parties intended the agreement to have effect. However, courts will not make a contract for the parties. Thus, courts may imply terms based on the supposed intention of parties, or based on trade custom or from a previous course of dealing between the parties. If a court does not have some acceptable basis to uphold a contract, the court will not do so. Note for reference that some contract terms are implied by statute, *e.g.*, the *Sale of Goods Ordinance* (Cap 26).

V. VITIATING FACTORS

This section presents the ways in which a legally binding agreement may be set aside, *i.e.*, made void or voidable.[154] This is known as "vitiating a contract" and the bases for doing so are known as "vitiating factors". The grounds for vitiating a contract concern a party's ability to enter knowingly and voluntarily into a legally binding agreement, for among the

---

> (1) As against a party to a contract for the supply of a service who deals as consumer, the other party cannot, by reference to any contract term, exclude or restrict any liability of his arising under the contract by virtue of this Ordinance.
>
> (2) Except as provided in subsection (1), where a right, duty or liability would arise under a contract for the supply of a service by virtue of this Ordinance, it may (subject to subsection (3) and the Control of Exemption Clauses Ordinance (Cap 71)) be negatived or varied by express agreement, or by the course of dealing between the parties, or by such usage as binds both parties to the contract.
>
> (3) An express term does not negative a term implied by this Ordinance unless inconsistent with it.

Supply of Services (Implied Terms) Ordinance, *supra* note 118, at section 8.

154. Note the differences between a "void" contract, a "voidable" contract and an "unenforceable" contract. A void contract has no legal effect. Strictly speaking, no contract has ever come into existence. For example, at common law, a contract formed by mistake is void. A voidable contract is valid until any party thereto raises a vitiating factor and wants to avoid it. A contract involving misrepresentation is an example of a voidable contract. An unenforceable contract is a valid contract but because of some reason the parties cannot enforce the contractual rights/duties by court action, *e.g.*, contract (not for necessity) with a minor or oral contract for sale of land. Ho, *supra* note 13, at 144.
Another source explains:

requirements for a valid contract is the capacity and the intent to enter into the agreement.

A. Lack of Capacity

This refers to the legal ability, competency, or fitness of a party to enter and be bound by a contract. A "party" may be a natural person, *i.e.*, an individual or a group of individuals. A "party" may also be a legal person, *i.e.*, a legal entity such as a company. A party to a legally binding agreement must have the ability to enter into a contract.[155] Without the ability to enter into a legally binding relationship, the party is considered to lack capacity. The general rule is that the law presumes that everyone has the capacity to contract unless falling within one of the following categories:

- a minor;[156]
- a person who is mentally disturbed;[157] or,
- a person who is intoxicated.

> The distinction between unenforceable and void agreements is potentially important. For instance, a landlord's claim for outstanding rent must fail if it is made under a lease which is unenforceable for non-conformity with section 3(1) of the Conveyancing and Property Ordinance. Equally, a tenant cannot recover rent already paid under the same lease merely because it does not conform to section 3(1); the lease will be legally valid and available as a defence, even if it is unenforceable. Similarly a vendor of land can resist a claim brought by a defaulting purchaser for return of a deposit on the purchase price notwithstanding the failure of the contract of sale to comply with the legislative requirements as to writing. A contract in non-compliance with section 3(1) is, therefore, available as a shield but not as a sword.

HALL, *supra* note 3, at 36.

The *BLIS Glossary*, *supra* note 2, translates "void" as 無效; "voidable" as 可使無效; and, "unenforceable" as 不能強制執行.

155. One source notes:

> In general, a valid contract may be made by any person recognised by law as having legal personality, that is natural persons, corporations and the Hong Kong Special Administrative Region. However, the following classes of persons are in law incompetent to contract, or are only capable of contracting to a limited extent or in a particular manner: (1) bankrupts; (2) minors; (3) persons of unsound mind; (4) alien enemies; (5) drunkards; (6) corporations; (7) companies; (8) partnerships; and (9) receivers of companies.

7(2) HALSBURY'S, *supra* note 1, at para. 115.025 (citations omitted).

156. *Interpretation and General Clauses Ordinance* (Cap 1) section 3, states in part: "'adult' (成人、成年人) means a person who has attained the age of 18 years".

See also *Age of Majority (Related Provisions) Ordinance* (Cap 410) section 2, which states in part: "a person shall attain full age on attaining the age of 18 years".

157. *See Mental Health Ordinance* (Cap 136) section 2 which states in part:

A minor may enter into a contract but the other party takes a risk that the minor may not fulfil the contract where it is for non-essential goods or for money. In Hong Kong, an exception exists under section 46 of the *District Court Ordinance* (Cap 336),[158] which provides that infancy (one younger than eighteen years) is no defence to a debt to the extent of $60,000. However, where a contract concerns land, company shares, partnership, or is of a similar long-term or continuing nature, that contract is voidable at the minor's option before coming of age and for a reasonable time afterwards.[159]

"mental disorder" (精神紊亂) means—
(a) mental illness;
(b) a state of arrested or incomplete development of mind which amounts to a significant impairment of intelligence and social functioning … associated with abnormally aggressive or seriously irresponsible conduct …
(c) psychopathic disorder; or
(d) any other disorder or disability of mind which does not amount to mental handicap,
…
"mental handicap" (弱智) means sub-average general intellectual functioning with deficiencies in adaptive behaviour, …
…
"mental incapacity" (精神上無行為能力) means—
(a) mental disorder; or
(b) mental handicap,
…
"mentally disordered person" (精神紊亂的人) means a person suffering from mental disorder;
…
"psychopathic disorder" (精神病理障礙) means a persistent disorder or disability of personality … which results in abnormally aggressive or seriously irresponsible conduct on the part of the person concerned;
…
"sub-average general intellectual functioning" (低於平均的一般智能) means an IQ of 70 or below according to the Wechsler Intelligence Scales for Children or an equivalent scale in a standardized intelligence test;

158. *District Court Ordinance* (Cap 336) section 46 states:

No person shall by reason of his not having attained the full age … be exempted from liability for any debt, damages or demand arising under an agreement … where the debt, damages or demand—
(a) does not exceed the sum of $60000; or
(b) has been reduced to a sum not exceeding $60000 by reason of the plaintiff having abandoned the amount in excess of $60000 in his cause of action.

See also Age of Majority (Related Provisions) Ordinance, *supra* note 156, at section 4.

159. Chui & Roebuck, *supra* note 3, at 11.3.3.
See also Chitty, *supra* note 2, at paras. 8–001 to 8–067.

A person either intoxicated or of unsound mind at the time of making a contract might lack the capacity to understand or appreciate the obligations of a contract and thus might lack the necessary willingness to enter into a contract. A person claiming intoxication at the time of entering into a contract bears the burden of satisfying two elements:

(a) intoxication to the level that prevented full appreciation of the nature of the contract and of the person's act in entering the agreement at the time; and
(b) the other party reasonably knew that the intoxicated person was unable to act in a reasonable manner.

Similarly, to vitiate a contract on the grounds of mental disability, a person of unsound mind, through his guardian or legal representative, must prove either that:

(a) this individual was too mentally incompetent to understand the nature and consequence of entering the contract at the time; or,
(b) the execution, *i.e.*, signing, of the contract was an uncontrolled reaction to a mental illness, and the other party had reason to know of this condition.

Capacity may also refer to the authority or power of a legal entity, in particular a company, to enter into contracts. A company's capacity to contract is determined by its constitution, *i.e.*, its Memorandum of Association and Articles of Association. A company may, but is not required to, state its objects in its Memorandum of Association. If the objects are so stated, the company's power is limited by its objects. If the company enters into a contract which is outside its stated objects and if the other party has actual knowledge of the circumstances, the contract would be invalid. The other party is not deemed to have notice of a company's capacity to contract merely because the objects are stated in the Memorandum and kept by the Registrar of Companies.[160]

B. Lack of Genuine Consent

In order to have a valid, legally binding agreement, the parties to the contract must be able to enter into the contract and be able to understand its obligations. Another essential requirement for a valid contract therefore

---

160. *See Companies Ordinance* (Cap 32) sections 5–5C, which respectively provides: requirements with respect to memorandum; powers of a company; power limited by memorandum, etc.; and, exclusion of deemed notice.

is that the parties voluntarily agree to accept the terms of and the responsibilities under that contract. In short, the parties must be able to comprehend the contractual provisions and be able to consent to the acceptance of these provisions. Where this consent is not genuine, *i.e.*, is not freely and voluntarily given based upon full and accurate knowledge of the contract's provisions, there might not be a valid, legally binding agreement. Situations which might prevent or preclude a party from exercising its free will, *i.e.*, genuine consent, are presented below.

i. Misrepresentation: Generally

Misrepresentation occurs when a party is enticed to enter into a contract by a factual statement, upon which it relied, and the statement was untrue.[161] If the recipient of the misrepresentation incurred damage arising from reliance on that statement, remedies may be available under several situations; these will be discussed later.[162] Firstly, however, the elements of misrepresentation will be presented. These elements can be found in the definition of "misrepresentation": a false statement of fact which causes the recipient to enter into a contract with the person making the statement.

- Falsehood: the statement must not be correct or true. Although a statement was made both honestly and reasonably, the statement may still be a misrepresentation if it is inaccurate.[163]
- Statement: this element may consist of written words, oral statements or conduct. For example, in the case of *Spice Girls Ltd v Aprilia World Service BV* [2000] EMLR 478 the court found an implied representation that the girl group would stay together as a singing group for the

---

161. For in-depth analysis, *see* CHITTY, *supra* note 2, at paras. 6–001 to 6–041, 6–094 to 6–102.
162. *Edgington v Fitzmaurice* (1885) 29 Ch D 459.
One authority defines misrepresentation as follows:

> A representation is a statement of fact made by one party to the contract (the representor) to the other (the representee) which, [while not part] of the contract, is yet one of the reasons that induces the representee to enter into the contract. A misrepresentation is simply a representation that is untrue. The representor's state of mind and degree of carefulness are not relevant to classifying a representation as a misrepresentation but only to determining the type of misrepresentation …

FURMSTON, *supra* note 45, at 332.
The *BLIS Glossary*, *supra* note 2, translates "innocent misrepresentations" as 無意的失實陳述; "fraudulent or reckless misrepresentation" as 有欺詐成分或罔顧後果的失實陳述; and, "negligent misrepresentation" as 疏忽的失實陳述.
163. FISHER & GREENWOOD, *supra* note 17, at 213.

duration of the advertising contract. However, as the group knew of the pending departure of one of its members, which would affect continuation of the advertising contract, the court found there had been misrepresentation on the part of the Spice Girls even though the group had said nothing.[164]

- There is a general rule that silence will not impose liability. One exception is where there is concealment of a fact. This concealment may be considered to be tantamount to an assertion that there is no defect. "Covering dry rot in a house so as to conceal its existence is equivalent to a 'statement' that the house is free from dry rot."[165] Another exception to the general rule concerns full disclosure. If a person begins to speak, the disclosure needs to be full and frank. In the case of *Dimmock v Hallett* (1866) 2 Ch App 21, the buyer of land wanted to know whether the farms on that land were leased. The seller said *yes*, which was true but the seller failed to state that all the tenants on that land had been given their notices to quit.[166] In this instance, the statement is literally true but is also false in the overall circumstances. The reason for this is because the statement implies other facts which are misleading or false, *i.e.*, that there will be rent from the tenants.
- Another exception to the rule is where silence amounts to a failure to correct a previous statement. The case of *With v O'Flanagan* [1936] Ch 575 concerned the sale of a medical practice. In the initial phase of negotiations, the doctor stated that the medical practice was worth £2000 per year. At the conclusion of the negotiations, the practice was worth substantially less as a result of the doctor's illness. The court found misrepresentation in the doctor's failure to disclose the change in value of the practice over the course of negotiations.

---

164. *See* Hall, *supra* note 3, at 488–490 wherein the author discusses two Hong Kong cases, both concerning misrepresentation by conduct. Both cases involved real estate agents showing property to potential purchasers. In both cases, the agents showed adjoining and separately owned property which was not included in the sale although it was reasonable for the purchasers to have concluded that the adjoining property was part of the estate being offered for sale. *Shum Kong v Chui Ting Lin* (2000) HCA 16227/1999, [2001] HKCU 531; *Green Park Properties Ltd v Dorku Ltd* [2000] 4 HKC 538.
165. Fisher & Greenwood, *supra* note 17, at 213.
166. Chui & Roebuck, *supra* note 3, at para. 5.2.1.

- There is one final exception to the general rule concerning silence. This exception is known as *uberrimae fidei* (translated as "of the utmost good faith").[167] Situations requiring *uberrimae fidei* are usually imposed by law and arises from fiduciary relationships such as insurance contracts, contracts between principal and agent, or solicitor and client relationships. In situations of *uberrimae fidei*, there is an obligation for full disclosure; silence or partial disclosure is unacceptable.

- Of Fact/Opinion/Intention: a false statement of a fact is misrepresentation. One should note that misrepresentation is limited to untrue statements of fact but not of opinion or intention. There would be misrepresentation of fact where a person pretended to hold an opinion which is not actually held. However, if a person actually held an opinion which turns out to be wrong, the representation would not be misrepresentation. Therefore, a false statement of an opinion, truly held, is not misrepresentation. An opinion may amount to a statement of fact where it can be proved that the person making the statement did not actually hold or believe in that opinion. In the case of *Smith v Land and House Property Corp* (1884) 28 Ch D 7 the seller of a hotel represented the property as being leased to "a most desirable tenant". At the time of the statement, the seller knew the tenant was frequently tardy in paying the rent. The court stated that:

  > if the facts are not equally known to both sides, then a statement of opinion by the one who knows the facts best involves very often a statement of a material fact, for he impliedly states that he knows facts which justify his opinion.[168]

  A statement of intention will not amount to misrepresentation should the intention change. However, a statement of intention, if not sincerely held at the time, would constitute a misrepresentation of an existing fact concerning the speaker's state of mind.[169]

- Inducement: the recipient of the misstatement must have been induced by the misstatement to enter into the contract. There would be no misrepresentation if the recipient did not receive the misstatement; ignored it; or, being aware of its falsehood, entered the contract nonetheless.

---

167. LexisNexis, *supra* note 140, at 1981, translates "*uberrimae fidei*" as 完全坦率真誠.
168. (1884) 28 Ch D at 12.
169. Chitty, *supra* note 2, at para. 6–010.

In Hong Kong, the legislation regulating misrepresentation is the *Misrepresentation Ordinance* (Cap 284) which is concerned with innocent misrepresentation. Despite this focus, there are sections of the Ordinance which refer to misrepresentations "other than fraudulent". This reference includes by inference negligent misstatement. Section 2 keeps the remedy of rescission (discussed below) for innocent misrepresentation even where the misrepresentation has become a contract term, or, where the contract has been performed.[170] Section 3(1) provides for damages as a remedy for non-fraudulent misrepresentation, unless the offending party proves that there had been reasonable grounds to believe that the representation was true and that the offending party believed the statement to be true when the contract was made. This section of the Ordinance, in effect, places the burden of proof upon the offending party to prove no misrepresentation occurred. Section 3(2) permits a court the discretion to grant damages rather than rescission. Damages may be awarded both under sections 3(1) and 3(2), but the award given under section 3(2) shall be taken into account when assessing damages under section 3(1). Section 4 invalidates any exemption clause in a contract seeking to restrict remedies and liability for pre-contractual misrepresentation, except to the extent that reliance on it is considered fair and reasonable.

With the *Misrepresentation Ordinance*'s implementation, the general opinion is that victims of misrepresentation should pursue an action under the Ordinance rather than pursuing the traditional remedies available under contract law or tort law. The major advantage for victims of misrepresentation proceeding under the Ordinance is that the burden of proof is shifted

---

170. "Rescission" is the right allowed in equity to the innocent party to cancel the contract, if it so chooses. If the injured party elects this option, the contract is rescinded and the parties are placed back into their pre-contract positions.

> Rescission is the name given to a process whereby an existing contract is brought to an end and the effects of its existence are cancelled or terminated. … it seems that where rescission is sought on equitable grounds its effect is to restore the parties to the position before the contract was entered into, whereas rescission at common law for breach simply discharges the parties from further obligations to perform the contract.

7(2) HALSBURY'S, *supra* note 1, at para. 115.345.
For further information, *see, e.g.*, *id.* at paras. 115.345 to 115.347; HO, *supra* note 13, at 169–175; CHITTY, *supra* note 2, at paras. 6–096 to 6–114 (discussing in part the application of the United Kingdom's *Misrepresentation Act* 1967 upon which the Hong Kong ordinance is based). *See also* CHITTY, *supra* note 2, at paras. 22–025 to 22–030.
The *BLIS Glossary*, *supra* note 2, translates "rescind the contract" as 撤銷合約; and, "rescission" as 撤銷.

from the victim/claimant to the offending party. The offender is to establish that its statement was honest and made reasonably. Under the Ordinance, the offending party thus has the responsibility to provide evidence that the statement involved neither fraud nor negligence.

Generally, misrepresentations fall into three categories: innocent, fraudulent and negligent. Each of these types of misrepresentation will be reviewed in turn. For the sake of completeness, the traditional remedies available to a victim of misrepresentation are also presented.

a. Innocent Misrepresentation

The first type of misrepresentation to be reviewed is innocent misrepresentation, which occurs where one party (the offending party) makes a false statement about a material fact believing that fact to be true.[171] A statement is considered to be "material" when the other party (the innocent party) is induced by that statement to enter into the contract. In other words, the innocent party would not have entered the contract but for that statement. In comparison with other types of misrepresentation, innocent misrepresentation is easier to prove because the innocent party need not establish the offending party's fraud or negligence in making the false statement. Where there has been innocent misrepresentation, the innocent party will have the right to cancel the contract. As such, the innocent party can terminate the contract (known as "rescission" or "rescinding" the contract), and have any

171. Ho, *supra* note 13, at 147 notes the term "innocent misrepresentation" should refer to misrepresentation made without fraud and without negligence. Chitty, *supra* note 2, at paras. 6–005, 6–094 defines the term "innocent misrepresentation" as a representation which is neither fraudulent nor negligent.

172. *See, e.g.*, Chitty, *supra* note 2, at para. 6–094, explaining:

> The term "innocent misrepresentation" is here used to mean a representation which is neither fraudulent nor negligent, and the general rule remains ... that no action for damages lies for a mere innocent misrepresentation ... a misrepresentation [may result in] a claim for damages if it can be construed as a contractual promise, and is either part of a wider contract, or is itself supported by consideration. This may happen in two principal types of case. First, where the representor and representee themselves enter into a contract after the misrepresentation was made. Here, if the misrepresentation becomes a term of the contract, an action for damages will lie, whether the misrepresentation was fraudulent, negligent or innocent. Secondly, the representee may enter into a contract with a third party as a result of the misrepresentation. Even in this situation, it is often possible to construe the misrepresentation as a collateral contract, the consideration for which is supplied by the fact that the representee enters into the contract with the third party.

property or money returned, so long as the innocent party can return any property in or near its original condition which was obtained under the contract. This is pursuant to a principle known as *restitutio in integrum*—that is, rescission, which might include indemnity for the expenses required by the contract. Thus, rescission is intended to return the parties to their pre-contractual positions.

Generally, no damages are recoverable for innocent misrepresentation.[172] The remedy of rescission may be lost if:

- the injured party states its intent to proceed with the contract after it has realised the misstatement of fact, *i.e.*, the innocent party affirms the contract;
- *restitutio in integrum* is impossible (*e.g.*, the goods are no longer in existence);
- *laches*, *i.e.*, too much time passed before the claim was made;[173]
- the contract was fully executed. However, this common law rule has been changed by section 2 of the *Misrepresentation Ordinance* (Cap 284);[174] or,
- a *bona fide* purchaser for value without notice of the dispute has intervened.[175]

b. Fraudulent Misrepresentation

Another category of misrepresentation involves fraud.[176] "Fraudulent misrepresentation" is where a contracting party gains an advantage:

- by lying about a material fact;
- the other contracting party relied on the lie; and,
- resulted in economic injury to that party.

---

173. What constitutes "too much time" depends upon the circumstances, according to the court in the case of *Leaf v International Galleries* [1950] 2 KB 86.
The *BLIS Glossary*, *supra* note 2, translates "equitable doctrine" as 衡平法則; and, "laches" as 就行使權利方面的疏忽延誤.

174. Section 2 of the *Misrepresentation Ordinance*, *supra* note 152, provides:

> Where a person has entered into a contract after a misrepresentation has been made to him, and—
> (a) the misrepresentation has become a term of the contract; or
> (b) the contract has been performed,
> or both, then, if otherwise he would be entitled to rescind the contract without alleging fraud, he shall be so entitled, subject to the provisions of this Ordinance, notwithstanding the matters mentioned in paragraphs (a) and (b).

175. The *BLIS Glossary*, *supra* note 2, translates "*bona fide* purchaser for value" as 付出價值的真誠購買人; and, "*bona fide* purchaser" as 真誠買方.

176. For an analysis, *see* CHITTY, *supra* note 2, at paras. 6–001 to 6–041, 6–042 to 6–066.

In order to successfully claim fraud, the innocent party's reliance on the alleged misrepresentation must have been reasonable.

"Fraud" is present when a false representation is made:

- knowingly:
- without belief in its truth; or,
- recklessly, careless of whether the representation was true or false.[177]

Fraudulent misrepresentation is not a dispute concerning a future promise or a future act, because this would be a claim for breach of contract. Rather, fraudulent misrepresentation must be a false representation of a present fact, and not future intent. To establish fraud, it is necessary to prove the lack of an honest belief in the truth of what was stated.[178]

> The converse of this is that however negligent a person may be, he cannot be liable for fraud, provided that his belief is honest; mere carelessness is not sufficient, although gross carelessness may justify an inference that he was not honest.[179]

Nonetheless, a mere allegation that the offending party never intended to perform a contract which the offending party made is insufficient to establish a claim for fraud.

Further, the misrepresentation must be made with the intent to defraud or mislead the innocent party. For example, assume a third party learnt of the misrepresentation, and subsequently relied on the misrepresentation.

177. *Derry v Peek* (1889) 14 App Cas 337, 374.
Ho, *supra* note 13, at 146 states:

> A fraudulent misrepresentation then is one made without honest belief in its truth. This dishonesty can be proved by showing that the representor knew of the falsity of his representation, or that he shut his eyes to the facts or purposely abstained from inquiry into them. The formulation connotes some moral blameworthiness, but it is not necessary to prove moral blame …

178. Chitty, *supra* note 2, at para. 6–043.
In order to establish fraudulent misrepresentation, the plaintiff needs to show the defendant's lack of an honest belief.

> The requirement of proof of the absence of honest belief does not, however, mean that the claimant must prove the defendant's knowledge of the falsity of the statement. It is enough to establish that the latter suspected that his statement might be inaccurate, or that he neglected to inquire into its accuracy, without proving that he actually knew that it was false. …
>
> Further, it is not necessary to establish that the defendant's motive was dishonest.

Id. at paras. 6–045 to 6–046.

179. *Id.* at para. 6–043.

The third party has no claim for loss against the fraudulent party, because the offending party had no intention or desire to defraud the third party.

If fraudulent misrepresentation is proven, there is no requirement for *restitutio in integrum*. The offending party must return any property of the innocent party which was obtained by the fraud. In addition, the innocent party may claim damages from the fraudulent party. Any party induced to enter a contract by misrepresentation concerning an essential term, upon which that party justifiably relied, may sue for economic damages in tort law by proving deceit. The innocent party may also sue in contract law to cancel or avoid[180] the contract for fraud, and recover any money expended by the plaintiff (*i.e.*, reliance damages). "Reliance damages" is the difference between the actual worth or value that the innocent party received and what the innocent party paid the offending fraudulent party. Alternatively, the innocent party may recover restitution damages to the extent that the offending party profited by the misrepresentation. If the property cannot be returned to the innocent party, the amount of damages will be increased to compensate for the loss.

> Fraudulent misrepresentation gives rise to a right to damages. Damages can be claimed whether or not rescission is claimed although obviously the plaintiff cannot recover twice.
>
> ... The representee is to be put in the position as if the representation had not been made and not as if the representation were true.[181]

c. Negligent Misrepresentation

The third category of misrepresentation is negligent misrepresentation.[182] A "negligent misstatement" is a representation made carelessly to a party who is induced by the statement to act to its detriment.[183] When an offending party makes a false statement honestly believed to be true but the statement was made without a reasonable ground for such a belief, there is negligent misrepresentation.

---

180. The *BLIS Glossary*, *supra* note 2, translates "avoid" as 廢止.

181. Ho, *supra* note 13, at 167.

182. For an in-depth analysis, *see* Chitty, *supra* note 2, at paras. 6–001 to 6–041, 6–067 to 6–093.

183. Ho, *supra* note 13, at 147 refers to this as "negligent misrepresentation", defined as "made without the maker exercising the standard of care owed to the representee."
In *Link Folk Ltd v Glorious Motors Ltd*, *supra* note 133, the court held that the vehicle seller's failure to verify the car's mileage before the sale to the buyer is negligent misrepresentation as the seller had no reasonable basis to believe the odometer reading to be accurate. The court allowed rescission of the contract while discussing exemption clauses, *contra proferentem* and *restitutio in integrum*.

Negligent misrepresentation arises usually where a professional, such as an accountant, lawyer or architect, breaches a duty owed to the innocent party to provide accurate information. The professional is not liable to everyone, but only to those whom a duty is owed. A duty arises under the privity of contract between the innocent party and the offending party, or the equivalent of privity for those who were the "end and aim" of the business transaction. Alternatively, an obligation arises where the recipient of the statement was within a group of persons to whom the statement was directed. There is some contact or awareness between the professional and the actual injured party.

The offending party may have failed to use reasonable care to determine the true facts, or failed to apply the skill and competence of a reasonable person in the offending party's profession. As such, an offending party who negligently supplies information may be liable for the economic or financial loss suffered by the recipient of that information.

In summary, the party making the negligent misrepresentation will be liable for any loss suffered if:

- the statement was untrue;
- the statement was material, *i.e.*, concerning matters relevant to some essential aspect or subject of pre-contractual negotiations;
- the maker of the statement owes a duty of care to the recipient of the statement;
- the maker of the statement did not exclude liability, or if the maker did exclude liability, the exemption clause is unreasonable;
- a reasonable person acting prudently and cautiously would not have made this statement; and,
- the recipient was acting reasonably by relying on this statement.

The remedy for economic or financial loss resulting from negligent misstatement is compensation known as "damages". (The topic of damages is discussed in section VIII.) Other possible remedies, depending upon the factual situation, might include bringing a case in tort (*e.g.*, claiming negligence in making the representation); rescission of the contract; or, damages under the *Misrepresentation Ordinance* discussed above.

ii. Mistake: Generally

The concept of "mistake" is a difficult topic. Academics have attributed this difficulty to the following disparate reasons:

- lacking conceptual unity;[184]
- overlapping with other areas of contract law such as offer and acceptance, misrepresentation, and, frustration;[185]
- being the most perplexing and academically complex topic found in contract law;[186] or,
- consuming inordinate amount of space in a textbook or class but not in real life.[187]

Reading some of the academic treatises on the subject of mistake reveals a lack of uniformity in the use of the terms associated with mistake. Despite the complexity and confusion, the concept of mistake remains important in contract law, because mistake is the only common law vitiating factor that renders the agreement void rather than voidable.[188] However, before proceeding to review this consequence of mistake, the definition of "mistake" and the different types are presented.

A mistake occurs when one party is wrong about some aspect of the proposed contract so that there is no actual agreement between the parties. In more technical language, a mistake is an erroneous belief, which is not in accordance with the facts. Mistake thus pertains to the formation of a legally binding agreement by preventing any "meeting of the minds" of the parties:

- Was there a lack of subject matter, that is, was there anything about which to make a contract?
- Was there a lack of agreement, that is, was there a lack of consent?

The law will provide a remedy only when the mistake (unilateral, common, or, mutual) is operative. An "operative" mistake pertains to the terms of the contract, and, whether a reasonable person would have made such a mistake.[189] The consequence of an operative mistake is that the contract is void *ab initio* (*i.e.*, void from the beginning).[190]

---

184. STONE, *supra* note 20, at 382; 385.
185. *Id.* at 382.
186. FISHER & GREENWOOD, *supra* note 17, at 245.
187. CHUI & ROEBUCK, *supra* note 3, at para. 5.4.
188. *Id.*
189. FISHER & GREENWOOD, *supra* note 17, at 245.
If a mistake is operative, the mistake is sufficiently serious to justify court intervention. STONE, *supra* note 20, at 385 n. 15.
190. The *BLIS Glossary*, *supra* note 2, translates "*ab initio*" as 一開始. ARJUNAN & NABI BAKSH, *supra* note 133, translates the term as 由最初開始.

Where mistake is proven, the remedy known as "rectification" is available. Rectification is an equitable remedy available where a written agreement can be proved not to reflect the prior oral agreement.[191] A court may then re-write the contract in order to represent the parties' true intentions.[192]

The court in *Codelfa Construction Proprietary Ltd v State Rail Authority of NSW* (1982) 149 CLR 337 explained the difference between an "implied term" (discussed in section IV.B.*ii*) and "rectification" as follows:

> In each case the problem is caused by a deficiency in the expression of the consensual agreement. A term which should have been included has been omitted. The difference is that with rectification the term which has been omitted and should have been included was actually agreed upon; with implication the term is one which it is presumed that the parties would have agreed upon had they turned their minds to it—it is not a term that they have actually agreed upon. Thus, in the case of the implied term the deficiency in the expression of the consensual agreement is caused by the failure of the parties to direct their minds to a particular eventuality and to make explicit provision for it. Rectification ensures that the contract gives effect to the parties' actual intention; the implication of a term is designed to give effect to the parties' presumed intention.[193]

The Hong Kong High Court in *Jardine Engineering Corporation Ltd v Shimizu Corporation* [1992] 2 HKC 271 cited this explanation with approval.[194]

At law, there are three types of mistakes that can vitiate a contract: unilateral, common and mutual mistake. The reader should be aware that mistake

---

191. *See* Ho, *supra* note 13, at 200–204.
    LexisNexis, *supra* note 140, at 1590, translates "rectification" as 糾正. The *BLIS Glossary*, *supra* note 2, translates "rectify" as 更正.
192. Chui & Roebuck, *supra* note 3, at para. 5.5.
    Rectification is:

    > where a contract has by reason of a mistake common to the contracting parties been drawn up so as to [be contrary to] ... the terms intended by both as revealed in their previous oral understanding, the court will rectify the document so as to carry out such intentions. Rectification will not be ordered if a written agreement fails to mention a matter because the parties simply overlooked it, having no intention on the point at all, nor if they decided deliberately to omit the issue. In such cases the written agreement must be construed as it stands.

    Chitty, *supra* note 2, at para. 5–108.
193. (1989) 149 CLR at 346.
194. [1992] 2 HKC at 310.

can also be categorized as one of fact or of law.[195] However, for the purposes of this chapter, only the first category containing the three types of mistakes is considered.

---

195. One authority explains:

> The error must have been present at the time of the contract's formation. An error of understanding which arises after the contract has been concluded cannot be an operative mistake.
>
> The error must also be one of fact. An error about the law, including the legal meaning or effect of a contractual term, is not a mistake for the purposes of the law of contract. (citation omitted)

HALL, *supra* note 3, at 515.

As for a mistake of fact:

> It has long been clear that money paid under a mistake of the payer as to a material fact is, in certain circumstances, recoverable. Mistake in this context means lack of knowledge of the absence of liability, but it is notoriously difficult to make an authoritative statement of the principles upon which recovery is based.

CHITTY, *supra* note 2, at para. 29–030.

As for a mistake of law, CHITTY, *supra* note 2, at para. 29–041 states:

> Despite a dubious legal foundation and the difficulty of drawing any clear dividing line between "law" and "fact" for many years, as a general rule money paid under a mistake as to the general law, or as to the legal effect of the circumstances under which it is paid, but with full knowledge of the facts, was irrecoverable.

Traditionally, payments made under mistake of law (as opposed to mistake of fact) were not recoverable. However, the general rule that mistake of fact is operative while mistake of law is inoperative is no longer followed in the United Kingdom. Several cases have recently abolished this distinction: *Kleinwort Benson Ltd v Lincoln City Council* [1999] 2 AC 349 (discussed in CHITTY, *supra* note 2, at paras. 29–045 to 29–046); *Pankhania v The London Borough of Hackney* [2002] EWHC 2441 (Ch); *Brennan v Bolt Burdon* [2003] EWHC 2493, [2004] 1 WLR 1240 (QB).

The *Brennan* court noted that:

> at common law a mistake of law did not vitiate a contract. A mistake of fact in some circumstances could vitiate the contract. The difficulty was in distinguishing between a mistake of law and a mistake of fact. In order to grant relief "mistakes of law" were sometimes described as "mistakes of fact" [2004] 1 WLR 1251, para. 45.
>
> …
>
> In my judgment the Courts should be very slow to set aside and declare compromise agreements void on the ground of alleged common mistakes of fact or law. Before declaring a compromise agreement void the court must be satisfied that the mistake, in this case of law, was both common and fundamental to the making of the compromise agreement … *Id.* at 1252, para. 50.

The *BLIS Glossary*, *supra* note 2, translates "mistake of fact" as 事實方面的錯誤. LEXISNEXIS, *supra* note 140, at 1216, translates "mistake of law" as 法律錯誤.

a. Unilateral Mistake

The first of these is termed "unilateral mistake", which occurs where only one party is in error. This party does not know the true state of affairs or makes an incorrect assumption in entering a contract and the other party is aware or ought to know of this mistake.[196] With unilateral mistake, consent between the parties is negated as the parties do not reach an agreement.

An example of unilateral mistake over a term of the contract can be found in the Hong Kong case of *Wong Tak-sing v Amertex International* [1988] HKLR 98. This case involved a $350,000 debt over which the parties' solicitors were negotiating a settlement. The plaintiff's lawyers offered in writing to accept $25,000 as settlement when the lawyers actually meant $250,000. Before any correction could be made, the defendant's solicitors claimed to accept the offer. The court found that there was an operative unilateral mistake, *i.e.*, "an attempt to accept an offer which the offeree knew the offeror never intended."[197]

Another frequently cited example of unilateral mistake concerns mistaken identity. This occurs when one party impersonates another person while negotiating in person with the innocent party. The innocent party has mistaken the identity of the pretender and enters into a contract with this

196. Chui & Roebuck, *supra* note 3, at para. 5.4.3 defines this as where "one party only has made a mistake, but a mistake of which the other knows or, on an objective test, ought to know."
As one authority has noted:

> No contract can be formed if there is no correspondence between the offer and the acceptance, or if the agreement is not sufficiently certain. ... If, however, one party claims that he did not intend to contract at all, or did not intend to contract on the terms which the other party claims were agreed, then the question is whether, there is a contract (or, as it is often put, whether or not the "contract is void"). The intention of the parties is, as a general rule, to be construed objectively ...

Chitty, *supra* note 2, at para. 5–067.
See also Fisher & Greenwood, *supra* note 17, at 248–249.

197. Chui & Roebuck, *supra* note 3, at para. 5.4.3.
For other examples of successful claims of unilateral mistake, *see, e.g.*, *Hartog v Colin and Shields* [1939] 3 All ER 566 (Seller mistakenly quoted the selling price as per pound rather than per piece. Buyer accepted the lower per pound price. The court held that Buyer could not claim a contract as the parties had negotiated the price on the per piece basis which was the trade standard and Buyer should have known of the mistake.); *Chwee Kin Keong v Digilandmall.com Pte Ltd* [2005] 1 SLR 502 (Seller mistakenly lists $3,900 product for sale at $66. Buyer claimed not to know of this mistake. Court found, based upon the number of orders placed and the time of placing the orders, Buyer had knowledge of the mistake.)

impostor. The court in *Lewis v Averay* [1972] 1 QB 198 held that, under this factual scenario, the mistake was not operative and the contract was not void. A more recent English case, *Shogun Finance Ltd v Hudson* [2004] 1 All ER 215, has confirmed that in situations where an imposter is negotiating face-to-face with an innocent party, the latter's claim of unilateral mistake likely will fail. The reasoning is that the innocent party's offer is made to the imposter, *i.e.*, the other party who is physically present rather than to the person the imposter is impersonating.

A unilateral mistake is generally no defence or excuse for the mistaken party to avoid performance of its contractual obligations. There is, generally, no requirement on the other party to correct the mistake of the mistaken party. Nonetheless, the other party must do nothing to mislead the mistaken party, whether actively or passively, even by silence. If the mistake is self-caused, and concerns the quality or characteristics of an object, the general rule is that there will be no remedy for the mistaken party. Where the mistake pertains to the scope of an offer, so that the mistaken party believes that the subject matter of the contract is essentially different in kind from what it actually is, and the other party is aware of this situation, there is a duty on the latter to correct the mistake. Should that party not correct the mistake, the contract will be void as there can be no acceptance of an offer not made.[198] Further, a unilateral mistake by one party as to the contract value (*i.e.*, the price being paid) or to the extent of the labour or materials required to perform the contract is considered to be an error of business judgment, which is not generally a ground to rescind the contract.

The case of *Yu Kam Por v New Central Ltd* [2005] 1 HKC 77 provides an example of these principles being applied. Yu sold his land in Sai Kung with a buy-back option agreement which would allow Yu to buy back a portion of the land if he complied with certain conditions. Yu passed away in August 2000; the plaintiff, as executor, sought to rectify the sale or the buy-back agreement on the basis of unilateral mistake. Alternatively, the plaintiff sought to rescind the sale and purchase agreement, again on the basis of unilateral mistake. The purported mistake is that Yu intended to sell

---

198. 7(2) HALSBURY'S, *supra* note 1, at para. 115.095 explains:

> A mistake as to the terms of the offer must be carefully distinguished from a mistake as to the quality of what is being offered. A mistake as to the terms which are being offered raises problems of offer and acceptance; but a mistake as to the quality of what is being offered usually does not. ... it is well-established that a mistaken motive of one party cannot prevent the formation of an agreement, even if realised by the other party.

only a 300 square feet portion of his parcel rather than the whole parcel of approximately 9,500 square feet.

The court followed and applied these principles in finding against the plaintiff:

1. a unilateral mistake is not a basis for rescission or rectification of a contract unless the other party actually knew of the mistake;[199]
2. proving the other party's actual knowledge of the mistake is a heavy evidentiary burden akin to the standard of convincing proof;[200]
3. the party, who is to benefit from an option, must conform strictly with the prerequisites stipulated for the exercise of that option;[201]
4. a court order to a party to perform the contract as specified should not be granted in respect of an unexercised option to purchase;[202]
5. and, the buy-back agreement was void for uncertainty as this agreement failed to indicate unambiguously the section of land to be retained by the defendant.[203]

199. [2005] 1 HKC at 88.
The court quotes 1 Chitty on Contracts (H.G. Beale, *et al.* eds., 29th ed. 2004) at para. 5–100 that:

> unilateral mistake is not by itself a ground for rescinding or rectifying a contract unless the other party knew of the mistake. It appears that the knowledge must be actual knowledge. It is not enough that the party against whom rectification is sought may have suspected that a mistake had been made …

200. [2005] 1 HKC at 88 citing to *Citilite Properties Ltd v Innovative Development Co Ltd* [1998] 4 HKC 62.

201. [2005] 1 HKC at 88.
The court referred to the judgment in *Hare v Nicoll* [1966] 2 QB 130, 146 which states:

> It is well established that an option for the purchase or repurchase of property must in all cases be exercised strictly within the time limited for the purpose. The reason for this, as I understand it, is that an option is a species of privilege for the benefit of the party on whom it is conferred. That being so, it is for that party to comply strictly with the conditions stipulated for the exercise of the option.

202. [2005] 1 HKC at 88.
The judge cites to *Alexander v Tse* [1988] 1 NZLR 318, 319 that:

> A decree for specific performance cannot be granted in respect of an option to purchase. Equity has never sought to enforce unexercised options by specific remedy, the aim of equity and the law being to enforce contracts not to make them.

This remedy is known as "specific performance" and is discussed in section VIII.C

203. [2005] 1 HKC at 94–95.

b. Common Mistake

"Common mistake" occurs when both parties make the same fundamental mistake concerning the contract; there is a want or lack of the subject matter of the contract.[204] With a common mistake, the parties have come to an agreement but that agreement was premised upon a common or shared error fundamental to the contract. Hence, a shared mistake nullifies the contract because the agreement is based on a falsehood. One frequently cited example of a common mistake nullifying consent is where the parties agree to the rental of a recital hall without realizing that the structure had burnt down.[205]

At common law, the contract will be void for common mistake if the mistake is sufficiently fundamental or extreme. In the case of *Great Peace Shipping Ltd v Tsavliris (International) Ltd* [2002] 4 All ER 689, the Court of Appeal stated the requirements in order for a common mistake to exist:

- There must be a common assumption as to the existence of a state of affairs;
- There must be no warranty by either party that that state of affairs exists;
- The non-existence of the state of affairs must not be attributable to the fault of either party;
- The non-existence of the state of affairs must render performance of the contract impossible; and,
- The state of affairs may be the existence, or a vital attribute, of the consideration to be provided or the circumstance which must subsist if performance of the contractual adventure is to be possible.[206]

---

204. FURMSTON, *supra* note 45, at 284 provides that:

> In common mistake, both parties make the same mistake. Each knows the intention of the other and accepts it, but each is mistaken about some underlying and fundamental fact. The parties, for example, are unaware that the subject matter of their contract has already perished.

FISHER & GREENWOOD, *supra* note 17, at 248 states that: "Common mistake arises when the parties are in agreement, but that agreement assumes some fact to be true when it is not." *See* CHUI & ROEBUCK, *supra* note 3, at para. 5.4.1.

205. Along similar, but not identical, lines to the consequences of common mistake is section 8 of the *Sale of Goods Ordinance*, *supra* note 66, which provides that:

> Where there is a contract for the sale of specific goods, and the goods, without the knowledge of the seller, have perished at the time when the contract is made, the contract is void.

206. [2002] 4 All ER at para. 76.

The consequence is unclear whether a common mistake as to the quality, rather than the existence, of an item will render a resulting contract void. The general rule is that there will be a valid contract and no operative common mistake. For the moment, the case of *Bell v Lever Brothers* [1932] AC 161 seems to be the authority. In this case, the court stated that a:

> mistake will not affect assent unless it is the mistake of both parties and is as to the existence of some quality which makes the thing without the quality essentially different from the thing as it was believed to be.[207]
>
> ...
>
> [For example,] A buys a picture from B; both A and B believe it to be the work of an old master, and a high price is paid. It turns out to be a modern copy. A has no remedy in the absence of representation or warranty.[208]

Equity may allow the remedy of rescission in situations where the contract is not void at common law. A court, in circumstances determined to be equitable, may declare the contract voidable, and either or both parties may seek to avoid this contract. Note that, under equity, this contract is not void *ab initio*, *i.e.*, void from the beginning. Thus, a court will impose whatever terms it considers to be fair before the contract may be avoided. In *Great Peace Shipping Ltd v Tsavliris (International) Ltd*, the court determined that if a contract is not void under the common law, equity will not be able to nullify this contract on the basis of common mistake. Consequently, this case from the United Kingdom has restricted the application of equity where common mistake is claimed.[209]

c. Mutual Mistake

"Mutual mistake" occurs when the parties are at cross-purposes; there is a complete want or lack of agreement. Unlike common mistake, each party makes a different mistake about the contract terms.[210] Consequently, there

---

207. [1932] AC at 218.
208. *Id.* at 224.
209. The impact of this case upon Hong Kong is unclear although there is a suggestion that Hong Kong courts would follow this narrowing of the application of common mistake. FISHER & GREENWOOD, *supra* note 17, at 246, 254–258.
See also CHITTY, *supra* note 2, at paras. 5–036, 5–060 to 5–061 for a discussion of this case; and, *id.* at paras. 5–057 to 5–063 for a discussion of the impact of this case upon the application of equity to common mistake.
210. There is divergence among the authorities as to the terminology. CHITTY, *supra* note 2, at para. 5–001 n. 3 states:

is no consent between the parties, as there is no "meeting of the minds" in that there has not been an acceptance of a corresponding offer. As one source explains, a mutual mistake can be viewed as "a question of ineffective offer and acceptance".[211] The result is the same as a unilateral mistake, *i.e.*, the consent of the parties in a mutual mistake is negatived or negated. The court will decide which version is more reasonable, based upon the facts, and will uphold the contract on this basis.[212]

d. *Non Est Factum*

The defence of *non est factum*[213] is available where the signer is an innocent victim of fraud or misrepresentation such that there is a radical difference between what was actually signed and what was thought to have been signed. The contract was signed by error, without knowledge of the agreement's meaning. However, this defence is not available to a signer who

---

> Earlier editions of this work used the phrase "mutual mistake", following the terminology used by Lord Atkin in *Bell v Lever Bros* [1932] A.C. 161, and some works adhere to this usage ... Other works refer to this type of mistake as "common mistake" ... and more recently the courts have also referred to common mistake ... One reason for using the phrase "common mistake" is to reduce the risk of confusion with what is termed here "mutual misunderstanding" (where the parties are at cross-purposes as to the terms of the contract) ...

FURMSTON, *supra* note 45, at 284 states:

> In mutual mistake, the parties misunderstand each other and are at cross purposes. A, for example, intends to offer his Ford Sierra car for sale, but B believes that the offer relates to the Ford Granada also owned by A.

FISHER & GREENWOOD, *supra* note 17, at 248 explains: "Mutual mistake arises when the parties are at cross purposes; each misunderstanding the other."

211. CHUI & ROEBUCK, *supra* note 3, at para. 5.4.2.

212. FURMSTON, *supra* note 45, at 284–285 notes in regard to mutual and unilateral mistakes:

> Where either mutual or unilateral mistake is pleaded, the very existence of the agreement is denied. The argument is that, despite appearances, there is no real correspondence of offer and acceptance and that therefore the transaction must necessarily be void.
>
> ... If mutual mistake is pleaded, the judicial approach ... is objective; the court, looking at the evidence from the standpoint of a reasonable third party, will decide whether any, and if so what, agreement must be taken to have been reached. If unilateral mistake is pleaded, the approach is subjective; the innocent party is allowed to show the effect upon *his* mind of the error in the hope of avoiding its consequences. (emphasis in original)

FISHER & GREENWOOD, *supra* note 17, at 249 comments that "Unilateral and mutual mistakes are instances where the mistake *negatives* consent; the parties never reach agreement." (emphasis in original)

213. ARJUNAN & NABI BAKSH, *supra* note 133, translates *non est factum* as 否定簽訂合約.

was negligent or careless in signing, *e.g.*, who did not read the document or signed it in blank, according to the court in *Saunders v Anglia Building Society* [1971] AC 1004. The court stated that there:

> must I think be a radical difference between what he signed and what he thought he was signing—or one could use the words "fundamental" or "serious" or "very substantial" ...[214]

Non est factum is thus difficult to establish, as no negligence on the part of the signatory is allowed. Yet, if the *non est factum* defence succeeds, the contract is void *ab initio* (from the beginning). This defence is available for situations involving mistake, duress and undue influence.

iii. Duress

A contract is voidable if a party proves the contract was induced by violence or unlawful restraint, or threats thereof, to the contracting party or to a member of that party's family. Accordingly, a contract is voidable if a party enters into an agreement involuntarily out of fear arising from:

- a threat of violence;
- actual violence;
- threat of arrest;
- false imprisonment;
- wrongful prosecution;
- blackmail;
- a threat to take goods; or,
- the actual seizure of the goods.

The party must have no alternative but to agree to enter the contract or to its modification. The party's assent to contract is thus involuntary; this party's consent is unfairly coerced so that free will has been overcome.

In order to be an operative vitiating factor, the duress must be an inducement, although it need not be the sole reason, to enter into a contract. Further, the coercion must be unlawful. For example, if the threatening party has a legitimate right to file a lawsuit, there is no duress by threatening a lawsuit if the other party does not enter into a contract. Note that the

214. [1971] AC 1017.

victim of the violence or the subject of the threat may be someone other than the contracting party, *e.g.*, a relative or friend.[215]

It was not until 1976 that the courts recognized economic duress[216] to be an operative factor.[217] Economic duress commonly occurs where a party is coerced into an unfavourable renegotiation of the contract. In these cases, consideration has been provided for the change, but that change has

---

215. Chui & Roebuck, *supra* note 3, at para. 5.6.1.

As noted in 7(2) Halsbury's, *supra* note 1, at para. 115.097:

> By duress is meant the compulsion under which a person acts through fear of personal suffering as from injury to the body or from confinement, actual or threatened. ... There is no duress simply because a party has to enter into a contract by reason of statutory compulsion, or the fact that the other party is a monopoly supplier. Moreover, as a general rule, a threat of civil proceedings or bankruptcy proceedings does not amount to duress, whether there is good foundation for the proceedings or not; but it may do so if it is intended and calculated ... to cause terror in the particular case. The question whether imprisonment or threatened imprisonment does or does not constitute duress depends upon whether the imprisonment is lawful or unlawful.
>
> A contract obtained by means of duress exercised by one party over the other is at very least voidable, and may perhaps be void; but if it is voluntarily acted upon by the party entitled to avoid, it will become binding on him. The duress must be actually existing at the time of the making of the contract; and the personal suffering may be that of the husband or wife or near relative of the contracting party, but that of a stranger or a master is not sufficient. (citations omitted)

See also Tam Lup Wai Franky v Vong Shi Ming Nicolas [2002] 4 HKC 135, where Tam had a 12-hour meeting with Vong to persuade the latter to make good the losses which Tam incurred in a business venture with Vong. Tam had two associates with him at this meeting where Tam threatened criminal charges against Vong, his wife and a friend of the Vongs with all the attendant publicity, particularly as Vong had previously been charged with indecent assault. The court held that Vong made out a claim of duress.

216. The concept of economic duress:

> amounts to recognising that certain threats or forms of pressure, not associated with threats to the person, nor limited to the seizure or withholding of goods, may give grounds for relief to a party who enters into a contract as a result of the threats or the pressure.

Chitty, *supra* note 2, at para. 7–014.

Fisher & Greenwood, *supra* note 17, at 277 explains:

> Economic duress occurs where some unfair and unlawful economic pressure is placed on a party to a contract. While it may sometimes be difficult to distinguish between duress and legitimate, hard bargaining, the key elements of economic duress are "illegitimate pressure" and lack of a practical alternative.

217. *Occidental Worldwide Investment Corporation v Skibs AS/Avanti* (The Siboen v the Sibotre) [1976] 1 Lloyd's Rep 293.

been against the free will of a party.[218] Economic duress renders a contract voidable, but not void. The factor in deciding whether there is duress is the existence of alternatives and the extent to which those alternatives have been considered.[219]

The case of *Pao On v Lau Yiu Long* [1980] AC 614, PC is a leading case in respect of economic duress. Plaintiff owned a private company whose principal asset was a building. Defendant was public company which wished to acquire the building. The parties respectively agreed to sell and purchase the subject building. Rather than a cash transaction, Defendant was to make the purchase by issuing shares in Defendant's company to Plaintiff. Under this main agreement, Plaintiff was to retain these shares for a specified period of time. To safeguard against a possible fall in these shares' value during this period of time, there was a subsidiary agreement whereby Defendant was to buy back from Plaintiff a majority of these shares at a set price. Plaintiff, concerned over incurring a loss in profits if the value of these shares rose above the set price, refused to continue with the main agreement unless Defendant cancelled the subsidiary agreement and agreed to an indemnity clause if the share price fell. Defendant refused to honour the clause when the share price fell, claiming that the indemnity clause was the result of duress. The Privy Council held that there had been no duress on the basis that there had to be coercion of will, rather than a change in circumstance, in order to vitiate consent.

A coerced transaction may be accepted after the coercion has ended. In other words, the coerced party may ratify the contract. The ratification may recognize the validity of the contract. The ratification may also prevent any

---

218. CHUI & ROEBUCK, *supra* note 3, at para. 5.6.2.

These authors explain economic duress through a review of the following case:

> For example, in *North Ocean Shipping v. Hyundai Construction: The Atlantic Baron* [1979] QB 705, the builders of a ship were to be paid in US dollars. At the time the dollar was dropping, they told the buyers that unless they increased the payment by 10%, there would be no delivery on the due date. The builders knew that the buyers had many commitments and needed the ship. The court was satisfied that there was economic duress. The renegotiation was prompted by coercion by the builders, who twisted circumstances under their power. This is why most cases have so far been about renegotiations–because there it is clear that it is not merely market forces which are involved. As it happens, the buyers still lost their case. They paid a final instalment after delivery, and this was held to be affirmation after duress had ceased.

Id.

219. *Atlas Express Ltd v Kafco Ltd* [1989] QB 833; CHITTY, *supra* note 2, at paras. 7–031 to 7–036.

See also HALL, *supra* note 3, at 582–593; HO, *supra* note 13, at 215–220.

claims for a remedy or for damages, if the party does not promptly move to have a court rescind the contract once the pressure is removed. Thus, whatever kind of duress is involved, a party must act quickly once the pressure is removed or risk losing any remedy.[220]

iv. Undue Influence

Undue influence is an equitable doctrine[221] and may be defined as the unconscionable use by one person of power over another individual in order to induce the other person to enter into a contract.[222] A party can avoid a contract into which it has been enticed by undue influence. Equitable relief is available where a party has been forced into an agreement without choice. A party entering into a contract as a result of undue influence has a voidable contract. The injured party may also claim rescission, subject to the usual equitable bars, as undue influence is a reflection of the maxims of equity.[223]

---

220. CHUI & ROEBUCK, *supra* note 3, at para. 5.6.2.
221. The *BLIS Glossary*, *supra* note 2, translates "undue influence" as 不當影響; and, "equitable doctrine" as 衡平法則.
222. HO, *supra* note 13, at 221 states:

> The underlying principle of the doctrine of undue influence is not that people should be saved from the consequences of their own folly, but that 'people should be protected from being forced, tricked or misled in any way by others into parting with their property'. Such an aim 'is one of the most legitimate objects of all law; and the equitable doctrine of undue influence has grown out of and been developed by the necessity of grappling with insidious forms of spiritual tyranny and with the infinite varieties of fraud'.

One source states that the doctrine of undue influence is equity's version of the common law's doctrine of duress. Undue influence relates to those circumstances where pressure of a more subtle nature than recognised by the doctrine of duress, has been used to persuade a party to enter into a contract. FISHER & GREENWOOD, *supra* note 17, at 277.

See 22 HALSBURY'S, *supra* note 100, at para. 340.152; CHITTY, *supra* note 2, at paras. 7–056 to 7–139.

The *BLIS Glossary*, *supra* note 2, translates "unconscionable" as 不合情理; and, "acted unconscionably" as 作出不合情理的作為.

223. CHITTY, *supra* note 2, at para. 7–097 notes:

> A transaction entered into as the result of undue influence is voidable and not void. The right to rescind on the ground of undue influence may be lost either by express affirmation of the transaction by the victim, by estoppel or by delay amounting to proof of acquiescence. ... to be of any value, the affirmation must take place after the influence has ceased ... Lapse of time in itself does not seem to constitute a bar to relief, but it will provide evidence of acquiescence if the victim fails to take any steps to set aside the transaction within a reasonable time after he is freed from the undue influence.

Undue influence is usually found in situations where a weaker party reposes trust and confidence in the stronger party. Traditionally, undue influence is presumed between parties of certain special relationships.[224] These special relationships overlap with, but are not identical to, fiduciary relationships.[225] For example, the presumption is applied between a spiritual adviser and advised, a doctor and patient (who do not have fiduciary relationships), but not between an agent and principal (who stand in a fiduciary relationship). The court held in *Royal Bank of Scotland v Etridge* [2001] 4 All ER 449 that the proper presumption in these situations is only that one party reposes trust and confidence in the other, but not that the confidence is abused. However, in certain circumstances, *e.g.*, where the transaction is manifestly disadvantageous to the weaker party, undue influence may be inferred as a matter of evidence, that the stronger party has exerted undue influence unless it proves otherwise. The stronger party may displace this inference by showing that the weaker party had obtained independent advice.[226]

A recent case involved similar facts as *Royal Bank of Scotland*. The UK case of *Hewett v First Plus Financial Group* [2010] EWCA Civ 312 involved the Hewetts who owned a home in which the husband, wife, her mother, and children lived. This property was remortgaged to First Plus Financial Group in part to pay the husband's credit card debts. The husband forged

---

224. 7(2) HALSBURY'S, *supra* note 1, at para. 115.099 states in part:

> If the parties at the time of the transaction or shortly before then were in a particular confidential relationship to each other, for example that of parent and child, or trustee and beneficiary, or solicitor and client, there is a further rule of equity which is that the existence of undue influence over the one party (namely the child, beneficiary or client) will be presumed unless it is shown by the other party that it did not exist; the burden of proving this has not uncommonly been discharged by showing that the transaction appeared fair and that the party who might have been subject to undue influence had competent independent advice. ... The power of the court to grant equitable relief on the ground of undue influence ... may be exercised in any case in which an unfair use has been made of influence possessed by one person over another. In this latter class of cases, where a confidential relationship of the class indicated above does not exist, the burden is on the party alleging undue influence affirmatively to prove that the contract was procured thereby.

225. For a discussion of these relationships, *see*, *e.g.*, HO, *supra* note 13, at 222–226; FURMSTON, *supra* note 45, at 392–403; CHITTY, *supra* note 2, at paras. 7–069 to 7–125.
The *BLIS Glossary*, *supra* note 2, translates "fiduciary relationship" as 受信關係.

226. Hong Kong has applied this test of presumed undue influence in the case of *Li Sau Ying v Bank of China (Hong Kong) Ltd* [2005] 1 HKLRD 106, CFA. *See* HALL, *supra* note 3, at 605–610; *Bank of China (Hong Kong) Ltd v China Hong Kong Textile Co Ltd* [2011] 4 HKLRD 457, CA.

his mother-in-law's signature to provide her consent to the remortgage. The court determined that Mr. Hewett made several misrepresentations to his wife to induce her to agree to the remortgage. One misrepresentation involved Mr. Hewett's failure to inform Mrs. Hewett of his infidelity.

> The third [misrepresentation] was his deliberate concealment of his affair, a highly material fact which his wife needed to know, if she were to make an informed decision whether or not to accede to his request.
>
> ...
>
> It is evident that Mrs. Hewett's decision to accede to her husband's request was based upon an assumption on her part that he was as committed as she was to the marriage, to the family and to the preservation of their home life in the future.

The court considered that the husband's concealment of the extra-marital affair amounted to the exercise of undue influence against Mrs. Hewett.

Undue influence may not only be exerted by the opposite party to the contract; it may also be exerted by a third party over a party to the contract. For example, a husband may, by means of undue influence, induce his wife to enter into guarantee contracts with a bank in order to secure his own debts. In such a case, the contract is voidable if the opposite party (the bank) has actual or constructive notice that the other party (the wife) entered into the contract under undue influence from a third party (the husband). In *Royal Bank of Scotland*, the court held that a bank is placed on notice if a wife offers to stand as surety for her husband's debt, as it is not to the wife's financial advantage and there is substantial risk that the husband has exercised undue influence. The bank has to take reasonable steps to ensure that the practical implications of the transaction are impressed upon the wife, *e.g.*, by ensuring that the wife has received independent legal advice. If the bank fails to do so and the husband has exercised undue influence, the bank will be considered to have had constructive notice.

A final example of undue influence is found in the case of *Diner's Club International v Ng Chi-sing* [1987] 1 HKC 78. The court determined that the credit card company had exercised improper pressure on the elder Mr. Ng to guarantee payment of credit card debts (HK$1,100,000+) of his son and his son's friend, by threatening to report the case to the police. As a result, the guarantee was voidable. The court found that:

> Ng Yan Kiang, a man of 60 and hard of hearing, was confronted at about 7 pm [in his home] by three men who were determined to persuade him to sign the guarantees. ... The three men did not leave until about 11 pm when they had achieved their object.

> … [Ng Yan Kiang] had been about to go out, with his wife, at the invitation of two relatives who were at his home. Because the uninvited and unexpected callers insisted on discussing their business, he was obliged to send his relatives ahead of him to a restaurant, from which during the remainder of the evening these relatives continually telephoned him to find out when he would join them.
>
> Ng Yan Kiang told his callers that he wanted to discuss the matter with his son before he signed but they would not allow him to do so. He had no opportunity to take independent advice, to consult his son or to think matters over and did not understand the full significance of what he was being asked to do. His visitors deliberately aroused anxiety in him (he called it fear) by suggesting that his son might be reported to the Commercial Crimes Bureau … with possible disastrous consequences for the son. …
>
> They deliberately sought to misrepresent the extent of the guarantees sought, implying that they would be of only temporary effect. They also deliberately attempted to mislead him as to the size of the financial commitment he was being asked to undertake.
>
> [He] was unwilling to sign, the two or three hours spent in overcoming his resistance testify to that. … Finally, under the pressure exerted upon him, his resistance collapsed. As he put it, he felt he had no choice. …
>
> [T]he signing of the forms could not be described as being based upon the free and voluntary agency of the individual.[227]

v. *Unconscionable Bargain*

This is a nebulous theory in that there is no universally accepted definition of the concept of unconscionable bargain.[228] Essentially, equity will set aside an agreement where a weaker party is victimized by a stronger party under circumstances that do not amount to coercion or undue influence. The theoretical doctrine of unconscionable bargain appears to be limited: firstly, the overall bargain must be oppressive to the weaker party; secondly,

227. (1986) CA 143/85 at 72.

228. Chui & Roebuck, *supra* note 3, at para. 5.7.

This term is identically defined both in section 2 of the Securities and Futures (Client Securities) Rules (Cap 571H) and in section 2 of the Securities and Futures (Client Money) Rules (Cap 571I):

> "unconscionable" (不合情理), in relation to a standing authority, means unconscionable having regard to the factors specified in section 6 of the Unconscionable Contracts Ordinance (Cap 458), as if the standing authority in question were a contract under that Ordinance;

the doctrine may only apply when the complaining party was suffering from certain types of bargaining weakness; and, thirdly, the stronger party must have acted unconscionably by having knowingly taken advantage of the weaker party.[229]

One authority describes the application of unconscionable bargain as follows:

> The usual requirements for showing a prima facie unconscionable bargain are that it was a purchase from a poor and ignorant or weak-minded person, that it was a purchase at a considerable undervalue and that the vendor had no independent advice. Where those requirements are satisfied the onus is on the purchaser to show that the purchase was fair, just and reasonable.[230]

Section 6 of the *Unconscionable Contracts Ordinance* (Cap 458) provides the criteria for finding an unconscionable agreement:

(1) In determining whether a contract or part of a contract was unconscionable in the circumstances relating to the contract at the time it was made, the court may have regard to (among other things)—
   (a) the relative strengths of the bargaining positions of the consumer and the other party;
   (b) whether, as a result of conduct engaged in by the other party, the consumer was required to comply with conditions that were not reasonably necessary for the protection of the legitimate interests of the other party;
   (c) whether the consumer was able to understand any documents relating to the supply or possible supply of the goods or services;
   (d) whether any undue influence or pressure was exerted on, or any unfair tactics were used against, the consumer or a person acting on behalf of the consumer by the other party or a person acting on behalf of the other party in relation to the supply or possible supply of the goods or services; and
   (e) the amount for which, and the circumstances under which, the consumer could have acquired identical or equivalent goods or services from a person other than the other party.

(2) In determining whether a contract or part of a contract was unconscionable in the circumstances relating to the contract at the time it was made—
   (a) the court shall not have regard to any unconscionability arising from circumstances that were not reasonably foreseeable at the time the contract was made; and
   (b) the court may have regard to conduct engaged in, or circumstances existing, before the commencement of this Ordinance.

(3) In considering the exercise of its powers under section 5 to grant relief in respect of a contract or part of a contract found to be unconscionable, the court may have regard to the conduct of the parties to the proceedings in relation to the performance of the contract since it was made.

229. Chitty, *supra* note 2, at para. 7–129.
230. 22 Halsbury's, *supra* note 100, at para. 340.153.

These guidelines appeared to have been applied in *Lo Wo v Cheung Chan Ka, Joseph and Bond Star Development Ltd* [2001] 3 HKC 70 which involved a claim of unconscionable contract. The court found that the plaintiffs, three elderly sisters (the youngest was approximately 78 years old), were simple country folk living in a remote part of Guangdong province. These three sisters were the heirs of a one-half interest in a North Point flat owned by their deceased sister. The defendants were involved in buying out all the owners of the building housing the subject flat for the purposes of redevelopment. The defendants approached the sisters offering them HK$870,000 on the basis that more cannot be paid for the property as it will be used for storing sand. The sisters entered into the sales contract by each making an "X" on the agreement. The defendants failed to inform the sisters that other comparable flat owners received HK$2.4 million and HK$300,000 removal expenses. The court found this contract to be unconscionable for reasons including but not limited to the following:

1. ensuring that the sisters entered into the contract unnecessarily hastily;
2. deliberately not informing the sisters as to the purchase prices of the other units;
3. Cheung lying to the sisters that the flat was to be acquired by the Developer to store sand rather than for property redevelopment;
4. dangling the cash deposit HK$50,000 before the sisters, knowing that to the rural Plaintiffs and their relatives this was a large sum;
5. by offering the Developer's agent Cheung to act as the sisters' attorney and the Administrator of their deceased sister's estate, thereby giving the defendants the advantage of depriving the sisters of the opportunity to have proper representation and proper independent advice and thereby minimising the chance that the sisters might wish to resile from the agreement;
6. by deliberately not informing the sisters that the nature of the transaction was such that they should have independent professional advice and not giving the sisters time to seek such advice;
7. by failing to explain to the sisters that the nature of the transaction they were to enter into with the defendants was extraordinarily disadvantageous to the plaintiffs and that they did not seem to be capable of making judgment of what was in their best interests; and,
8. by not giving a copy of the contract to the sisters.[231]

231. [2001] 3 HKC at 74–75.

Another Hong Kong example of unconscionability is found in the case of *Hang Seng Credit Card Ltd v Tsang Nga Lee* [2000] 3 HKC 269. The agreement between the bank and Tsang, the credit card holder, included a clause allowing the bank to recover from the credit card holder all the expenses and costs relating to enforcement of the agreement and the collection of debt from the credit card holder. There was no limitation on the amount of expenses and costs which could be recovered from the credit card holder. The court considered the following factors:

1. the relative strengths of the parties;
2. whether the credit card holder understood the clause;
3. whether a similar service was available to the credit card holder from another provider; and,
4. the effect of the clause itself.

After examining these factors, the court determined the clause used by Hang Seng to be unconscionable due to the following:

1. Hang Seng had a much stronger bargaining position;
2. a standard form contract was used by Hang Seng to which a credit card holder had no input;
3. the credit card application form did not mention the relevant clause;
4. a credit card holder had no practical choice in applying for a credit card as most credit card issuers used similar clauses;
5. the application of the clause was unrestricted; and,
6. the interest rate charged was extortionate.

A further instance of an unconscionable contract involved a foreign domestic helper. In *Semana Bachicha v Poon Shiu Man* [2000] 3 HKC 452, an employment dispute resulted in the parties signing an agreement arrived at with the assistance of a Labour Relations Officer of the Labour Department. This agreement provided that the plaintiff domestic helper would pay to the defendant employer the amount of $975. (The court, however, later found that the employer had breached the employment contract and had wrongfully dismissed the plaintiff. Consequently, it was the defendant who should have paid the plaintiff.) In relation to the issue of unconscionability, the judge held:

> [the Labour Relations Officer's] advice, which echoed the defendant's own assertions at the meeting, obviously failed accurately to convey the legal position. As a matter of commonsense, legal advice cannot be given on the foundation of only such part of the facts as may happen to be undisputed. The disputed facts, subsequently found by the Judge

> in our case to have been proved ... entirely changed the picture: the employee did not wrongfully walk out on her employers, she was unlawfully driven out of her job and so had been constructively dismissed.
>
> The plaintiff had been led to believe that she was in law taken to have walked out on her job and had consequently incurred a net liability to the defendant, her claim being disregarded. She therefore signed the compromise agreement in the mistaken belief that it represented a concession by her employer going beyond anything she was entitled to. She would not have signed the document if she had realised that her version of events would be entertained and if accepted, would lead to liability falling on the defendant.[232]
>
> ...
>
> In my judgment, such unconscionability was present in this case. Neither party was legally represented when the agreement was signed. The plaintiff was a person with an economic and social disadvantage, and with a marked inequality of bargaining power, when compared with her employer. At the meeting [before the Labour Relations Officer], the defendant, while knowing full well the circumstances which, as the Judge later found, led to the plaintiff being driven out of her job, contended that the plaintiff was liable to compensate him for walking out of the job and sought and obtained the [Labour Relations] Officer's support for his position. In consequence, the plaintiff was led to accept an improvident agreement limiting her compensation to a paltry $975 in purported full and final settlement of all claims against the defendant. The employer therefore took advantage both of the ignorance of the plaintiff and of the [Labour Relations] Officer's faulty advice to secure for himself an oppressive bargain by unconscionable means. To my mind, this suffices to bring the case into the exceptional class of cases where the court will intervene to set the bargain aside ...[233]

Note the effects of two Ordinances upon this area of contract law, namely, the *Supply of Services (Implied Terms) Ordinance* (Cap 457) and the *Unconscionable Contracts Ordinance* (Cap 458).[234] In relation to the latter

---

232. [2000] 3 HKC at 461.
233. *Id.* at 462.
234. Section 5(1) of the *Unconscionable Contracts Ordinance*, *supra* note 228, provides:

> If, with respect to a contract ... in which one of the parties deals as consumer, the court finds the contract or any part of the contract to have been unconscionable in the circumstances relating to the contract at the time it was made, the court may-

ordinance, a Hong Kong court has held that section 5 grants a court the authority to:

> refuse to enforce the contract, or to enforce the remainder of the contract without the unconscionable part, or to limit the application of, or revise or alter, any unconscionable part so as to avoid any unconscionable result[235]

if there existed unconscionability at the time the contract was made.

vi. *Illegal and Void Contracts*

This section examines situations where an agreement containing all the required elements to be a legally binding agreement is nonetheless unenforceable as a contract. Generally, the reasons for non-enforcement of these agreements are related to government policy.

On this subject, one authority has noted:

> There are several classes of contracts which, though perfect as to form, agreement and consideration, are not given full effect because they offend against the policy of the law. Some contracts may be illegal in the sense that they involve the commission of a legal wrong, whether by statute or the common law, or because they offend against fundamental principles of order or morality. Less objectionable contracts may be simply void by common law or statute.
>
> In respect of certain contracts invalidated under the above principles it is not absolutely clear whether they are illegal or void; but the distinction must be made, because there are differences between illegal and void contracts in respect of related agreements, severability and recovery of property transferred or money paid under such contracts.[236]

(a) refuse to enforce the contract;
(b) enforce the remainder of the contract without the unconscionable part;
(c) limit the application of, or revise or alter, any unconscionable part so as to avoid any unconscionable result.

Section 6 of the same Ordinance sets out the parameters to be considered by the courts in an action based upon the claim of an unconscionable contract. The provisions of section 6 are set out in full in *supra* note 228.

235. *Shum Kit Ching v Caesar Beauty Centre Ltd* [2003] 3 HKC 235, 239.

236. 7(2) HALSBURY'S, *supra* note 1, at para. 115.199 (citations omitted).

If a contract is illegal when formed, the whole purpose of the contract is illegal and the consideration is illegal.[237] Courts will not enforce the contract or provide any remedy. The contract is void and cannot be enforced by either party.[238] An example of an illegal contract is where the parties to a construction contract agree to by-pass the required approval from the Building Authority.[239]

Another example involves the interest charged on a loan. If the rate of interest charged exceeds the legal rate, the loan is considered to be usurious. This makes the loan void and unenforceable, resulting in the lender forfeiting the right to recover both the principal amount borrowed and the interest. Section 25(3) of the *Money Lenders Ordinance* (Cap 163) provides that a transaction shall be presumed to be extortionate if the effective rate of interest on a loan exceeds 48 per cent per annum. Such a transaction will be voided by a court only if the surrounding circumstances are considered unfair or unreasonable. Likewise, under section 24(1) of this Ordinance, "any person ... who lends money ... at an effective rate of interest which exceeds 60 per cent per annum commits an offence." Nonetheless, it is

---

237. For an example of an English court's approach in determining illegality of a contract, *see Craig Joseph v Jason Spiller* [2009] EWCA Civ 1075, 2010 ICR 642.

238. 7(2) HALSBURY'S, *supra* note 1, at para.115.238 notes:

> The general rule is that a contract involving the commission of a legal wrong or a contract with an unlawful purpose may not be enforced by either party at law or in equity. (citations omitted)

"An agreement to do that which is a crime or a tort is illegal and will not be enforced by the courts." *Id.* at para. 115.202 (citations omitted).

> Judges, in deciding the outcome of illegality cases, often draw a distinction between contracts which are illegal as *formed* and those illegal as *performed*. Thus, for example, a contract to jointly to rob a bank and then divide the proceeds is obviously illegal as formed. On the other hand a contract under which A agrees to ship B's goods is not, on the face of it, illegal but may be performed illegally if A decides to over-load the ship contrary to law.
>
> Generally, when contracts are illegal as formed, the courts refuse to allow enforcement by either party. However, they may allow limited enforcement of an illegally formed contract via the "severance" of the part that is illegal.
>
> When, however, the contract is illegally performed, the courts tend to permit enforcement by an "innocent" party (i.e. one who has not performed illegally) but not by the guilty. On rare occasions, even the guilty party may be allowed to enforce the contract if his action can be asserted without reference to the illegality of the contract. (emphasis in original)

FISHER & GREENWOOD, *supra* note 17, at 324.

239. For other examples of contracts to commit a crime or tort, *see, e.g.*, 7(2) HALSBURY'S, *supra* note 1, at paras. 115.202–115.203; CHUI & ROEBUCK, *supra* note 3, at paras. 10.5.1–10.5.6; FISHER & GREENWOOD, *supra* note 17, at 324–328.

not deemed usurious if *excessive* interest is charged after the loan or debt becomes past due because the law allows borrowers to avoid the excess interests by making timely payments under the loan contract.

Alternatively, a contract may be legally formed but be illegal as performed, *e.g.*, a contractor breaches the Building Regulations. The contract is not necessarily void if the work to be done is not essential to the contract as a whole. A client may be able to receive compensation for loss or damage as the contractor had agreed to comply with the Building Regulations. By contrast, as discussed later in section VI.D, if the contract becomes illegal due to changes in law after the contract was formed, performance is not required and is considered to be made impossible.

A contract may be found to be void as against "public policy".[240] An agreement which tends to be harmful to the public or against the public good would be invalidated on public policy grounds.[241] "The enforcement of contractual claims is in certain circumstances against public policy. The effects of public policy differ considerably depending upon the circumstances ..."[242] The doctrine of public policy is "open-textured and flexible"[243] as well as not being immutable.[244] Hence, the exact definition and application of the public policy doctrine is vague and subject to change. However, one authority has attempted to define public policy by delineating its scope as follows:

> Objects which on grounds of public policy invalidate contracts may, for convenience, be generally classified into five groups: first, objects which are illegal by common law or by legislation; secondly, objects injurious to good government either in the field of domestic or foreign affairs; thirdly, objects which interfere with the proper working of

---

240. CHUI & ROEBUCK, *supra* note 3, at para. 10.6 state:

> Contracts may be void because they are against public policy even though not illegal. The courts, while disapproving of them, do not regard them with the same severity as those which are strictly illegal.

The authors continue by noting:

> If merely one clause is void as against public policy, that clause may be severed, that is cut out, leaving the contract to stand without it ... Collateral contracts will be valid as long as they do not owe their existence only to the void part of the contract.

Id. at para. 10.6.2.

241. 7(2) HALSBURY'S, *supra* note 1, at para. 115.205.
242. CHITTY, *supra* note 2, at para. 16–001.
243. *Id.* at para. 16–003.
244. *Id.* at para. 16–004.

> the machinery of justice; fourthly, objects injurious to marriage and morality; and, fifthly, objects economically against the public interest.[245]

When a contract contains both lawful and unlawful objectives, a court may require the illegal portion to be severed, *i.e.*, removed, deleted, or, cut out. In situations where the lawful objectives have already been performed, payment for that performance can be enforced in a claim for restitution.

VI. DISCHARGE

"Discharge" of a contract refers to the termination of the contractual obligations between the parties. A contract ends when no further rights or obligations exist under the agreement. This occurs in one of the following ways.[246]

A. Performance

A contract ends when the parties have performed that which they promised to do under their contract. The general rule, though, is that the parties must execute precisely their promises before there can be discharge of a contract by performance.[247] There are some exceptions to this general

245. *Id.* at para. 16–005.

246. According to 7(2) HALSBURY'S, *supra* note 1, at para. 115.282:

> The ways in which a contractual promise may be discharged may be classified under two basic headings: discharge in accordance with the contract and discharge "against" the contract.
>
> The former covers (1) discharge by performance and (2) discharge as a result of an event stipulated in the contract. The latter covers (a) discharge by rescission for such matters as breach or misrepresentation or by subsequent agreement; (b) discharge by frustration; and (c) discharge as a result of certain miscellaneous events such as merger and (in some cases) death or bankruptcy. (citations omitted)

It is beyond the purview of this work to examine in depth each of these grounds for discharging a contract. Only the most common grounds will be presented in general.

247. *Id.* at para. 115.283 states in part:

> The basic rule is that a promisor must perform exactly what he undertook to do; and the question whether what has been done amounts to exact performance is a question in each case of the construction of the terms of the contract …
>
> … In all cases, however, the requirement of exact performance is qualified by the de minimis rule, that is that minute and unimportant deviations from exact compliance will be ignored. (citations omitted)

rule and the applicability of these exceptions might rest upon whether the contract is "entire" or "divisible":

> A contract is said to be "entire" when complete performance by one party is a condition precedent to the liability of the other; in such a contract the consideration is usually a lump sum which is payable only upon complete performance by the other party (hence, the reference is sometimes to a "lump sum contract"). The opposite of an "entire contract" is a "divisible contract", which is separable into parts, so that different parts of the consideration may be assigned to severable parts of the performance, *e.g.* an agreement for payment pro rata.[248]

i. Substantial Performance

One exception to the rule that "a party to a contract must perform exactly what he undertook to do" is where substantial performance of the contractual obligations has occurred.[249] "Substantial performance" occurs when one party has substantially performed or substantially completed an entire contractual obligation or obligations but has not completed full performance.[250] The doctrine of substantial performance is intended to prevent injustice where a contract is breached inadvertently and minor non-essential deficiencies are caused, which can be easily and inexpensively remedied. This doctrine is frequently raised in disputes involving construction contracts. However, substantial performance is not applicable to instances involving wilful or intentional breaches.

---

248. CHITTY, *supra* note 2, at para. 21–027.
In similar, but more detailed, language is this definition of entire and divisible contracts:

> Contracts are indivisible or entire when the consideration is one and entire; that is where ... no consideration is to pass from one party unless and until the whole of the obligations of the other party have been performed. Thus a party who has not completely performed cannot demand performance by the other party. If ... the contract resolves itself into a number of considerations for a number of acts (as, for example, in the case of a contract to deliver goods by instalments, the price being fixed per item or per instalment) the contract may be divisible (or alternatively it may constitute a series of separate contracts). If the contract is divisible the right to demand performance of the other party's obligations (for example, payment) arises as each part of the contract is performed and where there has been partial performance a proportionate part of the other party's performance may be demanded.

7(2) HALSBURY'S, *supra* note 1, at para. 115.284.

249. CHITTY, *supra* note 2, at para. 21–001 (citations omitted).

250. *Id.* at para. 21–032.

If the difference is minor between the work actually performed and the work contractually undertaken to be performed, the party committing this slight breach may be allowed to recover the contract price less an allowance for the difference between its substantial performance and the performance necessary to meet the contractual requirements.[251] Thus, the difference between substantial performance of the contractual obligations and complete performance of the contract terms is considered to be a breach of warranty. Damages for breach of warranty will be the value of the difference between what was bargained for and what was actually received. Breach with substantial performance results in damages, usually a reduction in price. Breach of a condition results in the injured party having the option to repudiate and to sue for damages.[252]

ii. *Severable Contracts*

Another exception to the general rule involves divisible or severable contracts. A "divisible" or "severable" contract is one in which separate "parts" are to be delivered or performed, and separately paid. Each instalment is considered to be independent of the others, and is separately enforceable regardless of performance or non-performance of the other instalments. In other words, each instalment is breached one at a time, unless the breach of one instalment shows an intent to repudiate the entire contract, or where the breached instalment substantially affects the value of the whole contract. The performing party does not have to prove substantial performance of the entire contract to recover for the performance of one instalment.

Should a court consider a contract to be severable, the party failing to perform all the promises can nevertheless recover a portion of the overall contract price for performing part of the contractual obligations. A wilfully defaulting party is permitted a partial payment for previously performed instalments of a severable contract, as each instalment of a severable contract is considered to be breached one at a time. The exceptions are where the breach of one instalment demonstrates an intent to repudiate the entire agreement, or, where the breached instalment substantially affects the value of the whole contract.

The presumption is against the existence of a divisible contract so that a party seeking to separate the individual terms of the contract must

251. Chui & Roebuck, *supra* note 3, at para. 6.2.1.
252. *Id.*

demonstrate that both parties intended a severable contract at the time of contracting. For example, the party may produce evidence that the parties intended instalment payments be made as work progressed in a building contract, as is the norm.[253]

iii. Part Performance

Another exception to the general rule that a promisor must perform fully its contractual undertaking is that of partial performance.

> Where a party has performed only part of an entire obligation he can normally recover nothing, neither the agreed price, since it is not due under the terms of the contract, nor any smaller sum for the value of his partial performance, since the court has no power to apportion the consideration. The refusal of pro rata payment is based on the inability of the court ... to add such a provision to the contract, and also upon the rule that ... part performance under an express contract cannot ... justify the imposition of a restitutionary obligation to pay on a quantum meruit basis.[254]

If the injured party had the effective option of refusing part performance but accepts part performance, there is a variation in the contract.[255] Partial performance need not be accepted or paid for unless the contract so provides. If partial performance is accepted, payment must be on a *pro rata* basis.

> [A] claim may be made by a party who has not completely performed if it can be inferred from the circumstances that there is a fresh agreement between the parties that payment will be made pro rata for work already done or goods already supplied under the original contract, as for example where a buyer of goods accepts less than the stipulated quantity. It is not, however, enough to bring this principle into play that the party from whom payment is demanded has received a benefit from the partial performance; he must have had, at the time when it became clear that there would not be exact performance, an opportunity to accept or reject the partial performance. Nor is it possible where that party had no such choice to bring an action upon a quantum meruit.[256]

---

253. *Id.* at para. 6.2.2.
254. CHITTY, *supra* note 2, at para. 21–030.
255. "Variation of a contract" refers to changes or amendments made to an existing contract and is discussed below in section VI.B.
See, e.g., CHITTY, *supra* note 2, at paras. 3–076 to 3–080, 22–032 to 22–039.
256. 7(2) HALSBURY'S, *supra* note 1, at para. 115.285.

iv. *Induced Non-performance*

Another exception to the general rule of full performance is found where one party prevents performance of the contract by the other party. In this event, the injured party may sue for the damages resulting from this breach of contract, repudiate the contract, or both.[257]

B. Agreement, Assignment and Novation

A contract can be varied or discharged by oral or written agreement.[258] A contract can be varied or discharged orally even if that contract was entered into in writing or by deed.[259] If the varying or discharging agreement is made by deed, there is no need to show consideration. A contract required to be in writing may be discharged orally, but cannot be varied unless evidenced by another contract in writing.[260]

Through an "assignment", the contractual rights, including options, may be transferred without the consent of the promisor.[261] However, liabilities under a contract and offers cannot be transferred without consent of the other party.[262] A contract right that has been assigned is irrevocable if consideration was paid for the assignment. The assignment extinguishes the right of the party making the assignment (referred to as the "assignor"). To revoke an assigned right, a court order for rescission is required. However, gratuitous assignments, similar to a promise to make a gift, in general can be freely revoked by the assignor.

> Assignment by act of the parties may be an assignment either of rights or of liabilities under a contract; or, as it is sometimes expressed, an assignment of the benefit or the burden of the contract.[263]

An assignment may also be effected through the operation of law, such as in the instance of a death or bankruptcy.[264]

257. CHUI & ROEBUCK, *supra* note 3, at para. 6.2.3.
258. See also CHITTY, *supra* note 2, at para. 22–001 (citations omitted).
259. CHUI & ROEBUCK, *supra* note 3, at para. 6.3.
260. *Id.*
261. 7(2) HALSBURY'S, *supra* note 1, at paras. 115.391, 115.395.
The *BLIS Glossary*, *supra* note 2, translates "assign a contract" as 轉讓……合約.
262. CHITTY, *supra* note 2, at para. 19–077.
See also CHUI & ROEBUCK, *supra* note 4, at para. 9.4.2.
263. 7(2) HALSBURY'S, *supra* note 1, at para. 115.136 (citation omitted).
264. *Id.* at para. 115.137.

"Novation", however, is with the consent or agreement of all the parties to the contract.[265] Novation is an act whereby a new contract is formed and substituted for an existing one which is discharged.[266] Generally, the purpose of novation is to allow the introduction of a new party to the new contract and the discharge of a party to the former contract.[267] Under the common law, novation was the only method of assigning a contractual right.[268]

C. Repudiation and Anticipatory Breach

"Repudiation" is the refusal by one of the contracting parties to be bound by the terms of the contract.[269] If a party repudiates a contract, that party demonstrates an intention no longer to be bound by the contract.

> Instead of merely failing to provide due performance at the stipulated time, a party may put himself in breach by evincing an intention, by words or conduct, of repudiating his obligations under the contract.[270]

---

265. *Id.* at para. 115.391.
For more detailed discussion, *see id.* at paras. 115.391–115.395.
266. *Id.* at para. 115.390.
The *BLIS Glossary*, *supra* note 2, translates "novation" as 約務更替.
267. 7(2) HALSBURY'S, *supra* note 1, at para. 115.391.
268. *Id.*
269. CHITTY, *supra* note 2, at para. 22–025 notes the distinction between rescission (*see supra* note 170) and repudiation:

> Where a contract is executory on both sides, that is to say, where neither party has performed the whole of his obligations under it, it may be rescinded by mutual agreement, express or implied. A partially executed contract can be rescinded by agreement provided that there are obligations on both sides which remain unperformed. Similarly, a contract which has been fully performed by one party can be rescinded provided that the other party returns the performance which he has received and in turn is released from his own obligation to perform under the contract. The consideration for the discharge in each case is found in the abandonment by each party of his right to performance or his right to damages, as the case may be. A rescission of this nature must be distinguished from a repudiation by one party, which the other party may elect to treat as a discharge of the obligation, and from the right to rescind which is given to one party in cases of fraud, misrepresentation, duress and undue influence, and in certain cases of mistake. It depends upon the consent of both parties, to be gathered from their words or conduct and not upon the intimation by one of them that he does not intend to be bound by the agreement. (citations omitted)

The *BLIS Glossary*, *supra* note 2, translates "rescind the contract" as 撤銷合約; "rescission" as 撤銷; "repudiates the contract" as 悔約; and, "repudiation of the contract" as 不履行……合約.
270. 7(2) HALSBURY'S, *supra* note 1, at para. 115.356.

Repudiation may occur when performance is due.

Repudiation also may take place before performance is due—this is also known as "anticipatory breach" or "anticipatory repudiation". Thus, repudiation by one party amounts to the wrongful refusal by that party to fulfil its contractual obligations. This act of repudiation would allow the innocent party to consider itself discharged from its obligations and sue for breach.[271] A party's request to renegotiate the contract or purchase price is not an anticipatory breach.

As explained by one source:

> Repudiation takes place where a party expressly or impliedly refuses to carry out duties under the contract. Parties may also make it impossible for themselves to carry out the contract. ... This is a kind of repudiation.
>
> ... The repudiation may take place before the time when performance is due. In such a case, the breach which repudiates the contract is called 'anticipatory breach'. Because a party cannot bring a contract to an end by breaking it, however fundamental the breach, unless the other party accepts that breach as repudiation, the injured party has a choice. When a breach is committed before the contract date of performance, it may be sufficiently serious to allow the injured party to treat it as repudiation. If it is bad enough to be treated as repudiation, the injured party may either treat the contract at once as discharged and sue for damages (and possibly some other remedy), or leave the contract in existence until the contract date for performance. If the injured party chooses to wait, the party in breach may carry out its part of the contract at any time until the contract date or the other's acceptance of the repudiation.
>
> ...

> Whether a party's conduct constitutes a repudiation of the contract is an objective question to be determined by reference to that party's conduct in the context of the contract as a whole. Ultimately the question is whether the party's conduct would convey to a reasonable person an intention not to comply with the party's obligations under the contract.

HALL, *supra* note 3, at 757 citing to *Creatiles Building Materials Ltd v To's Universe Construction Co Ltd* [2003] 2 HKLRD 309.

271. *See* 7(2) HALSBURY'S, *supra* note 1, at paras. 115.356–115.364 for a more detailed analysis of the intricacies of repudiation, particularly para. 115.357's proviso:

> Not every refusal to perform a part of the contract amounts to a repudiation which entitles the other party to treat the contract as at an end; there must be a refusal to perform something which goes to the root or essence of the contract. (citation omitted)

> ...
>
> ... If the term broken is a warranty, the breach is not a repudiation. Of course, a complete failure to perform, such as delivering a bicycle when the contract calls for a car—sometimes called fundamental breach—is also a repudiation.
>
> ... Unless the breach makes further performance of the contract impossible for the injured party, the injured party cannot be forced to accept the breach as repudiation but can go on performing the contract ...[272]

As previously mentioned, when an anticipatory breach occurs, the innocent party may either immediately sue for the breach, or wait and urge the breaching party to perform. Where the injured party affirms the continuation of the contract, the injured party cannot then decide later to rescind the contract. In *Long v Lloyd* [1958] 2 All ER 402 the plaintiff purchased a vehicle from the defendant. The vehicle had defects, allegedly known to the defendant at the time of the sale. Nonetheless, the plaintiff affirmed the contract after both parties agreed to share the costs of repairs to the vehicle. Subsequently, the vehicle broke down and the plaintiff attempted to rescind the contract. The court found that the plaintiff's previous decision to continue with the contract constituted an affirmation which deprived the plaintiff of the right to subsequently rescind the agreement.[273]

Damages for the breach of contract will be determined on the date of the anticipatory breach. This is the date the plaintiff first learned of the anticipatory breach and had the capability to sue in court. If a plaintiff buyer substantially delays in suing the defendant seller, then the plaintiff risks adverse price increases during the period of delay. However, anticipatory breach is not an available remedy, if the innocent party has fully performed under the contract. The performing party must wait for the future payment date fixed in the contract. To avoid this problem, some parties insert an "acceleration clause" to accelerate or make all future payments payable immediately, in the event that one payment instalment is breached. Acceleration clauses can be found in most mortgage contracts: the mortgagee bank fully performs by paying the loan in full, while the mortgagor repays the loan in instalments.

---

272. Chui & Roebuck, *supra* note 3, at paras. 6.5–6.5.2.

273. Fisher & Greenwood, *supra* note 17, at 226.

D. Frustration

"Frustration" of a contract[274] occurs whenever the law recognizes that, without either party being at fault, the contractual obligation has become incapable of being performed because the circumstances in which performance is required would render it radically different from that which was contemplated.[275] If, in the course of executing the contract, a fundamentally different situation arises for which the parties made no provision—so much so that it would not be just in the new situation to hold them bound to the contract terms—then the contract is ended.[276] Thus, the rationale of the doctrine of frustration is that it would be unjust to bind the parties to the contractual terms under the new circumstances and under an essentially different bargain.[277]

This principle of contract law has been summarized in the case of *National Carriers Ltd v Panalpina (Northern) Ltd* [1981] AC 675, HL:

> Frustration of a contract takes place when there supervenes an event (without default of either party and for which the contract makes no sufficient provision) which so significantly changes the nature (not merely the expense or onerousness) of the outstanding contractual rights and/or obligations from what the parties could reasonably have contemplated at the time of its execution that it would be unjust to hold them to the literal sense of its stipulations in the new circumstances; in such case the law declares both parties to be discharged from further performance.[278]

To determine whether a party may successfully claim frustration of contract:

- it is necessary to construe the contract terms in light of the contract's nature and relevant circumstances at the time of contracting in order to reveal the scope of the parties' obligations;

274. Frustration is a complicated area of contract law and as such an in-depth review is outside the purview of this work. *See* FISHER & GREENWOOD, *supra* note 17, at Chapter 14.4 ("Termination by Frustration"); 7(2) HALSBURY'S, *supra* note 1, at paras. 115.261–115.281; HO, *supra* note 13, at Chapter 17 ("Discharge by frustration"); FURMSTON, *supra* note 45, at Chapter 20 ("Discharge Under the Doctrine of Frustration"); CHITTY, *supra* note 2, at Chapter 23 ("Discharge by Frustration").
The *BLIS Glossary*, *supra* note 2, translates "frustration of contracts" as 合約受挫失效.
275. *Davis Contractors Ltd v Fareham Urban District Council* [1956] AC 696, 729.
276. *Ocean Tramp Tankers Corp v V/O Sovfracht, The Eugenia* [1964] 2 QB 226, 238.
See 7(2) HALSBURY'S, *supra* note 1, at para. 115.261 which offers one explanation of this doctrine.
277. *Ocean Tramp Tankers Corp*, *supra* note 276, at 238.
278. [1981] AC at 700.

- it is necessary to examine the situation after the frustrating event in order to determine the parties' obligations now if their contract were to be enforced; and,
- a comparison is then made between the original obligations and the new obligations in order to decide whether the new obligations are radically different from the original obligations.[279]

A claim of frustration of contract may arise from a multitude of causes. One authority has categorized the cases according to the types of frustrating events:

- Physical destruction of the subject matter of the contract.
- Cancellation of an expected event. Where an expected event is the foundation of the contract (as where the parties agree to provide and take seats to view a procession), the cancellation of that event will as a general rule frustrate the contract.
- Delay. Frustration very commonly arises through delay, attributable to the fault of neither party, of such a character that the fulfilment of the contract, in the only way or ways contemplated and practicable, is so inordinately postponed that the delayed fulfilment will involve something commercially or fundamentally different from that contemplated in the contract.
- Subsequent legal changes. Another familiar example of frustration is found where impossibility of performance arises through subsequent changes in the law. Where performance of the contract has been rendered impossible by legislation passed after the contract was made, the promisor is then excused from performing. The presumption is that the parties intend to contract with reference to the law existing at the time when the contract was made.

---

279. Chui & Roebuck, *supra* note 3, at para. 6.6.1.
In the case of *Li Ching Wing v Xuan Yi Xiong* [2004] 1 HKC 353, the tenant of a flat in Amoy Gardens failed in the attempt to avoid the lease on the basis of frustration as the building in which the flat was located was quarantined for ten days by the Hong Kong government during the SARS epidemic.

> The outbreak of SARS may arguably be an unforeseeable event however, such supervening event did not … significantly change the nature of the outstanding contractual rights or obligations from what the parties could reasonably have contemplated at the time of the execution of the tenancy agreement. Hence, the defence of frustration cannot possibly succeed in the present case …

[2004] 1 HKC at 358.

- Death or incapacity. Where personal obligations are the foundation of the contract, the death or incapacity of a party will generally discharge the contract.[280]

The grounds giving rise to a claim of frustration cannot be self-induced, *i.e.*, a party cannot render it impossible for itself to perform its contractual obligations.[281] Also note the consequences of frustration provided for under the *Law Amendment and Reform (Consolidation) Ordinance* (Cap 23) at sections 16–18. The fact that the contractual obligations are made more expensive or more difficult by a change in circumstances does not constitute frustration of a contract.[282]

280. 7(2) HALSBURY'S, *supra* note 1, at para. 115.264.

281. *Id.* at para. 115.262 notes:

> The doctrine of frustration is in all cases subject to the important limitation that the frustrating circumstances must arise without fault of either party. The defence of frustration can therefore be defeated by proof of fault, and the burden of proof of fault lies upon the party alleging it. Deliberate choice either not to perform or to put performance out of one's power will certainly be fault within this rule … (citations omitted)

CHITTY, *supra* note 2, at para. 23–061 states that:

> a contracting party cannot rely on "self-induced frustration, that is, on frustration due to his own conduct or to the conduct of those for whom he is responsible". …
>
> …
>
> … frustration has been held to be "self-induced" where the alleged frustrating event was caused by a breach or anticipatory breach of contract by the party claiming that the contract has been frustrated, where an act of the party claiming that the contract has been frustrated broke the chain of causation between the alleged frustrating event and the event which made performance of the contract impossible, and where the alleged frustrating event was not a supervening event or "something altogether outside the control of the parties". (citations omitted)

See also HALL, *supra* note 3, at 731–742.

282. In this regard, one source notes that:

> parties will not generally be released from their bargain on account of rises or falls in price, depreciation of currency or unexpected obstacles to the execution of the contract, for these are ordinary risks of business. In particular, a party's insolvency or inability to get finance will not discharge him, unless, of course, the parties have agreed otherwise.

7(2) HALSBURY'S, *supra* note 1, at para. 115.266.

VII. BREACH

A "breach" of contract occurs where one or more of the parties to a contract fail to fulfil the contract terms as and when required.[283] Breach must be evaluated to determine its effect on the rights and duties of the parties. This is done with reference to the contract as a whole, in light of the parties' intentions as expressed in the contract, or as the intentions may be inferred from the contract. A breach may arise in three ways: a repudiation of contract before performance is required; partial performance; or, incomplete or improper performance.

A party's failure to honour its contractual promise is a breach of contract. A breach may be of an express term or of an implied term.[284] This broken contractual promise may be a breach of warranty or a breach of condition. Recall that a breach of warranty only permits the innocent party the right to damages. There is no right to terminate the contract. As such, the innocent party is still required to comply with its contractual obligations.

Breach of condition, however, affords the innocent party the right to terminate the contract as well as the right to damages. Should the innocent party terminate the contract, that party is relieved of its obligation of fulfilling its duties under the contract. The innocent party also may retain any benefit obtained to the time of the termination, so long as the innocent party terminated as soon as possible and gave notice of the termination. Alternatively, the innocent party may decide to continue the contract rather than terminate the contract when a breach of condition occurs. In this event, the breach of condition will be treated as a breach of warranty.

As mentioned previously, anticipatory breach occurs where one party repudiates the contract before the due date of performance, or where some of the contractual obligations remain unperformed.[285] Repudiation may be expressed or implied, *e.g.*, the party states its intention not to perform, or the party by its conduct indicates its intention not to perform its obligations under the contract.

Under this situation, the injured party is excused from performing its obligations under the contract and may claim damages. The injured party

283. The topic of breach and the remedies available therefor have already been introduced to the reader in the context of topics discussed elsewhere in this work, *i.e.*, anticipatory breach, breach of condition, breach of warranty, fundamental breach, repudiation and rescission. Discussion of these topics will not be repeated in this section.

284. Express and implied terms are reviewed in section IV.B.*ii*.

285. This topic has been reviewed in section VI.C; consequently, only a brief summary is presented here.

must "mitigate" its damages, *i.e.*, minimize the losses. Alternatively, the injured party may refuse to accept the breach and affirm the contract's continuing existence, giving the other party an opportunity to change its position before the due date for performance

VIII. DAMAGES AND REMEDIES

This section reviews the recourse one party may have in instances where the other party to the contract has failed to honour its obligations or responsibilities.

> Whether or not a breach of contract gives rise to a right to rescind, it gives the injured party a right of action for damages. The object of damages in contract is to place the innocent party in the same position he would have been in had there been no breach; the innocent party must prove on the balance of probabilities both the breach itself and the amount of loss. The contract may provide for a sum payable as liquidated damages in the event of breach.
>
> In certain cases where damages would be an inadequate remedy application may be made for a decree of specific performance; or, where the obligation is a negative one, for an injunction to restrain breach of the contract. Certain types of contracts may give rise to special remedies, for example the rights of lien and resale under a contract for the sale of goods, or the right of repossession under a contract of hire purchase.[286]

A. Damages

Damages are awarded to compensate the innocent party for the incurred loss resulting from the other party's breach of contract.[287] Because damages are intended as recompense for the loss suffered by the injured party and to place the innocent party in the same position as if the contract had been

286. 7(2) HALSBURY'S, *supra* note 1, at para. 115.370, citing to *ICI Swire Paints Ltd v Techi Motor Engineering and Trading Co* [2003] 3 HKC 432, CFI. The remedies mentioned in the latter portion of the quotation will not be presented in this work. However, they are mentioned so the reader is made aware that remedies other than those presented in this section might be available to an injured party.

287. *See generally* HO, *supra* note 13, at Chapter 19 ("Remedies").
The purpose of damages is to compensate the plaintiff for the loss caused by the breach. Another purpose of damages is to put the injured party financially into the same position as if the contract had been performed. CHUI & ROEBUCK, *supra* note 3, at para. 7.3.2.

fully performed, an innocent party cannot generate a profit from an action for damages.[288] Damages generally are assessed by courts according to the following principles of remoteness of damage[289] and mitigation of loss. However, the parties are free to agree in the contract to change or limit the rules for damages. For example, the parties may agree to the use of exemption clauses and liquidated damages, as discussed in section IV.D and section VIII.B, respectively.

i. *Principles of Damages*

The principle of remoteness of damage provides that the innocent party can recover those losses which arise naturally from the breach, or losses which were in the reasonable contemplation of the parties as a probable result of a breach at the time the parties entered into the contract.[290] The defaulting

---

Likewise, traditionally:

> damages for a breach of contract committed by the defendant are a compensation to the claimant for the damage, loss or injury he has suffered through that breach, and this remains the normal rule. The claimant is, as far as money can do it, to be placed in the same position as if the contract had been performed.

CHITTY, *supra* note 2, at para. 26–001 (citation omitted).

288. *But see Attorney General v Blake* [2001] 1 AC 268, a court decision concerning the publication of the memoirs of a former British espionage agent in contravention of the Official Secrets Act 1989. The Attorney General claimed as damages the monies paid and to be paid to Blake by the publisher of his memoirs on the ground that Blake owed the Crown a fiduciary duty not to use his former position as a Secret Intelligence Service member so as to generate a profit for himself. The obstacle confronting the Attorney General was that the Crown had suffered no loss as a result of the publication and English law at that time did not permit damages for breach of contract to be measured by the financial benefits gained by the contract-breaker. The court overcame this obstacle by holding that damages for breach of contract could be assessed by reference to the benefits gained by the wrongdoer rather than the loss suffered by the innocent party. The impact of the *Blake* case is analyzed in 2003 *New LJ* 153.7079 (723); 2003 *Emp. Law & Lit.* 8.7 (33).

289. CHITTY, *supra* note 2, at para. 26–051 notes:

> The term "remoteness of damage" refers to the legal test used to decide which types of loss caused by the breach of contract may be compensated by an award of damages. (citation omitted)

The test is:

> A type or kind of loss is not too remote a consequence of a breach of contract if, at the time of contracting (and on the assumption that the parties actually foresaw the breach in question), it was within their reasonable contemplation as a not unlikely result of that breach.

Id. at para. 26–054 (citation omitted).

290. "The defendant does not have to pay damages for loss which was not caused by the breach." CHUI & ROEBUCK, *supra* note 3, at para. 7.3.3.

party will be liable for losses outside the natural course of events where the circumstances which caused the loss were within the knowledge of the defaulting party at the time of contract.

The case of *Hadley v Baxendale* (1854) 9 Ex 341 first stated the remoteness of damage principle. This case involved a mill. Due to a broken crankshaft, the mill's operation was brought to a halt. The defendant carriers failed to deliver the broken crankshaft to the manufacturer for repairs within the time promised. As a result, the plaintiff sued for loss of profits due to the delay. The plaintiff lost the case as the defendant's knowledge was insufficient to:

> show reasonably that the profits of the mill must be stopped by an unreasonable delay in the delivery of the broken shaft by the carriers to the third person.[291]

In other words, the defendant was unaware of the plaintiff's particular situation: that the plaintiff only had one crankshaft when it was the norm for mills to have spare crankshafts available for use while a broken crankshaft is undergoing repair.

The principle of mitigation requires the injured party to take all reasonable steps to minimize the loss suffered as a result of the other party's breach.

> There are three rules often referred to under the comprehensive heading of "mitigation" ... First, the claimant cannot recover damages for any part of his loss consequent upon the defendant's breach of contract which the claimant could have avoided by taking reasonable steps. Secondly, if the claimant in fact avoids or mitigates his loss consequent upon the defendant's breach, he cannot recover for such avoided loss, even though the steps he took were more than could be reasonably required of him under the first rule. Thirdly, where the claimant incurs loss or expense in the course of taking reasonable steps to mitigate the loss resulting from the defendant's breach, the claimant may recover this further loss or expense from the defendant.[292]

> The important issue in remoteness of damage in the law of contract is whether a particular loss was within the reasonable contemplation of the parties, but causation must first be proved: there must be a causal connection between the defendant's breach of contract and the claimant's loss. The claimant may recover damages for a loss only where the breach of contract was the "effective" or "dominant" cause of that loss.

CHITTY, *supra* note 2, at para. 26–032 (citations omitted).

291. (1854) 9 Ex at 355.

292. CHITTY, *supra* note 2, at para. 26–101.

ii. Types of Damages

There are different types of damages that the court may award the innocent party in a successful claim. The most common type of damages awarded for breaches of contract is "expectation damages". The courts determine the profits that would have been made if the contract had been fully performed. This method places the innocent party in the same financial position as if the contract had been fully performed. Damages are normally determined at the time of the breach for the loss of value to the innocent party. The courts would consider the value that the injured party should have received under the terms of the contract; the actual value received by that party; and, any incidental and foreseeable consequential damages. The courts would also reduce the damages awarded by any expenses that the innocent party would have had to incur to fully perform that contract.

In circumstances where determination or assessment of expectation damages is difficult, the courts may instead award "reliance damages" for breaches of contract. Reliance damages seek to compensate the innocent party for expenses incurred in performing the breached contract, and, do not include lost profits. Thus, reliance damages restore the innocent party to its original economic position, as if the contract had never been made. Courts may also award reliance damages where a party has suffered detrimental reliance from an unenforceable agreement.

The courts may also award "restitution damages" for partially performed contracts. Restitution damages are recoverable to the extent that a benefit was conferred on the defaulting party by the injured party's part performance. The measure of restitution damages is normally based on the market value of the services performed, *e.g.*, the price to obtain similar performance in the market. Alternatively, the damages may be measured by the extent to which the services performed increased the value of the defaulting party's property. Where there is the possibility, a court would award the greater value. A court award of restitution damages seeks to prevent an unfair benefit to the defaulting party by forcing that party to compensate the innocent party for the value of any performance that the defaulting party received. Restitution damages do not seek to enforce the contract.

In rare circumstances, courts may exercise their discretion to award either "nominal damages" or "punitive damages". Nominal damages are awarded when the injured party establishes a breach of contract claim against the defaulting party but fails to prove any damages. An award of punitive damages is intended to punish the defaulting party, and to deter others from engaging in similar reprehensible conduct, rather than to compensate the injured party. Punitive damages are generally not available for a breach of contract, unless the conduct of the defaulting party is considered so morally repugnant by the courts as to warrant punitive damages.

B. Liquidated Damages

"Liquidated damages" are the agreed sums which the parties stipulate in the contract as the amount of damages in the instances of breach.[293] Liquidated damages clauses are inserted into contracts to avoid the difficulty and expense of proving damages. To be enforceable, the liquidated damages must be a genuine pre-estimate of loss; the amount fixed in the clause must bear a reasonable relationship to any probable loss. A genuine pre-estimate of loss will be enforced even if the estimate is higher or lower than the actual loss.[294] This is to be contrasted with penalty clauses, which stipulate amounts *in terrorem*, *i.e.*, threatening, of the party in breach. Penalty clauses are not enforceable. Should a court invalidate a purported liquidated damages clause on the basis that it is a penalty, the innocent party may still sue for damages. The inclusion of a liquated damages clause in a contract does not necessarily preclude injunctive relief or specific performance, unless the contract explicitly so provides.

The distinctions between liquidated damages and penalties were considered in *Dunlop Pneumatic Tyre Co v New Garage Co* [1915] AC 79, from which the following principles may be deduced:

---

293. *See* Ho, *supra* note 13, at 469–478.

> The term liquidated damages is applied where the damages have been agreed and fixed by the parties (in respect of which the law has developed criteria for their validity), or fixed by statute … Unliquidated damages is the term applied where the damages are at large and are to be assessed by the court; the rules as to remoteness of damage are the main criteria for such damages.

CHITTY, *supra* note 2, at para. 26–010.

294. As noted by CHITTY, *supra* note 2, at para. 26–125:

> Where the parties to a contract agree that, in the event of a breach, the contract-breaker shall pay to the other a specified sum of money, the sum fixed may be classified by the courts either as a penalty (which is irrecoverable) or as liquidated damages (which are recoverable). The clause is enforceable if it does not exceed a genuine attempt to estimate in advance the loss which the claimant would be likely to suffer from a breach of the obligation in question: it is enforceable irrespective of the loss actually suffered.

- the labels which the parties attach to the clauses are not conclusive;
- whether a pre-agreed sum is a penalty or liquidated damages is to be judged according to the circumstances at the time of the making of the contract;
- a pre-agreed sum is a penalty if the amount is extravagant and unconscionable in comparison with the greatest loss conceivable;
- a pre-agreed sum is a penalty if the breach is a default of payment and the stipulated sum is higher than the defaulted payment; and/or,
- if a single sum is applied to various breaches with different degrees of seriousness, it is likely to be a penalty.[295]

The Supreme Court of Canada observed in *Elsey v JG Collins Insurance Agencies Ltd* (1978) 83 DLR (3d) 1:

> It is now evident that the power to strike down a penalty clause is a blatant interference with freedom of contract and it is designed for the sole purpose of providing relief against oppression for the party having to pay the stipulated sum. It has no place where there is no oppression.[296]

The court in *Philips Hong Kong Ltd v Attorney General of Hong Kong* (1993) 61 BLR 49, PC approved of the foregoing passage. Thus, where there is equal bargaining power between the parties, a court will not readily strike down a stipulated sum as a penalty. In *Polyset Ltd v Panhandat Ltd* [2000] 4 HKC 203, the Court of Appeal held that a forfeiture of deposit up to 35% of the purchase price in a land sale was not a penalty. This is because the parties had equal bargaining power and the amount was not out of proportion to the possible loss if the property market suddenly dropped, which was likely in the circumstances of the case.

C. Specific Performance

Equity provides an additional remedy known as "specific performance".[297] This equitable remedy is for cases where the contract's subject matter is considered to be unique, such as with land, so that damages paid as

295. [1915] AC at 86–88.
296. (1978) 83 DLR (3d) at 15.
297. Black's Law Dictionary, *supra* note 12, at 1297 defines "equitable remedy" as "a non-monetary remedy, such as an injunction or specific performance, obtained when monetary damages cannot adequately redress the injury." The term "equity" has been previously defined in *supra* note 42.

compensation would be inadequate.[298] Specific performance is discretionary upon the court. The claimant must have "clean hands", *i.e.*, must have acted in good faith, without any wrongdoing or moral turpitude. The claimant must plead specific performance without delay, as delay defeats the application of equitable remedies. Specific performance also requires consideration for the contract. The remedy of specific performance may not be granted if the contract lacks mutuality, even though the contract is made under seal. Consideration must be present.[299]

Specific performance will not be granted where:

- the remedy of specific performance is not available to both parties at the time the contract was made;[300]
- a court would find it impossible to supervise the performance of the contract, *e.g.*, where one party is bound by continuous duties, the performance of which might require constant court supervision;[301]
- the contract is too vague;[302]
- it is a contract of personal service, *e.g.*, an employment contract;[303] or
- the result would impose severe hardship upon the defendant.[304]

---

298. As for the inadequacy of monetary compensation resulting in the remedy of specific performance, one source notes:

> The historical foundation of the equitable jurisdiction to order specific performance of a contract is that the claimant cannot obtain a sufficient remedy by the common law judgment for damages. Hence the traditional view was that specific performance would not be ordered where damages were an "adequate" remedy.

CHITTY, *supra* note 2, at para. 27–005 (citation omitted).

299. CHUI & ROEBUCK, *supra* note 3, at 7.4.1.
As explained by CHITTY, *supra* note 2, at para. 27–034:

> On the principle that equity will not aid a volunteer, specific performance will not be ordered of a gratuitous promise even though it is binding at law because it is made by deed or supported by a nominal consideration so that an action at law for the agreed sum or for damages can successfully be brought upon it.

300. CHUI & ROEBUCK, *supra* note 3, at 7.4.1.

> "Mutuality" means that specific performance will not be awarded to a party if there is no possibility of specific performance being awarded against that party.

FISHER & GREENWOOD, *supra* note 17, at 141 n. 34.

301. CHITTY, *supra* note 2, at para. 27–026.
See also CHUI & ROEBUCK, *supra* note 3, at para. 7.4.1.
302. CHITTY, *supra* note 2, at para. 27–042.
303. CHUI & ROEBUCK, *supra* note 3, at para. 7.4.1.
See also CHITTY, *supra* note 2, at paras. 27–021 to 27–024.
304. CHITTY, *supra* note 2, at paras. 27–030 to 27–031.

D. Restrictions on Remedies

When considering the possible damages arising from a breach of a contractual promise, one also should be considering the possible constraints upon an innocent or injured party to recover such damages. The type of damages or the amount of damages recoverable by an injured party may be limited. Restrictions on the injured party's remedies may be imposed by the parties themselves under their contract or by law. A preliminary example of the restrictions upon an innocent party to recover for a breach concerns the doctrine of privity. The rules and the law governing the transaction are made by the parties to a contract; therefore, only those parties are bound by the responsibilities and receive the benefits of the contract. Thus, only parties to a contract may sue on that contract. However, this doctrine of privity might be avoided by finding the existence of a collateral contract. A party not involved in the main contract may sue one of the parties to the main contract under the collateral contract, thereby indirectly enforcing the main contract.

In the case of *Shanklin Pier v Detel Products* [1951] 2 KB 854, the plaintiff owned a pier. The defendant manufactured paint and made a representation to the plaintiff that its paint would last for approximately ten years. The plaintiff ordered its contractor to purchase paint from the defendant. The contractor duly complied, bought the paint and used it to paint the plaintiffs' pier. The paint lasted three months. As the main contract for the paint's purchase was between the contractor and the defendant, the plaintiff had no privity of contract with the defendant. The court held that a collateral contract existed between the plaintiff and the defendant in that consideration existed in the form of the plaintiff's instructions to its contractor to purchase the paint based upon the defendant's promise of the paint's durability.

The following are some examples of restrictions which may be imposed by the parties to the contract. The first example is liquidated damages, which was discussed above in section VIII.B. As previously noted, liquidated damages arise where the parties, at the time of entering into a contract, have incorporated into the agreement the price or the consequences in monetary terms of a breach of the contract. The courts will only examine whether the parties, at the time of contracting, made a genuine pre-estimate of the loss. The courts will not determine the accuracy of the estimate. Again, note that a liquidated damages clause cannot be used as a penalty clause. Penalty clauses generally are void as the parties to a contract are not permitted to impose punitive or unconscionable sanctions on each other.[305]

Another illustration of party imposed restrictions is the use of a deposit. The function of a deposit is similar to liquidated damages, except that a deposit is usually required at the commencement of the contract. With a deposit, some consideration, generally being money, is paid in advance and can be forfeited if the depositor fails to proceed with the contract. Deposits may be considered as a type of a guarantee of performance.[306]

A final example of party imposed restriction on recovery is the limitation or exemption clause, where one party to the contract attempts to exclude, limit, or exempt itself from liability. Exemption clauses were analyzed earlier in section IV.D.

Some examples of the statutorily imposed restrictions on liability include the *Control of Exemption Clauses Ordinance* (Cap 71), *Misrepresentation Ordinance* (Cap 284) and the *Sale of Goods Ordinance* (Cap 26), all of which have been mentioned earlier in this chapter.

Another example of a statutorily imposed restriction on an injured party's recovery is the *Limitation Ordinance* (Cap 347). This is a statute of limitations which bars a particular remedy after a specified time. For simple contract actions, the limitation period is six years from the date on which the cause of action accrues. If the contract is under seal, the limitation period is twelve years. The cause of action, *i.e.*, the right to sue, generally accrues at the time of a breach or when the cause of action was discovered or ought to have been discovered. No action may be brought after the limitation period expires.[307]

The remedy becomes time-barred after the limitation period expires, but the injured party's rights under the contract remain. For example, a time-barred debt remains payable. A creditor cannot sue on the debt to recover payment. However, should the debtor make a payment to the creditor to whom both time-barred and current debts are owed, without designating to which debt the payment should be allocated, the creditor may allocate the payment to the time-barred debt.[308]

305. *See, e.g.*, Chui & Roebuck, *supra* note 3, at paras. 8.1–8.2.1.
306. *See, e.g.*, *id.* at paras. 8.2.3–8.2.4.
307. *See, e.g.*, *id.* at paras. 8.11.1–8.11.2.
308. *Id.* at para. 8.11.1.

IX. CONCLUSION

This chapter concludes with a review of another case which also pertains to the sale of land. This case summarizes some of the principles presented in this chapter while also serving to introduce some concepts which overlap with the Property chapter. This case is *Lam Tin Hing v Lam Kwai Choi* [2009] 3 HKC 1 which involved issues pertaining to the sale of land in the New Territories, contracts required to be in writing, agency, part performance, limitation period and estoppel.

Lam Ting Hing, the plaintiff, purchased land and the building rights from Lam Kwai Choi, the defendant. Both parties are related to Lam Pak Ling, the builder. All purchasers of the defendant's various parcels of land were required to engage Lam Pak Ling as the builder. During the construction of the plaintiff's house, the builder proposed a larger garden and a vehicular access road to be built on land to be purchased from the defendant. The plaintiff agreed and made payment to the builder in mid-June 1990. A dispute arose when the defendant claimed that he did not agree to this proposal and that the builder had no authority to engage in the sale of the disputed land. The defendant claimed he did not object to the builder's actions due to the defendant's "awe and respect" for his relative. Another issue was whether the sale, made by an oral contract, was validly enforceable as the agreement was contrary to the *Conveyancing and Property Ordinance* (Cap 219) which requires transactions pertaining to land to be in writing.

The court held that the defendant failed to raise the in-writing requirement of the *Conveyancing and Property Ordinance* and therefore waived this ground. The court further noted that the defendant did not object or take action in relation to the disputed land sale for 17 years, from 1990 until 2007. Therefore, the court accepted the plaintiff's claim of part performance and estoppel by stating:

> If one party [Lam Kwai Choi] to an agreement stands by and lets the other party [Lam Tin Hing] incur expense or prejudice his position on the faith of the agreement being valid he [Lam Kwai Choi] will not then be allowed to turn round and assert that the agreement is unenforceable.[309]

309. [2009] 3 HKC at 9 quoting *Steadman v Steadman* [1976] AC 536, 540.

Chapter Two
Tort

This chapter is concerned with the law of tort. However, not all types of tort will be analysed. This chapter concentrates its review upon the types of tort that are generally governed by the common law. For those types of tort that are based upon statute, such torts will be reviewed briefly rather than exhaustively as the focus of this chapter is upon common law tort principles rather than statutory torts.

The first section of this chapter defines tort and discusses some of the purposes of tort law. The second section reviews the various types of torts most commonly encountered. It is here that the most common type of tort—negligence—is analysed. In addition, some of the liability theories are analysed to afford a better understanding of the reasoning upon which some tort actions are decided in the courts. The chapter concludes with a brief review of the compensation available to an injured party.

I. DEFINITION

There is no commonly agreed definition of the term "tort".[1] Generally, a tort is a type of civil wrong that has caused harm to an individual or to property. Tort is generally fault-based liability. A tort is an injury, caused

---

1. For example, one author has noted:

> The difficulty of defining the word "tort" is well recognised. In the words of an American authority (*Prosser on Torts* (4th ed.), p. 1), "the numerous attempts which have been made to define the term have succeeded only in achieving language so broad that it includes other matters than torts, or else so narrow that it leaves out some torts themselves." The main reason for this difficulty is the extreme variety of behaviour which may constitute a tort.

C. D. BAKER, TORT 1 (6th ed. 1996) [hereinafter BAKER]. Another authority has provided the definition that:

other than from a breach of contract, which the law will compensate by awarding damages to the injured party.[2] Dissimilar to criminal law, which involves enforcement of statutes by the government, tort actions generally involve court actions between private parties.[3] Although a tort action is different from a contract or criminal action, these different legal fields might overlap, and this overlap might arise from the same act by the defendant.[4]

The following are some of the differences between tort law and contract law:

> a tort is described as a form of wrongful conduct. In tort law, fault is generally taken to mean either a failure to take reasonable care for the safety of others or their property, or an intention to cause unwanted bodily contact or interference with property.
>
> Where tort law does recognise the right to compensation, that right is enforceable by the injured person through a civil court action against the person who caused the damage: the injured person can *sue* the wrongdoer. (emphasis in original)

RICK GLOFCHESKI, TORT LAW IN HONG KONG 1 (2nd ed. 2007) [hereinafter GLOFCHESKI]. The Hong Kong government's Bilingual Laws Information System's *The English-Chinese Glossary of Legal Terms* [hereinafter *BLIS Glossary*] translates "tort" as 侵權 and 侵權行為. "Tort law" is translated as 侵權法. *See* the *BLIS Glossary* website at: *http://www.legislation.gov.hk/eng/glossary/homeglos.htm* (last visited 26 Feb. 2011).

2. JOHN G. FLEMING, THE LAW OF TORTS, 3 (9th ed. 1998) [hereinafter FLEMING].
3. One source has noted:

> Intentionally or negligently to cause physical injury to another, to interfere with his enjoyment of his land, to defame him, or to conspire with another to cause him financial loss are examples of such behaviour. Such cases appear to have three elements. The first is behaviour by a human being (the defendant) considered by the law to be wrongful. Generally speaking torts are committed only by wrongful behaviour, *i.e.* by intentional wrongdoing or negligent conduct, but there are a few torts in which that is not so and in which the defendant is liable without fault. These are the so-called torts of strict liability. The second element is that the behaviour must infringe another human being's [the plaintiff's] interest, which the law regards as being worthy of protection against that form of behaviour. Some interests are regarded as so important by the law that they receive protection against both intentional and negligent infringement and even in some cases against conduct in which there is no element of fault. Such are the interests in the security of one's person and property. … The third element is that the plaintiff is entitled to obtain compensation from the defendants in the form of damages by taking action in a civil court.

BAKER, *supra* note 1, at 1–2.

4. For a further discussion as to the definition of tort or its overlap with other areas of law, *see, e.g.*, 25(1) HALSBURY'S LAWS OF HONG KONG para. 380.001 (2010) [hereinafter 25(1) HALSBURY'S]; ROBYN MARTIN, LAW OF TORT IN HONG KONG paras. 1.1–1.6 (1987) [hereinafter MARTIN].

- Tortious liability is not based on agreements between the parties, whereas contractual liability is based on legally binding agreements.[5]
- Tort obligations, *i.e.*, rights and duties, are owed to everyone whom the courts consider to be a neighbour, whereas contractual obligations or promises are owed only to those who have privity of contract.
- Tort obligations are imposed by law rather than by the parties themselves, whereas contractual obligations are created and decided voluntarily by the parties to those agreements.
- The basis of tort is to compensate the injured victim for loss or harm, *i.e.*, to return the injured party to the situation prior to the tortious act. The basis of a contract is to enforce the promises, rights or obligations of the parties; *i.e.*, the court attempts to place the parties in the position as if the contractual obligations were fulfilled.
- Damages in tort are an unliquidated sum, *i.e.*, the tortfeasor pays an amount which the court, in its discretion, thinks appropriate. Damages in contract may be either liquidated or unliquidated, *i.e.*, a pre-determined sum of money, depending on the facts of each case.[6]

As noted in 25(1) HALSBURY'S at para. 380.003:

> A crime is an unlawful act or default which is an offence against the public, and renders the person who is guilty of the act or default liable to legal punishment. The same act or omission may be both a crime and a tort, for the duty giving rise to a potential claim for damages against the tortfeasor may also be a duty imposed for the benefit of the public, a breach of which gives rise to a criminal offence. Where a person is convicted of a criminal offence the court of criminal jurisdiction may, in addition to passing such sentence as may otherwise by law be passed or making an order for costs, make an order requiring the offender to pay an aggrieved person compensation for any personal injury, loss or damage to property resulting from that offence or any other offence which is taken into consideration by the court. … (citations omitted)

5. One author comments that:

> A person who has been injured, or has suffered financial loss, or has suffered damage to his/her property, may have been in contractual relations with the wrongdoer, having paid for a particular service or product, or promise to perform. Such a person may have a right to sue for compensation under the law of contract if the contract was not performed according to its terms. Tort law is not concerned with this kind of a right. Tort law enforces duties independent of promises. The right to sue in tort is not dependent on prior agreement, nor on a prior payment of money.

GLOFCHESKI, *supra* note 1, at 2.

The *BLIS Glossary*, *supra* note 1, translates "civil proceedings" as 民事法律程序; "criminal proceedings" as 刑事法律程序; "liability in tort" as 侵權法律責任; and, "liable in tort" as 承擔侵權法律責任.

6. *See* MARTIN, *supra* note 4, at para. 1.4. For a similar comparison but in tabular form, see VIVIENNE HARPWOOD, LAW OF TORT 13 (1996). *See also* GLOFCHESKI, *supra* note 1, at 220–224

Some of the differences between tort law and criminal law are:

- In a court action based upon a tortious act, the proceeding is between private individuals, the plaintiff suing the defendant; in a proceeding based upon a criminal act, the action is prosecuted by the state or the government in lieu of a plaintiff.[7]
- The purpose of tort law is to compensate the injured party for the wrong suffered.[8] Criminal law aims, among other things, to punish the offender and deter future wrongful behaviour.[9]
- The burden of proof in tort actions generally is "on the balance of probabilities" or a "more likely than not" standard, whereas the evidential burden in criminal actions is generally the more onerous "beyond all reasonable doubt".[10]

---

for an exposition on the duty of care in a contractual context; and, 1 CHITTY ON CONTRACTS paras. 1–117 to 1–187 (H.G. BEALE, *et al* eds., 30th ed. 2008), on the relationship between tort and contract.

The *BLIS Glossary*, *supra* note 1, translates "tortfeasor" as 侵權人 and "liquidated or unliquidated damages" as 算定損害賠償或未經算定損害賠償.

7. The *BLIS Glossary*, *supra* note 1, translates "tortious act" as 侵權作為.
In Hong Kong, under exceptional circumstances, private individuals may prosecute offenders by way of private prosecution if the Secretary for Justice refuses to do so. For the distinction between tort and crime, *see* 25(1) HALSBURY'S, *supra* note 4, at para. 380.003.

8. An objective of tort law is stated by one source as endeavouring:

> as far as possible, to restore the person suffering injury or damage to the position that s/he would have been in had no tort been committed. … its fulfilment is normally attempted through an award of compensation referred to in law as *damages*. Occasionally, in those rare cases where the tort is continuing at the time of trial, the appropriate remedy is an *injunction*, an order of the court which requires the person committing the tort to stop the tortious activity. (emphasis in original)

GLOFCHESKI, *supra* note 1, at 2.
The *BLIS Glossary*, *supra* note 1, translates "injunction" as 強制令.

9. In distinguishing tort from criminal actions, one authority notes:

> A person may suffer injury or property damage as a result of a violation of the criminal law. This kind of conduct is often very similar to that of some torts. However, criminal law is primarily concerned with deterring such conduct and punishing a wrongdoer through the imposition of a prison sentence or other penalty. Tort law is not primarily concerned with any of these, but with compensation of the victim for the injury or damage suffered. Although the constituent elements of some crimes are similar to those of some torts, not all torts are crimes. At any rate, even for those torts that are crimes, the proceedings in tort for the recovery of compensation for the damage suffered are separate from and unconnected to any criminal law proceedings that may have been initiated.

GLOFCHESKI, *supra* note 1, at 2–3.

10. Note there are some statutory mandatory presumptions and strict liability offences. One should also note the existence of circumstances which might result in the relaxation of

- If the plaintiff establishes its case in tort, civil remedies, such as damages, are afforded to the injured party. If the government proves its case beyond reasonable doubt in the criminal proceeding, the defendant will be convicted and shall suffer a penalty such as a fine and/or imprisonment. Sometimes compensation, *e.g.*, restitution, is also ordered against the defendant.

Note that these distinctions can overlap, and a tortious act may also be a criminal offence. For example, the tortious liability of an accused, convicted of the criminal offence of battery, is not resolved by serving a prison sentence. The victim may additionally bring a civil action in tort against the accused who would be liable to pay damages for the victim's injuries.[11]

---

the rule that "to succeed in negligence, the plaintiff must prove on the balance of probabilities that the harm was caused by the defendant". TORT LAW AND PRACTICE IN HONG KONG para. 3.220 (JUSTICE KEMAL BOKHARY, *et al* eds., 2nd ed. 2011) [hereinafter BOKHARY]. For further detail, *see*, *e.g.*, GLOFCHESKI, *supra* note 1, at 114–131.

The *BLIS Glossary*, *supra* note 1, translates "strict liability" as 嚴格法律責任.

As noted by another source, a potential plaintiff may utilize the doctrine of *res ipsa loquitur* [the thing speaks for itself] in a situation where the facts of the case indicate negligence but actual negligence is difficult to prove. 25(1) HALSBURY'S, *supra* note 4, at para. 380.169.

The following cases are example of the application of this doctrine: *Wong Yiu Ming v To Chark Wah* [1993] 1 HKC 510 (window frame falling from the building); *Chung Man Yau v Sihon Co Ltd* [1996] 3 HKC 614 (collapse of balcony onto pavement injuring the plaintiffs); *Wong Sau Chun v Ho Kam Chiu* (2000) HCPI 872/1966, [2000] HKEC 109 (the deceased struck by a pane of glass while walking in a common area of a block of flats).

> The maxim *res ipsa loquitur* applies only where the causes of the accident are unknown but the inference of negligence is clear from the nature of the accident. If the causes are sufficiently known the case ceases to be one where the facts speak for themselves and the court has to determine whether or not, from the known facts, negligence is to be inferred. Where there is an unexplained occurrence which on the face of it is negligent, there is a presumption of negligence which can be rebutted only by express proof that the defendants exercised all reasonable care or that there is a likely explanation which does not connote negligence on their part. However, even where the defendant does give evidence relating to the possible cause of the damage and level of precaution taken, the court may still conclude that the evidence provides an insufficient explanation to displace the doctrine.

25(1) HALSBURY'S, *supra* note 4, at para. 380.170 (citations omitted). *See also* 25(1) HALSBURY'S, *supra* note 4, at paras. 380.171–380.173; MARTIN, *supra* note 4, at para.16.2.1–16.2.8.

The doctrine of *res ipsa loquitur* is discussed in more detail in section III.B.*i*.

11. Where one accused of committing a tort is acquitted in the criminal proceedings, this is not conclusive evidence in the civil action because the standard of proof in the criminal action is higher. *See Lam Kin Ping v Tsang Kam Cheong* (2002) HCPI 1458/2000.

Another example of this overlap may arise where the liability of a manufacturer of a defective product, which causes harm to person or property, is found both on the fault-based principles of tort law and the breach of warranty principles of contract law.

Whilst it is difficult to ascertain precisely the exact function lying behind tort law principles, two principal functions may be discerned: to compensate the victims of civil wrongs;[12] and, to deter people from committing wrongs which inflict injury upon others or damage upon their property.[13]

> A person convicted of a criminal offence will, for the purposes of a civil (eg tort) action arising from the same facts, be presumed to have committed that offence without the need for further proof. Documentary proof of the conviction is sufficient to give rise to the presumption. The plaintiff has the burden of proving the relevance of the conviction.

GLOFCHESKI, *supra* note 1, at 67 (citation omitted).

See also the *Evidence Ordinance* (Cap 8) section 62 which states in part:

> (1) In any civil proceedings the fact that a person has been convicted of an offence by or before any court in Hong Kong shall, subject to subsection (3), be admissible in evidence for the purpose of proving, where to do so is relevant to any issue in those proceedings, that he committed that offence, whether he was so convicted upon a plea of guilty or otherwise and whether or not he is a party to the civil proceedings; but no conviction other than a subsisting one shall be admissible in evidence by virtue of this section.
>
> (2) In any civil proceedings in which by virtue of this section a person is proved to have been convicted of an offence by or before any court in Hong Kong—
>
> (a) he shall be taken to have committed that offence, unless the contrary is proved; and
>
> (b) without prejudice to the reception of any other admissible evidence for the purpose of identifying the facts on which the conviction was based, the contents of any document which is admissible as evidence of the conviction, and the contents of the information, complaint, indictment or charge on which the person in question was convicted, shall be admissible in evidence for that purpose.
>
> (3) Nothing in this section shall prejudice the operation of section 64 or any other enactment whereby a conviction or a finding of fact in any criminal proceedings is for the purposes of any other proceedings made conclusive evidence of any fact.
>
> ...

12. The emphasis is upon compensation rather than upon punishment. The case of *Cassell v Broome* [1972] AC 1027 involved a defamation action where the House of Lords considered the availability of exemplary damages in tort. The function of exemplary damages is to punish the defendant for the wrong done rather than to compensate the plaintiff for the damage suffered. Lord Reid said at 1086 that tort damages have a compensatory aim and that to grant a plaintiff an award of exemplary damages against the defendant was to confuse the function of the civil law, which was to "compensate", with that of the criminal law, which was to "inflict deterrent and punitive penalties".

Therefore, the intent of tort law appears to include the following:

- to protect the physical integrity of people and property;
- to protect the enjoyment or use of property;
- to protect the reputation of a person or of things; and,
- generally to protect against economic or financial loss.

In summary, the purpose of tort law is to compensate the injured party for the unreasonable harm caused by the tortious acts of the person who is otherwise known as the tortfeasor. The law of tort thus provides a cause of action—a reason to sue—for the injured party seeking to protect one of the above interests or to redress a civil wrong suffered.

The law of tort in Hong Kong generally follows the case law in the United Kingdom with variations in interpretation necessitated by cultural differences.[14] Certain statutory provisions, such as Hong Kong's *Civil Liability (Contribution) Ordinance* (Cap 377), *Fatal Accidents Ordinance* (Cap 22) and the *Occupiers Liability Ordinance* (Cap 314), also play a role in tort law. In Hong Kong, the reality is that a person injured through a tortious act is more likely to seek and obtain compensation not through the tort system, but through one of the government administered no-fault schemes, such as those established under the *Employees' Compensation Ordinance* (Cap 282), the *Occupational Deafness (Compensation) Ordinance* (Cap 469), the *Pneumoconiosis and Mesothelioma (Compensation) Ordinance* (Cap 360), the *Traffic Accident Victims (Assistance Fund) Ordinance* (Cap 229), as well as the non-statutory Criminal and Law Enforcement Injuries Compensation Scheme. The awards under these no-fault schemes are much lower than those obtained from a tort action in court. Nonetheless, there are advantages to these schemes: the claimant is entitled to receive some compensation; the claimant does not have to commence a court action; and, the claimant has no obligation to prove fault.[15]

The *BLIS Glossary*, *supra* note 1, translates "civil action" as 民事訴訟; "civil suit" as 民事起訴; "civil wrong" as 民事過失; "exemplary damages" as 懲戒性的損害賠償; and, "punitive damages" as 懲罰性損害賠償.

13. For example, the tort of defamation has had an impact upon publishers and upon the conduct of the press. For a broader perspective on the functions of tort law, *see*, *e.g.*, GLOFCHESKI, *supra* note 1, at 4–9.

14. MARTIN, *supra* note 4, at para. 1.1. *See*, *e.g.*, 25(1) HALSBURY'S, *supra* note 4, at para. 380.002; GLOFCHESKI, *supra* note 1, at 3.

15. GLOFCHESKI, *supra* note 1, at 4–5.

II. TYPES

Tort may be categorized in several ways. For the purposes of this chapter, the different categories of tort are classified into the following three categories:

- Intentional tort: where a defendant intended the consequences of the act. Examples include assault, battery or false imprisonment.[16]
- Strict liability: where a defendant's conduct was neither intentional nor negligent, but the defendant is held liable without the plaintiff needing to prove the existence of fault. An example is the rule in *Rylands v Fletcher*.[17]
- Negligence: where a defendant is careless. For instance, if A deliberately throws a stone at B and hits B, A has committed an intentional tort. If A intentionally throws a stone at a tree, but misses and hits B, A may be negligent.[18] This will be discussed in detail in Section III.

---

16. MARTIN, *supra* note 4, at para. 2.1.7.
17. For further analysis of the *Rylands* holding and its application to tort law, *see* 25(1) HALSBURY'S, *supra* note 4, at paras. 380.250–380.256; GLOFCHESKI, *supra* note 1, at Chapter 21 ("Rylands v Fletcher").
    Note, too, the decision in *Cambridge Water Co Ltd v Eastern Counties Leather Plc* [1994] 2 AC 264 where Lord Goff of Chively stated:

    > We are concerned with the liability of a person where a nuisance has been created by one for whose actions he is responsible. … [I]t is still the law that the fact that the defendant has taken all reasonable care will not of itself exonerate him from liability, the relevant control mechanism being found within the principle of reasonable user. But it by no means follows that the defendant should be held liable for damage of a type which he could not reasonably foresee … such foreseeability should be a prerequisite of liability in damages for nuisance, as it is of liability in negligence. For if a plaintiff is in ordinary circumstances only able to claim damages in respect of personal injuries where he can prove such foreseeability on the part of the defendant, it is difficult to see why, in common justice, he should be in a stronger position to claim damages for interference with the enjoyment of his land where the defendant was unable to foresee such damage. Moreover, this appears to have been the conclusion of the Privy Council in *Overseas Tankship (U.K.) Ltd. v Miller Steamship Co. Pty. (The Wagon Mound (No 2))* [1967] 1 A.C. 617. The facts of the case … gave rise to a claim for damages arising from a public nuisance caused by a spillage of oil in Sydney Harbour. Lord Reid, who delivered the advice of the Privy Council, considered that, in the class of nuisance which included the case before the Board, foreseeability is an essential element in determining liability. …
    >
    > It is widely accepted that this conclusion, although not essential to the decision of the particular case, has nevertheless settled the law to the effect that foreseeability of harm is indeed a prerequisite of the recovery of damages in private nuisance, as in the case of public nuisance. …

    [1994] 2 AC at 300–301. *See also infra* note 233 and accompanying text.
18. *Id.*

A. Intentional Tort

An "intentional tort" is defined as an act or its consequences which are intended. Two types of intentional torts, trespass to the person (*e.g.*, assault, battery, and false imprisonment) and trespass to land, are addressed in more detail in sections V.F and V.G respectively. For present purposes, consider that trespass requires a direct act and that these intentional torts are also criminal acts.[19]

In relation to trespass to the person, the requirements are the intentional, direct and immediate application, or the threatened application, of force against the plaintiff.[20] In relation to trespass to land, the requirement is the deliberate intention to commit trespass rather than the actual act of trespassing on another's property.[21] For either type of trespass, there is no need to prove any loss or damage resulting from the trespass.

B. Strict Liability Tort

"Strict liability torts" are defined as acts which do not involve the intention to injure or any negligence.[22] Rather, the defendant is liable if the act occurs. Strict liability can be imposed in several categories. The first category relates to certain situations arising from ordinances which impose strict liability. This category may be referred to as "breach of statutory duty", because in this category are instances where legislation imposes strict liability upon a party for the occurrence of an event.[23] For example, in the case of *World Wide Stationery Manufacturing Co Ltd v Fong Chi Leung* [1994] 2 HKC 449 the court held that Regulation 4 of the Factories and Industrial Undertakings (Guarding and Operation of Machinery) Regulations (Cap 590) imposed absolute liability upon the employer when its employee was injured despite the employee's contributory negligence.

Another category of strict liability may apply where animals are involved. In Hong Kong, under certain circumstances, the "owner or keeper of an animal is strictly liable, that is without intention or negligence on his part,

19. Bokhary, *supra* note 10, at para. 9.037.
20. Glofcheski, *supra* note 1, at 500.
21. Bokhary, *supra* note 10, at para. 9.038.
22. The *BLIS Glossary*, *supra* note 1, translates "strict liability" as 嚴格法律責任.
23. A full discussion of this topic is outside the scope of this publication. For further information, *see* 25(1) Halsbury's, *supra* note 4, at paras. 380.191–380.198; Glofcheski, *supra* note 1, at Chapter 8 ("Breach of Statutory Duty"); Bokhary, *supra* note 10, at Chapter 14 ("Breach of Statutory Duty").

for any injury it causes ..."[24] Another source likewise states that the person who owns or keeps a dangerous animal may be liable for injuries or damages caused by that animal if the owner or keeper knows that the animal is dangerous or has a dangerous disposition. The owner or anyone in control of the animal may be sued for damage caused by the animal. Where the animal is harboured or controlled by a keeper, that individual has primary liability rather than the animal's owner.[25]

The final category where liability is strict so that no negligence needs to be proved is commonly known as the Rule in *Rylands v Fletcher*. Under this rule, a landowner is liable for keeping any non-natural thing on its land which is likely to cause damage should it escape. The purpose of this rule is to impose strict liability upon the occupant of land where a dangerous activity was being conducted, in order to compensate those injured off the premises.[26]

The rule is named after the case of *Rylands v Fletcher* (1868) LR 3 HL 330 which involved the defendant mill-owners wishing to improve the water supply to their mill. The defendant employed independent contractors to construct a reservoir on the defendant's land to supply the mill with water. During the course of the work, the independent contractors discovered underground passages and mines on the land where the reservoir was to be constructed. The independent contractors did not seal these mines and shafts properly with the result that the reservoir water burst through into the mines and shafts and flooded the plaintiff's coal mine, causing damage. The House of Lords approved the judgment of Blackburn J which stated:

> that the person who, for his own purposes, brings on his lands and collects and keeps there anything likely to do mischief if it escapes, must keep it in at his peril; and if he does not do so, is *prima facie* answerable for all the damage which is the natural consequence of its escape. He can excuse himself by showing that the escape was owing to the Plaintiff's default; or, perhaps, that the escape was the consequence of *vis major*, or act of God ...[27]

One authority provides the following distinction concerning absolute liability and the rule in *Rylands v Fletcher*:

> The liability for a breach of the rule in *Rylands v Fletcher* ... is strict but it cannot be equated with absolute liability; strict liability only arises if

24. Bokhary, *supra* note 10, at para. 8.004. *See generally id.* at Chapter 8 ("Animals").
25. 1(2) Halsbury's Laws of Hong Kong paras. 20.142–20.144 (2008).
26. Martin, *supra* note 4, at para. 12.1.4.
27. (1868) LR 3 HL at 336.

> the defendant knows or ought reasonably to foresee that the thing in question might, if it escapes, cause damage notwithstanding that the defendant has exercised all due care to prevent the escape occurring: see *Cambridge Water Co v Eastern Counties Leather* [1994] 2 AC 264, [1994] 1 All ER 53, HL. See also *ACL Electronics (HK) Ltd v Bulmer Ltd* [1992] 1 HKC 133, CA and *Wong Ching Chi v Full Yue Bleaching and Dyeing Co Ltd* [1994] 3 HKC 606 …[28]

The value of the rule in *Rylands v Fletcher* has not been settled. One source has stated that the rule in *Rylands v Fletcher* remains alive and well.[29] Other authorities are of the opinion that *Rylands v Fletcher* has become less important with the development of the law of negligence since the case of *Donoghue v Stevenson* in 1932.[30] In Australia, the rule in *Rylands v Fletcher* is said to have been overtaken by developments in the tort of negligence according to the case of *Burnie Port Authority v General Jones Pty Ltd* (1994) 179 CLR 520.[31]

III. TORT OF NEGLIGENCE

The broadest category of tort is the tort of negligence. This is the fastest growing category in tort law and the most frequently litigated type of tort.[32] The following sections concentrate on this category by first setting out the elements of the tort of negligence, then presenting the defences available against a claim of negligence. Finally, there will be discussion of several other types of torts which are anticipated to have the most impact upon the general public: vicarious liability, liability arising out of breach of statutory duty, occupier's liability, nuisance, trespass, and defamation.

---

28. 25(1) HALSBURY'S, *supra* note 4, at para. 380.103 n. 7.

29. BOKHARY, *supra* note 10, at para. 12.017 (citations omitted). *Id.* at para. 12.018 states:

> Thus, what must be recognised is that, following *Cambridge Water Co Ltd v Eastern Countries Leather Plc* and now *Transco Plc v Stockport Metropolitan Borough Council*, the rule [in *Rylands v Fletcher*] is firmly rooted in the tort of nuisance as a specialised form of nuisance involving a single escape. Further, what is required in future application of the law is a principled approach by reference to the elements of the rule as streamlined in the *Transco Plc* case.

30. GLOFCHESKI, *supra* note 1, at 639; MARTIN, *supra* note 4, at para. 12.1.5.

31. 25(1) HALSBURY'S, *supra* note 4, at para. 380.250.

32. MARTIN, *supra* note 4, at paras. 2.1.1–2.1.2. *See also* GLOFCHESKI, *supra* note 1, at 13; VIVIENNE HARPWOOD, MODERN TORT LAW 8 (7th ed. 2009) [hereinafter HARPWOOD, MODERN TORT]; FLEMING, *supra* note 2, at 114; BAKER, *supra* note 1, at 98.

The tort of negligence affords the right to protect oneself and one's property from harm caused by the unreasonable behaviour of another.[33] Negligence is interpreted to mean carelessness or lack of proper care and attention in the performance of some act.[34] A person is negligent even if that individual, as a tortfeasor, did not intend the consequences of the act, but instead acted indifferently to, or, was unaware of, the consequences.[35]

Legal negligence measures the tortfeasor's behaviour against an objective standard; if the actor's behaviour falls below that standard of the class of persons with the same level of knowledge or skills, the actor is negligent regardless of the care or skill exercised.[36] The court in *Blyth v Birmingham Waterworks Co* (1856) 11 Ex 781 defined legal negligence thus:

---

33. *See, e.g.*, John Cooke, Law of Tort 31–32 (9th ed. 2009) [hereinafter Cooke]; Harpwood, Modern Tort, *supra* note 32, at 8; Baker, *supra* note 1, at 1–2.
34. Martin, *supra* note 4, at para. 2.1.3 (citation omitted).
    The *BLIS Glossary*, *supra* note 1, translates "negligence" as 疏忽.
35. Martin, *supra* note 4, at para. 2.1.7 (citation omitted). Another authority has explained the nature of negligence thusly:

    > Negligence is a specific tort and in any given circumstances is the failure to exercise that care which the circumstances demand. What amounts to negligence depends on the facts of each particular case. It may consist in omitting to do something which ought to be done or in doing something which ought to be done either in a different manner or not at all. Negligence means more than heedless or careless conduct, whether in omission or commission: it properly connotes the complex concept of duty, breach and damage. An act of negligence may also constitute a nuisance where it occasions a dangerous state of affairs and satisfies the other requirements of that tort. Equally it may also be a breach of the rule in *Rylands v Fletcher* if it allows the escape of a dangerous thing which the defendant has brought onto his land. Negligent failure to maintain safety standards by an employer may give rise to both liability for negligence and for the tort of breach of statutory duty. Negligent harm to reputation may give rise to both liability for negligence where it occurs within a special relationship causing economic loss, and for defamation. Negligence liability may also overlap with non-tortious grounds of liability under contractual, equitable or public law principles. ...

    25(1) Halsbury's, *supra* note 4, at para. 380.103 (citations omitted).
    Glofcheski, *supra* note 1, at 14 provides that negligence is generally careless behaviour causing personal injury or property damage.
36. Martin, *supra* note 4, at para. 2.1.3. As for factors affecting the standard, *see, e.g.*, *id.* at paras. 3.3.1–3.3.20.
    Alan J. Pannett, Law of Torts 8 (8th ed. 1997) [hereinafter Pannett] noted:

    > Negligence is therefore measured by the conduct of the defendant relative to that of a notional moral exemplar, "the reasonable man". Negligence does not require "fault" on the part of the defendant, in the sense of moral blameworthiness, however it does require fault insofar as the defendant's conduct was not of the standard of a reasonable man.

> Negligence is the omission to do something which a reasonable man, guided upon those considerations which ordinarily regulate the conduct of human affairs, would do, or doing something which a prudent and reasonable man would not do.[37]

Legal negligence is not based upon the tortfeasor's state of mind. Negligence in itself does not give rise to liability. It is negligence causing injury or damage to another which is actionable and which may result in liability.[38] Only certain types of damage can result in a negligence action.[39]

Winfield and Jolowicz define the tort of negligence in the following terms: "negligence as a tort is breach of a legal duty to take care which results in damage to the claimant".[40] Therefore, this tort consists of four distinct elements. In order to prosecute a negligence action successfully, one needs to prove these four elements of negligence:

- the defendant owes a duty of care to the plaintiff, *i.e.*, a legal duty rather than a moral duty;
- the defendant breached the duty of care owed to the plaintiff;
- the plaintiff suffers injury or damage; and,
- the plaintiff's injury or damage is proximately caused by the defendant's breach of the duty of care.

A. Duty of Care

The first element of the tort of negligence is a duty of care.[41] This duty requires one to exercise reasonable care to avoid risks of injuring other

37. (1856) 11 Ex at 784.
38. MARTIN, *supra* note 4, at para. 2.1.4.
39. For example, some types of economic loss are not recoverable in tort. *See* section III.D.
40. WINFIELD & JOLOWICZ ON TORT 150 (W.V.H. ROGERS, 18th ed. 2010) [hereinafter WINFIELD & JOLOWICZ].
41. GLOFCHESKI, *supra* note 1, at 133:

> negligence liability does not attach for every wrongful act that a person commits. The plaintiff may have been injured by the defendant's carelessness, but will not succeed in an action in negligence unless s/he can also prove that the defendant owed him/her a duty of care.
>
> ...
>
> Duty of care is often described in terms of relationships: was the plaintiff who was injured by the defendant's carelessness in a sufficiently close relationship with the defendant such that the defendant should be made responsible for the harm caused? It might be thought ... that such a question is unnecessary, even artificial, and that it is enough that the plaintiff was injured by the defendant's carelessness, in order to justify holding the defendant accountable.

persons or their property. There can be no cause of action in negligence unless there is a duty of care owed by a tortfeasor to the injured victim.[42] The duty thus imposes an obligation or requirement to conform to a standard of conduct prescribed by law; the duty of reasonable care arises to prevent injury where one's acts or omissions create a foreseeable risk of harm to another.

An example of the common law's development can be seen in the evolution of the principle of the duty of care in the tort of negligence. There was no general principle of the duty of care in the tort of negligence[43] until the twentieth century, when the case of *Donoghue v Stevenson* [1932] AC 562, HL established a general principle for determining the exercise of a duty of care. The plaintiff in *Donoghue* suffered illness after drinking a bottle of ginger beer which contained a decomposed snail. The defendant brewery produced this beer. One issue was whether the defendant manufacturer owed a duty of care to the consumer in that the manufacturer sent the ginger beer to a wholesaler, who then sent the ginger beer to a retail store, then ultimately to the plaintiff's friend who purchased the ginger beer for the plaintiff. The plaintiff could not sue the defendant in contract because of a lack of privity of contract.

The court, nevertheless, found for the plaintiff, noting that the ginger beer bottle had been sealed at the brewery and was not opened until immediately before drinking. None of the intervening handlers of this product had an opportunity to inspect the bottle's contents until the ginger beer was

---

> But the tort of negligence has not evolved in that way. As stated by Esher MR in *Le Lievre v Gould* [1893] 1 QB 491, "a man is entitled to be as negligent as he pleases towards the whole world if he owes no duty to them".

GLOFCHESKI, *supra* note 1, at 138 continues:

> For many years, the neighbour principle has been accepted and applied by the courts of Hong Kong. It continues to form the basis of Hong Kong's product liability law. Moreover ... it now provides the sole determinant in cases in which the plaintiff has been the victim of the defendant's direct infliction of physical harm.

Consequently, due to the importance of this concept in Hong Kong tort law, this section will place emphasis on this legal concept.

42. As one source elaborates:

> The categories of negligence are never closed. When considering whether a notional duty of care applies in a particular situation, the courts will consider three questions: (1) whether the damage is foreseeable; (2) whether there is a relationship of proximity between the parties; and (3) whether the imposition of a duty would be fair, just and reasonable. There is no liability in an indeterminate amount for an indeterminate time to an indeterminable class.

25(1) HALSBURY'S, *supra* note 4, at para. 380.106 (citations omitted).

poured into a glass. The bottle was in any case opaque. The defendant, as the manufacturer of the ginger beer, owed a duty of care to the plaintiff, as the ultimate consumer of the ginger beer, to take reasonable care to ensure that the bottle did not contain any substance which was likely to cause injury to health. The court established the neighbour principle that where:

> in English law there must be, and is, some general conception of relations giving rise to a duty of care, of which the particular cases found in the books are but instances ... The rule that you are to love your neighbour becomes in law, you must not injure your neighbour; and the lawyer's question, Who is my neighbour? receives a restricted reply. You must take reasonable care to avoid acts or omissions which you can reasonably foresee would be likely to injure your neighbour. Who, then, in law is my neighbour? The answer seems to be—persons who are so closely and directly affected by my act that I ought reasonably to have them in contemplation as being so affected when I am directing my mind to the acts or omissions which are called in question.[44]

To summarize the principle set out in *Donoghue*:

- One owes a duty of care to those individuals who one ought reasonably to foresee might be harmed by one's actions.
- The manufacturer of the ginger beer knew that ultimately someone would consume the ginger beer. Although the manufacturer did not know who would consume the beer or when the beer would be consumed, the manufacturer knew that the ginger beer would be consumed eventually. Thus the manufacturer owed a duty of care to the ultimate consumer.

In *Anns v Merton London Borough Council* [1977] 2 All ER 492, HL the court re-formulated the principle of the duty of care into a two-stage test such that: the position has now been reached that in order to establish that a duty of care arises in a particular situation, it is not necessary to bring the facts of that situation within those of previous situations in which a duty of care has been held to exist. Rather the question has to be approached in two stages. First one has to ask whether, as between the alleged wrongdoer and the person who has suffered damage there is a sufficient relationship of proximity or neighbourhood such that, in the reasonable contemplation of the former, carelessness may be likely to cause damage to the latter, in which case a *prima facie* duty of care arises. Secondly, if the first question

---

43. *See* the case of *Heaven v Pender* (1883) 11 QBD 503.
44. [1932] AC at 580.

is answered affirmatively, it is necessary to consider whether there are any considerations which ought to negative, or to reduce or limit the scope of the duty or the class of person to whom it is owed or the damages to which a breach of it may give rise.[45]

Accordingly, pursuant to the two-stage test, one must establish that the damage was foreseeable based on a relationship of sufficient proximity, and whether any policy factors might affect a duty of care.[46] Policy factors include morality, sociology, economics, politics, common sense, logic, or administrative convenience. Different policy factors will be considered according to different types of damage, leading to different attitudes toward the feasibility of allowing a duty of care. The most overwhelming policy factor will be the possibility of opening up a floodgate of claims, *i.e.*, whether there will be an indeterminate number of possible plaintiffs, and, whether there will be liability for an indeterminate amount. This policy factor may be discerned in the following cases.

When applying the *Anns* two-stage test, courts should be cautious. In *Leigh and Sillivan Ltd v Aliakmon Shipping Co Ltd* [1985] 1 QB 350, CA[47] the judge stated that the courts were not free to evolve their own conception of policy without regard to established lines of authority, as it was not correct:

> to regard *Anns'* case … as establishing some new and revolutionary test of the duty of care the logical application of which is going to enable the court in every case to say whether or not a duty of care exists. Nor … can it properly be treated either as establishing some new approach to what the policy of the law should be or as conferring upon the court a free hand to determine for itself in each case what limits are to be set.[48]

---

45. [1977] 2 All ER at 498.
46. Glofcheski, *supra* note 1, at 141 opined:

> The immediate impact of the decision in *Anns v Merton* was to accelerate the trend of liberal interpretation of Lord Atkin's neighbour principle, and to expand the scope of the duty of care. That is, the number of situations that were now perceived to give rise to a duty of care relationship was further increased. This was because … [*Anns'*] emphasis on foreseeability of harm as the main, if not the sole determinant for duty [of care], unqualified by any other considerations, other than policy. In fact, most judges are rather reluctant to expressly decide a case on the basis of policy considerations and so, in practice, the second stage of … [the test in *Anns*] was rarely used to negate a *prima facie* finding of duty of care.

47. The plaintiff in this case is reported as *Leigh & Sillavan* in [1986] AC 785 and [1986] 2 All ER 145.
48. [1985] 1 QB at 373.

A few years later, the Privy Council decided *Yuen Kun Yeu v Attorney-General of Hong Kong* [1988] AC 175, a case which involved an action through the Attorney-General against the Commissioner of Deposit-Taking Companies for placing a deposit-taking company on the register pursuant to the *Deposit-taking Companies Ordinance* (Cap 328). The plaintiffs had placed money with such a deposit-taking company on the government's register and lost said money upon the company's liquidation. The plaintiffs sought to bring a negligence action against the Commissioner.[49] The issue considered here centred on the scope of the duty of care owed by the Commissioner. The Privy Council determined, in part, that:

> the two stage test formulated … [in *Anns*] for determining the existence of a duty of care in negligence has been elevated to a degree of importance greater than it merits, and perhaps greater than its author intended.[50]

The Privy Council continued by stating that in consideration:

> of the direction in which the law has since been developing … it should be recognized that the two-stage test in [*Anns*] is not to be regarded as in all circumstances a suitable guide to the existence of a duty of care.[51]

The Privy Council concluded that:

> there was clearly no voluntary assumption by the commissioner of any responsibility towards the plaintiffs … It was argued, however, that the effect of the Ordinance was to place such a responsibility upon him. Their Lordships consider that the Ordinance placed a duty on the commissioner to supervise deposit-taking companies in the general public interest, but no special responsibility towards individual members of the public. … While the investing public might reasonably feel some confidence that the provisions of the Ordinance as a whole went a long way to protect their interests, reliance on the fact of registration as a guarantee of the soundness of a particular company would be neither reasonable or justifiable, nor should the commissioner reasonably

---

49. In *Yuen Kun Yeu v Attorney-General of Hong Kong* [1988] AC 175, the Privy Council noted at 189–190:

> The foremost question … is whether … the commissioner owed to members of the public who might be minded to deposit their money with deposit-taking companies in Hong Kong a duty, in the discharge of his supervisory powers under the Ordinance, to exercise reasonable care to see that such members of the public did not suffer loss through the affairs of such companies being carried on by the managers in a fraudulent or improvident fashion.

50. *Id.* at 192.
51. *Id.* at 194.

> be expected to know of such reliance, if it existed. Accordingly their Lordships are unable to accept the plaintiffs' arguments about reliance as apt, in all the circumstances, to establish a special relationship between them and the commissioner such as to give rise to a duty of care.[52]

The House of Lords, in *Caparo Industries plc v Dickman* [1990] 2 AC 605 subsequently modified the *Anns* two-stage test into a three-stage test:

> since *Anns* case a series of decisions of the Privy Council and of your Lordships' House ... have emphasised the inability of any single general principle to provide a practical test which can be applied to every situation to determine whether a duty of care is owed and, if so, what is its scope ... What emerges is that, in addition to the foreseeability of damage, necessary ingredients in any situation giving rise to a duty of care are that there should exist between the party owing the duty and the party to whom it is owed a relationship characterised by the law as one of 'proximity' or 'neighbourhood' and that the situation should be one in which the court considers it fair, just and reasonable that the law should impose a duty of a given scope upon the one party for the benefit of the other.[53]

In *Murphy v Brentwood District Council* [1990] 2 All ER 908, the House of Lords overturned the decision in *Anns*. The *Murphy* case involved the original homeowner who purchased a newly constructed house and who subsequently brought an action against the district council for negligence. ABC Homes built the plaintiff's home over filled land on a concrete raft foundation which was designed by a firm of civil engineers. This design was submitted to the district council for its statutory approval. The district council sought the advice of independent consulting engineers as to the adequacy of this design. The independent consulting engineers advised that the design was appropriate for the ground conditions and that the district council could approve the design. Years after taking possession of the premises, the plaintiff noticed severe cracks in the foundation. Unable to afford the cost of repairs, the plaintiff sold the house unrepaired at a substantial discount to the market value of an equivalent house without defects. The plaintiff brought the action against the council in an attempt

---

52. *Id.* at 196–197. The implication of this case is that, although the injury to the plaintiffs were a reasonably foreseeable consequence of the defendant's failure to strike the company off the list, the parties did not have a sufficiently close relationship or proximity to give rise to a duty of care. GLOFCHESKI, *supra* note 1, at 142.
53. [1990] 2 AC at 617–618.

to recover the difference in price, alleging that the council was liable for the consulting engineers' negligence in recommending approval of the plans and that the plaintiff had suffered an imminent risk to health and safety because the foundation's settlement had broken gas and soil pipes, with a risk of further breaks.

The House of Lords stated:

> The present problem is concerned with the scope of the duty. The question is whether the defendant council owed the plaintiff a duty to take reasonable care to safeguard him against the particular kind of damage which he has in fact suffered, which was not injury to person or health nor damage to anything other than the defective house itself ...[54]
>
> ...
>
> The existence of a duty of that nature should not ... be affirmed without a careful examination of the implications of such affirmation. To start with, if such a duty is incumbent on the local authority, a similar duty must necessarily be incumbent also on the builder of the house. If the builder of the house is to be so subject, there can be no grounds in logic or in principle for not extending liability on like grounds to the manufacturer of a chattel. That would open on an exceedingly wide field of claims ...
>
> Liability under the *Anns* decision is postulated on the existence of a present or imminent danger to health or safety. But, considering that the loss involved in incurring expenditure to avert the danger is pure economic loss, there would seem to be no logic in confining the remedy to cases where such danger exists. There is likewise no logic in confining it to cases where some damage ... has been caused to the building, but refusing it where the existence of the danger has come to light in some other way ...
>
> ... it is clear that *Anns* did not proceed on any basis of established principle, but introduced a new species of liability governed by a principle indeterminate in character but having the potentiality of covering a wide range of situations, involving chattels as well as real property, in which it had never hitherto been thought that the law of negligence had any proper place.
>
> ...
>
> ... there can be no doubt that *Anns* has for long been widely regarded as an unsatisfactory decision. In relation to the scope of the duty owed by a local authority it proceeded on what must ... be regarded as a

54. [1990] 2 All ER at 917.

> somewhat superficial examination of principle and there has been extreme difficulty ... in ascertaining on exactly what basis of principle it did proceed. I think it must now be recognized that it did not proceed on any basis of principle at all, but constituted a remarkable example of judicial legislation. ... the case properly considered has potentiality for collision with long-established principles regarding liability in the tort of negligence for economic loss.[55]

Therefore, the present approach is that three requirements must exist before a duty of care is recognized:

1. foreseeability of harm or damage;
2. a sufficiently proximate relationship between the plaintiff and the defendant; and,
3. fairness, justice and reasonableness.

The difference between this test and the *Anns*' test is that under *Anns*, proximity between the parties was a test for reasonable foresight. Once foreseeability is established, there is a duty of care unless the duty is limited by policy considerations arising from concern about opening floodgates to unlimited liability. Under the three-stage test, the plaintiff must not only establish foreseeability of harm, but also the proximate relationship with the defendant, and justice and reasonableness[56] in imposing the duty.

The term "proximity" is difficult to define because it is a label for the circumstances which the court considers when attributing a duty of care.[57]

---

55. *Id.* at 921–923.
56. As explained by one authority:

> In *Peabody Donation Fund (Governors of) v Parkinson* [1985] AC 210, the plaintiff builders were constructing a residential development. One of their senior employees privately agreed with an inspector of the defendant local authority to deviate (without authorisation) from the approved plan of construction. This deviation subsequently proved to be unsuccessful, requiring the plaintiff to redo the work at considerable cost. The plaintiff sued, hoping to recover the loss from the defendant, but the House of Lords held that there was no duty of care owed. After rejecting the appropriateness of the *Anns v Merton* two-stage test as the determinant for duty of care, Lord Keith went on to say that in such circumstances, it would not be *just and reasonable* to impose a duty of care (in view of the plaintiff's having, through its employee, consented to the deviation).
>
> This seemingly casual phraseology came to be adopted by judges in a number of duty of care cases in the ensuing years, particularly those involving a contractual structure in which the plaintiff was seeking a tort remedy to supplant (or supplement) the terms of a contract. In these cases, the concept of justice and reasonableness has come to be treated as a precondition for a finding of duty of care. (emphasis in original)

Reasonable foreseeability focuses on the knowledge which someone in the defendant's position should possess, while proximity focuses on the broader relationship between the parties.[58] This relationship includes:

- physical proximity, *i.e.*, space and time;

GLOFCHESKI, *supra* note 1, at 145. This author continued:

> The justice and reasonableness principle was relied on for a finding of no duty of care in *Alcatel Cable Contracting Norway AS & Another v Titan Logistic(s) Pte Ltd & Another* [2000] 3 HKLRD 720. The plaintiff had contracted with the first defendant to organize the de-mobilisation of its offshore trenching equipment in Hong Kong and then ship the equipment to Oslo. The first defendant hired the second defendant as its subcontractor to discharge the cargo from a vessel and then to load and lash the cargo onto a flat-rack container. The flat-racks were later trans-shipped to a smaller feeder vessel in Hamburg. During the passage from Hamburg to Oslo, the vessel encountered severe weather conditions and the cargo was damaged and some of it lost overboard. The court held that it was not just and reasonable to impose a duty on the second defendant, since the second defendant did not have knowledge of how the cargo would be reloaded and shipped after departing Hong Kong.

Id. at 151.

Another authority comments:

> The criteria of foreseeability and proximity are derived from ... *Donoghue v Stevenson*. Reasonable foreseeability focuses on the knowledge that someone in the defendant's position would be expected to possess, whilst proximity focuses on the broader relationship between the parties from the perspective of both defendant and plaintiff, and may consist of various forms of closeness: physical, circumstantial, causal or assumed.
>
> Another requirement is that the court must be satisfied that in the circumstances it is fair, just and reasonable for a duty of care to be owned to the persons concerned. At its narrowest, the criterion focuses on the relationship between the parties and, in particular, the proportionality of the burden of liability in relation to the nature of the conduct. Assessing the burden may involve considering the relative exposure to risk of the class of plaintiff and defendant concerned and the availability of protection through insurance or contractual arrangements. At a broader level, the criterion may involve consideration of the so-called "floodgates argument", the overall framework of the legal system, and wider concerns about the evidentiary difficulties and length of litigation, following the imposition of a duty. At the broadest level, perceptions of community attitudes and goals, contemporary commercial practices and the general public good may also be relevant. ... However, judges are reluctant to consider broader consequential arguments when they have neither the full information nor the basis on which to evaluate the information that is presented.

25(1) HALSBURY'S, *supra* note 4, at para. 380.106 (citations omitted).

57. *Caparo Industries plc v Dickman* [1990] 2 AC 605, HL; *Murphy v Brentwood* [1990] 2 All ER 908.
58. CLERK & LINDSELL ON TORTS paras. 8–16 (ANTHONY M. DUGDALE, ed., 19th ed. 2006) [hereinafter CLERK & LINDSELL].

- circumstantial proximity, *e.g.*, an employer-employee relationship between the parties;
- causal proximity, *i.e.*, closeness and directness of causation; and,
- assumed proximity, *e.g.*, the defendant having undertaken to take care of the plaintiff.

There is overlap among the three requirements under the present test.

Despite a particular harm being reasonably foreseeable, there is no general duty to act to prevent that harm to others. Foreseeability of damage does not impose an obligation to act.[59] However, apart from the general duty of care imposed under the neighbour principle, tort law includes other types of duty. One of these duties concerns the omission[60] to act, referred to as "nonfeasance", as compared to a positive, negligent act which is referred to as "misfeasance".[61] To impose liability for an omission to act, there must be an overriding duty to act.[62] Special circumstances must exist to impose liability in negligence for damages arising under an omission to act. Such circumstances may include a special relationship between the plaintiff and

59. Bokhary, *supra* note 10, at para. 3.086; Pannett, *supra* note 36, at 42.

60. In this work, the definition of "omission" provided by Glofcheski, *supra* note 1, at 199 is adopted to refer to:

> omission in the purely passive sense, for instance, where a passerby fails to assist an injured pedestrian, or fails to warn a blind man of an excavation site that he is about to walk into. The term *nonfeasance* is sometimes used to describe this behaviour.

See also Martin, *supra* note 4, at paras. 2.3.1–2.3.9.

61. Misfeasance is defined by one source as being "concerned with activities that cause harm". Glofcheski, *supra* note 1, at 199. *See also* Martin, *supra* note 4, at para. 2.3.1.

62. As explained by Glofcheski, *supra* note 1, at 200, "In general, tort law does not impose liability for mere omission or nonfeasance. There is no duty to confer a benefit on another."

Bokhary, *supra* note 10, at para. 3.092, citing to *Barrett v Ministry of Defence* [1995] 1 WLR 1217, 1224, explains:

> Where relationships such as neighbouring occupiers; parent or school and child; employer and employee exist, the party who is in a better position is understood to have assumed certain responsibility and the other party is entitled to rely that its interest would be protected. Bedlam LJ, in *Barrett v Ministry of Defence*, said that:
>
> > "the mere existence of regulatory or public duties does not of itself create a special relationship imposing a duty of care in law for the safety of others. The characteristic which distinguished those special relations was the element of reliance, expressed or implied in the relationship, which the party to whom the duty was owed was entitled to place on the other party to make provision for his safety".

See also Bokhary, *supra* note 10, at paras. 3.086–3.100; Martin, *supra* note 4, at para. 2.3.2.

defendant: a defendant negligently creating a dangerous situation in which it was reasonably foreseeable that the intervention of a third party might cause damage;[63] and, where a defendant who knew or should have known that a third party created a danger on the defendant's property and failed to take reasonable measures to curtail that danger.

Where a special relationship exists there is an overriding duty to act in certain circumstances. Examples of these special relationships include:

- common carrier to passenger innkeeper (hotel, motel) to guest
- employer to employee[64]
- land owner or possessor to invitee[65]
- teacher to student[66]
- parent to child
- hospital to patients
- a professional person, such as a solicitor, to client[67]
- lifeguard to swimmers[68]

Because these special relationships involve an overriding duty to act, nonfeasance, rather than misfeasance, may result in liability. The duty in a special relationship is to use reasonable care to avoid injury, not to prevent injury. Where one negligently endangers another, the tortfeasor has entered into a relationship which gives rise to a duty to take reasonable steps to extricate the victim from danger.[69] For example, where one negligently sets a house on fire, one has a duty to the other occupants to minimize their danger.[70]

---

63. Alternatively, where:

> [o]ne who creates for persons a situation of danger likely to attract another as a rescuer may be found to be under a duty of care to that rescuer. … Foreseeability of the coming of a rescuer is the main determinant, without regard to any other specific proximity factors.

GLOFCHESKI, *supra* note 1, at 214. *See also* BOKHARY, *supra* note 10, at paras. 24.074–24.075; *Lai Tai Tai v Lam Pak Lo* [2000] 1 HKLRD 499.

64. *See, e.g.*, *Wong Wai Ming v Hospital Authority* [2000] 3 HKLRD 612.
65. Now generally superseded by the *Occupiers Liability Ordinance* (Cap 314). *See, e.g.*, GLOFCHESKI, *supra* note 1, at 200–201; Chapter 7 ("Occupiers' Liability"); and, the discussion of omissions in relation to property management in GLOFCHESKI, *supra* note 1, at 203.
66. *See, e.g.*, *T v Kan Ki Leung* [2002] 1 HKLRD 29.
67. *See, e.g.*, *Keep Point Development Ltd v Chan Chi Yim and Full Country Development Ltd (Third Parties)* [2000] 3 HKLRD 166.
68. *See generally* GLOFCHESKI, *supra* note 1, at 200–205 for a discussion of these relationships.
69. *See, e.g.*, GLOFCHESKI, *supra* note 1, at 201–202.
70. MARTIN, *supra* note 4, at para. 2.3.2. *See also Cutler v United Dairies (London) Ltd* [1933] 2 KB 297 where the court held that a rescuer may also be a plaintiff in a tort action against the defendant. Where a defendant negligently created a dangerous situation, it is foreseeable that a third party might attempt to rescue the victim. In these situations, the defences of *volenti non fit injuria* and *novus actus interveniens* are not available to a defendant.

B. Breach of Duty

The next element in this review of the tort of negligence is the breach of the duty of care. One authority explained that negligence is "conduct falling below the standard demanded for the protection of others against unreasonable risk of harm".[71] The breach of the duty of care occurs where the foreseeability of harm arising from a defendant's unreasonable conduct outweighs the burden upon the defendant to take precautions to prevent that harm, and where the defendant actually fails to take those precautions. The breach of duty is thus a negligent act or an omission to act.

Foreseeability is frequently one of the determining criteria whether there has been a breach of duty. Foreseeability may be interpreted as predictability because it is the scope of the risk and the likelihood of an event occurring. Factors affecting the scope of risk include:

- the lawfulness of the activity;[72]
- the gravity of injury;[73]
- the difficulty of eliminating a risk;[74] and,
- the usefulness of a defendant's conduct and the possible justification for the risk.[75]

An objective standard is used to determine foreseeability, that is, whether the defendant, as a reasonable person, knew or should have known of the harm. Foreseeability is determined before the occurrence by "turning back the clock" in order to identify the subject matter of the foreseeability question, *i.e.*, the act or the result, to be assessed.

Determining foreseeability may include consideration of the following factors:

- area: the location of the event and its physical nature;
- activity: the type of activities which were present leading up to the event;
- people: the type of individuals involved in those activities which led up to the event;
- human nature assumption: the type of behaviour which may be expected from those participating in the activities;

71. FLEMING, *supra* note 2, at 117.
72. *See, e.g.*, GLOFCHESKI, *supra* note 1, at 55 concerning standards imposed by legislation.
73. *See, e.g.*, *id.* at 40.
74. *See, e.g.*, *id.* at 42.
75. *See, e.g.*, *id.* at 45–46.

- preparation: the anticipatory or precautionary actions which were taken prior to the activities;
- historical data: whether there was any prior knowledge of similar or identical occurrences;
- specific sensory data: what the human senses perceived; and,
- common sense.[76]

Unknown risks or events which are extremely unlikely to occur might not result in liability for negligence, as one cannot take reasonable actions to avoid unknown risks. Events which are highly unlikely to occur generally will not result in liability because the purpose of tort law is not to render a potential tortfeasor an insurer.[77] A defendant must balance the risk against the precautions necessary to avoid that risk. Only reasonable precautions need to be taken.

Reasonable precautions were the issue in *Roe v Minister of Health* [1954] 2 QB 66. In 1947, the plaintiff entered hospital for a minor operation and became paralysed when a spinal anaesthetic the plaintiff received had become tainted from a syringe stored in phenol. At that time, medical science did not know that phenol could seep into a syringe through invisible cracks in the syringe and cause paralysis in some patients. Seven years later, when this case came before the court in 1954, the possibility of seepage of phenol into a syringe had become known. Denning LJ said that the court could not look at the 1947 incident "with 1954 spectacles". Thus, the defendant was not liable.

Another determining criteria for breach of duty is the concept of the "reasonable man". The reasonable man is a mythical creation that represents the standard of an average individual, the standard which the courts use to determine liability.[78] The reasonable man standard, however, may vary: for example, the standard of care required of a professional should be the standard of those trained in that profession. The breach of the duty of care is determined by whether a reasonable person in the particular circumstance would foresee the risk of injury. If the risk of injury is foreseeable, would a reasonable person in the defendant's position, with whatever special knowledge or skill the defendant possesses, have taken the risk? If a reasonable person of the defendant's experience would have foreseen the risk of injury

76. *See* William P. Statsky, Torts: Personal Injury Litigation 207–211(3rd ed. 1995).
77. *See, e.g.*, Glofcheski, *supra* note 1, at 38–46.
78. *See* Pannett, *supra* note 36, at 8 for a discussion of "reasonable man".

or damage, and would have decided that the risk was too great, then the defendant breached the duty of care to the plaintiff.[79]

The breach of duty is thus determined by means of the reasonable man test, which is the legal standard of care which everyone must reach. Failure to meet this standard results in liability, yet the standard varies according to the risk of damage and the capacity of a defendant. Again, the standard for a defendant as an ordinary citizen is different from the standard for a defendant as a professional.

The knowledge of a reasonable man, not the knowledge of the tortfeasor, determines foreseeability. If the tortfeasor has greater knowledge than a reasonable person, the tortfeasor must meet the standard of a reasonable man with that extra knowledge.[80] To reiterate, the knowledge of a reasonable person at the time of the act is relevant, not the knowledge at the time of trial.[81]

The application of this objective reasonable man test is demonstrated in the case of *The Lady Gwendolen* [1965] P 294. *The Lady Gwendolen*, on a voyage carrying beer from Dublin to Liverpool, travelled at full speed in dense fog without fully using its radar. She collided with and sank a ship anchored in the river. *The Lady Gwendolen*'s owners, a brewery, brought an action to limit their liability under the *Merchant Shipping Act* 1894, arguing that they should be judged by the standard of the reasonable brewers who, incidental to their primary business, owned several ships used to transport their alcoholic products. The owners argued that they should not be judged according to the standards of a reasonable shipowner. The court rejected this argument. The standard of care owed by the defendants was the same standard of care owed by every other shipowner. The court stated that:

> the law must apply a standard which is not relaxed to cater for their factual ignorance of all activities outside brewing; having become owners of ships, they must behave as reasonable shipowners.[82]

---

79. *See, e.g.*, 25(1) HALSBURY'S, *supra* note 4, at paras. 380.124–380.125.
80. *See, e.g.*, GLOFCHESKI, *supra* note 1, at 28–33.
81. One authority states:

> The determination of what is reasonable is made with reference to the state of knowledge at the time the act was committed and not at the time of trial. This point has repeatedly been made in Hong Kong in negligence actions against solicitors.

GLOFCHESKI, *supra* note 1, at 20–21 citing to *Foshan Hua Da Industrial Co v Johnson Stokes & Master* [1999] 1 HKLRD 418; *Whale View Investment Ltd v Kensland Realty Ltd* [2000] 2 HKLRD 261; *Feerni Development Ltd v Daniel Wong & Partners* [2001] 2 HKLRD 13. *See also* 25 (1) HALSBURY'S, *supra* note 4, at para. 380.125.

82. [1965] P at 350.

Likewise, the skill of a reasonable person, not the skill of the tortfeasor, determines foreseeability. If one possesses skills above those of the average reasonable man, the standard applied will be that of a skilled reasonable person.[83] In *Wharf Properties Ltd v Eric Cumine Associates, Architects, Engineers & Surveyors* [1991] 2 HKLR 6, the Privy Council found the defendant not liable for professional negligence as its performance had not fallen below the standards of a reasonably competent and skilful Hong Kong architect. However, skilled professionals are not expected to guard against unknown risks.

The common practice found in an industry might be an indicator of what a reasonable person in that trade might do. This common practice, however, is not conclusive as to reasonableness.[84] Where varying practices exist within a particular trade, members of that profession need only follow a practice accepted as proper by a responsible body of members of the profession.

---

83. MARTIN, *supra* note 4, at para. 3.3.3.
A learner, *i.e.*, a person training for a skill, trade or profession, must meet the same standard as a skilled person. In *Nettleship v Weston* [1971] 2 QB 691, the plaintiff, an experienced driver, agreed to give driving lessons to his friend, the defendant. On the third lesson, with the plaintiff moving the gear lever and the defendant steering the car, the defendant panicked and the car struck a lamp post. The plaintiff suffered injuries and sought to recover damages from the defendant. The defendant denied any negligence. The Court of Appeal found the defendant negligent: the standard of care required of a learner driver was the same as the standard required of an experienced driver, that standard being the standard of the reasonably competent and experienced driver. In other words, the court, at 699, said the learner's "incompetent best is not good enough". Megaw LJ also stated that the adoption of a variable standard would lead to unpredictability, uncertainty and the impossibility of arriving at fair and consistent decisions. He concluded, at 707, as a policy decision, that a general standard was preferable to "the vagaries of a fluctuating standard".
See also 25 (1) HALSBURY'S, *supra* note 4, at para. 380.126.
84. *Edward Wong Finance Co Ltd v Johnson Stokes & Master* [1984] AC 296, PC (on appeal from Hong Kong) involved a conveyancing transaction where the purchaser's mortgagee sued its solicitors for negligence. The solicitors followed the usual practice of paying the purchase price to the vendors' solicitor (who did not receive the money as agent for the vendor) against the latter's undertaking to forward the title documents. However the vendor's solicitor absconded with the money and the vendor refused to proceed. The Privy Council held that the risk of embezzlement by the recipient solicitor was foreseeable and the defendant solicitors were negligent in following such a practice.
See, e.g., GLOFCHESKI, *supra* note 1, at 46–55.

i. *Res Ipsa Loquitur*

The term "*res ipsa loquitur*" is Latin and can be translated to mean "the thing speaks for itself". This principle applies where a plaintiff may have difficulty meeting the burden of proving a case against the tortfeasor. In the case of *Li Kai Cheong v Lam Ying Wai* [2001] 3 HKLRD 48, the court stated that *res ipsa loquitur* is not a magic formula to assist a plaintiff in proving its case but is a rule of evidence. This rule of evidence applies in situations where the facts of a particular case indicate negligence but actual negligence is difficult to prove.

> Under the doctrine of *res ipsa loquitur* a plaintiff establishes a prima facie case of negligence where (1) it is not possible for him to prove precisely what was the relevant act or omission which set in train the events leading to the accident; and (2) on the evidence as it stands at the relevant time it is more likely than not that the effective cause of the accident was some act or omission of the defendant or of someone for whom the defendant is responsible, which act or omission constitutes a failure to take proper care for the plaintiff's safety. Where the thing which causes the accident is shown to be under the management of the defendant or his employees, and the accident is such as in the ordinary course of things does not happen if those who have the management use proper care, it affords reasonable evidence, in the absence of explanation by the defendant, that the accident arose from want of care.[85]

A hypothetical application of *res ipsa loquitur* would involve a plaintiff, who is a surgical patient, leaving an operating theatre with unnecessary medical equipment remaining inside the patient's body. As the equipment is unrelated to the patient's post-operative needs or care, the failure to remove the now embedded medical equipment would suggest negligence. However, as the patient was unconscious while under anaesthesia, the patient would have difficulty proving its case. The following cases are instances where plaintiffs successfully resorted to the use of *res ipsa loquitur*:

- *Wong Yiu Ming v To Chark Wah* [1993] 1 HKC 510, DC which involved a window frame falling from the building;

85. 25(1) Halsbury's, *supra* note 4, at para. 380.169. *See also id.* at paras. 380.170–380.173; Glofcheski, *supra* note 1, at 58–66; Bokhary, *supra* note 10, at paras. 3.224–3.238; Martin, *supra* note 4, at para. 16.2.1–16.2.8.
A recent case raising claims of negligence, *res ipsa loquitur* and occupier's liability is *Ho Ka Yin v Express Security Ltd* [2011] HKEC 975 where the plaintiff is a young wheel-chair bound woman who fell from her wheelchair while exiting the wheelchair lift operated by the defendant.

- *Chung Man Yau v Sihon Co Ltd* [1996] 3 HKC 614 involving the collapse of a balcony onto the pavement injuring the plaintiffs; and
- *Wong Sau Chun v Ho Kam Chiu* (2000) HCPI 872/1966, [2000] HKEC 109 where the deceased died when struck by a pane of glass while walking in a common area of a block of flats.[86]

ii. Egg-shell Skull Rule

Both the duty of care and damages are greater in circumstances where the "egg-shell skull" or "thin skull" rule applies. (The egg-shell skull rule will be encountered again in section VI.) This rule states that a defendant takes the victim as he finds him. This rule applies as follows: Assume a plaintiff had a skull as delicate as an egg-shell. A tortfeasor, unaware of this condition, taps the plaintiff's head, causing the skull unexpectedly to break. The tortfeasor would be liable for all damages arising from the battery, even though some of these damages were not foreseeable.

In other words, should a victim be predisposed to a particular injury or harm due to the victim's disposition or physical condition, the defendant would be responsible for any additional damages caused by the particular disposition or physical condition. Where some harm was reasonably foreseeable, the egg-shell skull rule would allow damages for harm that was greater than foreseen due to a peculiar vulnerability or predisposition of the plaintiff (*e.g.*, haemophilia), and also for harm that was not of a reasonably foreseeable "type".[87]

Thus, in *Dulieu v White & Sons* [1901] 2 KB 669, the court stated that:

> if a man is negligently run over or otherwise negligently injured in his body, it is no answer to the sufferer's claim for damages that he would have suffered less injury, or no injury at all, if he had not had an unusually thin skull or an unusually weak heart.[88]

In *Smith v Leech Brain and Co Ltd* [1962] 2 QB 405, the plaintiff worked in the defendant's factory. While at work, the plaintiff suffered a burn to the lower lip from a splash of molten metal. This burn caused a fatal cancer to develop in some pre-malignant tissue. The court determined:

---

86. 25(1) HALSBURY'S, *supra* note 4, at para. 380.169 n. 3. The *res ipsa loquitur* doctrine is also discussed in *supra* note 10.
87. GLOFCHESKI, *supra* note 1, at 126 (emphasis in original). For further discussion of the egg-shell skull rule, *see also* BOKHARY, *supra* note 10, at paras. 3.256–3.264. For discussion of the egg-shell rule's application to psychological or emotional damage, *see infra* note 110.
88. [1901] 2 KB at 679.

> The test is not whether these employers could reasonably have foreseen that a burn would cause cancer and that he would die. The question is whether these employers could reasonably foresee the type of injury he suffered, namely, the burn. What, in the particular case, is the amount of damage which he suffers as a result of that burn, depends upon the characteristics and constitution of the victim.[89]

In other words, the injury caused by the burn was reasonably foreseeable to the defendant. The defendant was thus liable even though the consequences of the plaintiff's ultimate demise, due to the susceptibility to cancer, were not reasonably foreseeable.

C. Causation

Another element required for the tort of negligence is causation, also known as "proximate cause". "Causation" references the physical connection between a defendant's negligence and a plaintiff's damage or injury. A defendant is not liable in negligence unless the plaintiff's loss was caused by that defendant's negligence.

A court needs to assess whether the defendant's negligent act caused the damage, or whether some prior unconnected factor or intervening event caused the damage. Courts tend to employ the notion of the chain of causation in ascertaining the connection between damage and the negligent act. If there is an unbroken chain of events between the act and the damage, the defendant will be liable, but if the chain of causation is broken by an intervening act, a *novus actus interveniens*,[90] the defendant "will be relieved of liability for the damage consequent upon the intervening negligence".[91]

---

89. [1962] 2 QB at 415.

90. BOKHARY, *supra* note 10, at paras. 1.124–1.126 comments:

> Where a defendant is negligent but before harm to the plaintiff results, an event, omission or act of a third party intervenes in the sequence of events, the question is whether the defendant remains responsible or whether the intervening act, event or omission, without which the plaintiff's damage would not have occurred, constitutes a novus actus interveniens such that it is regarded as breaking the chain of causation and relieving the defendant from liability. Both the defendant's wrongdoing and the intervening event may satisfy the "but for" test, however, the court considers whether in light of subsequent events, the defendant should still be held responsible for his/her original actions, notwithstanding the intervention of factors beyond his/her control. ...
>
> In order to break the chain of causation, a novus actus must be the sole or effective cause of the plaintiff's damage in that it overwhelms or eclipses the defendant's wrongdoing. ...

Such acts or omissions may be intentional, negligent or accidental. Generally, "deliberate acts are more likely to break the chain of causation than negligent ones".[92] Negligent acts are more likely to amount to a *novus actus* than mere accidents.[93] The general rule is that the chain of causation is broken where the intervening event is extraneous and disturbs the sequence of events. If the intervening event is foreseeable or follows naturally from the defendant's tort, the chain is not broken.

A distinction is often drawn between causation in fact and causation in law.[94] The former is concerned with whether, as a matter of fact, the defendant's negligence caused the plaintiff's loss. The test for causation in fact is whether the plaintiff's loss would have occurred but for[95] the defendant's negligence. Causation in law addresses whether the defendant can be held liable as a matter of law for the damage caused. The standard is whether the defendant's negligence is a real, substantial, direct or effective cause of the plaintiff's damage. The plaintiff must prove both causation in fact and causation in law in order to hold the defendant liable.

The "but for" test is one guideline used to determine factual causation.[96] This is a relatively simple test used to determine whether the conduct of a tortfeasor is the direct result of all of the damage or loss to another

---

> A novus actus may broadly take four forms:
> (1) A natural event occurring independently of any human action;
> (2) An act (or omission) by the defendant;
> (3) An act (or omission) by a third party;
> (4) The conduct of the plaintiff.

For an in-depth review of *novus actus interveniens*, *see*, *e.g.*, GLOFCHESKI, *supra* note 1, at 78–93; MARTIN, *supra* note 4, at Chapter 5 ("Negligence and Novus Actus Interveniens").

91. GLOFCHESKI, *supra* note 1, at 83.
92. BOKHARY, *supra* note 10, at para. 1.127.
93. *Id.*
94. One author expounds:

> Causation is typically explained by reference to two steps: factual causation and legal causation. However, the concept of legal causation as a separate component may be misleading, since the factual and legal matters are not discrete or fully separable. Bearing in mind that causation is always a matter of mixed fact and law … the defendant's breach must first be shown to be a factual cause of the damage; and then, that the breach must be shown to be an effective cause, sometimes referred to as proximate cause, such that legal responsibility for the damage will be attributed to the defendant.

GLOFCHESKI, *supra* note 1, at 71.

95. *McGhee v National Coal Board* [1973] 1 WLR 1. As noted in BLACK'S LAW DICTIONARY 381 (9th ed. 2009), the "but for" cause is the "cause without which the event could not have occurred.—Also termed *actual cause*; *cause in fact*; *factual cause*".
96. GLOFCHESKI, *supra* note 1, at 72 explains:

individual.[97] Where the plaintiff suffers successive injuries, with one of these injuries caused by the defendant's negligence, the extent of the defendant's liability is open to question, as a result of two conflicting decisions by the House of Lords.

The first of these decisions is *Baker v Willoughby* [1970] AC 467. In this case, the defendant driver accidentally knocked down the plaintiff, and the latter's leg injuries adversely affected his earning ability. The plaintiff assumed a new job after the accident, but while at work was shot in the same leg during an armed robbery. As a result, this leg had to be amputated. The defendant argued for a reduced level of liability: because the plaintiff's leg would be amputated eventually as a result of the robbery, the effect of the defendant's negligence had been obliterated. The House of Lords rejected this argument and found for the plaintiff, saying that the plaintiff was not being compensated for the physical injury itself but for the loss suffered as a result of that injury. The shooting incident had not diminished the plaintiff's pain and suffering, nor had it diminished the plaintiff's loss of earning capacity.

In the second decision, the House of Lords reached a different conclusion in *Jobling v Associated Dairies* [1982] AC 794. In 1973 the plaintiff injured his back while at work as a result of the defendant's breach of statutory duty. As a consequence of the injury, the plaintiff had to work a less strenuous job with a commensurate 50% reduction of earning capacity. Prior to trial in 1979, the plaintiff began to suffer from a crippling disease, myelopathy, which had rendered him totally unfit for work by the end of 1976. Their Lordships held that the defendant was not liable for any loss of earnings suffered by the plaintiff after 1976 when the myelopathy rendered the plaintiff totally incapacitated for employment purposes.

Both of these decisions followed from an application of the "but for" test. In *Baker*, but for the driver's negligence, the plaintiff would still have lost his leg from the shooting. In this sense, the loss after the shooting was

---

A device that is typically used by the courts at this preliminary stage has come to be known as the "but for" test. The question is posed: "But for the defendant's breach of duty, would the plaintiff have suffered the damage in question?" If the answer is yes, that is, the plaintiff would (on a balance of probabilities) have suffered the damage anyway, regardless of the defendant's breach, causation has not been proved. The defendant's conduct, however much it may have been a breach of duty, was not the cause.

See the recent Hong Kong cases cited to explain the application of the "but for" test in *id.* at 74–75.

97. If the damage is attributed to a pre-existing condition rather than to the negligence of the defendant, then the defendant will not be liable to the full extent of the damage. *See* the case of *Cutler v Vauxhall Motors Ltd* [1971] 1 QB 418.

not caused by the defendant. However, but for the robbery, the plaintiff would still have suffered from some degree of injury, such that the original injury after the date of the robbery was not caused by the robbers. If the robbers had been sued, they could only have been liable for the additional damage they caused to an already injured leg, because a defendant is to "take the victim as he finds him". Therefore, if the driver were liable only up to the date of the robbery, the victim would be under-compensated. The court thought that it was unfair that the victim should "fall between the two tortfeasors" and held the defendant liable to the full extent for the original injury. Similarly, in *Jobling*, but for the defendant's negligence, the victim would still have lost his earning capacity after 1976. Therefore the defendant did not cause the plaintiff's loss of earnings after 1976.

This conflict has not been resolved. Some suggest that *Baker* applies where the supervening event is a tort and *Jobling* applies where it is non-tortious. Another explanation is based upon the "vicissitudes of life" argument. In assessing damages for loss of earnings, the award is discounted for the possibility that any contingencies might reduce the victim's earning capacity in any event. Illness is an example of these vicissitudes of life and therefore should be taken into account. In this approach, supervening torts are not viewed as a vicissitude of life.[98]

More recently, the English Court of Appeal in *Rahman v Arearose Ltd* [2001] QB 351 suggested adopting a pragmatic approach:

> Once it is recognised that the first principle is that every tortfeasor should compensate the injured claimant in respect of that loss and damage for which he should justly be held responsible, the metaphysics of causation can be kept in their proper place: of themselves they offered in any event no hope of a solution of the problems which confront the courts in this and other areas. The law has dug no deeper in the philosophical thickets of causation than to distinguish between a *causa sine qua non* ['but-for' cause] and a *causa causans* [immediate or effective cause]. The latter is an empty tautology. The former proves everything, and therefore nothing: if A kills B by stabbing him, the birth of either of them 30 years before is as much a *causa sine qua non* of the death as is the wielding of the knife. So the law makes appeal to the notion of a proximate cause; but how proximate does it have to be? As a concept, it tells one nothing ... So in all these cases the real question is, what is the damage for which the defendant under consideration should be held responsible. The nature of his duty (here, the common

98. *See generally* Clerk & Lindsell, *supra* note 58, at paras. 2–72 to 2–77.

> law duty of care) is relevant; causation, certainly, will be relevant - but it will fall to be viewed, and in truth can only be understood, in light of the answer to the question: from what kind of harm was it the defendant's duty to guard the claimant? ... *Novus actus interveniens*, the eggshell skull, and (in the case of multiple torts) the concept of concurrent tortfeasors are all no more and no less than tools or mechanisms which the law has developed to articulate in practice the extent of any liable defendant's responsibility for the loss and damage which the claimant has suffered.[99]

In *Rahman*, the claimant suffered an assault at work, injuring his eye. A hospital's negligent treatment blinded him in that eye. The claimant sued the employer for failure to maintain a safe workplace and the hospital for negligent treatment. The appeal concerned the amount of damages for the psychiatric injury associated with the loss of the eye. The Court of Appeal apportioned the liability for the psychiatric injury between the two defendants. The hospital's later negligence did not absolve the employer's responsibility.

Where several individuals, not acting in together, each commits a tort against a victim at nearly the same time and causing the same or indivisible damage, each tortfeasor is liable for all the damage. Should each of several persons commits an independent tort consecutively against the victim, each is liable for the damage caused by his/her tortious act, assuming the damage caused by each tort is distinct. Thus, if the second tortfeasor's act caused no further damage or merely duplicated damage caused by the first tort, the second tortfeasor will not be liable; however, if the second tortfeasor's act aggravated merely the damage caused by the first tort, each tortfeasor will be liable only in respect of that part of the damage which his/her tort caused.[100]

D. Damage

"Damage" is the actual harm or loss suffered. "Damages" are the compensation which the injured party seeks from the tortfeasor. Damages frequently involve the issue of quantum, in other words, the actual amount of monetary loss of the plaintiff.[101] Generally, tort law is intended to make the

99. [2001] QB at 367–368.
100. 25(1) HALSBURY'S, *supra* note 4, at para. 380.066.
101. For a discussion of the different types of damages which may be awarded and the calculations thereof, *see*, *e.g.*, GLOFCHESKI, *supra* note 1, at Chapter 10 ("Damages for Personal Injury and Death"); BOKHARY, *supra* note 10, at Chapter 25 ("Damages").

injured party "whole" again, *i.e.*, to restore the victim to its position before the injury. This principle is known as *restitutio in integrum*, meaning full compensation or restitution.

As explained by one author:

> An award of damages is to serve as compensation for the losses, pecuniary and non-pecuniary, sustained by the plaintiff as a result of the tortious act of the defendant. Damages should be assessed to achieve *restitutio in integrum*. Litton V-P ... said that "the object of an award of damages is full restitution, compensating the victim for all the ill effects of the injury." In doing so, he echoed Lord Blackburn words, that the court should award "that sum of money which will put the party who has been injured, or who has suffered, in the same position as he would have been in if he had not sustained the wrong for which he is now getting his compensation or reparation."[102]

After establishing that the defendant owed the plaintiff a duty of care and that the defendant breached this duty of care causing loss to the plaintiff, the next issue to consider is whether the plaintiff's loss is recoverable in law.[103] The concept of remoteness of damage seeks to place limits upon a

---

102. Bokhary, *supra* note 10, at para. 25.002. *See also* Glofcheski, *supra* note 1, at 367–368.

103. Along with the consideration whether a loss is recoverable, a potential plaintiff also needs to consider the potential defendant or defendants who may be jointly or severally responsible for causing injury:

> Where injury or damage is caused to a plaintiff due to torts committed by two or more persons, they may either be joint tortfeasors or several tortfeasors. ... each of two or more joint tortfeasors, if sued alone, is liable for the entire damage resulting from the tort, though his contribution to the plaintiff's injury or damage was but a small part. ... under the Civil Liability (Contribution) Ordinance, judgment obtained against one joint tortfeasor in respect of the same damage is no bar to an action against other joint tortfeasors; and a release of, or accord with, a person liable in respect of any debt or damage, granted or made by a person to whom the debt is due or by whom the damage is suffered, does not discharge another person who is jointly liable in respect of the debt or damage unless the release or accord so provides. ...
>
> If each of several persons, not acting in concert, commits a tort against another person substantially contemporaneously and causing the same or indivisible damage, each several tortfeasor is liable for the whole damage. If each of several persons commits an independent tort consecutively against the same person, each is liable for the damage caused by his tortious act, assuming the damage proximately caused by each tort to be distinct. Thus, if the second tortfeasor's act caused no further damage or merely duplicated damage caused by the first tort, the second tortfeasor will not be liable; but, if his act merely aggravated the damage caused by the first tort, each tortfeasor will be liable only in respect of that part of the damage which his tort caused, assuming that it is possible to separate and quantify the aggravation of damage.

defendant's liability where the type of damage was unforeseeable or occurred in an unusual or unexpected way.[104]

> Related to the causation issue is the question of remoteness of damage. ... Normally, the defendant will be liable for all of the damage resulting from his/her negligent act. However, in some cases, some or all of the damage may be seen as "too remote" and therefore will not be shifted to the defendant. Legal principles have evolved to help determine the cut-off point, but these are not always easy to apply. Policy is implicit in this determination, as are notions of fault: should the plaintiff be held responsible for losses that could not have been reasonably foreseen?[105]

Re Polemis and Furness, Withy & Co [1921] 3 KB 560[106] first established the legal position in relation to remoteness of damage, and was later

---

25(1) HALSBURY'S, *supra* note 4, at paras. 380.065–380.066 (citations omitted). *See also id.* at para. 380.173. For a contemporary analysis, *see* MARC STAUCH, *Risk and Remoteness of Damage in Negligence*, 64 MLR 191 (2001).

The *BLIS Glossary*, *supra* note 1, translates "jointly and severally liable" as 負上共同及各別的法律責任.

104. GLOFCHESKI, *supra* note 1, at 119.

105. *Id.* at 71. *See also* BOKHARY, *supra* note 10, at para. 1.164–1.165.

106. The theory of "direct causation" was applied in the *Polemis* case where a plank dropped by one of the defendant's workers into the ship's hold caused a spark which exploded petroleum vapour in the cargo hold, thereby destroying the ship and its cargo. The arbitrators found that this was not a foreseeable result of the negligence; however, recovery was permitted because it was all "direct". WILLIAM L. PROSSER & W. PAGE KEETON, THE LAW OF TORTS 295 (5th ed. 1984) [hereinafter PROSSER & KEETON]. Under this theory of "direct causation", a defendant is liable for all the direct consequences of an act, however unforeseeable the extent or type of harm. HARPWOOD, MODERN TORT, *supra* note 32, at 179. Under the *Polemis* approach, therefore, a defendant was liable for all the damage which was the direct consequence of the wrongful act regardless whether the extent or the type of harm was foreseeable. HARPWOOD, MODERN TORT, *supra* note 32, at 179. *See also* GLOFCHESKI, *supra* note 1, at 119.

Lord Wright in *Liesbosch Dredger v SS Edison* [1933] AC 449 distinguished the *Polemis* approach. Presently, according to HARPWOOD, MODERN TORT, *supra* note 32, at 183:

> ... there is a view that the thin skull rule [discussed in *infra* note 110] would apply to property damage as well as to personal injury. As to economic loss, the authority is the *Liesbosch Dredger v SS Edison* [1933] AC 449. The defendants negligently caused the claimant's dredger to sink, and the claimants were forced to hire another vessel at an inflated rate in order to fulfil contractual obligations. They claimed that they were too poor to buy another dredger and for that reason had been forced into the hire contract. ... the House of Lords [held] that the claimants could not claim for the additional expense which they had incurred under the hire contract. That was the result of their own impecuniosity and was not foreseeable to the defendants.

superseded by *Overseas Tankship (UK) Ltd v Morts Dock & Engineering Co (The Wagon Mound (No 1))* [1961] AC 388, PC.[107]

> It has long been recognised that foreseeability has been used as a control to limit situations where there can be liability, both for omissions and commissions. It is a factor that has been considered in relation to whether a duty of care is owed … and it has featured in deciding whether the harm suffered is too remote. It is also relevant to whether a duty has been fulfilled, as what is reasonable to expect a party to have done will be linked to the harm that could be foreseen. However, it still seems to be the case that it is not crucial whether one looks at foreseeability in relation to whether a duty is owed at all or in relation to whether the harm suffered is too remote. …[108]
>
> … In reality it may be that it is not too important where foreseeability and policy factors come into the equation as they are both used

---

107. On 30 October 1951 the defendants' ship, the *Wagon Mound*, was loading oil in Sydney Harbour. Due to the negligence of the ship's engineers, a quantity of oil was spilt in the harbour and floated on the water's surface. The plaintiffs' vessels were undergoing repairs at a wharf approximately 200 yards distant. The spilt oil began to accumulate at the wharf where welding equipment was being used. Fearing the danger of fire, the plaintiffs' manager made enquiries and was informed it was safe to continue. On 1 November, the oil ignited and the fire severely damaged both the plaintiffs' ship and wharf. The wharf owners claimed damages for the wharf. The Privy Council held that the defendants were not liable. Viscount Simonds stated:

> a man must be considered to be responsible for the probable consequences of his act. To demand more of him is too harsh a rule, to demand less is to ignore that the civilised order requires the observance of a minimum standard of behaviour …

[1961] AC 388, 422–23.

Thus, the court repudiated the "direct causation rule", restricting liability to the foreseeable risk. PROSSER & KEETON, *supra* note 106, at 296. This case modified the previous rule in *Polemis*, which was that the defendant is liable for all the direct consequences of an act, however unforeseeable. HARPWOOD, MODERN TORT, *supra* note 32, at 179.

Six years later, in *Wagon Mound (No. 2)*, the Privy Council modified its earlier decision. The action in this case was for the damage to ships docked at the same wharf as in the *Wagon Mound (No. 1)* case. There was now evidence that the defendants were, or should have been, aware that there was some slight risk that the oil on the water would be ignited, even though it was a very unlikely event. The Privy Council held that as the defendants' had no justification or social value, they were not justified in neglecting even that slight risk, and they were therefore liable. This decision appears to have adopted the American formula of balancing the magnitude of the risk and the gravity of the harm against the utility of the conduct, and to have applied it to foreseeability in relation to "proximate cause". PROSSER & KEETON, *supra* note 106, at 296.

108. MAXINE WILLIAMS, *Case Comment: Foreseeability in duty or remoteness—still adrift on a sea of semantics?*, COVENTRY LAW JOURNAL 98, 101 (2000) [citations omitted].

> as limiting factors to control whether the defendant should or should not be held liable for the claimant's harm.[109]

Courts allow recovery for physical loss and personal injury, but are reluctant to allow recovery for nervous shock and economic loss.[110] The

---

109. *Id.* at 103.

See JENNY STEELE, *Pleural Plaques in the House of Lords: The implications for Page v Smith*, CAMBRIDGE LAW JOURNAL 28 (2008):

> In the combined appeals known as *In re Pleural Plaques* [2007] UHKL 39, [2007] 3 W.L.R. 876 the House of Lords has ruled that the development of symptomless pleural plaques (scarring of the lungs by asbestos fibres) does not constitute "damage" sufficient for a claim in negligence. Pleural plaques could be described as an "injury"; but the injury is too "trivial" to attract compensation. The addition of anxiety for the future, and of exposure to increased risk of future diseases–each unrecoverable in its own right–does nothing to alter this.

See also HARPWOOD, MODERN TORT, *supra* note 32, at 41.

The case of *Page v Smith* [1996] 1 AC 155, HL is cited for the principle that one who causes a foreseeable physical injury is also liable for any resulting psychiatric injury. GLOFCHESKI, *supra* note 1, at 128.

HARPWOOD, MODERN TORT, *supra* note 32, at 43 states that:

> it is now established that the claimant can succeed in obtaining damages for psychiatric injury as long as the court decides that it was reasonably foreseeable to the defendant that his actions could result in physical injury of some kind to the primary victim of his negligence.

See the case of *Simmons v British Steel Plc* [2004] ICR 585 as an example of the English courts' current approach on the issues of foreseeability and causation: victims must establish a causal connection between the incident and the damages, including psychiatric injuries, arising therefrom.

"Reasonable foreseeability" is a term which can give rise to confusion when applied to the concept of duty of care and to the concept of remoteness of damage:

> The adoption of reasonable foreseeability as the determinant for remoteness of damage may appear to conflate the function of remoteness of damage with that of duty of care, where reasonable foreseeability is also the main determinant ... However, the purpose of the inquiry is arguably different in each. In the duty of care issue, the court seeks to determine whether any harm is foreseeable, and to whom. At the remoteness of damage stage, a duty to take reasonable care is accepted, but now the court is concerned with the question whether the plaintiff's injury type was a foreseeable consequence of the defendant's negligence, that is, whether it actually comes within the specific foreseeable risk created by the defendant. However explained, the remoteness principle does involve some overlap with duty of care ...

GLOFCHESKI, *supra* note 1, at 122.

110. This also applies to the egg-shell skull rule in that its application:

> is not limited to the plaintiff's physical vulnerabilities. This much is clear from *White v Chief Constable of South Yorkshire* [1999] 1 All ER 1 ... Lord Goff said that the rule that permits a victim of personal injury to recover damages for accompanying psychiatric injury, whether or not reasonably foreseeable, is an application of the thin skull rule.

term "nervous shock" refers to a mental injury or psychiatric illness and not simply grief and sorrow.[111] It is the emotional trauma resulting from

---

...

In *Lam Wing Ming v Dragages et Travaux Publics (HK) Ltd* [1998] 2018 HKCU 1, the court applied the thin skull rule to the plaintiff's mental and psychological vulnerabilities that delayed his recovery from the physical injuries suffered. The court rejected the argument that damages should be assessed according to what a reasonable person would suffer, rather than what the plaintiff actually suffered.

... In *Yip Mau Leung v University of Hong Kong* [2000] 3 HKLRD 198, although a case concerned with the plaintiff's predisposition to physical injury to his wrist caused by an earlier sporting accident, the court adopted ... [the rule] that "the defendants must take the victim as they find him, that is to say, with his already vulnerable personality". On this basis, the defendant was held responsible for all of the damage resulting from a work-related accident, including a subsequent aggravation of the wrist injury before trial caused by another work-related incident.

In *Chun Yat-Nam v A-G for and on behalf of the Commissioner of Police* [1995] 1 HKLR 390 ... [the court allowed] the plaintiff's loss of earnings claim in full despite the plaintiff's decision to quit his menial post-accident job, on the basis that "a tortfeasor must take his victim as he finds him and the effect of the injury to this plaintiff was very different to another person of a different personality".

For this principle to operate, it is not necessary to show that the defendant was aware of the plaintiff's predisposition. In *T v Kan Ki Leung & Another* (2001) HCPI 443 of 2000, on the assumption that the plaintiff, a student who suffered schizophrenia as a result of the defendants' negligent disciplinary actions, was subject to a pre-disposition to schizophrenia, the court held that the "egg-shell" principle would apply whether or not the defendants were aware of the plaintiff's predisposition.

GLOFCHESKI, *supra* note 1, at 129–130.

111. For a more complete discussion, *see* 25(1) HALSBURY'S, *supra* note 4, at para. 380.115; GLOFCHESKI, *supra* note 1, at 163–173; *McLoughlin v O'Brian* [1982] 2 All ER 298, HL. *Jones v Wright* [1991] 3 All ER 88 arose out of the Hillsborough football disaster where the police allowed patrons into already fully occupied "pens" at the stadium. The crush of people forcing their way into the pens resulted in approximately 95 killed and 400 injured. Various persons alleging that they had suffered nervous shock as a result of this incident brought an action. It was also accepted that the plaintiffs had suffered psychiatric illness or nervous shock as a result of the disaster. The defendants admitted that they breached their duty owed to the dead and injured. The defendants, however, denied any duty of care to the plaintiffs. One of the issues related to the means which caused the shock. The trial court held that plaintiffs who witnessed the tragedy live on television were sufficiently proximate in time and space to justify the imposition of a duty of care. The court found that it was the "visual image" which was all important to the viewer; for the defendants, it was "not merely reasonably foreseeable that the television crews would be at Hillsborough for the semi-final"; and, the defendants had "full knowledge" that the TV crews would be there. [1991] 1 All ER 353, 380. The parties appealed this case, reported at [1991] 3 All ER 88, where the trial court's decision was partially reversed after a full discussion of the principles involved.

physical injury caused by the tort of another.[112] Courts are only willing to compensate for medically diagnosable nervous shock, *i.e.*, shock which results in medically recognisable physical or mental illness. Courts are less willing to compensate for emotional trauma unaccompanied by physical injury.[113]

Economic loss is another type of damages for which an injured party may seek compensation.[114] Economic loss resulting or arising from injury to the person or to property is a recoverable item of damage; however, there is generally no liability for pure economic loss.[115] *Spartan Steel & Alloys*

See White v Chief Constable of the South Yorkshire Police, *supra* note 110 (where the plaintiffs were police officers involved in rescue operations at the football disaster), and PAULA CASE, *Now you see it, now you don't: Black letter reflections on the legacies of White v Chief Constable of South Yorkshire Police*, 18(1) TORT LAW REVIEW 33 (2010).

112. 25(1) HALSBURY'S, *supra* note 4, at para. 380.115 remarks:

> A duty of care in relation to shock in the sense of psychiatric damage is owed to those foreseeably and directly involved in the horrific event caused by the defendant's negligence.

113. *See, e.g.*, 25(1) HALSBURY'S, *supra* note 4, at para. 380.115; MARTIN, *supra* note 4, at paras. 2.4.1–2.4.7.

114. *See Caparo Industries plc v Dickman*, *supra* note 57; *Murphy v Brentwood*, *supra* note 57. In-depth discussion on the recovery of economic loss is beyond the scope of this work. Readers may refer to BOKHARY, *supra* note 10, at para. 3.173; MARTIN, *supra* note 4, at paras. 2.6.1–2.6.14; CLERK & LINDSELL, *supra* note 58, at 1–36.

25(1) HALSBURY'S, *supra* note 4, at para. 380.116 defines the term:

> Pure economic loss refers to financial loss suffered by a plaintiff which does not flow from any injury to his own person or damage to property. Rather, the loss is caused through a web of economic relationships in which the plaintiff is involved. The pre-planned nature of these relationships frequently provides the plaintiff with an opportunity to seek protection through such measures as contract and insurance. The interlocking nature of the relationships means that the consequences of a single act of negligence may cause financial loss to numerous individuals. For both these reasons, it is not generally considered to be fair and just to allow recovery for pure economic loss however foreseeable it may have been. However, there are a number of situations where a pure economic loss is recoverable when it is truly consequent upon injury to the person or damage to the plaintiff's property.

25(1) HALSBURY'S, *supra* note 4, at para. 380.188 states:

> Damages may be awarded for pecuniary loss including future pecuniary loss, such as loss of profits or earnings, although a deduction may be made for benefits received. A person injured by another's wrong is entitled to general damages for non-pecuniary loss, such as pain and suffering and loss of amenity and enjoyment of life. Where the death of the deceased has been caused by the act or omission giving rise to the cause of action, damages may be awarded for the benefit of the estate. Dependants of the deceased may be able to claim compensation under the Fatal Accidents Ordinance. (citations omitted)

115. As explained by one authority:

Ltd v Martin & Co (Contractors) Ltd [1973] 1 QB 27, CA illustrates the distinction between pure and consequential economic loss. The defendant negligently damaged a power cable, cutting off the electricity supply to the plaintiff's factory. As a result, the plaintiff suffered damage to its property, loss of profit[116] and pure loss of profit during the interruption of electricity,

---

> It is important to learn to distinguish between pure economic loss on the one hand, and physical damage and economic loss consequent on physical damage, on the other. It is comparatively easy to prove a duty of care in respect of physical damage. Moreover, for duty purposes, economic loss consequent on physical damage is also treated as physical damage.
>
> Pure economic loss means a purely financial loss, independent from and not consequent upon any physical damage to the plaintiff or the plaintiff's property. …
>
> …
>
> The traditional position in negligence law has been that no duty of care is owed for purely financial losses, even where the loss is reasonably foreseeable.

GLOFCHESKI, *supra* note 1, at 175–176.

In *Murphy v Brentwood*, *supra* note 57, Lord Bridge stated that:

> if a manufacturer produces and sells a chattel which is merely defective in quality … the manufacturer's liability at common law arises only under and by reference to the terms of any contract to which he is a party in relation to the chattel; the common law does not impose on him any liability in tort to persons to whom he owes no duty in contract but who, having acquired the chattel, suffer economic loss because the chattel is defective in quality. If a dangerous defect in a chattel is discovered before it causes any personal injury or damage to property, because the danger is now known and the chattel cannot be safely used unless the defect is repaired, the defect becomes merely a defect in quality. The chattel is either capable of repair at economic cost or it is worthless and must be scrapped. In either case the loss sustained by the owner or hirer of the chattel is purely economic. It is recoverable against any party who owes the loser a relevant contractual duty. But it is not recoverable in tort in the absence of a special relationship of proximity imposing on the tortfeasor a duty of care to safeguard the plaintiff from economic loss. There is no such special relationship between the manufacturer of a chattel and a remote owner or hirer.
>
> I believe that these principles are equally applicable to buildings. If a builder erects a structure containing a letent [*sic*] defect which renders it dangerous to persons or property, he will be liable in tort for injury to persons or damage to property resulting from that dangerous defect. But, if the defect becomes apparent before any injury or damage has been caused, the loss sustained by the building owner is purely economic. … These economic losses are recoverable if they flow from a breach of a relevant contractual duty, but, here again, in the absence of a special relationship of proximity they are not recoverable in tort. …

[1990] 2 All ER at 925–926.

116. The damage claim of loss of profit arose from the plaintiff having to pump oxygen into its factory's furnace in order to keep the molten metal in it from solidifying, which reduced the value of the metal.

which caused lost production of metal alloy melts. The plaintiff succeeded on the first part of its claim, but failed to recover for loss of profit which it would have made but for the power loss caused by the defendant.[117]

Pure economic loss of this nature has generally been considered to be a business risk which every business bears. This attitude, together with the potential flood of claims, has been used as a policy reason not to find or to impose a duty of care. Economic loss involving negligent acts or negligent statements, *i.e.*, failure to take care in making statements,[118] causing financial loss is difficult to recover. *Hedley Byrne & Co Ltd v Heller & Partners Ltd* [1964] AC 465, HL involved the plaintiff advertising agent making enquiries concerning the creditworthiness of Easipower Ltd, in response to which the defendants, Easipower's bankers, gave favourable references. Relying upon this information, the plaintiffs incurred expenditure on Easipower's behalf and suffered a loss when Easipower went into liquidation. The House of Lords decided that the reference was negligent and the defendants would have been liable in negligence had the reference not been without an exemption clause, "without responsibility on the part of the bank or its officials", *i.e.*, the disclaimer protected the defendants so they were not liable.

Junior Books v Veitchi [1982] 3 All ER 201, HL limited recovery to cases of very close proximity where there is a special reliance on a defendant's skills.[119] The rule against recovery of pure economic loss has been expanded from the context of negligent statements to include now pure economic loss caused by negligent conduct, as opposed to words.[120]

---

117. *See* VERA BERMINGHAM & CAROL BRENNAN, TORT LAW DIRECTIONS 108 (2nd ed. 2010) [hereinafter BERMINGHAM & BRENNAN].
118. *See Derry v Peek* (1889) 14 App Cas 337; GLOFCHESKI, *supra* note 1, at 176–184; HARPWOOD, MODERN TORT, *supra* note 32, at 73–86.
119. In this case, the building owner sued a flooring sub-contractor for the economic loss suffered as a result of the flooring being improperly laid and having to be replaced. Since this decision, other courts have distinguished the holding in *Junior Books* on the bases of the close relationship between the sub-contractor and the main contractor as well as the evidence that the building owners had relied upon the sub-contractor's representations. *See* BERMINGHAM & BRENNAN, *supra* note 117, at 109.
120. GLOFCHESKI, *supra* note 1, at 185.
Id. at 220 states:

> However, if pure economic loss (only) has been suffered, a duty of care will not be found to have been owed … unless circumstances of reasonable reliance and close proximity as explained in *Hedley Byrne v Heller* are established. An example of such a case is *Linfield Ltd v Taoho Design Architects Ltd & Others* (2004) HCCT 68 of 2001. A duty of care was recognised as being owed by supervising architects to the developers of the property under construction, despite the fact that the architects had been engaged by another party to supervise the project. The court found that the dealings between the developer and the architects satisfied the criteria for a *Hedley Byrne* relationship.

See also the case of *White v Jones* [1995] 2 AC 207.

> Generally, courts will only allow recovery for pure economic loss where it can be said that the defendant has assumed a responsibility to the plaintiff and that the imposition of a duty would be fair ...[121]

IV. DEFENCES TO THE TORT OF NEGLIGENCE

The injured party must prove all the above elements of the tort of negligence on the balance of probabilities, otherwise the plaintiff has failed to prove its case and the defendant is absolved of liability. A tortfeasor may seek vindication by asserting a defence which would exonerate the defendant from full or partial liability for the injury caused to the plaintiff. Defences available to a defendant in the tort of negligence are mainly contributory negligence and *volenti non fit injuria*.[122]

---

121. 25(1) HALSBURY'S, *supra* note 4, at para. 380.116. *See id.* and GLOFCHESKI, *supra* note 1, at 185–198 for a discussion of cases where pure economic loss was allowed.

122. Other defences exist and will be presented below in sections IV.D and IV.E. One defence, that of illegality (*ex turpi causa non oritur actio*), is available. Another defence which might be available to a defendant in a tort action, although not limited to tort, is the limitation of actions.

Section 4 of the *Limitation Ordinance* (Cap 347) provides a general limitation period of six years:

> (1) The following actions shall not be brought after the expiration of 6 years from the date on which the cause of action accrued, that is to say—
> (a) action founded on simple contract or on tort;
> (b) actions to enforce a recognizance;
> (c) actions to enforce an award, where the submission is not by an instrument under seal;
> (d) actions to recover any sum recoverable by virtue of any Ordinance or imperial enactment, other than a penalty or forfeiture or sum by way of penalty or forfeiture:
>
> Provided that—
> (i) (Repealed 31 of 1991 s. 4)
> (ii) nothing in this subsection shall be taken to refer to any action to which section 6 applies.

Section 27 of the *Limitation Ordinance* applies to personal injury actions:

> (1) This section applies to any action for damages for negligence, nuisance or breach of duty (whether the duty exists by virtue of a contract or of provision made by or under an Ordinance or imperial enactment or independently of any contract or any such provision) where the damages claimed by the plaintiff for the negligence, nuisance or breach of duty consist of or include damages in respect of personal injuries to the plaintiff or any other person.
>
> ...
>
> (4) Except where subsection (5) applies, the said period is 3 years from—
> (a) the date on which the cause of action accrued; or
> (b) the date (if later) of the plaintiff's knowledge.

A. Contributory Negligence

At common law, the defence of contributory negligence acted as a complete bar to a plaintiff's action, provided that the plaintiff was unreasonable in avoiding risks for its own safety, and if this unreasonableness was a substantial factor in producing the plaintiff's own injury, even if the defendant was

---

(5) If the person injured dies before the expiration of the period in subsection (4), the period as respects the cause of action surviving for the benefit of the estate of the deceased by virtue of section 20 of the Law Amendment and Reform (Consolidation) Ordinance (Cap 23) shall be 3 years from—
(a) the date of death; or
(b) the date of the personal representative's knowledge,
whichever is the later.

(6) In this section, and in section 28, references to a person's date of knowledge are references to the date on which he first had knowledge of the following facts—
(a) that the injury in question was significant; and
(b) that that injury was attributable in whole or in part to the act or omission which is alleged to constitute negligence, nuisance or breach of duty; and
(c) the identity of the defendant; and
(d) if it is alleged that the act or omission was that of a person other than the defendant, the identity of that person and the additional facts supporting the bringing of an action against the defendant, and

knowledge that any acts or omissions did or did not, as a matter of law, involve negligence, nuisance or breach of duty is irrelevant.

...

Sections 31 and 32 of the *Limitation Ordinance* make provision for cases involving latent damages, *i.e.*, damage which does not become apparent until a considerable time after the breach of duty has been committed. Section 31 of the Ordinance provides:

(1) This section applies to any action for damages for negligence, other than one to which section 27 applies, where the earliest date on which the plaintiff or any person in whom the cause of action was vested before him first had both-
(a) the knowledge required for bringing an action for damages in respect of the relevant damage; and
(b) a right to bring such an action,
(referred to in this section as the "date of knowledge") falls after the date on which the cause of action accrued.

...

(4) That period is either—
(a) 6 years from the date on which the cause of action accrued; or
(b) 3 years from the date of knowledge, if that period expires later than the period mentioned in paragraph (a).

(5) In subsection (1) "the knowledge required for bringing an action for damages in respect of the relevant damage" (就有關損害而提出損害賠償訴訟所需的知悉) means knowledge—

also negligent.[123] In other words, if some contributory negligence could be established on the plaintiff's part, the plaintiff would not be able to claim any damages in a negligence action.[124]

(a) of such facts about the damage in respect of which damages are claimed as would lead a reasonable person who had suffered such damage to consider it sufficiently serious to justify his instituting proceedings for damages against a defendant who did not dispute liability and was able to satisfy a judgment;

(b) that the damage was attributable in whole or in part to the act or omission which is alleged to constitute negligence;

(c) of the identity of the defendant; and

(d) if it is alleged that the act or omission was that of a person other than the defendant, of the identity of that person and the additional facts supporting the bringing of an action against the defendant.

...

Section 32 of the *Limitation Ordinance* stipulates:

(1) An action for damages for negligence, other than one to which section 27 applies, shall not be brought after the expiration of 15 years from the date (or, if more than one, from the last of the dates) on which there occurred any act or omission—
(a) which is alleged to constitute negligence; and
(b) to which the damage in respect of which damages are claimed is alleged to be attributable (in whole or in part).

(2) This section bars the right of action in a case to which subsection (1) applies notwithstanding that—
(a) the cause of action has not yet accrued; or
(b) where section 31 applies to the action, the date which is for the purposes of that section the date of knowledge has not yet occurred,
before the end of the period of limitation prescribed by this section.

As noted by one authority:

> Generally speaking, for limitation purposes, time begins to run from the date when the cause of action *accrued*: from the earliest time at which the plaintiff had the right to sue. For most torts, including negligence, damage is the gist of the action so the action accrues and the limitation period begins to run when the damage occurred.
>
> Compare the situation in tort to that of contract law. In an action for breach of contract, the limitation period is six years, but the cause of action accrues not on the occurrence of damage, but on breach. This may mean that the limitation period in tort may be more favourable to the plaintiff ... The availability of concurrent actions in tort and contract then becomes an important issue for the plaintiff.

GLOFCHESKI, *supra* note 1, at 455 (emphasis in original).

123. For a detailed review of this topic, *see*, *e.g.*, 25(1) HALSBURY'S, *supra* note 4, at paras. 380.179–380.186.
The *BLIS Glossary*, *supra* note 1, translates "common law" as 普通法; "at common law" as 在普通法下; and, "contributory negligence" as 共分疏忽.

124. *See Butterfield v Forrester* (1809) 11 East 60; GLOFCHESKI, *supra* note 1, at 225–226.

In Hong Kong, the potentially harsh application of the common law rule has been ameliorated by the *Law Amendment and Reform (Consolidation) Ordinance* (Cap 23) which provides for apportionment of damages as the court thinks fit. Section 21(1) of the Ordinance provides that where a plaintiff suffers damage as the result of that person's own fault and of the fault of another, the damages recoverable shall be reduced having regard to the plaintiff's share in the responsibility for the damage.[125]

> In order to establish contributory negligence the defendant has to prove that the plaintiff's negligence was a cause of the harm which he has suffered in consequence of the defendant's negligence. The question is not who had the last opportunity of avoiding the mischief but whose act caused the harm. The question must be dealt with broadly and upon common sense principles. Where a clear line can be drawn, the subsequent negligence is the only one to be considered; however, there are cases in which the two acts come so closely together, and the second act of negligence is so much mixed up with the state of things brought about by the first act, that the person secondly negligent might invoke the prior negligence as being part of the cause of the damage so as to make it a case of apportionment. The test is whether in the ordinary plain common sense the plaintiff contributed to the damage.

25(1) HALSBURY'S, *supra* note 4, at para. 380.180 (citations omitted).

125. Section 21(1) states in full:

> (1) Where any person suffers damage as the result partly of his own fault and partly of the fault of any other person or persons, a claim in respect of that damage shall not be defeated by reason of the fault of the person suffering the damage, but the damages recoverable in respect thereof shall be reduced to such extent as the court thinks just and equitable having regard to the claimant's share in the responsibility for the damage:
> Provided that—
> (a) this subsection shall not operate to defeat any defence arising under a contract;
> (b) where any contract or enactment providing for the limitation of liability is applicable to the claim, the amount of damages recoverable by the claimant by virtue of this subsection shall not exceed the maximum limit so applicable.

Several definitions are provided in sub-section 10 of section 21:

> (10) In this section—
> "court" (法院) means, in relation to any claim, the court or arbitrator by or before whom the claim falls to be determined;
> "damage" (損害) includes loss of life and personal injury;
> "dependant" (受養人) means any person for whose benefit an action could be brought under the Fatal Accidents Ordinance (Cap 22);
> "fault" (過失) means negligence, breach of statutory duty or other act or omission which gives rise to a liability in tort or would, apart from this section, give rise to the defence of contributory negligence.

Law Amendment and Reform (Consolidation) Ordinance (Cap 23).

The *Law Amendment and Reform (Consolidation) Ordinance* alters only the legal consequences of contributory negligence.[126] The issue of whether there has been contributory negligence remains to be is determined by the common law. In *Nance v British Columbia Electric Railway Co Ltd* [1951] AC 601, the court stated that:

> when contributory negligence is set up as a defence, its existence does not depend on any duty owed by the injured party to the party sued and all that is necessary ... is to prove to the satisfaction of the jury that the injured party did not in his own interest take reasonable care of himself and contributed, by this want of care, to his own injury.[127]

Should a plaintiff's conduct be determined to have fallen below a reasonable standard of care and thus contributed to the claimed injuries, an apportionment of the damages will be made between the parties in an action for the tort of negligence. Section 21(1) of the *Law Amendment and Reform (Consolidation) Ordinance* provides that the damages recoverable shall be reduced as the court thinks just and equitable having regard to the claimant's share in the responsibility for the damage. One Hong Kong authority concludes that:

---

126. As noted by one source: "At the end of the day, the court assesses apportionment usually on the parties' respective responsibility for the damage, as opposed to simply assessing their comparative blameworthiness." BOKHARY, *supra* note 10, at para. 24.048. *See also* GLOFCHESKI, *supra* note 1, at 226.

127. [1951] AC at 611.
In Hong Kong, one source holds that:

> Section 21 will be activated when the plaintiff's conduct can be characterised as "fault" as defined in section 21(10). This entails taking into account the relevant standard of care ... Proof of causation is also necessary ... Fault, therefore, requires consideration of the standard of care, as well as causation.
>
> Moreover, the plaintiff's conduct in contributory negligence can take one of two forms. In most instances, the plaintiff's conduct will actually have been a cause of the accident itself that led to the injury. For instance, in crossing the road, the plaintiff may have failed to look to see if the road was clear. The plaintiff's conduct is a cause of the accident, as is the speeding car that runs the plaintiff down. However, it is not always necessary that the plaintiff's conduct be shown to be a cause of the accident in order for the defendant to rely on contributory negligence. ... in some cases, the plaintiff will be held to be contributorily negligent for failing to take precautions to minimise the injuries in the event that the defendant's negligence causes an accident. The classic example of this is where the plaintiff's injuries in the car accident are more serious as a result of the failure to wear a seat belt.

GLOFCHESKI, *supra* note 1, at 226.

> it is clear that this determination is a function of two factors: blameworthiness and causation. The court is engaged in a comparison of the plaintiff's conduct with the defendant's conduct, measuring their respective blameworthiness, and the degree to which their conduct caused the damage or injury.[128]

A Hong Kong case demonstrates the application of these rules. *Chau Fung Yee v Lee Chi Ming* [2000] 3 HKC 601 involved a first-time golfer whose ball struck the golfer's female caddie in the mouth. The caddie, knowing of the golfer's inexperience, had sought protection approximately 80 metres away amongst a grove of trees when struck by the golf ball. The court found both parties to be negligent. The golfer was negligent by failing to require all persons in front to be well out of the golfer's extreme range. The caddie was contributorily negligent for not exercising greater care for her own safety by moving to a safer position in the trees. The caddie's fault was in failing to take extra precautions for her safety and in failing to situate herself in the safest position despite her knowledge of the risk. Therefore, the court found the golfer to be two-thirds responsible for the injury and the caddie to be one-third responsible.[129]

---

128. GLOFCHESKI, *supra* note 1, at 239.

129. As the court stated:

> It was readily foreseeable that someone might be struck by the ball. It was far higher than the normal risk. He [the defendant golfer] should have taken the precaution of ensuring that no one was within range, and with his limitations, that range was very wide. He owed a duty of care towards the plaintiff. [2000] 3 HKC at 603.
>
> ...
>
> The defendant was wholly inexperienced. He should not in my view have been allowed on that course without proper precautions being taken for all concerned. Any one in front of him in a wide arc was at risk. ... He owed a duty of care to all in front of him, including the three caddies. ... He posed an obvious danger. He was negligent. [2000] 3 HKC at 606.
>
> The plaintiff was required to go in the area of trees as a matter of practice. That was not negligence on her part. She knew however the defendant's lack of experience and ability and the unpredictable nature of his play. She—as well as her colleagues—were at risk of being struck by a ball struck by the defendant ... She should have taken extra precautions for her own safety as she had advised her colleagues. She tried to do so late and may have misjudged the trajectory of the ball. I think she was negligent too ... [2000] 3 HKC at 606.

B. *Volenti Non Fit Injuria* (Assumption of Risk)

Volenti non fit injuria, or simply *volenti*, is a complete defence to a plaintiff's action.[130] This phrase is translated as: no injury is done to a person

---

130. 25(1) HALSBURY'S, *supra* note 4, at para. 380.174 states:

> Where a plaintiff relies on the breach of a duty to take care owed by the defendant to him, it is a good defence that the plaintiff consented to that breach of duty, or, knowing of it, voluntarily incurred the whole risk entailed by it. In such a case the maxim volenti non fit injuria applies. This defence is to be distinguished from the plea of contributory negligence, for a plaintiff may have voluntarily exposed himself to the risk of being injured while himself exercising the utmost care for his own safety; and, conversely, while knowledge of the risk may show contributory negligence, it does not prove voluntary assumption of risk. (citations omitted)

Another source explains:

> The defence of *volenti* is premised on the idea of consent or waiver, normally an implied consent or waiver. It requires proof that the plaintiff, with knowledge of risks to his/her safety created by the defendant's conduct, and acting voluntarily, agrees to take the risk and forego rights to compensation should the risk eventuate. The court will consider the nature of the plaintiff's conduct in drawing the necessary inferences: in the words of Lord Asquith in *Dann v Hamilton* [1939] 1 KB 509, was it like "engaging in an intrinsically and obviously dangerous occupation, intermeddling with an unexploded bomb or walking on the edge of an unfenced cliff"?
>
> The waiver of rights can be done expressly, as in writing, or more commonly, impliedly, by conduct. Where the "waiver" or "agreement" is express, the defence will be somewhat easier to establish, although even here, there are difficulties, including, importantly, some legislative restrictions on the availability of the defence (see the Control of Exemption Clauses Ordinance (Cap 71) ... and section 12 of the Motor Vehicles Insurance (Third Party Risks) Ordinance (Cap 272) ...).

GLOFCHESKI, *supra* note 1, at 245.

Relevant sections of the *Control of Exemption Clauses Ordinance* (Cap 71) are set out *infra* notes 136–141. Section 12(2) of the *Motor Vehicles Insurance (Third Party Risks) Ordinance* (Cap 272) provides:

> (2) Where a person uses, or causes or permits any person to use, a motor vehicle on a road in such circumstances that under section 4(1) there is required to be in force in relation to his use of it such a policy of insurance or such a security in respect of third party risks as complies with the requirements of this Ordinance, then, if any other person is carried in or upon the vehicle while the user is so using it, any antecedent agreement or understanding between them (whether intended to be legally binding or not) shall be of no effect so far as it purports or might be held—
>
> (a) to negative or restrict any such liability of the user in respect of persons carried in or upon the vehicle as is required by section 6(1) to be covered by a policy of insurance; or
>
> (b) to impose any conditions with respect to the enforcement of any such liability of the user, and

who consents to the risk of injury.[131] If a plaintiff knowingly and voluntarily accepts the risks of injury by the defendant's negligence, there is no recovery for any loss, damage or injury.[132] Courts generally construe this defence narrowly as they are reluctant on policy grounds to deprive a plaintiff of a remedy lightly.[133]

The plaintiff must voluntarily submit to the risk of injury. The plaintiff must actually know of the risk in addition to the nature of the risk and the extent of the risk. At issue will be the subjective state of mind of the plaintiff, "as opposed to the objective, reasonable standard required in (contributory) negligence".[134] In *Bowater v Rowley Regis Corporation* [1944] KB 476, the court found that:

> a man cannot be said to be truly "willing" unless he is in a position to choose freely, and freedom of choice predicates, not only full knowledge of the circumstances on which the exercise of choice is conditioned, so that he may be able to choose wisely, but the absence from his mind of any feeling of constraint so that nothing shall interfere with the freedom of his will.

In *Dann v Hamilton* [1939] 1 KB 509, the court held that mere knowledge of the danger is not sufficient to establish the defence of *volenti*. The defendant must prove that the plaintiff consented to the risk, not simply that the plaintiff had knowledge of the risk.[135]

> the fact that a person so carried has willingly accepted as his the risk of negligence on the part of the user shall not be treated as negativing any such liability of the user.

131. Note that some authorities refer to this defence as voluntary assumption of risk. GLOFCHESKI, *supra* note 1, at 245.
132. For an exposition on the application of this defence, particularly in relation to the tort of trespass to the person, discussed below in section V.F, *see* GLOFCHESKI, *supra* note 1, at 523–531. *See also* 25(1) HALSBURY'S, *supra* note 4, at paras. 380.175–380.176.
133. GLOFCHESKI, *supra* note 1, at 245. However, *see McGinlay v British Railways Board* [1983] 1 WLR 1427 where the defence of *volenti* was successful against a 15-year-old plaintiff who entered the defendant's rail line as a short cut. Compare this outcome with the decision in *British Railways Board v Herrington* [1972] AC 877 discussed below in section V.D in relation to occupier's liability.
134. GLOFCHESKI, *supra* note 1, at 245. *See also* BOKHARY, *supra* note 10, at para. 24.057–24.058.
135. [1944] KB at 479.
 See also the case of *Morris v Murray* [1990] 3 All ER 801, CA where the plaintiff was denied damages for his injury caused by an airplane crash because the pilot was drunk. There was evidence that the plaintiff had been out drinking with the pilot prior to the flight.
 BOKHARY, *supra* note 10, at paras. 24.060–24.062, says the following about the existence of agreement, that:

It should be noted that the *Control of Exemption Clauses Ordinance* (Cap 71) is a legislative attempt to restrict the use of exemption clauses by commercial enterprises in order to avoid business liability.[136] Section 7(3) of this Ordinance stipulates that one's agreement to or awareness of a contract provision limiting liability for negligence does not necessarily indicate that

---

the "agreement" aspect of the defence is probably the most controversial and this, in part, is due to different formulations of the defence of volenti by different judges. There is a line of authorities which suggest that nothing short of an agreement, express or implied, will suffice. In *Nettleship v Weston*, Lord Denning said:

> Now that contributory negligence is not a complete defence, but only a ground for reducing the damages, the defence of volenti non fit injuria has been closely considered and in consequence, it has been severely limited. Knowledge of the risk of injury is not enough. Nor is a willingness to take the risk of injury. Nothing will suffice short of an agreement to waive any claim for negligence. The plaintiff must agree, expressly or impliedly to waive any claim for any injury that may befall him due to the lack of reasonable care by the defendant.

Other cases suggest that the defence of volenti applies, in appropriate circumstances, where the plaintiff assumes a glaring and extreme risk akin to "tempering [sic] with a time bomb". Generally speaking, the authorities suggest that a full spectrum of the alternatives is possible: the agreement can be either express or implied, and can be reached either before or after the act of negligence in question.

In the case where the defendant seeks to establish an antecedent agreement, the following considerations come into play. Firstly, where the agreement is an express agreement, there is the issue of whether the agreement is subject to the CECO. Secondly, the defendant must establish that there is some form of relationship between the parties as a stranger cannot be deemed to have agreed to run the risk merely because he knows that the defendant has a propensity to act negligently. In any event, even if the defendant is able to show that there is such a relationship, only in very limited circumstances will the court be prepared to derive an implied agreement from the parties' conduct excusing the defendant's future negligent acts.

See also GLOFCHESKI, *supra* note 1, at 218.

136. *Control of Exemption Clauses Ordinance*, *supra* note 130, at section 2(2). Section 2 states:

(1) In this Ordinance—
"business" (業務) includes a profession and the activities of a public body, a public authority, or a board, commission, committee or other body appointed by the Chief Executive or Government;
"goods" (貨品) has the same meaning as in the Sale of Goods Ordinance (Cap 26);
"negligence" (疏忽) means the breach—
(a) of any obligation, arising from the express or implied terms of a contract,

person's acceptance of a risk.[137] Section 7(1)[138] of this Ordinance further stipulates that liability for death or personal injury resulting from negligence is not excludable. In respect of other property loss or property damage, section 7(2)[139] requires that the terms in the exemption clause limiting liability must meet a reasonableness requirement which is set out in section 3.[140] Section 5 of the Ordinance sets out the varieties of exemption clauses.[141]

(b) to take reasonable care or exercise reasonable skill in the performance of the contract; of any common law duty to take reasonable care or exercise reasonable skill (but not any stricter duty);

(c) of the common duty of care imposed by the Occupiers Liability Ordinance (Cap 314);

"notice" (告示) includes an announcement, whether or not in writing, and any other communication or pretended communication;

"personal injury" (人身傷害) includes any disease and any impairment of physical or mental condition.

(2) In the case of both contract and tort, sections 7 to 12 apply (except where the contrary is stated in section 11 (4)) only to business liability, that is liability for breach of obligations or duties arising—

(a) from things done or omitted to be done by a person in the course of a business (whether his own business or another's); or

(b) from the occupation of premises used for business purposes of the occupier,

and references to liability are to be read accordingly; but liability of an occupier of premises for breach of an obligation or duty towards a person obtaining access to the premises for recreational or educational purposes, being liability for loss or damage suffered by reason of the dangerous state of the premises, is not a business liability of the occupier unless granting that person such access for the purposes concerned falls within the business purposes of the occupier.

(3) In relation to any breach of duty or obligation, it is immaterial whether the breach was inadvertent or intentional, or whether liability for it arises directly or vicariously.

137. *Id.* at section 7(3) states in full:

> Where a contract term or notice purports to exclude or restrict liability for negligence a person's agreement to or awareness of it is not of itself to be taken as indicating his voluntary acceptance of any risk.

138. *Id.* at section 7(1) provides:

> A person cannot by reference to any contract term or to a notice given to persons generally or to particular persons exclude or restrict his liability for death or personal injury resulting from negligence.

139. *Id.* at section 7(2) states:

> In the case of other loss or damage, a person cannot so exclude or restrict his liability for negligence except in so far as the term or notice satisfies the requirement of reasonableness.

140. *Id.* at section 3 stipulates:

(1) In relation to a contract term, the requirement of reasonableness for the purposes of this Ordinance and section 4 of the Misrepresentation Ordinance (Cap 284) is satisfied only if the court or arbitrator determines that the term was a fair and reasonable one to be included having regard to the circumstances which were, or ought reasonably to have been, known to or in the contemplation of the parties when the contract was made.

(2) In determining for the purposes of section 11 or 12 whether a contract term satisfies the requirement of reasonableness, the court or arbitrator shall have regard in particular to the matters specified in Schedule 2; but this subsection does not prevent the court or arbitrator from holding, in accordance with any rule of law, that a term which purports to exclude or restrict any relevant liability is not a term of the contract.

(3) In relation to a notice (not being a notice having contractual effect), the requirement of reasonableness under this Ordinance is satisfied only if the court or arbitrator determines that it would be fair and reasonable to allow reliance on it, having regard to all the circumstances obtaining when the liability arose or (but for the notice) would have arisen.

(4) In determining (under this Ordinance or the Misrepresentation Ordinance (Cap 284)) whether a contract term or notice satisfies the requirement of reasonableness, the court or arbitrator shall have regard in particular (but without prejudice to subsection (2) to whether (and, if so, to what extent) the language in which the term or notice is expressed is a language understood by the person as against whom another person seeks to rely upon the term or notice.

(5) Where by reference to a contract term or notice a person seeks to restrict liability to a specified sum of money, and the question arises (under this Ordinance or the Misrepresentation Ordinance (Cap 284)) whether the term or notice satisfies the requirement of reasonableness, the court or arbitrator shall have regard in particular (but without prejudice to subsection (2) or (4)) to—

(a) the resources which he could expect to be available to him for the purpose of meeting the liability should it arise; and

(b) how far it was open to him to cover himself by insurance.

(6) It is for the person claiming that a contract term or notice satisfies the requirement of reasonableness to prove that it does.

141. *Id.* at section 5 states:

(1) To the extent that this Ordinance prevents the exclusion or restriction of any liability it also prevents—

(a) making the liability or its enforcement subject to restrictive or onerous conditions;

(b) excluding or restricting any right or remedy in respect of the liability, or subjecting a person to any prejudice in consequence of his pursuing any such right or remedy;

(c) excluding or restricting rules of evidence or procedure,

and (to that extent) sections 7, 10, 11 and 12 also prevent excluding or restricting liability by reference to terms and notices which exclude or restrict the relevant obligation or duty.

(2) An agreement in writing to submit present or future differences to arbitration is not to be treated under this Ordinance as excluding or restricting any liability.

C. Inevitable Accident

The defence of inevitable accident applies when injury or damage is caused by an unusual occurrence which cannot be prevented by use of ordinary care.[142]

> The defendant may escape liability by establishing that the cause of the claimant's injury was an accident rather than any wilful or negligent act on his part.
>
> An inevitable accident is one which no human foresight could have prevented, an accident which could not have been prevented by the exercise of reasonable care on the part of the defendant.
>
> ...
>
> Inevitable accident ... is a defence in which the burden of proof is on the defendant to show that what happened was an unforeseeable accident.[143]

This defence succeeded in *Stanley v Powell* [1891] 1 QB 86 when a bullet ricocheted off a tree and injured the plaintiff. For fault-based torts, *e.g.*, negligence, this defence is essentially a denial of fault or negligence. However, for torts of strict liability, this defence is not available because the defendant's fault is irrelevant.

However, as one authority notes:

> Inevitable accident no longer exists as a separate defence. A person is not liable in negligence unless the plaintiff proves that he failed to take reasonable care. In trespass, too, it now seems that the plaintiff fails unless he proves that the defendant either intentionally or negligently committed the wrongful act. Where the tort is one of strict liability, it will be no defence for the defendant to prove inevitable accident.[144]

D. *Ex Turpi Causa Non Oritur Actio*

This Latin term is translated as: no cause of action can be based upon an illegal act.[145] Thus, this defence to a tort of negligence action is also known

142. Bokhary, *supra* note 10, at para. 24.085; Pannett, *supra* note 36, at 219–220.
143. Harpwood, Modern Tort, *supra* note 32, at 485–486.
144. 25(1) Halsbury's, *supra* note 4, at para. 380.081 (citations omitted).
145. LexisNexis, Hong Kong English-Chinese Legal Dictionary (2005) translates "*ex turpi causa non oritur actio*" as 代價非法或不道德的，即不能據此而興訟.

as the illegality defence.[146] Under this defence, a plaintiff who was injured while committing an illegal act generally cannot recover damages from the tortfeasor. The following case is an illustrative example.

In *Pitts v Hunt* [1991] 1 QB 24, the plaintiff suffered injuries while being a passenger on a motorcycle being driven by a drunken friend who did not possess a licence and who did not carry the mandatory insurance coverage. The drunken plaintiff had encouraged this friend to drive at a high speed and in a way intended to frighten pedestrians. These two friends on the motorcycle collided with an automobile resulting in the death of the friend and injuries to the plaintiff.

Note, however, that the seriousness of the illegal act is a factor to be considered when applying this defence. If the illegality is a minor one, this defence might not apply. In the *Pitts* case mentioned above, the court held that the plaintiff was precluded from recovering damages for the injuries incurred during the course of very serious offences in which he was participating.

Another item to note about this defence is the requirement for a close connection between the illegal act and the damage suffered. Two cases illustrate this requirement. In the first case, *Leung Tsang Hung v Tse Yiu Pui* [2004] HKCU 515, an illegal hawker died as a result of the defendant's canopy falling upon her. *Ex turpi causa* would not apply in this case as there is an insufficient connection between the illegal act (hawking without a licence) and the accident.[147] In the second case, *Tsang Siu Hong v Kong Hoi For* [2003] 1 HKLRD D22, the plaintiff was working illegally in a Hong Kong garage when he was struck on the head by a falling iron rod. There was an insufficient connection between working illegally and the injury.

E. Statute of Limitations

Another defence possibly available to a tortfeasor is that the claim has become time barred, that is the time to bring a court case has expired. The

146. *Id.* translates "defence of illegality" as 以違法為理由的抗辯.
As this defence will not be examined in any substantive detail in this work, *see* GLOFCHESKI, *supra* note 1, at 254–265; BOKHARY, *supra* note 10, at paras. 3.065–3.067.
For recent applications of this defence in the United Kingdom, *see, e.g.*, *Stone & Rolls Ltd v Moore Stephens* [2009] 1 AC 1391, HL; *Gray v Thames Trains* [2009] 1 AC 1339. *See also* PO JEN YAP, *Rethinking the illegality defence in tort law*, 18(1) TORT LAW REVIEW 52 (2010).

147. GLOFCHESKI, *supra* note 1, at 260. This case was appealed to the Court of Appeal, reported at [2006] 4 HKLRD 714, and ultimately to the Court of Final Appeal, reported at [2007] 5 HKC 227 on the issue of the liability of the building's incorporated owners corporation —*see* section V.E.ii ("Public Nuisance") for further discussion.

injured party is barred or prevented from bringing a claim after a specified period of time. This is an example of a statutorily imposed restriction on an injured party's recovery. The *Limitation Ordinance* (Cap 347) is a statute of limitations which disallows a particular remedy after the passage of a specified time. For law suits concerning torts, the limitation period is either three years or six years from the date on which the reason to sue arises.[148] The cause of action, *i.e.*, the right to sue, generally arises or accrues at the time of injury or when the cause of action was discovered or should have been discovered. No action may be brought after the limitation period expires.

V. OTHER TORTIOUS LIABILITIES

There are various other forms of tortious liability not based upon the neighbour principle laid down in *Donoghue v Stevenson*:

(a) vicarious liability;
(b) breach of statutory duty;
(c) employer's liability to workers;
(d) occupier's liability;
(e) nuisance;
(f) trespass to the person;

---

148. For an analysis of the application of the *Limitation Ordinance*, *see* 25(1) HALSBURY'S, *supra* note 4, at paras. 380.094–380.099; 17(2) HALSBURY'S LAWS OF HONG KONG paras. 245.001–245.037; 245.050–245.069 (2008); GLOFCHESKI, *supra* note 1, at Chapter 13 ("Limitation of Action"); BOKHARY, *supra* note 10, at paras. 28.008–28.010.
Limitation Ordinance, *supra* note 122, at section 4(1) states in part:

> The following actions shall not be brought after the expiration of 6 years from the date on which the cause of action accrued, that is to say-
>
> (a) actions founded on simple contract or on tort;
>
> ...

Limitation Ordinance, *supra* note 122, at section 27(1) states in part:

> (1) This section applies to any action for damages for negligence, nuisance or breach of duty ... where the damages claimed by the plaintiff consist of or include damages in respect of personal injuries to the plaintiff or any other person.
>
> ...
>
> (9) For the purposes of this section "personal representative" (遺產代理人) includes any person who is or has been a personal representative of the deceased ... and regard shall be had to any knowledge acquired by any such person while a personal representative or previously.
>
> (10) If there is more than one personal representative, and their dates of knowledge are different, subsection (5)(b) shall be read as referring to the earliest of those dates.

(g) trespass to land; and,
(h) defamation.

Each one of these categories of tort is now reviewed in turn.

A. Vicarious Liability

Vicarious liability is not itself a tort, but is the basis upon which a person is held liable for the tortious acts of others.[149] "Vicarious liability is legal responsibility imposed on a person for the torts of others, regardless of any fault on the part of the non-tortfeasor".[150] Generally, vicarious liability arises where the tortious act of one person may be imputed to another, typically under a master and servant relationship where the employer shares in the liability of its servants' negligent acts committed in the course of employment.[151]

Vicarious liability under an employer-employee situation results in the employer's strict and joint liability for its employee's negligent acts

---

149. For an in-depth analysis of this topic, *see* P.S. ATIYAH, VICARIOUS LIABILITY IN THE LAW OF TORTS (1967). 25(1) HALSBURY'S, *supra* note 4, at para. 380.032 notes:

> An employer is liable for a tort committed by an employee against a third party or a fellow employee, provided that tort was committed by the employee in the course of his employment, or while he was engaged on his employer's business. (citations omitted)

The *BLIS Glossary*, *supra* note 1, translates "scope of employment" as 受僱範圍; and, "in the course of employment" as 受僱工作期間.

150. BOKHARY, *supra* note 10, at para. 2.001.

151. A source explains that:

> There are prohibitions which limit the sphere of employment, and prohibitions which only deal with conduct within the sphere of employment. A transgression of a prohibition of the latter class does not put the employee's act outside the course of employment. A transgression of the former class carries with it the result that the employee has gone outside the course of employment.

25(1) HALSBURY'S, *supra* note 4, at para. 380.041 (citations omitted).

Id. at para. 380.201 states:

> It is not yet settled whether an employer is liable vicariously for his employee's breach of statutory duty, where the duty is imposed on the employee and not on the employer but the act or omission which constitutes the breach of statutory duty may also amount to negligence at common law in the course of the employee's employment, and for that the employer will be vicariously responsible. However, there is no question of vicarious liability where the statutory duty is imposed on the employer and the only act or default bringing about the breach is that of an employee who then seeks to sue his employer on that breach. The employer cannot be liable for an employee's injuries caused by the employee himself. (citations omitted)

committed within the course of employment.[152] The employer's liability is not based on its personal fault; rather, the employer's liability is based upon the employment relationship between the employer and the tortfeasor, *i.e.*, the employee.[153] Accordingly, for an employer to be held jointly liable for its employee's tort under vicarious liability, the employee must be found to be at fault. If the employee is not at fault, neither is the employer. If the employee is found to be at fault, both the employee and the employer will be liable.

Tort actions for vicarious liability commonly involve an employer's liability for the actions of its employees. An independent contractor, however, is considered to be a completely separate entity from the employer and thus not under its control or supervision.[154] Consequently, as a general rule, if a party appoints an independent contractor, the consequences of any damages arising from the independent contractor's negligence belong solely to the independent contractor. The exception to this general rule is where an employer has:

> negligently engaged an incompetent contractor, or employed too few men, or has interfered with the way the work had to be carried out or has authorised or ratified the negligent act.[155]

One author stated that there are various policy reasons for vicarious liability:

- One motive is tort law's quest to find "deep pockets" in order to ensure compensation to the victim.
- Another is a moral element that holds that one who profits from the accident-causing activity should pay the injured party.
- Further, vicarious liability has a loss distribution function in that vicarious liability provides a mechanism for spreading the loss beyond the immediate tortfeasor.[156]

As vicarious liability is usually raised in situations involving employees, this topic is reviewed in detail in the Employment chapter. That chapter discusses the status of a worker as either an employee or independent contractor; the factors which assist in determining the status; the scope of employment and an employer's liability for its independent contractor(s).

---

152. The *BLIS Glossary*, *supra* note 1, translates "strict liability" as 嚴格法律責任; and, "employee" as 僱員.
153. GLOFCHESKI, *supra* note 1, at 407.
154. The *BLIS Glossary*, *supra* note 1, translates "independent contractor" as 獨立承辦商.
155. GLOFCHESKI, *supra* note 1, at 439 (citation omitted).
156. *Id.* at 407.

In *Kwong Kwok Kin v Observatory Watch & Jewellery Co Ltd* [1987] 3 HKC 138, the Court of Appeal considered vicarious liability in a situation other than in an employment relationship. In 1982, Kwong lent his car to his friend who allegedly caused damage to the jewellery company's vehicle. In 1986, Kwong received a writ from the plaintiff alleging negligence on his part or on that of his servant or agent. Kwong's friend had disappeared in the interim. The District Court found the driver to be Kwong's agent, thus rendering Kwong vicariously liable. The Court of Appeal, in reversing the trial judge's decision, quoted the test put forward in *Launchbury v Morgans* [1973] AC 127 that:

> in order to fix vicarious liability upon the owner of a car in such a case as the present it must be shown that the driver was using it for the owner's purposes, under delegation of a task or duty.[157]

B. Breach of Statutory Duty

Apart from the general duty for a person to take reasonable care, legislation may impose particular duties on individual persons or businesses.[158]

---

157. [1973] AC at 135.

158. As explained by one author:

> Although based on the breach of a legislative provision, breach of statutory duty is a common law tort action. Moreover, it is separate and distinct from an action in negligence or occupiers' liability. It may be brought alone, or in addition to negligence or occupiers' liability.

GLOFCHESKI, *supra* note 1, at 305. This source further explains that:

> in many cases, the plaintiff brings actions in both of breach of statutory duty and negligence, and is often able to succeed in both. Since proof of a breach of a statutory standard is likely to be taken by the court in a negligence action as strong proof of a failure to meet the reasonable standard of care, why does the tort exist?
>
> ... before the decision in *Donoghue v Stevenson* [1932] AC 562, an action for breach of statutory duty was sometimes the only means of redress by persons injured as a result of the defendant's failure to meet the statutory standard. It was generally thought that legislation that required a specified standard of behaviour must give rise to a right to sue for damages in the event of a failure to meet that standard ... and the tort of negligence was not yet sufficiently developed to ensure a remedy to all persons so injured. This was particularly so regarding workplace injuries, where a number of now-defunct defences were at one time available to an employer. However today, the action for breach of statutory duty has been largely overtaken by modern developments expanding the reach of the tort of negligence, and the need for a separate tort action for breach of statutory duty is questionable.

Id. at 308.

For example, the Factories and Industrial Undertakings (Guarding and Operation of Machinery) Regulations (Cap 59Q) require employers to provide safety equipment or to ensure that dangerous machine parts are equipped with guarding devices.[159] The breach of statutory duty provides an additional cause of action in tort to parties injured as a result of such failure.

> Where an Ordinance requires someone to do a particular act, the obligation is personal and cannot be delegated to another. So, even if the person under the statutory mandate employs an independent contractor to perform the task and the contractor fails to execute the mandated task, the person upon whom the duty is laid remains liable and cannot escape liability. In such circumstances the person upon whom the statutory duty rests will be vicariously liable and, more often than not, the party in primary breach will also be liable ...[160]

Whether the breach of statutory duty confers a cause of action in tort is generally determined by the courts resorting to statutory construction, *i.e.*, ascertaining whether the law confers upon the plaintiff a right of action in tort for the breach of the statute.[161] If the law is silent on this issue, the

---

For an analysis of this topic, *see*, *e.g.*, 25(1) HALSBURY'S, *supra* note 4, at paras. 380.191–380.211; GLOFCHESKI, *supra* note 1, at Chapter 8 ("Breach of Statutory Duty"); KEITH STANTON, PAUL SKIDMORE, MICHAEL HARRIS & JANE WRIGHT, STATUTORY TORTS (2003).

In Hong Kong, "'statutory duty' (法定責任) means any duty imposed by or under any Act of Parliament or Ordinance." *Crown Proceedings Ordinance* (Cap 300) section 2(2).

159. *See*, *e.g.*, Regulation 5 which provides in part:

> (1) Subject to paragraph (3), effective guarding of a dangerous part shall be achieved either by any one of the following methods or by a combination of any of them—
> (a) by a fixed guard;
> (b) by an interlocking guard;
> (c) by an automatic guard;
> (d) by a trip guard;
> (e) by a two-hand control device.
>
> (2) Subject to paragraph (3), every guard or device used pursuant to paragraph (1) shall be—
> (a) of substantial construction;
> (b) maintained in an efficient condition; and
> (c) kept in its proper position while the machinery or plant is in motion.
>
> ...

Factories and Industrial Undertakings (Guarding and Operation of Machinery) Regulations (Cap 59Q).

160. BOKHARY, *supra* note 10, at para. 2.068.

161. *See* the case of *Cutler v Wandsworth Stadium Ltd* [1949] AC 398.

25(1) HALSBURY'S, *supra* note 4, at para. 380.195 explains:

courts have to discern the legislative intent.[162] The leading case is *Lonrho Ltd v Shell Petroleum Co Ltd (No 2)* [1982] AC 173 where Lord Diplock stated that:

> the initial presumption was that, where the Act creates an obligation and enforces the performance in a specified manner, namely a criminal penalty, that performance cannot be enforced in any other manner.[163]

Lord Diplock went on to discuss the two main exceptions to the initial presumption. The first arose where the statute was enacted for the benefit of a particular class of individuals. The second arose where the statute created a public right and the plaintiff had suffered special damage—damage over and above the damage suffered by the public at large.

Therefore, a statutory obligation coupled with a criminal sanction is generally considered to be criminal in nature and is not a cause of action in

---

> An individual may sue for a breach of statutory duty only if the statute imposes a duty enforceable by a party aggrieved. The answer to the question whether the statute imposes a duty so enforceable does not necessarily depend on whether the statute was intended to protect a limited class of persons or the public as a whole. Nevertheless it is of importance to determine what was the intention of the statute in this respect, because, if the statute on its true construction is intended to protect a particular class, it is some indication that members of that class are intended to have a right of action (for example in the case of statutes for the protection of factory workers, mine workers, building workers, merchant seamen, dock labourers and shipyard workers, or intended for the protection of the public when exposed to certain dangers). On the other hand, if the statute is intended to protect the public as a whole, it will not usually be construed as giving a right of action in individual members of a particular class. In any case in which a class of individuals has a common law right to action in respect of the breach of a duty imposed by a statute, a plaintiff to succeed must show that he is within the class of persons which is intended to be protected and to which the duty is therefore owed. A private right of action may be fairly readily constituted where legislation prescribes safety and health standards of a class of persons rather than where they have merely suffered economic loss. (citations omitted)

162. Legislative intention is becoming more important and in limited circumstances the court will look at minutes of the Legislative Council to ascertain such intention. *See* the case of *Pepper (Inspector of Taxes) v Hart* [1993] 1 All ER 42.

> Where the statute or regulation is silent on the issue of a cause of action, a breach of its provisions does not in itself give rise to a cause of action for breach of statutory duty. The plaintiff must prove a legislative intention to create a civil cause of action for damages. In function (although not in technique) this process is similar to the establishment of a duty of care in the tort of negligence.

GLOFCHESKI, *supra* note 1, at 310.

163. [1982] AC at 185.

tort, unless the obligation falls within the two exceptions. Again, the first exception is where the statute is passed for the benefit of a particular class of individuals as opposed to the public as a whole.[164] For example, industrial safety legislation is intended to protect employees and the employer's breach would constitute a tort.[165] The second exception is where the statute creates a public right and the plaintiff suffers particular damage from its breach. Thus, in *Lonrho*, the court held that an embargo is merely a prohibition on the public and does not create public rights. Therefore its breach is not a tort.

If a statute were to create a liability in tort, the damage that the plaintiff suffers must be of the type that the statute is intended to prevent. The classic case is *Gorris v Scott* (1874) LR 9 Ex 125. The defendant was in breach of the statutory duty to import animals in pens on board ship, the purpose of which was to prevent the spread of disease. The plaintiff's sheep were washed overboard in a storm because the defendant's ship did not have pens. The court found the defendant's breach was not actionable in tort as the loss was different from that contemplated by the statute.

After establishing that the breach of the statutory duty is actionable in tort, a plaintiff needs to establish that the statutory duty was in fact breached. In *Gitsham v CH Pearce & Sons plc* (1991) The Times, February 11, the plaintiff, in the course of his employment, fell on a roadway which was covered with ice and snow. This roadway connected two buildings occupied by his employer. The plaintiff brought an action against his employer alleging that

---

164. *See* GLOFCHESKI, *supra* note 1, at 314.

165. BOKHARY, *supra* note 10, at para. 2.067 explains that in:

> *Wong Chi Wing v Chun Wo Building Construction Ltd* it was held that the employer's non-delegable duty to provide a safe place of work had been fulfilled even though the court found that the workplace was unsafe. The plaintiff was employed by a company that supplied and serviced mobile lavatories to construction sites. In the course of emptying one such lavatory the plaintiff fell off the unguarded edge of the open floor of the building under construction. His employer was held to have met his non-delegable duties by having inspected the construction site some three weeks prior to the accident. This decision conflicts with the basic rule that no matter who is actually responsible for the negligent conduct leading to the damage, the employer upon whom a non-delegable duty rests cannot discharge his personal duty of care to the claimant by contracting it out. A logical extension to this rule can be seen in the case of *MTM Construction Ltd v William Reid Engineering Ltd* where an independent sub-contractor himself appointed a sub-sub-contractor who undertook some inherently dangerous work and performed it negligently. The principal—as the ultimate employer—and the sub-sub-contractor were held liable but not the sub-contractor.

it was in breach of its statutory duty under section 29 of the *Factories Act* 1961 which provides:

> There shall, so far as reasonably practicable, be provided and maintained safe means of access to every place at which any person has at any time to work …

The employer was thus to ensure that all means of access to the place of work had been gritted by the start of the working day. The Court of Appeal found that the employer had an extensive procedure for clearing snow and ice which was being properly carried out on the morning of the accident, and that the defendant had done all that was reasonably practicable in the severe weather conditions to ensure that the access roads were safe.

The defences available to a defendant in this type of tort are contributory negligence, *volenti non fit injuria* and statute of limitations.[166] Also available as a defence to an action for breach of statutory duty is:

> novus actus interveniens, that is to say that the damage suffered by the plaintiff was due not to a breach of duty by the defendant but to some independent act of a third person which the defendant could not reasonably foresee … Whether it is available in any particular action depends, it seems, on the construction of the particular statute imposing the duty.[167]

An act of God may likewise be a defence:

> Where an injury results due to natural causes, directly and exclusively without human intervention which could not by any amount of ability have been foreseen or if foreseen could not by the exercise of all reasonable skill and care have been avoided, it may be said to result from an act of God. The mere fact that it has happened before, and may happen again, does not prevent it from being an act of God. It must however not be an ordinary accidental circumstance. It must be something

166. These defences were discussed earlier in sections IV.A; IV.B; IV.E; and, *supra* note 135. As noted in 25(1) HALSBURY'S, *supra* note 4, at para. 380.206:

> As a general rule a defendant, who is in breach of a statutory duty cannot escape liability. Where a defence rests upon an agreement between the parties, such a defence cannot be applied as an agreement of this kind to contract out of a statutory duty is void. However where the plaintiff who knows of the breach of statutory duty by the defendant encounters the risk, the defence of volenti non fit injuria can succeed, for in this case the only effective cause of the injury or damage suffered by him was his own negligence. The defence might also succeed where it is proved that it was impracticable for the defendant to guard against the risk.

167. 25(1) HALSBURY'S, *supra* note 4, at para. 380.209 (citations omitted).

> overwhelming. An act of God is merely a type of inevitable accident, but its particular quality is that it affords a defence to common law torts involving strict liability whereas other categories of inevitable accident do not.[168]

In essence, act of God is a defence that claims the incident happened naturally, without human cause. Alternatively, this defence claims that the incident could not have been prevented by the use of reasonable care.[169]

> The defence of act of God may apply for a failure to fulfil an obligation created by statute, but whether it does apply depends on the construction of the particular statute. ... In the case of a statute which is to be construed as creating an absolute duty or imposing on any person liability for the damage occasioned by a particular state of circumstances, the defence is as a rule no excuse. ...[170]

C. Employer's Liability to Workers

The decision in the case of *Wilsons & Clyde Coal Co Ltd v English* [1937] 3 All ER 628, stated that an employer owes an affirmative duty of care to its employees. This affirmative duty requires positive action by an employer to ensure its workers' safety.[171] The duty has four distinct elements:

- to provide competent staff;
- to provide adequate material, including the duty to maintain the equipment;
- to provide a proper system of work and effective supervision; and,
- to provide a safe place of work.

An employer breaches its obligation to an employee where the standard of care falls below that of the reasonable employer, considering all the circumstances, including the individual characteristics of the worker, particularly any susceptibility of which the employer was or ought to have been aware.[172]

168. *Id.* at para. 380.082.
169. This defence is discussed further in section V.E.*ii*.
170. 25(1) HALSBURY'S, *supra* note 4, at para. 380.210 (citations omitted).
171. GLOFCHESKI, *supra* note 1, at 350. The author explains:

> In *Ho Ying Wai v Keliston Marine (Far East) Limited & Another* [2003] 1 HKLRD 343, the duty required the employer, a diving company, to conduct a proper inquiry of the employee's medical history at the time of his employment, in order to ensure that the work as a deep sea diver did not unreasonably endanger the employee.

172. *Id.* at 351–352.

This four-element duty of an employer is personal. The duty an employer owes to employees is to provide effective supervision and a safe system of work.[173] Once an employer is aware of, or suspects, danger in the work site, the employer must take reasonable actions to protect the employees. Statutory safety standards generally apply to anyone working in a factory or undertaking, regardless of the precise nature of the worker's contractual relationship with the employer. This duty is non-delegable in the sense that this duty cannot be fulfilled by assigning the responsibility to another.[174]

However, the non-delegable aspect of this duty might be lessened when the worker is sent to another employer's premises to perform work.[175] In the case of *Wong Chi Wing v Chun Wo Building Construction Ltd* (2001) HCPI 1476 of 2000, the plaintiff worker was sent to a client's site to do toilet extraction work and where the worker was injured due to unsafe conditions. The court found that the employer had discharged its non-delegable duty. The employer had "taken reasonable steps to ensure that there is a safe place of work by inspecting the site and ensuring that the occupiers were responsible and competent". The court's reasoning suggests that where workers perform their work at another employer's site, the non-delegable aspect of the duty of care is diluted.[176]

An employer also owes a general common law duty of care to an independent contractor whom the employer has retained. The duty an employer owes to employees is more extensive, in that the employer is required to provide effective supervision and a safe system of work.[177] Once an employer

173. In *Inglefield v Macey* (1967) 2 KIR 146, the injured worker claimed that he was a servant of the defendant and sued the latter for failure to provide a safe system of work. The court held that the worker was self-employed and said that the duty to provide a safe system of work was inherent in a master-servant relationship. However, the employer of an independent contractor only had a duty to ensure that the equipment supplied to the independent contractor was safe.

In *Gauchan Som Prasad v Hin Wah Construction Co Ltd* [2011] HKEC 1011 the Plaintiff worker was injured while removing the metal frames from formwork used for pouring concrete. The court held that:

> 21. .. it is clear that the accident was caused by the breach of duty of care on the part of his employer, the 1st Defendant, to provide sufficient manpower and mechanical aid to lift the metal frames. Further, the 1st Defendant was also in breach of its duty to provide a safe system of work by ensuring that there would not be excess flow of concrete in the formwork of the ditch causing the metal frames to get stuck in the concrete. As the 1st Defendant had failed in such duties, it is liable to the Plaintiff for the accident.

174. GLOFCHESKI, *supra* note 1, at 350.

175. *Id.* at 359.

176. *Id.*

177. *See* the case of *Inglefield v Macey*, *supra* note 173.

is aware of, or suspects, danger in the work site, the employer must take reasonable actions to protect the employees. Statutory safety standards generally apply to anyone working in a factory or undertaking, regardless of the precise nature of the worker's contractual relationship with the employer.

D. Occupier's Liability

This type of tort concerns the liability of an occupier of premises to persons who are on the premises and who suffer injury caused by some defects in the condition of the premises. The occupier's duty is not to keep the premises safe but to keep a visitor safe.[178] The main issue therefore is the venue where the damage or the injury occurred—the victim must be on the premises. The legal definition of "premises" in Hong Kong is broad, with the duty imposed by the *Occupiers Liability Ordinance* upon the occupier extending to fixed and movable structures including any vessel, vehicle or aircraft on the land which the visitor has been invited to use. Thus, the term "premises" has been held to cover a pleasure boat,[179] a train, a streetcar,

---

178. As explained in greater detail by one authority:

> Occupiers' liability is the term commonly used to describe that branch of negligence law regulating the duty owed by an occupier of premises to visitors. It is concerned with injuries to visitors or damage to their property arising out of the occupier's failure to maintain premises in a condition that is safe for visitors. Occupiers' liability is a commonly litigated tort action in Hong Kong, as a surprisingly large number of injuries occur as a result of the defective state of premises.
>
> . . .
>
> The need for a separate occupiers' liability law arises primarily because the tort of negligence is not wide enough to cover the circumstances encountered in an accident caused by an occupier's negligence. ... the tort of negligence imposes no legal responsibility for a failure to take affirmative action in favour of persons at risk of injury. Yet this is the very kind of duty needed to protect visitors injured as a result of the poor maintenance of premises. After all, a negligent occupier is one who does nothing to maintain his premises. Hence the need for a separate liability regime that imposes an affirmative duty on occupiers to provide for the safety of visitors.

GLOFCHESKI, *supra* note 1, at 267.
See id. at 284 concerning the nature and extent of the common duty of care. *See also* 25(1) HALSBURY'S, *supra* note 4, at para. 380.137.
For discussion of Hong Kong's *Occupiers Liability Ordinance*, *see* BOKHARY, *supra* note 10, at Chapter 10 ("Occupier's Liability"). *See generally* 25(1) HALSBURY'S at paras. 380.134–380.151.

179. *See, e.g.*, *Marlene Susanne Courbet v Divers Mandarin Services Limited* (2001) HCPI 677 of 2000.

a scaffold,[180] an apron at an airport, a petrol station, toilets in a building, an illegal structure adjoining property and an unfenced roof. Whether the application of this Ordinance includes ladders and similar items is unclear. The issue is whether the owner is considered to have given up possession of the premises. However, a claim under the tort of negligence may be sufficient to establish liability under such circumstances.[181] If a person were to be injured by the state of the premises while standing in the street or on neighbouring premises, the appropriate action would be in nuisance or negligence. If a person were to be injured on the premises by an activity or chattel unconnected with the premises, the action would be in negligence.[182]

As previously mentioned, occupier's liability in Hong Kong is governed by the *Occupiers Liability Ordinance* (Cap 314). However, the Ordinance does not define the terms it uses, therefore requiring reference to the common law. Section 2(2) states that this Ordinance regulates the duty imposed by law arising from a person's occupation or control of premises and of any invitation or permission this person expressly or impliedly gives to another to enter or use the premises, but these rules shall not alter the rules of the common law.[183]

---

180. *See, e.g.*, *Ta Xuong v Incorporated Owners of Sun Hing Building* [1997] 4 HKC 171; *Sanfield Building Contractors Ltd v Li Kai Cheong* [2003] 3 HKLRD 48.

181. Bokhary, *supra* note 10, at para. 10.023. *See also* Glofcheski, *supra* note 1, at 284. *Occupiers Liability Ordinance*, *supra* note 65, at section 2(3) provides:

> (3) The rules so enacted in relation to an occupier of premises and his visitors shall also apply, in like manner and to the like extent as the principles applicable at common law to an occupier of premises and his invitees or licensees would apply, to regulate—
> (a) the obligations of a person occupying or having control over any fixed or movable structure, including any vessel, vehicle or aircraft; and
> (b) the obligations of a person occupying or having control over any premises or structure in respect of damage to property, including the property of persons who are not themselves his visitors.

182. Glofcheski, *supra* note 1, at 268 states that occupier's liability is only concerned with the occupancy duty (*i.e.*, injuries arising from the defective condition of the premises) and not with the activity duty.

183. *Occupiers Liability Ordinance*, *supra* note 65, at section 2(2) states in full:

> The rules so enacted shall regulate the nature of the duty imposed by law in consequence of a person's occupation or control of premises and of any invitation or permission he gives (or is to be treated as giving) to another to enter or use the premises, but they shall not alter the rules of the common law as to the persons on whom a duty is so imposed or to whom it is owed; and accordingly for the purpose of the rules so enacted the persons who are to be treated as an occupier and as his visitors are the same as the persons who would at common law be treated as an occupier and as his invitees or licensees.

The *BLIS Glossary*, *supra* note 1, translates "rules of the common law" as 普通法規則; "at common law" as 在普通法下; and, "licensees" as 獲……特許的人.

One authority comments:

> The common law duty of an occupier was limited to "occupancy duty" dangers, that is dangers arising from the state of the premises or the static condition of the land. Where the nature of the land permitted some dangerous activity being carried on there, for example rock climbing, this did not mean that there was a danger because of the state of the premises. ... the statutory provisions retain the common law distinction between "occupancy duty" and "activity duty", and that the Ordinance has no application in relation to the latter. ... Under the Ordinance, the substance of an occupier's liability has become much more like the ordinary law of negligence. ... there is a duty to use reasonable care. Under the Ordinance, the duty is owed to those lawfully coming onto the premises.[184]

Since the Ordinance does not define its terms, it is thus necessary to mention certain aspects about the common law rules, which were dependent upon a highly technical classification of the injured party. The common law rules attribute a different standard of care according to the different categories of entrant to the premises:

- Contractual entrant: a contractual entrant is a person authorized by contract, or obliged by some right conferred in a contract, to enter the premises, *e.g.*, movie-goer or cleaning staff. The occupier owes the highest degree of care to contractual entrants, that being the general duty of care in negligence. A contractual entrant may become a trespasser if that individual goes beyond the conferred contractual right to enter the premises.
- Lawful invitee: a lawful invitee is a person using the premises by express or implied invitation with a common purpose with the occupier, *e.g.*,

184. Bokhary, *supra* note 10, at para. 10.030.
The case of *Gauchan Som Prasad v Hin Wah Construction Co Ltd*, *supra* note 173, reiterated these principles:

> 30. ... the accident was caused by the "current operation" and the defective system of work rather than by the unsafe condition of the premises, and the present case is one concerning "activity duties" rather than "occupancy duties". The Plaintiff injured himself whilst lifting and removing the metal frame [of the formwork]. He knew that the frame was partly stuck in the concrete and so it required greater strength to remove the frame. The Plaintiff asked for help but none was provided by his employer. Further, no lifting equipment was provided. The Plaintiff was therefore compelled to undertake the work himself on behalf of his employer. In such circumstances, the injury was caused by the work activity or defective system of work rather than occupancy or the condition of the premises *per se*. Hence, the 2nd Defendant is not liable simply because it was one of the occupiers of the Site.

lobbies of buildings or shops. The occupier owes a duty to warn a lawful invitee of any unusual dangers of which the occupier knows or ought to know.

- Licensee: a licensee is a person who has permission to enter the premises but who has no common purpose with the occupier, *e.g.*, food stall operators, salespersons or visitors to a public park. The occupier owes a licensee a lesser duty, that being a duty to warn of dangers actually known to the occupier.
- Trespasser: a trespasser is a person who has no right to enter or remain on the premises. Such person is owed virtually no duty other than a duty not to harm by wilful or reckless misconduct, *e.g.*, assault or traps.[185]

The *Occupiers Liability Ordinance* provides that an occupier owes a common duty of care to all lawful visitors.[186] Section 2(2) of the Ordinance does not define occupier but states that the definition remains the same as at common law.[187] The original common law test considered the level of control over the premises in order to identify the occupier who had the power to control entry to the premises.[188] In *Wheat v E Lacon and Co Ltd* [1966] AC 522, the House of Lords rejected this approach. The court held that some degree of control is sufficient to render one to be an occupier:

> Whenever a person has a sufficient degree of control over premises that he ought to realise that any failure on his part to use care may result in injury to a person coming lawfully there, then he is an "occupier" and the person coming lawfully there is his "visitor".[189]

Accordingly, there could be more than one occupier of premises; every person with sufficient degree of control over the premises is an occupier.[190]

---

185. *See, e.g.*, 25(1) HALSBURY'S, *supra* note 4, at paras. 380.136–380.145.
186. *Occupiers Liability Ordinance*, *supra* note 65, at section 3(1) states:

> An occupier of premises owes the same duty, the "common duty of care", to all his visitors, except in so far as he is free to and does extend, restrict, modify or exclude his duty to any visitor or visitors by agreement or otherwise.

For a discussion of the scope of this duty of care, *see, e.g.*, 25(1) HALSBURY'S, *supra* note 4, at para. 380.137; BOKHARY, *supra* note 10, at paras. 10.025–10.059.
The *BLIS Glossary*, *supra* note 1, translates "common duty of care" as 一般謹慎責任.

187. *See, e.g.*, GLOFCHESKI, *supra* note 1, at 273.
188. *Cavalier v Pope* [1906] AC 428. *See also* GLOFCHESKI, *supra* note 1, at 273.
189. [1966] AC at 578.
190. *See AMF International Ltd v Magnet Bowling Ltd* [1968] 1 WLR 1028; *Collier v Anglian Water Authority*, The Times, 26 March 1983.
As explained by one source:

Furthermore, the occupier does not need to be present on the premises in order to qualify as an occupier, so that independent contractors and landlords may be considered as occupiers.[191]

Section 2(1) of the *Occupiers Liability Ordinance* provides that sections 3 and 4, in place of the common law rules, form the basis of the liability of an occupier to a visitor in respect of dangers due to the state of the premises or to things done or omitted to be done.[192] Under section 3, an occupier

---

> The occupier is that person who has a sufficient degree of control over premises to put him under a duty of care towards those who come lawfully upon the premises. "The answer in each case depends on the particular facts of the case and especially on the nature and extent of the occupation or control in fact enjoyed or exercised by the defendants on the premises." While the owner-occupier is plainly an occupier, an owner who has demised the premises to another and parted with possession is not. In *Wan Tsz Nok v Hung Fai Electrical Engineering Ltd* a fatal accident took place at the Baptist University during construction of construction of a 21 storey student hostel. The Court found that the University had relinquished all authority and control to their contractors, who were solely responsible for the management of the site.
>
> Someone with immediate supervision and control of premises may be an occupier, even if he does not have the power to permit or prohibit entry. However, the person who does have the legal right to invite or permit others to enter will be an occupier. Occupiers may include building contractors carrying out work on another's land, managers of a building and the incorporated owners of a building. A factory owner who had no immediate supervision or control over the only access path was held not to be an occupier. A highway authority is not considered to be the occupier of a public road or pedestrian walkway. Neither is the owner of the underlying soil. It has been suggested that the occupier's control need not be lawful, so that a squatter might be liable under the Ordinance, *qua* occupier. When no one is in physical control of premises, the person who has the legal title should be deemed to be the occupier.
>
> Possession or control need not be entire or exclusive and there may be two or more persons in occupation at the same time, even if both in fact have separate premises which overlap. In this case, each owes the common duty of care to a visitor.

BOKHARY, *supra* note 10, at paras. 10.003–10.005 (citations omitted). *See also* GLOFCHESKI, *supra* note 1, at 273.

191. For an analysis of the situation in Hong Kong, *see* GLOFCHESKI, *supra* note 1, at 276–279 and the Hong Kong cases cited therein.

192. *Occupiers Liability Ordinance*, *supra* note 65, at section 2(1) stipulates:

> The rules enacted by sections 3 and 4 shall have effect, in place of the rules of the common law, to regulate the duty which an occupier of premises owes to his visitors in respect of dangers due to the state of the premises or to things done or omitted to be done on them.

owes the same duty, the common duty of care, to all lawful visitors.[193] This duty is regardless of the common law classification of different entrants, in order to ensure that the visitor will be reasonably safe in using the

193. *Id.* at section 3 provides:

(1) An occupier of premises owes the same duty, the "common duty of care", to all his visitors, except in so far as he is free to and does extend, restrict, modify or exclude his duty to any visitor or visitors by agreement or otherwise.

(2) The common duty of care is a duty to take such care as in all the circumstances of the case is reasonable to see that the visitor will be reasonably safe in using the premises for the purposes for which he is invited or permitted by the occupier to be there.

(3) The circumstances relevant for the present purpose include the degree of care, and of want of care, which would ordinarily be looked for in such a visitor, so that (for example) in proper cases—

(a) an occupier must be prepared for children to be less careful than adults; and

(b) an occupier may expect that a person, in the exercise of his calling, will appreciate and guard against any special risks ordinarily incident to it, so far as the occupier leaves him free to do so.

(4) In determining whether the occupier of premises has discharged the common duty of care to a visitor, regard is to be had to all the circumstances, so that (for example)—

(a) where damage is caused to a visitor by a danger of which he had been warned by the occupier, the warning is not to be treated without more as absolving the occupier from liability, unless in all the circumstances it was enough to enable the visitor to be reasonably safe; and

(b) where damage is caused to a visitor by a danger due to the faulty execution of any work of construction, maintenance or repair by an independent contractor employed by the occupier, the occupier is not to be treated without more as answerable for the danger if in all the circumstances he had acted reasonably in entrusting the work to an independent contractor and had taken such steps (if any) as he reasonably ought in order to satisfy himself that the contractor was competent and that the work had been properly done.

(5) The common duty of care does not impose on an occupier any obligation to a visitor in respect of risks willingly accepted as his by the visitor (the question whether a risk was so accepted to be decided on the same principles as in other cases in which one person owes a duty of care to another).

(6) For the purposes of this section, persons who enter premises for any purpose in the exercise of a right conferred by law are to be treated as permitted by the occupier to be there for that purpose, whether they in fact have his permission or not.

For further information of common duty of care, *see supra* note 186 and accompanying main text.

premises.[194] According to section 2(2), the term "visitors" includes invitees and licensees.[195]

By virtue of section 3(3),[196] an occupier must be prepared for children[197] to be less careful than adults and the occupier may expect that persons, in the exercise of their trade or business, will be aware of, and take precautions

---

194. The nature and extent of this obligation is described as:

> The same duty is now owed to all lawful entrants, the common duty of care (section 3(1)). The duty is one of reasonable care in the circumstances, and is circumscribed according to the purposes for which the visitor is invited or permitted to be on the premises (section 3(2)).
>
> ...
>
> The common duty of care is an affirmative one, requiring the occupier to actively take measures to see that the visitor will be reasonably safe in using the premises. ... *Wong Tung Ming v Kwok Chiu Hung & Others* ... demonstrates that the duty is breached when active steps are not taken to prevent risks created by family members over whom he has control. In *Chan Chum Kam v Chu Nga Kam & Others* ... the deceased, a guest in the defendant's guest house, was killed in a fire for which the defendant was not responsible, the defend ant was nonetheless found in breach of the common duty of care for having failed to provide and maintain adequate escape routes in the event of fire. And in *Kwong Chiu v Sunshine Heights Limited & Others* ... an action brought on behalf of the estates of 12 persons killed by arsonists in a karaoke lounge, the owner and manager of the building were found to be in breach of the common duty of care in failing to provide an adequate sprinkler system in all areas, in failing to maintain the sprinkler system that was installed, in failing to maintain a proper alarm system, in failing to prevent the tenant karaoke lounge operator from using and furnishing lift lobbies and other common parts with highly combustible and toxic furniture, and generally in turning a blind eye to how a tenant paying a "good rent" was using the premises. Somewhat surprisingly, Justice Seagroatt imposed the common duty of care on the owner and building manager even as regards the leased premises, although it is not clear whether this was pursuant to a landlord's obligation to repair under section 5.

GLOFCHESKI, *supra* note 1, at 284–285. *See also* BOKHARY, *supra* note 10, at paras. 10.025–10.027.

Section 5 of the *Occupiers Liability Ordinance* is set out in part in *infra* note 204.

195. *See* GLOFCHESKI, *supra* note 1, at 279 which summarizes the definition of "visitor" thus:

> To bring an action under the OLO, the plaintiff must show that s/he was a visitor. This term is not defined in the OLO. Under section 2(2) of OLO, the term visitor subsumes all those categories of persons who were protected at common law. Put simply, visitors are persons permitted by the occupier to be on the premises. Persons not permitted to be there are trespassers and are owed no duty under OLO.

See also BOKHARY, *supra* note 10, at para.10.013.

196. For the text of section 3 of the *Occupiers Liability Ordinance*, *see supra* note 193.

197. *See, e.g.*, GLOFCHESKI, *supra* note 1, at 282, 287.

against, any special risks ordinarily incidental thereto.[198] Whether an occupier has discharged this duty under section 3(2) is to be considered in all the circumstances. [199] For example, where a visitor has been warned of a particular danger, the warning, without more, does not absolve the occupier from liability unless in all the circumstances it was enough to enable the visitor to be reasonably safe.[200] Again, an occupier would not be liable to any damage due to the faulty execution of any maintenance or repair of the property where such work was entrusted to an independent contractor, if the occupier can show that he had acted reasonably in entrusting the work to the independent contractor; and the occupier was reasonably satisfied that the contractor was competent and that the work had been properly done.[201]

---

198. *See, e.g., id.* at 287–288.

199. The text of section 3 of the *Occupiers Liability Ordinance* has been set out in *supra* note 193.

200. *Occupiers Liability Ordinance*, *supra* note 65, at section 3(4)(a).

 See, e.g., GLOFCHESKI, *supra* note 1, at 289, where it is stated:

> For the warning to be sufficient, the specific danger must be identified, and it must be possible for the visitor to avoid the danger. The warning will be insufficient to discharge the duty if it offers no safe alternative, or where the notice is posted in an unsuitable place.

 See also 25(1) HALSBURY'S, *supra* note 4, at para. 380.137; BOKHARY, *supra* note 10, at para. 10.045.

201. *See, e.g.*, 25(1) HALSBURY'S, *supra* note 4, at para. 380.146; GLOFCHESKI, *supra* note 1, at 290–291.

 However, in relation to injuries suffered by workers on the site:

> In the case of workers' injuries, a common area of occupiers' liability in Hong Kong, the issue often presents itself thus: Did the injury arise from a use of the premises, or from an unsafe system of work? Hence, an occupier who had subcontracted demolition work to a contractor was not liable for the injury of a workman resulting from dangerous demolition techniques (*Ferguson v Welsh* [1987] 1 WLR 1553). … And in *Lau Kam Tai v United Soundfair Engineering Co Ltd & Others* [1999] 2 HKC 299, where a worker who without his employer's knowledge constructed a wooden ramp on which to unload concrete, and which became slippery resulting in injury to the worker, the action succeeded in negligence and was not even argued in occupiers' liability.
>
> However, there is a discernible tendency in Hong Kong toward expanding the reach of OLO to apply to work site injuries that arise from activities, including the system of work. In *Wong Kwok Tung v Tsang Hin Ping & Others* (2000) HCPI 725 of 1997, the occupier, who was not the employer, was found liable under OLO for injuries to a scaffolding workman caused by the absence of safety harnesses.

 GLOFCHESKI, *supra* note 1, at 268.

Under section 3(6) of the *Occupiers Liability Ordinance*, persons entering the premises under a right conferred by law are treated as visitors, regardless of whether they have the occupier's permission.[202] Section 4 of the Ordinance addresses an occupier's liability to persons whom an occupier is bound by contract to permit to enter or use the premises.[203]

In section 5 of the *Occupiers Liability Ordinance*, a landlord may be considered an occupier of the premises if under the tenancy agreement the landlord has the obligation for the maintenance or repair of the premises.[204] A landlord may also be an occupier in respect of the common area of the premises. The owner of the premises is necessarily the occupier. Other

---

202. For example, the police making an arrest or a firefighter attending to a fire.

203. *Occupiers Liability Ordinance*, *supra* note 65, at section 4 states:

> (1) Where an occupier of premises is bound by contract to permit persons who are strangers to the contract to enter or use the premises, the duty of care which he owes to them as his visitors cannot be restricted or excluded by that contract, but (subject to any provision of the contract to the contrary) shall include the duty to perform his obligations under the contract, whether undertaken for their protection or not, in so far as those obligations go beyond the obligations otherwise involved in that duty.
>
> (2) A contract shall not by virtue of this section have the effect, unless it expressly so provides, of making an occupier who has taken all reasonable care answerable to strangers to the contract for dangers due to the faulty execution of any work of construction, maintenance or repair or other like operation by persons other than himself, his servants and persons acting under his direction and control.
>
> (3) In this section "stranger to the contract" (合約的局外人) means a person not for the time being entitled to the benefit of the contract as a party to it or as the successor by assignment or otherwise of a party to it, and accordingly includes a party to the contract who has ceased to be so entitled.
>
> (4) Where by the terms or conditions governing any tenancy (including a statutory tenancy which does not in law amount to a tenancy) either the landlord or the tenant is bound, though not by contract, to permit persons to enter or use premises of which he is the occupier, this section shall apply as if the tenancy were a contract between the landlord and the tenant.
>
> (5) This section, in so far as it prevents the common duty of care from being restricted or excluded, applies to contracts entered into and tenancies created before the commencement of this Ordinance, as well as to those entered into or created after its commencement; but, in so far as it enlarges the duty owed by an occupier beyond the common duty of care, it shall have effect only in relation to obligations which are undertaken after that commencement or which are renewed by agreement (whether express or implied) after that commencement.

204. *Id.* at section 5 provides:

people who might be considered to be in control of the premises, depending upon the circumstances, include a tenant or a party placed in control by agreement.

The occupier may discharge the duty imposed by this statue by undertaking one or more of the following acts:

---

(1) Where premises are occupied by any person under a tenancy which puts on the landlord an obligation to that person for the maintenance or repair of the premises, the landlord shall owe to all persons who or whose goods may from time to time be lawfully on the premises the same duty, in respect of dangers arising from any default by him in carrying out that obligation, as if he were an occupier of the premises and those persons or their goods were there by his invitation or permission (but without any contract).

(2) Where premises are occupied under a sub-tenancy, subsection (1) shall apply to any landlord of the premises (whether the immediate or a superior landlord) on whom an obligation to the occupier for the maintenance or repair of the premises is put by the sub-tenancy, and for that purpose any obligation to the occupier which the sub-tenancy puts on a mesne landlord of the premises, or is treated by virtue of this provision as putting on a mesne landlord, shall be treated as put by it also on any landlord on whom the mesne landlord's tenancy puts the like obligation towards the mesne landlord.

(3) For the purposes of this section, where premises comprised in a tenancy (whether occupied under that tenancy or under a sub-tenancy) are put to a use not permitted by the tenancy, and the landlord of whom they are held under the tenancy is not debarred by his acquiescence or otherwise from objecting or from enforcing his objection, then no persons or goods whose presence on the premises is due solely to that use of the premises shall be deemed to be lawfully on the premises as regards that landlord or any superior landlord of the premises, whether or not they are lawfully there as regards an inferior landlord.

(4) For the purposes of this section, a landlord shall not be deemed to have made default in carrying out any obligation to the occupier of the premises unless his default is such as to be actionable at the suit of the occupier or, in the case of a superior landlord whose actual obligation is to an inferior landlord, his default in carrying out that obligation is actionable at the suit of the inferior landlord.

(5) This section shall not put a landlord of premises under a greater duty than the occupier to persons who or whose goods are lawfully on the premises by reason only of the exercise of a right of way.

(6) Nothing in this section shall relieve a landlord of any duty which he is under apart from this section.

(7) For the purposes of this section, obligations imposed by any enactment in virtue of a tenancy shall be treated as imposed by the tenancy, and "tenancy" (租賃) includes a statutory tenancy which does not in law amount to a tenancy, and includes also any contract conferring a right of occupation, and "landlord" (業主) shall be construed accordingly.

...

- Remove the risk: this will depend on the cost, utility and perception of the danger.
- Warn the visitor: the warning must be sufficient to enable a visitor to be reasonably safe.
- Agree to modify, extend, restrict or exclude this duty: it is not possible to exclude liability for negligence in cases involving death or personal injury. It is however possible to exclude liability in other cases even if negligence exists, if the exclusion satisfies the reasonableness test contained in the *Control of Exemption Clauses Ordinance*.[205]

One source concludes that this subsection of the Ordinance allows an occupier to modify its obligations with such modifications being limited by the *Control of Exemption Clauses Ordinance* (Cap 71), which is the major legislation restricting an occupier's ability to modify its common duty of care to lawful visitors.[206] This source further states:

> It may be clarified that section 7 [of the *Control of Exemption Clauses Ordinance*] talks of three things. First, an occupier cannot exclude or modify his liability for death or personal injury arising from his negligence in any circumstances. Secondly, although he may exclude or restrict his liability for other loss or damage, such exclusion or restriction must satisfy the test of reasonableness. Thirdly, even where the plaintiff has agreed to or was aware of an exempting condition or notice, such agreement or awareness by itself is not sufficient indication of his voluntary acceptance of the risk. The consent must be real.[207]

In situations where the *Control of Exemption Clauses Ordinance* does apply, the statute imposes two major restrictions upon the use of exemption provisions. As mentioned previously, the first limitation is that this law prohibits the use of exemption clauses to avoid liability for injury or death. Section 7(1) of this Ordinance prohibits exclusion or restriction of liability for negligence resulting in personal injury or death.

The other major restriction upon the use of exemption clauses pertains to the reasonableness of the exclusion.[208] In other words, in order for an

205. Section 3 of the *Control of Exemption Clauses Ordinance*, concerning reasonableness, has been set out *supra* note 140.

206. D. K. Srivastava & A. D. Tennekone, The Law of Tort in Hong Kong 518 (2nd ed. 2005).

207. *Id.* at 518–519.
Section 7 of the *Control of Exemption Clauses Ordinance* has been set out *supra* notes 137–139.

208. *See, e.g.*, section 3 of the *Control of Exemption Clauses Ordinance* in *supra* note 140.
See also the Ordinance Schedule 2 which provides additional guidelines for determining "reasonableness":

exemption clause to be valid, the clause must be reasonable. The guidelines for reasonableness are set out in section 3 and in Schedule 2 of the statute. This test is flexible and will be fact-dependant.[209]

Damages recoverable under the *Occupiers Liability Ordinance* include:

- recovery for personal injury;
- nervous shock; and,
- property damage.

Defences to claims for occupier's liability can be found in several provisions of the *Occupiers Liability Ordinance*.[210] For example, section 3(1)[211] permits an occupier to extend, restrict, modify, or exclude a duty to any visitors by agreement or otherwise, subject to the *Control of Exemption Clauses Ordinance*.[212] Under section 3(2),[213] an occupier's duty only extends

---

(a) the strength of the bargaining positions of the parties relative to each other, taking into account (among other things) alternative means by which the customer's requirements could have been met;
(b) whether the customer received an inducement to agree to the term, or in accepting it had an opportunity of entering into a similar contract with other persons, but without having to accept a similar term;
(c) whether the customer knew or ought reasonably to have known of the existence and extent of the term (having regard ... to any custom of the trade and any previous course of dealing between the parties);
(d) where the term excludes or restricts any relevant liability if some condition is not complied with, whether it was reasonable at the time of the contract to expect that compliance with that condition would be practicable;
(e) whether the goods were manufactured, processed or adapted to the special order of the customer.

209. 7(2) HALSBURY'S LAWS OF HONG KONG para. 115.196 (2007) states that the *Control of Exemption Clauses Ordinance* also prevents:

- making the liability or its enforcement subject to restrictive or onerous conditions;
- excluding or restricting any right or remedy in respect of the liability, or subjecting a person to any prejudice as a consequence of pursuing any such right or remedy; and
- excluding or restricting rules of evidence or procedure.

Other examples of statutory control of exemption clauses may be found in the:

- *Sale of Goods Ordinance* (Cap 26) section 57
- *Misrepresentation Ordinance* (Cap 284) section 4
- *Supply of Services (Implied Terms) Ordinance* (Cap 457) section 8.

210. *See, e.g.*, GLOFCHESKI, *supra* note 1, at 293, 296.
211. The full text of section 3 of the *Occupiers Liability Ordinance* is found in *supra* note 193.
212. *See* 25(1) HALSBURY'S, *supra* note 3, at para. 380.143.
213. The full text of section 3 of the *Occupiers Liability Ordinance*, is set out in *supra* note 193.

to what is reasonable in order to ensure a visitor's safety and is confined to the purpose or purposes for which that visitor is invited onto the premises.[214]

Section 3(3) implies that contributory negligence is a partial defence by stating that the determination of liability depends on the circumstances, including the degree of care exercised by the injured visitor. [215] Section 3(4)(a)[216] provides that any warning of risk or hazard will not exonerate an occupier from liability unless in all the circumstances the warning was specific enough to enable a visitor to be reasonably safe.[217] Section 3(5) provides an occupier with the defence of assumption of risk.[218]

Pursuant to section 4(1)[219] an occupier cannot exclude liability to visitors whom that occupier is obligated to admit by contract.[220] A landlord of a

---

214. *See, e.g.*, GLOFCHESKI, *supra* note 1, at 296. Note, too, that an occupier's liability may be limited to areas to which a visitor may be restricted.

> The common duty of care owed to a visitor might be limited to those places in the premises where the visitor may reasonably be expected to go. Permission to enter one part of the occupier's premises cannot be interpreted as permission to enter other parts. ... [A visitor's reasonable belief] is that he is entitled to be in certain parts of the premises may prevent him from becoming a trespasser. Thus, a customer of a public establishment remains a lawful visitor while making a reasonable search for the lavatory in it and does not become a trespasser if he accidentally enters a prohibited area. A visitor does not necessarily become a trespasser if he enters a part of a building by mistake. However, if entry has been forbidden, expressly or by clear and sufficient notice, he becomes a trespasser. The permission to enter might also be limited by time, so that a visitor must leave within a reasonable time after his permission to remain is revoked. Thus, if a customer fails to leave a shop after it has closed, or remains in the bar of a public entertainment establishment after hours, knowing full well that his permission to remain must have been revoked, he will become a trespasser when his permission is in fact terminated. Similarly, permission to enter might be limited as to purpose and a person will be considered a trespasser if he enters for a purpose not contemplated by the occupier.

BOKHARY, *supra* note 10, at para. 10.016 (citations omitted). *See also* GLOFCHESKI, *supra* note 1, at 282.

215. *See Occupiers Liability Ordinance*, *supra* note 65. Section 3's text is set out at *supra* note 193.
216. The relevant provisions of section 3 can be found in *supra* note 193.
217. *See* 25(1) HALSBURY'S, *supra* note 4, at para. 380.139.
218. The full text of section 3 of the *Occupiers Liability Ordinance* is provided in *supra* note 193.
219. The relevant provisions of section 4 of the *Occupiers Liability Ordinance* are set out in full in *supra* note 203. Relevant text of *id.* at section 4(1) provides:

> Where an occupier ... is bound by contract to permit ... strangers to the contract to enter or use the premises, the duty of care which he owes ... cannot be restricted or excluded by that contract ...

220. *See, e.g.*, 25(1) HALSBURY'S, *supra* note 4, at paras. 380.141–380.142.

block of flats, who occupies common parts of the building, cannot exclude liability to the tenants' visitors even if the lease with the tenants includes a liability exclusion clause.[221]

An occupier's liability to a trespasser, one who goes onto the land of another without permission, is not subject to the *Occupiers Liability Ordinance*. An occupier's liability to a trespasser is thus governed by the common law. Under the common law, an occupier is liable to a trespasser only for intentional or reckless injuries inflicted by the occupant.[222]

In *British Railways Board v Herrington* [1972] AC 877, a six-year-old boy frequently played in a field next to the railway line. The fence between the field and the railway line was in need of repair where people had broken through the fence to cross the railway. Some weeks after British Railways became aware of the presence of children on the rail line, the boy passed through the fence and was electrocuted on the live rail. The House of Lords held that the railroad company owed the boy a duty of common humanity, as opposed to a general duty of care. Although a trespasser, the boy was entitled to recover damages. Lord Morris of Borth-y-Gest said:

> The duty that lay on the railways board was a limited one. There was no duty to ensure that no trespasser could enter upon the land. And

---

221. MARTIN, *supra* note 4, at para. 11.6.11.

222. *See, e.g.*, GLOFCHESKI, *supra* note 1, at 297.

As explained by another source:

> The liability of an occupier of premises to trespassers or others who are not visitors is unaffected by the Occupiers Liability Ordinance. It is only to some trespassers that occupiers owe any duty of care at all 'to take steps as common sense or common humanity would dictate to exclude or to warn or otherwise within reasonable and practicable limits to reduce or avert the danger'. A duty is owed if the occupier knows of the trespasser's presence … No duty is owed to other trespassers. The occupier is entitled to neglect a bare possibility that trespassers may come to a particular place on his land but is bound at least to give consideration to the matter when he knows facts which show a substantial chance that they may come there. Moreover, the occupier cannot set a trap with the deliberate intention of injuring a trespasser.
>
> The duty of care owed is not the same as the standard of care generally applied in negligence. … It is merely a duty of common humanity or 'humanitarian duty' to act in a humane manner or with common or ordinary humanity. There is no duty to inspect or survey the land; the duty exists only in respect of physical facts in relation to the land or activities on it of which the defendant knows and which constitute a serious danger to those who are unaware of those facts. The duty of common humanity is somewhat different from the common duty of care owed to lawful visitors in that the duty of common humanity is based more on subjective considerations.

25(1) HALSBURY'S, *supra* note 4, at para. 380.145 (citations omitted).

> certainly an occupier owes no duty to make his land fit for trespassers to trespass in. Nor need he make surveys of his land in order to decide whether dangers exist of which he is unaware. The general law remains that one who trespasses does so at his peril. But in the present case there were a number of special circumstances—(a) the place where the fence was faulty was near to a public path and public ground; (b) a child might easily pass through the fence; (c) if a child did pass through and go on to the track, he would be in grave danger of death or serious bodily harm; (d) a child might not realise the risk involved in touching the live rail or being in a place where a train might pass at speed. Because of these circumstances (all of them well known and obvious) there was, in my view, a duty which, while not amounting to the duty of care which an occupier owes to a visitor, would be a duty to take such steps as common sense or common humanity would dictate; they would be steps calculated to exclude or to warn or otherwise within reasonable and practicable limits to reduce or avert danger.[223]

The court decided that an occupier must observe the common duty of humanity. This duty is not the same as the common duty of care.[224] The duty of humanity is limited to instances where an occupier which has the knowledge, skill, and, resources to avoid an accident is obligated as a humane person to take steps to do so.[225]

The local case of *Chan Yan Nam v Hui Ka Ming t/a Kar Lee Engineering* [2003] 1 HKC 341 followed the precedent set by the English case above.[226] A balance between policy factors and the circumstances of each case needs to be achieved. To summarize, the existence and nature of the duty of humanity is determined by:

- the occupier's knowledge of the presence of a trespasser;
- the effort and expense involved in making the premises safe;
- the character of the occupier;
- the character of the trespasser;
- the gravity of the danger presented; and,
- the nature of the danger.

223. [1972] AC at 909.
224. *See, e.g.*, GLOFCHESKI, *supra* note 1, at 297–303.
225. HARPWOOD, MODERN TORT, *supra* note 32, at 218.
226. *See also Wong Wing Ho v The Hong Kong Housing Authority and Kai Shing Management Services Ltd* (2006) HCPI 558/2004, [2006] HKEC 2355, appeal dismissed in *Wong Wing Ho v Housing Authority* [2008] 1 HKLRD 352, CA which also followed the precedent set out in the *Herrington* case.

E. Nuisance

The definition of "nuisance" is the indirect and unreasonable interference by a defendant:

- with the use and enjoyment of, or interest in, the plaintiff's land; or
- with the protection of the environment; or,
- with the comfort and convenience of life for a class of persons.[227]

The essence of nuisance may be found in the maxim *sic utere tuo ut alienum non laedas*: no one's land is allowed to be used in such a way as to injure another.[228] This doctrine determines whether one person's use of land in a manner which might not, of itself, be unlawful, might become a nuisance when the consequences of pursuing that use extend onto a neighbour's

227. *See generally* BERMINGHAM & BRENNAN, *supra* note 117, at Chapter 13 ("Nuisance"). Another source defines the term "nuisance" as protecting:

> the right to the use and enjoyment of one's land from substantial and unreasonable interference by neighbouring land users. It seeks to strike a balance … in which one person may wish to use his/her land and the interests of that person's neighbours. Conflicts can arise not only between neighbouring households (for instance, over the use of a barbecue or the playing of mahjong), but also between … land users, such as stadiums or factories and the occupants of nearby residential areas. … How much importance is to be attached to a clean, quiet living environment when the effect of achieving such an environment may be to close down a factory or a development project?

GLOFCHESKI, *supra* note 1, at 575.
Yet another source states:

> The term "nuisance" as used in law is not capable of exact definition. Although most nuisances arise from a long continuing condition, a single isolated happening is sufficient if it arises from a continuing condition on land in the control of the defendant.
>
> Nuisances may be broadly divided into: (1) acts or omissions generally connected with the user or occupation of land which cause damage to another person in connection with that other's user [*sic*] of land or interference with the enjoyment of land or of some right connected with the land; (2) acts not warranted by law or omissions to discharge a legal duty, which obstruct or cause inconvenience or damage to the public in the exercise of rights common to the public and; (3) acts or omissions which have been designated or treated by statute as nuisances.

25(1) HALSBURY'S, *supra* note 4, at para. 380.212.
The *BLIS Glossary*, *supra* note 1, translates "nuisance" as 滋擾 or 妨擾.

228. GLOFCHESKI, *supra* note 1, at 576 explains that liability in nuisance requires a balancing of the interests of competing land users. For the nuisance to be actionable, the interference must be substantial and unreasonable. A generally objective criteria is used to determine whether the interference is substantial and unreasonable. *See also* BOKHARY, *supra* note 10, at paras. 11.022–11.023.

land.[229] The unreasonable use of one's land which causes damage to another is prohibited. In short, nuisance amounts to an annoyance.[230]

Nuisance compared to the tort of negligence is narrower as nuisance applies to one's interest in land whereas negligence can involve other interests. Despite this narrower focus than negligence, nuisance has a broader claim for damages. For example, a nuisance action can claim for physical damage and amenity damage arising from interferences such as noise, smells, smoke, vibrations, etc. Nuisance does not require proof of negligence. Rather, as discussed below, nuisance requires the interference to be unreasonable. Therefore, a defendant who proves that reasonable care was taken may still be liable for a nuisance. The focus is less on a defendant's conduct than on whether that conduct is an unreasonable interference with another's use and enjoyment of land. Fault of some type is becoming important to prove nuisance.[231] As the court stated in the case of *Lau Chun Wing v Incorporated Owners of Po On Building* [2006] HKEC 1516:

> It is settled law that the exercise of care and skill by a competent contractor or every effort made by the Defendant to prevent a nuisance afford no defence to an action on nuisance.[232]

Nuisance generally is not a strict liability tort.[233] Again, reasonableness in nuisance is not the same as reasonableness in the tort of negligence.

229. Direct interference would constitute a trespass action rather than a nuisance action.
230. MARTIN, *supra* note 4, at para. 13.1.2.
231. GLOFCHESKI, *supra* note 1, at 576.

> There is increasing overlap between nuisance and negligence. Actions are routinely brought in both torts where physical damage is concerned, and the boundaries of the two tort actions are becoming increasingly blurred. This trend is most evident in the commonest case of nuisance in Hong Kong, the case of water leakage from the flat above. In *Born Chief Co (t/a Beijing Restaurant) v Tsai George & Another* [1996] 2 HKLR 188, the defendant left the sliding door to his rooftop flat open by 12 inches. The rainwater that flooded his flat flowed into the plaintiff's premises below causing extensive damage. The case seemed better characterised as one of negligence, since a duty of care was self-evident and the defendant's behaviour involved unnecessary risk-taking and resulted in a one-off incident of physical damage. The defendant was found liable in nuisance (in addition to negligence), despite the fact that the interference did not arise from the defendant's "use" of his property or from a "state of affairs" (conditions traditionally required by the tort action), but a single act of inadvertence.

Id.

See also 25(1) HALSBURY'S, *supra* note 4, at para. 380.213.

232. [2006] HKEC at para. 120.
233. *See Cambridge Water Co Ltd v Eastern Counties Leather Plc*, *supra* note 18, at 304–306, where the court stated that the defendant's use of the land as a tannery was not a nuisance, but that such use of the land constituted a non-natural land use.

Reasonableness in nuisance is determined by whether the activity and the interference or damage caused is reasonable.[234] Nuisances may be divided into two categories: private and public. The importance of this division of nuisances into public and private categories is based, in part, upon the different remedies and defences applicable to each. The importance of the distinction is also based, in part, on the fact that a private individual cannot file a law suit based on a public nuisance unless this individual can show some special damage over and above that suffered by the community at large.[235]

> Perhaps the most fundamental distinction is that private nuisance is a tort: a civil area of law where actions are commenced in a District Court or High Court. Public nuisance, on the other hand, is primarily a crime.[236]

i. *Private Nuisance*

Nuisance may be either private or public.[237] Private nuisance is a tort in which a plaintiff must prove actual damage.[238] A plaintiff will have a private

---

234. MARTIN, *supra* note 4, at para. 13.1.4.

> Where the interference is … more in the way of inconvenience or irritation, the determination of substantial and unreasonable interference will involve a balancing … of factors, including, among others: the nature, extent, timing and duration of the interference; any peculiarity or sensitivity of the plaintiff; the nature of the locality; and the purpose of the defendant's activity and its social utility. Given the range of these factors and their indeterminacy, it is not surprising that the outcome of a nuisance action cannot easily be predicted, and often depends more on intuition than principled reasoning.

GLOFCHESKI, *supra* note 1, at 579.

235. 25(1) HALSBURY'S, *supra* note 4, at para. 380.219. *See infra* note 254 which sets out in relevant part the decision in *Leung Tsang Hung v Incorporated Owners of Kwok Wing House* [2007] 5 HKC 227, CFA. The court in this case provides an extensive review of the various principles relating to tort law and nuisance.
236. BOKHARY, *supra* note 10, at para. 11.248.
237. One source comments that:

> Nuisances are divisible into common law and statutory nuisances. A common law nuisance is one which, apart from statute, violates the principles which the common law lays down for the protection of the public and of individuals in the exercise and enjoyment of their rights. A statutory nuisance is one which, whether or not it constitutes a nuisance at common law, is made a nuisance by statute either in express terms or by implication.

25(1) HALSBURY'S, *supra* note 4, at para. 380.215 (citations omitted).

238. The traditional view is that liability for a private nuisance is strict. Private nuisances which interfere with the enjoyment of land require no proof of financial or physical loss.

nuisance action if there is some legal right in the land and the defendant has, by some act, interfered with the plaintiff's enjoyment of this right and the interference is unreasonable. Only those who have a right in the land may sue in nuisance.[239] This traditional approach is set out in *Malone v Laskey* [1907] 2 KB 141, where the defendant let a house to a tenant who then sub-let it to a company.[240] The managing director of the company and his wife then lived in the house. Due to the vibrations caused by the defendant's machinery in adjacent premises, a bracket belonging to the water cistern fell off the wall, injuring the wife who was using the lavatory at the time. The court held that the wife was unable to sue in nuisance as she had neither proprietary nor possessory interest in the land as the court considered her to be a licensee.

> Nuisances of this type [interference with the enjoyment of land] require no proof of actual financial or physical damage. …
>
> Where the nuisance is caused by smell or noise, the damage in such a case consists of discomfort or annoyance to the occupier of the premises.

BOKHARY, *supra* note 10, at para. 11.051–11.052 (citation omitted).

In general, however, while there are court decisions asserting the proposition that liability in nuisance is "strict", few cases have defined this term. "It is impossible to reconcile everything that has ever been said on this subject." WINFIELD & JOLOWICZ, *supra* note 40, at 726. These authors continue by stating that "it does therefore seem difficult to support the proposition that in the modern law nuisance involves any general rule of strict liability". *Id.* at 731. GLOFCHESKI, *supra* note 1, at 576 states "whether nuisance can still be described as a tort of strict liability is becoming increasingly doubtful … Fault in some form is becoming increasingly important". *See also* 25(1) HALSBURY'S, *supra* note 4, at paras. 380.213, 380.223–380.224; GLOFCHESKI, *supra* note 1, at 577.

239. *See, e.g.*, *Hunter v Canary Wharf Ltd* [1997] 2 All ER 426, holding that in order to sue on a private nuisance, a plaintiff must have a proprietary interest in the land upon which the nuisance occurs.

240. Other cases have broadened the restriction that for one to sue in nuisance, one had to have at least exclusive right of possession. *See, e.g.*, *Khorasandjian v Bush* [1993] QB 727 and *Motherwell v Motherwell* (1976) 73 DLR (3d) 62 [Supreme Court of Alberta, Canada]. However, the House of Lords declined to follow this line of cases, in part for policy reasons: that of expanding the scope of the tort and opening the floodgates of litigation.

> Ordinarily, such a person can only sue if he has the right to exclusive possession of the land, such as a freeholder or tenant in possession, or even a licensee with exclusive possession. Exceptionally however … this category may include a person in actual possession who has no right to be there; and in any event a reversioner can sue in so far his reversionary interest is affected. But a mere licensee on the land has no right to sue.
>
> The question therefore arises whether your Lordships should be persuaded to depart from established principle, and recognize such a right in others who are no more than mere licensees on the land. At the heart of this question

lies a more fundamental question, which relates to the scope of the law of private nuisance. ... although, in the past, damages for personal injury have been recovered at least in actions of public nuisance, there is now developing a school of thought that the appropriate remedy for such claims as these should lie in our now fully developed law of negligence, and that personal injury claims should be altogether excluded from the domain of nuisance. ... Furthermore, it is now being suggested that claims in respect of physical damage to the land should also be excluded from private nuisance ... it is right for present purposes to regard the typical cases of private nuisance as being those concerned with interference with the enjoyment of land and, as such, generally actionable only by a person with a right in the land. Characteristic examples of cases of this kind are those concerned with noise, vibrations, noxious smells and the like. ...

For private nuisances of this kind, the primary remedy is in most cases an injunction, which is sought to bring the nuisance to an end, and in most cases should swiftly achieve that objective. The right to bring such proceedings is, as the law stands, ordinarily vested in the person who has exclusive possession of the land. He or she is the person who will sue, if it is necessary to do so. Moreover he or she can, if thought appropriate, reach an agreement with the person creating the nuisance, either that it may continue for a certain period of time, possibly on the payment of a sum of money, or that it shall cease ... An agreement of this kind was expressly contemplated by Fletcher Moulton LJ in his judgment in *Malone v Laskey* [1907] 2 KB 141 at 153. But the efficacy of arrangements such as these depends upon the existence of an identifiable person with whom the creator of the nuisance can deal for this purpose. If anybody who lived in the relevant property as a home had the right to sue, sensible arrangements such as these might in some cases no longer be practicable.

Moreover, any such departure from the established law on this subject ... faces the problem of defining the category of persons who would have the right to sue. The Court of Appeal [in the present cases] adopted the not easily identifiable category of those who have a "substantial link" with the land, regarding a person who occupied the premises "as a home" as having a sufficient link for this purpose. But who is to be included in this category? It was plainly intended to include husbands and wives, or partners, and their children, and even other relatives living with them. But is the category also to include the lodger upstairs, or the au pair girl or resident nurse caring for an invalid who makes her home in the house while she works there? If the latter, it seems strange that the category should not extend to include places where the people work as well as places where they live, where nuisances such as noise can be just as unpleasant or distracting. In any event, the extension of the tort in this way would transform it from a tort to land into a tort to the person, in which damages could be recovered in respect of something less serious than personal injury and the criteria for liability were founded not upon negligence but upon striking a balance between the interests of neighbours in the use of their land. This is, in my opinion, not an acceptable way in which to develop the law.

Hunter v Canary Wharf Ltd [1997] AC 655, 692–693. The Court of Appeal decision in this case is reported at [1996] 2 WLR 348. The Hong Kong case of *Artco Properties Ltd v Yau Chun Wing* [2000] 1 HKLRD 697 followed the holding in *Hunter*, by finding the plaintiff failed to prove it had exclusive possession and hence the right to sue the defendants for the nuisance of disrupting the plaintiff's property exhibition at a hotel.

Private nuisance regulates the unreasonable interference with an occupier's beneficial use of land committed by:

- the creator of the nuisance; or,
- the occupier of premises from which the nuisance is emitted; or,
- anyone who adopts or continues the nuisance.

In private nuisance, the defendant's activity may be lawful, but when this activity unreasonably interferes with another party's enjoyment of its land, the activity may become a nuisance. Unreasonableness is determined by the standard of whether the defendant's conduct unreasonably interferes with the plaintiff's use and enjoyment of the land, having regard to the defendant's activities. Thus, in a private nuisance action, the focus is not on the defendant's acts but on the consequences of the acts.[241]

In a private nuisance action, a court balances a defendant's rights to use its land with the right of a plaintiff to have unimpeded use of its land. The determination of reasonableness depends on the type of damage caused. In a private nuisance action, the damage may consist of both personal discomfort and physical damage, including personal injury and property damage. Physical damage claims involve a presumption in favour of the plaintiff, as the plaintiff has a right to expect protection from physical damage by the defendant's activities.[242] Personal discomfort claims involve a balancing test and the court will consider a number of factors, including:

- the plaintiff's locality;
- the plaintiff's sensitivity to the activity;[243]
- the duration of the defendant's interference;[244]
- the public benefit of the defendant's activity;[245]

---

241. As noted by one authority:

> Although nuisance contains an element of reasonableness, the "reasonable" requirement here is not the same as the "reasonable care" requirement in negligence ... Reasonable care in negligence is determined by what a reasonable person would foresee as the consequence of the act and whether a reasonable person would take the risk of damage ... Reasonableness in nuisance is determined by whether the activity and the interference or damage were reasonable.

MARTIN, *supra* note 4, at para. 13.1.4.

242. *See Southport Corporation v Esso Petroleum* [1954] 2 All ER 561.
243. A person cannot increase a neighbour's liability merely because that person puts the land to some special use. In *Robinson v Kilvert* (1889) 41 Ch D 88, the court held the defendant, who heated up the cellar to a temperature of 80 degrees Fahrenheit, was not liable for the damage caused to the sensitive paper stored upstairs on the floor of the plaintiff's premises. The court held that the heat was not of such a character as would ordinarily interfere with the normal use of the premises.
244. *See Harrison v Southwark and Vauxhall Water Co* [1891] 2 Ch 409 where the court held that some interference which was of a temporary nature did not amount to nuisance.
245. The more useful or beneficial the conduct of the defendant, the more reasonable is the defendant's action.

- the defendant's malice or intent;[246] and,
- the natural conditions of the land.

A plaintiff in a private nuisance action may seek damages and/or an injunction in order to prevent the nuisance. An injunction will only be granted where damages are considered to be an inadequate remedy. The liable parties may include one or more of the following: the creator of the nuisance and/or the occupier of the land and/or the landlord.[247]

---

246. There is a case showing the significance of a malicious motive on a nuisance case. In *Hollywood Silver Fox Farm Ltd v Emmett* [1936] 2 KB 468, the defendant intentionally caused guns to be fired on his own land which lies close to the plaintiff's land. The purpose of the shooting was to scare the plaintiff's silver foxes, which were very sensitive during breeding season. Loud noise would deter the foxes from breeding, produce a miscarriage, or cause them to kill and devour their young. The plaintiff obtained an injunction and was awarded damages, even though the shooting took place on the defendant's land, where he was entitled to shoot.

247. As one authority has summarized liability thus:

> Typically it is the creator of the nuisance who is liable. Traditionally, it was thought that the creator need not be the occupier of the land from which the nuisance emanates, and that the nuisance need not originate on the plaintiff's land. …
>
> … However, this position appears to have changed. In *Hussain & Another v Lancaster City Council* [1999] 4 All ER 125, the plaintiffs, who owned a shop and residential property on a council housing estate, brought an action in nuisance and negligence against the council. They alleged that the council had failed … to prevent its tenants and/or members of the tenants' households from committing criminal acts of harassment against the plaintiffs. In the Court of Appeal, Hirst LJ held that a nuisance action could not succeed [as the acts complained of did not involve the tenants' use of the land] … *Hussain* was applied in Hong Kong in *Artco Properties Ltd v Yau Chun Wing* [2000] 1 HKLRD 697 … In rejecting the plaintiff's action in nuisance, Deputy Judge Chu said:
>
>> Another essential element for the tort of nuisance is that the acts complained of must involve the defendant's use of his land: see *Hussain & Another v Lancaster City Council* [1999] 4 All ER 125 at p 144D–G. In this case, even accepting the evidence of Mr Koo, the interference with the plaintiff's enjoyment of the hotel lobby is not occasioned by the defendant's use of his land. The case is thus outside the scope of the tort or private nuisance.
>
> The requirement imposed in *Hussain* and applied in *Artco Properties Ltd* represents a major restriction on … the nuisance tort action … The range of interferences caused by persons not on their own land is limitless, but protection against those interferences by the law of nuisance appears to have been curtailed, if not removed … Together with the requirement from *Hunter v Canary Wharf Ltd* that a plaintiff can sue only if he/she has exclusive possession of the land, the nuisance action has a greatly diminished potential as a means of securing a liveable home environment.

GLOFCHESKI, *supra* note 1, at 595–596.

A recent case, *Hu Wei Hsin v Ma Hung Wing* [2011] HKEC 736, applied these principles: definition and purpose of nuisance, reasonable or average man standard, damages and injunction. This case involved the burning of incense in the corridor of a residential building by the defendant. The plaintiff, pregnant at the time, was the occupant of a neighbouring flat. The plaintiff's complaints resulted in the defendant using loud noise and foul language in the course of the incense-burning ritual, sweeping the ashes from the burnt incense towards the door of the plaintiff's flat as well as the corridor, and, threw some white powder of an unknown nature towards the plaintiff's main door. As a result of such alleged nuisance, the Plaintiff claimed that the smell and the smoke from the incense sticks entered the Plaintiff's flat. Consequentially, the Plaintiff, the Plaintiff's husband and their new-born baby all suffered discomfort in breathing, with the adults also suffering headaches and choking.

In deciding this dispute, the court stated:

> 13. It is a nuisance if a defendant unduly interfered with his neighbour in the comfortable and convenient enjoyment of his land. ...
>
> 14. The following principles are clear from the said passage:
>
> - (i) there is no precise or universal formula for determining whether there is an actionable nuisance, and it is always a question of degree whether the interference with comfort or convenience is sufficiently serious to constitute a nuisance;
> - (ii) everyone must put up with a certain amount of discomfort and annoyance caused by the legitimate activities of his neighbours;
> - (iii) the court has to strike a balance between the right of the defendant to use his property for his own lawful enjoyment and the right of the claimant to the undisturbed enjoyment of his property;
> - (iv) a nuisance, to be actionable, must be such as to be a real interference with the comfort or convenience of living according to the standards of the average man, and an interference which alone causes harm to something of abnormal sensitiveness does not of itself constitute a nuisance; and
> - (v) once the nuisance is established, the court can take into account the delicate and sensitive characteristics of the plaintiff in determining the issue of remedy.
>
> ...

22. ... In determining the issue of nuisance, the court is not applying the standard of the Plaintiff but that of an average person.

...

36. ... There is also concrete evidence to show ... Defendant was sweeping the dust resulting from the burning of the incenses out to the corridor sometimes in the direction of [Plaintiff's flat]. To me, such act alone constituted a nuisance. ... in my judgment, the smoke, the smell and the dust produced by the burning of the incenses ... had exceeded the tolerance that the law would expect from an average person, and hence the Plaintiff has successfully established [its case] ...

...

43. In determining the issue of nuisance, the court is not applying the standard of that set by the Plaintiff or her witnesses. Instead, the law requires the court to apply the standard of an average person. ... one should not lose sight of the "average man" test as mentioned above, and the Plaintiff therefore has to put up with a certain amount of discomfort and annoyance caused by the burning of the new kind of incenses.

...

51. The smoke and smell had caused the Plaintiff to suffer headaches and difficulty in breathing. ... Although there is no evidence to support the causal link between the nuisance and the dysmaturity complicating pregnancy suffered by the Plaintiff, I accept that the nuisance was causing a lot of psychological stress on the part of the Plaintiff ... . The nuisance was made worse when the Defendants were reacting in a hostile manner against the Plaintiff and she was pregnant at the relevant time. ... once an actionable nuisance is established, the court can take into the personal circumstances of the individual plaintiff in assessing ... damages. When the flat she was living in was flooded with smell and smoke caused by the burning of incenses, it was only natural that the Plaintiff had genuine concern for her own health and the health of her baby, and one should not underestimate the distress suffered by the Plaintiff during such difficult time.

....

59. By reason of the aforesaid, I grant judgment in favour of the Plaintiff against all 3 Defendants in the sum of $75,000. I would also grant an injunction restraining the Defendants from burning incenses unless under the conditions mentioned in paragraph 39 above. I direct the parties to submit to the Court the terms of the injunction for approval within 14 days.

ii. *Public Nuisance*

Public nuisance is a tort as well as a crime, usually consisting of some activities which cause inconvenience or annoyance to members of the general public.[248]

> A wide range of conduct which has in the past been the subject of prosecution at common law for the offence of public nuisance is now regulated by statute. Thus, there are statutes concerned with the following matters: food, water, clean air, noise, vehicle and aircraft pollution, waste disposal, offensive trades, health and safety at work, highways, hygienic conditions in dwellings, trade premises and factories, cemeteries, animals, agriculture, medicines, transport, mines, the countryside and village greens and the protection of the environment generally. The statutes create many offences; in certain cases, the proscribed conduct is simply described as a "nuisance" without really defining it (for example regulations and by-laws under the Public Health and Municipal Services Ordinance); in others, the definition of the statutory offence incorporates the common law notion of nuisance; and in others, there is no reference to nuisance (for example under the Summary Offences Ordinance (Cap 228)), but the activity in question is nonetheless the type of activity which has formerly been held to be a nuisance.[249]

Examples of a public nuisance include: obstructing the highway, throwing fireworks into the street, maintaining a brothel, or erecting a factory which emits excessive noise, smoke and fumes.

---

248. ARCHBOLD HONG KONG: CRIMINAL LAW, PLEADING, EVIDENCE AND PRACTICE para. 33–32 (JUSTICE KEMAL BOKHARY, *et al* eds., 2012) defines public nuisance in the following terms:

> Public nuisance is an offence at common law. A person is guilty of a public nuisance (also known as common nuisance), who (a) does an act not warranted by law, or (b) omits to discharge a legal duty, if the effect of the act or omission is "to endanger the life, health, property, morals, or comfort of the public, or to obstruct the public in the exercise or enjoyment of rights common to all Her Majesty's subjects" ... The common law remains important because of its flexibility in adapting to those areas not covered by special legislative schemes. ...
>
> Although many forms of nuisance can now be punished summarily under statutes or by-laws, many of them created under the Summary Offences Ordinance (Cap 228), the remedy by indictment is preserved, with few, if any, exceptions.

249. *Id.* at para. 33–31. *See also* GLOFCHESKI, *supra* note 1, at 612.

There are two elements which are essential for establishing the tort of public nuisance. First, the alleged nuisance must affect the public or a section of the public rather than merely a private individual or group of individuals. In *Attorney General v PYA Quarries* [1957] 2 QB 169, the Court of Appeal held that a public nuisance was a nuisance which "materially affects the reasonable comfort and convenience of a life of a class of Her Majesty's subjects".[250] Lord Denning declined to specify the number of people required to constitute a "class of Her Majesty's subjects", explaining that it was not simply a question of numbers and that the effect of the nuisance had also been taken into account. A public nuisance was a nuisance which was so widespread that it was not reasonable to expect one individual to bring an action to put a halt to it, but rather that it was the responsibility of the whole community to bring the action.[251]

The second element relates to the proof of special damage. An individual can only seek legal recourse if that person has suffered special damage which exceeds the annoyance and inconvenience suffered by the rest of the general public. This damage must differ both in degree and in kind from that damage suffered by the remainder of the public. Note that where the damage suffered interferes with the comfort and convenience of a number of persons, those persons may seek an injunction. One authority notes:

> There is no need to have an interest in land to maintain a tort action in public nuisance. The claimant merely needs to establish that, as a result of the actions of the defendant, he or she has suffered particular damage over and above the damage caused to the public in general: *Tarry v Ashton*, a pedestrian who was injured by a falling lamp was able to recover for particular damage, i.e. personal injury, suffered as a result of the public nuisance that had been created by the hazard. However, having an interest in land is no bar to an action in public nuisance if the claimant suffers particular damage.[252]

The obstruction of a highway, whether whole or partial, constitutes a public nuisance. The collection or gathering of a crowd onto a highway may also be a public nuisance. Note that a higher duty is imposed upon an occupier of premises compared with persons on a highway. Where dangers spread onto a highway, strict liability is imposed on the occupier, so that a plaintiff need not prove unreasonableness to succeed in a law suit.

---

250. [1957] 2 QB at 184.
251. *See* Glofcheski, *supra* note 1, at 611–612.
252. Bokhary, *supra* note 10, at para. 11.250.

Premises on a highway may become a nuisance due to a lack of repair. Should this nuisance cause injury to a passerby or an adjoining owner, the occupant or the owner if it has assumed the duty to repair is liable. This liability is imposed regardless of the occupant's or owner's knowledge of the danger. In the case of *Chung Man Yau v Sihon Co Ltd* [1996] 3 HKC 614, the court found liability where a concrete balcony collapsed, injuring pedestrians passing by below.[253] A later case, *Leung Tsang Hung v Incorporated Owners of Kwok Wing House* [2007] 5 HKC 227, CFA involved similar facts: a concrete block fell off of an illegal extension of a flat's balcony killing a hawker on the street below. The court found the incorporated owners liable in public nuisance, along with the flat's owners and the flat's tenant. The Court of Final Appeal in its decision made an extensive review of the legal principles governing public nuisance which, due to its length, is set out below in a footnote.[254]

---

253. GLOFCHESKI, *supra* note 1, at 613.

254. *Leung Tsang Hung v Incorporated Owners of Kwok Wing House* [2007] 5 HKC 227, CFA provides an extensive review of the various principles relating to tort law and nuisance:

> 12. Public nuisance is a common law offence. ... the Secretary for Justice may also move to restrain a public nuisance ... on behalf of the public at large. Public nuisance is further actionable as a tort by an individual who has been caused particular damage over and above the damage suffered by the public at large. ... The ingredients of a public nuisance are the same for both the crime and the tort.
>
> 13. While there is an overlap between the elements of public and private nuisance, they are causes of action which are different in kind. Private nuisance is a tort protecting property rights. It is concerned with the activities of the owner or occupier of property within the boundaries of his own land which may harm the interests of the owner or occupier of other land. ... an interest in land is not an essential element of the tort. Neither the plaintiff ... nor the defendant ... need have any interest in or relationship with any land or building. ...
>
> 14. ... a public nuisance is one which endangers the lives, safety, health, property or comfort of the public; or obstructs the public in the exercise or enjoyment of any right that is common to members of the public. ...
>
> 15. A defendant may be held liable for public nuisance on the basis of his positive act or his omission. ... In each case, the nuisance hazard which arises from the act or omission must be causative of particular injury to a member of the public. Certain differences necessarily exist in the rules applicable to acts and to omissions respectively. ...
>
> 16. Where a nuisance hazard results from a positive act by the defendant, the basis of liability is relatively straightforward. But before a defendant's omission is actionable, he must first have been under a legal duty to eliminate the nuisance hazard or to prevent it from causing harm to the public. The law then must recognize an entitlement on the part of an injured plaintiff to compensation for the defendant's omission, which entitlement does not follow as a matter of course.

17. The modern case-law establishes that a defendant can only be liable for public nuisance if he knew or ought reasonably to have known (in that the means of knowledge were reasonably available to him) that his act or omission would result in a nuisance hazard presenting a real risk of harm to the public. Where a defendant ought reasonably to have known of the risk, he may be said to have the necessary "presumed knowledge". …
18. It is furthermore established that, as with the tort of negligence, a defendant is not liable in public nuisance unless the injury caused to the plaintiff is of a foreseeable type.
19. It follows from the above that it is now recognized that liability in public nuisance is not "strict" or "absolute". Cases suggesting the contrary should no longer be followed. …

…

23. In my view, the law has now evolved to the point where the question is simply whether the defendant knew or ought to have known of the relevant nuisance hazard. Thus, it must be shown that a defendant whose positive act creates the hazard knows or ought to know that it is the likely consequence of his act. And a defendant who is potentially liable on the basis of an omission must be shown to have had knowledge or presumed knowledge that a nuisance hazard is the likely consequence of his failure to carry out his applicable duty.
24. … negligence is not an essential element of public nuisance. However, this does not mean that liability is strict or absolute. It means that where a defendant does an act with knowledge or presumed knowledge that it may result in a nuisance hazard causing injury to the public, it is no answer for him to say that he took all reasonable care to avoid causing injury if his act turns out to be causative of a foreseeable type of harm. …
25. It is also important not to confuse strict liability or absolute liability with liability arising under a non-delegable duty. Where a defendant is under a duty to nullify a nuisance … that duty is non-delegable. He remains liable even though he has engaged an apparently competent independent contractor to eliminate the nuisance hazard if, through the latter's negligence or otherwise, the hazard is not in fact removed, resulting in injury to the plaintiff.
26. The frequently cited case of *Tarry v Ashton* is properly understood as illustrating the foregoing proposition and not … as an authority for strict liability in relation to injury caused by structures projecting over the highway. It was a case involving injury to a passer-by when a heavy gas lamp overhanging the pavement fell on her. The defendant occupier knew or ought to have known of the potentially dangerous condition of the lamp and was held liable because of his duty was non-delegable, not because the liability was strict. …

…

28. Where alleged liability is based on a positive act, the defendant is liable if the act is his own or the act of someone for whom his is vicariously liable. … no liability arises unless the independent contractor was engaged by the defendant with a view to discharging a non-delegable duty resting upon the defendant.

29. … an omission is only actionable in public nuisance if the defendant is under a duty to neutralise the nuisance hazard and fails to do so in circumstances where the law confers on the injured plaintiff the right to compensation from the defendant. … A prerequisite of liability must be the identification of a duty on the defendant to prevent the nuisance from causing harm. That duty must then be one which the law regards as actionable on behalf of the injured plaintiff …

30. In one class of cases, the liability on the basis of an omission—that is, of having done nothing—is clearly established. Occupiers of land generally come under a duty to remove a nuisance hazard on or emanating from the land of which they have knowledge or presumed knowledge, or at least to prevent such hazard from injuring members of the public. If they fail to do so and injury results, they are liable in public nuisance for such omission. The law imposes that duty because occupation generally gives such immediate and practical control over the property that the occupier is justifiably made liable on the basis of omission.

…

33. … The paradigm instance where liability for omission is established involves owners in actual occupation of their land. Such persons can plainly be expected to have effective control, both physically and legally, over the property in question. Such an owner-occupier is subject to a duty to nullify the hazard if he knows or ought to know of its existence, even though he has done nothing to create it. …

34. An owner may have left his land vacant. In such cases, although he is factually not in occupation, he is still regarded, by virtue of his ownership, as having sufficient control of the land to be made subject to liability on the basis of omission if he has the requisite knowledge or presumed knowledge.

…

36. Another sub-category within this class involves land, not occupied by the owner but by a tenant (by which term I include any sub-tenant or licensee who may be in actual occupation). It is clear that the tenant, as occupier and therefore presumptively in immediate control of the premises, is in principle subject to liability by way of omission. …

37. However, it may be quite unrealistic to expect the tenant, who may merely be a weekly or monthly tenant with modest resources to have the means to eliminate a nuisance hazard of which he knows or ought to know. The courts have therefore been ready to hold that the owner or landlord remains liable even though he has parted with possession to the tenant. …

…

41. … in the context of liability by omission, a particular defendant's resources are relevant to his potential liability. The law adopts the criterion of what is reasonable in all the circumstances. In asking whether a defendant ought to have known of a nuisance hazard, the financial and other resources realistically available to him are taken into account in deciding whether he ought reasonable in all the circumstances be regarded as having had the means of knowledge. Similarly, such resources are taken into account in deciding whether in all the circumstances he ought reasonably be held responsible for failing to neutralise a nuisance hazard of which he had knowledge or presumed knowledge.

…

Section 4 of the *Summary Offences Ordinance* (Cap 228) contains a long list of activities and situations considered to be nuisances under the law.[255]Violations of this Ordinance are crimes, but a person can only sue if incurring special damage.[256] Under section 4(7), it is an offence if an occupier or owner of any house, building or other erection, neglects to repair or remove the property when it is in a ruinous or unsafe state, and when it endangers or may endanger passers-by in any public place.[257]

Section 4B(1) of this Ordinance makes it an offence to drop anything or allow anything to fall from any building to the danger or injury of any person in or near a public place.[258] The penalty for an infringement consists of a fine and/or imprisonment. Section 4B(2) makes the principal contractor and subcontractor liable if anything is dropped from any building which is being constructed, repaired or decorated.[259] The penalty for an infringement of this section is a fine and imprisonment.

> 45. As we have seen, in omission cases, effective practical control over the property in which the nuisance hazard arises is the criterion for imposing a duty to remove the hazard in the class of cases mentioned above. It is consistent to regard a defendant's lack of the resources objectively required to gain knowledge or and/or to eliminate the hazard a negating such control and so removing the basis of the duty.

Id. at 235–247 (citations omitted).

255. These activities include littering, spitting, obstructing public property, driving recklessly, negligently discharging firearms or fireworks. For a complete list, *see Summary Offences Ordinance* (Cap 228) section 4.

256. *See* GLOFCHESKI, *supra* note 1, at 615.

257. Section 4(7) of the *Summary Offences Ordinance*, *supra* note 255, states:

> Any person who without lawful authority or excuse ... being the occupier or owner of any house, building or other erection, neglects to repair or remove the same when in a ruinous or unsafe state, and when it endangers or may endanger the passers-by in any public place ... shall be liable to a fine of $500 or to imprisonment for 3 months.

258. *Id.* at section 4B(1) provides:

> If anything is dropped or allowed to fall from any building to the danger or injury of any person in or near a public place, the person who drops that thing or allows it to fall commits an offence and is liable to a fine of $10000 and imprisonment for 6 months.

259. *Id.* at section 4B(2) states:

> If anything is dropped or allowed to fall from any building in the course of the construction, repair or decoration of the building or part thereof, to the danger or injury of any person in or near a public place, the principal contractor on the site and the contractor carrying out the construction, repair or decoration commits an offence and is liable to a fine of $50000 and imprisonment for 1 year.

For other examples of statutory regulation of nuisances, the reader may refer to the *Air Pollution Control Ordinance* (Cap 311), *Noise Control Ordinance* (Cap 400), *Public Health and Municipal Services Ordinance* (Cap 132), *Waste Disposal Ordinance* (Cap 354) and the *Water Pollution Control Ordinance* (Cap 358).

Defences available for both categories of nuisance actions include the defence of statutory authority. If a statute authorizes an act, the act will not usually give rise to a tort action. Thus, if the activity which gives rise to the nuisance was authorized by law and the defendant can show that the nuisance is, either expressly or impliedly, permitted by the wording in the statute, the defendant will not be liable. For example, if the nuisance is an inevitable result of performing that activity, then the statute affords a good defence to a nuisance action. The assertion of statutory authority is the most important defence to a nuisance action.[260]

Another defence available to a defendant in a nuisance action is the claim of "act of God" or "act of trespasser". An act of God is some event against which no human foresight can guard.[261] This defence appears to require

260. *See* GLOFCHESKI, *supra* note 1, at 599; BOKHARY, *supra* note 10, at paras. 11.213–11.214. 25(1) HALSBURY'S, *supra* note 4, at para. 380.278 notes:

> Although the Government cannot grant to a person a right to commit a public nuisance, an act or omission may have been specifically authorised by statute, and may, therefore, not be actionable either as a public or as a private nuisance. For the defence of statutory authority to be successfully raised, however, it must be shown that the act was within the powers conferred by the statute. A local highway authority or the conservators of a navigable river can therefore legalise an obstruction or encroachment to the public right of passage providing they are authorised by statute to give their consent to what would amount to a nuisance in the absence of such statutory powers.
>
> If a nuisance is the inevitable consequence of what has been authorised, the defence will be available by necessary implication even if the statute does not expressly authorise the commission of a nuisance in so many words. If, on the other hand, the statute authorises a particular act only if no nuisance is caused, statutory authority will be no defence to a claim in nuisance. However, a body acting under a statutory duty, as distinct from a mere power, will not be liable for nuisance, even if such liability is expressly preserved by the statute, unless the nuisance was caused negligently. A grant of planning permission under statutory powers must not be confused with statutory authority, since such a grant cannot license nuisances. In exceptional cases, however, it is possible that planning permission might enable the whole character of a neighbourhood to be changed and thereby render innocent activities which would previously have constituted nuisances. (citations omitted)

261. *Greenock Corp v Caledonian Railway* [1917] AC 556.
Act of God is also discussed in section V.B. *See also* 25(1) HALSBURY'S, *supra* note 4, at para. 380.082.

that the event be an exceptional and unexpected natural event.[262] *Nichols v Marsland* (1876) 2 Ex D 1, where sudden floods were caused by violent storms, is an example of the act of God defence. Similarly, in *Noble v Harrison* [1926] 2 KB 332, the court held that a tree branch which overhung the highway and caused injury did not constitute any tort because it was simply an act of God.

Born Chief Co v Tsai George [1996] 2 HKC 282, CA[263] is an example of an unsuccessful plea of the act of God defence. The plaintiff sued a neighbour for leaving open the sliding door between the latter's flat and the flat's roof. During a heavy rain, water ran into the defendant's flat through the door, then flowed into and flooded the plaintiff's flat. The defendant argued that the flooding was an act of God because October, the month in which the heavy rain occurred, was known to be a dry month in Hong Kong. The court held that the heavy rainfall was not so exceptional as to constitute an act of God. Should the rainfall had been an act of God, the fact that water would accumulate and would flood the flats was nevertheless foreseeable, and the defendant should have taken the time to close the door.

The mere fact that an event occurred in the past and may occur again in the future does not prevent the event from being raised as an act of God defence.[264] Unlike the defence of inevitable accident, the defence of act of God is an excuse to torts of strict liability. A defendant in a nuisance action who successfully raises the defence that the event was caused by an act of God will have a complete defence.[265] This is a viable defence provided that the defendant has not adopted or continued the nuisance.

Also available is the defence known as "act of a stranger" or "act of a trespasser". This assertion would be a successful defence if the interference can be proved to be caused by someone other than the defendant or by someone not under the control of the defendant. This principle was acknowledged in *Ideal Consolidators Ltd v Maeda Corporation* [1992] 1 HKC 528. In this case, a passing motorist negligently dislodged a barrier on a flyover being constructed by the defendant. A short time later, the plaintiff motorist was injured by the barrier. The defendant claimed the act-of-a-stranger defence to the public nuisance claim. The court said that the passing motorist's act did not constitute a defence because the defendant failed to show that the

---

262. *See also* 25(1) HALSBURY'S, *supra* note 4, at para. 380.082.

263. *See supra* note 238 where this case is discussed in terms of negligence and nuisance. This case is also discussed in relation to the defences to a nuisance action in GLOFCHESKI, *supra* note 1, at 602.

264. 25(1) HALSBURY'S, *supra* note 4, at para. 380.082; GLOFCHESKI, *supra* note 1, at 603.

265. GLOFCHESKI, *supra* note 1, at 602.

act could not reasonably have been anticipated. The court found that the passing motorist's act was reasonably foreseeable.[266]

Two other defences are available in a nuisance action. The first is known as "prescription".[267] Under this principle, a nuisance that continues for 20 years will, by prescription, become legal. This legalization applies only to a private nuisance but not a public one.[268] The second is where the plaintiff had consented to the nuisance. This defence of consent is confined to private nuisance actions.

F. Trespass to the Person

Trespassory torts, such as trespass to the person or trespass to land, are less frequently litigated than the negligence-based torts. This is particularly true for the tort of trespass to the person because, when committed, this type of tort often also constitutes a criminal offence for which the wrongdoer is prosecuted and imprisoned. Acts such as murder, rape, battery, assault and false imprisonment are examples of such trespassory torts, but are usually only dealt with as crimes by the criminal courts. On a more pragmatic consideration, generally, such tortfeasors often have no assets. Therefore, a potential plaintiff would not undertake the inconvenience of a civil action, although the right to sue exists. An exception might arise in relation to medical treatment where the wrongdoer might have assets.[269]

Battery,[270] assault[271] and false imprisonment[272] are acts classified under the category "trespass to the person", that is torts committed against the person, because these torts involve the direct and immediate application

---

266. *Id.*

267. BLACK'S LAW DICTIONARY, *supra* note 95, at 1302 defines "prescription" as:

> ...
>
> (3) The effect of the lapse of time in creating and destroying rights.
>
> (4) The extinction of a title or right by failure to claim or exercise it over a long period.—Also termed *negative prescription*; *extinctive prescription*.
>
> (5) The acquisition of title to a thing (esp. an intangible thing such as the use of real property) by open and continuous possession over a statutory period.—Also termed *positive prescription*; *acquisitive prescription*.
>
> ...

The *BLIS Glossary*, *supra* note 1, translates "prescription" as 時效歸益權.

268. *See* 25(1) HALSBURY'S, *supra* note 4, at para. 380.279.

269. GLOFCHESKI, *supra* note 1, at 497. For another analysis of the subject of trespass to the person, *see* 25(1) HALSBURY'S, *supra* note 4, at paras. 380.308–380.382.

270. One source notes:

> Battery involves the intentional, direct and immediate infliction of unwanted harmful or offensive bodily contact. ...

or the threatened application of force. The common features of these three torts are that they are intentionally committed and are committed through direct and immediate means.[273] With these three torts, an action may be brought even in the absence of injury or damage suffered by the plaintiff,

---

> The requirement of directness ... should not be taken too literally. For instance, pouring water over the plaintiff, throwing an object at the plaintiff, or pulling a chair from beneath the plaintiff are sufficiently direct for this purpose. ...
>
> ... Note that the "intention" necessary for this tort relates to the contact with the plaintiff and not to the infliction of injury. Intention to injure is not a requirement of battery ...

GLOFCHESKI, *supra* note 1, at 500 (citation omitted).

271. This tort of trespass to the person is explained as follows:

> Like battery, it is actionable *per se*. Unlike battery, assault involves no bodily contact. Rather, it involves the apprehension of imminent bodily contact. The tort consists of the intentional creation in another person of an apprehension of imminent harmful or offensive bodily contact. ...
>
> This tort can be committed in a number of ways. Pointing a gun at the plaintiff, raising a fist as if to strike a blow at the plaintiff, or throwing an object at the plaintiff (even if no contact is made) are all examples of assaults. Subjective fear for one's safety is not a requirement of the tort. Mere apprehension (with or without such fear) of imminent harmful or offensive bodily contact will complete the tort. Of course, as the tort of assault involves apprehension, no tort is committed if the victim is unaware of the threat, as where he/she is asleep, or did not otherwise see the attacker. It should be noted that where the plaintiff apprehends the attack and if actual bodily contact occurs, the victim would have actions in both battery and assault.

Id. at 507.

272. This tort is defined as:

> when the defendant intentionally causes the plaintiff to be restrained or confined within a particular limited area. The tort can be committed in various ways, for instance by making a wrongful arrest, by detaining a person for longer than is justifiable, or by simply preventing a person from leaving a flat.

Id. at 515.

273. In relation to battery, intention is interpreted in such a way that the:

> conduct must be intentional. This means that the relevant consequence must have been desired. ...
>
> In battery, the consequence is bodily contact. Therefore, to succeed in battery, the plaintiff must show that the bodily contact was desired by the defendant. This can be termed actual intention. However, where the bodily contact is not specifically desired, but is substantially certain to result from conduct that the defendant has knowingly undertaken, the necessary intention for the battery is also established. This can be termed imputed or oblique intention. ... Similar, but not identical, is the situation where A, intending to strike B, but having a bad aim, in fact strikes C. Here, the necessary intention is sometimes described as being transferred.

Id. at 502.

i.e., these torts are "actionable *per se*". Most other tort actions require actual damage in order for the action to be sustained.[274]

The tort of battery is the intentional and direct making of any unwanted physical contact on another person. The required intention is making the physical contact, not that of inflicting injuries. Thus an "intention to injure is not essential to an action of trespass to the person. It is the mere trespass by itself which is the offence".[275] Examples of battery include the splashing of sulphuric acid on a person as in the case of *Ng Chung Ying v Lee Siu Yeung & Another* [2002] 1 HKC 154; or, the unjustified handcuffing by a police officer as in the case of *Crawley v AG* [1987] HKLR 379. If a soldier intended to shoot at one rioter but hit another rioter, the shooting is considered to be intentional. Intention here is assumed as the bodily contact is certain to happen.[276]

Assault does not involve the actual use of physical force but its intention. The victim has to be aware of the offender's intention. When the victim is unaware of such an intention, there is no assault. The offender's intention is not to invoke the victim's fear but to cause an expectation that force is about to be used. An assault could only be committed by an offender with the apparent ability immediately to carry out the threat.[277]

The tort of false imprisonment involves the complete restriction of a person's movement without lawful justification. The person is not required to be confined to a fixed and enclosed space. With this tort, it is the denial of freedom of movement which is important. The denial of freedom of movement can be brought about through the use of physical force, the knowledge of the threat of the use of such force and even the submission of legal process. In the case of *R v Chan Wing Kuen* [1995] 1 HKC 470, the court decided that the offence can be committed without a threat of force. The deprivation of freedom of movement has to be total in the sense that the victim's freedom of movement is limited in every direction. When a road was blocked and a road user was thus compelled to turn back, the circumstances did not amount to imprisonment.[278]

In relation to false imprisonment, one source notes:

> Some of the criminal cases are illustrative of acts that may constitute false imprisonment: persons seeking repayment of a gambling debt

274. *Id.* at 500. *See also* 25(1) HALSBURY'S, *supra* note 4, at para. 380.009.
275. *Wilson v Pringle* [1986] 2 All ER 440 at 495.
276. BOKHARY, *supra* note 10, at para. 5.010. *See also* GLOFCHESKI, *supra* note 1, at 500.
277. BOKHARY, *supra* note 10, at para. 5.009. *See also* GLOFCHESKI, *supra* note 1, at 507.
278. BOKHARY, *supra* note 10, at para. 5.020. *See also* GLOFCHESKI, *supra* note 1, at 515.

taking that person from Macau to Hong Kong and guarding him whilst he made telephone calls trying to obtain money see *R v Chan Wing Kuen*; and forcibly detaining employees suspected of theft and subjecting them to threats and beatings, *HKSAR v Ma Hoi Ching*.[279]

G. Trespass to Land

Trespass to land is a tort.[280] Although it is often thought of as a crime, trespass to land constitutes a criminal offence only in some exceptional circumstances.[281] Winfield and Jolowicz define the phrase "trespass to land"

---

279. BOKHARY, *supra* note 10, at para. 5.022 (citations omitted). *See also* GLOFCHESKI, *supra* note 1, at 515.
280. For an in-depth review of this subject, *see*, *e.g.*, 25(1) HALSBURY'S, *supra* note 4, at paras. 380.383–380.409.
281. *See Summary Offences Ordinance*, *supra* note 255, at section 4.
Violation of the by-laws of some public bodies may give rise to a criminal penalty. *See*, *e.g.*, Ocean Park Bylaw (Cap 388B) section 5 which states in part:

> ...
> (3) A person shall not—
> ...
> (b) without authority granted by the Corporation, enter or remain in Ocean Park or a part of Ocean Park when it is closed to the public;
> ...
> (e) except as permitted by notice to the contrary, walk, run, stand, sit or lie in Ocean Park upon any grass, flower-bed or ground in the course of preparation as a flower-bed or for the planting of trees, shrubs or other plants;
> ...
> (m) without authority granted by the Corporation, enter a part of Ocean Park which is designated by the Corporation by notice as a restricted area;
> (4) A person who contravenes subsection (3) commits an offence and is liable on conviction to a fine at level 1.
> ...

Ocean Park Corporation Ordinance (Cap 388) section 39 provides in part:

> ...
> (2) Any by-law made under this section may provide that a contravention of specified provisions thereof shall be an offence and may prescribe penalties therefor not exceeding a fine of $2000 and imprisonment for 3 months.
> (3) Without prejudice to any Ordinance relating to the prosecution of criminal offences or to the powers of the Secretary for Justice in relation to the prosecution of criminal offences, prosecutions under any by-law made under this section may be brought in the name of the Corporation.
> ...

as the unjustifiable interference with the possession of land.[282] It is a tort which is actionable *per se*, meaning that it is not dependent upon the plaintiff showing actual damage resulting from the trespass.[283] This tort requires the trespasser's intent to enter the land; if a person's entry on to the land was involuntary, no trespass was committed.[284]

In protecting the plaintiff's interest in the peaceful enjoyment of property, trespass performs a function similar to the function of the tort of nuisance. The two torts differ in that proof of damage is normally required in nuisance, whereas such proof is not required in trespass. On the other hand, trespass requires proof of the defendant's intention of entry, though not knowledge that the land belongs to the plaintiff, whereas intention is not relevant for nuisance. Additionally, trespass, unlike nuisance, does not require a balancing of interests. Trespass is concerned with the direct interference with the plaintiff's enjoyment of property, whereas nuisance is concerned with indirect or consequential damage to the property. A court has to determine whether a defendant's use of its own land is reasonable.[285]

Trespass to land arises from interference with possession, thus only those who are in possession can sue. Ownership, however, does not give rise to a cause of action. A landlord, an owner or even a tenant may sue, provided that at the time the damage is caused to the property the plaintiff had possession of the land.[286]

---

282. Winfield & Jolowicz, *supra* note 40, at 685.
283. Glofcheski, *supra* note 1, at 617 defines trespass to land:

> Like nuisance, trespass to land is concerned with the right to be free from interference with one's land ... However, unlike nuisance, this tort action is not premised on the unreasonableness of the interference, but with the fact of unauthorised entry. Although trespass requires an actual physical intrusion, a single intrusion will suffice to establish the action. Moreover, trespass is actionable *per se*. That is, it is actionable without proof of damage.

284. One source explains:

> The necessary intention does not require that the defendant knows the entry or intrusion to be unauthorised. The defendant need only be desirous of making an entry. Put another way, the entry must be voluntary and affirmative. For instance, falling onto or being pushed onto the land of another does not constitute trespass.

Id. at 618. *See also* Bokhary, *supra* note 10, at paras. 9.038–9.039.

285. *See, e.g.*, Glofcheski, *supra* note 1, at 617–618 for a discussion of the similarities and differences between these two torts.
286. *Id.* at 617 states that:

> possession, not ownership, is the key. In *Yeung Wah James v Alpha Sea Ltd* [1993] 1 HKC 440 ... the defendant was the owner of the flat that was the subject of the trespass. The defendant was found liable for a trespass to the plaintiff, its tenant in possession, when it instructed the entry by contractors to conduct renovations without obtaining the plaintiff's consent.

There must be some interference with the plaintiff's possession of the property. For example, the most common way of committing trespass is for the defendant to enter the land without the landowner's permission. In *Westripp v Baldock* [1938] 2 All ER 799, the court determined that the placement of a ladder without permission against the plaintiff's wall constituted a trespass. The fact that the defendant had the plaintiff's permission for the initial entry is irrelevant; trespass is committed if the defendant acted beyond that permission or the permission is revoked.[287]

Such interference need not be of a one-off nature; the interference can be of a continuing nature if the trespass results from the failure to remove a person or item so that a new cause of action arises from day to day. In *Holmes v Wilson* (1839) 10 A & E 503, the defendant trespassed on the plaintiff's land and, without permission, installed buttresses on the plaintiff's land in order to prop up a road. The plaintiff successfully sued the defendant in trespass and obtained £25 damages. When the defendant failed to remove the buttresses after the first action, the plaintiff brought a further action in which the defendant contended that this action was time-barred. The court held that this was a case of continuing trespass, *i.e.*, a new cause of action arising daily, so that the plaintiff could bring an action in trespass until the defendant removed the buttresses.

If the trespass arises from the failure to restore or to repair the land to its previous condition, the trespass is not continuing and there is only one cause of action.[288]

Some particular forms of interference include:

- Trespass on the highway
  A person can use the highway for the purpose of passage and for travelling from one point to another. However, where the highway is used for some purpose which is not reasonably incidental to the purpose of passage, the highway's user may commit the tort of trespass.[289]

> Possession implies a sufficient degree of physical control exercised by the plaintiff over the property (*Lam Wing Ching & Others v Chow Kum Wing* [1985] 1 HKC 189). ... For trespass, possession is probably satisfied if it entails physical control in the sense of the ability to exclude others, and the intention to exercise that control. The possessor need not be the owner, and an owner not in possession has no right to sue a trespasser ... However, it has been held that the owner of a vacant house is in possession, and may maintain trespass against anyone who invades it ...

See also BOKHARY *supra* note 10, at paras. 9.001–9.025.

287. *Robson v Hallett* [1967] 2 QB 939. *See also* BOKHARY *supra* note 10, at paras. 9.001–9.025.
288. *See* the case of *Clegg v Dearden* (1848) 12 QB 576.
289. *See Hickman v Maisey* [1900] 1 QB 752.

- Trespass to airspace
  Formerly, the supposition was that trespass could not be committed in airspace unless there was contact with the plaintiff's land. *Kelsen v Imperial Tobacco Co Ltd* [1957] 2 QB 334 rejected this view. The current proposition requires a demonstration that the infringement was at such a height that the intrusion interfered with the ordinary use and enjoyment of the land and/or any structures erected on the land.[290]
- Trespass to the subsoil
  In *Cox v Moulsey* (1848) 5 CB 533, the court held that trespass to land may be committed against the subsoil. The defendant in this case was held liable in trespass to the plaintiff when the defendant drove a stake into the subsoil owned by the plaintiff. The subsoil may be composed of subterranean rights, *e.g.*, mining rights.

A number of remedies against trespassers to land are available to the successful plaintiff:

- Damages: as trespass is actionable *per se*, where no special damage is proved and the trespass is a trivial one, damages will be nominal.
- Injunction: where the trespass is of a continuing nature or the trespass has been threatened but not yet committed, an injunction to restrain the trespass or to restrain any further trespasses is useful to the plaintiff.
- Action for recovery of land: this remedy is available to those who can show that they have an immediate right to possession of the land.
- Mesne profit: a plaintiff who has been wrongfully dispossessed of land may claim for mesne profits.[291]
- Re-entry: the remedy to expel a trespasser by the use of reasonable force.

There are several defences available against a claim of trespass. One is the defence of statutory authority. The defence of statutory authority is commonly used in trespass actions and applies most often to the acts of police officers and other officials.[292]

290. *See Lord Bernstein of Leigh v Skyviews & General Ltd* [1978] QB 479.

291. Mesne profits are the profits which the defendant has obtained from occupation of the plaintiff's property. Black's Law Dictionary, *supra* note 95, at 1329 provides this definition: "The profits of an estate received by a tenant in wrongful possession between two dates.—Also termed (archaically) *medium tempus*."
The *BLIS Glossary*, *supra* note 1, translates "mesne profits" as 中間收益.

292. 25(1) Halsbury's, *supra* note 4, at para. 380.083 states:

> No liability in tort can arise from acts done in pursuance, and within the scope, of statutory powers where the powers are exercised in good faith, reasonably, without negligence and for the purpose for which, and the manner which, the statute provides. (citations omitted).

See also Glofcheski, *supra* note 1, at 534–547; Bokhary, *supra* note 10, at para. 24.083.

There is another defence available to a defendant in a trespass action. This is the defence of necessity,[293] which, if successful, is a complete defence. The defence of necessity may apply, for example, when a defendant's action, causing harm to a plaintiff, was necessary to prevent greater harm to the defendant or another.[294] In *Leigh v Gladstone* (1909) 26 TLR 139, the court found that necessity was a valid excuse for the defendants when a Suffragette was on a hunger strike while in prison. She complained of assault and battery during force-feeding by the defendant prison officers.

This defence is limited by the requirement that the defendant acted reasonably, under the conditions existing at the time of the act, to avoid a real and imminent danger. Necessity will not succeed as a defence if the need to act is the result of the defendant's negligence, or where this negligence creates or contributes to the necessity.[295] In the case of *Rigby v Chief Constable of Northamptonshire* [1985] 2 All ER 985, the court stated that where the defendant's negligence caused the need to act, necessity would not be a valid defence. Thus, necessity cannot be a defence to negligence.

Courts, in general, find that where personal injury is threatened, any necessary damage to property is justified. Where damage to property is threatened, the issue is whether the defendant acted in a reasonable manner. However, courts are very hesitant to allow a defence of necessity, as a successful defence would result in loss to the plaintiff.[296]

Another possible defence to a trespass action is that of self-defence. If a person, while using reasonable force to defend life or property, including

---

293. This defence:

> may justify an intentional interference with persons or property where it is necessary to prevent greater damage to the public, a third party of the defendant, provided always that the necessity is not created by the defendant's own wrongful conduct. Implied in the defence is that the defendant chose the lesser of two evils … the court has to make a value judgment as to whose interests are to be preferred. In so doing, one of the foremost considerations in the court's mind is whether the defendant has acted reasonably in the circumstances.
>
> The defence of necessity usually plays a role in cases involving protecting persons and properties, and in either instance, the test is whether the act is reasonably necessary to prevent harm. Some examples are committing a trespass to prevent fire from spreading, or shooting an animal to prevent harm to livestock. Since necessity, if established, provides a complete defence, the court has placed close scrutiny to it.

Bokhary, *supra* note 10, at paras. 24.076–24.077.

294. Cooke, *supra* note 33, at 507. *See also* Glofcheski, *supra* note 1, at 533–534.

295. Golfcheski, *supra* note 1, at 623–624.

296. Cooke, *supra* note 33, at 507.

animals, causes injury to another, a court will be unlikely to impose liability although that injury would otherwise be a tort.

> A person in fear of being struck has a right to counter the attack or ward off the blow. The privilege arises whenever there is an honest and reasonable apprehension of physical aggression ... Mere provocation, not threatening to physical security, is not a defence.[297]

The force used must not be disproportionate to the force exerted by the plaintiff on the defendant. Self-defence is a complete defence once the defendant proves that the situation warranted defensive action and that such action was not excessive.[298] In *Harrison v Duke of Rutland* [1893] 1 QB 142 the plaintiff deliberately disturbed grouse on the Duke's land while a shooting party was hunting. The Duke's servants restrained the plaintiff to prevent further disturbances, *i.e.*, further trespasses by the plaintiff. The court dismissed the plaintiff's claim of trespass to the person on the ground that the Duke and his servants were entitled to use reasonable force to prevent a tort.[299]

The defence of legal authority may absolve a defendant of liability:

> A defendant in an action for battery, false imprisonment, trespass to land or even trespass to goods will have a complete defence if the defendant can show that he/she was acting pursuant to some legal

297. GLOFCHESKI, *supra* note 1, at 531.

298. *See, e.g.*, *id.* at 532.

299. Two other defences are available to an action of trespass to the person, both of which are premised upon a principle similar to self-defence: defence of others and defence of property.

> If another's life is threatened or physical safety jeopardised, reasonable force may be used to prevent the attack. As with self-defence, the conduct of the defendant must be reasonable in all of the circumstances, and the force used not excessive. ...
>
> Historically, the class of persons who could rely on this defence was limited by precedent: a servant could justify a battery in defence of his master, and one member of a household or family could act to defend another. However, there is no reason in principle why any citizen should not be entitled to protect his fellow citizen from an aggressor without incurring liability. At any rate, in view of the defence of legal authority ... citizens are statutorily empowered to assist others within the parameters of the legislation relied on.
>
> ... One may use reasonable force to defend land or goods in one's possession against any person threatening to commit or committing a trespass to property. Again, the amount of force that may be used to exclude or expel a trespasser must be reasonable in the circumstances.

Id. at 532. *See also* 25(1) HALSBURY'S, *supra* note 4, at paras. 380.317–380.319 (citations omitted); BOKHARY, *supra* note 10, at para. 5.026.

> authority, usually of arrest. ... An arrest is lawful if authorised by common law or by legislation, and if not so authorised will constitute false imprisonment. ... There are numerous Hong Kong ordinances, specific and general, which confer powers of arrest on the police and/or citizens to make an arrest with or without warrants.[300]

H. Defamation

Defamation is a tort action for the protection of one's reputation. To establish defamation, a plaintiff has to prove that the defendant has published, or is responsible for the publication of, defamatory material that is reasonably understood to refer to the plaintiff. Generally, for liability purposes, a defendant's motive is not a factor unless the situation calls for a consideration of "qualified privilege" or "fair comment", both of which is discussed below. Whether defamation exists is dependent upon determining the natural tendency of the publication in the surrounding circumstances rather than the defendant's intention. A plaintiff needs to allege that the imputation is false but need not prove the statement to be untrue. The right to sue does not extend beyond the death of the plaintiff.[301]

i. *Libel and Slander*[302]

Tort law also protects a person's reputation from disparagement by:
(i) defamatory statements;
(ii) of and concerning the plaintiff; and,

---

300. GLOFCHESKI, *supra* note 1, at 534.

301. GLOFCHESKI, *supra* note 1, at 646; BOKHARY, *supra* note 10, at para. 20.001.
The *Law Amendment Reform (Consolidation) Ordinance*, *supra* note 125, at section 20(1) provides in part:

> Subject to the provisions of this section, on the death of any person after 26 October 1951, all causes of action subsisting against or vested in him shall survive against, or, as the case may be, for the benefit of, his estate:
> Provided that this subsection shall not apply to causes of action for defamation or seduction or for inducing one spouse to leave or remain apart from the other or to claims for damages on the ground of adultery.

See, *e.g.*, 25(1) HALSBURY'S, *supra* note 4, at para. 380.524. For the related torts (*i.e.*, slander of title, slander of goods and malicious falsehood), *see* 25(1) HALSBURY'S, *supra* note 4, at paras. 380.527 and 380.638; GLOFCHESKI, *supra* note 1, at 647–648; BOKHARY, *supra* note 10, at paras. 20.012–20.013.

302. For further information on this topic, *see*, *e.g.*, 25(1) HALSBURY'S, *supra* note 4, at paras. 380.524–380.652; GLOFCHESKI, *supra* note 1, at Chapter 22 ("Defamation"); BOKHARY, *supra* note 10, at Chapter 20 ("Defamation") and Chapter 21 ("Malicious Falsehood"); MARTIN, *supra* note 1, at Chapter 14 ("Defamation").

(iii) published to a third party or parties.

Each of these elements will be discussed in turn after examining the two types of defamatory statements: libel and slander.[303] Statements of fact, *i.e.*, statements that can be proved true or false, are actionable. Statements of opinions mixed with fact are also actionable. The law presumes that the statements were published falsely, intentionally and without lawful excuse.[304]

A defamatory statement made in a permanent form, including printed words, is known as "libel".[305] Libel claims are actionable without proof of injury or damage. The *Defamation Ordinance* (Cap 21) in Section 2 defines "words" as including "pictures, visual images, gestures and other methods signifying meaning". Consequently, if libel is established, the law generally presumes that damage will result.[306]

A defamatory statement made in a transient form, including spoken words, looks and gestures, is known as "slander".[307] A claim of slander

---

303. The *BLIS Glossary*, *supra* note 1, translates "defamation" as 誹謗; "slander" as 短暫形式誹謗; and, "libel" as 永久形式誹謗.

304. *Tai Yip Dyeing Factory Ltd v Kong Hoi Sang* [2007] 1 HKLRD 608. *C.f. Hong Kong Wing On Travel Service Ltd v Hung Thai Citizens Travel Services Ltd* [2001] 2 HKLRD 481.

305. Apart from printed words, libels may be in the form of statue, caricature, effigy, chalk marks on a wall, signs or pictures. *See* 25(1) HALSBURY'S, *supra* note 4, at para. 380.525 n. 1.

306. *Yu Kwong Chiu v Consolidated Newspapers Ltd* [1987] 2 HKC 351.

307. *Gregory v Duke of Brunswick* (1844) 6 Man & G 953, 959; *Cook v Cox* (1814) 3 M & S 110, 114.

BOKHARY, *supra* note 10, at para. 20.004 notes the difference between libel and slander:

> The distinction is often explained by reference to slander being in transient form, and defamation in permanent form is libel. Libel is usually something that is written or printed … One of the important differences between slander and libel is that in order to succeed in an action for slander, the plaintiff must prove special damage, unless the case falls within one of four exceptions. This reflects the commonly accepted position that libel is in permanent, hence more durable form, more likely to damage reputation. But it has been said that the proposition that libel is actionable per se should not be "pressed too far"; that although the presumption of damage has been defended as pragmatic good sense, the court may strike out a trivial claim without apparent proof of any damage as an abuse of process if the accusation was not serious and was not published to a significant number of people on the ground that the cost of the proceedings will be out of all proportions to what would have been achieved. The four classes of slander that are actionable per se without the need to prove special damage are cases where the defamatory allegations impute a criminal offence, that a plaintiff is suffering from certain contagious diseases, the unchastity of a woman, and where the allegations are likely to damage the plaintiff's reputation in his profession, trade or office. (citations omitted)

See also GLOFCHESKI, *supra* note 1, at 648–649.

requires proof of actual damage or loss, also known as "special damage". However, the *Defamation Ordinance* permits claims of slander without proof of damage in several cases: where the words are used to impute unchastity to a girl or woman; and, where the words are calculated to "disparage a person in any office, profession, calling, trade or business held or carried on by him at the time of the publication".[308]

A statement has a defamatory character[309] if it tends to injure a person's reputation by:

---

308. *Defamation Ordinance* (Cap 21) sections 21, 23 and 24 provide:

> 21. Words imputing unchastity to woman or girl per se actionable
> Words spoken and published which impute unchastity or adultery to any woman or girl shall not require special damage to render them actionable:
> Provided that, in any action for words spoken and made actionable by this Ordinance, a plaintiff shall not recover more costs than damages, unless the judge at the trial certifies that there was reasonable ground for bringing the action.
>
> ...
>
> 23. Slander affecting official, professional or business reputation
> In an action for slander in respect of words calculated to disparage the plaintiff in any office, profession, calling, trade or business held or carried on by him at the time of the publication, it shall not be necessary to allege or prove special damage, whether or not the words are spoken of the plaintiff in the way of his office, profession, calling, trade or business.
>
> 24. Slander of title, etc
> (1) In an action for slander of title, slander of goods or other malicious falsehood, it shall not be necessary to allege or prove special damage—
> (a) if the words upon which the action is founded are calculated to cause pecuniary damage to the plaintiff and are published in writing or other permanent form; or
> (b) if the said words are calculated to cause pecuniary damage to the plaintiff in respect of any office, profession, calling, trade or business held or carried on by him at the time of the publication.
> (2) Section 22 shall apply for the purposes of this section as it applies for the purposes of the law of libel and slander.

See also GLOFCHESKI, *supra* note 1, at 649 and BOKHARY, *supra* note 10, at para. 20.004, both of whom would include the following as slander actionable *per se*:

1. the plaintiff is suffering from contagious disease(s)
2. the plaintiff has committed a criminal offense

For further discussion, *see* GLOFCHESKI, *supra* note 1, at 649.

309. BOKHARY, *supra* note 10, at para. 20.017 states that:

> There are two general questions to be answered before deciding whether a statement ... is defamatory. The first one is what meaning could be conveyed

- lowering the public's esteem of that person;[310]
- exposing that person to public contempt or ridicule;[311] or
- affecting adversely that person's general character or standing within a business, profession or trade.[312]

A court would examine whether the words have a defamatory effect by considering their natural and ordinary meaning,[313] and the inferences

---

> to an ordinary and reasonable person. Secondly, the court has to consider whether that meaning is defamatory. ... when there would be no doubt as to whether a statement is defamatory, like when someone calls another a thief or adulterer, but if such remarks would have been taken by the hearer as "mere abuse" and not seriously meant, it may not be defamatory. Whilst it may be clear as to what is meant when someone is referred to as "horrendously ugly", it may be open as to whether such a statement is defamatory. … a statement may be defamatory in being calculated to hold the plaintiff up to "hatred, contempt, or ridicule". But this test is not exhaustive.

See also GLOFCHESKI, *supra* note 1, at 652–653.

310. *See, e.g.*, *Bell v Stone* (1798) 1 Bos & P 331 (imputation of dishonesty); *Stephens v Avery* [1988] Ch 449 (imputation of sexual immorality); *Watkin v Hall* (1868) LR 3 QB 396 (imputation of physical or mental illness); *Brown v Smith* (1853) 13 CB 596 (imputation of insolvency).
311. *Chan Kwong Wai v Lo Sau King* [1963] HKLR 692; *Chu Siu Kuk Yuen v Apple Daily Ltd* [2002] 1 HKLRD 1.
    BOKHARY, *supra* note 10, at para. 20.021 states:

    > In *Li Yau Wai, Eric v Genesis Films Ltd* the plaintiff succeeded in a defamation claim where his photograph was featured in a film as the dead husband of a character, ... and where the "son" in the film had accused his "father" of not returning to visit his wife in erotic dreams. Rhind J said a person may be exposed to light-hearted banter without defamation becoming present, but "[w]here exposure to innocent banter ends and ridicule of a type giving rise to defamation begins is a question of degree and depends on context and circumstances". … Exposing a person to mere ridicule may not be defamatory, but if the plaintiff is exposed to ridicule of sufficient magnitude, defamation can occur.

312. *Next Magazine Publishing Ltd v Ma Ching Fat* [2003] 1 HKLRD 751.
313. *Peregrine Investments Holdings Ltd v Associated Press* [1997] HKLRD 1073. In *Oriental Daily Publisher Ltd v Ming Pao Holdings Ltd* [2011] 3 HKLRD 393, the court stated:

    > Where a person repeats a defamatory statement made by another person, generally the person is liable as if he is the author of the statement. … This is known as the "repetition rule".
    >
    > The repetition rule applies to a newspaper. … the repetition rule is subject to the general principle that the entire statement must be considered as a whole and in its proper context, in order to determine whether it bears the defamatory meaning alleged … *Id.* at 401 (citations omitted).
    >
    > I am prepared to accept that very few people would believe the allegations. But I cannot go so far as to say that the article was so incredible that no reasonable reader could believe it.

which a reasonable person would draw from the entire publication.[314] The words may also have an additional meaning, or innuendo, which may have been popularized from words that once held a special meaning to certain people.[315] Innuendo may give rise to a separate action.[316]

> ... it is only if we could conclude that no reasonable reader of the article could possibly believe ... [the] allegations we could find that the article is not defamatory. ...
>
> But adoption of the truth of the allegation is not essential to liability under the repetition rule, as the following citation shows ... *Id.* at 402.
>
> The fact that the defendant expressed a doubt or disbelief as to the truth of defamatory assertions which he repeats will not relieve him of liability. ... It is not therefore necessary that the defendant should have adopted the statement ... *Id.* at 403 (citations omitted).

314. *Hung Yuen Chan Robert v Hongkong Standard Newspaper Ltd* [1996] 4 HKC 519; *Oriental Daily Publisher Ltd v Easy Finder Ltd* [1998] 1 HKC 546.
BOKHARY, *supra* note 10, at para. 20.018 notes:

> Whilst words apparently defamatory may be proved to be understood in its innocent meaning in the circumstances, words which are not apparently defamatory may become so if the circumstances are taken into account. In *Co* [*sic*] the jury found the statement that the male plaintiff gave "personalised massages" in his health spa was defamatory, as in its ordinary and natural meaning the phrase meant he provided sexual services. Statements as to conduct may be defamatory, but since certain conduct may be viewed differently in different times; the relevant time in considering whether a statement is defamatory is the time of publication. Further, a person may be defamed by juxtaposition, where the circumstances in which the matter is exhibited makes it defamatory. In *Monson v Tussauds Ltd* a wax figure resembling the plaintiff was placed at the entrance to the "Chamber of Horrors" at Madame Tussauds. *Dwek v Macmillan Publishers Ltd* is another example where the plaintiff was shown in a photograph, sitting beside a known prostitute. It was held that the publication was capable of being defamatory. (citations omitted)

315. *See* GLOFCHESKI, *supra* note 1, at 656–657 for an analysis of "innuendo".
BOKHARY, *supra* note 10, at para. 20.030 states:

> In order to succeed, the plaintiff must present additional facts and circumstances to establish the meaning he relies upon. This, a gloss on the words used, amounts to a true innuendo. ... A true innuendo is thus an innuendo by which the plaintiff says a special defamatory meaning of the words distinct from their ordinary meaning and arising by reason of surrounding facts or circumstances known to the recipients has been attached to those words. ... The innuendo must be specific, referable to a special meaning which is actionable. Ironical words may be used exactly opposite to their natural meaning, and may carry an imputation that is altogether unconnected with their apparent meaning.

316. *Ming Kee Manufactory Ltd v Man Shing Electrical Manufactory Ltd* [1992] 2 HKLR 357.
BOKHARY, *supra* note 10, at para. 20.030.

The defamatory statement must be of and concerning the plaintiff, although it need not expressly refer to the plaintiff. The fact that a reasonable viewer would infer that the statement concerns the plaintiff is sufficient.[317] Defamatory statements must also be published or caused to be published.[318] Publication of a libellous statement requires that it is first reduced to permanent form.[319] Publication must be made to a third party or parties, such as the plaintiff's spouse, the plaintiff's employee, or the defendant's employee. Indeed, anyone other than the plaintiff himself or the defendant's own spouse is sufficient. Publication means making known the statement, or causing its publication, or failing to prevent its publication.[320] However, a defendant must be aware of or has reason to know the defamatory nature of the statement at the time of publication.[321] Further, the publisher is liable, even if it published at the request of another person and believed the statement to be true, unless the defence of a recognized privilege applies.[322]

---

317. *See Knupffer v London Express Newspaper Ltd* [1944] 1 All ER 495, 497; *Morgan v Odhams Press Ltd* [1971] 2 All ER 1156; *Jones v Skelton* [1963] 3 All ER 952, [1963] 1 WLR 1362, PC.

318. Bokhary, *supra* note 10, at para. 20.033 states:

> A plaintiff must prove that the libel or slander has been ... communicated by the defendant to another person other than the plaintiff. ... And, spouses are treated as one and no publication will be regarded as made between them concerning a third person, but the defamatory matter could be published to the spouse of the person the subject of the defamation. Nowadays there is potentially a difficult case for internet service providers in monitoring what are posted on bulletin boards on the internet, as people may find it easy to post messages on the internet that may carry defamatory meanings. One example of an action in Hong Kong relating to defamatory emails is *Drummond v Kwaku* where, however, only the writer was sued, and liability was found. (citations omitted)

See also the case of *Dr Ki Ping Ki v Next Magazine Publishing Ltd* [2004] 1 HKLRD B21.

319. *Defamation Ordinance*, *supra* note 308, at section 22 treats broadcasting of words as permanent publication.

320. *Tarpley v Blabey* (1936) 2 Bing NC 437. "Causing publication" includes accidental and negligent publication, and delivery of publication. Consequently, an internet service provider may be liable for publication. The defamatory statement must be posted on the internet in Hong Kong or downloaded in Hong Kong, and was uploaded by the provider or passed through the provider's possession, *e.g.*, server. *See Investasia Ltd v Kodansha Co Ltd* [1999] 3 HKC 515. *See also* the available statutory defence in section 25 of the *Defamation Ordinance*, set out in *infra* note 329.

321. *Pullman v Walter Hill & Co Ltd* [1891] 1 QB 524.

322. *De Crespigny v Wellesley* (1829) 5 Bing 392. *See, e.g., Citizens' Life Assurance Co Ltd v Brown* [1904] AC 423, 427–428.

ii. *Defences*

A claim of defamation is unsuccessful where there is a lawful excuse or defence. The following are some common defences:

- "Justification" is a complete defence, even if the defamatory words were motivated by ill will or malice.[323] The defendant must establish that the words, particularly the "sting" of the defamatory statements, were true.
- "Privilege" protects the communication of facts that should be known for public interest. There are two types. "Absolute privilege" includes judicial, parliamentary, or official statements.[324] "Qualified privilege" is attached to occasions where the communicator has an interest or duty, such as legal, social, or moral, to convey the statement to the receiver, who has a legitimate interest or duty to receive the communication, *e.g.*, news reports.[325] The difference between absolute and qualified privilege is that the former would protect statements made with malicious intent, but the latter would not. As explained by one authority:

> In the case of absolute privilege, it is the occasion which is privileged, and every communication on that occasion is protected ... As for qualified privilege, however, the defendant does not establish privilege until he has shown how the occasion was used. ... The privilege is qualified ... [and] would be lost if the defendant was malicious. A privileged communication means that the occasion on which the communication was made rebuts the inference *prima facie* arising from a statement

323. BOKHARY, *supra* note 10, at para. 20.044 states:

> A plea of justification, that is, that the statement in an action for defamation is true is a complete defence, and generally no interlocutory injunction would be granted against a defendant pleading justification. A defendant who pleads justification must have clear evidence to support such a defence.

See also GLOFCHESKI, *supra* note 1, at 670–671.

324. *See* BOKHARY, *supra* note 10, at paras. 20.055–20.058. For example, *id.* at para. 20.054 explains "witnesses must be free to testify in courts or tribunals without fear that legal action may entail examining their motives for performing their public duty". *See also* GLOFCHESKI, *supra* note 1, at 672.
In the case of *Wong Shui Kee Roger v Victor LL Chu* [2001] 3 HKC 589 both parties were opposing solicitors in a case. The plaintiff claimed defamation in that the defendant wrote a letter asserting the plaintiff to be "intellectually dishonest". The defendant raised the defence of absolute privilege in legal proceedings. The court ruled that the letter was prepared and published in the course of and for the purpose of legal proceedings in that the letter, under the circumstances, was seeking to advance the client's interest in the case.

325. *Lee York Fai v Ho Hau Cheung* [2007] 4 HKC 455. *See also* GLOFCHESKI, *supra* note 1, at 675–684.

> prejudicial to the character of the plaintiff and puts it upon him to prove that ... the defendant was actuated by motives of personal spite or ill-will independent of the occasion on which the communication was made.[326]

- "Fair comment" protects statements of public interest that are made fairly and honestly.[327] The defence applies to comments or value judgements about facts, but not mere representations of facts.

  In the case of *Cheng Albert v Tse Wai Chun Paul* [2000] 4 HKC 1, the court listed the five elements to the defence of fair comment.

  1. The comment must be a matter of public interest. Public interest is not to be confined within narrow limits.
  2. The comment must be recognisable as a comment rather than an imputation of fact.
  3. The comment must be based upon a fact or facts which are true or which are protected by privilege.
  4. The comment must indicate the facts on which the comment is being made.
  5. The comment must be one which could have been made by an honest person. The comment must pertain to the subject matter being criticized. For example, a dislike of an artist's style would not justify an attack upon that person's morals or manners.[328]

- "Unintentional defamation" is a defence under Section 25 of the *Defamation Ordinance*. The unintentional defamation defence allows a publisher to make an offer of "compensation" by publicly withdrawing innocently published defamatory words in order to avoid liability. Under this section of the ordinance, the person making the defamatory statement can make amends by offering to correct the words and to

---

326. Bokhary, *supra* note 10, at para. 20.059.
327. *See also* Glofcheski, *supra* note 1, at 692–699.
Bokhary, *supra* note 10, at para. 20.081 states:

> Even if imputing on the characters of individuals, fair comment and criticism on matters which have become public property are protected. An editor has only the general right that belongs to the public to comment upon public matters. So long as it is within the limit of fair and proper comment, it is no libel. The onus is on the defendant to prove that the comment is fair.

See the case of *British Chiropractic Association v Dr Simon Singh* [2010] EWCA Civ 350, CA for a discussion of fair comment involving Dr. Singh's written commentary that the British Chiropractic Association "happily promotes bogus treatments".
328. [2000] 4 HKC at 8–9.

apologize to the injured party. If the injured party accepts this offer, the injured party is barred from bringing court proceedings against the offending publisher. If the offer is not accepted, the offending publisher making the offer may raise and prove the defence that the statement was innocently and unintentionally published, that the offer was made as soon as possible after the offending publisher learned the statement might be defamatory, and that if the offending publisher was not the author, the statement was made without any malice by the author.[329]

---

329. BOKHARY, *supra* note 10, at para. 20.042.
Defamation Ordinance, *supra* note 308, at section 25 provides in part:

(1) A person who has published words alleged to be defamatory of another person may, if he claims that the words were published by him innocently in relation to that other person, make an offer of amends under this section; and in any such case—
(a) if the offer is accepted by the party aggrieved and is duly performed, no proceedings for libel or slander shall be taken or continued by that party against the person making the offer in respect of the publication in question (but without prejudice to any cause of action against any other person jointly responsible for that publication);
(b) if the offer is not accepted by the party aggrieved, then, except as otherwise provided by this section, it shall be a defence, in any proceedings by him for libel or slander against the person making the offer in respect of the publication in question, to prove that the words complained of were published by the defendant innocently in relation to the plaintiff and that the offer was made as soon as practicable after the defendant received notice that they were or might be defamatory of the plaintiff, and has not been withdrawn.

...

(3) An offer of amends under this section shall be understood to mean an offer—
(a) in any case, to publish or join in the publication of a suitable correction of the words complained of, and a sufficient apology to the party aggrieved in respect of those words;

...

(5) For the purposes of this section words shall be treated as published by one person (... the publisher) innocently in relation to another person if and only if the following conditions are satisfied, that is to say—
(a) that the publisher did not intend to publish them of and concerning that other person, and did not know of circumstances by virtue of which they might be understood to refer to him; or
(b) that the words were not defamatory on the face of them, and the publisher did not know of circumstances by virtue of which they might be understood to be defamatory of that other person,
and in either case that the publisher exercised all reasonable care in relation to the publication; and any reference in this subsection to the publisher shall be construed as including a reference to any servant or agent of his who was concerned with the contents of the publication.
(6) Subsection (1)(b) shall not apply in relation to the publication by any person of words of which he is not the author unless he proves that the words were written by the author without malice.

iii. Remedies

Generally, there is no need to prove actual damage in actions for defamation. The exception is slanders not actionable *per se* which require the proof of special damage.[330] Whether aggravated damages are awarded will depend on:

> the circumstances of the publication, and on any evidence of the motives and conduct of the defendant, as well as the effect which the defamatory matter has produced.[331]

There are also exemplary or punitive damages if compensatory damages are not sufficient. For example, if there has been abuse of power by a civil servant or if the defendant is aware that the conduct can make a profit well beyond the damages payable to the plaintiff.[332] Damages could be awarded on the grounds that there could be consequences injurious to the plaintiff resulting from the defamation.[333] "Special damage" is "the loss of some specific thing or temporal advantage capable of being estimated at a money value, if it is not actual pecuniary loss".[334] For a slander action, a plaintiff must prove special damage generally.[335] If the defendant is considered likely to continue the defamation, a court may grant an injunction to prevent further publication.[336]

VI. DAMAGES

In previous sections of this chapter, various types of torts were introduced and the duties and obligations arising under these torts were analysed. The breach of these duties or obligations was presented along with an analysis of possible defences available to the defendant. In this section, a brief introduction is made as to the types of damages which a successful plaintiff can recover against a defendant in a tort action.[337]

> [T]he overriding principle in the award of damages in tort law (whether for personal injury or property damage) is *restitutio in integrum*. This simply means full compensation—that the plaintiff should be restored,

330. *See* Glofcheski, *supra* note 1, at 701–702; Bokhary, *supra* note 10, at para. 20.091.
331. Bokhary, *supra* note 10, at para. 20.092.
332. *See id.* at para. 20.095; Glofcheski, *supra* note 1, at 707.
333. *See* Bokhary, *supra* note 10, at para. 20.097.
334. *Id.* at para. 20.099.
335. Glofcheski, *supra* note 1, at 701.
336. *Id.* at 707–708.
337. One authority notes:

in so far as money can do so, to the position s/he was in before the tort occurred. …

Notice how the approach differs with that in contract law, where, on a breach of contract, the court aims to put the innocent party into the position … as if the contract had been performed. Contract law looks forward, imagining the contract had been fulfilled, while tort law looks back, to the pre-accident position.[338]

As negligence constitutes the largest and fastest growing sector of tort law, emphasis will be placed on personal injury awards.[339] An award of damages for personal injury may be divided into:

In the torts of negligence and nuisance (whether or not negligence is an ingredient in the nuisance) the wrongdoer is responsible and responsible only for any type of damage which should have been foreseen by a reasonable man as being something of which there was a real risk, even though the risk would actually occur in very exceptional circumstances, or in the most unusual case, unless the risk was so small that the reasonable man would feel justified in neglecting it or brushing it aside as far-fetched. The magnitude of the risk, namely the likelihood of the occurrence and the gravity of potential results, must be weighed against the expense of eliminating it.

In the tort of negligence the degree of likelihood relevant to the measure of damages is the same as the degree of likelihood relevant to the existence of a duty. A plaintiff recovers damages in respect of a foreseeable accident, even though only an accident of that type and not the precise circumstances were foreseeable, for an unforeseeable form of a foreseeable type of injury, and for unforeseeable consequences of a foreseeable type of injury. The degree of likelihood required in the torts of negligence and nuisance is lower than in contract, and this is probably true for most torts, at least for those which are of a non-deliberate or non-malicious nature.

22 HALSBURY'S LAWS OF HONG KONG para. 340.181 (2008) (citations omitted) [hereinafter 22 HALSBURY'S].

Fatal accidents are not covered in this chapter. The recovery of damages arising from fatalities is briefly presented in the Employment chapter, section III.F. For further information, *see* 25(1) HALSBURY'S, *supra* note 4, at paras. 380.127–380.132; 10(2) HALSBURY'S LAWS OF HONG KONG paras. 145.614–145.645 (2009) [hereinafter 10(2) HALSBURY'S]; GLOFCHESKI, *supra* note 1, at 389–406; 22 HALSBURY'S paras. 340.213–340.221. *See generally* BOKHARY, *supra* note 10, at Chapter 25 ("Damages").

338. GLOFCHESKI, *supra* note 1, at 367–368 (citation omitted).

339. For example, as noted by one source: "Cases involving personal injuries, usually those due to negligence, constitute the majority of civil cases in the courts." 22 HALSBURY'S, *supra* note 337, at para. 340.189. Consequently, the damages which a successful plaintiff may recover from the defendant in a defamation action will not be analyzed further. For further information on this subject, *see* GLOFCHESKI, *supra* note 1, at 701–707; 22 HALSBURY'S, *supra* note 337, at para. 340.238. For actions relating to fatal accidents, *see* the Employment chapter, section III.D; GLOFCHESKI, *supra* note 1, at 389–405; 22 HALSBURY'S, *supra* note 337, at paras. 340.213–340.221.

> those damages awarded for the pecuniary and non-pecuniary loss which the plaintiff would expect to suffer in the future from the date of trial (general damages) and those losses which have accumulated from the date of the accident to the date of the trial (special damages).[340]

Accordingly, there are two types of damages recoverable:

> "general" and "special" damages. The distinction affects the form of the award and in pleading and proof. "General damage" is damage said to be the result of the tortious act complained of and need not be specifically pleaded. "Special damage" means "the particular damages (beyond the general damage), which results from the particular circumstances of the case, and of the plaintiff's claim to be compensated … Generally, "special damages" refer to losses that can be arithmetically calculated to a more or less exact amount, namely pre-trial pecuniary loss; and "general damages" refer to non-pecuniary loss and future pecuniary loss.[341]

Other types of damages which may be recoverable in a tort action include aggravated damages and exemplary damages. The former allows a court to factor into a plaintiff's award the behaviour of the defendant.

> Aggravated damages are designed to compensate the plaintiff for his wounded feelings; they must be distinguished from exemplary damages which are punitive in nature and which may only be awarded in a limited category of cases.[342]

---

340. MARTIN, *supra* note 4, at para. 15.2.1. The author of 22 HALSBURY'S, *supra* note 337, at para. 340.191 states:

> Special damages mean the actual pecuniary loss suffered by the plaintiff up to the date of the trial resulting from the wrongful act of the defendant. They must be specially pleaded. The plaintiff is entitled to interest on special damages between the date of the accident and the date of trial or assessment.
>
> General damages are those losses which are not capable of precise quantification: future pecuniary loss, and past and future non-pecuniary loss. General damages do not need to be specifically pleaded. However, the plaintiff must plead any material facts giving rise to a claim for general damages, and must provide such evidence as is necessary and appropriate to support a claim.
>
> Interest is awarded on special damages from date of accident to date of judgment at half judgment rate. Interest is awarded on general damages for pain, suffering and loss of amenities at two percent per annum from date of service of writ to date of judgment. (citations omitted)

The *BLIS Glossary*, *supra* note 1, translates "special damages" as 專項損害賠償.

341. BOKHARY, *supra* note 10, at paras. 25.007–25.008. *See also* GLOFCHESKI, *supra* note 1, at 370.
342. 22 HALSBURY'S, *supra* note 337, at para. 340.345 (citation omitted). *See also id.* at para. 340.168.

Exemplary damages are those damages awarded in order to punish the defendant and vindicate the strength of the law.[343] Exemplary damages may only be awarded in tort claims and only in three types of cases:

1. The first category of cases involves actions by government servants which were oppressive, arbitrary or unconstitutional.
2. The second category of cases involves acts by the defendant calculated to make a profit for himself which may exceed the compensation payable to the plaintiff.
3. The third category of cases is where exemplary damages are authorized by statute.[344]

A. Personal Injury

As noted earlier, general damages consist of pecuniary and non-pecuniary loss. The former refers to the amount of money which the plaintiff:

> was financially disadvantaged by the accident, including the plaintiff's loss of future earnings and earning capacity, cost of future medical care and attention, and loss of ability to render services to members of the family.[345]

---

343. *Id.* at para. 340.346 (citation omitted). *See also id.* at para. 340.168.
The *BLIS Glossary*, *supra* note 1, translates "exemplary damages" as 懲戒性的損害賠償.

344. 22 Halsbury's, *supra* note 337, at para. 340.346 (citations omitted). This source continues:

> Where exemplary damages may be awarded the court should ask itself whether the sum it proposes to award as compensatory damages, which may include an element of aggravated damages, is adequate not only for the purpose of compensating the plaintiff but also for the purpose of punishing and deterring the defendant. Only if it is inadequate for the latter purpose should the court consider awarding additionally exemplary damages.
>
> The following considerations should be borne in mind: (1) that the plaintiff cannot recover exemplary damages unless he is the victim of the punishable behaviour; (2) that the power to award exemplary damages is a weapon to be used with restraint; and (3) that the parties' means are relevant.
>
> Exemplary damages may not be awarded in actions for breach of contract. Exemplary damages may be awarded for nuisance, but never in straightforward allegation of negligence nor deceit.

Id. (citations omitted). *See* Glofcheski, *supra* note 1, at 556; Bokhary, *supra* note 10, at paras. 9.080–9.081.

345. Martin, *supra* note 4, at para. 15.2.8.
As stated by another authority:

> the plaintiff is entitled to recover damages in respect of pecuniary loss, past and future, such as loss of earnings, medical expenses and cost of nursing care, and for loss of earning capacity where he is handicapped in the labour market.

22 Halsbury's, *supra* note 337, at para. 340.190 (citations omitted). *See generally* Glofcheski, *supra* note 1, at 369–377.

"Loss of future earnings" refers to the earnings which are expected to be lost from the date of the trial, along with future medical care and attention.[346]

"Non-pecuniary loss" is the loss which cannot be rectified by a financial payment by the tortfeasor.

> The category of pain, suffering and loss of amenities is the most important basis of an award for non-pecuniary loss. An amount is awarded to cover past and future pain and suffering, whether physical, mental or emotional.[347]

"Special damages" are:

> awarded to cover those costs which have been accrued by the date of trial, including medical expenses, loss of earnings between accident and trial, and damage to clothing or goods in the accident. The courts in Hong Kong have recognized the importance of traditional chinese [*sic*] medicine and traditional foods to accident victims in Hong Kong ...

Local courts have allowed such claims where there is evidence of such expenses.[348]

Note that in tort law, as in contract law, there is the obligation upon an injured party to take reasonable measures to mitigate the loss. If the defendant establishes that the plaintiff failed to mitigate the loss, that part of the loss that could have been reasonably avoided will be deducted from the plaintiff's recovery of damages.[349]

---

346. MARTIN, *supra* note 4, at para. 15.2.9. *See also* GLOFCHESKI, *supra* note 1, at 370–373.
347. MARTIN, *supra* note 4, at para. 15.2.3.
"Loss of amenities" refers to "the loss of ability to enjoy life, in view of the injuries". GLOFCHESKI, *supra* note 1, at 321. For further discussion on the topic of recovery of damages for pain, suffering and loss of amenities, *see* GLOFCHESKI, *supra* note 1, at 321–327.
Another authority has noted:

> A person injured by another's wrong is entitled to general damages for non-pecuniary loss such as his pain and suffering, past and future, and his loss of amenity and enjoyment of life. Even in cases where he is unconscious and will remain so for the rest of his life he is entitled to substantial damages for the invasion of his body.

22 HALSBURY'S, *supra* note 337, at para. 340.190.
348. MARTIN, *supra* note 4, at para. 15.2.13. *See* GLOFCHESKI, *supra* note 1, at 369 which adds that interest on the award of special damages calculated from the date of loss to the date of trial is allowed under section 48(c) of the *High Court Ordinance* (Cap 4) and section 49(4) of the *District Court Ordinance* (Cap 336).
349. 22 HALSBURY'S, *supra* note 337, at para. 340.188.

> The plaintiff is said to be under a duty to mitigate the losses resulting from the defendant's tort. … The extent of the duty to mitigate depends on what the court considers to be "reasonable" in the circumstances for the plaintiff to mitigate his loss. The courts are concerned that requiring the plaintiff to do what is reasonable would not amount to excessive demands. A string of Hong Kong authorities held that a surgical operation involving substantial risk but uncertain outcome may not be a necessary part of the medical treatment for an injured plaintiff. There are also English cases holding that a plaintiff are [*sic*] not expected to commence a law suit with uncertain prospects against a third party, or to risk capital in a speculative venture, or to destroy his own property, or to put his good public relations at risk.[350]

i. Pecuniary Loss

The principle governing the recovery of damages for pecuniary loss is the principle of *restitutio in integrum*, where the injured party is placed in the position in which this party would have been if the injury had not occurred.[351] Therefore, the injured plaintiff may be entitled to recover expenditures incurred as a result of the injury.[352] The plaintiff bears the burden of proving, through the balance of probabilities, the pecuniary loss, failing which, nominal damages will be awarded.[353]

---

350. BOKHARY, *supra* note 10, at para. 25.009. *See also* 22 HALSBURY'S, *supra* note 337, at para. 340.188.

351. 22 HALSBURY'S, *supra* note 337 at para. 340.197.

352. *Id.* at para. 340.205. This source continues:

> Such reasonable expenditure may include medical and nursing expenses, the cost or value of carers (including in some cases unpaid care), special equipment, special food, the cost of travel to and from hospital (for the plaintiff and his family) and costs of investment advice.
>
> The plaintiff must prove that the expense is caused by the accident, that it is necessary or reasonable and that the amount claimed is a reasonable cost. The plaintiff is usually entitled to a high standard of post-accident care. A subjective test is adopted when determining the reasonableness of any needs claimed or expenses incurred by the plaintiff. The plaintiff's personal circumstances, race, personality and belief should be taken into account. The psychological benefit to the plaintiff will make an expense reasonable, even though it does not bring about any physical benefit.

Id. (citations omitted).

353. *Id.* at para. 340.197 (citations omitted).

ii. Non-pecuniary Loss

The principles regulating the recovery of damages for non-pecuniary loss are that:

> the figure awarded must be basically a conventional figure derived from awards in comparable cases and the damages must be assessed by reference to the value of money at the date of trial and not at some other and lower sum calculated by reference to an earlier and higher value of the dollar.[354]

Pain and suffering may be recovered against a defendant in a negligence action. An injured plaintiff may claim for damages, both physical and mental distress, caused by the defendant. The damages may be calculated from the date of the injury into the future. This category of damages includes pain caused by the injury, any pain incurred in treating the injury, embarrassment at the disability or disfigurement, or suffering resulting from anxiety that the plaintiff's condition may worsen in the future. Also included in this category is the distress caused to the plaintiff by not being able to tend to the plaintiff's children or to tend to an aged or ill relative.[355]

Pain and suffering must be proved. An award of damages under this category depends upon the plaintiff's knowledge of its suffering. Unlike loss of amenity, which is discussed below, pain and suffering is a subjective loss. Where the plaintiff's life expectancy has been reduced by the defendant's act, a court must consider any suffering caused or likely to be caused by the plaintiff's awareness that the expectation of life has been reduced. The plaintiff's age may also be a factor to be considered.[356]

Also recoverable under the grouping of non-pecuniary loss is the loss of amenity. The loss of amenities is the plaintiff's damages resulting from the injuries affecting the ability to enjoy life, participate in pleasurable activities, etc.[357] This type of damages or injuries may include the loss of:

- the ability to walk;
- eyesight;
- a limb or its use;
- employment;

---

354. *Id.* at para. 340.193.
355. *Id.* at para. 340.194. *See also* GLOFCHESKI, *supra* note 1, at 378–388; BOKHARY, *supra* note 10, at para. 25.019.
356. 22 HALSBURY'S, *supra* note 337, at para. 340.194.
357. GLOFCHESKI, *supra* note 1, at 378. For further discussion on the topic of recovery of damages for pain, suffering and loss of amenities, *see id.* at 378–384; 22 HALSBURY'S, *supra* note 337, at paras. 340.190; 340.194; 340.195.

- pride and pleasure in one's work product;
- marriage prospects;
- sexual function;
- the ability to have children;
- the ability to give natural childbirth; or,
- mental abilities.

Included in this list of losses is a change in personality as a result of the injury or injuries suffered. The award of damages under this category does not depend upon the plaintiff's knowledge of the loss. Damages are awarded for the deprivation itself rather than knowledge of the deprivation. The amount to be awarded is objectively calculated based upon similar precedent. The precise amount, however, is subjective to reflect the impact of the loss upon the particular plaintiff.[358]

B. Joint Tortfeasors

When two or more wrongdoers commit a tort causing the same damage to the plaintiff the wrongdoers are referred to as "joint tortfeasors".[359] Joint tortfeasors may be found in all types of torts.[360] In Hong Kong, the *Civil Liability (Contribution) Ordinance* (Cap 377) permits a court to apportion damages between the joint tortfeasors.[361] The apportionment would be done with regard to each tortfeasor's responsibility for the damage, and to be just and equitable. Both causation and the relative blameworthiness of the parties would be taken into consideration by the court.[362] Under this law, any person who is liable for damages may recover a contribution from any other tortfeasor who is jointly liable for the damages.[363] The court may exempt any person from having to make any contribution.[364]

358. 22 HALSBURY'S, *supra* note 337, at para. 340.195. *See also* GLOFCHESKI, *supra* note 1, at 378–388; BOKHARY, *supra* note 10, at para. 25.020.

359. BOKHARY, *supra* note 10, at para. 27.037.

360. 25(1) HALSBURY'S, *supra* note 4, at para. 380.065.
See also STAUCH, *Risk and Remoteness of Damage in Negligence*, *supra* note 103.

361. *Civil Liability (Contribution) Ordinance* (Cap 377) section 4(1) states:

> Subject to subsection (3), in any proceedings for contribution under section 3 the amount of the contribution recoverable from any person shall be such as may be found by the court to be just and equitable having regard to the extent of that person's responsibility for the damage in question.

362. 25(1) HALSBURY'S, *supra* note 4, at para. 380.071.

363. *Civil Liability (Contribution) Ordinance*, *supra* note 361, at section 3(1) provides:

> Subject to the following provisions of this section, any person liable in respect of any damage suffered by another person may recover contribution from any other person liable in respect of the same damage (whether jointly with him or otherwise).

Examples of joint tortfeasors include:

1. employer and employee where the employer is vicariously liable for the employee's tort;
2. principal and agent where the principal is liable for the agent's tort;
3. employer and independent contractor where the employer is liable for the independent contractor's tort;
4. a person who causes another to commit a tort and that person then commits the tort; and,
5. persons who take collaborative action for a common purpose and in the course of executing that joint purpose commit a tort.[365]

C. Nuisance

In an instance where nuisance causes damage to land, the purpose of recovering damages is to protect the amenity value of the land.[366] Thus, only the person with a proprietary or possessory interest in the land can bring an action for damages and the wrongful acts involved the defendant's use of the plaintiff's land.[367]

> If only physical damage to land is caused, the measure of damages is the diminution of the value of the land. This may be the cost of repair or restoration but if that exceeds the diminution of the value of the land … the higher amount will be awarded if the plaintiff reasonably intends to repair and occupy the property, the lower if it is to be sold in its damaged state.[368]

D. Trespass to the Person

Trespass to the person, *i.e.*, assault, battery or false imprisonment, is actionable without proof of actual damage. Therefore, at the least, nominal damages are recoverable. Substantial damages are recoverable for discomfort

---

See also 10(2) HALSBURY'S, *supra* note 337, at para. 145.038. GLOFCHESKI, *supra* note 1, at 446.

The *BLIS Glossary*, *supra* note 1, translates "jointly liable" as 共同有責.

364. 25(1) HALSBURY'S, *supra* note 4, at para. 380.071.
365. *Id.* at para. 380.065.
366. 22 HALSBURY'S, *supra* note 337, at para. 340.236. *See* GLOFCHESKI, *supra* note 1, at 603–605.
367. 22 HALSBURY'S, *supra* note 337, at para. 340.236. *See* BOKHARY, *supra* note 10, at paras. 11.011–11.029.
368. 22 HALSBURY'S, *supra* note 337, at para. 340.236.

and inconvenience, or injury to dignity, even where no physical injury is proved.[369] Where physical harm or injury is involved, the ordinary principles of assessment of damages apply. The plaintiff will be compensated for both special damages and general damages.[370] Aggravated damages may be available dependent upon the circumstances.[371]

> In *A v Director of Immigration*, Andrew Cheung J, when assessing damages for unlawful detention by the Immigration Department of persons who made a claim for non-refoulement under the Convention Against Torture and Other Forms of Cruel, Inhuman or Degrading Treatment or Punishment, indicated that aggravated damages may be awarded where there are aggravating features about the case which result in the victim not receiving sufficient compensation for the injury suffered if the award were restricted to basic award. Aggravated damages are essentially compensatory in nature, but nonetheless contains also a penal element as far as the wrongful party is concerned. Earlier, in *Achacoso v Liu Man Kuen*, Master Hui applied the well-known dicta that aggravated damages refer to the higher than conventionally calculated damages for a tortuous [*sic*] act that are awarded in cases where the manner of commission of the tort was such as to injure the plaintiff's proper feelings of dignity and pride. In that case, a domestic helper was awarded aggravated damages against her employer after she accidentally damaged a piece of clothing, and her employer punished her for this minor mistake by running the iron over the helper's hands causing grievous bodily harm. Awards of aggravated damages have been made for several types of tort, such as defamation, assault and battery; breach of confidence; trespass to land; conversion; deceit; sex discrimination; disability discrimination; and false imprisonment and malicious prosecution. Equal opportunities and data privacy legislations in Hong Kong

---

369. *Id.* at para. 340.222.

370. GLOFCHESKI, *supra* note 1, at 553.
Although not discussed in this work, one should note the existence of the Hong Kong Criminal Injuries and Law Enforcement Compensation Scheme which offers:

> financial assistance to persons (or to their dependants in cases of death) who are injured as a result of a crime of violence, or by a law enforcement officer using weapon in the execution of his duty. The scheme is non-contributory and non-means tested. …

See the Scheme's website at: *http://www.swd.gov.hk/doc/social-sec/CLEICL1107.pdf* (last visited 26 Feb. 2011).

371. As GLOFCHESKI, *supra* note 1, at 554 states:

> The circumstances in which the tort was committed can be taken into account, and if they are seen as having aggravated the tort, in the sense of injuring the plaintiff's feelings of dignity and pride, then further "aggravated" damages can be awarded. In function and effect, these damages appear to be compensatory.

> authorize the awarding of damages for injury to feelings and in the assessment of those damages, case law on the principles for awarding aggravated damages is followed.[372]

Should the case fall within one of the three categories which allow recovery of exemplary damages, this may also be recovered against the defendant.[373]

E. Trespass to Land

A trespass to land allows the injured party to claim nominal damages for the trespass even though no damage or loss has been incurred.[374] It is immaterial that the plaintiff was not hindered or prevented from using its own land.[375] If damage or loss arises from the defendant's trespass, the plaintiff is entitled to compensatory damages, generally considered to be the diminution in the value of the land.[376] This diminution may be the costs of repair and reinstatement of the land to its condition immediately prior to the trespass. Consequential losses, exemplary and aggravated damages may also be available to the plaintiff.[377]

---

372. BOKHARY, *supra* note 10, at para. 25.099 (citations omitted). *See also* GLOFCHESKI, *supra* note 1, at 554.
373. 22 HALSBURY'S, *supra* note 337, at para. 340.222. *See also* BOKHARY, *supra* note 10, at para. 9.081.
374. *See generally* GLOFCHESKI, *supra* note 1, at 624.
375. 22 HALSBURY'S, *supra* note 337, at para. 340.234.
376. GLOFCHESKI, *supra* note 1, at 624–627; 22 HALSBURY'S, *supra* note 337, at para. 340.234.
377. 22 HALSBURY'S, *supra* note 337, at para. 340.234. The term "consequential damages" refers to the "pecuniary loss consequential on physical damage, such as loss of profit sustained due to fire damage in a factory". *Id.* at para. 340–170.

Chapter Three
Employment

This chapter considers several matters relating to employment law.[1] The first concerns the classification of a worker as an employee, for this classification governs the responsibilities and liabilities of the parties between themselves and others. The second is a review of relevant ordinances and their subsidiary regulations controlling the employer-employee relationship. Finally, this chapter proffers some general comments concerning employment contracts.

I. STATUS OF A WORKER

The status of a worker as an employee or as an independent contractor is important as this distinction determines an employer's obligations and responsibilities to those retained by the employer, and to those affected by the employee's acts. The parties in an employer-employee relationship are also affected by the application of certain ordinances,[2] the jurisdiction of

---

1. This work will not consider agency law, that is, the law regulating the relationship between a principal and its agent who may act on behalf of and bind the principal. For a review of agency law in Hong Kong, *see*, *e.g.*, 1(2) HALSBURY'S LAWS OF HONG KONG paras. 15.001–15.108 (2008); BETTY HO, HONG KONG AGENCY LAW (1991). For an analysis of the impact of vicarious liability upon an agency relationship, *see*, *e.g.*, RICK GLOFCHESKI, TORT LAW IN HONG KONG 439–442 (2nd ed. 2007) [hereinafter GLOFCHESKI–TORT].
   The Hong Kong government's Bilingual Laws Information System's *The English-Chinese Glossary of Legal Terms* [hereinafter *BLIS Glossary*] translates "law of agency" as 代理法; and, "agents" as 代理人. *See* the *BLIS Glossary* website at: *http://www.legislation.gov.hk/eng/glossary/homeglos.htm* (last visited 26 Feb. 2011).
2. For example, the *Employment Ordinance* (Cap 57); the *Employees' Compensation Ordinance* (Cap 282); the *Companies Ordinance* (Cap 32); and, the *Bankruptcy Ordinance* (Cap 6) only apply to instances where an employer-employee relationship exists.

the employment regulatory agencies,[3] the higher duty of care which exists towards employees under the law of tort,[4] the existence of vicarious liability,[5] the terms of the employment contract,[6] the taxation system,[7] the operation of the Mandatory Provident Fund Schemes,[8] and, an employer's insolvency.[9]

---

3. For instance, the Labour Tribunal can only hear claims relating to a contract of employment. The *Labour Tribunal Ordinance* (Cap 25) section 7 provides that the Tribunal has exclusive jurisdiction to hear the claims specified in the Schedule, which relates to employment contracts only.
   Section 7 provides:
   > (1) The tribunal shall have jurisdiction to inquire into, hear and determine the claims specified in the Schedule.
   > (2) Save as is provided in this Ordinance, no claim within the jurisdiction of the tribunal shall be actionable in any court in Hong Kong.
   > (3) Subsection (2) shall not operate to prevent the transfer of any claim to the tribunal in accordance with any rules made under section 73B of the District Court Ordinance (Cap 336).
   > (4) Subsection (2) shall not operate to prevent the transfer of any claim to the tribunal in accordance with any rules made under section 73C of the District Court Ordinance (Cap 336).
   > (5) Subsection (2) shall not operate to prevent the transfer of any claim to the tribunal in accordance with any rules made under section 73D of the District Court Ordinance (Cap 336).
   > (6) Subsection (2) shall not operate to prevent the transfer of any claim to the tribunal in accordance with any rules made under section 73E of the District Court Ordinance (Cap 336).
4. Common law requires an employer to take reasonable care for the employee's safety, whereas these duties are not normally applicable to independent contractors.
   The *BLIS Glossary*, *supra* note 1, translates "common law" as 普通法; "employee" as 僱員; and, "independent contractor" as 獨立承辦商.
5. Employers are vicariously liable for the tortious acts of their employees if these acts occur while the employees are serving in the course of their employment.
   The *BLIS Glossary*, *supra* note 1, translates "tortious act" as 侵權作為; "tort" as 侵權; and, "vicariously" as 因他人作為而.
6. Implied terms of an employment contract impose obligations upon employers and upon employees which obligations may not be owed to or by an independent contractor. *See also* the obligations imposed by the *Employment Ordinance*, *supra* note 2.
7. Different assessments and different reporting requirements are imposed upon the parties, *e.g.*, an employee is liable to pay salaries tax whereas an independent contractor is liable to pay profits tax. For details, *see* Part 3 ("Salaries Tax") and Part 4 ("Profits Tax") of the *Inland Revenue Ordinance* (Cap 112).
8. Under an employer-employee relationship, both the employer and the employee must contribute to the employee's Mandatory Provident Fund Scheme. An independent contractor is a self-employed person, and is required to contribute to the Mandatory Provident Fund Scheme. For details, *see* the *Mandatory Provident Fund Schemes Ordinance* (Cap 485).
   For example, the Hong Kong government's web site contains the following definitions:
   > **Relevant Employee:** A relevant employee means an employee aged 18 to aged below 65. A relevant employee may be a regular employee or a casual employee.

The classification of a worker as either an employee or as an independent contractor is therefore an important matter for the parties involved. Distinguishing between an employee and an independent contractor can be a difficult task.[10] This section sets out the differentiation between the

---

> **Regular Employee:** A regular employee refers to any full-time and part-time worker who is aged 18 to aged below 65 employed under an employment contract for a continuous period of not less than 60 days.
> **Casual Employee:** A casual employee is an employee aged 18 to aged below 65 working in the construction or catering industries under an employment contract of less than 60 days. Industry Schemes of the MPF System are established specially for employees in the two industries.
> **Employer:** An employer means a person who has entered into a contract of employment to employ another person as his or her employee.
> **Self-Employed Person (SEP):** A self-employed person is a person aged 18 to aged below 65 whose income is derived from the production of goods or services in Hong Kong, or from trading in goods or services in or from Hong Kong. To put it simply, a self-employed person is one that works for himself or herself and is not employed as an employee. Essentially, if you are a sole proprietor, or partner of a partnership type business, you will be regarded as a self-employed person covered by the MPF System.

http://www.mpfa.org.hk/english/abt_mpfs/abt_mpfs_fms/abt_mpfs_fms_def/abt_mpfs_fms_def.html (last visited 6 Jan. 2011).

9. When an employer becomes insolvent, the unpaid wages and salary of its employees stand in priority to other debts, that is, the employees will be paid out of the employer's assets before other creditors. The contract fees for independent contractors, if unsecured, will have the lowest priority in cases of insolvency. *See, e.g.*, the *Bankruptcy Ordinance*, *supra* note 2, at section 38.

10. For example, in the case of *Chan Sik Pan v Wylam's Services Ltd* [2000] 1 HKLRD 687, 689 the court stated that this case "would be a mundane personal injury claim but for issues relating to employment of the plaintiff at the time of the accident." The judge continued:

> ... Windsor House in Causeway Bay, was being re-fitted ... The general contractor had a main sub-contractor for electrical and mechanical work. This main sub-contractor further sub-contracted the fire installation work to the first defendant. According to the first defendant, it appointed one Joe Wong trading in the name of United Company as its agent for such work. Joe Wong on behalf of the first defendant "sub-delegated" part of the work to the second defendant. The second defendant says that he sub-sub-contracted work to the third defendant and so he (the second defendant) had no relationship with the workers like the plaintiff. The third defendant says he was at the material time not a sub-sub-contractor. He (the third defendant) merely supervised the workers like the plaintiff and the work at site.
>
> The plaintiff ... had no idea as to all the contractual relationships between the defendants and other superior contractors. According to him, an old friend telephoned him about work available at the site. He went and reported to the third defendant. He regarded the third defendant as the foreman. It was the third defendant who handed him wages in cash twice a month on pay day. The plaintiff had no dealing or knowledge of the other defendants until after the accident. It is undisputed fact that after the accident the first defendant filed a statutory industrial accident report (Form II) with the Labour Department.

two classifications and the guidelines for determining the actual status of a worker.[11]

A. Employee or Independent Contractor

Historically, an employer and an employee were considered to have a master-servant relationship, but today this affiliation has become commonly

---

> This Form II is the form that an employer must file on every industrial accident that has occurred to a worker under his employ. After filing the report, months later, the first defendant twice reached a written agreement with the plaintiff on the amount of allowance payable under the Employees' Compensation Ordinance (Cap 282). And the allowance was paid to the plaintiff as agreed.
>
> ...
>
> To complicate matters further, neither the second defendant nor the third defendant is covered by any employee compensation insurance. Only the first defendant took out compulsory employee compensation insurance; but because there is evidence that the first defendant sub-contracted work to other parties, the insurers of the first defendant deny that the plaintiff is covered by the insurance of the first defendant. ...

Id. at 690–691.

For a practical guide to employment agreements, *see, e.g.*, DRAFTING EMPLOYMENT CONTRACTS (MICHAEL PATTERSON, ed., 1993).

11. As noted earlier in this work, frequently the fields of law, in this instance contract, tort and employment, overlap and each should not be viewed in isolation. This section is a prime example in that while discussing employment relationships in order to determine tort liability, contract matters arise:

> A point that should not be overlooked in the contract of service/independent contract determination is the intention of the parties. A contract for work, whether as servant or independent contractor, is a contract all the same. The intention of the parties in forming their legal relationship will be given due and normally considerable weight. Where the parties have entered into a written contract, the determination is, in the first instance at least, one of construction of the contract. However ... it is the substance of the agreement that will be determinative, so much so that even an apparently agreed designation as independent contractor will, in appropriate circumstances, be set aside by the court ...

GLOFCHESKI–TORT, *supra* note 1, at 413.

Likewise, 10(2) HALSBURY'S LAWS OF HONG KONG para. 145.001 (2009) [hereinafter 10(2) HALSBURY'S] notes that the:

> legal basis of employment remains the contractual relationship between the employer and the employee. The contract of employment is important in itself, in that it may give rise to a common law or equitable action for its enforcement or for damages for its breach but it is equally important in areas of statutory employment law because the expressions 'employee', 'employer' and 'contract of employment' are defined by reference to the contractual relationship between the parties as recognized at common law. (citations omitted)

See 10(2) HALSBURY'S, *supra*, at paras. 145.019–145.026 for a review of the formalities of an employment contract and paras. 145.027–145.033 concerning the terms of employment.

known as an employer-employee relationship. In this relationship, the employee undertakes to provide labour or services in exchange for regular remuneration by the employer. This relationship is created by a contract *of* service through which the employer retains the worker. Employees dedicate themselves exclusively to their employer's business for the duration of the employment contract.[12]

An independent contractor is retained under a contract *for* services, *e.g.*, for the provision of a particular service. The independent contractor is employed from outside the employer's organization for the purpose of producing a specific result, for which the independent contractor is generally paid a lump sum fee. The independent contractor's performance of the assigned task need not be supervised by the employer. Generally, there is no obligation upon the independent contractor to provide services exclusively to the employer.[13]

B. Criteria for Determining Status

Several criteria are used to distinguish between an employee and an independent contractor. Nevertheless, despite these indicators, ascertaining the parties' relationship can be complicated. At times, it is difficult to draw a distinction between an employee and an independent contractor. For example, chauffeurs, ships' captains, or staff reporters on a newspaper are generally considered to be employees. Yet taxi drivers, ship's pilots, or newspaper columnists who contribute regular articles may be independent contractors.[14]

Several court cases demonstrate the difficulty in determining whether a worker is an employee or is an independent contractor. The first of these cases is *Mersey Docks & Harbour Board v Coggins & Griffiths* [1947] AC 1. The court used the control test to ascertain the employment relationship between the parties. According to this test, there is an employer-employee relationship if an employer exercises control over what a worker can do and how that work is done. An independent contractor relationship exists where an employer assigns a task to a person but does not determine the manner in which the work is executed. The control test is whether the

12. *See* Hong Kong Employment Law Manual (Michael Downey, gen. ed., 2010) [hereinafter Downey] §§A.7–A.12 ("Who Is An Employee?") and §§A.13–A.15 ("Who Is An Employer?"). *See also* Employment Law and Practice in Hong Kong para. 2.005 (Rick Glofcheski, *et al.* eds., 2010) [hereinafter Glofcheski–Employment].
13. *See, e.g.*, Glofcheski–Employment, *supra* note 12, at paras. 2.006, 2.010.
14. *Stevenson, Jordan & Harrison v McDonald & Evans* [1952] 1 TLR 101, 111.

employer has the right of ultimate control in instances where the nature of a person's work is too technical or skilful for an employer to exercise day-to-day control.[15]

The second case is *Stevenson, Jordan & Harrison v McDonald & Evans* [1952] 1 TLR 101, where the court used the integration test, also known as the organization test, to determine the parties' relationship.

> His Lordship pointed out that under a contract of service, a man is employed as part of the business, and his work is done as an integral part of the business; whereas under a contract for services, his work, although done for the business, is not integrated into it but is only accessory to it.[16]

Thus, under a contract of service, the person is employed as part of the business organization; under a contract for services, the worker is not integrated into the business but is only supplementary thereto.

In the third case, *Wong Po-Sin v New Universal Paper Co Ltd* [1973] HKLR 59, 72–73, the court provided factors to be considered in ascertaining the type of employment relationship between the parties:

- Selection: if an employer has the power or the right to select the individual to work for the employer, whether the selection is made personally by the employer or through the hiring party's agent, the relationship is likely to be that of a master-servant.

---

15. For further discussion of the control test, *see, e.g.*, GLOFCHESKI–EMPLOYMENT, *supra* note 12, at para. 2.015.
16. KRISHNAN ARJUNAN & ABDUL MAJID BIN NABI BAKSH, BUSINESS LAW IN HONG KONG 561–562 (2nd ed. 2009) [hereinafter ARJUNAN & NABI BAKSH].
    As noted by one authority:

    > Subsequently, the "organisation" approach came to be preferred by the courts, partly as a response to changes in management and organisational structures. Many workers in more advanced work settings exercised a high degree of independence and judgment in their work, but nonetheless did not enjoy the kind of managerial autonomy and self-determination associated with true independent contractors. Under the organisation approach, a contract of service would be found if the work was done as "part and parcel of the employer's organisation" subject perhaps to control of the employer as to when and where, although not necessarily as to how, the work would be done. ... This approach, although a helpful addendum to the control approach, ran the risk of including too many, for example, subcontractors repeatedly employed on the employer's building sites.

    GLOFCHESKI–EMPLOYMENT, *supra* note 12, at para. 2.016 (citations omitted). *See also* GLOFCHESKI–TORT, *supra* note 1, at 409.

- Power of dismissal: if an employer has the power to dismiss a person, this power is more likely to indicate an employer-employee relationship.
- Remuneration: if a worker is paid periodic wages or a salary which is calculated by reference to piece work or time worked, the relationship is likely to be that of an employer-employee. If a worker is paid a commission or a lump sum, that person is more likely to be considered to be an independent contractor.
- Performance: if at least part of the work is performed by the individual alone or independently, *i.e.*, if a worker could delegate the entire performance of work to another person, this would indicate the existence of a contract for services.
- Exclusive services: an employer may require the exclusive services of its employees. A person is thus likely to be an employee if while at work there is only one employer. If an individual simultaneously works for several employers, that person is likely to be an independent contractor.
- Place of work: if an individual's services are to be performed at the employer's premises rather than at the worker's premises, the individual is more likely to be an employee.
- Where a person's services cannot be considered to be conducted as part of an independent business would suggest the status of an employee rather than an independent contractor.
- Supply of equipment: the obligation to provide tools or equipment for a worker indicates an employer-employee relationship whereas an independent contractor would provide its own tools.
- Hours of work: if the employer determines the working hours, the worker is likely to be an employee. If the individual determines the working hours, the worker is likely to be an independent contractor.
- Type of work: where the worker is engaged generally without reference to any particular task or outcome, the relationship is more likely to be that of an employer-employee.[17]

17. To this list, one might add another factor: internal rules such as a personnel manual. If the worker is subjected to the internal rules of the business organization, then that person is likely to be an employee.
For another, but similar, list of factors or guidelines, *see* GLOFCHESKI–EMPLOYMENT, *supra* note 12, at paras. 2.021–2.041; 10(2) HALSBURY'S, *supra* note 11, at para. 145.003; DMITRI M.A. HUBBARD, HONG KONG EMPLOYMENT LAW 32 (2009) [hereinafter HUBBARD].

The classification which the parties give to their relationship may also be a factor which courts may consider in establishing the employment relationship. The parties' contract might contain terms which would indicate the intention to create either a contract of service or a contract for services. However, the classification is not conclusive unless the labelling indicates the parties' genuine intention at the time of making the contract.

> Although a term in a written contract will carry considerable weight in the court's determination of the plaintiff's status, it will not be conclusive. The court will look to the substance of the arrangement, and have close regard to the circumstances of the making of the contract. The court will not enforce a sham contract, particularly where the sole purpose appears to be the employer's avoidance of liabilities.[18]

Whether part-time interviewers of a company were employees of that company was the issue in the case of *Market Investigations Ltd v Minister of Social Security* [1969] 2 QB 173. The judge introduced the economic reality test: whether the person engaged to perform services will be performing these services as a person in business on his/her own account. The Hong Kong Court of Appeal in *Wong Man-luen v Hong Kong Wah Tung Stevedore Co* [1971] HKLR 390 followed the decision in *Market Investigations*. Control of the individual, although a factor, was not decisive. The fundamental test was whether a person was performing the services as a "person in business on his own account" and thus under a contract for services. The status of being in business on one's own account implies the possibility of loss as well as profit in the enterprise.

These criteria do not provide definitive determinations; the criteria serve merely as guidelines. A court needs to consider all the relevant factors,

18. GLOFCHESKI–TORT, *supra* note 1, at 349. *See, e.g.*, GLOFCHESKI–EMPLOYMENT, *supra* note 12, at paras. 2.004, 2.039–2.041.
In the case of *Ready Mixed Concrete (South East) Ltd v Minister of Pensions and National Insurance* [1968] 2 QB 497, 512, the court stated that whether:

> the relation between the parties to the contract is that of master and servant or otherwise is a conclusion of law dependent upon the rights conferred and the duties imposed by the contract ... it is irrelevant that the parties have declared it to be something else ... If it were doubtful what rights and duties the parties wished to provide for, a declaration of this kind might help in resolving the doubt and fixing them in the sense required to give effect to that intention.

See also the Hong Kong case *Young and Woods Ltd v West* [1980] IRLR 201. However, note that the matter remains unsettled as two Privy Council cases each came to a different conclusion. *See* the cases of *Lee Ting Sang v Chung Chi-keung* [1990] 2 AC 374; *Cheng Yuen v Royal Hong Kong Golf Club* [1997] 2 HKC 426. *See also* the case of *Poon Chau Nam v Yim Siu Cheung* [2007] 1 HKLRD 951; ARJUNAN & NABI BAKSH, *supra* note 16, at 566–572.

including the totality of the facts of each particular case.[19] Courts emphasize that there is no comprehensive list of factors and that this list excludes other considerations or indicia.[20] Ascertaining a worker's employment status cannot be made by compiling a checklist or by tallying the factors falling in one category or the other.[21]

---

19. As noted by one authority:

> Today, the courts are inclined toward a more flexible, pragmatic approach in characterising the relationship as one of contract of service or independent contract. The court will look into the substance of the relationship, taking into consideration the peculiarities of the work and the realities of the workplace, even to the point where apparent "agreements" between worker and employer, purporting to designate the relationship as one of independent contract, will be disregarded. Control is probably in most cases still the single most important consideration, but the court will look at all the circumstances of the relationship between defendant and worker in deciding this issue. ... Particular attention will be paid to economic considerations, such as the worker's opportunity to control the rate of income or profit by virtue of his/her own efforts. The relevant question becomes: Is the worker a businessperson? Is the worker in business on his/her own account?

GLOFCHESKI–TORT, *supra* note 1, at 409–410.

GLOFCHESKI–EMPLOYMENT, *supra* note 12, at para. 2.027 provides clarification of "being in business on one's own account":

> Financial risk and the prospect of profit is an often misunderstood head. It does not normally include a piece-worker's opportunity to increase his income by working harder. Nor should it be understood as meaning that a worker with management responsibilities is self-employed. It means expending one's own energies and putting one's own financial resources as risk in the business enterprise, with the possibility of financially benefitting of suffering from one's own management decisions. (citations omitted)

In determining whether a worker is an employee or an independent contractor, another authority opines:

> There is no single test for determining whether a person is an employee. The test which used to be considered adequate, that is to say the control test, can no longer be considered sufficient, especially in the case of the employment of highly skilled individuals. The control test is now only one of the particular factors which may assist a court or tribunal in deciding the point. The question whether the person was integrated into the enterprise or remained apart from and independent of it has been suggested as an appropriate test, but is likewise only one of the relevant factors, for the modern approach is to examine all the features of their relationship against the background of the indicia of employment with a view to deciding whether, as a matter of overall impression, the relationship was one of employment.

10(2) HALSBURY'S, *supra* note 11, at para. 145.003 (citations omitted).

20. GLOFCHESKI–EMPLOYMENT, *supra* note 12, at para. 2.017.

21. *Id.*

> it is impossible to *define* a contract of service in the sense of stating a number of conditions which are both necessary to, and sufficient for, the existence of such a contract.[22]

After the decision in *Wong Sai-yee v Kong Kwan* [1988] 1 HKLR 367, the Court of Appeal seems to emphasize the following criteria as the more important of the many tests for ascertaining contracts of service:

- the power of control, as distinct from the actual exercise in fact of control;
- the "part and parcel of the organization" test;
- the financial risk, if any, of the worker; and,
- as a corollary of the financial risk aspect, any indicia as to whether the worker was carrying on business for his/her own account.[23]

Courts presently adopt a pragmatic test of considering all features of the particular relationship in determining the parties' employment relationship. Some Hong Kong court cases follow the approach in *Wong Po-sin v New Universal Paper* of examining all the indicia as a whole rather than applying any particular test.[24] However, other court decisions, such as *Lee Ting Sang v Chung Chi-keung* [1990] 2 AC 374, PC and *Chan Shui Man v Tsang Hing Shan* [1991] 2 HKC 243, CA, suggest that the economic reality test used in the *Market Investigations* case represents the correct current approach. The economic reality test contributes to the task of distinguishing between employees with contracts of service and independent contractors with contracts for services. In the circumstances of individuals carrying on a profession or vocation, the courts will review the extent to which an individual relies upon a particular paymaster for the financial exploitation of the worker's talents.[25] Since the importance to be given to the various factors depends on the facts of each case, the approach is therefore flexible, but vague.

The case of *Cheng Yuen v Royal Hong Kong Golf Club* [1997] 2 HKC 426 is an example illustrating the difficulty in classifying a worker's status. The golf club assigned a number, a locker and a uniform to the plaintiff caddie. He could work when he wished. However, the plaintiff caddie went to the

---

22. P.S. Atiyah, Vicarious Liability in the Law of Torts 38 (1967) [hereinafter Atiyah] (approved in *Construction Industry Training Board v Labour Force Ltd* [1970] 3 All ER 220, 226).
23. G.R. McCormick, *Employees' Compensation: Employee or Independent Contractor*, 21 HKLJ 109, 111 (1991).
24. *See* the cases of *Poon Chau Nam v Yim Siu Cheung*, *supra* note 18; *Li Chung-i v Li Man-yuen* [1991] 2 HKLR 138; *Wong Sai-yee v Kong Kwan* [1988] 1 HKLR 367.
25. *Hall v Lorimer* [1994] 1 All ER 250.

club daily where he offered his services to golfers. The golf club did not guarantee that the caddie would receive any work, although it was agreed that he would average two rounds a day. At the end of each day he was paid in cash by the club. The club then debited the member concerned who repaid the club.

The Labour Tribunal determined that the golf club exercised control over the caddie by providing him a uniform, giving instructions as to his duties and the disciplinary power to reduce a caddie in grade or to dismiss him. The club benefited indirectly from the payment and collection of fees paid to the caddie. These factors outweighed the inference to be drawn from the fact that he did not receive benefits normally provided by an employer to an employee, *e.g.*, insurance coverage, holidays, sick leave, and, pension scheme. The Labour Tribunal concluded that the caddie was an employee of the golf club.

Ultimately, the Privy Council determined the arrangement between the parties to be a licence by the club to allow the caddie to offer his services on terms dictated by the administrative convenience of the club and its members. The controls were merely the club's administrative measures. There was no obligation between the parties such that the club would employ the caddie and that he would work for the club in return for a wage. On the contrary, the individual golfers were responsible for the caddie's fees; although as a convenience the club collected the fees and paid them to the caddie. It was the golfers who instructed the caddie as to his tasks during the round of golf. Therefore, the Privy Council held the caddie to be an independent contractor rather than a club employee. Lord Hoffman dissented from the majority opinion, stating that the caddie, though not under continuous employment, ought to be considered a casual employee rather than an independent contractor as the caddie could claim payment from the golf club even if the golfer did not pay the club.

In the case of *Wong Ki v Shun Tak Electrical Mechanical and Engineering (Hong Kong) Co Ltd* [2009] HKEC 595, the court, in deciding whether the injured plaintiff was an independent contractor or an employee, stated:

> 7. The parties in this case, as laymen, have expressed confusion and bewilderment over the question of when a worker is, in law, an employee, and when he is an independent contractor. They may get some comfort from the fact that often, lawyers are just as confused, and that the question cannot be easily answered by the courts.
>
> 8. The modern approach to the question whether a person is an employee, as adopted in the case of *Poon Chau Nam* [v. *Yim Siu Cheung* (2007) 10 HKCFAR 156] itself, is to examine all the

> features of their relationship against the background of the indicia of employment with a view to deciding whether, as a matter of overall impression, the relationship was one of employment, bearing in mind the purpose for which the question is asked.
>
> ...
>
> 42. The authorities are clear that it is for the court and not the parties to evaluate the facts and determine the legal relationship between them, such that the parties' own description of their relationship is not determinative (Chan Kwok Kin v. Kwok Kwan Hing [1991] HKLR 631).

The case of *Leung Suk Fong Peggy v Prudential Assurance Co Ltd* [2011] HKEC 1297 involved the issue of whether the defendant insurer's engagement of the plaintiff amounted to an employer/employee relationship. The court determined the plaintiff's status to be an independent contractor upon an analysis of the following criteria:

- extent of control;
- prospect of profit return and risk of loss;
- integral part of the organization;
- provision of equipment;
- incidence of taxation and insurance;
- the parties' view of the relationship; and,
- the traditional structure of the particular trade.

Distinguishing between an employee and an independent contractor is also important as an employer has liability for certain acts committed by its employees. This accountability rests upon one of two bases. The first basis upon which an employer might be found liable is for the breach of a non-delegable duty owed to an employee. This personal duty imposes upon an employer the obligation to take reasonable care for the employee's safety.[26] An employer ought to undertake precautions which a reasonable employer would assume in order to ensure that the employee is not exposed to unreasonable risks. The second basis of employer liability might arise under the head of vicarious responsibility to another party for the employee's negligence. The two following sections review these liabilities in the above order.

26. *See, e.g.*, 10(2) HALSBURY'S, *supra* note 11, at paras. 145.051–145.053 (employers' obligations for employees' safety), 145.589–145.595 (compensation for injuries and employers' bankruptcy) and citations contained in those two sections. Vicarious liability and non-delegable duties are also discussed in the Tort chapter, sections V.A and V.C respectively. Vicarious liability is discussed in this chapter's section II.C. Non-delegable duties are discussed in this chapter's section II.D.

II. EMPLOYER'S LIABILITY

In this section, an employer's liability is examined in relation to its employees in the torts of negligence and breach of statutory duty, in relation to an employer's vicarious liability to parties injured by the employer's workers, and, in relation to an employer's liability for independent contractors.

A. Liability in Negligence to Employees

In *Wilsons & Clyde Coal Co Ltd v English* [1937] 3 All ER 628, the court held that an employer owes an affirmative duty of care to its employees, requiring positive action by an employer to ensure the workers' safety.[27] This duty has four distinct elements:

- to provide competent staff;
- to provide adequate material, including the duty to maintain equipment;
- to provide a proper system of work and effective supervision; and,
- to provide a safe place of work.[28]

This four-element duty of an employer is personal or non-delegable in the sense that this duty cannot, generally, be discharged by delegating the responsibility to another.[29] However, the non-delegable aspect of this duty might be ameliorated when the worker is sent to another employer's premises to perform work.[30] An employer breaches this obligation to an employee where the standard of care falls below that of the reasonable employer, having regard to all the circumstances, including the individual

---

27. GLOFCHESKI–TORT, *supra* note 1, at 350.
The author further explains:

> The four-fold duty postulated in *Wilsons and Clyde Coal v English* is an affirmative duty, requiring positive action by the employer to ensure the safety of workers. In *Ho Ying Wai v Keliston Marine (Far East) Limited & Another* [2003] 1 HKLRD 343, the duty required the employer, a diving company, to conduct a proper inquiry of the employee's medical history at the time of his employment, in order to ensure that the work as a deep sea diver did not unreasonably endanger the employee.

Id.
See also GLOFCHESKI–EMPLOYMENT, *supra* note 12, at paras. 10.006–10.008.

28. For discussion of these four elements, *see, e.g.*, GLOFCHESKI–EMPLOYMENT, *supra* note 12, at paras. 10.014–10.024.
29. GLOFCHESKI–TORT, *supra* note 1, at 350. *See also* GLOFCHESKI–EMPLOYMENT, *supra* note 12, at paras. 10.009–10.010.
30. GLOFCHESKI–TORT, *supra* note 1, at 350.

worker's characteristics, in addition to any particular susceptibility of which the employer was or ought to have been aware.[31]

For example, the case of *Chow Po v Chow Hau Man* [2010] HKEC 349, illustrates the employer's duty to provide a safe system of work. The plaintiff suffered injuries when he, as instructed, attempted to lift the end of some metal boards to enable these boards to be loaded onto a lorry. The Court of Appeal considered the issue and decided that:

> 5. Under common law, the contract of employment between an employer and an employee contains an implied term that the employer would take reasonable care for the safety of the employee (Wilsons and Clyde Coal Co. Ltd. v. English [1938] AC 57, HC). This level of duty is the same as that of an employer's common law duty of care in the law of negligence. Such duty includes the provision of a safe system of work.
> 6. The Defendant did not give the Plaintiff any warning about the risks in carrying out the Defendant's instruction. He also walked away after giving his instructions. So he did not supervise the Plaintiff in carrying out the work. If he had supervised the work, he would have detected any risk that may come and warn the Plaintiff of it. He did not provide adequate and competent fellow staff to assist the Plaintiff. Mr. Chow Ching Cheung [Plaintiff's co-worker] was there, but he shrinked [*sic*] away from giving assistance to the Plaintiff. All these factors contribute to the occurrence of the Accident.

In another example, the case of *Lam Fong & Ho Kok Keong v So Hoo Yuen* [1990] HKLY 1209 illustrates the first three elements of an employer's duty of care. The plaintiffs were the personal representatives of the deceased, who was employed by the first defendant on a building site. The deceased

---

In support of this proposition, the author propounds:

> In *Wong Chi Wing v Chun Wo Building Construction Ltd* (2001) HCPI 1476 of 2000, where the plaintiff was sent to a client's site to do toilet extraction work and was injured due to unsafe conditions there, the court found that the employer had discharged its non-delegable duty, having earlier "taken reasonable steps to ensure that there is a safe place of work by inspecting the site and ensuring that the occupiers were responsible and competent". This reasoning suggests that where workers are required to perform their work off-site, the non-delegable aspect of the duty of care is diluted.

Id. at 359.

See also GLOFCHESKI–EMPLOYMENT, *supra* note 12, at paras. 10.027–10.028.

31. GLOFCHESKI–TORT, *supra* note 1, at 351–352.

See also GLOFCHESKI–EMPLOYMENT, *supra* note 12, at paras. 10.008, 10.010.

wore no safety belt at the time of the accident. The negligence of the deceased's co-workers resulted in a putlog hitting the deceased, causing him to fall and to sustain fatal injuries. The parties agreed that the fall caused the deceased's demise and that a safety belt–if he had worn one—would have saved him. The court held the first defendant vicariously liable for the negligence of its workers who caused the deceased to be struck by the putlog.[32] Additionally, the court found the first defendant failed to take reasonable care of the deceased's safety by failing to provide enough safety belts for its workers. Finally, the court found the first defendant again failed to take reasonable care for the deceased's safety by failing to issue instructions to use safety belts.[33]

The court in *Wong Chick v Swire Pacific Ltd* [1992] 1 HKC 571 considered the fourth duty of care owed by an employer to its employee. In this case, the defendant employed the plaintiff between 1935 and 1971, first as an apprentice and eventually as a boiler-maker. The noise at the defendant's dockyard where the plaintiff worked exceeded 90 decibels. Noise at this level could cause hearing loss. The judge concluded that the plaintiff's deafness was attributable to the constant loud noise encountered at work. The failure to provide a safe working environment would have rendered the defendant liable. However, in this particular case, the claim was struck out because of the time bar under the *Workmen's Compensation Ordinance* of 1969—in other words, the plaintiff waited too long to sue.[34]

An employer also owes a general common law duty of care to an independent contractor whom the employer has retained. However, the duty an employer owes to employees is more extensive, in that the employer is required to provide effective supervision and a safe system of work.[35] Once an employer is aware of, or suspects, danger in the work site, the employer must take reasonable actions to protect the employees. Statutory safety

32. For the discussion on vicarious liability, *see* section II.C.
33. *See also Chui Yu Yau v Chan Pak Luk* [1987] 3 HKC 339, where the judge followed *Wilson v Tyneside Window Cleaning Co* [1958] 2 QB 110, in holding that it was essential for employers to provide adequate instructions concerning the proper and safe method of performing a task and also the dangers of deviating from that prescribed method. However, there was no duty on the part of employers to give instructions or warnings to experienced workers.
34. This was the predecessor to the *Employees' Compensation Ordinance*, *supra* note 2.
35. In *Inglefield v Macey* (1967) 2 KIR 146, the plaintiff, injured at work, alleged that he was a servant of the defendant and sued the latter for failure to provide a safe system of work. The court held that the plaintiff was self-employed and said that the duty to provide a safe system of work was inherent in a master-servant relationship. However, the employer of an independent contractor only had a duty to ensure that the equipment it supplied to the independent contractor was safe.

standards generally apply to anyone working in a factory or undertaking, regardless of the precise nature of the worker's contractual relationship with the employer.[36]

The *Employees' Compensation Ordinance* (Cap 282) provides compensation from the employer to employees injured or killed in the course of

---

36. The topic of safety-related ordinances will be presented later in this chapter.
An example of legal provisions imposing safety-related obligations is regulation 38AA of the Construction Sites (Safety) Regulations (Cap 59I) set out below:

(1) Without prejudice to the other provisions of this Part, any contractor who has direct control over any construction work shall, so far as reasonably practicable—
  (a) identify the hazardous conditions of persons working at a height in the construction work;
  (b) rectify any hazardous conditions of persons working at a height in the construction work; and
  (c) safeguard any person working at a height in the construction work against all hazardous conditions.

(2) Any contractor who has direct control over any construction work shall ensure that, so far as is reasonably practicable, suitable and adequate safe access to and egress from every place of work where the construction work is being carried out is provided and properly maintained.

(3) Subject to paragraph (4), any contractor who has direct control over any construction work shall take suitable and adequate steps to ensure that, so far as is reasonably practicable, no person gains access to any place which is within the place of work where the construction work is being carried out and where any hazardous conditions are present.

(4) Paragraph (3) shall not apply in relation to a person engaged in work for the purpose of rectifying any hazardous conditions if all reasonably practicable steps have been taken to ensure the safety of that person whilst engaged in that work.

(5) For the purpose of this regulation, "hazardous conditions" (危險狀況) includes the following conditions that may give rise to a risk of persons falling from a height—
  (a) unprotected edge or opening at a place of work;
  (b) improper design and construction of a place of work;
  (c) inadequate or insecure support or anchoring of a place of work;
  (d) improper maintenance of a place of work;
  (e) any working platform (other than a suspended working platform) that fails to comply with the provisions of the Third Schedule applicable to it.

(6) For the avoidance of doubt, it is hereby declared that—
  (a) paragraph (5) does not prejudice the generality of paragraphs (1), (3) and (4);
  (b) the reference to working platform in paragraph (5) does not prejudice the operation of the provisions of the Factories and Industrial Undertakings (Suspended Working Platforms) Regulation (Cap. 59 sub. leg. AC) in relation to a working platform which is a suspended working platform.

employment regardless of fault.[37] Independent contractors are excluded from the coverage of this compensation scheme, and must resort to tort remedies in order to recover compensation. In *Yeung Kam Fuk v Len Shing Construction Co Ltd & Others* [1986] HKC 160, the plaintiff suffered injuries at work when a platform on which he was working collapsed, causing him to fall approximately ten feet. The plaintiff brought an action against the first defendant alleging that it was his employer and that it also owed a duty to him as the occupier of the site. The court found the plaintiff to be a self-employed sub-contractor. Therefore, the claims based on an employment relationship failed. However, the first defendant remained liable by reason of breach of statutory duty and negligence. The first defendant's defence, based on the *Occupiers Liability Ordinance* (Cap 314), that it had acted reasonably in entrusting the works to another, did not succeed on the facts of this particular case.[38]

B. Breach of Statutory Duty

Breach of statutory duty is a common law tort action against an employer for breaching the work place safety laws and regulations.[39] Breach of statutory duty is a distinct and separate cause of action from negligence to which an employee may resort for injuries incurred while at work.[40] A claim of breach of statutory duty affords an injured employee another basis to claim for damages for the injuries suffered.[41]

Whether an injured worker may claim breach of statutory duty will depend upon the relevant legislation which may:

- expressly provide for such a claim;
- expressly preclude such a claim; or,
- be silent on whether such a claim may be brought in court.

Where an ordinance is silent on the matter, courts will require evidence that the legislature intended such a remedy be available for a breach or violation of the relevant ordinance. "This is an open-ended, largely intuitive process."[42] Some guidelines which courts follow in ascertaining whether a

37. This statute is discussed in greater detail in section III.F.
38. For a review of occupier's liability, *see* the Tort chapter, section V.D.
39. GLOFCHESKI–EMPLOYMENT, *supra* note 12, at para. 10.050.
40. *Id.* at para. 10.049.
41. For detailed analysis of this subject, *see, e.g.*, *id.* at paras. 10.049–10.078; GLOFCHESKI–TORT, *supra* note 1, at Chapter 8 ("Breach of Statutory Duty").
42. GLOFCHESKI–EMPLOYMENT, *supra* note 12, at para. 10.052.

claim of breach of statutory duty is available to the injured worker includes the following:

- whether the purpose of the relevant ordinance is intended to protect a particular class of persons rather than the general public;[43]
- whether the ordinance provides for any other remedy for contravention of its provisions; and,
- whether a claim of breach of statutory duty is the only civil remedy available to the injured worker.

There are several advantages to bringing a claim under breach of statutory duty rather than in negligence. One advantage is that the provisions of health and safety related ordinances are often worded in such a way that there is strict liability for a breach or contravention of the legislation.[44] Another advantage is that a statutory duty is non-delegable. Employers cannot avoid liability by delegating to the worker or a subcontractor the responsibility of fulfilling the obligations or requirements imposed by the statute. "Moreover, it is not sufficient for employers, after instructing employees on safety, to leave employees to choose whether or not to follow the regulations."[45]

A case which applies the principles reviewed so far in this chapter and the previous chapter and which foreshadows other principles to be reviewed in this chapter is *Ng Chun Mo v Waihong Environment Services Ltd* [2011] HKEC 897. The plaintiff was employed by the defendant cleaning company [hereafter referred to as "D1"] which was contracted the cleaning works for a residential estate managed by the second defendant, the property management company [hereafter referred to as "D2"].

The facts involved the plaintiff cleaning the roof of a glass canopy over a pedestrian walkway when he fell approximately 3.6 meters to the ground. As a result of the fall, the plaintiff became an incontinent paraplegic. There was no safety railing on the roof. There was no safety platform. Neither defendant provided a safety harness nor anchor points for a safety harness. The court decided three issues:

---

43. *Id.* at paras. 10.052, 10.057–10.061.
44. *Id.* at para. 10.055.
45. *Id.* at para. 10.056.
See also id. at paras. 10.074 ("Defence of contributory negligence available but reluctantly applied"), 10.075 ("Contributory negligence assessed less severely than in an ordinary negligence action"), 10.076 ("No or reduced contributory negligence in cases of momentary inadvertence"), 10.077 ("Where worker disregards employer's express safety instructions").

- D2's liability;
- the apportionment of liability between the joint tortfeasors, if any, under the *Civil Liability (Contribution) Ordinance* (Cap 377);
- and, whether the plaintiff was contributorily negligent for his own safety.

The court found that D2 had sub-contracted its cleaning responsibilities to D1 while retaining an amount of control in relation to matters such as supervision of the cleaning activities and instructing which tools or equipment would be used by D1 for cleaning. The court decided that despite the sub-contract, D2 remained responsible for the management of the estate, including ensuring that there would be a safe and secure environment under the *Occupiers Liability Ordinance* (Cap 314). In reaching its conclusion, the court stated:

> 63. … By employing an independent contractor the occupier does not avoid all liability. He cannot turn round and say this is not my responsibility at all; it is the independent contractors alone. Equally he is not directly responsible for an independent contractor as though that man were his own servant … the test is whether the contractor himself took reasonable care in the respects identified.
>
> …
>
> 65. … the attention of D2 had already been drawn to the potential dangers to workmen cleaning the ceiling of the walkway. They were fully aware of the position and took no effective action either to make good the deficiencies or to order that no workers were to work on the ceiling until it was safe for them to do so.
>
> …
>
> 69. In addition to this detailed provisions are contained in the Construction Sites (Safety) Regulations which are subsidiary legislation to the Factories and Industrial Undertaking Ordinance Cap. 59, which are relevant to this case.
>
> 70. The cleaning work on the walkway comes within the definition in s. 2 of "Construction Work" in the Regulations.
>
> …
>
> 72. … D2 has failed to comply with these requirements and accordingly it is jointly and severally liable for this accident.
>
> 78. … However what is abundantly clear is that if the worker is performing his duties in the way he is instructed to do he will not be held to be contributorily negligent.
>
> 79. Here there was no suggestion of any misconduct disobedience or impropriety on the plaintiff's part.

> 81. The overwhelming reason for this accident was that the plaintiff was being required to work in an unsafe place of work and no blame whatever attaches to him.
>
> 82. D2's claim that the plaintiff contributed to this accident is dismissed.
>
> ...
>
> 85. ... both D1 and D2 were failing in their duties and responsibilities to a serious extent and that it was on account of this that the accident occurred.
>
> 86. While both parties realised that it was dangerous for workers to work on the ceiling without safe guards being provided in some form neither of them took prompt action to remedy the defects or to issue instructions that no worker was to work on the ceiling until the situation had been rectified.
>
> 87. In addition to this ... both defendants equally owed a responsibility for ensuring that the workplace was safe.
>
> 88. ... I have come to the conclusion that the fairest result is to hold that D1 and D2 are equally to blame for this accident.
>
> 89. Accordingly I apportion the liability between them 50/50.

C. Vicarious Liability

The preceding section discusses an employer's liability to its employees. In this section, a survey is provided of an employer's liability to another potential plaintiff—a party, uninvolved in the master-servant relationship, who is injured by the acts of the employer's servant, including a co-worker.[46] "Vicarious liability means that a person otherwise free from blame may be held liable for the tort of another."[47]

---

46. *See generally id.* at paras. 10.040–10.048; 10(2) HALSBURY'S, *supra* note 11, at paras. 145.636–145.652; HUBBARD, *supra* note 17, at Chapter 13 ("Vicarious Liability"); ATIYAH, *supra* note 22. *See also* the Tort chapter, section V.A.
47. GLOFCHESKI–TORT, *supra* note 1, at 407.
    This author states that there are various policy reasons for vicarious liability:
    - One is tort law's quest to find "deep pockets" in order to ensure compensation to the victim.
    - Another is a moral element that holds that one who profits from the accident-causing activity should pay the injured party.
    - Further, vicarious liability serves as a deterrent.
    - Finally, vicarious liability has a loss distribution function in that vicarious liability provides a mechanism for spreading the loss beyond the immediate tortfeasor.

    Id.
    See HUBBARD, *supra* note 17, at 388–389.

Vicarious liability is imposed upon an employer for its employee's negligence committed within the course of employment.[48] An employer's liability is not dependent upon the employer's personal fault. Rather, liability is vicariously imposed based upon the employment relationship between the defendant employer and the negligent party, the employee. Liability is not premised upon any breach of a duty of care by the defendant employer to an injured plaintiff.[49]

Thus, an employer's liability is completely contingent upon the employee's liability. An employee must be shown to be at fault in order for an employer to be vicariously liable. Vicarious liability co-exists with the tortfeasor's liability.[50] If an employee is found to be not liable, then the employer cannot be vicariously liable.

Finding an employer vicariously liable does not displace an employee's liability.[51] Both the employer and the employee may be held liable as joint tortfeasors. In Hong Kong, the *Civil Liability (Contribution) Ordinance* (Cap 377) permits a court under section 4(1) to allocate the responsibility and the damages between the joint tortfeasors.[52] Under section 3(1), any person who is liable for damages may recover a contribution from any other person who is jointly liable for those damages.[53]

---

48. The *BLIS Glossary*, *supra* note 1, translates "in the course of … employment" as 受僱工作期間.
49. GLOFCHESKI–TORT, *supra* note 1, at 407.
50. *Id.*
51. *Id.* at 408 explains that a finding of vicarious liability on the part of the employer does not relieve the immediate tortfeasor (the employee) of responsibility. The employee is jointly and severally liable with the employer. Vicarious liability gives the injured victim a right to sue another party, in addition to the party actually causing the injury, for the damages suffered.

    The *BLIS Glossary*, *supra* note 1, translates "jointly and severally liable" as 負上共同及各別的法律責任.
52. Section 4(1) states:

    > Subject to subsection (3), in any proceedings for contribution under section 3 the amount of the contribution recoverable from any person shall be such as may be found by the court to be just and equitable having regard to the extent of that person's responsibility for the damage in question.

    Civil Liability (Contribution) Ordinance (Cap 377).
53. Section 3(1) provides:

    > Subject to the following provisions of this section, any person liable in respect of any damage suffered by another person may recover contribution from any other person liable in respect of the same damage (whether jointly with him or otherwise).

    The *BLIS Glossary*, *supra* note 1, translates "jointly liable" as 共同有責.

Course of employment is a criterion to be satisfied in a vicarious liability claim. As one authority states:

> Nonetheless, the course of employment concept is interpreted to include not only those wrongful acts authorised or instructed by the employer (a relatively straightforward proposition, and anyway, arguably a form of primary liability), but also the more common occurrence of a lawful act authorised by the employer, but done in a wrongful and unauthorised way. ... This second category includes an employee's negligent performance of normal work duties, which causes injury to another. This inquiry requires the court to identify the scope of the employment duties.
>
> Moreover, as regards the second category, an employer is liable even for acts which he or she has not authorised, provided they are so connected with acts which s/he has authorised that they may rightly be regarded as modes–although improper modes–of doing them (*Lister & Others v Hesley Hall Ltd* [2001] 2 WLR 1311).
>
> It follows, then, that if, during the course of work, the employee engages in a diversion, going on "a frolic of his own", engaging in an unauthorised act not connected with the authorised act, he will be deemed to have stepped out of the course of employment. That is, where the employee's activity is a very clear departure from the scope of employment, there will be no vicarious liability.[54]

The following case demonstrates the application of some of these principles. *Ming An Insurance Co (HK) Ltd v Ritz-Carlton Ltd* [2002] 3 HKLRD 844, CFA involved the issue of the hotel's vicarious liability as determined by its employee's scope of employment. The hotel hired limousines and drivers from a third party for the convenience of the hotel's guests. The hotel employee in question served as a doorman at the hotel. This employee also had the responsibility of keeping the hotel's forecourt unobstructed by moving the limousines when the drivers were off-duty. The employee would undertake this task sometimes by driving the limousines along a particular route on the public roads. At the time of the vehicular accident, which injured two pedestrians, the employee was driving along this particular route accompanied by a bellboy to collect food for the hotel staff. The

54. GLOFCHESKI–TORT, *supra* note 1, at 415–416.
See also GLOFCHESKI–EMPLOYMENT, *supra* note 12, at paras. 10.042–10.044; HUBBARD, *supra* note 17, at 409 (concerning deviation from the original undertaking, usually pertaining to the driving route travelled by vehicles), 414 (prohibitions concerning scope of employment versus sphere of employment).

act of collecting meals for hotel staff was not a course of conduct authorized by the hotel.

In making its decision, the court made the following observations:

- Employers are liable for the torts committed by their employees in the course of their employment. And an employee's tort is deemed to have been committed in the course of his employment if it is either (a) something authorised by the employer or (b) an unauthorized mode of doing something authorised by the employer.[55]
- The "unauthorized mode" can give rise to difficulty in its application. The UK House of Lords adopted a new test under which the question is whether the defendant employee's tort was so closely connected with its employment that the employer should be held vicariously liable. An employer is liable even for acts which it has not authorized, provided these acts are so connected with the acts which it has authorized, that these unauthorized acts may rightly be regarded as methods, although improper methods, of doing the authorized acts. By "close connection" is meant a connection between the employee's unauthorized tortious act and the employment which is so close as to make it fair and just to hold the employer vicariously liable.[56]
- "Close connection" is the basic criterion for vicarious liability in regard to all torts committed by an employee during an unauthorized course of conduct, whether intentional wrongdoing or mere inadvertence is involved. The application of this criterion is always to be undertaken in the context of each individual case. The disposal of each case will always turn ultimately on its own facts and the particular considerations raised by these facts.[57]
- In considering the scope of the employment, a broad approach should be undertaken. Concerning vicarious liability, the nature of the employment is not to be ascertained merely by tabulating the employee's duties. It is necessary to review the mode in which the employer's activities were carried out and how the manner of carrying out the activities exposed others to the employee's tortious harm.[58]
- In this case, the defendant employee was driving a limousine for the purpose of collecting food, which does not appear to be an authorized act. It is a fact that, albeit driven by their chauffeurs rather than the

55. [2002] 3 HKLRD at 851.
56. *Id.* at 851–852 (citations omitted).
57. *Id.* at 854 (citations omitted).
58. *Id.* at 855 (citations omitted).

hotel's employees, the limousines were sometimes used for the purpose of collecting food. This apparently impliedly authorized activity existed. Collecting food was a purpose not only of the hotel's staff but also of the hotel itself. The collection of food was obviously in the business interests of the hotel that its staff be adequately fed despite the inadequacy of the hotel canteen. Consequently, under the then-prevailing practice, collecting food was properly to be considered as incidental to the employment of the hotel staff involved. The defendant employee's tort was so closely connected to its employment that court's decision would be fair and just to find the hotel vicariously liable.[59]

To conclude, the requirements for vicarious liability are:

- the tortfeasor is retained by the employer as an employee;[60]
- the employee committed the tortious act; and,
- the employee's tortious act was in connection with, or, in the course of employment. This act may be either expressly or impliedly authorized, even if it were careless or mistaken. A wrongful way or an unauthorized mode of performance, even if the act is contrary to the master's instructions, will render the employer liable. An employee's act which is outside the scope of employment will not subject the employer to liability. Whether the tortious act is incidental or necessary to employment is also a factor.

The prohibition of the act does not necessarily result in that act being outside the scope of employment.[61] An employer cannot escape liability by prohibiting negligent acts or any acts outside of direct instructions. A prohibition is effective only where it limits the scope of employment.[62] Liability

---

59. *Id.* at 855–856.
60. The *BLIS Glossary*, *supra* note 1, translates "tortfeasor" as 侵權人.
61. 10(2) HALSBURY'S, *supra* note 11, at para. 145.639 notes:

> The employer cannot escape responsibility where the act is otherwise one for which the employer is responsible, on the ground that the employer had forbidden the employee to do the act in the manner which produced the injury.

Another source states:

> It seems correct that an express prohibition does not necessarily absolve the employer of vicarious liability. If it did, an employer would be forever absolved of vicarious liability by simply passing a general prohibition on his servants to not perform any negligent acts, or any acts outside of express instructions. A prohibition will be effective only if it limits the scope of the employment.

GLOFCHESKI–TORT, *supra* note 1, at 418.

62. GLOFCHESKI–TORT, *supra* note 1, at 418.

depends upon one of two situations. The first is whether the prohibited act restricts the scope of employment, *i.e.*, an act which is outside the scope of employment. Alternatively, the second situation concerns whether the prohibited act limits the conduct within the sphere of employment, *i.e.*, an act which is within the scope of employment. There will be no liability where the prohibited act limits the sphere of employment, an act which is outside the scope of employment. There will be liability where the prohibition limits the conduct within the sphere of employment, an act which is within the scope of employment. An employer will be vicariously liable if its employee's act is an unauthorized mode of performing an authorized act connected to the employment relationship.[63]

D. Liability for Independent Contractors

Employers are not, in general, vicariously liable for torts committed by their retained independent contractors.[64] In some circumstances, however, an employer will be liable. In these instances, the employer's liability is based not on vicarious liability but on the employer's personal duty to the injured plaintiff, a duty that the employer breaches through the independent

63. *Id.* at 417 states:

> Where the diversion involves the employee's breach of the employer's express instructions, the employee will only be outside the course of the employment if the instructions truly delimit the scope of the employment. If the conduct can still be characterised as a merely unauthorised way of doing an authorised task, or … as sufficiently connected to the employment, vicarious liability will be imposed.

The *BLIS Glossary*, *supra* note 1, translates "scope of … employment" as 受僱範圍.

64. *See, e.g.*, 25(1) HALSBURY'S LAWS OF HONG KONG para. 380.019 (2010) [hereinafter 25(1) HALSBURY'S]. As explained in *id.* at paras. 380.048–380.049:

> The general rule is that an employer of an independent contractor is not liable for torts committed by the contractor or his employees in the course of employment. A contractor as an employer may be vicariously liable for a tort committed by his employees. The original employer however may be liable for torts committed by the contractor or by the contractor's employees which is attributable to the negligence or other personal fault of the original employer. A distinction however has to be made where a person agrees merely as agent of a party to arrange for services to be provided by others. An employer will not be liable for the torts of an Independent [*sic*] contractor where in all the circumstances of the particular case the employer has i) acted reasonably in entrusting the work to the independent contractor, ii) used reasonable care in selecting the contractor, iii) taken reasonable steps (if any are possible) to supervise the carrying out of the work and iv) used reasonable steps (if this is possible) to ensure that the work has been properly done.

contractor.[65] An employer has primary liability in these instances, whereas an employer's vicarious liability for the acts of its servant is secondary liability.

Where the law imposes a strict or absolute duty or a non-delegable duty upon a person, he cannot discharge that duty by delegating the performance of work to an independent contractor. ... if the contractor wrongfully performs a delegated duty then the employer is liable. Whether a duty is a non-delegable duty or not depends on the facts of each case. There is also a non-delegable duty at common law to provide a safe system of work. A person who fails to do so will be liable for the plaintiff's injury notwithstanding that an independent contractor was employed to do his work. While a person is liable for an imperfect performance of his non-delegable duty by the contractor, he is not liable for the contractor's contractual or casual negligence: such negligence cannot be regarded as being the performance of his non-delegable duty.

An occupier of premises owes certain duties under the Occupiers Liability Ordinance towards visitors ... His duties continue to exist ... notwithstanding that he has entrusted some work on the premises to be performed by an independent contractor. ... the independent contractor is also under duty to provide a safe system of work. In a case where an employee of the independent contractor is injured at the premises he may in some situations be allowed to sue the occupier as well as the independent contractor, his employer, who sent him to work there ... (citations omitted).

Another source states that:

> an employer is not liable for the torts of an independent contractor–that is, unless the employer is negligent in his/her own right, for instance, where the employer has "negligently engaged an incompetent contractor, or employed too few men, or had interfered with the way the work had to be carried out or has authorized or ratified the negligent act": *Shan He Electronic Components Co Ltd v Skybo International Food Co Ltd & Another* (2002) HCA 4568 of 2000, per Deputy Judge Gill ... After all, an independent contractor is a completely separate entity, not under the control or supervision of the employer. As a general rule, if one appoints a competent independent contractor to perform a task, the consequences of any injury arising from the contractor's negligence will be borne by the contractor alone.

GLOFCHESKI–TORT, *supra* note 1, at 439 (citation omitted).

> For some types of work delegated by an employer to an independent contractor, the employer may still be found liable for damage caused by the independent contractor's negligence. This occurs only in the category of so-called non-delegable duties, which include operations carried on by the employer on or adjoining a highway that may cause injury to persons using the highway; extra-hazardous activities (a broad, open-ended category); and, in particular, an employer's duty to provide safe working conditions for workers.

GLOFCHESKI–EMPLOYMENT, *supra* note 12, at para. 10.045 (citation omitted).

65. GLOFCHESKI–TORT, *supra* note 1, at 439 notes:

> But it must be pointed out that these exceptions are not really instances of vicarious liability. They are more properly characterised as a personal "non-delegable duty" on the part of the employer to take care in respect of those exposed to the possibility of harm by the work of the employer's independent contractor. It has been described as a "duty to provide that reasonable care is taken" (*The Pass of Ballater* [1942] P 112). It is a personal duty owed by the employer to the plaintiff.

Where a personal duty is owed to another by an employer, that duty cannot be delegated to an independent contractor.[66] Should that other person be injured by the independent contractor's negligence, the employer of the independent contractor would be liable. For example, a hospital's duty to tend to a patient cannot be delegated to a medical professional who is not on the hospital's staff. A school's duty to its pupil is another example of a non-delegable duty where the school may be liable for the negligence of a child who causes injury to another, or for the negligence of a teacher who causes injury to a pupil.[67]

---

66. *Id.* at 439 states that: "It is a personal duty owed by the employer to the plaintiff." *See, e.g.*, 10(2) HALSBURY'S, *supra* note 11, at para. 145.654; GLOFCHESKI–EMPLOYMENT, *supra* note 12, at para. 10.045.

As one source has noted:

> As to the engagement of independent contractors, the rule is that the "employer" may be liable if he has himself been negligent, for example in selecting the contractor, or if he has authorized the tort or if the law imposes upon him a "non-delegable" duty of care, as in the case of inherently hazardous activities.

RICHARD KIDNER, CASEBOOK ON TORTS 239 (11th ed. 2010).

67. As one authority notes:

> Examples of activities for which the defendant will be liable if carried out negligently by the independent contractor to whom the work has been delegated include:
>
> (a) the withdrawal of support from land;
> (b) the escape of dangerous substances which have been brought onto the land (the rule in *Rylands v Fletcher* ...);
> (c) medical treatment provided by a hospital (but administered by doctors as independent contractors);
> (d) a school's supervision of its students;
> (e) an employer's provision of safe working conditions for workers (servants) ...
> (f) operations on (or adjoining) the highway that may cause injury to persons using the highway;
> (g) an occupier's maintenance of premises on the highway;
> (h) extra-hazardous activities (a broad category, which is by no means closed); and
> (i) duties imposed by statute that have been long recognized as non-delegable (an employer's statutory duties under workers' safety legislation being an obvious example).
>
> This list is not exhaustive.
>
> In each of these, the employer will not be absolved from liability to an injured plaintiff merely because he or she had entrusted the work to a competent contractor. It is in this sense that the duty is non-delegable. Both employer and independent contractor are liable.

GLOFCHESKI–TORT, *supra* note 1, at 440.

Dangerous activities may also give rise to non-delegable duties.[68] Where an employer engages in tasks which are dangerous, the employer owes a duty to take reasonable care towards those who may be endangered that the work is performed safely. Conducting a hazardous activity may require the employer to ensure the safety of that activity.

Operations on or adjoining a highway require special duties.[69] Whenever an employer hires an independent contractor to perform work on a building or construction project adjoining a highway, or on the highway itself, the employer is under a non-delegable duty to observe that the work does not endanger the public.

---

68. 10(2) HALSBURY'S, *supra* note 11, at para. 145.655.
25(1) HALSBURY'S, *supra* note 64, at para. 380.050 states:

> An employer who employs an independent contractor to carry out some extra hazardous or unlawful activities cannot relieve himself of any liability for injury or damage caused by the independent contractor in the course of execution of such activities by establishing that he had delegated their performance to the independent contractor or an independent person. In such cases the employer has not merely a duty to take care himself but also a duty to see to it that independent contractor takes care. It is a question of law whether a given duty is non-delegable or not. And the categories of such duties are never closed. The provider or organizer of a service is also being subjected to a non-delegable duty and made liable for negligence of independent contractors who render such service. The employer's liability extends not only to negligence of his independent contractor but he can also be sued for the negligence of his independent contractor's sub-contractor or sub-subcontractor. (citations omitted)

69. 10(2) HALSBURY'S, *supra* note 11, at para. 145.657 explains:

> With regard to roads and highways a distinction must be drawn between the exercise of the public right to pass and trespass, on the one hand, and the execution of work upon the highway, on the other. The employer is not answerable where exercise of his right of passage occasions danger to other persons on the highway owing to the negligence of a contractor, such as a hired driver, a hired drover or motor repairer. Where, however, the employer contracts for the execution of fixed works on the highway or on a navigable river, even though the works themselves are lawful, the employer is liable if a contractor occasions dangers there, for example from heaps of soil, or an open cellar flap, or overhead objects insecurely fixed. The liability is not restricted to persisting dangers in the nature of nuisance, but extends to isolated events, such as the explosion of a benzoline lamp or the falling of a brick.
>
> Even in those cases where the employer is under a personal duty, he is not liable for every negligent act of an independent contractor. The employer is responsible only where the contract which he had made is one by which the employer entrusts any duty to the independent contractor. Again, the employer has been held not liable for damage resulting from the casual or collateral negligence of an independent contractor, or of the latter's employees, while doing the work contracted to be done. (citations omitted)

An employer's liability to its own employees for the acts of an independent contractor may also be non-delegable. An employer who hires an independent contractor to work alongside the employees may be liable to those employees for the negligent acts of the independent contractor.[70]

III. STATUTORY REQUIREMENTS

Differentiation between an employee and an independent contractor is also important in respect of Hong Kong's employment-related legislation, which is designed to protect the employee rather than the independent contractor. This section examines some important provisions of the major employment-related ordinances.[71] This section begins with the ordinance which dictates a minimum wage in Hong Kong. This section continues with the statute regulating payment of wages and employment-related benefits. As the same statute regulates termination of employees, this topic will be analysed next. The fourth and fifth sections address employees' health, safety, and compensation for injuries or death arising from employment. This is followed by the law relating to employees' wages in the event of the bankruptcy of the employer. This section concludes with a review of employment-related ordinances which impact the employee.

A. Minimum Wage Ordinance

The Legislative Council passed the *Minimum Wage Ordinance* (Cap 608)[72] on 17 July 2010. The Secretary for Labour and Welfare appointed 12 November

---

70. *See id.* at para. 145.654.

71. As this work is concerned with presenting an introduction, rather than an in-depth analysis, certain aspects concerning employment law will not be covered. Two areas not covered in this work concern casual and part-time employees, and, children. *See generally* DOWNEY, *supra* note 12, §§C.4–C.18 (discussing employment of children and young persons), C.19–C.22 ("Casual and Part-time Employment"); GLOFCHESKI–EMPLOYMENT, *supra* note 12, for a discussion of these particular areas of employment law.

72. Text of *Minimum Wage Ordinance* (Cap 608) can be found at: *http://www.gld.gov.hk/egazette/pdf/20101429/es12010142915.pdf* (last visited 3 Jan. 2011). Section 2 of this Ordinance provides that "'wages' (工資), subject to section 6, has the same meaning as in the Employment Ordinance (Cap. 57)".
Section 6 of the *Minimum Wage Ordinance* provides:

> (1) A deduction from the wages of an employee made under section 25(3) or 32(2)(b), (c), (d), (e), (f), (g), (h) or (i) of the Employment Ordinance (Cap. 57) in respect of any wage period must be counted as part of the wages payable in respect of that period.

2010 as the day on which the following provisions of the Ordinance came into operation:

- section 1 ("Short title and commencement")
- section 2 ("Interpretation")
- section 16 ("Amendment of Schedule 3"—which specifies the minimum wage)
- Part 3 ("Minimum Wage Commission")
- Schedule 4 ("Minimum Wage Commission")[73]

The remainder of the *Minimum Wage Ordinance*, except those provisions mentioned above, came into operation on 1 May 2011.[74] Schedule 3 has been amended to reflect the prescribed statutory minimum hourly wage of HK$28.00.[75]

With the implementation of the Ordinance, the statutory minimum hourly wage applies to employees with the exception of those categories of workers which are set out in section 7:

> 1. Subject to this section, this Ordinance applies to every employee, his or her employer and the contract of employment under which he or she is engaged.
> 2. This Ordinance does not apply to a person to whom the Employment Ordinance (Cap 57) does not apply because of section 4(2) of that Ordinance or who is engaged under a contract of apprenticeship registered under the Apprenticeship Ordinance (Cap 47).

---

(2) A payment made to an employee in any wage period for any time that is not hours worked by the employee must not be counted as part of the wages payable in respect of that or any other wage period.

(3) An advance or over-payment of wages made to an employee in any wage period must not be counted as part of the wages payable in respect of that period.

(4) A payment of arrears of wages in respect of an earlier wage period made to an employee in any wage period must not be counted as part of the wages payable in respect of the wage period in which it is paid.

(5) Despite subsections (1), (3) and (4), for the purposes of this Ordinance, any commission paid, with the prior agreement of the employee, at any time after the first 7 days of a wage period but before the end of the 7th day immediately after that period must be counted as part of the wages payable in respect of that period irrespective of when the work is done or the commission is otherwise payable under the contract of employment.

73. *http://www.legco.gov.hk/yr10–11/english/subleg/negative/ln146–10-e.pdf* (last visited 3 Jan. 2011).
74. *http://www.legco.gov.hk/yr10–11/english/subleg/brief/145–148_brf.pdf* (last visited 3 Jan. 2011).
75. *Id.*

3. This Ordinance does not apply to a person who is employed as a domestic worker in, or in connection with, a household and who dwells in that household free of charge.
4. This Ordinance does not apply to a student intern.
5. This Ordinance does not apply to a work experience student during a period of exempt student employment.[76]

Another category of employees exempted from the application of this Ordinance is the category of employees with disabilities.[77] The purpose of excluding this category of employees is to prevent discrimination by acknowledging that in certain circumstances, a person's disability would impede production output of the worker. In such a situation, a person with a disability would be disadvantaged in competing with a non-disabled person for the same position.[78] Persons with disabilities may undergo an assessment to determine whether the statutory minimum hourly rate is to apply or a rate proportional to the individual's productivity would apply.[79] Schedule 2 of the Ordinance, "Assessment of Degree of Productivity of PWDS" [殘疾人士], is the primary section pertaining to this assessment.

The application of the provisions of the *Minimum Wage Ordinance* is mandatory. Parties are not allowed to reduce or to eliminate any rights, benefits or protections offered by this Ordinance.[80]

---

76. *Minimum Wage Ordinance*, *supra* note 72, at section 7.
See also id. at section 3.
GLOFCHESKI–EMPLOYMENT, *supra* note 12, at para. 4.006 n. 14 explains:

> A "work experience student" is defined to mean a student who is enrolled in an accredited programme or is resident in Hong Kong and enrolled in a non-local education programme, and who is engaged under a contract of employment at the beginning of which he is under the age of 26. Section 3 of the [*Minimum Wage Ordinance*] provides that, subject to certain conditions, a work experience student may agree with his employer to treat a continuous period of up to 59 days during a contract of employment as a period of exempt student employment.

For the government's position on these exemptions from the application of the Ordinance, *see, e.g.*, *http://archive.news.gov.hk/isd/ebulletin/en/category/ontherecord/090928/html/090928en11002.htm* (last visited 3 Jan. 2011).

77. *See, e.g.*, *http://www.legco.gov.hk/yr10–11/english/panels/mp/papers/mp1216cb2–533-5-e.pdf* (last visited 3 Jan. 2011).
78. *See* GLOFCHESKI–EMPLOYMENT, *supra* note 12, at para. 4.007.
79. *See http://www.legco.gov.hk/yr10–11/english/panels/mp/papers/mp1216cb2–533-5-e.pdf* (last visited 3 Jan. 2011); GLOFCHESKI–EMPLOYMENT, *supra* note 12, at para. 4.007.
80. *Minimum Wage Ordinance*, *supra* note 72, at section 15 states:

> A provision of a contract of employment (whether the contract was entered into before, on or after the commencement of this section) that purports to extinguish or reduce any right, benefit or protection conferred on the employee by this Ordinance is void.

B. Employment Ordinance

The *Employment Ordinance* (Cap 57) is one of the principal statutes regulating the relationship between an employer and an employee. As noted in the introductory section to this legislation, the purpose of the statute is to "provide for the protection of the wages of employees, to regulate general conditions of employment and employment agencies, and for matters connected therewith."[81] As summarized by one authority:

81. The *Employment Ordinance*, *supra* note 2, in particular, contains the following major provisions:

- Contracts Of Employment (Part II, sections 5–11)
- End Of Year Payment (Part IIA, sections 11A–11F)
- Maternity Protection (Part III, sections 12A–15C)
- Rest Days (Part IV, sections 16–21 with section 16 repealed)
- Protection Against Anti-Union Discrimination (Part IVA, sections 21A–21J with sections 21D–21J repealed)
- Payment Of Wages (Part V, sections 22–31)
- Severance Payment (Part VA, sections 31A–31I with sections 31A and 31H repealed)
- Long Service Payments (Part VB, sections 31R–31ZE with section 31X repealed)
- Employment Protection (Part VIA, sections 32A–32Q with section 32H repealed)
- Deduction From Wages (Part VI, section 32)
- Sickness Allowance (Part VII, sections 33–38)
- Holidays With Pay (Part VIII, sections 39–41)
- Annual Leave With Pay (Part VIIIA, sections 41A–41G)
- Liability To Pay Wages Of Sub-Contractor's And Nominated Sub-Contractor's Employees (Part IXA, sections 43A–43M)
- Offence Of Employer's Failure To Pay Any Sum Payable Under Award Of Labour Tribunal Or Minor Employment Claims Adjudication Board (Part IXB, sections 43N–43S)
- Information Respecting Conditions Of Service (Part X, sections 44–46)
- Records, Forms And Returns (Part XI, sections 47–49A)
- Employment Agencies (Part XII, sections 50–62)
- Offences And Penalties (Part XIII, sections 63–65)
- Miscellaneous (Part XIV, sections 66–76)

As many of the terms used in this chapter are found in this Ordinance, some of the terms and their definitions are set out below:

(1) In this Ordinance, unless the context otherwise requires—
"alternative holiday" (另定假日) means a holiday granted or to be granted under section 39(2) and (2A);
"annual leave" (年假) means the annual leave provided for in Part VIIIA;
"annual leave pay" (年假薪酬) means the annual leave pay required by this Ordinance to be paid in respect of a period of annual leave and any sum required to be paid under section 41D;
"business" (業務) includes a trade or profession and any like activity carried on by a person;

"cease" (停止), in relation to Part VA, Part VB, the Third Schedule and the Sixth Schedule, means cease either permanently or temporarily and from whatsoever cause, and "diminish" (縮減) has a corresponding meaning;
"child" (兒童) means a person under the age of 15 years;
...
"confinement" (分娩) means the delivery of a child;
"contract of employment" (僱傭合約) means any agreement, whether in writing or oral, express or implied, whereby one person agrees to employ another and that other agrees to serve his employer as an employee and also a contract of apprenticeship;
...
"domestic servant" (家庭傭工) includes a garden servant, chauffeur and boat-boy and any other personal servant of a like class;
"employee" (僱員) means an employee to whom, by virtue of section 4, this Ordinance applies;
"employer" (僱主) means any person who has entered into a contract of employment to employ any other person as an employee and the duly authorized agent, manager or factor of such first mentioned person;
"holiday" (假日) means—
(a) a statutory holiday;
(b) an alternative holiday;
(c) a substituted holiday; or
(d) a day on which an employee is required by section 39(4) to be granted a holiday;
"holiday pay" (假日薪酬) means the holiday pay provided for by section 40;
...
"Labour Tribunal" (勞資審裁處) means the Labour Tribunal established by section 3 of the Labour Tribunal Ordinance (Cap 25);
"lock-out" (閉廠) has the meaning assigned to it by section 2 of the Trade Unions Ordinance (Cap 332);
"long service payment" (長期服務金) means the long service payment payable by an employer to an employee under section 31R or to a person entitled to such payment under section 31RA;
"mandatory provident fund scheme" (強制性公積金計劃) means a provident fund scheme registered under the Mandatory Provident Fund Schemes Ordinance (Cap 485);
"maternity leave" (產假) means absence from work, in accordance with the provisions of Part III, by a female employee because of her pregnancy or confinement;
"maternity leave pay" (產假薪酬) means pay in respect of maternity leave payable to a female employee under section 14;
...
"occupational retirement scheme" (職業退休計劃) means a scheme or arrangement under which benefits, based on length of service, are payable in respect of employees on retirement, death, incapacity or termination of service, but does not include a mandatory provident fund scheme;

"outworker" (外發工) means a person to whom articles or materials are, for payment or reward, given out to be made up, cleaned, washed, altered, ornamented, finished or repaired, or adapted for sale, in his own home or on other premises not under the control or management of the person who gave out the articles or materials;
"paid sickness day" (有薪病假日) means a sickness day in respect of which an employee is entitled to be paid sickness allowance;
...
"relevant date" (有關日期), in relation to the termination of employment of an employee, means—
(a) where the employee's contract of employment is terminated by notice in accordance with section 6, the date on which that notice expires;
(b) where the employee's contract of employment is terminated by payment in lieu of notice in accordance with section 7, the date up to which such wages are calculated;
(c) where the employee terminates his contract of employment without notice or payment in lieu in accordance with section 10, the date on which termination takes effect;
(d) where the employee is employed under a contract for a fixed term and that term expires, the date on which that term expires;
(e) where a continuous contract of employment specifies an age of retirement and the employee retires at that age, the date of retirement;
(f) where the employee dies, the date of his death; and
(g) where the employee's contract of employment is terminated other than in accordance with the provisions of this Ordinance, the date of termination;
"relevant mandatory provident fund scheme benefit" (有關強制性公積金計劃權益), in relation to an employee, means the accrued benefits of the employee held by the approved trustee of a mandatory provident fund scheme in respect of the employee, but does not include any part of the benefit that is attributable to the contributions paid to the scheme by the employee;
"relevant occupational retirement scheme benefit" (有關職業退休計劃利益), in relation to an employee, means a benefit payable under an occupational retirement scheme on the retirement, death, incapacity or termination of service of the employee, but does not include any part of the benefit that is attributable to the contributions paid to the scheme by the employee
...
"rest day" (休息日) means a continuous period of not less than 24 hours during which an employee is entitled under Part IV to abstain from working for his employer;
"severance payment" (遣散費) means the severance payment payable by an employer to an employee under section 31B(1);
"sickness allowance" (疾病津貼) means the sickness allowance provided for by section 33;
"sickness day" (病假日) means a day on which an employee is absent from his work by reason of his being unfit therefor on account of injury or sickness;
...

The Employment Ordinance (EO) regulates the conditions under which payment of wages and certain other contractual benefits … must be made. It also prescribes the manner and form of wage payments. In order to ensure that wage payments in full are made by employers promptly, the EO sets the parameters within which an employer is entitled lawfully to make deductions from an employee's wages.[82]

"statutory holiday" (法定假日) means a holiday specified as a statutory holiday in section 39(1);
"strike" (罷工) has the meaning assigned to it by section 2 of the Trade Unions Ordinance (Cap 332);
"substituted holiday" (代替假日) means a holiday granted or to be granted under section 39(3);
…
"wage period" (工資期) means the period in respect of which wages are payable under a contract of employment or under section 22;
"wages" (工資) subject to subsections (2) and (3), means all remuneration, earnings, allowances including travelling allowances and attendance allowances, attendance bonus, commission, overtime pay, tips and service charges, however designated or calculated, capable of being expressed in terms of money, payable to an employee in respect of work done or to be done under his contract of employment, but does not include-
…
"week" (星期), for the purposes of section 11 and Parts VA and VB, means the period between midnight on Saturday night and midnight on the succeeding Saturday night;
"young person" (青年) means a person who has attained the age of 15 years but not the age of 18 years.

Id. at section 2(1).
See DOWNEY, *supra note* 12, at §§A.1–A.2 on employment contracts.

82. GLOFCHESKI–EMPLOYMENT, *supra* note 12, at para. 4.001.
For a discussion concerning the payment of wages, *see id.* at paras. 4.041–4.072. For a discussion concerning deduction from wages, *see id.* at paras. 4.073–4.097.

83. Section 4 of the *Employment Ordinance*, *supra* note 2, provides in full:

(1) Subject to subsection (2) and section 69, this Ordinance applies to every employee engaged under a contract of employment, to an employer of such employee and to a contract of employment between such employer and employee.
(2) Subject to Part IVA, this Ordinance does not apply—
  (a) (Repealed 41 of 1990 s. 3)
  (b) to a person who is a member of the family of the proprietor of the business in which he is employed and who dwells in the same dwelling as the proprietor;
  (c) to an employee as defined in the Contracts for Employment Outside Hong Kong Ordinance (Cap 78);
  (d) to a person who is serving under a crew agreement within the meaning of the Merchant Shipping (Seafarers) Ordinance (Cap 478), or on board a ship which is not registered in Hong Kong.
  (e) (Repealed 8 of 1976 s. 49)

Section 4 delineates the application of the Ordinance.[83] Excluding the exceptions set out in this section, the Ordinance "applies to every employee engaged under a contract of employment, to an employer of such employee and to a contract of employment between such employer and employee." This section thus provides coverage to employees and to certain apprentices in the private sector. The Hong Kong government is not considered to be bound by this Ordinance.[84] An employee must normally serve a minimum qualifying period under a continuous contract in order to derive

---

(2A) This Ordinance shall not apply to contracts of apprenticeship registered under the Apprenticeship Ordinance (Cap 47) except to the extent provided in that Ordinance.

(3) For the avoidance of doubt it is hereby declared that the provisions of section 5(3) shall not apply to any contract of employment made before 1 April 1965.

84. One authority puts it thusly:

> In the absence of either an express or an implied term to the contrary, statutory employment provisions do not apply to the Government. As a result, legislation applying to employment protection, labour relations, health and safety, employee training and employee's compensation has not been expressly applied to the Government. By way of limited exception, some provisions have been made expressly applicable to civil servants rather than the Government as such. More usually, legislation will apply to civil servants in their capacity as individuals rather than as agents of the Government. This distinction can in some instances become somewhat finely drawn.

10(2) HALSBURY'S, *supra* note 11, at para. 145.008 (citations omitted).
Another source notes:

> Although the relationship between civil servants and the Government ... is based on the employment contract, the terms of such employment are also governed by various regulations and instructions which come from within the Government departments. While the provisions of the Employment Ordinance do not apply to civil service employment, an increasing number of employment-related Ordinances have been extended to apply to civil servants.
>
> The relationship between civil servants and the Government ... is an employment relationship. ...
>
> ...
>
> Statutory provisions do not apply to the Government ... unless the statute in question has been expressly (or implicitly) applied to the Government: Interpretation and General Clauses Ordinance s 66.
>
> The Employment Ordinance does not apply to the employment of civil servants. In addition, the following enactments have not been expressly applied to the Government ... [*Apprenticeship Ordinance* (Cap 47), *Contracts for Employment Outside Hong Kong Ordinance* (Cap 78), *Employees' Compensation Assistance Ordinance* (Cap 365), *Employees' Compensation Insurance Levies Ordinance* (Cap 411), *Employees' Retraining Ordinance* (Cap 423), *Employment Ordinance* (Cap 57), *Employment of Young Persons at Sea Ordinance* (Cap 58), *Factories and Industrial Undertakings Ordinance* (Cap 59), *Labour Relations*

various entitlements from this Ordinance.[85] Sufficiency of this continuity of contract is determined by the length of employment and the number of hours worked per week.

Section 3(1) defines a continuous contract as "a contract of employment under which an employee is deemed ... to be in continuous employment."[86] An employee is deemed to be in continuous employment if employed under a contract of employment for a period of not less than four weeks, and in each of those weeks has worked eighteen hours or more, while the hours need not be consecutive.[87]

> *Ordinance* (Cap 55), *Labour Tribunal Ordinance* (Cap 25), *Minor Employment Claims Adjudication Board Ordinance* (Cap 453), *Occupational Safety and Health Ordinance* (Cap 509), *Pneumoconiosis (Compensation) Ordinance* (Cap 360), *Protection of Wages on Insolvency Ordinance* (Cap 380), *Trade Union Ordinance* (Cap 332).]
>
> More recently, a number of employment related statutes have been expressly applied to the employment of civil servants. These are ... [*Disability Discrimination Ordinance* (Cap 487), *Employees' Compensation Ordinance* (Cap 282), *Family Status Discrimination Ordinance* (Cap 527), *Personal Data (Privacy) Ordinance* (Cap 486), *Race Discrimination Ordinance* (Cap 602), *Sex Discrimination Ordinance* (Cap 480).]

DOWNEY, *supra* note 12, at §§C.1–C.3.

See also GLOFCHESKI–EMPLOYMENT, *supra* note 12, at para. 2.052, Chapter 15 ("Government Employment Contracts").

85. Workers failing to satisfy the "continuous contract" requirement are entitled only to the basic legal protection:

> Basic entitlements include payment of wages, restrictions on deductions from wages, granting of statutory holidays, protection against anti-union discrimination, and employment protection in respect of unreasonable and unlawful dismissal. Those working under a continuous contract of employment are entitled to further benefits such as rest days, paid statutory holidays, annual leave, sickness allowance, severance payment, long service payment and the like, subject to the specific longevity requirements for each.

GLOFCHESKI–EMPLOYMENT, *supra* note 12, at para. 2.042 n. 122.

86. Section 3 of the *Employment Ordinance*, *supra* note 2, provides in full:

> (1) In this Ordinance, "continuous contract" (連續性合約) means a contract of employment under which an employee is deemed by virtue of the provisions of the First Schedule to be in continuous employment.
>
> (2) In any dispute as to whether a contract of employment is a continuous contract the onus of proving that it is not a continuous contract shall be on the employer.

See generally DOWNEY, *supra* note 12, at §A.22.

87. Paragraphs 2 and 3 of the First Schedule, entitled "Continuous Employment", provide:

> 2. Subject to the following provisions, where at any time an employee has been employed under a contract of employment during the period of 4 or more weeks next preceding such time he shall be deemed to have been in continuous employment during that period.

Periods are calculated in weeks ending on Saturday.[88] If a particular week does not count to an employee's credit, the required continuity is broken and the value of all service prior to the period of discontinuity is lost. Work performed under successive contracts is considered to be continuous, so that an employee's rights are unaffected by promotion or the fact that employment was on a casual, daily basis.[89]

Paragraph 5 of the First Schedule protects employees in the event of a transfer of ownership of the business.[90] Any transfer of business does

---

> 3. (1) For the purposes of paragraph 2, no week shall count unless the employee has worked for 18 hours or more in that week, and in determining whether he has worked in any hour the provisions of sub-paragraph (2) shall apply.
>
> (2) If in any hour the employee is, for the whole or part of the hour-
>
> (a) incapable of work in consequence of sickness or injury; provided that any such incapability in excess of 48 hours is supported by a certificate issued by a registered medical practitioner or registered dentist; or
>
> (b) absent from work in circumstances such that, by law, mutual arrangement or the custom of the trade, business or undertaking, he is regarded as continuing in the employment of his employer for any purpose,
>
> then, save as provided in paragraph 4, that hour shall count as an hour in which he has worked.

Employment Ordinance, *supra* note 2, at Schedule 1.

See generally DOWNEY, *supra* note 12, at §§A.22–A.23 ("Continuous Employment").

88. Schedule 1 states:

> In this Schedule, unless the context otherwise requires-
>
> "lock-out" (閉廠) and "strike" (罷工), respectively, have the meanings assigned to them in the Trade Unions Ordinance (Cap 332);
>
> "week" (星期) means a week ending with Saturday.

Employment Ordinance, *supra* note 2, Schedule 1, at para. 7.

89. *See*, *e.g.*, 10(2) HALSBURY'S, *supra* note 11, at para. 145.058 and cases cited therein. *See also* DOWNEY, *supra* note 12, at §A.22.

The statute provides:

> For the purposes of this Schedule, any reference to hours in which an employee has worked shall mean hours in which he has worked for his employer whether or not the hours were worked under the same or another contract of employment with that employer and whether or not they were consecutive hours.

Employment Ordinance, *supra* note 2, Schedule 1, at para. 6.

90. *Employment Ordinance*, *supra* note 2, Schedule 1, at para. 5 states:

> If a trade, business or undertaking is transferred from one person to another, the period of employment of an employee in the trade, business or undertaking at the time of the transfer shall count as a period of employment with the transferee, and the transfer shall not break the continuity of the period employment..

not break the continuity of service; the period of employment with the former employer counts as a period with the new employer.[91] In the event a business is transferred to an associated company, section 31K of the Ordinance affords similar protection. Again, the employee's continuity of service with both companies is regarded as unbroken. "Two companies shall be taken to be associated companies if one is a subsidiary of the other, or both are subsidiaries of a third company."[92] Section 31E(2)[93] provides that the continuity of an employment contract is unaffected by any lay off where no severance payment has been made.[94]

---

91. *See, e.g.*, DOWNEY, *supra* note 12, at §§A.24–A.28 ("Business Ownership Transfer"); 10(2) HALSBURY'S, *supra* note 11, at para. 145.058.

92. *Employment Ordinance*, *supra* note 2, at section 31K(5) provides:

> For the purposes of this section 2 companies shall be taken to be associated companies if one is a subsidiary of the other, or both are subsidiaries of a third company, and "associated company" (相聯公司) shall be construed accordingly.

93. Section 31E states in full:

> (1) Where an employee is employed under a contract on such terms and conditions that his remuneration thereunder depends on his being provided by the employer with work of the kind he is employed to do, he shall for the purposes of section 31B(1) be taken to be laid off where the total number of days on each of which such work is not provided for him by the employer exceeds-
> (a) half of the total number of normal working days in any period of 4 consecutive weeks; or
> (b) one-third of the total number of normal working days in any period of 26 consecutive weeks,
> and he is not paid a sum equivalent to the wages which he would have earned if work had been provided on the days on which no work was provided.
>
> (1A) Notwithstanding subsection (1), any period during which an employee is not provided with work because of a lock-out by his employer, or as a result of a rest day, a statutory holiday or a day of annual leave, shall not be taken into account as normal working days in determining whether an employee has been laid off.
>
> (2) The continuity of a contract of employment of an employee shall not be treated as broken by any lay-off as a result of which no severance payment has been made.
>
> (3) For the purposes of this Part the "relevant date" (有關日期) in respect of the right of an employee to a severance payment arising by reason of lay-off means any day on which the period of 4 consecutive weeks or 26 consecutive weeks, as the case may be, referred to in subsection (1) has expired.

Id.

94. *See, e.g.*, 10(2) HALSBURY'S, *supra* note 11, at para. 145.058.

Continuous contract status can easily be lost.[95] This status will be lost when an employee works less than 18 hours in any week and the absent hours do not fall within the exceptions provided by law.[96] In any dispute as to whether a contract of employment is a continuous contract, section 3(2) imposes the onus upon the employer of proving that the contract is not a continuous one.[97]

Some benefits under this statute are available regardless of length of service. For example, all employees under a continuous contract are entitled to one statutory rest day in each seven-day period, irrespective of the length of time their continuous contract has existed.[98]

In other instances, service under a continuous contract for a specified time is necessary before an entitlement or benefit becomes available, *e.g.*, maternity leave and holiday pay. Other benefits increase commensurately

---

95. *See, e.g., Fong Anne v Hong Kong Adventist Hospital* [2010] HKEC 985 where the issue was whether the plaintiff was in situation of casual employment or continuous employment. In this case, the court needed to consider the plaintiff's working hours: whether her "stand-by" time was to be included in calculating the minimum 18 hours; and, whether the periods where the plaintiff had no patients and hence no work disrupted the continuous contract requirement.
96. For further discussion, *see, e.g.*, 10(2) HALSBURY'S, *supra* note 11, at para. 145.058 listing exceptions such as illness, injury, or "circumstances such that, by law, mutual arrangement or the custom of the trade, business or undertaking, he is regarded as continuing in the employment of his employer".
    See also GLOFCHESKI–EMPLOYMENT, *supra* note 12, at para. 2.044 and the accompanying n. 129.
97. Section 3 of the *Employment Ordinance* is set out in full in *supra* note 86.
98. As noted by 10(2) HALSBURY'S, *supra* note 11, at para. 145.061:

    > Limited statutory protection extends to all employees in respect of the payment of wages; deduction from wages; rest day entitlement; holiday leave; trade union protection; information concerning employment; and protection from prolonged suspension, irrespective of whether the employment is continuous or not.
    >
    > Employees who are engaged under a continuous contract will be presumed to be employed for a specific duration and entitled to various statutory rights and protection in relation to the minimum notice of termination; protection from wrongful termination; end of year payment protection; and sickness allowance.
    >
    > Other benefits and entitlements will only be awardable where an employee has been continuously employed for a specific period. As a result benefits in the form of maternity leave; protection from termination on taking maternity leave; end of year payment; maternity allowance; annual leave; severance payment; long service payments; paid holidays; and pro rata payments on termination will only be payable to employees who have been continuously employed for a specified duration. (citations omitted)

    See also DOWNEY, *supra* note 12, at §A.22 (explaining that where continuity of service is preserved, an employee is entitled to all statutory benefits).

with the total accumulated amount of continuous service, *e.g.*, sickness allowance and long service payment.[99]

---

99. *See* 10(2) HALSBURY'S, *supra* note 11, at para. 145.061 (citations omitted). *See also* ARJUNAN & NABI BAKSH, *supra* note 16, at 598–600, 629–634.

100. *Employment Ordinance*, *supra* note 2, at section 31B provides in part:

> (1) Where an employee who has been employed under a continuous contract for a period of not less than 24 months ending with the relevant date-
> (a) is dismissed by his employer by reason of redundancy; or
> (b) is laid off within the meaning of section 31E,
> the employer shall, subject to this Part and Part VC, be liable to pay to the employee a severance payment calculated in accordance with section 31G.

Section 31G(1) of the Ordinance provides:

> (1) Subject to this Part, the amount of a severance payment to which an employee is entitled in any case shall be calculated by allowing-
> (a) in the case of a monthly rated employee, two-thirds of this last full month's wages, or two-thirds of $22500, whichever is less; and
> (b) in any other case, 18 days' wages based on any 18 days chosen by the employee and occurring during his last 30 normal working days, or two-thirds of $22500, whichever is less,
> for every year (and pro rata as respects an incomplete year) of employment under a continuous contract by his employer subject in all cases to a maximum payment not exceeding, where the relevant date occurs in a period specified in column 1 of Table A in the Seventh Schedule, the amount specified in column 2 of that table opposite to the period.

In another example of proportional end of year payments, the Ordinance provides in part:

> (2) The proportion of the end of year payment payable under subsection (1) shall be-
> (a) the proportion specified in that behalf in the contract of employment; or
> (b) if a proportion is not so specified, the sum which bears the same proportion to a full month's wages of the employee as his period of service under the contract of employment in the payment period bears to that payment period.
> (3) The proportion of the end of year payment payable under subsection (1) shall become due to the employee-
> (a) under paragraph (a) of that subsection-
> (i) on the day on which the contract of employment terminates; or
> (ii) in the case of a proportion of an end of year payment that falls to be calculated by reference to any profits of the employer, on the day on which the profits of the employer are ascertained; or
> (b) under paragraph (b) of that subsection-
> (i) subject to subsection (4), on the day specified in the contract of employment as the day on which the end of year payment becomes due; or
> (ii) if a day is not so specified, on the last day of the payment period,
> and shall be paid as soon as is practicable but in any case not later than 7 days after that day …

The total length of service defines the extent of some of the entitlements; *e.g.*, redundant workers need two years' continuous service at the date of dismissal to be eligible for severance pay, while the actual amount of severance pay is proportional to the period of continuous employment worked.[100]

The parties cannot contract out of any benefit, right or protection conferred by this Ordinance.[101] Section 70 mandates that "any term of a contract of employment which purports to extinguish or reduce any right, benefit or protection conferred upon the employee by this Ordinance shall be void." Accordingly, only the terms in a contract of employment which attempt to circumvent the statute are invalid. For instance, an agreement in which a company offered to its workers compensation during a six-week closure of its factory was held void by virtue of section 70 of the *Employment Ordinance*. In *Cheung Sau-ching v Fashion Garment Manufactory Ltd* [1988] 2 HKLR 430, the court considered the agreement to be in conflict with the entitlement of the workers under section 31E of the *Employment Ordinance* as the workers were worse off under the agreement. Therefore, the court found the agreement to be void. Likewise, a similar decision was reached by the court in *Hang Fook Lau Seafood Restaurant v Kwok Sik Yuen* [2001] 2 HKC 69 where the employment contract attempted to reduce the employee's statutory entitlement to rest days. The court decided that such an attempt was contrary to section 70.

Section 70 does not apply to the settlement of disputed claims arising out of a contract.[102] Section 8(a) allows either party to a contract to forgo its right to notice or wages in lieu of notice at the time of termination, though not before.[103] An employer may better an employee's minimum statutory

---

> (4) Where the contract of employment of an employee to whom subsection (1)(b) applies is terminated after the expiry of the payment period but before the end of year payment becomes due on the day specified in the contract, the proportion of the end of year payment payable under subsection (1) shall, notwithstanding that a day is so specified, become due to the employee—
> (a) on the day on which the contract of employment terminates; or
> (b) in the case of a proportion of an end of year payment that falls to be calculated by reference to any profits of the employer, on the day on which the profits of the employer are ascertained,
>
> and shall be paid as soon as is practicable but in any case not later than 7 days after that day.

Id. at section 11F.

101. *See generally* GLOFCHESKI–EMPLOYMENT, *supra* note 12, at para. 3.064; DOWNEY, *supra* note 12, at §§B.13-B.14 ("Contracting Out of Minimum Statutory Terms and Conditions").
102. *See* the case of *Lee King v Gammon-Leighton Joint Venture*, LT Appeal 29 of 1982.
103. *Employment Ordinance*, *supra* note 2, at section 8(a) provides:
Nothing in section 6 or 7 shall be taken—

entitlements or agree to qualify or abandon the employer's own statutory rights.

Certain provisions of the Ordinance provide for the parties' employment agreement to be contrary to those provisions, *i.e.*, these matters may be considered to be negotiable. Some other sections permit the parties to negotiate some variation to the statutory requirements, *i.e.*, these matters are regarded as semi-negotiable. The remaining provisions of the Ordinance are mandatory; under the application of section 70, these remaining matters are non-negotiable.[104]

C. Lawful Termination

A contract of employment may be terminated by the following methods:[105]

(1) Agreement: where the contract is for a fixed term or for a particular task, and the fixed term has expired or the task has been

---

(a) to prevent either party to a contract of employment from waiving, at the time notice is required to be given for the purposes of section 6(2), (3) or (3A), his right to notice or to payment in lieu of notice;

104. For example, fully negotiable terms include:

- duration of the employment contract may be agreed upon a different length than month-to-month: section 5(1)
- end-of-year payment (*e.g.*, Chinese New Year bonus): Part IIA (sections 11A-11F)
- annual leave notice: section 41AA(4)

Semi-negotiable terms include:

- duration of manual employee's contract: section 5(3)
- agreement for different termination notice period: section 6(2)
- probationary period: section 6(3A)
- limitations on agreed lay-offs: section 11
- voluntary work on rest days: section 20
- agreement to pay by cash, cheque or autopay: section 26(2)
- alternative or substituted holidays: section 39
- timing for annual leave: section 41AA(3)
- payment in lieu of annual leave days which exceed the statutory ten days: section 41E

See, e.g., Downey, *supra* note 12, at §§A.3 ("Statutory Provisions"), A.16-A.19 (discussing employment terms).

105. For further discussion of termination and related matters, *see, e.g.*, Glofcheski–Employment, *supra* note 12, at Chapter 6 ("Termination of Employment"); 10(2) Halsbury's, *supra* note 11, at paras. 145.532–145.580; Termination & Altering Contract Terms (Milena Hertell, ed., 1999).

For a discussion on remedies for unreasonable dismissal, *see generally* Downey, *supra* note 12, at Part O, ("Termination"); 10(2) Halsbury's, *supra* note 11, at paras. 145.581–145.589, 145.665–145.671.

completed; or, where the parties have mutually agreed to terminate the contract.[106]

The statutory provision may be found in the *Employment Ordinance*, *supra* note 2, at section 31D which states in full:

(1) For the purposes of and subject to this Part, an employee shall be taken to be dismissed by his employer if, but only if—
   (a) the contract under which he is employed is terminated by the employer with or without notice or payment in lieu thereof other than in accordance with section 9;
   (b) where under that contract he is employed for a fixed term, that term expires without being renewed under the same contract; or
   (c) the employee terminates that contract with or without notice or payment in lieu, in circumstances such that he is entitled to terminate it without notice or payment in lieu in accordance with section 10 by reason of the employer's conduct.

(2) An employee shall not be taken for the purposes of this Part to be dismissed by his employer if—
   (a) his contract of employment is renewed, or he is re-engaged by the same employer under a new contract of employment; and
   (b) the renewal or re-engagement takes effect immediately on the ending of his employment under the previous contract.

(3) For the purposes of the application of subsection (2) to a contract under which the employment ends on a rest day or holiday, the renewal or re-engagement shall be treated as taking effect immediately on the ending of the employment under the previous contract if it takes effect on or before the next day after that rest day or holiday.

The text of section 9 of the *Employment Ordinance* may be found at *infra* note 114. Section 10 of the *Employment Ordinance* provides:

An employee may terminate his contract of employment without notice or payment in lieu—
(a) if he reasonably fears physical danger by violence or disease such as was not contemplated by his contract of employment expressly or by necessary implication;
(aa) if—
   (i) he has been employed under the contract for not less than 5 years; and
   (ii) by a certificate in the form specified by the Commissioner under section 49 and issued by a registered medical practitioner, he is certified as being permanently unfit for a particular type of work specified in the certificate for a reason or reasons stated therein; and
   (iii) he is engaged in that type of work under the contract;
(b) if he is subjected to ill-treatment by the employer; or
(c) on any other ground on which he would be entitled to terminate the contract without notice at common law.

106. *See generally* GLOFCHESKI–EMPLOYMENT, *supra* note 12, at paras. 6.004–6.017; DOWNEY, *supra* note 12, at §§B.9-B.10 ("Termination"); 10(2) HALSBURY'S, *supra* note 11, at paras. 145.534–145.535.

(2) Notice,[107] or by payment in lieu of notice:[108] the notice period imposed by agreement, or, as stipulated by statute.

(a) A contract with no fixed duration is ended by reasonable notice under the common law. If a contract of employment is fixed for a particular period only, at common law the contract will end automatically at the expiration of the agreed period.[109]

---

107. *See generally* Glofcheski–Employment, *supra* note 12, at paras. 6.040–6.063; 10(2) Halsbury's, *supra* note 11, at paras. 145.536–145.537.

One source summarizes the procedure as follows:

> The Employment Ordinance allows either party to terminate an employment contract by giving the other party notice of termination. There are four possible situations:
>
> 1. Employment may be terminated by either party giving not less than one month's notice where:
>   - an employee is employed for not less than 18 hours for four or more weeks;
>   - the contract is not for a fixed term; and
>   - the contract makes no express provision for termination by notice.
> 2. Employment may be terminated by one party giving the agreed notice (but not less than seven days' notice) where:
>   - an employee is employed for not less than 18 hours for four or more weeks;
>   - the contract is not for a fixed term; and
>   - the contract makes express provision of not less than seven days' notice for termination by notice.
> 3. Employment may be terminated by the one party giving the agreed notice (but not less than seven days' notice) where:
>   - an employee is employed for not less than 18 hours for four or more weeks;
>   - the contract is for a fixed term; and
>   - the contract makes express provision of not less than seven days' notice for termination by notice.
> 4. Employment may be terminated by one party giving the agreed notice (no minimum) where:
>   - an employee is employed for less than 18 hours every week;
>   - the contract is not for a fixed term; and
>   - the contract makes express provision for termination by notice.

Downey, *supra* note 12, at §B.9.

108. *See generally* Glofcheski–Employment, *supra* note 12, at paras. 6.067–6.082; Downey, *supra* note 12, at §B.9; 10(2) Halsbury's, *supra* note 11, at para. 145.538. *See also* Arjunan & Nabi Baksh, *supra* note 16, at 580–581.

109. Downey, *supra* note 12, at §B.9 states:

> There are at least two types of employment contracts that are not terminable in accordance with the provisions of the Employment Ordinance.
>
> 1. Employment may not be terminated prior to the fixed-term where:
>   - the contract is for a fixed-term; and
>   - the contract makes no express provision for termination by notice.

(b) Section 6(1) provides that either party to a contract of employment may at any time terminate the contract by giving notice (written or verbal) to the other party.[110] Section 6(2) states the notice period required under section 6(1):
- in a contract for one month, renewable from month to month, and which does not make any provision for the length of notice required to terminate—the notice period shall not be less than one month;

---

2. Employment may be terminated by giving reasonable notice at common law where:
   - an employee is employed for less than 18 hours every week; and
   - the contract makes no express provision for termination by notice.

110. Section 6 states:
(1) Subject to subsections (2), (2A), (2B), (3) and (3A) and sections 15 and 33, either party to a contract of employment may at any time terminate the contract by giving to the other party notice, orally or in writing, of his intention to do so.
(2) The length of notice required to terminate a contract of employment shall be—
(a) in the case of a contract which is deemed by ... section 5 to be a contract for 1 month renewable from month to month and which does not make provision for the length of notice required to terminate the contract, not less than 1 month;
(b) in the case of a contract which is deemed by ... section 5 to be a contract for 1 month renewable from month to month and which makes provision for the length of notice required to terminate the contract, the agreed period, but not less than 7 days;
(c) in every other case, the agreed period, but not less than 7 days in the case of a continuous contract.
(2A) Without prejudice to section 41D, annual leave to which an employee is entitled under section 41AA shall not be included under subsection (2) in the length of notice required to terminate a contract of employment.
(2B) The period of maternity leave to which a female employee is entitled under section 12 shall not be included under subsection (2) in the length of notice required to terminate a contract of employment.
(3) Where in any contract of employment, whether in writing or oral, it has been expressly agreed that the employment is on probation and the contract does not make provision for the length of notice required for its termination such contract may be terminated-
(a) by either party at any time during the first month of such employment without notice or payment in lieu;
(b) by either party at any time after the first month of such employment by giving to the other party notice of not less than 7 days.
(3A)Where in any contract of employment, whether in writing or oral, it has been expressly agreed that the employment is on probation and the contract makes provision for the length of notice required for its termination such contract may be terminated-

- in a contract for one month, renewable from month to month, and which makes provision for length of notice—the notice period shall be the agreed period, but not less than seven days;
- in every other case, the agreed period shall be the notice period, but not less than seven days in the case of a continuous contract.

Termination by payment in lieu of notice is found in section 7.[111] Subject to section 33(4B),[112] either party may end the contract without notice by paying a sum equal to the amount of wages which would have accrued to the employee during the notice period required by section 6 of this Ordinance. Either party, having given proper notice, may terminate the contract by agreeing to pay to the other party such proportion of the sum referred to in subsection (1) as is proportionate to the period between the termination of the contract and the time when the given notice would have expired.

(a) notwithstanding the length of notice provided for in the contract, by either party at any time during the first month of such employment without notice or payment in lieu;

(b) by either party at any time after the first month of such employment by giving to the other party notice of the agreed period, but not less than 7 days.

(4) For the purposes of this section the expression "month" (月) means a period of time commencing on the day when notice of termination of a contract of employment is given or when employment begins, as the case may be, and ending at the end of the day before the corresponding date in the following month or, where there is no corresponding date in the following month or where the commencing day is the last day of a month, at the end of the last day of the following month.

Employment Ordinance, *supra* note 2.

111. Section 7 provides in full:

(1) For the purposes of subsections (1A), (1B) and (1C), "wages" (工資) includes any sum paid by an employer in respect of-

(a) a day of maternity leave, a rest day, a sickness day, a holiday or a day of annual leave taken by the employee;

(b) a day of leave taken by the employee with the agreement of his employer;

(c) a normal working day on which the employee is not provided with work;

(d) a day of absence from work of the employee due to temporary incapacity for which compensation is payable under section 10 of the Employees' Compensation Ordinance (Cap 282).

(1A) Subject to sections 15 and 33, either party to a contract of employment may at any time terminate the contract without notice by agreeing to pay to the other party—

(a) where the length of notice required to terminate the contract under section 6 is a period expressed in days or weeks, a sum calculated by multiplying the number of days in the period for which wages would normally be payable to the employee by the daily average of the wages earned by the employee during—
  (i) the period of 12 months immediately before the date on which the party terminating the contract gives notice of the termination to the other party ("date of notification"); or
  (ii) if the employee has been employed by the employer concerned for a period shorter than 12 months immediately before the date of notification, the shorter period; or
(b) where the length of notice required to terminate the contract under section 6 is a period expressed in months, a sum calculated by multiplying the number of months required by the monthly average of the wages earned by the employee during—
  (i) the period of 12 months immediately before the date of notification; or
  (ii) if the employee has been employed by the employer concerned for a period shorter than 12 months immediately before the date of notification, the shorter period.

(1B) In calculating the daily average or monthly average of the wages earned by an employee during the period of 12 months or the shorter period—
(a) any period therein for which the employee was not paid his wages or full wages by reason of—
  (i) any maternity leave, rest day, sickness day, holiday or annual leave taken by the employee;
  (ii) any leave taken by the employee with the agreement of his employer;
  (iii) his not being provided by his employer with work on any normal working day; or
  (iv) his absence from work due to temporary incapacity for which compensation is payable under section 10 of the Employees' Compensation Ordinance (Cap 282); and
(b) any wages paid to him for the period referred to in paragraph (a), are to be disregarded.

(1C) For the avoidance of doubt, if the amount of the wages paid to an employee in respect of a day specified in subsection (1) is only a fraction of the amount earned by the employee on a normal working day, the wages and the day are to be disregarded in accordance with subsection (1B).

(1D) Despite subsection (1A), if for any reason it is impracticable to calculate the daily average or monthly average of the wages earned by an employee in the manner provided in that subsection, the amount may be calculated by reference to the wages earned by a person who was employed at the same work by the same employer during the period of 12 months immediately before the date of notification, or, if there is no such person, by a person who was employed in the same trade or occupation and at the same work in the same district during the period of 12 months immediately before the date of notification.

(2) Either party to a contract of employment, having given proper notice in accordance with section 6, may at any time thereafter terminate the contract by agreeing to pay to the other party such proportion of the sum referred to in subsection (1) as is proportionate to the period between the termination of the contract and the time when the notice given would have expired.

(3) (Repealed 7 of 2007 s. 3)

(4) For the purposes of this section, and notwithstanding any other provision of this Ordinance, the term "wages" (工資)—

(a) includes overtime pay of a constant character or the monthly average of which over a period of 12 months (or if not applicable, such shorter period of employment) immediately preceding the date on which the termination takes effect is equivalent to or exceeds 20% of his monthly average wages during the same period;

(b) except as provided in paragraph (a), shall be deemed not to include overtime pay.

Id.

112. The relevant provisions of this section provide:

(4B) Subject to subsection (4BAA), an employer shall not terminate a contract of employment of an employee otherwise than in accordance with section 9 on any sickness day taken by the employee in respect of which sickness allowance is payable under this section.

(4BAAA) For the purposes of subsections (4BA)(b), (4BAAB) and (4BAAC), "wages" (工資) includes any sum paid by an employer in respect of—

(a) a day of maternity leave, a rest day, a sickness day, a holiday or a day of annual leave taken by the employee;

(b) a day of leave taken by the employee with the agreement of his employer;

(c) a normal working day on which the employee is not provided with work;

(d) a day of absence from work of the employee due to temporary incapacity for which compensation is payable under section 10 of the Employees' Compensation Ordinance (Cap 282).

(4BA) An employer who contravenes subsection (4B) shall be liable to pay to the dismissed employee—

(a) the sum which would have been payable if the contract had been terminated by the employer under section 7; and

(b) a further sum equivalent to 7 times the daily average of the wages earned by the employee during—

(i) the period of 12 months immediately before the date of termination of the contract of employment; or

(ii) if the employee has been employed by the employer for a period shorter than 12 months immediately before the date of termination of the contract, the shorter period.

(4BAAB) In calculating the daily average of the wages earned by an employee during the period of 12 months or the shorter period—

(a) any period therein for which the employee was not paid his wages or full wages by reason of—

(i) any maternity leave, rest day, sickness day, holiday or annual leave taken by the employee;

(ii) any leave taken by the employee with the agreement of his employer;

(3) Summary dismissal: where the employee is guilty of serious misconduct or serious breach of contract.[113] Summary dismissal of an employee is provided for in section 9.[114] An employer may terminate the contract of employment without notice or payment in lieu of notice:

(iii) his not being provided by his employer with work on any normal working day; or

(iv) his absence from work due to temporary incapacity for which compensation is payable under section 10 of the Employees' Compensation Ordinance (Cap 282); and

(b) any wages paid to him for the period referred to in paragraph (a), are to be disregarded.

(4BAAC) For the avoidance of doubt, if the amount of the wages paid to an employee in respect of a day specified in subsection (4BAAA) is only a fraction of the amount earned by the employee on a normal working day, the wages and the day are to be disregarded in accordance with subsection (4BAAB).

(4BAAD) Despite subsection (4BA)(b), if for any reason it is impracticable to calculate the daily average of the wages earned by an employee in the manner provided in that subsection, the amount may be calculated by reference to the wages earned by a person who was employed at the same work by the same employer during the period of 12 months immediately before the date of termination of the employee's contract of employment, or, if there is no such person, by a person who was employed in the same trade or occupation and at the same work in the same district during the period of 12 months immediately before the date of termination of the employee's contract of employment.

(4BAA) An employer who terminates the continuous contract of employment of an employee on any sickness day taken by the employee in respect of which sickness allowance is payable under this section shall be taken for the purposes of subsection (4B) to terminate the contract otherwise than in accordance with section 9—

(a) unless the contrary is proved; or

(b) subject to subsection (4BAB), unless the employer proves that—

(i) he purported to terminate the contract in accordance with that section; and

(ii) at the time of such termination, he reasonably believed that he had a ground to do so.

(4BAB) Subsection (4BAA)(b) shall not apply in the case of civil proceedings.

(4BB) Any employer who contravenes subsection (4B) shall be guilty of an offence and shall be liable on conviction to a fine at level 6.

Id. at sections 33(4B)–33(4BB).

113. *See generally* 10(2) HALSBURY'S, *supra* note 11, at paras. 145.539–145.546. *See also* DOWNEY, *supra* note 12, at §O.13 (listing several common law circumstances, now recognized in the *Employment Ordinance*, allowing an employer to summarily dismiss an employee).

114. This provision provides in full:

(1) An employer may terminate a contract of employment without notice or payment in lieu—

(a) under s 9(1)(a), if an employee, in relation to his employment:
- wilfully disobeys a lawful and reasonable order; or
- misconducts himself, where such conduct is inconsistent with the due and faithful discharge of his duties; or
- is guilty of fraud or dishonesty; or
- is habitually neglectful in his duties; or

(b) under s 9(1)(b), on any other ground on which the employer would be entitled to terminate the contract without notice at common law. This part of subsection (1) is intended to cover all other breaches of duty not already covered by subsection (1)(a).

(4) Resignation without notice: where the employee is guilty of serious misconduct or serious breach of contract.

(5) Wrongful termination:[115] either party may terminate the contract at any time; but wrongful termination entitles the injured party to claim damages for breach of contract under section 8A of the Ordinance.[116] Wrongful termination occurs where a party's termination of the employment is not in accordance with the contract terms, *i.e.*, without serious misconduct on the part of the employer as provided by section 9

(a) if an employee, in relation to his employment—
(i) wilfully disobeys a lawful and reasonable order;
(ii) misconducts himself, such conduct being inconsistent with the due and faithful discharge of his duties;
(iii) is guilty of fraud or dishonesty; or
(iv) is habitually neglectful in his duties; or
(b) on any other ground on which he would be entitled to terminate the contract without notice at common law.

(2) The fact that an employee takes part in a strike does not entitle his employer to terminate under subsection (1) the employee's contract of employment.

Employment Ordinance, *supra* note 2, at section 9.

115. For terminations other than in a manner recognized by law, *see supra* note 105. *See generally* 10(2) HALSBURY'S, *supra* note 11, at paras. 145.548, 145.557.

116. Section 8A states:

(1) Without prejudice to section 9, 10 or 11(2), where a contract of employment is terminated otherwise than in accordance with section 6 or 7, a sum equal to the amount of wages which would have accrued to the employee during the period of notice required by section 7 shall be payable by the party terminating the contract to the other party.

or without giving the required period of notice or payment in lieu or without proper cause.

(6) Operation of law: where external events make it impossible for the employment to continue; or where the employment is rendered illegal; or because of death[117] or insolvency[118] of the employer or the business is transferred to a new owner.[119]

An employer may terminate an employment contract as a form of disciplinary action, except in instances where such action would constitute wrongful termination.[120] Other than regulating the termination of employment contracts, section 11 of the *Employment Ordinance* also provides for suspension from employment for a period not exceeding 14 days, either with pay or without pay, where an employer is entitled to dismiss an employee under section 9.[121] An employer may also suspend an employee

---

> (2) Without prejudice to section 9, 10 or 11(2), where a party to a contract of employment, having given proper notice in accordance with section 6 thereafter terminates the contract before the expiry of the period of notice otherwise than in accordance with section 7, such proportion of the sum equal to the amount of wages which would have accrued to the employee during the period of notice as is proportionate to the period between the termination of the contract and the time when the notice given would have expired shall be payable by the party terminating the contract to the other party.
>
> (3) For the purpose of calculating the sum referred to in subsection (1), where the party terminating the contract has not given notice of the termination to the other party, in calculating the daily average or monthly average of the wages earned by the employee in accordance with section 7, the reference in that section to the date on which the party or to the date of notification is to be constructed as a reference to the date of termination of the contract.

Employment Ordinance, *supra* note 2, at section 8A.
See generally 10(2) HALSBURY'S, *supra* note 11, at paras. 145.665–145.671 for a discussion of damages recoverable for wrongful dismissal.

117. *See generally* 10(2) HALSBURY'S, *supra* note 11, at para. 145.553 ("Dissolution of a partnership"), 145.432 ("Effect of death of employer").
118. *See generally id.* at para. 145.554.
119. *See generally id.* at para. 145.550.
120. *See generally id.* at paras. 145.550–145.557.
121. Section 11 provides:

> (1) Notwithstanding any other provision of this Ordinance or of any other law, an employer may without notice or payment in lieu suspend from employment any employee for a period not exceeding 14 days—
> (a) as a disciplinary measure for any reason for which the employer could have terminated the contract of employment under section 9;
> (b) pending a decision by the employer as to whether or not he will exercise his right to terminate the contract of employment under section 9; or

where criminal proceedings are pending against the employee. Any other form of suspension, even if expressly incorporated into the employment contract, is void under section 70 of the *Employment Ordinance*. Failing to provide work or wages in circumstances not authorized by the contract and the Ordinance will entitle the affected workers to consider themselves dismissed. It will also trigger application of the severance pay provisions.[122]

The employer has limited use of other disciplinary action where the employee's misconduct does not warrant dismissal or suspension. Examples of possible disciplinary action are as follows:

- not granting future pay increases, or delaying the same;
- not granting future promotions;
- withholding a bonus if the contract states that a bonus is at the employer's discretion or that a bonus is subject to overall satisfactory performance and conduct;
- withdrawing fringe benefits; however, this is only possible if the contract provides for this action by the employer; or,
- assigning different duties to the employee, provided the transfer is within the scope of the original employment.

(c) pending the outcome of any criminal proceedings against the employee arising out of or connected with his employment:
Provided that where such criminal proceedings are not concluded within the period of 14 days such suspension may be extended till the conclusion of the criminal proceedings.

(2) An employee who is suspended from employment under subsection (1) may at any time during the period of his suspension, notwithstanding sections 6 and 7, terminate his contract of employment without notice or payment in lieu.

(3) Without prejudice to the provisions of subsection (1), an employer may lay-off an employee for such periods as are expressly agreed in, or may be implied from, the contract of employment.

(4) Notwithstanding subsection (3), the period of lay-off shall in no case exceed-
(a) a total of half of the total number of normal working days in any period of 4 consecutive weeks; or
(b) a total of one-third of the total number of normal working days in any period of 26 consecutive weeks.

Employment Ordinance, *supra* note 2.
See, e.g., GLOFCHESKI–EMPLOYMENT, *supra* note 12, at paras. 6.152–6.156; DOWNEY, *supra* note 12, at §B.47 for further review of this topic.

122. On the topic of severance pay, *see generally* GLOFCHESKI–EMPLOYMENT, *supra* note 12, at paras. 7.095–7.156; DOWNEY, *supra* note 12, at §§B.41–B.42; 10(2) HALSBURY'S, *supra* note 11, at paras. 145.567–145.580.

Warham v Cathay Pacific Airways Ltd [2009] HKEC 1848 involved some of the matters presented above. The defendant airline allegedly dismissed a group of its pilots without cause but with three month's salary in lieu of notice. The pilots contended that their dismissal by the airline was wrongful, alleging that the dismissal was in part the result of the pilots' union activities and in part the result of a breach of their contract's disciplinary and grievance procedures. In the conclusion of its decision, the court found:

(1) Unfair dismissal:-
  (a) The predominant reason for the Plaintiffs' termination by Cathay was their perceived participation in union activities.
  (b) The Plaintiffs were unfairly dismissed.
(2) Wrongful termination:-
  (a) The reasons which Cathay publicly gave when dismissing the Plaintiffs in July 2001 amounted to accusations of 'gross misconduct' within the terms of the contract's disciplinary and grievance procedures.
  (b) The Plaintiffs' employments with Cathay were wrongly terminated since the procedures mandated by the contract's disciplinary and grievance procedures were not followed.

D. Annual Leave

The *Employment Ordinance* provides annual leave with pay to an employee working under a continuous contract for a period of twelve months.[123] Many

123. The provisions of section 41AA of the *Employment Ordinance*, *supra* note 2, stipulate in part:
(1) Subject to this Part, every employee who has been in employment under a continuous contract for not less than 12 months shall, in respect of each leave year, be entitled to paid leave (in this Part referred to as "annual leave") calculated in accordance with subsection (2).
(2) Where an employee has been in employment under a continuous contract for a period specified in column (1) of the Table to this section, the amount of annual leave to which he shall be entitled in respect of any leave year in that period shall be the number of days specified in column (2) of such Table in respect of the period.
(3) Subject to subsection (5)(c), times at which annual leave is granted shall be determined by the employer after consultation with the employee concerned or his representatives.
(4) An employer shall give an employee not less than 14 days' notice in writing of the time he has determined for the grant of a period of annual leave, except where a shorter period of notice is agreed to by the employer and employee.

employees have annual leave benefits which exceed the minimum statutory entitlements. As the Ordinance addresses only minimum entitlements, any annual leave benefits exceeding the Ordinance's minimum will fall outside the statute's regulatory ambit. Therefore, the parties to an employment contract may structure any excess annual leave as they wish.[124]

Annual leave is granted in addition to rest days, holidays and maternity leave to which an employee may be entitled under the Ordinance. Should a rest day or statutory holiday fall within any period of annual leave, another holiday or rest day must be substituted, in accordance with section 41AA(6) of the *Employment Ordinance*.[125]

If at the commencement of a scheduled annual leave, an employee suffers a total incapacity through illness or injury, the period of such incapacity is not calculated as part of the annual leave entitlement. In these situations, an employee can defer the annual leave until after the employee has recovered.

---

(5) Annual leave to which an employee is entitled—
  (a) shall be granted by his employer and be taken by the employee within the period of 12 months beginning immediately after the expiration of the leave year to which it relates;
  (b) subject to paragraph (c), shall be for an unbroken period; and
  (c) subject to subsection (9), shall, if the employee so requests his employer, be divided as follows—
    (i) where the leave entitlement does not exceed 10 days, it shall be granted on consecutive days except that not more than 3 days of the period of leave may be granted on any day or days (whether consecutive or not); and
    (ii) where such entitlement exceeds 10 days, 7 days of the period of leave shall be granted on consecutive days and the remaining leave may be granted on any day or days (whether consecutive or not).

(6) If a rest day or holiday falls within any period of annual leave granted in accordance with this section, it shall be counted as annual leave and another rest day or holiday shall be substituted in accordance with section 18(5) or section 39(2), (2A), (3) or (4), as the case may require.

(7) No period of total incapacity for work by reason of sickness or injury occurring during a period of annual leave shall count as part of that annual leave unless it commences after the commencement of the period of annual leave.

...

(10) For the avoidance of doubt it is declared that annual leave is, and shall be granted, in addition to the rest days, holidays and maternity leave to which an employee is entitled under this Ordinance.

See also Arjunan & Nabi Baksh, *supra* note 16, at 597–598.

124. Downey, *supra* note 12, at §B.17.

125. The provisions of section 41AA of the *Employment Ordinance* can be found in *supra* note 123.

Note that if the incapacity arises after the commencement of the annual leave, the sick days will be considered to be part of the annual leave.[126]

Section 67[127] of the *Employment Ordinance* provides that if an employer intends to leave Hong Kong in order to evade payment of monies owed to any of its employees under a contract of employment, an employee may petition the District Court to issue an arrest warrant for the employer.[128] In addition to the arrest power conferred under section 67, it may also be possible to restrain an employer by a *Mareva* injunction from removing assets outside the jurisdiction.[129]

In order to prevent malicious applications, section 67(2) of the Ordinance stipulates that an employee must have reasonable cause before applying for a warrant under section 67(1). Section 63(3)[130] imposes criminal liability on wilful contravention of section 67(2) and any person convicted of this offence is liable to a fine.

An employee's burden in a section 67 action is to persuade the court that the sole reason for the employer's relocation from Hong Kong is its intention to avoid the payment of wages or other monies owed under the employment contract. Section 67 is infrequently used because this requirement is a heavy burden upon the employee.[131]

---

126. Section 41AA(7) of the *Employment Ordinance*, *supra* note 2.
127. The full text of this provision follows:

    > (1) If an employer or former employer is about to leave Hong Kong with intent to evade payment of—
    > (a) any wages earned by any of his employees and owed by the employer, whether or not the payment of such wages is yet due; or
    > (b) any other moneys owed by the employer under a contract of employment to any of his employees,
    > any of his employees may apply to a District Judge to issue a warrant in accordance with the Second Schedule, and in respect of any such application the Second Schedule shall apply.
    > (2) No person shall make an application under subsection (1) unless he has reasonable grounds for making such application.

    Id. at section 67.
128. *See id.* at Schedule 2 "Procedure for Apprehension of Absconding Employer".
129. A Mareva injunction (also known as a freezing order) is an order prohibiting the defendant from disposing of its assets so as to avoid the risk of having to satisfy a judgment. It is named after the case *Mareva Compania Naviera SA v International Bulk Carriers SA* [1980] 1 All ER 213. For an example of invoking a Mareva injunction against an employer, *see* the case of *Ireland v Canton Fitzgerald (HK) Ltd* [1988] 1 HKC 493.
130. This section provides: "Any person who wilfully contravenes section 67(2) shall be guilty of an offence." *Employment Ordinance*, *supra* note 2, at section 63(3).
131. HONG KONG STAFF EMPLOYMENT MANUAL, vol. 1, 1 (Robert Lewington, gen. ed., 4th ed. 1997) [hereinafter LEWINGTON]. *See generally* DOWNEY, *supra* note 12.

E. Health and Safety Related Ordinances

In regards to this subject, this section reviews the three main statutes affecting work place safety.[132] The first of these laws is the *Occupational Safety and Health Ordinance* (Cap 509) which comprises 51 sections and five Schedules, although three sections and two Schedules are omitted as spent. This Ordinance applies to the Hong Kong government although the government and its officers are not liable to prosecution for contraventions of this statute.[133]

The rationale of this legislation is found in section 2:

(a) to ensure the safety and health of employees when they are at work;
(b) to prescribe measures that will contribute to making the workplaces of employees safer and healthier for them;
(c) to improve the safety and health standards applicable to certain hazardous processes, plant and substances used or kept in workplaces;
(d) generally to improve the safety and health aspects of working environments of employees.

This Ordinance applies to employees at the workplace rather than independent contractors.[134]

---

132. For an in-depth review of occupational safety and health in Hong Kong, *see, e.g.*, GLOFCHESKI–EMPLOYMENT, *supra* note 12, at Chapter 9 ("Health and Safety at Work I–The Safety Legislation Regime, the Inspectorate, Enforcement and Penalties"), Chapter 10 ("Health and Safety at Work II–Civil Liabilities"), Chapter 11 ("Health and Safety at Work III–Statutory Compensation for Work-Related Injury, Disease and Death"); DOWNEY, *supra* note 12, at Part K ("Health and Safety"); THE HANDS ON GUIDE: OSH LEGAL GUIDE: HONG KONG (2002); *Occupational Safety and Health Ordinance* (Cap 509) sections 6(1)-6(2).
See also Ian Wolfe, *Those Were the Days … A brief account on OSH development in Hong Kong after World War II* at *http://www.hkosha.org.hk/Paper%201st.pdf* (last visited 3 March 2011).

133. *Occupational Safety and Health Ordinance*, *supra* note 132, at section 5 provides:

> (1) This Ordinance binds the Government.
> (2) Neither the Government nor any public officer in the officer's capacity as such is liable to be prosecuted for an offence against this Ordinance.

See also id. at section 28.
For in-depth analysis of the *Occupational Safety and Health Ordinance*, *supra* note 132, and the Occupational Safety and Health Regulation (Cap 509A), *see* GLOFCHESKI–EMPLOYMENT, *supra* note 12, at paras. 9.011–9.042; DOWNEY, *supra* note 12, at Part K ("Health and Safety").

134. The exception is found in the *Occupational Safety and Health Ordinance*, *supra* note 132, at section 4:

> This Ordinance applies to independent contractors and self-employed persons only in their capacity as employers or as occupiers of premises where workplaces are located.

For the sake of completeness, some of the relevant provisions pertaining to interpretation of the Ordinance are set out below. Note the overlap with tort law concepts such as strict liability and occupier's liability.

(1) In this Ordinance, unless the context otherwise requires—

"activity" (活動) includes operation and process;

...

"bodily injury" (身體傷害) includes injury to health;

...

"dangerous occurrence" (危險事故) means an occurrence of a kind specified in Schedule 1;

"domestic premises" (住宅處所) means premises occupied as a private dwelling;

"domestic servant" (家庭傭工) has the same meaning as in the Employment Ordinance (Cap 57);

"employee" (僱員) means a natural person who works under a contract of employment or apprenticeship, but does not include a domestic servant;

"employer" (僱主) means a person who employs natural persons under contracts of employment or apprenticeship;

"function" (職能) includes a power and a duty;

...

"occupier" (佔用人), in relation to any premises or workplace, includes a person who has any degree of control over the premises or workplace and, in particular, includes a person to whom subsection (5) or (6) applies;

"offence of strict liability" (嚴格法律責任罪行) means an offence in relation to the prosecution of which it is not necessary for the prosecutor to prove-

(a) that the defendant did the act or omission constituting the offence intentionally, knowingly or recklessly; or

(b) that the defendant had knowledge of any specific ingredient of the offence;

"person responsible" (負責人), in relation to a workplace, has the meaning given by subsection (2);

"plant" (作業裝置) includes machinery, equipment, appliances, furniture, furnishings and fittings;

"premises" (處所) includes any vehicle and any public place, and also includes a part of particular premises;

...

"public place" (公眾地方) means-

(a) any public street, pier or public garden; or

(b) the permanent way of a railway; or

(c) any part of the territorial sea or any publicly navigable waterway; or

(d) any part of the airspace above Hong Kong; or

(e) any other place to which people are entitled to have access whether with or without payment;

...

"serious bodily injury" (嚴重身體傷害), in relation to a person, includes any bodily injury that results in the person's admission at a hospital or clinic for treatment or observation;

"substance" (物質) means a natural or artificial substance, whether in the form of a solid, liquid, gas or vapour;

. . .

"work" (工作) means work as an employee;

"workplace" (工作地點) means any place where employees work, but does not include any of the following-

(a) an aircraft or vessel when located in a public place;

(b) when a vehicle that is designed or used for the carriage of people, animals or goods is located in a public place, the seat or position normally occupied by the driver of the vehicle;

(c) domestic premises at which the only employees are domestic servants;

(d) a place at which only self-employed persons work;

(e) any other place of a kind prescribed by a regulation for the purposes of this paragraph;

"workplace code of practice" (工作地點工作守則) means a code of practice issued under section 40(1) and, if such a code has been amended, means the code as amended.

(2) For the purposes of this Ordinance, the person responsible for a workplace is the employer of the employees who are employed to carry out work there, or if the employer does not exercise any degree of control over the relevant part or aspect of the workplace, means the occupier of the workplace.

(3) For the purposes of this Ordinance, risks arising out of the activities of persons at work are taken to include risks attributable to the manner of conducting an undertaking, risks attributable to the plant or substances used in connection with an undertaking and risks attributable to the condition of premises so used.

(4) For the purposes of this Ordinance, a person is at work only during the time when the person is actually at a workplace. However, a person is not to be regarded as being at work at a workplace for those purposes when the person is being conveyed as a passenger in a vehicle referred to in paragraph (b) of the definition of "workplace" in circumstances no different from those applicable to persons being so conveyed who are not at work at a workplace.

(5) A person who, under a lease or contract, has an obligation for—

(a) the maintenance or repair of premises; or

(b) the safety of, or the absence of risks to health arising from the condition or use of, any plant or substance located on premises,

is taken to be an occupier of the premises for the purposes of this Ordinance.

(6) A person who, under a lease or contract, has an obligation to provide, maintain or repair a means of access to, or egress from, premises is taken to be an occupier of the premises for the purposes of this Ordinance.

(7) Subsections (5) and (6) do not apply to persons in their capacity as occupiers of domestic premises.

Id. at section 3. The definitions of the other terms used in this Ordinance may be found in sections 17 and 22 thereof.

Part II of the Ordinance, entitled "Responsibility for Safety and Health of Employees at Work", comprising three sections, imposes health and safety obligations upon the employer, occupier of the workplace and the employees, respectively. For example, Section 6 of Part II requires an employer, so far as is reasonably practicable, to guarantee its employees' health and safety.[135] The following section imposes, so far as is reasonably practicably, similar safety requirements upon an occupier of a building in which the workplace is located, namely, that the building and the machinery therein offer no threats to the employees' health and safety.[136] Finally, Section 8 of Part II mandates that employees at work are to take care for their own safety and the safety of others at the work site, and, to cooperate with the employer in relation to health and safety matters.[137]

---

135. *Id.* at section 6 provides in part:

(1) Every employer must, so far as reasonably practicable, ensure the safety and health at work of all the employer's employees.

(2) The cases in which an employer fails to comply with subsection (1) include (but are not limited to) the following—

(a) a failure to provide or maintain plant and systems of work that are, so far as reasonably practicable, safe and without risks to health;

(b) a failure to make arrangements for ensuring, so far as reasonably practicable, safety and absence of risks to health in connection with the use, handling, storage or transport of plant or substances;

(c) a failure to provide such information, instruction, training and supervision as may be necessary to ensure, so far as reasonably practicable, the safety and health at work of the employer's employees;

(d) as regards any workplace under the employer's control—

(i) a failure to maintain the workplace in a condition that is, so far as reasonably practicable, safe and without risks to health; or

(ii) a failure to provide or maintain means of access to and egress from the workplace that are, so far as reasonably practicable, safe and without any such risks;

(e) a failure to provide or maintain a working environment for the employer's employees that is, so far as reasonably practicable, safe and without risks to health.

136. The pertinent sub-section provides:

(1) If an employee's workplace is located on premises that are not under the control of the employee's employer, the occupier of the premises must ensure that—

(a) the premises; and

(b) the means of access to and egress from the premises; and

(c) any plant or substances kept at the premises,

are, so far as reasonably practicable, safe and without risks to health.

Occupational Safety and Health Ordinance, supra note 132, at section 7.

137. *Id.* at section 8 which provides in part:

(1) An employee while at work—

(a) must, so far as reasonably practicable, take care for the safety and health of persons (including the employee) who are at the employee's workplace and who may be affected by the employee's acts or omissions at work; and

This section now reviews several other pieces of legislation which pertain to health and safety related matters: the *Factories and Industrial Undertakings Ordinance* (Cap 59) and some of the ordinances related to payment for an employee's illness, injury or demise, *e.g.*, *Employment Ordinance* (Cap 57). The former, similar to the *Occupational Safety and Health Ordinance*, regulates general health and safety issues, while the latter ordinances relate to compensation for accidents causing sickness, injury or mortality.

Another legislative scheme concerning health and safety generally is found in the *Factories and Industrial Undertakings Ordinance* (Cap 59) and in the regulations made under section 7 of this Ordinance.[138] The Labour

---

(b) as regards any requirement imposed in the interests of safety or health on the employee's employer or any other person by this or any other Ordinance, must, so far as reasonably practicable, co-operate with the employer or other person so far as may be necessary to enable the requirement to be complied with.

138. Section 7(1) of the *Factories and Industrial Undertaking Ordinance* (Cap 59) provides in part:

(1) The Commissioner may in respect of industrial undertakings by regulation prescribe or provide for—
(a) prohibiting or controlling the employment of all persons or any class of persons in dangerous trades or scheduled trades;
(b) prohibiting or controlling the employment of women, young persons and children in industrial undertakings, and requiring registers to be kept of women, young persons and children employed in industrial undertakings;
(c) imposing obligations for securing compliance with the provisions of this Ordinance upon persons who employ women, young persons or children in industrial undertakings and upon the agents and servants of such persons;
(d) defining the duties and powers of all officers appointed under section 3;
(e) exempting any industrial undertaking from the operation of this Ordinance or any part thereof;
(f) the forms to be used for the purposes of this Ordinance and the manner of publishing such forms;
(g) means of securing hygienic conditions;
(h) means of ensuring the safety of persons in industrial undertakings and of relieving persons suffering from the effects of accidents in industrial undertakings;
(i) means of securing the removal of any danger or defect;
(j) requiring notifications to be made in relation to accidents and such dangerous occurrences as may be specified in the regulations;
(k) precautions to be taken against fire and providing for means of escape from fire;
(l) the taking for purposes of analysis of samples of materials or substances used or handled;

Department's Occupational Safety Service, formerly the Factory Inspectorate Division, enforces the *Factories and Industrial Undertakings Ordinance* and its subsidiary regulations. The Service seeks to ensure the safety, health and welfare of workers through the enforcement of law, through education and through publicity. The Occupational Safety and Health Training Centre, formerly the Industrial Safety Training Centre, is operated by the Service and proffers training courses occupational safety and health.

The *Factories and Industrial Undertakings Ordinance* requires every proprietor to ensure the health and safety at work of all those employed in an industrial undertaking. A general duty is also levied on employees to avoid harming others. These statutory duties, unlike those imposed by the common law, are fortified by criminal penalties. These obligations are similar to those imposed by the *Occupational Safety and Health Ordinance*.

Paralleling Section 6 of the *Occupational Safety and Health Ordinance*, Section 6A(1) of the *Factories and Industrial Undertakings Ordinance* imposes a duty upon every proprietor of an industrial undertaking to ensure, so far as is reasonably practicable, the health and safety at work of all persons employed at the industrial undertaking. Section 6A(2) extends this accountability to include the following obligations:

(m) requiring notifications to be made in relation to the occurrence amongst person who have been or are employed in industrial undertakings of such diseases as may be specified in such regulations;

(n) requiring the medical inspection by a Health Officer or by a medical practitioner employed by the proprietor of the industrial undertaking concerned of any person or of any class of person employed or intended to be employed in any industrial undertaking, and the keeping of records of any such inspections;

(o) imposing duties on proprietors, contractors and persons employed;

(oa) without prejudice to the generality of paragraph (o), requiring proprietors and contractors (including any class of proprietors and contractors)—

(i) to develop, implement and maintain any management system that relate to the safety of personnel in their industrial undertakings;

(ii) to prepare and revise safety policy statements in relation to the general safety policy of their industrial undertakings and make such statements available to persons employed;

(iii) to establish safety committees to identify, recommend and review measures to improve the safety and health of persons employed;

(iv) to employ, or otherwise use the services of, persons specified in regulations made under this section to assess the effectiveness of any management system referred to in subparagraph (i) as implemented;

...

- the provision and maintenance of plant and systems of work that are, so far as is reasonably practicable, safe and without risks to the health of the workers;
- the procedures for ensuring, so far as is reasonably practicable, the safe use, handling, storage and transport of articles and substances;
- the dissemination of such information, training and supervision as is necessary to ensure, so far as is reasonably practicable, the health and safety of employees;
- the maintenance of any part of an industrial undertaking controlled by the proprietor in a condition that is safe and without risks to health and the provision and maintenance of access to and egress from it that are safe and without such risks, so far as is reasonably practicable;
- the provision and maintenance of a working environment for all employees that is, so far as is reasonably practicable, safe and without risks to health.

Note that the duty imposed under section 6A of this Ordinance is not absolute, as the duty is qualified by the phrase "so far as is reasonably practicable."[139]

---

139. Section 6A of the *Factories and Industrial Undertakings Ordinance*, *supra* note 138, states:

(1) It shall be the duty of every proprietor of an industrial undertaking to ensure, so far as is reasonably practicable, the health and safety at work of all persons employed by him at the industrial undertaking.

(2) Without prejudice to the generality of a proprietor's duty under subsection (1), the matters to which that duty extends include in particular—

(a) the provision and maintenance of plant and systems of work that are, so far as is reasonably practicable, safe and without risks to health;

(b) arrangements for ensuring, so far as is reasonably practicable, safety and absence of risks to health in connection with the use, handling, storage and transport of articles and substances;

(c) the provision of such information, instruction, training and supervision as is necessary to ensure, so far as is reasonably practicable, the health and safety at work of all persons employed by him at the industrial undertaking;

(d) so far as is reasonably practicable as regards any part of the industrial undertaking under the proprietor's control, the maintenance of it in a condition that is safe and without risks to health and the provision and maintenance of means of access to and egress from it that are safe and without such risks; and

(e) the provision and maintenance of a working environment for all persons employed by him at the industrial undertaking that is, so far as is reasonably practicable, safe, and without risks to health.

(3) Subject to subsection (4), a proprietor of an industrial undertaking who contravenes this section commits an offence and is liable to a fine of $500000.

Section 6B(1) provides that it is an offence for every person employed at an industrial undertaking to fail to take reasonable care for the health and safety of themselves or of others while in the course of employment.[140] The employee should also co-operate with the proprietor so far as necessary to enable the duty or requirement securing health and safety at the industrial undertaking to be observed. The failure to use or the wilful misuse of safety equipment constitutes a separate offence under Regulation 21(1) of the Factories and Industrial Undertakings Regulations (Cap 59A).[141]

---

(4) A proprietor of an industrial undertaking who contravenes this section wilfully and without reasonable excuse commits an offence and is liable to a fine of $500000 and to imprisonment for 6 months.

See also the *Occupational Safety and Health Ordinance*, *supra* note 132, at sections 6 and 7 which contain near identical phraseology.

The *BLIS Glossary*, *supra* note 1, translates "so far as is reasonably practicable" as 在合理地切實可行的範圍內.

140. Section 6B stipulates:

(1) It shall be the duty of every person employed at an industrial undertaking while at work—

(a) to take reasonable care for the health and safety of himself and of other persons who may be affected by his acts or omissions at work; and

(b) as regards any duty or requirement imposed on a proprietor of the industrial undertaking or on any other person by this Ordinance for securing the health and safety of persons employed at the industrial undertaking, to co-operate with him so far as is necessary to enable that duty or requirement to be performed or complied with.

(2) A person who contravenes subsection (1) commits an offence and is liable to a fine at level 4.

(3) A person employed at an industrial undertaking who wilfully and without reasonable excuse does anything while at work likely to endanger himself or other persons commits an offence and is liable to a fine of $50000 and to imprisonment for 6 months.

Factories and Industrial Undertakings Ordinance, *supra* note 138.

Similar language is found in the *Occupational Safety and Health Ordinance*, *supra* note 132, at section 8.

141. Regulation 21 of the Factories and Industrial Undertakings Regulations (Cap 59A) provides:

(1) No person employed in an industrial undertaking shall wilfully interfere with or misuse any means, appliance, convenience or other thing provided in pursuance of the Ordinance for securing the health, safety or welfare of the persons employed in the industrial undertaking, and where any means or appliance for securing health or safety is provided for the use of any such person under the Ordinance, he shall use the means or appliance.

(2) (Repealed 71 of 1989 s. 13)

Section 7 empowers the Commissioner for Labour to make detailed rules relating to, among others: the control or regulation of dangerous trades; the regulation of the industrial employment of women, young persons and children; the assurance that precautions are taken in relation to safety, welfare and hygiene, including fencing, cleanliness, ventilation and lighting; the imposition of duties on proprietors, contractors and persons employed; and, the requirement of notification of accidents, dangerous occurrences and specified industrial diseases.[142] Construction work must be notified separately under Part VIII of the Construction Sites (Safety) Regulations.[143] Section 7(4) of the Ordinance authorises the Commissioner to demand the adoption of special precautions in addition to any precautions required by any regulation.[144]

In relation to an employee's illness, Section 33 of the *Employment Ordinance* stipulates that a sickness allowance shall accrue at the rate of two paid sickness days for each completed month of an employee's employment under a continuous contract with the employer during the first 12 months of such employment; and four paid sickness days for each such month thereafter, and may be accumulated from time to time up to a maximum of 120 paid sickness days.[145]

---

142. A portion of section 7 of the *Factories and Industrial Undertaking Ordinance* is set out *supra* note 138.
143. *See, e.g.*, regulation 56 of the Construction Sites (Safety) Regulations, *supra* note 36.
144. Sections 7(4) and 7(4A) of the Ordinance state:

> (4) The Commissioner in such cases as he shall think fit may, for such period and subject to such conditions as he may specify, exempt any industrial undertaking from any regulation made under this Ordinance and the Commissioner, or any officer authorized in writing by him, may order the adoption of special precautions in addition to any precautions required by any regulation made under this Ordinance.
>
> (4A) Any person aggrieved by an exemption or order made under subsection (4) may, within 28 days of being notified of such exemption or order, appeal to the Administrative Appeals Board.

Factories and Industrial Undertakings Ordinance, *supra* note 138.

145. The relevant portion of the law specifies:

> (2) Subject to subsection (2A), an entitlement to sickness allowance shall accrue at the rate of—
> (a) 2 paid sickness days for each completed month of the employee's employment under the continuous contract with his employer during the first 12 months of such employment; and
> (b) 4 paid sickness days for each such month thereafter,
> and may be accumulated from time to time up to a maximum of 120 paid sickness days.

Section 33(4B) of the *Employment Ordinance* provides that an employer shall not terminate an employee's contract of employment on any day that sick leave is taken by the employee.[146] Any employer who contravenes section 33(4B) shall be guilty of an offence and shall be liable on conviction to a fine.[147] This section is intended to protect an employee's interest by preventing the employer from dismissing an employee merely due to illness.

Employees' compensation or sickness allowance generally is paid in the event of an employment-related injury. Where compensation is payable under the *Employees' Compensation Ordinance*, section 33(5)(e) of the *Employment Ordinance* excludes the payment of a sickness allowance.[148] The payment of a sickness allowance under the *Employment Ordinance* depends upon an employee's continuity of service. The payment of compensation under the *Employees' Compensation Ordinance* does not depend upon an employee's continuity of service.

Section 15 of the *Employees' Compensation Ordinance*[149] and paragraph 4 of the Employees' Compensation Regulations[150] also impose obligations upon the employer to report injuries or deaths to the Commissioner of Labour. The failure to meet these reporting obligations amounts to an offence and may result in a possible fine.

> (2A) In the case of an employee who has been employed by his employer under a continuous contract for a period of 1 month or more immediately preceding the commencement of the Employment (Amendment) Ordinance 1983 (57 of 1983), the employee's entitlement to sickness allowance shall, with effect from and without prejudice to the entitlement to sickness allowance accrued at such commencement, accrue at the rate prescribed by subsection (2) as amended by that Ordinance, and his employment for part of a month (if any) at such commencement shall be taken into account in calculating his entitlement to sickness allowance under and at the rate prescribed by that subsection.

Employment Ordinance, *supra* note 2, at sections 33(2) and 33(2A).

146. The relevant provisions of *id.* at section 33 can be found in *supra* note 112.
147. *Id.* at section 33(4BB), the text of which is set out *supra* note 112.
148. *Id.* at section 33(5)(e) provides:

> An employer shall not be liable to pay sickness allowance to an employee in respect of any sickness day—
>
> ...
>
> (e) if the unfitness for work of the employee is on account of an injury or occupational disease in respect of which compensation is payable in accordance with the Employees' Compensation Ordinance (Cap 282)

149. *See* DOWNEY, *supra* note 12, at §§K.142-K.146 (delineating the circumstances under which notice to the Commissioner of Labour must be made, the time limits for notice to be given, and the particulars of the notice). Section 15 of the *Employees' Compensation Ordinance*, *supra* note 2, states in part:

(1) Notice of any accident which results in the death of the employee within 3 days after the accident shall be given in the prescribed form to the Commissioner by the employer not later than 7 days after the accident irrespective of whether the accident gives rise to any liability to pay compensation.

(1A) Notice of any accident which results in the total or partial incapacity of the employee shall be given to the Commissioner by the employer not later than 14 days after the accident, irrespective of whether the accident gives rise to any liability to pay compensation, and shall be given—

(a) in the prescribed form, if the accident results in the total or partial incapacity of the employee for a period exceeding 3 days immediately following the accident; or

(b) in the form specified by the Commissioner, if the accident results in the total or partial incapacity of the employee for a period not exceeding 3 days immediately following the accident.

(1B) If the happening of such accident was not brought to the notice of the employer or did not otherwise come to his knowledge within such periods of 7 and 14 days respectively referred to in subsections (1) and (1A) then such notice shall be given not later than 7 days or, as may be appropriate, 14 days after the happening of the accident was first brought to the notice of the employer or otherwise came to his knowledge.

(1BA)Where—

(a) an employer has given notice of an accident in the form specified by the Commissioner for the purposes of subsection (1A)(b); and

(b) the total or partial incapacity of the employee resulting from the accident extends beyond the period referred to in that subsection,

the employer shall give further notice of the accident to the Commissioner in the form prescribed for the purposes of subsection (1A)(a) not later than 14 days after the extension of the incapacity beyond the period referred to in subsection (1A)(b) was first brought to the notice of the employer or otherwise came to his knowledge.

...

(2) When the death of an employee in any circumstances other than those specified in subsection (1) is brought to the notice of, or comes to the knowledge of, his employer, the employer shall, not later than 7 days after the death, give notice thereof in the prescribed form to the Commissioner, irrespective of whether the death gives rise to any liability to pay compensation:

Provided that if the death was not brought to the notice of the employer or did not otherwise come to his knowledge within such period of 7 days then such notice shall be given not later than 7 days after the death was first brought to the notice of the employer or otherwise first came to his knowledge.

(2A) The notice of accident referred to in subsections (1), (1A) and (2) shall contain such matters relating to the accident, the employer, the employee, any compensation agreed, paid or payable, and any matters incidental thereto as may be prescribed or, where the notice of accident is required to be given in the form specified by the Commissioner for the purposes of subsection (1A)(b), as may be specified by the Commissioner.

150. Regulation 4 of the Employees' Compensation Regulations (Cap 282A) states:

Notice of an accident required by section 15(1), (1A)(a), (1B), (1C) or (2) of the Ordinance to be given by an employer to the Commissioner for Labour shall be in writing and—

Where a person becomes deceased, an action may be brought for the benefit of or against the deceased's estate under section 20 of the *Law Amendment and Reform (Consolidation) Ordinance* (Cap 23).[151] Damages may be awarded for:

- the deceased's pain and suffering;
- funeral expenses; and,
- loss of earnings to the time of death, and the value of any savings that the deceased would probably have accumulated had the decedent died in the normal course of events.

(a) if the notice is required under section 15(1), (1A)(a), (1B), or (2), shall be in Form 2 in the Schedule where the accident caused personal injury and in Form 2A in the Schedule in the case of incapacity or death due to an occupational disease; and
(b) if the notice is required under section 15(1C), shall be in Form 2 or Form 2A, as the case may be, in the Schedule.

151. Section 20 of the *Law Amendment and Reform (Consolidation) Ordinance* (Cap 23) states:

(1) Subject to the provisions of this section, on the death of any person after 26 October 1951, all causes of action subsisting against or vested in him shall survive against, or, as the case may be, for the benefit of, his estate:

...

(1A) The right of a person to claim under section 4 of the Fatal Accidents Ordinance (Cap 22) (for bereavement) or under section 20C(1) of this Ordinance (for loss of society) shall not survive for the benefit of his estate on his death.

(2) Where a cause of action survives as aforesaid for the benefit of the estate of a deceased person, the damages recoverable for the benefit of the estate of that person—

(a) shall not include any exemplary damages;
(b) shall, where the death of that person has been caused by the act or omission which gives rise to the cause of action-
(i) be calculated without reference to any loss or gain to his estate consequent on his death, except that a sum in respect of funeral expenses may be included;
(ii) not include any damages in respect of loss of ability to render services after his death;
(iii) not include any damages for loss of property, whether income or otherwise, in respect of any period after his death, except in so far as the court is satisfied that, but for the act or omission that gave rise to the cause of action, the deceased would have achieved an accumulation of wealth by the time that he would otherwise have died, in which case damages may be awarded in respect of the loss of that wealth:

Provided that damages awarded under this sub-paragraph shall be subject to such deduction as the court considers it just to make in the circumstances of any particular case on account of the accelerated receipt of that wealth and in order to avoid over-compensation.

Under the *Fatal Accidents Ordinance* (Cap 22), a separate cause of action may be brought for the loss of financial support by certain dependants of a person wrongfully killed.[152] Monetary benefits which accrued to the deceased's dependants, other than charitable payments, insurance

...

(4) Where damage has been suffered by reason of any act or omission in respect of which a cause of action would have subsisted against any person if that person had not died before or at the same time as the damage was suffered, there shall be deemed, for the purposes of this section and sections 21 and 22, to have been subsisting against him before his death such cause of action in respect of that act or omission as would have subsisted if he had died after the damage was suffered.

(5) The rights conferred by this section and sections 21 and 22 for the benefit of the estates of deceased persons shall be in addition to and not in derogation of any rights conferred on the dependants of deceased persons by the Fatal Accidents Ordinance (Cap. 22) and so much of this section and sections 21 and 22 as relates to causes of action against the estates of deceased persons shall apply in relation to causes of action under the said Ordinance as it applies in relation to other causes of action not expressly excepted from the operation of subsection (1).

...

See also the Tort chapter, section IV.A where this Ordinance is discussed.

152. For example, section 3 of the *Fatal Accidents Ordinance* (Cap 22) states:

> If death is caused to any person ("the deceased") by any wrongful act, neglect or default which is such as would (if death had not ensued) have entitled the deceased to maintain an action and recover damages in respect thereof, then subject to section 4(2) an action for damages may be brought for the benefit of the dependants of the deceased against the person who would have been liable in damages to the deceased in respect of that wrongful act, neglect or default.

Section 4 of the *Fatal Accidents Ordinance* provides in part:

(1) An action under this Ordinance may consist of or include a claim for damages for bereavement unless, by reason of the act, neglect or default referred to in section 3, any person has recovered, by action or otherwise, a sum in respect of loss of the deceased's society under section 20C(1) of the Law Amendment and Reform (Consolidation) Ordinance (Cap 23).

(2) A claim for damages for bereavement shall only be for the benefit of such of the following persons as survive the deceased for not less than 30 days—

(a) the wife or husband of the deceased, unless they had been living apart for a continuous period of at least 2 years immediately preceding the death of the deceased; or

(b) where there is no spouse by or for whom a claim can be made under paragraph (a), the children of the deceased; or

(c) where there is no person by or for whom a claim can be made under paragraph (a) or (b), the wife or husband of the deceased (notwithstanding that they had been living apart); or

monies and pensions, must be taken into account in awarding damages.[153] Therefore, where only the deceased's dependant, *e.g.*, spouse, inherits the deceased's estate, the *Fatal Accidents Ordinance* award is set off against the award to the estate under the *Law Amendment and Reform (Consolidation) Ordinance* and effectively disappears.

Separate from, and in addition to, any dependency claim based on loss of material support is a bereavement award which is made to acknowledge the grief, sorrow and loss of society resulting from death. Those qualifying for a

---

(d) where there is no person by or for whom a claim can be made under paragraph (a), (b) or (c), any concubine taken by the deceased before 7 October 1971; or

(e) where there is no person by or for whom a claim can be made under paragraph (a), (b), (c) or (d), any person who-

(i) was living with the deceased in the same household immediately before the date of his death; and

(ii) had been living with the deceased in the same household for at least 2 years before that date,

as the husband or wife of the deceased; or

(f) where there is no person by or for whom a claim can be made under paragraph (a), (b), (c), (d) or (e), the parents of the deceased or (if the deceased was illegitimate) his mother; or

(g) where there is no person by or for whom a claim can be made under paragraph (a), (b), (c), (d), (e) or (f), but the deceased was at the date of his death a minor, any person who during any marriage to which that person was a party treated the deceased as a son or daughter of the family in relation to that marriage; or

(h) where there is no other person by or for whom a claim can be made under this subsection, any brother or sister of the deceased.

(3) Subject to subsection (4), the sum to be awarded as damages under this section shall be $150000.

For further discussion of the recovery of damages for fatal injuries, *see* GLOFCHESKI–EMPLOYMENT, *supra* note 12, at Chapter 9 ("Health and Safety at Work I–The Safety Legislation Regime, the Inspectorate, Enforcement and Penalties"), Chapter 10 ("Health and Safety at Work II–Civil Liabilities"), Chapter 11 ("Health and Safety at Work III–Statutory Compensation for Work-Related Injury, Disease and Death"); 10(2) HALSBURY'S, *supra* note 11, at paras. 145.619–145.620; GLOFCHESKI–TORT, *supra* note 1, at 384–404; 25(1) HALSBURY'S, *supra* note 64, at paras. 380.114–380.118; 22 HALSBURY'S LAWS OF HONG KONG paras. 340.213–340.222 (2008).

153. *See*, *e.g.*, section 6 of the *Fatal Accidents Ordinance*, *supra* note 152, which provides for the following assessment of damages:

(1) In the action, such damages, other than damages for bereavement, may be awarded to dependants in such proportions as reflect their respective injuries as a result of the death.

(2) Where damages are awarded under subsection (1), any costs not recovered from the defendant shall be deducted from those damages and thereafter those damages shall be divided among the dependants in such proportions as has been decided under that subsection.

bereavement award are ranked by section 4 of the *Fatal Accidents Ordinance*, so that the surviving spouse exclusively is entitled to this award, unless the couple had been living apart for two or more years prior to the decedent spouse's death.[154]

Sections 27–28 of the *Limitation Ordinance* (Cap 347) require any action for damages for personal injury or death to be brought within three years.[155] Should a plaintiff bring a lawsuit after the three-year limit provided by this ordinance, the action will not be allowed by the court.

---

(3) In an action under this Ordinance, or under the Carriage by Air Ordinance (Cap 500), where there fall to be assessed damages payable to a widow in respect of the death of her husband there shall not be taken into account the re-marriage of the widow or her prospects of re-marriage.

(4) In an action under this Ordinance where there fall to be assessed damages payable to a person who is a dependant within the meaning of paragraph (c) of the definition of that term in section 2, in respect of the death of the person with whom the dependant was living as husband or wife, there shall be taken into account (together with any other matter that appears to the court to be relevant to the action) the fact that the dependant had no enforceable right to financial support by the deceased as a result of their living together.

(5) In assessing damages in any action brought under this Ordinance the funeral expenses of the deceased person, if such expenses have been incurred by the parties for whose benefit the action is brought, shall be taken into account.

(6) Money paid into court in satisfaction of a cause of action under this Ordinance may be in one sum without specifying any person's share.

154. Section 4 of the *Fatal Accidents Ordinance* is set out in part at *supra* note 152.

155. Section 27 of the *Limitation Ordinance* (Cap 347) states in part:

(1) This section applies to any action for damages for negligence, nuisance or breach of duty (whether the duty exists by virtue of a contract or of provision made by or under an Ordinance or imperial enactment or independently of any contract or any such provision) where the damages claimed by the plaintiff for the negligence, nuisance or breach of duty consist of or include damages in respect of personal injuries to the plaintiff or any other person.

(2) Section 4 shall not apply to an action to which this section applies.

(3) Subject to section 30, an action to which this section applies shall not be brought after the expiration of the period specified in subsections (4) and (5).

(4) Except where subsection (5) applies, the said period is 3 years from-
   (a) the date on which the cause of action accrued; or
   (b) the date (if later) of the plaintiff's knowledge.

(5) If the person injured dies before the expiration of the period in subsection (4), the period as respects the cause of action surviving for the benefit of the estate of the deceased by virtue of section 20 of the Law Amendment and Reform (Consolidation) Ordinance (Cap 23) shall be 3 years from—

To summarize, a person who suffers personal injury may bring a civil action for damages based on breach of the statutory safety duty. An injured plaintiff will succeed only if this individual:

- is within that class of persons for whose benefit the duty is imposed;
- has suffered harm of the type the legislation intended to prevent; and,
- can show that the breach of duty caused the injury.

All employers, including the government, owe employees a duty of care at common law, the breach of which gives rise to an action for damages for death or injury. Since 1984, employers have been required to insure against their potential liability to pay damages in tort. Failure to insure is a criminal offence.

Employers must select and, where necessary, train their staff so that they are competent to work alongside others. Employers must provide and properly maintain necessary equipment. However, there is generally no employer liability if the equipment, made or supplied by a reputable third

---

(a) the date of death; or
(b) the date of the personal representative's knowledge,
whichever is the later.

Section 28 of the *Limitation Ordinance* states:

(1) This section has effect subject to section 30.
(2) An action under the Fatal Accidents Ordinance (Cap 22) shall not be brought if the death occurred when the person injured could no longer maintain an action and recover damages in respect of the injury (whether because of a time limit in this Ordinance or in any other Ordinance, or any other reason); and where any such action by the injured person would have been barred by the time limit in section 27, no account shall be taken of the possibility of that time limit being overridden under section 30.
(3) An action under the Fatal Accidents Ordinance (Cap 22) shall not be brought after the expiration of 3 years from—
(a) the date of death; or
(b) the date of knowledge of the person for whose benefit the action is brought,
whichever is the later.
(4) Subsection (3) shall not apply to an action for which a period of limitation is prescribed by or under any Ordinance other than this Ordinance, and section 27 shall not apply to an action under the Fatal Accidents Ordinance (Cap 22).
(5) An action under the Fatal Accidents Ordinance (Cap 22) shall be one to which section 22 applies, but otherwise sections 22 to 26, inclusive, and Part IV shall not apply to the action.

For an analysis of the application of the *Limitation Ordinance*, *see*, *e.g.*, 17(2) HALSBURY'S LAWS OF HONG KONG paras. 245.001–245.036, 245.060–245.062 (2008).

party and provided by that third party, unexpectedly breaks or otherwise malfunctions, causing injury to the employees.

An employer is liable both to its own employees and to lawful visitors if the premises under the employer's control are unsafe.

F. Employees' Compensation Ordinance

Another form of statutory protection for an employee in Hong Kong is found in the *Employees' Compensation Ordinance* (Cap 282), to which reference was made in the preceding section. The function of this law is to "provide for the payment of compensation to employees who are injured in the course of their employment."[156] Employers are required to maintain insurance coverage under the Ordinance so that employees injured in the course of their employment may receive compensation from the employer or its insurer. Pursuant to section 40, no employer shall employ any individual unless there is an insurance policy for the amount of the employer's liability for any injury arising out of and in the course of employment.[157]

---

156. For in-depth analysis, *see, e.g.*, GLOFCHESKI–EMPLOYMENT, *supra* note 12, at paras. 11.002–11.154; HUBBARD, *supra* note 17, at Chapter 14 ("Employees' Compensation").

157. The section states in relevant part:

> (1) Subject to subsections (1B) and (1C), no employer shall employ any employee in any employment unless there is in force in relation to such employee a policy of insurance issued by an insurer for an amount not less than the applicable amount specified in the Fourth Schedule in respect of the liability of the employer.
>
> (1A) Subsection (1) does not require an employer to obtain insurance for any liability he may have in respect of damages awarded by a court outside Hong Kong to an employee referred to in section 30B.
>
> (1B) A principal contractor who has undertaken to perform any construction work may, in compliance with subsection (1), take out a policy of insurance issued by an insurer for an amount not less than the amount specified in the Fourth Schedule in relation to a principal contractor in respect of the liability of the principal contractor and the liability of his sub-contractor.
>
> (1C) A group of companies may, in compliance with subsection (1), take out a policy of insurance issued by an insurer for an amount not less than the amount specified in the Fourth Schedule in relation to a group of companies in respect of the liabilities of the companies, bodies corporate and corporations in the group specified in the policy.
>
> (1D) For the purpose of this section, section 44B and the definition of "the available amount covered by the policy of insurance" (可得的保險單承保款額) in section 38, "accident" (意外) means an accident or a series of accidents arising out of one event, and in relation to an occupational disease—

Accordingly, private sector employers must insure against their potential liability to pay compensation and common law damages under section 40. Where there is an insurance policy, sections 42–44 confer an absolute right on the injured employees, or their dependants, to recover directly from the insurer any amount to which they are entitled from the employer.[158] This

---

(a) where incapacities or deaths of more than one employee are attributable to a cause that does not arise out of a sudden and identifiable event, the incapacities or deaths of such employees are regarded as being caused by separate accidents arising out of separate events; and

(b) where incapacities or deaths of more than one employee are attributable to a cause that arises out of a sudden and identifiable event, the incapacities or deaths of such employees are regarded as being caused by an accident or a series of accidents arising out of one event.

...

(2) An employer who contravenes subsection (1) commits an offence and is liable—

(a) on conviction upon indictment to a fine at level 6 and to imprisonment for 2 years; and

(b) on summary conviction to a fine at level 6 and to imprisonment for 1 year.

Employees' Compensation Ordinance, *supra* note 2, at section 40.

158. These sections of the *Employees' Compensation Ordinance*, *supra* note 2, provide in part:

42. Insurer's liability:

(1) Notwithstanding anything in a policy of insurance issued for the purposes of this Part, an insurer is liable, in a proceeding under section 36LA or 44, for the amount of the liability of the employer not exceeding the available amount covered by the policy of insurance.

(1A) For the avoidance of doubt, it is declared that an insurer is liable, in a proceeding under section 36LA or 44, for the amount of the liability of the employer not exceeding the available amount covered by the policy of insurance issued for the purposes of this Part notwithstanding the obligation imposed upon the employer by section 40 to insure for an amount in excess of the amount insured.

...

43. Condition under which liability for payment by insurer arises:

(1) Subject to this section, where in relation to an employee there is in force a policy of insurance issued for the purposes of this Part and the employer of the employee becomes liable to pay any sum under this Ordinance or independently of this Ordinance in respect of an injury to the employee arising out of and in the course of his employment, such sum shall forthwith become due and payable by the insurer, including any sum payable in respect of interest and costs, notwithstanding anything to the contrary in the policy of insurance.

...

44. Right of injured party to proceed against insurer:

right to recover payment is a separate and a distinct right which is vested in the injured employee. This right is not subject to, or dependent upon, the employer possessing a valid indemnification claim against the insurer.[159]

The *Employees' Compensation Ordinance* entitles accident victims, killed or injured in the course of employment, to compensation from their employers, regardless of fault.[160] The employees' compensation is in addition to,

---

(1) Every policy of insurance issued for the purposes of this Part shall be deemed to provide that any employee or other person having a claim against the person insured in respect of the liability in regard to which such policy was issued shall, subject to section 42, be entitled to recover in his own name, as though he were a party to the policy, directly from the insurer any amount which he would have been entitled to recover from the person insured.

(2) An employee or other person having a claim against the person insured under a policy of insurance issued for the purposes of this Part shall not commence proceedings against the insurer unless he also commences or has commenced proceedings against the person insured.

Id.

159. LEWINGTON, *supra* note 131, vol. 1, at 146.
See generally DOWNEY, *supra* note 12, at §K.172.

160. DOWNEY, *supra* note 12, at §K.61 which states "No statutory compensation is payable where the accident does not incapacitate the employee from earning full wages for work the employee was employed to perform."
Section 5(4) of the *Employees' Compensation Ordinance*, *supra* note 2, provides:

(4) For the purposes of this Ordinance—
(a) an accident arising in the course of an employee's employment shall be deemed, in the absence of evidence to the contrary, also to have arisen out of that employment;
(b) an accident to an employee shall be deemed to arise out of and in the course of his employment, notwithstanding that the employee was at the time when the accident happened acting in contravention of any statutory or other regulation applicable to his employment, or of any orders given by or on behalf of his employer, or that he was acting without instructions from his employer, if such act was done by the employee for the purposes of and in connection with his employer's trade or business;
(c) an accident to an employee shall be deemed to arise out of and in the course of his employment if it happens—
(i) while, with the consent of his employer, the employee is being trained in first aid, ambulance or rescue work or engaged in any competition or exercise in connection therewith;
(ii) in, at or about any premises other than his employer's while, with the consent of his employer, the employee is engaged in any first aid, ambulance or rescue work or in any competition or exercise in connection therewith; or
(iii) in, at or about his employer's premises while the employee is engaged in any first aid, ambulance or rescue work,

notwithstanding that in the case of rescue work the employee was acting in contravention of any statutory or other regulation applicable to his employment, or of any orders given by or on behalf of his employer, or that he was acting without instructions from his employer, if when such act was done the employee reasonably acted in order to rescue, succour or protect any other person who had suffered, or who was reasonably believed to be in danger of, injury, or to avert or

(d) an accident to an employee shall be deemed to arise out of and in the course of his employment if it happens to the employee while he is with the express or implied permission of his employer, travelling as a passenger by any means of transport to or from his place of work and at the time of the accident, the means of transport is being operated—
 (i) by or on behalf of his employer or by some other person pursuant to arrangements made with his employer; and
 (ii) other than as part of a public transport service;

(e) an accident to an employee shall be deemed to arise out of and in the course of his employment if it happens to the employee while he is driving or operating any means of transport arranged or provided by or on behalf of his employer or by some other person pursuant to arrangements made with his employer between his place of residence and his place of work, travelling by a direct route—
 (i) to his place of work for the purposes of and in connection with his employment; or
 (ii) to his place of residence after attending to those purposes;

(f) an accident to an employee shall be deemed to arise out of and in the course of his employment if it happens to the employee when, within the duration of a gale warning, or of a rainstorm warning, he is travelling between his place of residence and his place of work—
 (i) to his place of work, by a direct route within a period of 4 hours before the time of commencement of his working hours for that day or to his place of residence, within a period of 4 hours after the time of cessation of his working hours for that day, as the case may be; or
 (ii) in such other circumstances as the Court thinks reasonable, and for the purposes of this paragraph—
  (A) "gale warning" (烈風警告) means a warning of the occurrence of a tropical cyclone in, or in the vicinity of, Hong Kong by the use of the tropical cyclone warning signals issued by the Director of the Hong Kong Observatory to the effect that any of the tropical cyclone warning signals commonly referred to as No. 8NW, 8SW, 8NE, 8SE, 9 or 10 is in force;
  (B) "rainstorm warning" (暴雨警告) means a warning of a heavy rainstorm in, or in the vicinity of, Hong Kong by the use of the heavy rainstorm warning signals issued by the Director of the Hong Kong Observatory to the effect that any of the heavy rainstorm warning signals commonly referred to as Red or Black is in force;

and does not replace, the right to common law damages where negligence or other breach of duty can be shown.[161]

Most employees and apprentices are covered by the *Employees' Compensation Ordinance*, regardless of earnings, length of service or type of work.[162] Compensation is paid when a "personal injury by accident arising

---

> (g) an accident to an employee shall be deemed to arise out of and in the course of his employment if it happens to the employee while he is, with the express or implied permission of his employer, travelling by any means of transport for the purposes of and in connection with his employment between Hong Kong and any place outside Hong Kong or between any place outside Hong Kong and any other such place.

See also ARJUNAN & NABI BAKSH, *supra* note 16, at 622–625.

161. LEWINGTON, *supra* note 131, vol. 1, at 148.
See generally DOWNEY, *supra* note 12, at Part K ("Health and Safety").
Cheung Shuk Wah Jessica v Wong Kang Hung Darwin involved two cases arising from the same incident. In both cases Cheung, the widow of Man Chung Wah, filed a law suit against Wong, who owned a pub and employed Man in the capacity of bartender. One night at the pub, there was an altercation between a waitress and some patrons in which Man intervened. Later that evening after the pub closed, Man escorted this waitress to her destination. Upon arrival at the destination, two of the patrons involved in the altercation attacked and fatally injured Man. The first case, before the District Court DCEC 842/2007, [2009] HKEC 1105, involved employees' compensation and whether Man's murder occurred in the course of his employment. The District Court determined that Man accompanying the waitress to her destination after they both finished work at the pub was incidental to Man's responsibility to ensure the waitress would be safe leaving work. [2009] HKEC at para. 42. The court followed the principle that where "the activity upon which the workman is engaged is reasonably incidental to the work that he is employed to do, his course of employment can extend beyond the normal hours or place of work." [2009] HKEC at para. 17 (citations omitted). The second case, before the Court of First Instance HCPI 12/2009, [2010] HKEC 909, involved a tort action by the widow Cheung against Wong. The court found the employer was negligent and breached its common law duty of care as an employer. The court determined that Wong owed a duty to Man to ensure that he would be safe while discharging his duty of protecting the waitress. Wong knew that an attack might follow the altercation between the waitress and patrons. Wong also could foresee that Man would escort the waitress in the course of his employment. [2010] HKEC at para. 49.

162. "So long as the accident arises out of and in the course of employment, it makes no difference whether the employee caused or even contributed to the accident." DOWNEY, *supra* note 12, at §K.57.
Id. at §K.49 notes:

> Employees, including civil servants, are entitled to receive employees' compensation for injuries arising out of their employment.
>
> An employee means any person who has entered into or works under a contract of service or apprenticeship with an employer in any employment, whether by way of manual labour, clerical work, or other form of employment, and whether the contract is expressed or implied, oral or in writing.

See GLOFCHESKI–EMPLOYMENT, *supra* note 12, at paras. 11.015–11.022. *See also* the first case of *Cheung v Wong*, *supra* note 161.

out of and in the course of employment" is determined to exist.[163] Accidents arising out of and in the course of employment include situations where the employee was acting for the purposes of and in connection with his employer's trade or business at the time of the accident.[164] This definition applies even to situations where, at the time of the accident, the employee was acting contrary to law or regulations applicable to his employment, or to any orders given by or on behalf of the employer, or the employee was acting independently without his employer's instructions.[165]

The phrase "in the course of employment" is frequently litigated. In *Check Chor-ching v Wik Far East Ltd* [1991] 2 HKLR 224, a vehicle knocked down the plaintiff when she was changing buses, as she had boarded the wrong bus. The defendant employer provided both buses free of charge. Section 5(4)(d) of the *Employees' Compensation Ordinance* provides that while a person is "travelling as a passenger" in his employer's transport, any accident would be deemed to arise out of and in the course of employment.[166] The Court of Appeal held that the provision gave an artificial extension of the meaning of "in the course of employment" and should be construed narrowly. Accordingly the section would only apply if the plaintiff had been injured when she was actually being carried in the bus.

---

163. For an analysis of the definition of "accident", *see, e.g.*, GLOFCHESKI–EMPLOYMENT, *supra* note 12, at paras. 11.023–11.033.

164. For an analysis of "arising out of and in the course of the employment", *see, e.g.*, GLOFCHESKI–EMPLOYMENT, *supra* note 12, at paras. 11.034–11.043.

165. *Employees' Compensation Ordinance*, *supra* note 2, at section 5(4), text of which is set out in *supra* note 160. DOWNEY, *supra* note 12, at §§K.42–K.43 states:

> An employer is liable to pay compensation whenever an employee suffers personal injury arising out of and in the course of employment. Personal injury includes injuries resulting in death. An accident arising in the course of an employee's employment is regarded, in the absence of evidence to the contrary, as having arisen out of that employment …
>
> An accident will be regarded as having arisen out of an employee's employment irrespective of whether at the time of the accident, the employee was acting in contravention of any:
>
> - statutory or other regulation applicable to the employee's employment; or
> - orders given by or on behalf of the employee's employer.
>
> The law also assumes the accident to be employment-related where an employee was acting without instructions from the employer, where such an act was done by the employee for the purposes of and in connection with the employer's trade or business …

166. The text of section 5(4)(d) of the *Employees' Compensation Ordinance*, *supra* note 2, is set out in *supra* note 160.

Similarly, the court was required to interpret section 5(4)(g) of the *Employees' Compensation Ordinance* in a case involving employees injured in a traffic accident returning to Hong Kong from their company's annual dinner in Shenzhen. In the case of *Chan Ho Yuen v Multi-Circuit Board (China) Ltd* [2011] 5 HKLRD 554, [2011] HKEC 1282, two of the employer's Hong Kong employees returning to Hong Kong were injured in a vehicle driven by a colleague based in Shenzhen after these three employees visited a karaoke lounge upon the conclusion of the company's annual dinner. The issues in this case involved two questions:

(1) Did the two injured plaintiffs have the employer's express or implied permission to return to Hong Kong in the third employee's car?
(2) Did the detour to the karaoke lounge render the return journey outside the course of employment?

The court made the following analysis and decision:

> 38. Whether an employee can be said to have the implied permission of his employer to travel by a particular means of transport for the purposes of and in connection with his employment is … determined by … all the surrounding facts. … the question is to be answered objectively by a review of whether those facts, including the past history between the particular employer and his employees, would reasonably lead an employee to believe that he is permitted by his employer to travel by the particular means of transport.
>
> …
>
> 42. In the light of that body of evidence, I would conclude … that an employee … would reasonably conclude that he had the implied permission of the … [employer] to travel from ... the annual dinner … back to the border by … [the third employee's] car. … the majority of the Hong Kong-based employees … would likely have travelled in the … [employer's] 7-seater vehicle which had travelled that day from Hong Kong or in one of the two vehicles of the … [employer's] Shenzhen factory, but it is important … that the … [employer] never sought to make those means of transport compulsory or to issue any directive prohibiting the taking of any other form of transport.
>
> …
>
> 61. … I do not accept … that the detour to the karaoke parlour here was of such a character or duration as to prevent the resumption of [the] journey in [the] car from being a continuation of the course of their employment. ... the detour was for a period of approximately 2½ hours. I would not regard this as being of such

> a lengthy period as to constitute more than a temporary interruption to a journey undertaken in the course of employment. I see no reason to regard the visit to the karaoke parlour as any different to a visit to a cinema, café or restaurant for the purposes of entertainment, a drink or a meal before commencing or resuming a work-related journey. ... a detour ... merely incidental to the journey (for example, a stop for a cup of coffee at a roadside petrol station) would not interrupt the course of employment. ... the detour to the karaoke parlour did interrupt the journey undertaken in the course of employment ... it did so only on a temporary basis until the return journey was resumed. That resumed journey was on precisely the same route that [the] car would have taken if he had driven them straight from the annual dinner to the border without making the detour to the karaoke parlour and therefore it was, in my judgment, undertaken in the course of ... employment.
>
> ...
>
> 64. ... On the facts of the present case, once the detour was over, the return journey continued and their course of employment resumed.
>
> ...
>
> 69. ... I would conclude that the detour to the karaoke parlour only operated as a temporary interruption to the journey undertaken in the course of ... employment and did not mean that they were no longer in the course of their employment when they resumed their journey ... and when the accident occurred.

The duty to pay compensation rests upon the employer, although sub-contractors' employees may also make a claim from the principal contractor, who then may seek indemnification from the sub-contractor.[167] Section 31 of the *Employees' Compensation Ordinance* prohibits employers from

167. *See* Glofcheski–Employment, *supra* note 12, at para. 11.006; Downey, *supra* note 12, at §K.45.

The pertinent section of the ordinance states in part:

> (1) Where any person (in this section referred to as the principal contractor), in the course of or for the purposes of his trade or business, contracts with a sub-contractor for the execution by or under the sub-contractor of the whole or any part of any work undertaken by the principal contractor, the principal contractor shall be liable to pay to any employee employed by that sub-contractor or by any other sub-contractor in the execution of the work any compensation under this Ordinance which the principal contractor would have been liable to pay if that employee had been immediately employed by him; and where compensation is claimed from or proceedings are taken against the principal contractor,

contracting-out of this duty to remove or reduce the liability of any person to pay compensation.[168] However, under exceptional circumstances, in accordance with section 31(2), the Commissioner for Labour may allow the employee and employer to enter into any agreement to contract out of the duty to compensate if the Commissioner is satisfied that by reason of old age or serious physical defect or infirmity, a person, if employed as an employee, is especially liable to meet with an accident.[169] The court held in

---

then, in the application of this Ordinance, references to the principal contractor shall be substituted for references to the employer, except that the amount of any compensation calculated by reference to earnings shall be calculated by reference to the earnings of the employee under the employer by whom he is immediately employed.

(1A) Where a principal contractor is liable to pay compensation under this section, he shall be liable for the offences under sections 6C(15), 6D(10), 6E(16), 10(10), 16A(12) and 16I(6) as if he were an employer.

(2) Where the principal contractor is liable to pay compensation under this section, he shall be entitled to be indemnified by any person who would have been liable to pay compensation to the employee independently of this section.

...

(8) Nothing in this section shall be construed as preventing an employee recovering compensation under this Ordinance from a subcontractor instead of the principal contractor.

Employees' Compensation Ordinance, *supra* note 2, at section 24.

168. Section 31 mandates:

(1) Any contract or agreement whether made before or after the commencement of this Ordinance, whereby an employee relinquishes any right to compensation from an employer for personal injury by accident arising out of and in the course of his employment, shall, subject to subsection (2), be null and void in so far as it purports to remove or reduce the liability of any person to pay compensation under the provisions of this Ordinance.

(2) The Commissioner may, if satisfied that, by reason of old age or serious physical defect or infirmity, a person, if employed as an employee, is specially liable to meet with an accident, or, if he meets with an accident is specially liable to sustain injury, in connection with any contract of such employment, authorize the person and the employer to enter into an agreement in writing reducing or giving up the right of such person to compensation under the provisions of this Ordinance in respect of any accident which is caused or contributed to by the old age or serious physical defect or infirmity.

(3) An agreement entered into under subsection (2) shall be ineffective unless the Commissioner certifies that in his opinion such agreement is fair and reasonable.

Id.

169. Section 31(2) of the *Employees' Compensation Ordinance* is set out in *supra* note 168.

Shiu Ying-kwong v Po On [1990] HKDCLR 15, 19 that section 31 did not disable:

> the parties from coming to a settlement whereby the employee obtains compensation in an amount in excess of the *minimum*, if any stipulated by the Ordinance ... but conceivably less than he or she might obtain after a full hearing. If the disputed issue of fact is one which gives the Court the alternative of making *no award at all* ... a settlement which gives the employee *some* compensation would be consistent with the general policy of the Ordinance ... [Section 31(1)] does not prohibit any agreement which seeks to establish and determine the amount of a disputed claim, so long as the agreed amount is not less than would be due to the employee under the various provisions of the ordinance *on the basis of the facts agreed between the parties*. (emphasis in original)

Compensation payable by an employer will be for loss of earning capacity,[170] total incapacity[171] and death.[172] It is age- and wage-related to reflect the level of pecuniary loss. Medical expenses are also recoverable to specified limits,[173] as are costs of any prostheses or surgical appliances.[174]

---

170. Section 9 of the *Employees' Compensation Ordinance*, *supra* note 2, provides for permanent partial incapacity:

> (1) Subject to subsection (1A), where permanent partial incapacity results from the injury the amount of compensation shall be—
> (a) in the case of an injury specified in the First Schedule, such percentage of the compensation which would have been payable in the case of permanent total incapacity as is specified therein as being the percentage of the loss of earning capacity caused by that injury;
> (aa) in the case of a combination of injuries specified in the First Schedule, the aggregate of the compensation which would have been payable in respect of the injuries; and
> (b) in the case of an injury not specified in the First Schedule, such percentage of the compensation which would have been payable in the case of permanent total incapacity as is proportionate to the loss of earning capacity permanently caused by the injury in any employment which the employee was capable of undertaking at that time: Provided that—
> (i) in the case of injury to any part of the body specified in the First Schedule not amounting to the loss of that part, the loss of earning capacity permanently caused by that injury, expressed as a percentage, shall not exceed the appropriate percentage specified in the First Schedule in respect of the loss of such part;
> (ii) in the case of injury not specified in the First Schedule, the loss of earning capacity permanently caused by such injury shall be assessed as a percentage having regard so far as possible to the scale of percentages specified in that Schedule and to the Note thereto.

(1A) Where—
(a) permanent partial incapacity results from an injury or a combination of injuries (whether or not specified in the First Schedule); and
(b) the percentage of the loss of earning capacity specified or assessed in relation to that injury or combination of injuries in accordance with subsection (1) would be substantially less than the percentage of the loss of earning capacity permanently caused by the injury or injuries in the special circumstances of the employee, including, without limiting the generality of the foregoing—
(i) the nature of the injury or injuries in relation to the nature of his former usual employment; and
(ii) his qualifications, previous training and experience,
the amount of compensation shall be such percentage of the compensation which would have been payable in the case of permanent total incapacity as is proportionate to the loss of earning capacity permanently caused by the injury or injuries in any employment which, having regard to those special circumstances, the employee was capable of undertaking at that time.
(2) Where more injuries than one are caused by the same accident, the amount of compensation payable under the provisions of this section shall be aggregated, but not so in any case as to exceed the amount which would have been payable if permanent total incapacity had resulted from the injuries.
(3) For the purposes of this section, permanent partial incapacity shall be deemed to result from an injury where the percentage or aggregate percentage of the loss of earning capacity amounts—
(a) in the case of an incapacity of a permanent nature which results from an injury specified in the First Schedule, to less than 100 per cent as specified in that Schedule; or
(b) in the case of an incapacity of a permanent nature which results from an injury not specified in the First Schedule, to less than 100 per cent as assessed by an Ordinary Assessment Board, a Special Assessment Board or the Court,
and a reference in this subsection to an injury shall include a reference to a combination of injuries whether they are mentioned in paragraph (a) or (b) or in both those paragraphs.

...

See GLOFCHESKI–EMPLOYMENT, *supra* note 12, at paras. 11.110–11.112.

171. In situations involving permanent total incapacity, section 7 of the *Employees' Compensation Ordinance*, *supra* note 2, stipulates:

(1) Where permanent total incapacity results from the injury, the amount of compensation shall be—
(a) in the case of an employee under 40 years of age at the time of the accident, a lump sum equal to 96 months' earnings or 96 times the amount specified in the second column of the Sixth Schedule shown opposite section 7(1)(a) specified in the first column of that Schedule, whichever is the less;
(b) in the case of an employee of or over 40 years of age but under 56 years of age at the time of the accident, a lump sum equal to 72 months' earnings or 72 times the amount specified in the second column of the Sixth Schedule shown opposite section 7(1)(b) specified in the first column of that Schedule, whichever is the less;

(c) in the case of an employee of or over 56 years of age at the time of the accident, a lump sum equal to 48 months' earnings or 48 times the amount specified in the second column of the Sixth Schedule shown opposite section 7(1)(c) specified in the first column of that Schedule, whichever is the less.

(2) The amount of compensation payable under subsection (1) shall in no case be less than the amount specified in the second column of the Sixth Schedule shown opposite section 7(2) specified in the first column of that Schedule.

...

See GLOFCHESKI–EMPLOYMENT, *supra* note 12, at paras. 11.107–11.109.
Section 10 provides for compensation in situations of temporary incapacity. Section 10(1) provides:

(1) Where temporary incapacity whether total or partial results from the injury, the compensation shall be the periodical payments hereinafter mentioned, or a lump sum calculated accordingly, having regard to the probable duration, and probable changes in the degree, of the incapacity. Such periodical payments shall be, or shall be at the rate proportionate to, a monthly payment of four-fifths of the difference between the monthly earnings which the employee was earning at the time of the accident and the monthly earnings which he is earning, or is capable of earning, in some suitable employment or business during the period of the temporary incapacity after the accident.

See GLOFCHESKI–EMPLOYMENT, *supra* note 12, at paras. 11.113–11.119.

172. Section 6 regulates compensation in instances of fatality, providing in part:

(1) Where death results from the injury, then, subject to section 6A, the amount of compensation payable to the members of the family of the employee shall be—

(a) in the case of an employee under 40 years of age at the time of the accident, a lump sum equal to 84 months' earnings or 84 times the amount specified in the second column of the Sixth Schedule shown opposite section 6(1)(a) specified in the first column of that Schedule, whichever is the less;

(b) in the case of an employee of or over 40 years of age but under 56 years of age at the time of the accident, a lump sum equal to 60 months' earnings or 60 times the amount specified in the second column of the Sixth Schedule shown opposite section 6(1)(b) specified in the first column of that Schedule, whichever is the less;

(c) in the case of an employee of or over 56 years of age at the time of the accident, a lump sum equal to 36 months' earnings or 36 times the amount specified in the second column of the Sixth Schedule shown opposite section 6(1)(c) specified in the first column of that Schedule, whichever is the less.

(2) The amount of compensation payable under subsection (1) shall in no case be less than the amount specified in the second column of the Sixth Schedule shown opposite section 6(2) specified in the first column of that Schedule.

Employees' Compensation Ordinance, *supra* note 2.
See GLOFCHESKI–EMPLOYMENT, *supra* note 12, at paras. 11.101–11.106; DOWNEY, *supra* note 12, at §§K.66–K.69 ("Compensation for Fatal Cases").

173. Section 10A provides in part:

(1) ... if, in any employment, personal injury is caused to an employee by accident ... and arising out of and in the course of his employment his employer shall be liable to pay the medical expenses for the medical treatment in respect of such injury.

(1A) Medical expenses which an employer is liable to pay under subsection (1) shall, unless otherwise provided by agreement in writing entered into by the employer with the employee, not include those in respect of medical treatment given outside Hong Kong in relation to an accident occurring in Hong Kong.

(2) Medical expenses which an employer is liable to pay under subsection (1) shall be payable in addition to any other compensation which the employer is liable to pay under this Ordinance.

(3) Medical expenses which the employer is liable to pay under subsection (1) shall be payable in accordance with the Third Schedule in respect of the period during which the employee receives medical treatment until the attending registered medical practitioner, registered Chinese medicine practitioner or registered dentist certifies that in his opinion no further treatment is required.

(4) An employer shall not be liable to pay medical expenses under subsection (1)-

(a) if the employer has provided adequate free medical treatment to the employee; or

(b) if, by a written undertaking given in accordance with subsection (5), the employer has agreed to provide adequate free medical treatment and the employee fails, without reasonable excuse, to submit himself for such medical treatment.

Employees' Compensation Ordinance, *supra* note 2.
See GLOFCHESKI–EMPLOYMENT, *supra* note 12, at para. 11.120.

174. Section 36B states in part:

(1) Subject to the provisions of this section, if, in any employment, personal injury is caused to an employee by accident arising out of and in the course of the employment, the employer shall, notwithstanding any other compensation he may be liable to pay under this Ordinance, be liable to pay for the cost of supplying and fitting to the employee a prosthesis or surgical appliance required by him as a result of his injury.

(1A) Notwithstanding anything in section 5(2)(a), the employer shall be liable under subsection (1) whether or not the injury has resulted or is likely to result in any temporary incapacity or permanent incapacity causing a loss of earning capacity.

Section 36C limits the employer's obligation under section 36B:

The amount of the cost which the employer is liable to pay under section 36B shall not, in the case of any one employee, exceed an aggregate of the amount specified in the second column of the Sixth Schedule shown opposite section 36C specified in the first column of that Schedule in respect of any one accident.

Employees' Compensation Ordinance, *supra* note 2.
See GLOFCHESKI–EMPLOYMENT, *supra* note 12, at para. 11.121.

Family members of the deceased are entitled to a lump sum payment under section 6 of the *Employees' Compensation Ordinance*.[175] The amount of the lump sum compensation depends on the age of the employee at the time of the death.

"Permanent total incapacity" is provided as a lump sum payment under section 7[176] and the Sixth Schedule of the Ordinance. The maximum lump sum payment that an employee under the age of 40 at the time of accident shall receive is ninety-six months' earnings or ninety-six times the amount specified in the second column of the Sixth Schedule, whichever is less.[177] Where an injured person needs constant attention to perform essential life functions, a court may make an additional award of periodical or lump sum payment by virtue of section 8 and the Sixth Schedule of the Ordinance.[178]

Permanent partial incapacity is addressed in section 9 of the Ordinance.[179] The amount of compensation shall be: (i) in case of an injury specified in

---

175. Section 6 of the *Employees' Compensation Ordinance* is set out in part in *supra* note 172. *See, e.g.*, section 11(1) of the Ordinance; DOWNEY, *supra* note 12, at §§K.70 (definition of "family members"), K.73 ("Compensation for death to be calculated by reference to deceased's earnings"), K.74 ("Calculation of earnings for computing compensation for death").

176. Section 7 of the *Employees' Compensation Ordinance* is set out in part in *supra* note 171. *See also* DOWNEY, *supra* note 12, at §§K.86–K.103 ("Compensation for Permanent Total Incapacity: s 7").

177. *See* DOWNEY, *supra* note 12, at §K.89.

178. Section 8 of the *Employees' Compensation Ordinance*, *supra* note 2, provides in relevant part:

> (1) Where permanent incapacity which results from the injury is of such a nature that the employee is unable to perform the essential actions of life, without the attention of another person the compensation payable under this section for and in relation to such attention shall, in addition to any compensation payable under other provisions of this Ordinance, be—
>
> (a) such amount not exceeding the amount specified in the second column of the Sixth Schedule shown opposite section 8(1)(a) specified in the first column of that Schedule as the Court considers necessary to meet the cost of such attention; or
>
> (b) an amount of the amount specified in the second column of the Sixth Schedule shown opposite section 8(1)(b) specified in the first column of that Schedule payable pursuant to an agreement entered into by the employer with the injured employee and approved by the Commissioner under this section.

The *BLIS Glossary*, *supra* note 1, translates "essential actions of life" as 日常生活所需活動.

179. The text of section 9 of the *Employees' Compensation Ordinance* is set out in *supra* note 170.

See DOWNEY, *supra* note 12, at §§K.108–K.123 ("Compensation for Permanent Partial Incapacity: s 9").

the First Schedule, such percentage of the compensation as is specified in the schedule as being the percentage of the loss of earning capacity caused by that injury; and (ii) in the case of an injury not specified in the First Schedule, such percentage of the compensation as is proportionate to the loss of earning capacity permanently caused by the injury in any employment which the employee was capable of undertaking at that time.

Temporary incapacity is covered in section 10.[180] The employer is to make a lump sum payment or regular periodical payments in lieu thereof at four-fifths of the difference between the employee's monthly earnings at the time of the accident and monthly earnings thereafter. Incapacitation beyond twenty-four months results in the injury's classification as permanent and the provisions of section 7 or section 9, as the case may be, shall apply to the employee. Should the injured person receiving periodical payments die or be found to be permanently incapacitated, a lump sum compensation is payable in addition to the sums due previously.[181]

G. Protection of Wages on Insolvency Ordinance

In 1985, the *Protection of Wages on Insolvency Ordinance* (Cap 380) created the Protection of Wages on Insolvency Fund.[182] With the establishment of

180. The text of section 10(1) of the *Employees' Compensation Ordinance* is set out in *supra* note 171.
See DOWNEY, *supra* note 12, at §§K.124–K.137 for an illustration of the calculation of periodical payments for temporary incapacity.

181. *See, e.g.*, DOWNEY, *supra* note 12, at §§K.74–K.75 ("Calculation of earnings for computing compensation for death").

182. Section 6 of the *Protection of Wages on Insolvency Ordinance* (Cap 380) which established the Fund states:

> The fund known as the Protection of Wages on Insolvency Fund established under the provisions of section 21 of the Business Registration Ordinance (Cap 310) in force immediately before the commencement of this Ordinance shall be deemed to be established and continue in existence under this section, and shall consist of—
> (a) moneys that are paid by the Commissioner of Inland Revenue under that section whether paid before or after the commencement of this Ordinance;
> (b) moneys recovered under Part VI;
> (c) interest and other income derived from the moneys and investments comprising the Fund; and
> (d) other moneys lawfully paid into the Fund.

For additional information, reference may be made to the *Guide to the Protection of Wages on Insolvency Ordinance and Points to note for making application to the Protection of Wages on Insolvency Fund. See: http://www.labour.gov.hk/eng/public/wsd/Guide_PWI_and_Points_to_Note_Application.pdf* (last visited 7 Sept. 2012).

this Fund, under certain conditions, payments may be made to employees of an insolvent employer.[183] The intention is to provide limited but immediate relief to affected employees by:

- eliminating the need for completion of the employer's insolvency proceedings before receiving preferential payments with regard to wages, wages in lieu of notice and severance pay; and
- affording preferential payments regardless of the employer's assets.[184]

---

183. The conditions are stipulated in the *Protection of Wages on Insolvency Ordinance*, *supra* note 182, at sections 15–16 which provide in part:

> 15. Entitlement to apply for ex gratia payment
> (1) Subject to this Part, an applicant to whom—
> (a) wages are due and unpaid;
> (b) wages in lieu of notice are due and unpaid; or
> (c) the liability to be paid a severance payment has arisen and the severance payment is unpaid, whether or not the severance payment is then due,
>
> may apply for an ex gratia payment from the Fund in respect of the wages, wages in lieu of notice or the severance payment, as the case may be, or all or any of them.
>
> ...
>
> 16. Payment
> (1) Subject to subsections (1B) and (2) where it appears to the Commissioner that an employer has failed to pay any wages, wages in lieu of notice or severance payment, as the case may be, or all or any of them to an applicant and that—
> (a) in the case of an employer who is not a company—
> (i) a bankruptcy petition has been presented against him; or
> (ii) he would, but for the existence of section 6(2)(a) of the Bankruptcy Ordinance (Cap 6), be liable to have a bankruptcy petition presented against him; or
> (b) in the case of an employer who is a company, a winding-up petition has been presented against that employer,
>
> he may make an ex gratia payment to the applicant out of the Fund of the amount of the wages, wages in lieu of notice or severance payment, as the case may be, or all or any of them.
>
> (1A) When the Commissioner makes a payment under subsection (1)(a)(ii), he shall give notice of the payment and the reasons therefor in the Gazette.
> (1B) Where an application has been made in respect of a severance payment which is not due at the date of the application, the Commissioner may defer consideration of the application until the severance payment becomes due.
> (2) The Commissioner shall not make any payment under subsection (1)—
> (a) to the applicant unless the applicant has verified his application by a statutory declaration in a form approved by the Commissioner;
> (b) of an amount exceeding $36,000 in respect of wages;
> (c) (Repealed 15 of 1993 s. 3)
> (d) in respect of wages—
> (i) for services rendered more than 4 months prior to an applicant's last day of service; or

This Fund is not intended to guarantee that workers' claims against the insolvent employer will be paid in full. If an employee's claim exceeds the preferential payment amount allowed by the Protection of Wages on Insolvency Fund Board, that employee retains the right to seek payment from the employer for the excess claimed.[185] Where an employee's claim

---

(ii) for which an application is made to the Fund more than 6 months after the applicant's last day of service;

(e) in respect of wages in lieu of notice—

(i) of an amount exceeding—

(A) the equivalent of 1 month's wages of the applicant; or

(B) $22,500,

whichever is the lesser; or

(ii) subject to subsection (2A), which became due more than 6 months prior to the date of application; or

(f) in respect of a severance payment—

(i) of an amount exceeding the aggregate of $50,000 and half of that part of the applicant's entitlement to severance payment in excess of $50,000; or

(ii) the liability for payment of which arose more than 6 months prior to the date of application.

184. LEWINGTON, *supra* note 131, vol. 1, at 263.
See, e.g., DOWNEY, *supra* note 12, at §P.14 ("Wage Payment Claims for Ex-gratia Payments").
For an extensive review of the Fund and the Board's operation, *see* 10(2) HALSBURY'S, *supra* note 11, at paras. 145.590–145.613.
In the event of an employer's bankruptcy, *see also* GLOFCHESKI–EMPLOYMENT, *supra* note 12, at paras. 14.059; 14.066 ("Payments that will be paid in priority to all other debts"); DOWNEY, *supra* note 12, at §P.18 ("Preferential Claims of Employees") in the event of an employer's bankruptcy.

185. The Board is established under section 3 of the *Protection of Wages on Insolvency Ordinance*, *supra* note 182:

(1) There is hereby established a board to be known as the Protection of Wages on Insolvency Fund Board and in the Chinese language as "破產欠薪保障基金委員會" which shall be a body corporate.

(2) The Board shall consist of a Chairman appointed under the Schedule and not more than 10 members appointed by the Chief Executive as follows-

(a) subject to paragraph (b) not more than 4 public officers;

(b) equal numbers of persons who, in his opinion, represent employers and persons who, in his opinion, represent employees.

...

The functions and powers of this Board are set out in *id.* at section 4:

(1) The Board shall have the following functions—

(a) to administer the Fund;

(b) to make recommendations to the Chief Executive with respect to the rate of levy; and

(c) to perform such other duties as are imposed or other powers as are conferred on it by this Ordinance.

has been fully or partially satisfied, that employee's right to payment from the insolvent employer is assigned to the Board which then assumes the employee's position as a creditor of the employer to the extent of the Board's award to the employee under section 24 of the Ordinance.[186]

Section 16(2) of the statute stipulates the following maximum payments:

- wages to a maximum of HK$36,000 for each employee for wages owed during the previous four months;
- wages in lieu of notice equivalent to one month's wages or HK$22,500, whichever is the lesser;

---

(2) The Board may do all such things as are necessary for, or incidental or conducive to, the better carrying out of the functions of the Board and may in particular, but without prejudice to the generality of the foregoing—
(a) hold, acquire or lease all kinds of property whether movable or immovable;
(b) sell or otherwise dispose of all kinds of property whether movable or immovable;
(c) subject to section 10, invest its funds in such manner and to such extent as it thinks necessary or expedient; and
(d) with the prior consent of the Financial Secretary, borrow money in such manner and on such securities or terms as it thinks expedient.

186. LEWINGTON, *supra* note 131, vol. 1, at 263.
Section 24 of the Ordinance states in part:

(1) Where a payment is made under section 16 to an applicant in respect of wages due to him, or in respect of any liability to pay him a severance payment, whether or not the severance payment is due when that payment under section 16 is made, all his rights and remedies with respect to those wages or severance payment, as the case may be, existing immediately before that payment under section 16 shall, to the extent of the amount of that payment under section 16, be transferred to and vest in the Board for the benefit of the Fund and the Board may take such steps as it considers necessary to enforce those rights and remedies.
(2) The rights and remedies of an applicant in respect of a severance payment transferred to and vested in the Board pursuant to subsection (1) shall include the rights and remedies of the applicant in respect of so much of that severance payment as the applicant would, on the winding up of a company, be entitled to priority under section 265(1)(ca) of the Companies Ordinance (Cap 32) or would, on a bankruptcy, be entitled to priority under section 38(1)(ca) of the Bankruptcy Ordinance (Cap 6).
(2A) Where—
(a) the amount of any wages due to an applicant exceeds the amount of any payment made to him under section 16 in respect of those wages, nothing in this section shall affect the rights or remedies of the applicant in respect of the amount of the excess;

Protection of Wages on Insolvency Ordinance, *supra* note 182, at section 24.

- severance pay exceeding the aggregate of $50,000 for each employee, and half of that part of the employee's entitlement to severance payment in excess of $50,000.[187]

H. Miscellaneous Ordinances

There are many other Ordinances which directly or indirectly affect the employer-employee relationship. A thorough discussion of these statutes and their provisions is beyond the scope of this work. However, due to the impact of these statutes, they are listed here for the reader's reference. One such ordinance is the *Employees Compensation Assistance Ordinance* (Cap 365). The "Long title" of this statute indicates its purpose is:

> to provide for the protection of the entitlement of employees and others to compensation or damages for employment-related injury; for the protection of employers against default under policies of insurance in respect of their liability for such compensation or damages; for the establishment of a board and a fund for those purposes; and for incidental or connected matters.

In addition to the ordinances mentioned earlier in this chapter, the following laws also have a substantial effect upon employers and employees: *Companies Ordinance* (Cap 32), *Employees Retraining Ordinance* (Cap 423), *Employment of Young Persons and Children at Sea Ordinance* (Cap 58), *Labour Relations Ordinance* (Cap 55), *Mandatory Provident Fund Schemes Ordinance* (Cap 485), *Occupational Retirement Schemes Ordinance* (Cap 426), and *Personal Data (Privacy) Ordinance* (Cap 486).[188] Others are presented below in the following section.

IV. THE EMPLOYMENT CONTRACT

Various laws impact upon the parties' agreement and their obligations toward each other under the employment contract. These matters are presented below, firstly with a review of the statutory requirements, followed by the parties' obligations under an employment contract and finally the requirement of confidentiality during and after the conclusion of the

187. A portion of the text of section 16 of the *Protection of Wages on Insolvency Ordinance* is set out in *supra* note 183.

188. For a more comprehensive listing of laws affecting employment, *see* DOWNEY, *supra* note 12, at §§C.4–C.9 ("Employment of children").

employment agreement. It should be noted that an employment contract is a legally binding agreement and is therefore subject to the usual rules of contract law.[189]

A. Statutory Implications

Four anti-discrimination ordinances apply in Hong Kong. The four laws which are in force are: the *Sex Discrimination Ordinance* (Cap 480);[190] the *Disability Discrimination Ordinance* (Cap 487);[191] the *Family Status Discrimination Ordinance* (Cap 527);[192] and, the *Race Discrimination Ordinance* (Cap 602).[193] Part III of each of these four Ordinances contains anti-discrimination provisions in relation to employment.[194] These provisions concern the offer of employment, opportunities for promotion, transfer

189. *See id.* at §§B.1–B.7 for a thorough discussion of terms and conditions of an employment contract under the *Employment Ordinance*, *supra* note 2; 10(2) HALSBURY'S, *supra* note 11, at paras. 145.019–145.026 for a review of the formalities of an employment contract and paras. 145.027–145.033 concerning the terms of employment. *See also* ARJUNAN & NABI BAKSH, *supra* note 16, at 575; GLOFCHESKI–EMPLOYMENT, *supra* note 12, at Chapter 3 ("Contract of Employment").

190. The *Sex Discrimination Ordinance* (Cap 480) is discussed in detail by 10(2) HALSBURY'S, *supra* note 11, at paras. 145.125–145.180. *See also* GLOFCHESKI–EMPLOYMENT, *supra* note 12, at Chapter 8 ("Discrimination Law"); DOWNEY, *supra* note 12, at §§F.2–F.18 ("Discrimination on the Basis of Gender"), Part F generally for a review of all matters pertaining to discrimination.

191. The *Disability Discrimination Ordinance* (Cap 487) is presented in greater detail in 10(2) HALSBURY'S, *supra* note 11, at paras. 145.181–145.238. *See also* GLOFCHESKI–EMPLOYMENT, *supra* note 12, at Chapter 8 ("Discrimination Law"), particularly paras. 8.097–8.101; DOWNEY, *supra* note 12, at §§F.35–F.42 for discussions, examples, and explanations on the protections afforded by the *Disability Discrimination Ordinance*.

192. *See* 10(2) HALSBURY'S, *supra* note 11, at paras. 145.239–145.292 for an in-depth analysis of this Ordinance. *See also* GLOFCHESKI–EMPLOYMENT, *supra* note 12, at Chapter 8 ("Discrimination Law"), particularly para. 8.102; DOWNEY, *supra* note 12, at §§F.43–F.53 ("Discrimination on the Basis of Family Status").

193. The *Race Discrimination Ordinance* (Cap 602) is reviewed in detail at GLOFCHESKI–EMPLOYMENT, *supra* note 12, at paras. 8.103–8.108. *See also* DOWNEY, *supra* note 12, at §§F.34.1–F.34.5 ("Discrimination on the Basis of Race").

194. *See, e.g.*, section 11 of the *Sex Discrimination Ordinance*, *supra* note 190, which, for example, provides in part:

> (1) It is unlawful for a person, in relation to employment by him at an establishment in Hong Kong, to discriminate against a woman—
> (a) in the arrangements he makes for the purpose of determining who should be offered that employment;
> (b) in the terms on which he offers her that employment; or
> (c) by refusing or deliberately omitting to offer her that employment.
>
> (2) It is unlawful for a person, in the case of a woman employed by him at an establishment in Hong Kong, to discriminate against her-

or training; the provision of benefits, facilities or services, or the refusal or deliberate omission of access to those benefits; terms of employment; and, dismissal and other detrimental acts. Furthermore, these Ordinances also contain provisions regulating discriminatory advertising, such as gender-specific employment advertisements.[195] As a result of the enactment of these four Ordinances, it is unlawful to treat a person less favourably than others on the basis of gender, marital status, pregnancy, disability, race or family status, *e.g.*, having responsibility for the care of an immediate family member. There is, however, no legislation presently in force in Hong Kong that outlaws discrimination on the basis of religion or gender orientation.

(a) in the way he affords her access to opportunities for promotion, transfer or training, or to any other benefits, facilities or services, or by refusing or deliberately omitting to afford her access to them;
(b) in the terms of employment he affords her; or
(c) by dismissing her, or subjecting her to any other detriment.

(3) Except in relation to discrimination falling within section 9, subsections (1) and (2) shall not apply to employment where the number of persons employed by the employer, added to the number employed by any associated employers of his, does not exceed 5 (disregarding any persons employed for the purposes of a private home).

See, e.g., section 8 of the *Family Status Discrimination Ordinance* (Cap 527), which provides a prohibition against discrimination based on family status in language essentially identical to the above.
See also Hubbard, *supra* note 17, at 483.

195. *See, e.g.*, section 31 of the *Family Status Discrimination Ordinance*, *supra* note 194, which states:

(1) It is unlawful to publish or cause to be published an advertisement which indicates, or might reasonably be understood as indicating, an intention by a person to do any act which is or might be unlawful by virtue of Part III or IV.
(2) Subsection (1) shall not apply to an advertisement if the intended act would not in fact be unlawful.
(3) For the purposes of subsection (1), use of a job description which is specific to a particular family status or the absence of family status shall be taken to indicate an intention to discriminate, unless the advertisement contains an indication to the contrary.
(4) The publisher of an advertisement made unlawful by subsection (1) shall not be subject to any liability under that subsection in respect of the publication of the advertisement if he proves-
(a) that the advertisement was published in reliance on a statement made to him by the person who caused it to be published to the effect that, by reason of the operation of subsection (2), the publication would not be unlawful; and
(b) that it was reasonable for him to rely on the statement.
(5) A person who knowingly or recklessly makes a statement of the kind referred to in subsection (4) which in a material respect is false or misleading commits an offence and is liable on conviction to a fine at level 4.

Section 21B[196] of the *Employment Ordinance* makes it an offence for employers, or anyone acting on their behalf to prevent or deter individuals from exercising their trade union rights once hired. Section 21C[197] of the Ordinance makes it a criminal offence to offer employment contingent upon the applicant's status as a non-trade union member, or to impede this individual's enrolment or participation in a union, or this person's association with others for the purpose of forming a union.[198]

Another restriction upon employment bias arises out of the *Rehabilitation of Offenders Ordinance* (Cap 297), which aims to protect first-time offenders

---

196. Section 21B provides in part:

> (1) Every employee shall as between himself and his employer have the following rights—
> (a) the right to be or to become a member or an officer of a trade union registered under the Trade Unions Ordinance (Cap 332);
> (b) where he is a member or an officer of any such trade union, the right, at any appropriate time, to take part in the activities of the trade union;
> (c) the right to associate with other persons for the purpose of forming or applying for the registration of a trade union in accordance with the provisions of the Trade Unions Ordinance (Cap 332);
>
> ...
>
> (2) Any employer, or any person acting on behalf of an employer, who—
> (a) prevents or deters, or does any act calculated to prevent or deter, an employee from exercising any of the rights conferred on him by subsection (1); or
> (b) terminates the contract of employment of, penalizes, or otherwise discriminates against, an employee by reason of his exercising any such right,
>
> shall be guilty of an offence and shall be liable on conviction to a fine at level 6.

Employment Ordinance, *supra* note 2.

197. Section 21C states:

> Any person who, acting on his own or another's behalf, in the engagement of persons for employment includes in an offer of employment to any person a condition or requirement that the person to whom the offer is made shall undertake—
> (a) if he is a member or officer of such a trade union, that he will relinquish his membership thereof or office therein;
> (b) not to become a member of, or officer in, such a trade union; or
> (c) not to associate with other persons for the purpose of forming or applying for the registration of a trade union in accordance with the provisions of the Trade Unions Ordinance (Cap 332),
>
> shall be guilty of an offence and shall be liable on conviction to a fine at level 6.

198. *Id.*

For further discussion of this topic, *see* 10(2) HALSBURY'S, *supra* note 11, at paras. 145.104–145.105; GLOFCHESKI–EMPLOYMENT, *supra* note 12, at paras. 16.052–16.061.

from discrimination based upon a minor conviction in their past. Section 2(1)(iii) provides that subject to sections 3 and 4 neither the conviction itself nor any failure to disclose it shall be "a lawful and proper ground for dismissing or excluding that individual from any office, profession, occupation or employment or for prejudicing him in any way."[199]

No party who is aware that its employment contract is tainted by illegality, can enforce the agreement or any statutory rights based on or arising from that contract.[200] Nonetheless, section 2(2) of the *Employees' Compensation Ordinance* expressly grants the courts discretion to ignore an illegality, whether in the formation of the contract or in its performance, when the courts hear compensation claims under this Ordinance.[201]

---

199. *See, e.g.*, section 2(1) which mandates in part:

> (1) Where—
> (a) an individual has been convicted in Hong Kong (before or after the commencement of this Ordinance) of an offence in respect of which he was not sentenced to imprisonment exceeding 3 months or to a fine exceeding $10000;
> (b) he has not been convicted in Hong Kong on any earlier day of an offence; and
> (c) a period of 3 years has elapsed without that individual being again convicted in Hong Kong of an offence,
>
> then—
> (i) subject to section 3(3) and (4), no evidence shall be admissible in any proceedings which tends to show that that individual was so convicted in Hong Kong;
> (ii) any question asked of that individual or any other person relating to, or any obligation imposed on that individual or any other person to disclose, that individual's previous convictions, offences, conduct or circumstances shall be treated as not referring to that conviction; and
> (iii) that conviction, or any failure to disclose it shall not be a lawful or proper ground for dismissing or excluding that individual from any office, profession, occupation or employment or for prejudicing him in any way in that office, profession, occupation or employment.

Rehabilitation of Offenders Ordinance (Cap 297).

200. *See, e.g.*, Downey, *supra* note 12, at §§A.5.1 ("Illegality and Unenforceability of Contract"), A.10–A.11 (discussing contractual terms and illegal terms).

201. Section 2(2) of the *Employees' Compensation Ordinance*, *supra* note 2, states in full:

> If, in any proceedings for the recovery of compensation under this Ordinance, it appears to the Court that the contract of service or apprenticeship under which the injured person was working, at the time when the accident causing the injury happened, was illegal, the Court may, if having regard to all the circumstances of the case it thinks proper so to do, deal with the matter as if the injured person had at the time aforesaid been a person working under a valid contract of service or apprenticeship.

See Downey, *supra* note 12, at §A.5.1 ("Illegality and Unenforceability of Contract").

Certain types of contracts are subject to special rules:

- The *Apprenticeship Ordinance* (Cap 47) regulates the employment and work parameters of persons over the age of fourteen years and under the age of nineteen years.[202] The purpose of this Ordinance is to promote and regulate the training of apprentice craftsmen and technicians. No employer in any of forty-three "designated trades" may employ a young person over the age of fourteen years and under the age of nineteen years of age except by a written and signed apprenticeship contract registered with the Director of Apprenticeship. No contract can be registered unless it contains appropriate terms and conditions concerning hours of work, rest days, training, payment of wages, and so on. This contract must be explained to, and understood by, both the apprentice and the guardian of the apprentice.[203]
- *Contracts for Employment Outside Hong Kong Ordinance* (Cap 78) protects manual workers and domestic servants recruited in Hong Kong to work overseas for non-Hong Kong individuals or for companies not conducting business in the territory.[204] The "Long title" of this Ordinance states its purpose is to:

  > control contracts of employment entered into in Hong Kong by employees performing primarily manual work and certain other employees who are proceeding outside Hong Kong for employment.

  This Ordinance establishes an institutional structure to prevent exploitation of workers who contract in Hong Kong to work abroad. With the exception of certain categories of employees, such as air crew and emigrants, all such contracts must be in a standard form,[205] signed by both

202. On the matter of employment training of apprentices, *see* 10(2) HALSBURY'S, *supra* note 11, at paras. 145.408–145.456. In relation to the employment of minors, *see*, *e.g.*, the Employment of Children Regulations (Cap 57B) and Employment of Young Persons (Industry) Regulations (Cap 57C). For an analysis on the subject of employment of children and young persons, *see* 10(2) HALSBURY'S, *supra* note 11, at paras. 145.344–145.351, 145.363–374; DOWNEY, *supra* note 12, at §§C.4–C.18.
203. For a review of this Ordinance and the obligations entailed therein, *see* GLOFCHESKI–EMPLOYMENT, *supra* note 12, at para. 2.055; 10(2) HALSBURY'S, *supra* note 11, at paras. 145.011, 145.408–145.456.
204. For a discussion of this Ordinance and the obligations entailed therein, *see* GLOFCHESKI–EMPLOYMENT, *supra* note 12, at paras. 2.056–2.057; 10(2) HALSBURY'S, *supra* note 11, at para. 145.010; DOWNEY, *supra* note 12, at §§C.23–C27 ("Employment Outside of Hong Kong").
205. *See Contracts for Employment Outside Hong Kong Ordinance* (Cap 78) section 4:

parties and attested by the Labour Department prior to the worker's departure overseas.[206] This Ordinance specifies that the contract is void as against the worker should the contract fail to comply with the statutory requirements. Section 7 provides that where the omission to make the contract in writing or to present the contract for attestation is due to the employer's wilful omission or neglect, the employee may, without prejudice to any right to sue for damages for breach of contract, sue the employer for expenses incurred in returning along with family to Hong Kong.[207]

> (1) Subject to subsection (2), this Ordinance applies to contracts of employment entered into in Hong Kong after the commencement of this Ordinance, by which a person in Hong Kong enters or agrees to enter into the service of another person who is not in Hong Kong and not carrying on a business in Hong Kong where the contract is to be performed, whether wholly or partially, outside Hong Kong.
> (2) This Ordinance shall not apply in respect of—
> (a) persons employed for service as members of the crews of ships or aircraft;
> (b) (Repealed 56 of 2000 s. 3)
> (c) any person or class of persons migrating for employment whose admission to the place of immigration will be granted on a permanent basis.
> (d) any person who does not perform primarily manual work and whose wages exceed an amount set by the Secretary for Labour and Welfare by notice in the Gazette.

206. *Id.* at section 6 provides: "Every contract to which this Ordinance applies shall be presented to the Commissioner for attestation before the departure of the employee from Hong Kong."

207. Section 7 states in full:

> Where a contract to which this Ordinance applies—
> (a) is not in writing in accordance with section 5(1); or
> (b) has not been presented to the Commissioner for attestation before the departure of the employee from Hong Kong,
>
> it shall not be enforceable against the employee and no action shall be maintainable against the employee for breach or non-fulfilment thereof, and, where the omission to make the contract in writing or to present the contract for attestation, as the case may be, is due to wilful omission or neglect on the part of the employer or any person acting on the employer's behalf, the employee may, without prejudice to any right he may have to sue for damages for breach of contract, sue the employer or such person for any expenses reasonably incurred by him in the return of himself and any dependants accompanying him to Hong Kong.

Id.

- *Merchant Shipping (Seafarers) Ordinance* (Cap 478) regulates the hiring and employment of seafarers in matters such as recruitment fees, discharge and removal of discharged seafarers, crew agreements, regulations in relation to crew agreements, payment and account of wages, wage dispute resolution, powers of the court, and, protection of rights and remedies.[208]

B. The Parties' Obligations

Having earlier considered some of the statutory obligations of both the employer and employee, this section reviews the general common law obligations of the parties arising from an employment contract. As each employment contract contains its own express provisions concerning the working relationship between the parties, this section will not analyse any particular type of employment contract.

i. *Employee's Obligations*

The right of employers to command and the duty of employees to obey are fundamental elements of an employment contract. Employees must undertake tasks which are within their job description and obey an employer's instructions which are lawful and reasonable.[209] The job description and definition of "lawful and reasonable orders" are questions of fact to be ascertained by a court considering all the circumstances of a particular case.[210]

---

208. 10(2) HALSBURY'S, *supra* note 11, at para. 145.014.
A related statute is the *Employment of Young Persons and Children at Sea Ordinance* (Cap 58) which is reviewed at 10(2) HALSBURY'S, *supra* note 11, at paras. 145.344–145.351. *See also* DOWNEY, *supra* note 12, at §K.59 for a brief discussion of compensation for persons employed on ships.

209. 10(2) HALSBURY'S, *supra* note 11, at para. 145.036 notes that an employee "is under a [*sic*] implied contractual obligation to carry out lawful orders given by and employer."
See also DOWNEY, *supra* note 12, at §§B.69–B.70 (analysing the scope and application of job descriptions).

210. One authority states in relevant part:

> Lawfulness is determined by reference to instructions which are within the scope of the contract of employment. There is, however, an implied obligation on the employer not to give the employee orders which are illegal or, in some cases, dangerous. An employee cannot lawfully be ordered to work beyond the terms of employment, or to vary such terms against an employee's consent, in order to cover new duties. Insistence on such an order could found a claim of constructive dismissal.

Wilful disobedience of a lawful and reasonable order shows a complete disregard of a condition essential to the contract of service so as to warrant dismissal. So, while an isolated incident of lateness may not warrant dismissal, persistent and repeated lateness that had been warned against has been held to be a sufficient ground for summary dismissal by reason of disobeying a lawful order. Holding a stop work meeting to discuss pay conditions has been held to be wilful disobedience of an employer's lawful and reasonable orders. Whether an order is reasonable will need to be assessed in the context in which it is given. The employee has the burden of establishing a reasonable excuse in not obeying a *prima facie* lawful and reasonable instruction of the employer. Where an employer gives a direction to an employee that is both lawful and within the scope of the employee's employment, the employee is obliged to comply with such direction.[211]

Should an employee's act amount to improper disobedience, the employer is entitled to refuse to pay wages in full, to discipline the worker or to dismiss the worker summarily upon a deliberate flouting of this basic obligation.[212] An employee may refuse an employer's instruction if that order

---

> A breach of the obligation to carry out a lawful order may mean that the employee may be lawfully dismissed at common law. The common law right to dismiss for failing to carry out a lawful order has been given statutory recognition.

10(2) HALSBURY'S, *supra* note 11, at para. 145.036 (citations omitted).
See also DOWNEY, *supra* note 12, at §B.69.

> While an employer can require an employee to undertake a lawful order relating to employment, an employee is not entitled to refuse to carry out any duty that falls within the scope of his or her employment duties. Even where an order to undertake specific work is lawful, there is judicial authority to suggest that such a direction must also be reasonable.
>
> By contrast, if a direction to undertake work falls outside the scope of employment, such an order will not be regarded as lawful. In such circumstances, an employee will be entitled to refuse.

DOWNEY, *supra* note 12, at §B.70.

211. GLOFCHESKI–EMPLOYMENT, *supra* note 12, at para. 3.034 (citations omitted).

212. One authority states in relation to remedies for the failure by an employee to observe employment obligations:

> An employer is entitled to resort to various remedies on failure on the part of an employee to observe the terms of the contract of employment. Where such a failure amounts to a repudiatory breach, an employer may terminate the employment summarily. In the event of suffering any loss from such a breach, an employer is entitled to sue an employee both at common law and under statute for damages and a compensation award. In addition, an employer may apply for an injunction to restrain any further breach.

10(2) HALSBURY'S, *supra* note 11, at para. 145.045 (citations omitted).
See also DOWNEY, *supra* note 12, at §O.13 ("Summary Dismissal").

would require an unlawful act, would expose the employee to physical dangers not contemplated by the employment contract, or would otherwise require the employee to go beyond the parties' contractual undertaking.[213]

An employee is obligated to provide faithful service to the employer such that certain activities are prohibited, including but not limited to:[214]

- Misappropriation: the misuse of the worker's position in the company to take secret profits, commissions or bribes.[215] Such conduct would justify the employee's summary dismissal. In *GSL Engineering Ltd v Yau Hon-yin Sammon* [1991] 1 HKLR 199, the plaintiff obtained injunctions against the defendant, a former managing director of the plaintiff company. The defendant applied to set aside the injunctions. The defendant admitted that in breach of duty he had wrongfully diverted business from the plaintiff. Through this diversion of business, the defendant had made secret profits. The court followed the precedent established in *Thomas Marshall (Exports) Ltd v Guinle* [1979] 1 Ch 227 and refused the application. The court stated:

  > it is true that here the defendant is no longer in the employ of the plaintiff, but ... by the way of his acting as managing director of the company ... the defendant had established his relationship with the suppliers and customers of the company, so that, even if he ceased to be managing director of the company he could not claim instant freedom to use for himself the relationship which he had established on behalf of the company. [1991] 1 HKLR at 204.

"Repudiatory breach" is defined as a breach of contract which "must evidence either a failure to comply with or an intention not to comply with an essential term of a contract." ARJUNAN & NABI BAKSH, *supra* note 16, at 379–380.

An "injunction" is defined as "an order of court to prohibit threatened or continuing illegal conduct of certain kinds." ARJUNAN & NABI BAKSH, *supra* note 16, at 446.

Section 9 of the *Employment Ordinance* is set out in *supra* note 114.

213. *See* DOWNEY, *supra* note 12, at §B.70 ("Definition and Scope").

10(2) HALSBURY'S, *supra* note 11, at para. 145.036 states in part:

> It is an implied term of a contract of employment that an employee must not be required by an employer to do an unlawful act. A dismissal for refusing to obey an order to do such an act is likely to amount to a constructive dismissal. Similarly, an employer may not order an employee into danger, though this is clearly a more vague rule than that against illegality; and it seems that, in order to justify refusal to obey such an order, the danger must be immediate and personal. (citations omitted)

214. An employee's duty of fidelity and good faith is reviewed in GLOFCHESKI–EMPLOYMENT, *supra* note 12, at paras. 3.028–3.032; DOWNEY, *supra* note 12, at §§B.64–B.66 ("Exclusivity of Employment"). For an analysis of other activities in which an employee should not engage, *see, e.g.*, 10(2) HALSBURY'S, *supra* note 11, at paras. 145.038–145.039.

215. *See, e.g.*, 10(2) HALSBURY'S, *supra* note 11, at para. 145.040 and citations therein.

- Competition: an employee may not compete with the employer during the period of the contract.[216]
- Confidential information and trade secrets: information which is imparted or gained in confidence during the employee's tenure may not be disclosed or otherwise misused, whilst employed. Once an employee has left the company, this information may be used freely despite a restrictive covenant in the employment contract unless the information constitutes a trade secret.[217] In *Ho Wing-cheong v Graham Margot* [1991] 1 HKLR 245, the court agreed with the decision in *Putsman v Taylor* [1927] 1 KB 637 that not only information in the nature of trade secrets but also information which can be acquired by the employee from contact with customers is capable of protection. The Hong Kong court stated at 248:

---

216. *See GSL Engineering Ltd v Yau Hon-yin Sammon* [1991] 1 HKLR 199; 10(2) HALSBURY'S, *supra* note 11, at para. 145.040 and citations therein; DOWNEY, *supra* note 12, at §§B.64–B.66 ("Exclusivity of Employment").

217. L.B. CURZON & P.H. RICHARDS, THE LONGMAN DICTIONARY OF LAW 582 (7th ed. 2007), defines "trade secret" as:

> Some manufacturing or productive process, knowledge of which has economic value in that it is generally confined to a business which has a proprietary interest in it and utilisation of which provides an advantage over competitors. Disclosure of such information, as the result of a breach of confidence or where it has resulted from employment under contract, can be prevented by injunction.

Thus a trade secret must be respected during and after employment has ended. A trade secret is difficult to define; some considerations include: nature of employment, nature of information, extent to which confidentiality stressed and how easily the alleged trade secret can be separated from other unprotected knowledge. A secret and highly advantageous process of manufacture would be an example of a trade secret.

See also 10(2) HALSBURY'S, *supra* note 11, at para. 145.044 and citations therein; DOWNEY, *supra* note 12, at §§B.67–B68 ("Restrictive Agreements"); HUBBARD, *supra* note 17, at 342, 367.

> It is very common for employers to attempt to restrict the manner in which employees are employed after their employment is terminated. Contractual terms that restrict the manner of employment with third parties are commonly referred to as agreements in restraint of trade. The general term 'restrictive agreements' will be used here.
>
> A restrictive agreement between an employer and an employee are generally unenforceable unless such an agreement applies to some tangible subject matter that belongs to the employer and any such restraint is regarded by a court as both reasonable between the parties and reasonable by reference to the public interest. The onus of proving whether a term is reasonable rests with the person relying on the restraint.

DOWNEY, *supra* note 12, at §B.68.

> The reason ... is that the employer's customer connection belongs to the employer, not the employee, although it may be the employee who has built it up or maintained it. If the law were to permit the employee, who has built up or maintained the employer's customer connection, to walk off with it ... in the face of restrictions entered into by the employee to protect the employer against just such a risk and going no further than reasonably necessary for that purpose, the employer would have just cause for complaint. The risk is that the employee "might obtain such personal knowledge of and influence over the customers of his employer ... as would enable him, if competition were allowed, to take advantage of his employer's trade connection."—see Herbert Morris Ltd. v. Saxelby [1916] AC 688 *per* Lord Parker of Waddington at page 709. Such restrictions, then, will be enforced if "the protection sought is reasonably necessary to ... prevent some personal influence over customers being abused in order to entice them away." (citations omitted)

Another authority has compiled a similar list of an employee's implied duties:

- Duty of fidelity and good faith, including the obligation not to persuade customers of the current employer to move with the employee to the new employer; not to be in business in competition with the employer; to disclose misconduct of fellow employees; and, not to disrupt the business operations of the employer. [218]
- Duty to exercise reasonable skill and competence in executing the duties and tasks of the employer.[219]
- Duty not to disclose the employer's confidential information or the employer's trade secrets.[220]
- Duty to account for the employer's property provided to the employee or to account for profits made during the course of employment.[221]
- Duty to indemnify the employer in the event of the employer's vicarious liability for the tortious act of the employee.[222]

---

218. GLOFCHESKI–EMPLOYMENT, *supra* note 12, at paras. 3.028–3.032.
219. *Id.* at para. 3.033.
220. *Id.* at paras. 3.035–3.038.
The subjects of confidentiality and trade secrets are discussed in further in section IV.C.
221. GLOFCHESKI–EMPLOYMENT, *supra* note 12, at para. 3.039.
222. *Id.* at para. 3.040.
See section II.C for an analysis of vicarious liability.

- Duty not to participate in industrial action which would disrupt the business of the employer.[223]

ii. *Employer's Obligations*

The preceding section reviewed the worker's obligations in an employment agreement. In this section, the employer's obligations under a contract is presented.[224] The employer's obligations may be classified under three broad categories: pay, employee safety, and, legal. It should be noted that the last category has significant overlap with the first two categories in that there exist legal requirements in relation to the payment of wages or other remuneration and employee safety.[225]

Generally, under a contract of employment, an employer's basic obligation is the payment of remuneration, rather than the provision of work.[226]

---

223. GLOFCHESKI–EMPLOYMENT, *supra* note 12, at para. 3.041.

> Industrial action that falls short of a strike (*e.g.* work to rule) can amount to a breach of contract. Any action of an employee designed to disrupt the business of the employer will breach the implied duty of good faith. This extends to a restriction on taking industrial action designed to damage the employer. So, an employee participating in a strike may be in breach of his contract of employment. However, the employer would be prohibited from summarily dismissing the employee under [section 9 of the *Employment Ordinance*]. Where industrial action takes the form of a refusal to undertake certain actions that would fall within the normal course of employment, then this will be a breach of contract where the refusal contravenes a direct order from the employer. …

Id. (citations omitted)

224. Similar to the difficulties in ascertaining the status of a worker, one's status as an employer is at times difficult to determine. *See, e.g.*, 10(2) HALSBURY'S, *supra* note 11, at paras. 145.016–145.018.

225. Accordingly, some of these relationships have already been discussed in preceding sections and will not be repeated here.

226. 10(2) HALSBURY'S, *supra* note 11, at para. 145.046 notes:

> The rate of remuneration usually depends upon the terms of the contract and the obligation to pay may be express or implied.
>
> …
>
> Even where there is a definite requirement of remuneration, this does not necessarily mean that there must be a regular wage. There may be a valid contract of employment where the employee is to be rewarded only by fees or commission, or by the receipt of tips from customers, or by being given the chance to earn a salary.

For the purposes of this work, the term "remuneration" includes indemnification or reimbursements owed by the employer to the employee. *See* DOWNEY, *supra* note 12, at §§G.1–G.2 ("Wages and Salaries").

As one source states:

Even this basic obligation is not without controversy. Another authority notes:

> Where an employee's level of remuneration is dependent on the number of hours worked (or amount of work performed in respect of piece rate employees) the law will imply an obligation on the employer to provide the employee with the opportunity to earn a reasonable wage. However, whether this right to earn wages truly amounts to a right to be given work independent of payment of remuneration (i.e. the question of whether an employer is obliged to provide work for an employee in addition to paying the agreed salary) is less clear.[227]

As with most general rules, there are exceptions. In this instance, one exception might include situations where the performance of the work, and the attendant publicity, are as important to the employee as the remuneration, as in the case of an actor or singer.[228] Other exceptions might include instances where it is necessary for the employer to provide work in order for the employee to earn the remuneration, *e.g.*, the employee is paid on a commission basis or a piece-work basis, or where the employee is engaged to fill a particular office.[229]

> An employer is under an implied duty to indemnify or to reimburse the employee, as the case may be, against all liabilities and losses and in respect of all expenses incurred by the employee either in consequence of obedience to orders, or incurred by the employee in the execution of the employee's authority, or in the reasonable performance of the duties of employment. Notwithstanding the fact that an employee was acting in the course of employment, such an employee may lose any right of indemnity or reimbursement where the liabilities or expenses did not arise out of the nature of the transaction which the employee was employed to carry out, but were solely attributable to the default or breach of duty of the employee, or where, by reason of the employee's conduct, the employee has forfeited any right to receive any remuneration for such services.
>
> If the employer requires the employee to perform an act which, unknown to the employee, is unlawful, the employee is entitled to be indemnified by the employer against any damage suffered in consequence of its unlawful nature. Even where the transaction is prima facie unlawful, an employee is entitled to be indemnified if the employee was led to believe by the employer, and was justified in believing, that in the circumstances of the case the transaction was one in which the employee might lawfully engage.

10(2) HALSBURY'S, *supra* note 11, at para. 145.055 (citations omitted).

227. GLOFCHESKI–EMPLOYMENT, *supra* note 12, at para. 3.042 (citations omitted).

228. 10(2) HALSBURY'S, *supra* note 11, at para. 145.050 (citation omitted).
See generally DOWNEY, *supra* note 12, at Part G ("Remuneration and Benefits"), Part B ("Terms and Conditions of Employment under the Employment Ordinance").

229. 10(2) HALSBURY'S, *supra* note 11, at para. 145.050 (citations omitted).

As noted earlier in this chapter, an employer has both a common law duty as well as a statutory law duty to take reasonable care of its employee's safety.[230] Accordingly, should an employer fail in this obligation to keep an employee safe in the course of employment, the injured employee may be able to bring an action against the employer both in negligence and for breach of contract.[231] This obligation has been summarized as follows:

> At common law, an employer is under a duty to take reasonable care for the safety of employees in all the circumstances of the case so as not to expose them to an unnecessary risk. The duty to exercise reasonable care is, however, personal to the employer. If the employer entrusts its performance to some other person, the employer will be vicariously liable for any negligence on the part of the person so appointed in performing the duty. The duty may vary with the employee's particular circumstances which are known, or ought reasonably to be known, to the employer.
>
> An employer's duty to take reasonable care to carry on operations so as not to subject employees to unnecessary risks is a single and continuing duty, applicable in all circumstances. For convenience, in applying the principle in particular cases, however, the employer's obligation has long been recognised as threefold in character, that is to say, to provide (1) a competent staff of employees; (2) adequate material; and (3) a proper system and effective supervision. In addition, it is the employer's duty to take reasonable care to provide and maintain a reasonably safe place of work for employees and reasonably safe access to it.[232]

---

230. *See, e.g.*, *id.* at para. 145.053; DOWNEY, *supra* note 12, at §§K.1–K.2 (reviewing an employer's duties in relation to health and safety of the workplace).
231. 10(2) HALSBURY'S, *supra* note 11, at para. 145.051 (citations omitted).
232. *See id.* at para. 145.052 (citations omitted); DOWNEY, *supra* note 12, at §§K.1–K.2. GLOFCHESKI–EMPLOYMENT, *supra* note 12, at para. 3.043 notes:

> An employer must ensure that the plant, tools, equipment, premises and systems of work used in the employer's business are safe. …
>
> …
>
> So the employer's duty does not extend to an absolute duty to warrant the safety of an employee. The employer will not be liable for an injury caused by a latent defect in machinery reasonably chosen by the employer. In addition, an employer is not under any duty to protect the belongings of an employee. (citations omitted)

C. Non-competition Clauses/Restrictive Covenants

The protection of the employer's proprietary interest in its business or company might also affect the employment relationship. Non-competition clauses in employment contracts prevent an employee, on leaving a company, from competing with that company, thereby restricting the employee's ability to compete in the future. This restraint must be no wider than is necessary in order to protect the employer's legitimate interests. A non-competition clause cannot be used to stifle competition; otherwise, such a clause would be void for restraint of trade under contract law principles.[233] Restrictive covenants in employment contracts operate in a similar manner as non-competition clauses and are subject to the same limitations imposed by law.

> Restrictive covenants are void for being in restraint of trade and contrary to public policy unless the employer can show that the provision is reasonable in all the circumstances to protect a legitimate business interest. Legitimate business interests have been held to include the protection of trade connections and goodwill, the protection of confidential information and trade secrets and maintaining a stable workforce. The reasonableness of such a restrictive covenant is generally considered by reference to the duration, geographical scope and nature of the activities restrained. The most common forms of restrictive covenant are non-disclosure of confidential information, non-solicitation of customers, non-solicitation of work colleagues and non-competition clauses.[234]

The use of these types of clauses in an employment contract is intended to protect the confidential aspects of the employer's business operations. Employees have an obligation of good faith and fidelity to their employers. This obligation includes nearly all types of information concerning the employer. Unauthorized use or disclosure of an employer's information for another business constitutes a breach of this obligation.[235]

Former employees have a more restricted obligation of confidentiality. This obligation extends only to trade secrets, *i.e.*, information which

233. *See, e.g.*, 10(2) HALSBURY'S, *supra* note 11, at paras. 145.042–145.044. *See supra* note 217 and accompanying main text.

234. GLOFCHESKI–EMPLOYMENT, *supra* note 12, at para. 3.068 (citations omitted).
See HUBBARD, *supra* note 17, at 359 (discussing the main principles governing the valid use of restrictive convenants).

235. *See, e.g.*, 10(2) HALSBURY'S, *supra* note 11, at paras. 145.040, 145.042.

has a high level of confidentiality and importance. The obligation upon ex-employees does not extend to information which becomes part of the employee's skill, knowledge and experience.

Courts currently favour the inclusion of an express restrictive covenant in the employment contract restraining competitive activities immediately following termination of employment. The courts prefer to enforce restrictive covenants, subject to the reasonableness test, rather than to enforce confidentiality obligations.[236]

GSL Engineering Ltd, discussed earlier, also concerns misuse of confidential information by ex-employees. Godfrey J at 201–02 cited *Mauriello (HK) Ltd v Julie Chen Soo-lee (t/a The Bohemian Shop)*, unreported, (1989) A7088/87 in which the judge summarized the law on this issue:

> the court will look unfavourably on an employee who steals his employer's goodwill. If, during … your employment, you use your position and your employer's time for your own benefit you cannot expect any sympathy from the court. Every employee owes to his employers a duty of fidelity. If, after your employment is terminated, you steal your employer's trade connection by under-hand and dishonest conduct … again you cannot expect any favourable treatment from the court. If, whether before or after the termination of your employment, you set about, knowing of your employer's contracts with other people, to induce those other people to break their contracts with your employer and to do business with you, then again you can expect no sympathy from the court. All these things are actionable wrongs … This is trite law; but so is the proposition that an employee who leaves an employer and enters into a business competing with his employer does not per se

236. One authority comments:

> There is a fundamental issue which is usually addressed by the courts before the question of reasonableness of a restrictive agreement is considered. A term restricting employment is enforceable only if it protects an interest that can either be regarded as belonging to the employer or in respect of which the employer can be considered to have sufficient interest. As a general rule, such a proprietary interest will normally include property in the form of trade secrets or recognized customer connections, but not mere competition. Terms that expressly restrain employees or former employees from enticing, soliciting or employing employees currently employed or formerly employed by an employer are usually only enforceable in the event of a court being satisfied that such employees might have access to (and misuse) trade secrets or customer connections.

Downey, *supra* note 12, at §B.68.

See the table of the types of information which is protected by restrictive covenants during and after employment in Hubbard, *supra* note 17, at 333.

> do anything wrong at all, no matter how damaging to the interest of the employer that course of conduct may prove to be. Every one is entitled to use or sell his or her own labour.

In this case, the defendant's knowledge of the plaintiff's business practices, customers' requirements, prices to its customers and of suppliers and their prices to the plaintiff, all of which were obtained as a result of the defendant's service as the plaintiff's managing director, were held not to be information of a confidential character.

The common law principles governing obligations of confidentiality in an employment context may be summarized as follows:

(1) The obligations are determined by the contract of employment.
   (a) While the employment continues, an express term imposing obligations of confidentiality will be fully enforceable for most practical purposes.
   (b) After the employment is terminated, an express undertaking of confidentiality will be enforceable subject to the following reservations:
      (i) The undertaking must specify the information or types of information protected. If the express term broadly refers to confidential information generally, the courts are likely to find only a breach in relation to information considered to be a trade secret or its equivalent.
      (ii) Equitable remedies are available where such information can be easily separated from the employee's own skill, knowledge and experience.[237]
      (iii) If there is no express term in the contract governing confidentiality, the employee's obligations will be governed by implied terms.

(2) During employment, the obligations are included in the implied term which imposes a duty of good faith or fidelity on the employee.[238] Information which becomes part of the employee's own skill, knowledge and experience would fall within the duty of good faith and

237. *E.g.*, an injunction, an account of profits and/or an order for delivery up of confidential property.
The *BLIS Glossary*, *supra* note 1, translates "equitable relief" as 衡平法濟助; and, "injunction" as 強制令.

238. An employee's duty of fidelity and good faith is presented in GLOFCHESKI–EMPLOYMENT, *supra* note 12, at paras. 3.028–3.032; DOWNEY, *supra* note 12, at §§B.64–B.66 ("Exclusivity of Employment"). *See also* ARJUNAN & NABI BAKSH, *supra* note 16, at 636–638.

fidelity while the employment continues, but would not normally be restricted by an implied term after termination of employment.[239]

(3) After termination of the employment, the implied term's application becomes more restricted. The implied term extends to information that is of a sufficiently high degree of confidentiality. All information protected by the duty of good faith or fidelity during the term of the contract will not be regarded as capable of protection after termination of the employment. The information must be a trade secret or its equivalent, although there is no set list of trade secrets.

(4) To determine whether an item of information is within the scope of protection upon the contract's termination, all the circumstances of the case, including the following would be considered:

   (a) The nature of the employment: whether the employee routinely processed confidential and sensitive information, or only came across such information occasionally and had incidental access to this information.

   (b) The nature of the information itself: whether the information is a trade secret or the equivalent of a trade secret.

   (c) Whether the employer impressed upon the employee the confidential nature of the information. This information is unlikely to be a trade secret if the employer did not treat the information as such.

   (d) Whether the information can be easily isolated from other information which the employee is free to use or disclose. An employee is generally free to use the skill, knowledge and experience gained in the course of previous employment, but an employee is not free to use a trade secret or its equivalent.

The court in *Faccenda Chicken Ltd v Fowler* [1986] 1 All ER 617 expressed a policy preference for the use of restrictive covenants rather than confidentiality clauses in employment contracts.[240] Under a restrictive covenant, an

239. Such information would include, *e.g.*, customer information, pricing and operating procedures which an employee would acquire in the course of employment and which the employee would possess without recourse to confidential documents or extraordinary efforts of memorization.

240. The plaintiff in *Faccenda Chicken* was a company marketing fresh chicken. The company employed the defendant as its sales manager, and implemented a system suggested by the defendant. Later, the defendant left the company and set up a similar business in the same area, employing a number of the plaintiff's staff. There was no contractual agreement governing the activities of employees after their cessation of employment. The plaintiff sought an injunction restraining the defendant from using its confidential sales information but was unsuccessful. The Court of Appeal dismissed the plaintiff's appeal, holding that:

ex-employee may be prohibited from using trade secrets, provided that the extent of this restriction is reasonable in terms of time, place and the scope of activities. This policy preference recognizes that the purpose of enforcing confidentiality obligations after termination of employment may be to restrain competition and such restraints should be reasonable.

Where the information is confidential and sufficiently important to qualify as a trade secret, an injured party has several remedies. The employer may seek an injunction to prevent present and former employees from using or disclosing trade secrets. A court may order an employee or ex-employee to pay to the previous employer any gains or profits from the unauthorized use of a trade secret. The employer may recover compensation for any loss by suing for damages, and may obtain an order for the return of any confidential materials or items. These remedies will also apply against a third party who obtains a trade secret from an employee or ex-employee where the third party knew that the information was confidential.[241]

These principles of law provide no clear guidelines concerning the type of information regarded as a trade secret. An employing company may undertake some practical measures to obtain a level of confidentiality which the courts will protect. Some procedures which an employing company may implement include:

- A valuable trade secret should be treated as such in the daily operations of the company. It should be labelled "confidential" and its access limited.
- Employees with access to confidential information should have a confidentiality clause in their employment contract. This clause should be as specific as possible as to the information covered.

- an ex-employee did not owe the same duty of fidelity as an employee and confidential information short of a trade secret was not protected, so long as the ex-employee had not abused his duty of fidelity whilst an employee by memorising or recording said data. Furthermore, such information short of a trade secret could not be protected by a restrictive covenant; and
- in considering whether information was a trade secret or the equivalent of a trade secret, the court should have regard to a number of factors, including whether the employer had stressed the confidentiality of the information to the employee, *i.e.*, the existence of a restrictive covenant.

241. Although not concerning trade secrets, the House of Lords case of *Attorney General v Blake* [2001] 1 AC 268 concerned the recovery of profits from a former British espionage agent made from the sale of his memoirs in which the defendant divulged state secrets in violation of his written undertaking and the Official Secrets Act 1989. For further analysis of the import of this decision and its application to *Experience Hendrix LLC v PPX Enterprises Inc and Another* (2003) The Times, April 19, CA, *see, e.g.*, 2003 *Emp. Law & Lit.* 8.7(33); 2003 NLJ 153.7073(723); 1 CHITTY ON CONTRACTS paras. 26–020 to 26–028 (H.G. BEALE, *et al.* eds., 30th ed. 2008).

- An express restrictive covenant should be included in the contract when an employee first joins the company.
- Upon notice of termination, the employee's access to confidential information should be limited.
- Terminated employees' activities should be monitored and an inventory of company papers in their possession should be requested prior to departure.
- Upon providing or receiving the notice of termination, the company should assume contacts with customers or clients in order to offset the risk of a wholesale transfer of business.
- The employee should be reminded in writing of the contractual covenants to which he is bound and the continuing duty of confidentiality.

The notion of restraint of trade gives rise to these procedures.[242] Contract provisions restraining a separated employee from competing with the employer are enforceable only if these provisions protect a legitimate interest of the employer and the degree of constraint imposed on the employee is reasonable.

In ascertaining whether the restraint protects an employer's legitimate interest, courts search for proprietary interests in goodwill, trade secrets or confidential information. The interests that the courts protect include matters such as customer contact lists, supplier lists, secret formulas and processes, confidential business know-how, and the like. The courts will enforce restraints considered reasonable both in terms of the parties' interests and the public's interest.

Non-competition clauses are intended to prevent an employee, after separation, from improperly exploiting the business connections forming the goodwill of the employer's business. As one source notes:

---

242. As explained by one authority:

> It is not uncommon for employers to restrict the way in which employees and former employees use property, including information, belonging to the employer. Such restrictions normally take the form of a contractual obligation agreed to by an employee. Employers also frequently attempt to contractually restrain employees from maintaining contact with, or having access to, the employer's clients, customers and even employees after the employment has ended. Some employers go further by contractually precluding a former employee from working for competitors for a certain period. All of the above restrictions are commonly referred to as 'restraint of trade' clauses.
>
> While the law permits an employer to protect itself against misuse of property belonging to the employer eg trade lists and confidential information, the law treats as *prima facie* unenforceable any attempt on the part of an employer to protect itself against mere competition.

DOWNEY, *supra* note 12, at §B.67.

> Customer contacts are particularly important. A key employee who is introduced to the customers or clients of the business or who develops relationships with such customers at the employers' [*sic*] expense may be in a position to detract from the goodwill of the business if he/she sets up in direct competition. In some businesses, supplier contacts are equally important.[243]
>
> ...
>
> Some businesses have secret recipes, formulas, processes or business know-how that a competitor may seek to obtain by hiring a key employee who is familiar with the trade secrets. The courts will usually enforce contractual restraints to the extent that they provide reasonable protection against the loss of those secrets.[244]

The courts must balance the employer's interest in protecting its business against the employee's right to use the knowledge and experience gained in the workplace. Thus, the types of trade secret likely to be protected by the courts would be those of a confidential nature, the release of which may be injurious to the employer or advantageous to the employer's rivals and not generally known in the public domain.

> Depending on the interest to be protected, the courts will not enforce any restrictive agreement that goes beyond the proper scope of the interest being protected. Rather than rewriting a term which is defective, the courts often refuse to enforce the entire restraint where the interest that is purporting to be protected does not amount to a proprietary interest. Even where an interest belonging or relating to the employer is the proper subject matter of a restraint, the courts will refuse to enforce such terms where they are excessive either in terms of duration, scope or geographical restriction.[245]

The courts will make such determinations considering the usages and practices of the particular industry or trade concerned, as in *Gilman Engineering Ltd v Simon Ho Shek-on* (1986) 8 IPR 313. In *Gilman*, the defendant managed the plaintiff's contracting division for electrical supplies. When the defendant left the job, the plaintiff sued, asking for an interlocutory order with general terms restraining the defendant from disclosing any confidential information related to the plaintiff's business. The court found

243. LEWINGTON, *supra* note 131, vol. 2, at 446.

244. *Id.* at 448.

245. DOWNEY, *supra* note 12, at §B.68.
See also, HUBBARD, *supra* note 17, at 370–372 (tables detailing cases where duration were challenged and the factors which the courts used to decide those cases).

that such a general order was too broad to be practical because, while the defendant had access to the plaintiff employer's confidential information during employment, the plaintiff offered no specific evidence of abuse by the defendant, and because the names of companies with which the plaintiff did business were those of known suppliers in the plaintiff's field.

To summarize, reasonableness is assessed in terms of time, geographical scope and the activities restrained. The courts will also consider the particular industry context, whether the employee received an extra payment as consideration for accepting the constraint and the amount of such consideration. In *Kao, Lee & Yip v John Richard Edwards* [1993] 1 HKC 314, CA, the court held that in considering a restrictive covenant in employment contracts, the court would review, in addition to the reasonableness of the terms and the legitimacy of the interests seeking protection, the bargaining power of the covenantor and of the covenantee and whether there was mutuality between them. The Court of Appeal recognized that the goodwill of a solicitor firm took time to establish. Despite its refusal to uphold the covenant in this case, the Court of Appeal agreed with *Bridge v Deacons* [1984] AC 705 that a restrictive covenant for a five-year duration was reasonable under the circumstances

HSBC Bank Plc v Wallace [2008] 1 HKLRD 613 is a case where the plaintiff bank's restrictive convenant, an anti-competition clause, was upheld. The defendant's employment contract required six months' notice to terminate employment and included a post-termination non-compete clause. The non-competition clause applied to the Asia-Pacific region, for a period of six months after the termination date. The defendant served as the Head of Investment Banking division of the plaintiff bank. On 29 June 2007, the defendant resigned from HSBC and accepted the position of Managing Director and Head of Mergers and Acquisitions in Asia with Citigroup in Hong Kong. The court held that the plaintiff bank's contract provisions were reasonable, in that the duration was not unreasonably long and that the geographic scope was not unreasonably wide.[246]

246. The court stated in particular the principles which it considered and applied in this case:

> 40. A restrictive covenant in a contract of employment which restrains the employee from undertaking certain activity post-contract is *prima facie* unenforceable. It becomes enforceable only if it is reasonable having regard to the interests of the parties concerned and of the general public. It is said of the doctrine of restraint in trade that it "is one to be applied to factual situations with a broad and flexible rule of reason" per Lord Wilberforce in *Esso Petroleum Co Ltd v Harper's Garage (Stowaport) Ltd* [1968] AC 269 at p.331.
>
> ...

In *Wealthy Realty Ltd v Cheng Yung* [2008] 2 HKLRD 425, the court struck down the anti-competition clause in the parties contract as being too broad in its geographic scope. In this case, the plaintiff employed the defendant as senior sales manager. The parties' contract contained a six-month anti-competition clause in respect of the 'district' in which the defendant had been assigned to work immediately preceding the termination. The defendant worked at the Austin Road office; however, the defendant was also assigned to work at six other districts. After four months with the plaintiff, the defendant left to join China Group Property Agency Co,

---

56. What is apparent and not in dispute is that Mr Wallace was employed to head a division in the Bank whose primary function is to provide advisory services which include mergers and acquisitions, leveraged and acquisition finance, and strategic finance for major commercial corporate and institutional clients including governments. Mr Wallace was required to have a knowledge of the identity of these clients and their areas of growth actual and potential, and an intimate knowledge of the financial products developed and made available by the Bank for the purpose.
57. ... as I have said, the role he played will require to be determined after trial, there is no serious challenge to the proposition that what he came to be told and to learn was information equivalent to the Bank's trade secrets.
58. It is in the context of that that I have to decide whether the non-compete clause post termination (less the period of garden leave) is likely to be found to be no more than is reasonably necessary for the protection of the Bank.

...

62. ... the case *TFS Derivatives v Morgan* [2005] IRLR 246, in which the Court was asked to grant injunctive relief to enforce a non-compete clause in a contract of employment, post termination of the contract. ... Mrs Cox J stated at para.37:

> Firstly, the court must decide what the covenant means when properly construed. Secondly, the court will consider whether the former employers have shown on the evidence that they have legitimate business interests requiring protection in relation to the employee's employment. In this case, as will be seen later on, the defendant concedes that TFS have demonstrated on the evidence legitimate business interests to protect in respect of customer connection, confidential information and the integrity or stability of the workforce, although the extent of the confidential information is in dispute in relation to its shelf life and/or the extent to which it is either memorable or portable.

And at para.75:

> The third and final question to be answered in the process is, therefore, whether the covenants ... are no wider than is reasonably necessary for the protection of those interests.

which assigned the defendant to its Austin Road office. The court found in favour of the defendant, holding the term "district" was undefined and to allow the plaintiff's definition to apply would preclude the defendant from employment in all the various districts where the defendant had previously worked for the plaintiff.[247]

247. In its decision, the court stated:

> … the well-established principle [is] that this Court should have regard to such factors as the circumstances under which the Clause was agreed to, the object sought to be attained by it and the position of both parties. If this Court forms the view that its meaning is ambiguous and there are two possible constructions of the Clause, one of which would lead to a conclusion that it is unreasonable restraint of trade and thus unlawful, but the other would lead to the opposite result, then the latter construction should be adopted (Fall-back Construction). [2008] 2 HKLRD at 429.
>
> …
>
> … the word 'district' may have different meanings to different people for obvious reasons. I think the parties would be at a loss as to what 'district' meant at that time. There is no evidence that the plaintiff had demarcated 'district' for the purpose of the Agreement at that time. On this footing alone, the plaintiff must fail because this Clause is too wide to be reasonable. There is no Fall-back Construction to save it. *Id.* at 429–430.
>
> …
>
> The plaintiff's [alternative] argument necessarily means that the Clause could stop the defendant from working in all those [six] districts as well. There is only one construction, namely that all such districts are no doubt included in the restraint of trade. The fact that the plaintiff is now asking for an injunction only for Kowloon West has no bearing on the construction of the Clause. The Clause is likewise too wide to be reasonable. There is no Fall-back Construction to save it. On this footing, the plaintiff must also fail. *Id.*

Chapter Four
Property

This chapter is concerned with property, its definition and the general principles of property law. Both personal and real property will be examined. The chapter consists of two major sections: The first section focuses both on personal and on real property. This discussion regarding real property includes a review of freehold and leasehold estates, and co-ownership. Subsequently, the second section focuses on land-related issues, such as fixtures, adverse possession, servitudes and mortgages. These issues are followed by a detailed reference to conveyancing: the process of creation and transfer of interests in real property. This chapter concludes with an overview of the new land registration system under development in Hong Kong.

In preparing this work, it is assumed that the reader has some knowledge of contract law as most transactions concerning property involve legally binding agreements.

I. PROPERTY GENERALLY

This section is the introduction to property in general. Here the matters relating to property are reviewed: definition of property; ownership of property; acquisition and disposition of property; and, some general rules about property. Later, the detailed aspects of what is commonly known as real estate are reviewed.

The definition of "property" used in this chapter is: title to, or, rights of, ownership in goods or other valuables. "Title" means one's right to property, or the evidence of that right to property. "Ownership" means the complete and the exclusive right to control property, subject to law.[1]

---

1. For a general introduction to personal property, *see*, *e.g.*, Bruce Welling, Property in Things in the Common Law System (1996); Michael Bridge, Personal Property Law (3rd ed. 2002); Sarah Worthington, Personal Property Law: Text and Materials (2000); Simon Gleeson, Personal Property Law (1997).

In Hong Kong, the *Interpretation and General Clauses Ordinance* (Cap 1) provides the following definitions:

> "immovable property" (不動產) means –
> (a) land, whether covered by water or not;
> (b) any estate, right, interest or easement in or over any land; and
> (c) things attached to land or permanently fastened to anything attached to land;
>
> "movable property" (動產) means property of every description except immovable property;
>
> "property" (財產) includes –
> (a) money, goods, choses in action and land;
> (b) and obligations, easements and every description of estate, interest and profit, present or future, vested or contingent, arising out of or incident to property as defined in paragraph (a) of this definition.[2]

The concept of property includes the notion of ownership or title. Ownership involves certain rights.[3] Someone who owns property has the following rights:

- to use the property
- to enjoy the property aesthetically (*e.g.*, works of art)
- to destroy the property
- to dispose of the property
  - by gift
  - by succession,[4]
  - through a testamentary document known as a will made by the testator[5] or by intestacy,[6] through the probate court's application of the laws of intestate succession[7]

---

2. *Interpretation and General Clauses Ordinance* (Cap 1) section 3.
   The *Official Solicitor Ordinance* (Cap 416) section 2(6) translates "property vested in" as 轉歸予… 的財產.
3. *See* 20 HALSBURY'S LAWS OF HONG KONG para. 295.027 (2010) [hereinafter 20 HALSBURY'S].
4. L.B. CURZON & P.H. RICHARDS, THE LONGMAN DICTIONARY OF LAW 560 (7th ed. 2007) [hereinafter CURZON] defines "succession" as:

   (1) The order in which persons succeed to property, or some title.
   (2) Term applied to the estate of a deceased person.
   (3) Process of becoming entitled to property of a deceased by the operation of law or will.

5. *Wills Ordinance* (Cap 30) section 2 provides: "'will' (遺囑) includes a codicil and any other testamentary instrument or act, and 'testator' (立遺囑人) shall be construed accordingly."

- by sale
- by abandonment[8]

These rights of ownership of property may be acquired through one of the following methods:

- original, *i.e.*, taking possession of property which has never been owned[9]
- taking property which has been abandoned by the original owner
- creation or invention, *i.e.*, creating property such as when a carpenter creates a piece of furniture from raw materials[10]
- derivatively:
  - by sale/purchase of the property
  - by gift of the property
- succession: either in accordance with a will or the laws of intestacy if the person died without a will

Note that some methods of disposing of property by one person may also be the manner through which property is obtained by another person. For example, property may be disposed of by gift and can be acquired by gift. The sale of property by the original owner may result in the purchase of the same property by a new owner. As a final example, a person may come into ownership of property abandoned by the original owner.

With ownership comes the right of control. However, ownership and possession may be exercised independently. Property may thus be controlled by a person who exercises fewer rights than an owner, but who nonetheless may control access to and use of the property. This person has possession of the property. This concept of possession of personal property is discussed immediately below. Real property is discussed in section II below.

---

6. *See generally Intestates' Estates Ordinance* (Cap 73). *Id.* at section 2(1) translates "intestate" as 無遺囑者.
7. The Hong Kong Government's *Bilingual Laws Information System's English-Chinese Glossary of Legal Terms* [hereinafter *BLIS Glossary*] translates the term "succession" as 死亡繼承. *See http://www.legislation.gov.hk/eng/glossary/homeglos.htm* (last visited 26 Feb. 2011).
   See also the Law Reform Commission of Hong Kong, Report on Law of Wills, Intestate Succession and Provision for Deceased Persons' Families and Dependents (Topic 15) (1990).
8. "Abandonment of goods takes place when possession of them is quitted voluntarily without any intention of transferring them to another." 20 HALSBURY'S, *supra* note 3, at para. 295.025.
9. Defined as "occupancy". *See id.* at para. 295.036.
10. *See also id.* at para. 295.037.

A. Possession and Bailment

"Possession" is the actual physical control of that property or the intent to possess exclusively that property with the intent to prevent others from using the property. The word "possession":

> may mean effective, physical or manual control, or occupation, evidenced by some outward act, sometimes called *de facto* possession or detention as distinct from a legal right to possession. This is a question of fact rather than of law.[11]

When an owner of property lawfully parts temporarily with possession of property, one of two situations may result. In the first situation, if the owner has no intention for any other person to have exclusive control, then this other person has no rights to possess the property. This person is a custodian. "Custodian" is defined as a "person or institution that has charge or custody of property, papers, or other valuables" while "custody" is defined as:

> care and control of a thing or person. The keeping, guarding, care, watch, inspection, preservation or security of a thing, carrying with it the idea of the thing being within the immediate personal care and control of the person to whose custody it is subjected. Immediate charge and control, and not the final, absolute control of ownership, implying responsibility for the protection and preservation of the thing in custody.[12]

In the second situation, if the owner, upon parting with possession, gives full control over the property to another person, a bailment is created. A "bailment" is a transaction under which goods are delivered by one party, the "bailor", to another party, the "bailee", on terms which normally require the bailee to hold the goods and ultimately to return the property to the bailor or to dispose of the property according to the bailor's instructions.[13]

---

11. *Id.* at para. 295.011. This section continues by stating:

> "Possession" may mean legal possession: that possession which is recognised and protected … by law. The elements … of legal possession are an intention of possessing together with that amount of occupation or control of the entire subject matter of which it is practically capable and which is sufficient for practical purposes to exclude strangers from interfering.

12. BLACK'S LAW DICTIONARY 384 (6th ed. 1990). The *BLIS Glossary*, *supra* note 7, translates the term "custodian" as 保管人.

13. P.S. ATIYAH, THE SALE OF GOODS 12–13 (11th ed. 2005). *See* CURZON, *supra* note 4, at 51. The *BLIS Glossary*, *supra* note 7, translates "bailment" as 委託保管; "bailee" as 受託保管人; and, "bailor" as 委託保管人.

> Acts as diverse as lending a book to [a] friend, leaving luggage in a storage area at a train station, and renting a car are all bailments. ... in a bailment one person is entitled to ownership of the chattel but a different person has lawful possession of the good. In general, the good is to be held for a purpose and to be returned or redelivered when the purpose for which it was delivered is accomplished. The quintessential characteristic of a bailment, however, is a change in possession (control) over the good with the result that two sets of property rights exist in the same object—those arising from the bailor's title and those resulting from the bailee's possession.[14]

A bailment is usually based upon a contract. Three elements are required for the creation of a bailment. First, the bailee is to take care of the goods and return them in accordance with the bailor's instruction. The extent of the duty of care varies, depending upon whether the bailment is for payment or free. Second, the bailee is liable for the loss or damage of the property should the bailee be negligent. Finally, the bailee cannot deny the bailor's ownership of the goods.[15] Thus, the bailee is given both physical and legal possession over the goods but does not become the owner of the goods. The bailor keeps the ownership or title to the goods, and, may recover possession upon the end of the bailment.

B. Possession and the Finder Doctrine

Where an owner is unintentionally separated from its property, the common law[16] recognizes the Finder Doctrine.[17] Under this doctrine, if the owner loses or misplaces property, the finder has better rights to the found object than anyone except the owner. The case of *Armory v Delamirie* (1722) 93 ER 664 introduced this doctrine that a finder:

> does not by such finding acquire an absolute property or ownership. Yet he has such a property as will enable him to keep it against all but the rightful owner.

14. Derek Mendes Da Costa, Richard Balfour & Eileen Gillese, Property Law: Cases, Text and Materials para. 4.1 (2nd ed. 1990) [hereinafter Property Law: Cases, Text and Materials].
15. Judith Sihombing, Goods: Sales and Securities 2 (3rd ed. 1997).
16. "Common law" is defined as: "(普通法) means the common law in force in Hong Kong". *Interpretation and General Clauses Ordinance*, *supra* note 2, at section 3.
17. For further analysis of this topic, *see* 20 Halsbury's, *supra* note 3, at para. 295.020.

Thus a finder has a right in the found property that is good against the whole world except the owner.[18] Some examples include the following:

- in a public place, such as a park, a person who finds an object is entitled to the item unless it is claimed by the owner
- in a private place where the public is invited, such as a store, mall, or restaurant, a person who finds an object is entitled to the item unless it is claimed by the owner
- in a private place where the public is not invited, the object becomes the property of the owner of the land where the item is found
- if the owner was never in actual possession of the land, then the person who finds an object thereon will obtain lawful possession, except against the lawful owner

Parker v British Airways Board [1982] 1 QB 1004 is a case that applied the Finder Doctrine. The claimant, a passenger of the respondent airline, found a bracelet in the respondent's international executive lounge which only specific classes of passengers are permitted to use. The claimant handed over the bracelet to the respondent's employee, requesting that if the bracelet remained unclaimed, it should be returned to him. The respondent sold the bracelet for £850 and kept the proceeds. The claimant sued and was awarded the proceeds with interest. The court held that the claimant acted properly. The respondent did not show an intention to exercise control over the lounge such that the bracelet was in its possession before the claimant found this piece of jewellery.[19]

The Finder Doctrine illustrates the common law's concept of relativity of property: the law determines which claimant of particular property has better title, rather than determining the true owner. Thus, in an action for conversion,[20] the claimant only needs to prove better title than the respondent. The respondent cannot rely on the defence that a third party has a better title than the claimant.[21] This common law rule still applies in Hong Kong. Further, at common law, possession is assumed as evidence of title.

18. For a detailed discussion, *see* PROPERTY LAW: CASES, TEXT AND MATERIALS, *supra* note 14, at Chapter 3 ("Finding Lost Personal Property"); 20 HALSBURY'S, *supra* note 3, at para. 295.020. Note that under the *Limitation Ordinance* (Cap 347) sections 4(1)(a) and 5, the owner of goods must bring an action within six years to recover the goods converted by another, or where the owner was wrongfully deprived of the goods by other means.
19. *See* 1 QB at 1017–18 for discussion of the finder's rights and obligations, and, the occupier's rights and liabilities.
20. "Conversion" is defined by BLACK'S LAW DICTIONARY 381 (9th ed. 2009) [hereinafter BLACK'S LAW DICTIONARY] as the "wrongful possession or disposition of another's property as if it were one's own …".
21. This is known as the plea of *jus tertii*. As explained by 20 HALSBURY'S, *supra* note 3, at para. 295.024:

> The right to have legal and de facto possession is a normal but not necessary incident of ownership. Such a right may exist with, or apart from, de facto or legal possession, and in different persons at the same time in virtue of different proprietary rights. Thus, when an owner has been wrongfully dispossessed of his goods by theft, or has lost them, he retains the right to possess them; but, where he has bailed them for a term or by way of pledge, this right is temporarily suspended.[22] …
>
> …
>
> The presumption of law is that the person who has de facto possession also has the property, and accordingly, such possession is protected, whatever its origin, against all who cannot prove a superior title. This rule applies equally in criminal and civil matters. Thus, as against a stranger or a wrongdoer, a person in actual or apparent possession, but without the right to possession, has all the rights and remedies of a person entitled to and able to prove a present right to possession.[23]

C. Classification of Property

The classification of property may be done in a multitude of ways, some of which may overlap. Thus, it is possible that a particular type of property could be classified under more than one heading.

One method of classification designates property as either "tangible" property or "intangible" property. Tangible property includes goods or other items that have a physical shape or a physical being, *i.e.*, items which can be touched. Intangible property refers to things that do not have a physical shape or being, such as rights arising under a contract.

Another method of classification designates property into the categories of "realty", also known as real property; or, "personalty", also known as personal property. Realty includes all items such as freehold estates and interests in land; trees and other plants which grow in the land; and, items that are permanently affixed to the land, such as buildings, structures and plant. Real property can be further sub-divided into corporeal hereditaments and incorporeal hereditaments. "Corporeal" refers to something which has a physical being, in other words, tangible property. "Incorporeal" refers to rights over objects rather than the property itself. "Hereditament"

> If the plaintiff was in possession of goods at the time of the act complained of, the defendant in an action for wrongful interference with goods is not entitled to show that a third party, under whom he did not claim, has a better right than the plaintiff …

22. *Id.* at para. 295.016.
23. *Id.* at para. 295.022.

means those rights which are capable of being inherited. Corporeal hereditaments thus consist of physical objects over which rights may be exercised and incorporeal hereditaments are intangible rights over objects. Therefore, an incorporeal hereditament means any rights attached to, arising out of, or exercisable within a corporeal hereditament, *e.g.*, a right of way. "Personalty" is all other types of property. Personalty sometimes is referred to as "chattels".

These classifications of property originated from historical legal developments concerning the treatment of property by the courts. In the past, an individual's status depended upon that person's relationship to the land. Thus, it was deemed essential that someone who lost land should be able to recover that land rather than settling for monetary compensation. The courts would protect real property by requiring that the realty be returned or restored to the dispossessed owner. Thus, a court action concerning land is known as a "real" action, which is sometimes termed an action "*in rem*".[24] A legal right in land is a right *in rem*. This right *in rem* attaches to the land, binding upon all those who come into ownership or possession of that land. Land, even today, is considered to be unique in its character. On the other hand, a lawsuit against a person for loss or damage to property other than land would be an action *in personam*, that is, a court action against the wrongdoer. The claimant in an action *in personam* would generally seek monetary payment for damages resulting from the wrongdoer's acts rather than the property's return.

---

24. Real property evolved because historically enforcement was by real actions which were only available to holders of freehold estates. Thus, leasehold estates are technically only personal property, as they were only regarded as a personal right and enforced by the leaseholder bringing a personal action against the lessor. As there is no freehold estate in Hong Kong (except St. John's Cathedral), there is virtually no realty. Nevertheless, in order to distinguish leasehold interests from other types of personal property, leaseholds have come to be described as "chattels real", as opposed to other personal property which are called "chattels personal". Today, the technical distinctions between chattels real and realty have disappeared, and it is accepted in Hong Kong to describe land as real property. For further historical information *see, e.g.*, 20 HALSBURY'S, *supra* note 3, at para. 295.001 where it is stated in part:

> In England, the distinction between personal and real (or freehold) property was manifested in the early rule that freehold estates and interests in land were specifically recoverable, by a 'real' action, from a wrongful taker, whereas no action lay to compel restitution of other forms of property, the appropriate remedy for such cases being a mere 'personal' action for damages …

See generally S.H. GOO & ALICE LEE, LAND LAW IN HONG KONG (3rd ed. 2010) Chapter 1 ("Tenures, Estates, Land and Property") [hereinafter GOO & LEE].

Another historical development involved the common law being more concerned with the form and with the strict application of law. As a result of the harsh application of the statutes by the courts of law, notions of equity began to be applied by certain courts, known as the courts of equity. Equity sought to ameliorate the severity of the common law in order to make the law more fair and just.[25] An equitable right is a right *in personam* which can be enforced against the whole world except a person who acquired the land in good faith,[26] for value and without notice of the equitable interest.

Equitable remedies apply in property law and are discussed in further detail in the following sections. Presently, as an example, equity may be discussed in terms of trusts involving land.[27] Equity permits the creation of a "trust" where the legal title is in one person while another person enjoys the beneficial, or equitable, interests in that property.[28] With a trust involving land, the common law recognizes that one party owns the land. This person has the legal estate in the land. If a trust is created allowing another person to enjoy the land and its benefits, then this other person, referred to as the "beneficiary", has an equitable interest in the land. This equitable interest in the land is also referred to as an "equitable estate". Equity would protect the interests of the beneficiary against those of the legal owner, the "trustee".

---

25. Common law and equity are conceptually two separate and parallel sets of law. In Hong Kong, there is a unified court system which operates both the common law and equitable rules. The parallel but separate system in the UK has never been introduced to Hong Kong. There are thus no separate courts of common law and courts of equity (*i.e.*, Chancery) in Hong Kong. Consequently, the rules and remedies of both are operated in and available from the same judiciary in Hong Kong.
    The *BLIS Glossary*, *supra* note 7, translates "rules of the common law" as 普通法規則; and, "rules of equity" as 衡平法 or 衡平法規則. *See also* the explanation at *supra* note 16.
26. *I.e.*, without any evil intent or purpose, fraud, conspiracy or collusion.
27. JUDITH-ANNE MACKENZIE & MARY PHILLIPS, TEXTBOOK ON LAND LAW 11 (12th ed. 2008) [hereinafter MACKENZIE & PHILLIPS]. The essential characteristic of the trust is the separation of the property's title from the right to use and enjoy the property. The trustee is the owner of the property but holds this property for the beneficiary. *Id.* at 192. *See also* SARAH NIELD, HONG KONG LAND LAW 28 (2nd ed. 1997) [hereinafter NIELD].
28. The law of trusts may be considered, and is usually studied, as a separate area of law due to its complexity. The law of trusts will not be discussed further. *See*, *e.g.*, GOO & LEE, *supra* note 24, at Chapter 4 ("Trust"); 26(2) HALSBURY'S LAWS OF HONG KONG (2009); LAWRENCE MA, EQUITY AND TRUSTS LAW IN HONG KONG (2009); JOHN THURSTON & DEBORAH ANNELLS, A PRACTITIONER'S GUIDE TO TRUSTS – HONG KONG EDITION (2007).

II. REAL PROPERTY: DEFINITIONS

The definition of "land" under the common law includes the surface of the earth, together with all things of a physical nature above and below the land surface, such as buildings, trees and minerals.[29] In Hong Kong, there are several statutory definitions of real property. One set of definitions is found in the *Interpretation and General Clauses Ordinance* which was provided earlier.[30]

Another set of definitions is provided in Section 2 of the *Conveyancing and Property Ordinance* (Cap 219), which sets out the definitions pertaining to conveyancing and property matters. As these definitions are used in this book, section 2 is set out in full as follows:

> In this Ordinance, unless the context otherwise requires—
>
> "assignment" (轉讓、轉讓契) includes–
>
> (a) the transfer of the whole of the interest in land held under a Government lease;
>
> (b) a legal charge;
>
> (c) a lease (other than a Government lease);
>
> (d) a surrender;
>
> (e) an assent; and
>
> (f) every other assurance or conveyance of land by any instrument;
>
> "bankruptcy" (破產) includes winding up;
>
> "borrower" (借款人), where used in the First, Second and Third Schedules, includes "mortgagor";
>
> "encumbrance" (產權負擔) includes a legal and equitable mortgage, a trust for securing money, a lien, a charge of a portion, annuity, or other capital or annual sum; and "encumbrancer" (產權負擔人) … includes every person entitled to the benefit of an encumbrance, or to require payment or discharge thereof;
>
> "equitable interest" (衡平法權益) means any estate, interest or charge in or over land which is not a legal estate or a freehold;
>
> "instrument" (文書) means any document having legal effect except a will;
>
> "land" (土地) includes—

29. *See*, *e.g.*, 16 HALSBURY'S LAWS OF HONG KONG para. 230.043 (2010) [hereinafter 16 HALSBURY'S].
30. Section 3 of the *Interpretation and General Clauses Ordinance*, *supra* note 2.

(a) land covered by water;

(b) any estate, right, interest or easement in or over any land;

(bb) the whole or part of an undivided share in land and any estate, right, interest or easement in or over the whole or part of an undivided share in land; and

(c) things attached to land or permanently fastened to anything attached to land;

"legal charge" (法定押記) means a mortgage expressed to be a legal charge;

"legal estate" (法定產業權) means—

(a) a term of years absolute in land;

(b) the legal interest in any easement, right or privilege in or over land for an interest equivalent to a term of years absolute; and

(c) a legal charge;

"lender" (貸款人), where used in the First, Second and Third Schedules, includes "mortgagee";

"mortgage" (按揭) means a security over land for securing money or money's worth;

"mortgage money" (按揭金) means the money, or money's worth, secured by a mortgage;

"mortgagee" (承按人) includes any person claiming under a mortgagee;

"mortgagor" (按揭人) includes any person claiming under a mortgagor;

"sale" (售賣), in relation to the sale of land, includes the disposition of all or part of the vendor's estate and interest under a Government lease; …

"term of years absolute" (絕對年期), includes a term for less than a year, for a year or years and a fraction of a year and from year to year

The *Conveyancing and Property Ordinance*, defines "land" in sections (a) and (c). Intangible rights which might exist over or in the land are defined in sections (b) and (bb).

These definitions include concepts which might be unfamiliar. The following section explains the application of these concepts to land law. The section also presents a brief exposition on the doctrine of estates, examines the principles involving rights and interests in land, and reviews the nature of objects fastened or attached to the land. Servitudes and mortgages are discussed in sections VI.C.*iv*.c and VI.F respectively.

III. ESTATES

An "estate" is an interest in land. This interest in land entitles its owner to exercise rights over that land for a period of time.[31] There are two types of estates: freehold and leasehold. The differing types of freehold estates are examined below before proceeding to a discussion of leasehold estates.

It should be noted that the freehold estates are practically irrelevant to Hong Kong, but their discussion assists in the analysis of leasehold estates, which are the predominant form of estate in Hong Kong.

A. Freehold Estate

Traditionally, there are three types of freehold estate: (i) fee simple, (ii) fee tail and (iii) life estate. These are discussed below. Here, however, two terms are introduced: grantor and grantee. A "grantor" is the entity who grants, gives or sells a property or a property right. This entity may be a person, a company, or a trustee. A "grantee" is the entity, *e.g.* person, company, or trustee, receiving the property or property right.[32]

i. *Fee Simple*

The first type of freehold estate is known as a fee simple estate. The term "fee simple" is the shortened version for the proper name of this estate: fee simple absolute in possession. The word "fee" signifies an estate which can be passed to another person. The word "simple" indicates that the estate can be passed on to anyone, that there are no restrictions upon who can take possession or ownership of the land. The term "absolute" denotes an unlimited or unrestricted time period of ownership. An absolute interest is an interest in an estate which "is not determinable or conditional, *i.e.*, it is not granted on such terms that it is liable to end prematurely on the occurrence of some specified event."[33] The term "possession" is self-explanatory. The owner of the estate is entitled to possess the estate, *i.e.*, to live on the premises or to rent the premises. Thus, a fee simple estate is the highest and most unrestricted form of ownership.

31. MacKenzie & Phillips, *supra* note 27, at 610. *See also* Goo & Lee, *supra* note 24, Chapter 1, section 2 ("Estates").
32. The *BLIS Glossary*, *supra* note 7, translates "grant" as 補助, "grantor" as 授予人; and, "grantee" as 承授人.
33. MacKenzie & Phillips, *supra* note 27, at 609.

There are two sub-types of fee simple estates, neither of which has an absolute interest. One sub-type is known as a "conditional fee simple" where the person granting or creating this estate may re-enter or re-take possession of the property in the future when a specified event either takes place or does not take place. A conditional fee simple requires the event, *i.e.*, the condition, to occur after the granting of the estate rather than as a pre-condition, which is a requirement to be satisfied before the granting of the estate.

> A conditional interest arises where a fee simple is granted subject to a limitation which provides that the grantor will be able to re-enter the property at some date in the future on the occurrence (or non-occurrence) of specified events. In such a case the grantor appears initially to be giving a fee simple absolute, but then reserves the right to recover the land (right of re-entry).[34]

For example, a grantor grants a fee simple estate to a grantee on the condition that the grantee will not marry someone with red hair. If the grantee does marry an individual with red hair, the grantor has the option of taking back the estate. Note however that this fee only gives the grantor the option to re-enter the estate. The estate does not terminate until the grantor actually exercises the right of re-entry into the estate.

The other sub-type of fee simple estate is known as a "determinable fee simple", where the grant of the interest in the land lasts until a specified event occurs or does not occur. The fee is a determinable estate even where a specified event is unlikely to occur. This is because, from the beginning of the grant, the period of the interest in the estate has been reduced. For example, a grantor grants a determinable fee simple estate to a grantee until such time as the grantee buys a flat in Causeway Bay. When and only if the grantee buys such a flat, the grantee's interest in the estate terminates. A determinable fee simple automatically ends, or "determines", when the specified event occurs.

At times, it is difficult to discern whether a conditional fee simple or a determinable fee simple is being created as the end result, return of the estate to the grantor, known as "reversion", is quite similar. However, the wording used in the grant might assist in classifying whether the estate is of one sub-type or the other.[35]

---

34. *Id.* at 156.
35. *See id.* at 157. *See also* MEGARRY'S MANUAL OF THE LAW OF REAL PROPERTY 42 (A.J. OAKLEY, ed., 8th ed. 2002) [hereinafter MEGARRY'S MANUAL]; SIR ROBERT MEGARRY & WILLIAM WADE, THE LAW OF REAL PROPERTY para. 3–056 (7th ed. 2008) [hereinafter MEGARRY & WADE].

Conditional Fee Simple:	Determinable Fee Simple:
on condition that	until
providing that	as long as
but if	or the duration of
	while

The role of equity as it relates to land was reviewed earlier. The common law and equity affect these sub-types of fee simple in different ways. A conditional fee takes effect as a legal estate, while a determinable fee exists only as an equitable interest.

ii. Fee Tail

The second type of freehold estate is the fee tail estate. This estate continues so long as the original tenant or any of the tenant's descendants survives. Once the family line is broken, the fee tail estate ends. Thus, the grantee cannot sell the land and only familial descendants may inherit the estate. Once the fee tail ends, the estate reverts back to the grantor.

iii. Life Estate

The third type of traditional freehold estate is the life estate which is measured by the life of a person. Thus, this estate exists only for the duration of someone's lifetime. The life estate may be granted for the life of the tenant or the grant may be based on the life of any another individual.

B. Co-ownership: Types[36]

Having reviewed the types of estates which a person may possess, presented below are the ways in which those estates may be held by more than one grantee, *i.e.*, co-ownership. Depending upon the laws of the location of the realty, there are various types of co-ownership. The two types of co-ownership most commonly encountered in Hong Kong are joint tenancy and tenancy in common. Here, the terms "tenant" or "tenancy" refer to ownership rather than to someone who rents property under a lease.[37]

---

36. *See* Goo & Lee, *supra* note 24, at Chapter 10 ("Co-Ownership"); M.P. Thompson, Co-ownership (1988), Megarry's Manual, *supra* note 35, at Chapter 8 ("Co-ownership").
37. *See* Nield, *supra* note 27, at 228.

i. *Joint Tenancy*

Joint tenancy is the method of co-ownership of an estate where each owner is entitled to the whole property, rather than to an undivided share in the estate. A joint tenant, thus, does not hold any interest in the property as an individual. The interest is held equally and jointly with the other joint tenant(s).[38]

> A joint tenant is said to hold the whole [estate] with another but nothing of himself. There is thus only one estate in the land which is held jointly and, although the joint tenants as between themselves have distinct rights, to everyone else they are like a sole owner.[39]

A joint tenancy as a form of co-ownership also:

> dictates that no co-owner is entitled to the possession of any particular part of the land to the exclusion of his fellow co-owner. He is entitled to the possession of the whole, with and not to the exclusion of his fellow co-owners. If A and B are co-owners of a flat they are both entitled to occupy the whole flat. Neither A nor B can exclude the other from the kitchen, bathroom, 'their' respective bedrooms, or any other part of the flat.[40]

The right of survivorship, known as *jus accrescendi*, applies: the last survivor among all the joint tenants becomes entitled to the whole property. The heirs of the joint tenants who predecease the surviving joint tenant have no share in the property. For example, assume there are three friends, Au, Chan and Tang, who own a flat as joint tenants. When Au passes away Au's ownership interest in the property will pass to Chan and Tang. Au's family will receive nothing from Au's share in this flat. The same result will happen when Chan passes on. In the end, Tang will solely own the whole property.

The premise underlying the joint tenancy form of co-ownership is that each joint tenant has no individual interest in the realty. The only interest a joint tenant has is held jointly with fellow joint tenants. Although the joint tenants as between themselves have separate rights and obligations, the joint tenants are regarded as a sole owner to the world at large.

Because of this premise that a joint tenant holds the property with others as a single owner, the requirements for the creation of a joint tenancy reflect

38. *Id.* at 230.
39. *Id.*
40. *Id.* at 231.

this premise. Thus, provided no words of severance are present,[41] there will be a joint tenancy if the four "unities" are present, namely:

1. unity of possession: each owner has possession of the whole, and none of the joint tenants may claim possession of any particular part of the estate
2. unity of interest: the interest of each joint tenant is equal both in quantity and quality in terms of nature, extent and duration, so that no share is larger or smaller than another
3. unity of title: each co-owner derives title from the same document
4. unity of time: the interest of each co-owner vests at the same time

Formerly, a joint tenancy at law must always remain a joint tenancy. Dividing the ownership, referred to as "severance", was not possible. Equity recognized instances of injustice might arise and allowed severance under the rules established in the case of *Williams v Hensman* (1861) 1 John & H 546:

> a joint tenancy may be severed in three ways; in the first place, an act of any one of the persons interested operating upon his own share may create a severance as to that share (*e.g.*, selling his "share") … Secondly, a joint tenancy may be severed by mutual agreement. And, in the third place, there may be a severance by any course of dealing sufficient to intimate that the interests of all were mutually treated as constituting a tenancy in common. When the severance depends on an inference of this kind without any express act of severance, it will not suffice to rely on an intention, with respect to the particular share, declared behind the backs of the other persons interested. You must find in this class of cases a course of dealing by which the shares of all the parties to the contest have been affected …[42]

The statutory provision in Hong Kong regarding severance of a joint tenancy is found in section 8 of the *Conveyancing and Property Ordinance*[43] which provides for severance by instrument or by notice.[44]

---

41. *See* the following section on the creation of co-ownership.
42. (1861) 1 John & H at 557. *See generally* Goo & Lee, *supra* note 24, Chapter 10, at section 7 ("Severance of joint tenancy").
43. Section 8 of the *Conveyancing and Property Ordinance* (Cap 219) provides:

    (1) A joint tenancy of an estate or interest in land may be severed at law only by
        (a) a notice served by a joint tenant on the other joint tenants; or
        (b) an instrument.

The main characteristics of a joint tenancy are:

- A joint tenancy has a right of survivorship. "Survivorship" means that the interest of the deceased joint owner is acquired by the surviving joint tenant or tenants. The deceased owner's interest does not pass to its heirs. Title in a joint tenancy passes upon death and by the process of elimination. The last joint tenant to survive acquires the sole ownership of the property.
- The interest of a joint tenant is extinguished upon death and is incapable of being passed on to an heir under a will or on intestacy.
- Each joint owner has the legal right to equal participation in the land's actual profits, a right which may be enforced by a court action for an accounting of the profits.

ii. *Tenancy in Common*

A tenancy in common is another form of co-ownership in which each owner has a notional, although undivided, share in the property which passes with the estate at the time of death.[45] The right of survivorship does not apply to this form of co-ownership. Accordingly, a deceased tenant's interest or share in a tenancy in common can be inherited by the heirs. Unity of possession must exist in a tenancy in common, because all co-owners are entitled to possession of all parts of the land. However, the unities of interest, title and time are not required for a tenancy in common.

Historically, joint tenancies were favoured over other forms of co-ownerships. This common law preference may be the result of the feudal system that simplified the collection of taxes by concentrating land holdings in the hands of a few and the right of survivorship tended to accomplish this end.

---

(2) A joint tenancy of an estate or interest in land may be severed in equity by a notice served by a joint tenant on the other joint tenants or by any other method that is effective in equity or that would, but for subsection (1), be effective at law.

44. The notice must be served by a joint tenant on the other joint tenants. But the case of *Re 88 Berkeley Road, London NW9, Rickwood v Turnsek* [1971] 1 All ER 254 held that written notice of severance is effective once delivered even if not received by the addressee(s). *See also Ho Nga Sheung v Ma Fook Leung* [1993] 2 HKC 647 (joint tenancy severed by divorce proceedings).

45. "Estate" in this sense refers not to an estate in land, but, rather, to the assets of a deceased person's total property, the realty as well as the personalty. *See* BLACK'S LAW DICTIONARY, *supra* note 20, at 626. The *Intestates' Estates Ordinance*, *supra* note 6, at section 2 provides that "estate" (遺產) refers to both real estate and personal estate. The *BLIS Glossary*, *supra* note 7, translates the term "tenancy in common" as 分權共有.

With the decline of feudalism, however, joint tenancies became disfavoured. Lord Denning MR in *Burgess v Rawnsley* [1975] Ch 429, 438, CA stated that "the thing to remember today is that equity leans against joint tenants and favours tenancies in common ..." Today, section 9 of the *Conveyancing and Property Ordinance* expresses a legal preference in favour of a tenancy in common rather than a joint tenancy.[46] Section 9 states:

> (1) Where a tenancy in the same estate or interest in land vests in two or more persons under an instrument or a will, it shall be presumed, unless the contrary intention is expressed in that instrument or will, that the tenancy vests in those persons as tenants in common rather than as joint tenants.[47]
>
> (2) This section shall not apply to any instrument or will made before the commencement of this section.
>
> (3) This section shall not apply to a tenancy vesting in trustees or personal representatives.

The important points to note about the tenancy in common form of co-ownership are:

- Each tenant owns an individual portion. The portions are not physically divisible but each tenant has an undivided share. Portions need not be equal so long as together they make up the whole. In the above example of the three friends jointly owning a flat, in a tenancy in common situation, it would be possible for Au to have a 65 percent share in that flat, Chan to have a 30 percent share and Tang to have a 5 percent share.
- Each tenant may deal with its individual interest or share in the property, e.g. a tenant in common may sell its share.
- There is no right of survivorship in a tenancy in common. If a tenant in common dies, that tenant's share in the land will pass to the beneficiaries by will or under the rules of intestacy. Again using the previous example, should Au pass away where the ownership of the flat is under a tenancy in common, Au's heirs, *e.g.*, spouse and children, will become tenants in common with a 65% share in that flat with Chan and Tang.

C. Co-ownership: Creation

The following is a brief discussion on the creation of co-ownership, reviewing the guidelines used to determine whether a co-ownership is a joint

46. Section 9 of the *Conveyancing and Property Ordinance*, *supra* note 43.
47. The *BLIS Glossary*, *supra* note 7, translates the term "vest" as 歸屬.

tenancy or a tenancy in common in instances where the documents are ambiguous. Where the co-ownership is silent as to whether the property is held either at law or in equity, a court will look to the presumptions that arise both at law and in equity.

If one or more of the four unities is absent, then the co-owners must hold the realty as tenants in common both at law and in equity. Additionally, where all four unities are present, the existence of a joint tenancy or a tenancy in common will depend on whether the relationship came into existence before or after the implementation of the *Conveyancing and Property Ordinance* on 1 November 1984.

Prior to enactment of the Ordinance, the common law favoured a joint tenancy in order to avoid the fragmentation of the property's title that results from a tenancy in common, where there were multiple owners with each owner's share being disposed of separately from the other owners. If an intention is to create a tenancy in common, indicated by using words of severance, this intention will be recognized by the common law. Therefore, the words used in the grant will determine if there is an intention to sever or divide the shares in the estate. If there are words of severance, the grant will be a tenancy in common. If there are no words of severance, the grant will be a joint tenancy.[48]

A tenancy in common is created by words in the grant of title which indicate each grantee will take a distinct share in the property, *i.e.*, the words in the grant amount to words of severance. Words or phrases which have been held to have this effect include: "equally"; "between"; "share and share alike"; and, "to be divided amongst". Additionally, words showing that the grantees were to take unequal interests or shares in the realty create a tenancy in common.[49]

As noted above, section 9 of the *Conveyancing and Property Ordinance* overturned the common law presumption, so that at law, co-owners are presumed to hold an estate as tenants in common even if no words of severance are used. In order to create a joint tenancy, the document by which

48. *Mole v Ross* (1951) 24 ALJ 356 held that it was unnecessary to use the precise words "as joint tenants" to create a joint tenancy, but that any clear and plain language expressing an intention to do so will suffice, despite the fact that the words "as joint legatees" were held to create a joint tenancy in that case. *See* MEGARRY & WADE, *supra* note 35, at paras. 13-014 to 13-035. *See generally* GOO & LEE, *supra* note 24, Chapter 10, at section 3 ("How to Distinguish Between Joint Tenancy and Tenancy in Common").
The *BLIS Glossary*, *supra* note 7, translates the term "legatee" as 受遺贈人.

49. MACKENZIE & PHILLIPS, *supra* note 27, at 296–297; MEGARRY'S MANUAL, *supra* note 35, at 308; MEGARRY & WADE, *supra* note 35, at para. 13–017.

the co-owners acquire their interest in the property must express a clear intention against a tenancy in common.

Because equity favours fairness rather than conveyancing convenience, equity prefers a tenancy in common. Although a legal estate might be held by joint tenants, equity will presume an intention to create a tenancy in common and actually impose a tenancy in common in three situations:

1. Unequal contributions: where the money used to purchase the land is provided in unequal shares, the parties providing the funds are presumed by equity to be tenants in common in the same proportions as their contributions to the purchase price.[50] "If two or more persons together purchase property and provide the money in equal shares they are presumed in equity to be joint tenants."[51] These presumptions may be rebutted by evidence that the parties intended to hold as joint tenants despite unequal contributions, or that they intended a tenancy in common despite equal contributions.[52]

---

50. *See, e.g.*, *Lake v Gibson* (1729) 1 Eq Ca Abr 290, 291.
51. MEGARRY & WADE, *supra* note 35, at para. 13–022. *See also* MEGARRY'S MANUAL, *supra* note 35, at 314.
52. In the case of *Bull v Bull* [1955] 1 QB 234, the son, who is the claimant in this case and his mother, who is the respondent, together purchased a house. The son contributed a larger part of the purchase price than his mother. The conveyance was taken in the son's name. The parties agreed that the mother should occupy two rooms of the house and that the son and his wife occupy the rest of the house. Differences arose between the parties and the son sued for possession of the rooms occupied by the mother. The court ruled in favour of the mother, an equitable tenant in common who should be entitled to share the proceeds of sale of the property. The court ordered that the house be sold and the proceeds be divided between them in the proper proportions:

> The son is, of course, the legal owner of the house; but the mother and son are, I think, equitable tenants in common. Each is entitled in equity to an undivided share in the house, the share of each being in proportion to his or her respective contribution ... My conclusion, therefore, is that when there are two equitable tenants in common, then, until the place is sold, each of them is entitled concurrently with the other to the possession of the land and to the use and enjoyment of it in a proper manner: and that neither of them is entitled to turn out the other.

[1955] 1 QB at 236–238.
NIELD, *supra* note 27, at 241–242 states that:

> while co-owners may be joint tenants at law, they may hold that legal estate on trust for themselves as either joint tenants or tenants in common in equity. The reverse result does not, however, follow. Co-owners who hold as tenants in common at law will hold as tenants in common in equity, for equity leans in favour of a tenancy in common and will follow the law in this respect.

2. Money advanced on a mortgage: where two or more people lend money for a mortgage they are presumed to have advanced the loan as tenants in common, unless the contrary can be shown.

> So if two people join in lending money upon a mortgage, Equity says, it could not be their intention, that the interest in that should survive. Though they take a joint security, each means to lend his own and take back his own.[53]

Again, this presumption may be countered by evidence showing the contrary intention.

3. Business assets: the concept of survivorship does not generally apply to the commercial field. Equity will presume a tenancy in common over partnership assets or the assets of a joint business, or where the premises are held jointly for several individual business purposes.[54]

D. Co-ownership: Determination

Co-ownership of an estate may be terminated by one of several methods. The first method of termination of co-ownership is by union into a sole owner, where one person becomes the sole owner of the estate, *e.g.*, by purchasing it from the other co-owner or is gifted the share from another co-owner. Co-ownership among joint tenants can be terminated by death. As

---

53. *Morley v Bird* (1798) 3 Ves. Jr. 628, 631.
Section 48 of the *Conveyancing and Property Ordinance*, *supra* note 43, provides:

> Where any mortgage effected after the commencement of this section is expressed to be made to 2 or more persons jointly, the mortgage money shall (if and so far as the contrary intention is not expressed in the mortgage), as between them and the mortgagor, be deemed to be owing to these persons on a joint account and the receipt of the survivors or the last survivor of them or of the successor or personal representative of the last survivor shall be a complete discharge.

This section is intended to simplify the mechanism of discharging the mortgage as the presumption between the borrower(s) and the lender(s), the lender(s) are usually deemed to be jointly entitled to the loan by virtue of the "joint account" clause normally inserted in mortgages to make the lender(s) appear as joint tenants to the outside world.

54. The Privy Council held in the case of *Malayan Credit Ltd v Jack Chia MPH Ltd* [1986] 1 All ER 711 that there was an equitable presumption in favour of a tenancy in common where the co-owners held for their various business purposes: "where premises are held by two persons as joint tenants at law for their several business purposes, it is improbable that they would intend to hold as joint tenants in equity." *Id.* at 715.

the term implies, survivorship occurs where the co-ownership is ended by the demise of the other joint tenant(s), leaving one remaining joint tenant. In the third method, co-ownership may be terminated by severance, when a joint tenant changes the relationship with the other co-owners to that of a tenant in common. The joint tenant maintains an undivided share in the property but is no longer affected by the right of survivorship.[55] Severance results in the conversion of a joint tenancy into a tenancy in common. Any act destroying one or more of the four unities results in a severance, as will the intention by the joint tenants to exclude the operation of survivorship. However, the unity of time cannot be destroyed; and, the destruction of the unity of possession results in partition.

Partition is a procedure available to end either type of co-ownership of land. Partition may be done voluntarily by a conveyance of a part by all of the co-owners jointly to each one individually. Partition can be compulsory through an application to a court. Hong Kong's *Partition Ordinance* (Cap 352) gives a court the power to partition or to sell jointly owned property. For example, the Ordinance allows a court to partition the realty in one of the following ways:

(i) into parcels to be held by the single owners individually;
(ii) into parcels held by two or more persons as joint tenants; or,
(iii) into parcels held by two or more individuals as tenants in common.[56]

In conclusion, this section has reviewed briefly the types, creation and determination of freehold estates.

E. Licence and Leasehold Estate: Introduction

Having concluded the review of freehold estates, attention now focuses on the other type of estate: leasehold. Leasehold estates are estates that do not rise to the level of freehold estates. Leasehold estates are held for a certain duration "and usually involve a continuing relationship between the grantor and the grantee, such as the grantee's (*e.g.*, lessee's/tenant's) obligation to pay rent to the grantor (*e.g.*, lessor/landlord)."[57]

---

55. *See, e.g.*, the preceding section on joint tenancy; MacKenzie & Phillips, *supra* note 27, at 295–297.
56. *Partition Ordinance* (Cap 352) section 4.
57. Daniel P. McLoughlin, Principles of Real Estate Law 30 (1992).
See also 17(1) Halsbury's Laws of Hong Kong para. 235.483 (2007) [hereinafter 17(1) Halsbury's] as to the definition of "tenancy". *See generally* Goo & Lee, *supra* note 24, at Chapter 7 ("Leases").

> Generally, the relationship of landlord and tenant arises as a rule when one person ('the landlord') grants to another ('the tenant') a right to the exclusive possession of land for a term less than that which the landlord has in the land ... and it usually carries with it the right to receive from the tenant payment of rent for the use of the property.[58]

Leases were not considered to be a legal right to real property. Leases were regarded as commercial contracts creating *in personam* rights between the parties. Unlike freehold estates, leases historically did not affect the tenants' position on the feudal ladder and were not subject to a real action. A dispossessed tenant could not recover the land from the landlord but would only be awarded damages for breach of contract. Since the interests contained in a lease were protected only by an action *in personam*, the lease was regarded as personal property. After the passage of time, a tenant was enabled to recover the land by an action *in rem*, whether dispossessed of the land by a landlord or by some third party. However, by this time, the classification of the lease had become fixed as personalty.

In *Street v Mountford* [1985] AC 809, the court stated that "to constitute a tenancy the occupier must be granted exclusive possession for a fixed or periodic term certain in consideration of a premium or periodical payments."[59] Yet, not all occupiers of land are tenants. Whereas a tenant holds a legal estate, some occupants of land only have a licence or permission to use the premises which creates no interest in the land.[60] Thus, there are differences between a lessee and licensee. For example, the tenant of a shop in an arcade is different from a licenced hawker set up in a marketplace. In this example, the hawker has a licence, but not a lease. The hawker pays for the space, but the hawker gains no interest in the premises.

---

58. 17(1) HALSBURY'S, *supra* note 57, at para. 235.001.

59. [1985] AC at 818. *See also* 17(1) HALSBURY'S, *supra* note 57, at para. 235.001; MALCOLM MERRY, HONG KONG TENANCY LAW: AN INTRODUCTION TO THE LAW OF LANDLORD AND TENANT 1–10 (5th ed. 2010) [hereinafter MERRY].

> an agreement creates the relationship of landlord and tenant and not that of licensor and licensee where there is the grant of exclusive possession for a fixed or periodic term at a stated rent.

17(1) HALSBURY'S, *supra* note 57, at para. 235.008.

60. 17(1) HALSBURY'S, *supra* note 57, at para. 235.007 states that:

> There can be no tenancy without the grant of exclusive possession. Exclusive possession enables the tenant to exclude strangers and to exclude also the landlord unless the landlord is exercising rights to enter the land granted to him under the tenancy agreement. ...

See generally GOO & LEE, *supra* note 24, Chapter 7, at section 3 ("Basic Requirements for a Lease and Distinction Between Lease and Licence"), Chapter 9 ("Licences").

A licence is revocable, whereas a lease is not. A licensee whose licence is illegally revoked will need to pursue remedies in court for damages arising from a breach of contract rather than for possession of the land. Furthermore, leases can be assigned to third persons whereas licences are generally personal and not assignable.

Thus, "a licence is a permission to use land, without which an occupier would be a trespasser."[61] The distinction between a lease and a licence is important because the *Landlord and Tenant (Consolidation) Ordinance* (Cap 7) applies only to the former. This classification assists in determining whether a covenant against subletting has been broken and determining the manner in which an occupation can be brought to an end. A tenant may also be entitled to statutory benefits.

> There is, therefore, an incentive for owners to grant licences rather than leases, and in many cases the court has to determine whether a document before it, which is expressed to be a licence, is in fact a tenancy either mislabelled or disguised as a licence.[62]

As both licences and leases are routinely encountered, the topic of licences is set out briefly below, followed by an introduction to leases.

F. Licence: Types[63]

The case of *Thomas v Sorrell* provides the classic definition of "licence":

> A dispensation or licence properly passeth no interest, nor alters or transfers property in anything, but only makes an action lawful, which without it had been unlawful.[64]

Another source states that:

> a licence creates no interest or estate in the land. It is merely a personal right providing a remedy only against the licensor and not against the land. Nor is the licensee considered to be in possession of the land, and he is unable to sue in either trespass or nuisance. However, in recent

61. NIELD, *supra* note 27, at 487.
62. Chancery Practice, Inns of Court 1990/91.
63. *See* I.J. DAWSON & ROBERT A. PEARCE, LICENCES RELATING TO THE OCCUPATION OR USE OF LAND (1979) [hereinafter DAWSON & PEARCE], for a detailed discussion. *See also* MERRY, *supra* note 59, at 4–10.
64. (1673) Vaugh 330, 351.
See also 17(1) HALSBURY'S, *supra* note 57, at para. 235.010.

years the status of licences as lying purely within the realm of personal rights has been challenged.[65]

In addition to the criteria set out in *Street v Mountford*, the courts may consider the following factors in determining whether there is a licence or a lease:

- The power to grant a lease
  This rule is similar to the *nemo dat quod non habet* principle that a seller cannot give a better title than the seller possesses. If the grantor has no interest or estate in land, the grantor cannot grant a lease to others. In *Torbett v Faulkner* [1952] 2 TLR 659, the court found a lease agreement between an occupant and a company to be invalid as the director of the company, rather than the company, was the true owner of the house in question.[66]
- The substance of the agreement
  The parties cannot create a licence simply by labelling the agreement a licence. The courts will look at the substance, rather than the form, of the agreement. In *Addiscombe Garden Estates Ltd v Crabbe* [1958] 1 QB 513, 522, the court stated:

  > It does not necessarily follow that a document described as a licence is, merely on that account, to be regarded as amounting only to a licence

65. Nield, *supra* note 27, at 487.
    In a recent case, the court stated:

    > The main difference between a lease and a licence are best summarized in the following passage in *Woodfall's Law of Landlord and Tenant*, 2008 ed., vol. 1, at para. 1.020:
    >
    > > A lease or tenancy confers on the grantee an interest in the land demised but a licence confers no such interest. It is a mere personal privilege; it merely makes lawful that which would otherwise be unlawful. … All lessees and tenants necessarily have exclusive possession of the demised premises. Some licensees have exclusive possession; some do not. Contractual licences do not constitute equitable interests in the land, and consequently do not bind a successor in title of the original grantor.
    > >
    > > However, a licensee with a right to occupy land has a sufficient interest to be entitled to maintain an action for trespass if it is necessary to do so in order to give effect to his rights under the licence.
    >
    > From this passage, it is clear that a licensee does not enjoy any estate in the land. However, that does not necessarily mean that he has no right whatsoever, at least he has sufficient interest to maintain a claim for trespass to give effect to his right under the licence.

    Ricas Properties Ltd v Armed Forces Trading, unreported, DCMP 75/2008 at paras. 37–38.
66. *See also Attorney General v Chiu Pak-yue* (No.2) [1963] HKLR 544.

> in law. The whole document must be looked at; and if, after it has been examined, the right conclusion appears to be that, whatever label may have been attached to it, it in fact conferred and imposed on the grantee in substance the rights and obligations of a landlord, then it must be given the appropriate effect, that is to say, it must be treated as a tenancy as distinct from a mere licence.

For example, clauses such as "the landlord reserves the right to enter and inspect the state of repair of the premises" or "the tenant is forbidden to transfer his interest" suggest that exclusive possession has been granted. Accordingly, a lease is created.

- Family arrangements, acts of friendship or generosity
  Where the parties have no intention to create any legal relationships, no lease is created.

A detailed analysis of licences is beyond the scope of this work. Below is an introduction to different types of licences most commonly encountered. Megarry J classified licences thus: "The threefold classification of licences is well known. There are licences coupled with an interest, contractual licences and bare licences."[67] Presented first is the lowest form of licence which affords licensees the minimum protection under the law.

i. *Bare Licence*

A bare licence is permission to enter land without any consideration or payment provided by the entrant. For instance, a visitor's entry onto land is allowed with the owner's permission. The visitor, with this permission, is a licensee and not a trespasser. Should the owner request the visitor to depart and, failing to do so after being afforded a reasonable time, the visitor will become a trespasser.

A bare licence can be created expressly or impliedly. For example, a dinner guest will have express permission to attend; a postman has an implied permission to come to a home's front door to deliver the mail; the public has an implied licence to come up to the entrance of privately owned land for any lawful business.

A bare licence can be revoked by either party. Revocation may be made by express notice or by any act inconsistent with the continuance of the licence. For instance, the express licence of dinner guests ends when they

67. *Hounslow London Borough Council v Twickenham Garden Development Ltd* [1971] Ch 233, 243.

leave. Another example involves the cessation of the implied licence of members of the public when they are asked, by words or conduct, to leave. The death of one of the parties or the assignment by the licensor of their interest in the land will also terminate a bare licence.

ii. Licence Coupled with an Interest

A licence coupled with an interest is comprised of two components: a licence and an interest.[68] A licence coupled with an interest occurs where a right to enter land is granted in order to support an interest in that land. Thus, the grantee of a *profit à prendre* is entitled to enter the land of another person to take its natural products such as wild animals, soil, or minerals. For instance, a right to fish is of little value unless permission is also given to reach the source of the fish. Licences coupled with an interest are uncommon in Hong Kong because some of the natural products entitled to one who holds a *profit à prendre* are in low abundance.

iii. Contractual Licence

A contractual licence arises where the permission to use or to occupy land is made pursuant to a contract. Contractual licences serve many functions. Contractual licences are found in the right to enter a cinema, concert hall, sports venue, or in the right to park a vehicle in a commercial car park. Contractual licences may govern the right of a building contractor to enter a building site to execute the building works. Contractual licences may also govern the right to use and to enjoy the facilities of a club.

The creation and the terms of contractual licences may be express or implied. Termination of a contractual licence will depend on the terms of the licence.

> For instance, the length of the licence may be expressly stated, but in many cases the courts will have to ascertain the parties' intention from the terms of the licence and the surrounding circumstances.[69]

---

68. Dawson & Pearce, *supra* note 63, at 44.
    See also 17(1) Halsbury's, *supra* note 57, at para. 235.014.
69. Nield, *supra* note 27, at 489.
    See also 17(1) Halsbury's, *supra* note 57, at para. 235.011.

G. Leases: Definition

Distinguishing between leases and licences can be difficult. Conceptually, the distinction is clear, but its application is difficult. Each situation is judged on a case-by-case basis. Since the mid-1980s, the decision in the case of *Street v Mountford* [1985] AC 809 has been the authority: to be a lease, every tenant must have exclusive possession for a fixed duration.[70]

i. *Exclusive Possession*

A tenant must have the right to take possession and to exercise all the rights associated with possession.[71]

> Exclusive possession enables the tenant to exclude strangers and to exclude also the landlord unless the landlord is exercising rights to enter the land granted to him under the tenancy agreement.[72]

A tenant's exclusive possession is the basis for the recognition of the tenant's estate or interest in the land. If the tenant's occupation does not include exclusive possession, there is no estate in the real property.

As in the situation of determining whether an agreement is a lease or a licence, in determining whether the occupants are granted exclusive possession, the courts will look to the substance, rather than to the form, of the agreement. Thus, the parties cannot create a licence simply by labelling it a licence. Some terms in the agreement may indicate that exclusive possession has been granted, for example, where the landlord reserves the right to enter and inspect the condition of the premises, or to restrict the occupant's right to transfer any interest in the property.

Formerly, exclusive occupation meant exclusive possession. In *Street v Mountford*, the court made a clear distinction between a tenant and a lodger. An occupant with exclusive occupation is not considered to be in overall control of the premises. The provision of services to an occupant or the restriction of access to the premises may indicate that the occupant does not have exclusive possession.

---

70. *See generally* Goo & Lee, *supra* note 24, Chapter 7, at section 3 on requirements for a lease and distinctions between a lease and a licence.
As discussed in more detail later in this section, a lease is considered to be a transaction affecting land. 17(1) Halsbury's, *supra* note 57, at para. 235.050. *See also id.* at paras. 235.051–235.052, 235.054.
71. The *BLIS Glossary*, *supra* note 7, translates the term "exclusive possession" as 獨有管有.
72. 17(1) Halsbury's, *supra* note 57, at para. 235.007.

The court in *Lam Man-yuen v Lucky Apartment* [1964] HKLR 689 held that the degree of control is a factor in deciding the existence of exclusive possession. In this case, the respondent owned three floors of a building. Each floor was divided into rooms which were hired out to various occupants including the claimant. The rooms were furnished, bed linen provided, and rooms and linen were cleaned by an amah. Electricity was supplied at no extra charge. Keys to the rooms were kept at the building's entrance. The gate to the building's entrance was locked after midnight. The occupants had no key to the gate; if they returned late, they had to summon the watchman. In the lobby and in each room was a notice with the title "Regulations for guests". These regulations concerned such matters as noise after midnight and the keeping of pets. New occupants had to complete a registration card. Rooms could be hired at a daily rate. A manager, who was a partner of the respondent, lived on the premises.

The claimant refused to leave the room, contending he was protected by legislation concerning tenants' security of tenure and could do what he liked in his room, *e.g.*, have as many visitors or occupants as he wished. Further, the claimant asserted the respondent was concerned only with the payment of rent. All these factors indicated a landlord-tenant relationship according to the claimant. Nonetheless, the respondent asserted that the claimant was not a tenant but a licensee. The respondent won the case by showing that it maintained some control over the property and that the occupants' interests were too transient to be a lease.

In *May King Development Co v Young Ching Huo Ltd* [1981] HKLR 280, the developers of a building assigned the flats in the building to the respondent. The assignment stated that the premises were for residential purposes. There was a similar stipulation in the Crown lease to the claimant developers. An agreement between the developer and the assignees, including the respondent, required that the building not be used for boarding or lodging. The respondent hired individual rooms in the flats to largely short-term occupants.

The issue was whether the respondent had retained enough control over the flats to make the occupants only licensees. The following facts in this case made it different from the *Lam Man-yuen* case:

- no shared facilities with the other occupants of other rooms;
- no cooking was allowed in the rooms;
- rooms were furnished as bedrooms with their own telephones;
- each occupant had its own key to its room and to the flat in which it was situated;
- cleaning and linen services were provided and were charged to the occupant;

- rooms were hired on a weekly or a monthly basis and a deposit was required;
- the management staff registered occupants and visitors, and collected payments;
- the management staff were not present on the premises between 7:00 pm and 10:00 am; and
- there were no regulations or rules except that occupants should not create any disturbance.

Despite the foregoing, the court found that the respondent did not retain sufficient control of the premises because:

- occupants kept their own keys and therefore had ready access to their rooms at all times (in the *Lam Man-yuen* case, the room keys were kept at the entrance and the front gate, to which the occupants had no key, was locked at night);
- there were no regulations (there were regulations in the *Lam Man-yuen* case); and
- management did not live on the premises (they did in the *Lam Man-yuen* case).

Thus the occupants did not have a licence but a lease. As the court stated in the case of *Marchant v Charters* [1977] 1 WLR 1181:

> What is the test to see whether the occupier of one room in a house is a tenant or a licensee? ... the answer depends on the nature and quality of the occupancy. Was it intended that the occupier should have a stake in the room or did he have only permission for himself personally to occupy the room ...[73]

ii. *Fixed Duration*

The length or duration of the lease period must be ascertainable at the commencement of the lease.[74] The duration may be stated as a fixed term, *e.g.*, 1 April 2008 to 31 March 2012. Alternatively, the duration may be stated as a periodic term (*e.g.*, weekly, monthly or yearly). In either event, there must be certainty of duration of the lease; there must be a fixed period of time.

A lease "for the duration of the war" failed to meet this requirement in the case of *Lace v Chantler* [1944] KB 368 where the court stated that:

73. [1977] 1 WLR at 1185.
74. *See* KATHERINE LYNCH, *Leaseholds: Certainty Principle Prevails, But For How Long?* HKLJ 234 (1993).

> a term created by a leasehold tenancy agreement must be expressed either with certainty and specifically or by reference to something which can, at the time when the lease takes effect, be looked to as a certain ascertainment of what the term is meant to be. In the present case, when this tenancy agreement took effect, the term was completely uncertain. It was impossible to say how long the [war] ... would last.[75]

H. Types of Leases

In this section, the different categories of leases are presented. Included in this discussion is an analysis of the components which distinguishes the different categories of leases.

i. *Fixed-term Lease*

A fixed-term lease is for a specified duration. The length or duration of the lease is fixed to end at a specified time. The key points to note about a fixed-term lease are the following: a lease for a fixed term is created by an express agreement; the commencement and termination dates of the fixed-term lease must be stated or ascertainable; and, under the common law, no notice to quit is required for the fixed-term lease as it will expire at the end of the fixed term.

A yearly lease continues from year to year.[76] In order to terminate this lease, the required period for the notice to quit, unless expressly agreed otherwise, is six months, which expiration coincides with the end of one of the years of tenancy.[77]

---

75. *Lace v Chantler* [1944] KB at 370. This case is frequently quoted as authority. A more recent case is *Ashburn Anstalt v WJ Arnold* [1988] 2 WLR 706.

76. 17(1) HALSBURY'S, *supra* note 57, at para. 235.160 observed:

> A tenancy from year to year arises either by express agreement or by implication of law. It differs from a tenancy at will in that it may be determined only by notice duly given except where there is a stipulation for determination without notice. The appropriate words for the express creation of the tenancy are "from year to year". ...

See also MERRY, *supra* note 59, at 43–44; MEGARRY'S MANUAL, *supra* note 35, at 347. The *BLIS Glossary*, *supra* note 7, translates the term "tenancy from year to year" as 按年計算的租賃.

77. For further information on this procedure, *see* 17(1) HALSBURY'S, *supra* note 57, at paras. 235.166, 235.169, 235.176–235.178.

ii. Periodic Lease

Another type of lease is a periodic lease, which consists of an initial period of time and automatically renews for successive periods until notice to terminate the lease is given by one of the parties.[78] Examples of periodic leases include quarterly, monthly or weekly tenancies. Periodic leases are created by express agreement, *e.g.*, by deed, or by implication of law, or where no intention to create a particular form of lease has been expressed.[79] Unless otherwise agreed, periodic leases can only be terminated at the end of one of the periods of tenancy. Periodic leases require notice of one full period in order to terminate the lease. In other words, a weekly periodic tenancy will, unless otherwise agreed, require one week's notice. Likewise, a monthly tenancy will require one month's notice to quit in order to determine the lease.

iii. Tenancy at Will

Another type of lease is a tenancy at will.[80] To classify this type of tenancy as a proper lease might be misleading because of its unknown or uncertain duration. Nonetheless, this tenancy is more than a contractual relationship because the parties' relationship is one of landlord and tenant. A tenancy at will may be likened to a tenure with no estate.[81]

A tenancy at will arises when a tenant takes possession of the landlord's land with consent and understanding that the tenancy might be terminated

---

78. *E.g.*, yearly, quarterly or monthly. *See also* MEGARRY & WADE, *supra* note 35, at para. 17–072; MEGARRY'S MANUAL, *supra* note 35, at 348–349.

79. *See Conveyancing and Property Ordinance*, *supra* note 43, at section 6, which provides:

> (1) All interests in land created by parol and not put in writing and signed by the persons creating the same, or by their agents thereunto lawfully authorized in writing, have, notwithstanding any consideration having been given for the same, the force and effect of interests at will only.
>
> (2) Nothing in section 3 or 5 or in subsection (1) shall affect the creation by parol of leases taking effect in possession for a term not exceeding 3 years (whether or not the lessee is given power to extend the term) at the best rent which can be reasonably obtained without a premium.

80. The *BLIS Glossary*, *supra* note 7, translates the term "tenancy at will" as 隨意終止的租賃.

81. NIELD, *supra* note 27, at 277.

17(1) HALSBURY'S, *supra* note 57, at para. 235.003 notes:

> Like a licensee, the tenant at will has no estate in land. However, a tenancy at will is different from a license in that the tenant at will is in 'possession' of the land, and may bring an action in trespass against a stranger.

at any time.[82] In the case of *Errington v Errington and Woods* [1952] 1 KB 290 the court said, "it is of the essence of a tenancy at will that it should be determinable by either party on demand."[83] This type of tenancy arises when a person occupies land as a tenant, with the owner's consent, and, with the understanding that either party may determine the tenancy at any time.[84] This occupation might be the result of an expressed or an implied tenancy.[85] If expressed, the rent should be stipulated, although the tenancy at will can be rent-free. The offer and acceptance of rent generally converts a tenancy at will into a periodic tenancy unless stated otherwise.

Frequently, a tenancy at will is created when a tenant remains in possession of the estate after the end of lease, with the landlord's permission. This will not be the case if the tenant is relying on the *Landlord and Tenant (Consolidation) Ordinance*.[86] There is no tenancy at will where the original tenancy is for a one-year period, which, upon expiry, will result in another tenancy from year to year.

No formal notice to quit is required. A tenancy at will may be ended at any time when either party gives notice, or either party may commit an act which is inconsistent with the continuation of the tenancy.[87] For example, a purported transfer of either party's interest would end a tenancy at will.

---

82. *Id. See also* 17(1) HALSBURY'S, *supra* note 57, at para. 235.003; MERRY, *supra* note 59, at 45–47.
83. [1952] 1 KB at 296.
84. MEGARRY & WADE, *supra* note 35, at para. 17–075; MEGARRY'S MANUAL, *supra* note 35, at 349.
85. An implied tenancy is addressed in 17(1) HALSBURY'S, *supra* note 57, at para. 235.151:

    > A tenancy at will is implied where a person is in possession by the owner's consent, and his possession is not as employee or agent or as a licensee holding under an irrevocable licence, and is not held in virtue of any freehold estate or of any tenancy for a certain term. Such a tenancy is implied accordingly in cases of mere permissive occupation without payment of rent.

86. As explained in *id.* at para. 235.153, this situation arises when:

    > A tenant who, with the landlord's consent, remains in possession after his lease has expired is a tenant at will until some other interest is created, either by express grant or by implication by the payment and acceptance of rent. … The terms of a tenancy at will which arises in this way will be those of the expired lease unless inconsistent with the nature of a tenancy at will and unless there is evidence of a contrary intention.

    The amendments in the *Landlord and Tenant (Consolidation) (Amendment) Ordinance 2004* which came into effect 9 July 2004. The amendments removed the security of tenure provisions from the *Landlord and Tenant (Consolidation) Ordinance* (Cap 7). These changes as they pertain to domestic tenancies are reviewed in section III.N and the changes as they affect commercial premises are presented at section III.O.
87. *See* 17(1) HALSBURY'S, *supra* note 57, at para. 235.154 where it is stated:

Finally, as the relationship between the parties to a tenancy at will is a personal one, the tenancy at will ends if either party becomes deceased.

iv. *Tenancy at Sufferance*

Another type of lease is a tenancy at sufferance. Tenancy at sufferance is not a true lease as there is no tenure of the land and no estate in the land.

> A tenancy at sufferance arises where a tenant wrongfully holds over on termination of a previous tenancy without the landlord's consent or dissent. The absence of the landlord's consent distinguishes a tenancy at sufferance from a tenancy at will.[88]

The term "tenancy" is used because the occupier was originally a tenant who entered the land with the owner's permission, and in this respect the tenant differs from a trespasser. A tenancy at sufferance may be terminated at any time by the landlord suing for possession of the property or otherwise evicting the tenant.[89]

In sum, tenancies at sufferance arise by operation of law, without any agreement between the landlord and the tenant, where a tenant originally had a tenancy but then continues to occupy the property after the expiry of that tenancy. This occupation must be without the landlord's consent; otherwise, the occupant becomes a tenant at will rather than a tenant at sufferance. If the landlord dissents, the tenant is considered to be a trespasser.[90]

> A tenancy at will is determinable by either party on his expressly or impliedly intimating to the other his wish that the tenancy should be at an end. Until the intimation is thus given, the tenant is lawfully in possession ... the landlord may not recover the premises ... without a previous demand of possession or other determination of the tenancy. A demand for possession by the landlord which determines the tenancy at will is not a notice to quit. The issue of a writ claiming possession is a sufficient demand for possession to bring the tenancy to an end.

88. *Id.* at para. 235.004.
89. NIELD, *supra* note 27, at 278. *See also* MERRY, *supra* note 59, at 42–43.
90. As explained by one authority:

> A person who enters on land by a lawful title and, after his title has ended, continues in possession without statutory authority and without obtaining the consent of the person then entitled, is said to be a tenant at or on sufferance, as distinct from a tenant at will who is in possession with the landlord's consent. This is so whatever the nature of the tenant's original estate, whether he was tenant for years, or the subtenant of a tenant for years, or a tenant at will. A tenancy at sufferance arises by implication of law and may not be created by contract between the parties.
>
> There can be no tenancy at sufferance against the Government. In such a case, the person holding over is a mere trespasser.

17(1) HALSBURY'S, *supra* note 57, at para. 235.158.

I. Formal Requirements of Leases

Under the *Conveyancing and Property Ordinance*, a lease is defined as a type of legal estate.[91] Section 4 of the Ordinance requires that a legal estate be created, extinguished or disposed of by deed.[92] There are some exceptions. One of these exceptions to the general rule is: the grant, disposal or surrender of a lease taking effect in possession for a term not exceeding three years (whether or not the lessee is given power to extend the term) at the best rent which can reasonably be obtained without a premium.[93]

> In calculating the three-year term of a lease, any option to renew is disregarded. Thus, a monthly periodic lease is for a term of less than three years. Where an oral lease does not satisfy the exemption requirements, a tenancy at will is created.[94]

Leases and agreements for lease are subject to an *ad valorem* stamp duty calculated on the average annual rent.[95] The rate or amount of the stamp duty depends upon the length of the lease term. The stamp duty should be paid within 30 days after the lease is signed. Pursuant to the *Stamp Duty Ordinance* (Cap 117), both landlord and tenant are responsible for the duty but frequently a lease will specify which party is to pay. A premium paid for the grant of a lease attracts *ad valorem* duty, presently at the rate of 2.75 percent. An unstamped agreement can neither be used in court proceedings nor registered.

Only leases that are both stamped and written can be registered in the Land Registry. Written leases for a period longer than three years must

---

91. *See* Tenancy (Notice of Termination) (Exclusion) (Consolidation) Order (Cap 7A) para. 2:

    Tenancies held from—

    (a) the Hong Kong Housing Authority,

    (b) the Hong Kong Housing Society, and

    (c) (Repealed L.N. 164 of 1992)

    (d) the Hong Kong Settlers Housing Corporation Limited,

    are excluded from the further application of Part V of the Landlord and Tenant (Consolidation) Ordinance (Cap 7).

92. The *BLIS Glossary*, *supra* note 7, translates the term "deed" as 契據.
    See generally Goo & Lee, *supra* note 24, Chapter 7, at sections 5 ("Creation of Leases"), 7 ("Determining a Lease").

93. *Conveyancing and Property Ordinance*, *supra* note 43, at section 4(2)(d).

94. *See Landlord and Tenant (Consolidation) Ordinance*, *supra* note 86, at section 6(1).

95. *See Stamp Duty Ordinance* (Cap 117) Schedule 1.
    The *BLIS Glossary*, *supra* note 7, translates the term "*ad valorem*" as 從價費; and, "stamp duty" as 印花稅.

be registered to protect their priority. As with title documents and mortgages, in order to be prioritized by the day of signing, *i.e.* execution date rather than the date of registration, leases must be registered within one month of signing.[96] A lease which should be, but is not, registered is void against a *bona fide* purchaser or mortgagee for value, regardless of notice.[97] A written lease for a term of three years or less at rack rent does not need to be registered.

A lease option is considered to be a disposition of an interest in land. An option to renew a lease is an interest in land that is independent of the lease itself.[98] In order to be enforceable, the option to renew must be in writing and signed by the party against whom enforcement is sought.[99] The instrument creating the option must be registered to bind a subsequent purchaser or mortgagee for value.

Domestic tenancies must be notified to the Commissioner of Rating and Valuation.[100] For each new letting or renewal, Form CR109 needs to be completed, signed and lodged, in triplicate, by the landlord. The Commissioner endorses two copies, returns one to the landlord and sends the other to the tenant. There is no time limit for filing but a charge is made if not done within one month. More importantly, if the filing is not made, the landlord or principal tenant cannot maintain a court action for unpaid rent unless Section B of Form CR109 is endorsed by the Commissioner which cannot be done until the form has been filed.[101]

J. Obligations of Landlords and Tenants

Having discussed the types of tenancies under a leasehold estate, the manner by which the landlord and the tenant's rights and obligations are allocated now follows. A leasehold estate is governed by the agreement made between

96. *Land Registration Ordinance* (Cap 128) section 5, the text of which is set out *infra* note 445.
97. *Id.* at section 4.
The *BLIS Glossary*, *supra* note 7, translates "*bona fide* purchaser" as 真誠買方; and, "*bona fide* purchaser for value" as 付出價值的真誠購買人.
98. For more details on options to renew, *see*, *e.g.*, 17(1) HALSBURY'S, *supra* note 57, at paras. 235.106–235.107.
99. *Conveyancing and Property Ordinance*, *supra* note 43, at section 3(1).
100. Tenancies where the premises are let wholly or primarily as a residence. MERRY, *supra* note 59, at 45. *See also Landlord and Tenant (Consolidation) Ordinance*, *supra* note 86, at section 2.
101. *See* Note 9 of Form CR109; *Landlord and Tenant (Consolidation) Ordinance*, *supra* note 86, at section 119L.

the parties. This agreement provides the rights and the responsibilities between the parties. The following section presents some of those benefits and burdens.

A "covenant" is a promise made by one party, the "covenantor", for the benefit of another party, the "covenantee".[102] The covenant or covenants are contained in a deed which is signed, witnessed and delivered by the covenantor to the covenantee. As all leases for more than three years should be made by deed, the promises made in the lease will be covenants.[103]

Covenants should be differentiated from "conditions", which may also impose obligations on a tenant. If a tenant breaks a lease condition, the landlord will have an automatic right to end the tenancy. The landlord does not automatically have such a right for a breach of a covenant. The landlord must make an express provision in the lease for automatic termination. In a lease, this provision is usually known as a "forfeiture clause". The parties' intentions determine whether a term in a lease should be construed as a covenant or a condition. A condition exists where it is clear that the continuance of the lease is premised upon the tenant fulfilling its obligations. Generally, courts presume lease provisions are covenants unless the obligations are clearly expressed to be conditions. Most obligations[104] will thus be considered as covenants rather than as conditions.[105]

Usually, the parties will negotiate the provisions governing their relationship as landlord and tenant. In leases, these provisions are usually referred to as covenants. Leasehold covenants consist of three categories:

---

102. Covenants may be positive, *e.g.*, a covenant to repair. Covenants may also be negative, *e.g.*, a covenant not to assign. *See* 17(1) HALSBURY'S, *supra* note 57, at para. 235.424. *See generally* GOO & LEE, *supra* note 24, Chapter 8 ("Leasehold Covenants").
The *BLIS Glossary*, *supra* note 7, translates "covenant" as 契諾.

103. *See Conveyancing and Property Ordinance*, *supra* note 43, at sections 4(1) and 4(2)(d) which state:

> (1) A legal estate in land may be created, extinguished or disposed of only by deed.
> (2) This section does not apply to—
> ...
> (d) the grant, disposal or surrender of a lease taking effect in possession for a term not exceeding 3 years (whether or not the lessee is given power to extend the term) at the best rent which can be reasonably obtained without a premium;
> ...

104. This includes even the most fundamental of covenants, including the one to pay rent.

105. For further analysis on the topic of remedies for breaches of covenant or condition, *see* GOO & LEE, *supra* note 24, Chapter 8 at section 7 ("Remedies for Breach of Covenants"); 17(1) HALSBURY'S, *supra* note 57, at para. 235.100.

- implied covenants: those terms so essential to the landlord-tenant relationship that they are implied by law into the lease
- express covenants: the expressed provisions agreed between the parties
- usual covenants: those covenants imposed where a lease agreement provides that the usual covenants are to be given

In Hong Kong, implied covenants are particularly important because of the small number of express covenants usually made by a landlord. The Hong Kong government makes no express covenants in a Government lease. In short-term tenancy agreements, the landlord usually provides only an express covenant for quiet enjoyment and an express covenant for the payment of the Government rent due under the Government lease. The established test for the implication of terms is the business efficacy test. The rules to be applied are the same as the rules which govern the implication of terms into contracts generally. A court has no right to imply into an agreement any term:

> unless, on considering the terms of the contract in a reasonable and business manner, an implication necessarily arises that the parties must have intended that the suggested stipulation should exist. It is not enough to say that it would be a reasonable thing to make such an implication. It must be a necessary implication in the sense that I have mentioned.[106]

i. Landlord's Implied Covenants

A landlord's implied covenants or obligations include the following:

(1) Quiet enjoyment: a lessee, that is a tenant, shall have quiet enjoyment and use of the premises, free from any interference with the tenant's use of the premises by the landlord or the landlord's agent or any person claiming any interest in the realty through the landlord.[107] The case of *Kenny v Preen* [1963] 1 QB 499, CA considered the covenant of quiet enjoyment. The landlord supposedly gave the female tenant a valid

---

106. *Hamlyn & Co v Wood & Co* [1891] 2 QB 488, 491.
See also Hang Tak Co Ltd v Attorney General, unreported, (1986) HCA 2567/83 where the court applied the business efficacy test.
See also JUDITH SIHOMBING & MICHAEL WILKINSON, A STUDENT'S GUIDE TO HONG KONG CONVEYANCING 83–122 (5th ed. 2007) [hereinafter SIHOMBING, STUDENT'S GUIDE] on Government leases.

107. In Hong Kong, *see Landlord and Tenant (Consolidation) Ordinance*, *supra* note 86, at section 119V which provides in part:
> (1) Any person who unlawfully deprives a tenant or sub-tenant of occupation of any premises commits an offence …
> (2) Subject to subsection (3), any person who, in relation to any premises

notice to quit. Thereafter the landlord threatened, both by letters and by shouting at the tenant and banging on her door, to physically evict the tenant and remove her belongings from the premises. The tenant succeeded in court against the landlord for breach of covenant for quiet enjoyment and for a court order preventing the landlord from further interference with her enjoyment of the premises.[108]

In *Yeung Wah James v Alfa Sea Ltd* [1993] 1 HKC 440, the court found the respondent landlord liable to the claimant tenant for breach of the covenant of quiet enjoyment. The claimant was away from Hong Kong for work for three months during which time renovation was carried out. The claimant later found the flat full of debris and waste materials and the bedroom was no longer fit for that purpose. The court awarded the claimant $50,000 general damages for the discomfort, inconvenience and distress caused and an additional $50,000 exemplary damages for the respondent's harassment of the tenant with the intention of eviction.

Other examples of breach of the quiet enjoyment covenant include:

- scaffolding: *Owen v Gadd* [1956] 2 QB 99
- foul air: *World Realty v Kwan Ngar Kin* [1987] 3 HKC 148
- frequently changing the name of the building: *Union Assurance Society of Canton v Hong Kong Land Co Ltd* [1977] HKLR 597

(2) Derogation from grant: a landlord must not do anything which might cause the premises to become unfit for the purpose for which it was let to the tenant.[109] This obligation may overlap with the covenant for quiet enjoyment, but applies even when there is no physical interference. The court will consider the purpose(s) for which the premises are let. If that purpose is frustrated or made impossible by the landlord's

---

(a) either—
(i) does any act calculated to interfere with the peace or comfort of the tenant or sub-tenant or members of his household; or
(ii) persistently withdraws or withholds services reasonably required for occupation of the premises as a dwelling; and
(b) knows, or has reasonable cause to believe, that that conduct is likely to cause the tenant or sub-tenant—
(i) to give up occupation of the premises; or
(ii) to refrain from exercising any right or pursuing any remedy in respect of the premises,

commits an offence …

See generally Goo & Lee, *supra* note 24, Chapter 8 at section 2 ("Covenants by the Landlord").

108. *But see Wise Stand Ltd v United Pentatcostal Church of Hong Kong Ltd* (2003) DCCJ 19369/2001; [2003] HKEC 296. *See, e.g.*, Merry, *supra* note 59, at 55–57.

109. *See, e.g.*, Merry, *supra* note 59, at 57–60.

action, there will be derogation. There might not be any derogation, however, when that purpose is made more difficult, more expensive or less profitable.

In the case of *Aldin v Latimer Clark, Muirhead & Co* [1894] 2 Ch 437, an assignee of the landlord built on adjacent land in such a way as to obstruct the flow of air to the drying sheds in the tenant's timber yard, the purpose for which the tenant had let the premises. The court held that the covenant had been breached and awarded damages to the tenant.

In *Wisename Ltd v Secretary for Justice* [1998] 1 HKC 128, the court held that the government derogated from its grant where it granted an easement, which included vehicular use, and subsequently executed works such that vehicular use was no longer possible. However, in the case of *Lam Kwok-leung v Attorney General* [1979] HKLR 145, the court found no derogation where the erection of a latrine adjacent to the granted realty adversely affected the classification of the subject realty.

(3) Condition of premises: generally, there are no implied obligations upon the lessor that the premises are fit for habitation,[110] or will remain fit for that purpose, unless the house or flat let is furnished, in which case there is an implied covenant of habitability.[111] A landlord is not under

110. On the subject of habitability, 17(1) HALSBURY'S, *supra* note 57, at para. 235.292 states that:

> on the letting of an unfurnished dwelling house or flat there is no implied warranty on the part of the landlord that it is in a reasonably fit state for habitation … The intending tenant is presumed to make his own inquiries as to its condition … he takes the house as it stands. … If the house is, in fact, uninhabitable, then, after accepting the lease, the tenant is without remedy except where he has obtained a warranty of fitness, or where he has been induced to take the lease by misrepresentation … [by] the landlord, in which case the tenant may be entitled to rescission or damages. The mere omission of the landlord to disclose defects is not such misrepresentation but the deliberate concealment of some defects may be conduct equivalent to a fraudulent misrepresentation. …

111. Regarding furnished premises:

> On the letting of a furnished house, there is an implied condition that it is in a fit state for habitation … and, if this condition is not fulfilled, the tenant is entitled to repudiate the contract at once. He need not wait to give the landlord an opportunity for effecting repairs. … To fulfil the condition it is not enough that the landlord believes the house to be in a fit state for habitation; it must in fact be reasonably habitable. The implied condition may be treated also as a warranty, and the tenant may recover damages for the breach. The condition and warranty relate, however, only to the state of the premises at the commencement of the tenancy; and there is no implied condition or warranty that they are to continue fit for habitation throughout the term.

Id. at para. 235.294.
See also MERRY, *supra* note 59, at 60–62.

any implied obligation to carry out repairs on the leased premises unless it is expressly agreed otherwise.[112]

ii. Tenant's Implied Covenants

A tenant's implied covenants or obligations include the following:

(1) To repair: the tenant is to use the premises in a tenant-like manner.[113]
   (a) At common law, a tenant is liable for "waste", which is an act or omission that alters the condition of the land.[114] The standard "to use in a tenant-like manner" might vary with the type of the tenant and the length of tenancy.
   There are various categories of waste:
      (i) Equitable waste: equity will not excuse acts of wanton destruction even if an agreement purports to exclude a tenant's liability for waste.
      (ii) Voluntary waste: voluntary waste is a positive act, which does not amount to wanton destruction, but which nevertheless harms the property. "'voluntary waste'... consists of doing something which should not be done (*e.g.*, knocking down a wall)".[115] Voluntary waste occurs when a tenant deliberately or negligently commits an act which destroys or diminishes the property's value.[116] All tenants are liable for voluntary waste unless their liability is expressly excluded.

---

112. *See* the discussion below concerning repairs. For a discussion of a landlord's liability to make repairs, *see* 17(1) HALSBURY'S, *supra* note 57, at paras. 235.289–235.290.

113. *See* MERRY, *supra* note 59, at 63–65, Chapter 9 ("Repairs"). *See generally* GOO & LEE, *supra* note 24, Chapter 8 at section 3 ("Covenants by the Tenant").

114. 17(1) HALSBURY'S, *supra* note 57, at para. 235.298 states:

> Waste consists of any act or omission which causes a lasting alteration to the nature of the land in question to the prejudice of the person who has the remainder or reversion of the land. The obligation not to commit waste is an obligation in tort, and is independent of contract or implied covenant.

115. MACKENZIE & PHILLIPS, *supra* note 27, at 215.

116. MERRY, *supra* note 59, at 64 states that voluntary waste:

> occurs when the tenant does an act, whether deliberate or negligent, which tends to destroy or diminish the premises. A clear instance would be pulling down a building (even if it is replaced by a building of greater value). More common examples are the removal of fixtures and the alteration of the premises …

(iii) Ameliorating waste: ameliorating waste consists of a positive act that alters the premises but in such a way as to improve the realty.[117]

(iv) Permissive waste: permissive waste is the failure to repair or to do what ought to be done in order to maintain the property. "Permissive waste implies an omission through which damage results to the premises, as, for example, where houses are allowed to fall into decay."[118] The duties of a particular tenant vary according to the type of leasehold interest held, particularly the length of tenancy. The longer the tenancy, the higher the duty imposed upon the tenant.[119]

(b) The tenant's liability for waste depends upon the lease involved. A weekly tenant must take proper care of the property.[120] Yearly tenants must carry out minor repairs but they are not responsible for any substantial repairs, *e.g.*, mending the roof or fixing the foundation. A fixed-term tenant must carry out all the repairs that are necessary to enable the rendering up of the premises at the end of the term in the same condition as when occupation commenced, normal wear and tear excepted.[121]

(c) Trespassers, tenants at will, tenants at sufferance and short-term periodic tenants are not liable for permissive waste. Tenants at will

---

117. On occasions, it is difficult to distinguish between voluntary waste and ameliorating waste where the alterations might be considered an improvement. The case of *Cheung Yeung-kan v Lui Kwan* [1973–1976] 1 HKC 237 held the alteration of the character of the premises to be a decisive factor. *See also* 17(1) HALSBURY'S, *supra* note 57, at para. 235.299.

118. *See* 17(1) HALSBURY'S, *supra* note 57, at para. 235.298.

119. A tenant for a fixed-term of years is liable for permissive waste. Many fixed-term leases contain an express obligation to repair that supersedes the duty not to commit waste. Yearly tenants must keep the premises wind-and water-tight but will not be liable for fair wear and tear—the gradual deterioration caused by normal use or the normal action of weather. Weekly or monthly tenants must keep the premises in "a tenant-like manner" by "doing the little jobs about the place that a reasonable tenant would do" like cleaning the windows, mending a fused light, clearing a blocked sink, etc. NIELD, *supra* note 27, at 288.

120. MACKENZIE & PHILLIPS, *supra* note 27, at 216 explains:

> Generally the rule is that a weekly tenant is liable for voluntary waste but not for permissive waste: in other words he may not knock a wall down but he can let it fall down ... The duty is increased ... that he must use the premises in a 'tenant-like manner' ... This means that the tenant must clean the premises, mend the electric light if it is fused, unstop blocked sinks and generally 'do the little jobs about the place which a reasonable tenant would do'.

121. 17(1) HALSBURY'S, *supra* note 57, at para. 235.301.
For a review of "fair wear and tear", *see id.* at para. 235.310. For a review of the remedies available for the failure to repair, *see id.* at para. 235.302.

and tenants at sufferance are not liable for voluntary waste, but such acts would end the tenancy and make the tenants liable for the damages as trespassers.

(2) To pay rent: the rent must be paid promptly.[122] An assignee of a lease must also pay rent even though there still is an obligation to pay the rent on the part of the original tenant. Privity of contract exists between the original tenant and the landlord.[123] Privity of estate exists between the under-lessee and the original tenant.[124] A tenant is also under an implied covenant to permit the lessor to re-enter and take possession when in arrears of rent.

(3) Not to repudiate the landlord's title: a tenant may not commit any acts which might prejudice the landlord's title.[125]

(4) To pay rates, management fees and other taxes: in the absence of any agreement to the contrary, a tenant is liable to pay management fees, rates, and other taxes.[126]

(5) To allow the landlord entry and inspection: where the landlord is responsible for internal repairs, the right to enter the premises to inspect and/or make repairs will be specifically stated in the lease. If not, it will be an implied term.

(6) To deliver up the premises at the termination of the lease: it is implied that the tenant should return possession of the premises in good condition at the lease's end.[127]

(7) Not to assign or to under-let/sublet or to depart with possession of the leased premises without the landlord's consent.[128]

(8) To insure.

---

122. *See, e.g.*, MERRY, *supra* note 59, at 63.

123. BLACK'S LAW DICTIONARY, *supra* note 20, at 1320, defines "privity of contract" as "[t]he relationship between the parties to a contract, allowing them to sue each other but preventing a third party from doing so". LEXISNEXIS, HONG KONG ENGLISH-CHINESE LEGAL DICTIONARY 1478 (2005) [hereafter LEXISNEXIS] translates this term as 契約之相互關係.

124. BLACK'S LAW DICTIONARY, *supra* note 20, at 1434, defines "privity of estate" as "[a] mutual or successive relationship to the same right in property, as between grantor and grantee or landlord and tenant". LEXISNEXIS, *supra* note 123, at 1478 translates this term as 出租人與承租人的相互關係.

125. *See, e.g.*, MERRY, *supra* note 59, at 65.

126. *See, e.g.*, *id.* at 63.

127. *See, e.g.*, *id.* at 65.

128. 17(1) HALSBURY'S, *supra* note 57, at para. 235.333 states:

> In the absence of a provision to the contrary, a tenant for years or a tenant from year to year or other term has the right to assign his term or tenancy, or to create underleases or subtenancies. A restraint on assignment or underletting is, however, valid, and may be created either by condition or by covenant.

iii. Usual Covenants

"Usual covenants" will be read into a lease if the lease is stated to be subject to the usual covenants or if the lease is an open contract where only the basic terms are recorded, *i.e.*, parties, rent, premises, length of term, and commencement date.[129] Usual covenants may be divided into two classes.

The first category consists of covenants regarded as usual in every lease. These include the following covenants:

- by the landlord
  - for quiet enjoyment
- by the tenant
  - to pay rent and rates
  - to keep the premises in repair
  - to permit the landlord to enter and inspect where the landlord is liable for effecting repairs
  - a condition for re-entry for non-payment of rent

The second class of usual covenants consists of promises considered to be usual in a particular letting. This class varies according to the area, nature of the premises, and, the length and purpose of the lease. However, a covenant which commonly appears in leases of a particular nature might not be classified as a usual covenant. Courts hesitate to find a covenant to be a usual covenant if it limits or qualifies the estate granted to the tenant. For this reason, covenants against assignment or subletting, and covenants against carrying on a specified trade or usage for certain purposes, have not been regarded as usual covenants.

iv. Remedies for Breach of Covenants

A tenant may seek damages, injunction and declaration for any breach of covenant by the landlord.[130] A landlord may seek the same for a tenant's

---

> If it is created by a condition, the condition will express the lease to be void upon those events, but it will be construed as making the lease subject to re-entry at the election of the landlord. More usually the restraint will be imposed by the tenant's covenanting not to assign or underlet. An assignment in breach of such a covenant or condition is not void but is effective subject to the landlord's right to forfeit the lease.

See generally id. at paras. 235.330–235.339.

129. *See, e.g., id.* at para. 235.055. *See generally* Goo & Lee, *supra* note 24, Chapter 8 at section 4 ("Usual Covenants").

130. "Damages" generally refer to monetary compensation. "Injunction" is a court order either ordering a person or prohibiting a person from performing a particular act.

breach of covenant. In certain circumstances, a tenant may make repairs for which the landlord is responsible and deduct the repair costs from the rent. A landlord has additional remedies for non-payment of rent and breach of covenant, including deductions from the security deposit, forfeiture and distress, which are discussed below.

K. Alienation of Leases

A tenant may assign or sublet the premises unless expressly prohibited. Most written Hong Kong leases restrict sublets, assignments or licences.[131] Breach of the prohibition by a tenant could result in the premises' forfeiture to the landlord for breach of covenant. A landlord can assign its reversionary interest subject to the lease. Assignments and sublets are considered to be dispositions of an interest in land so that the requirements of the *Conveyancing and Property Ordinance* need to be observed.[132] The practice is for the lease to prohibit subletting and assignment without the landlord's consent, such consent not to be unreasonably withheld.

L. Transfer of Deposits

Usually, a tenant pays a deposit to the landlord as security for the fulfilment of the tenant's obligations. The landlord agrees to return the money at the end of the lease term when the tenant has surrendered the premises. A common provision allows the landlord to deduct any loss or damage resulting from the tenant's breach of any lease covenants. Any remaining funds from the deposit will then be returned to the tenant.[133]

> A declaration of legal rights is really a polite alternative to an order for specific performance. Where the plaintiff is confident that the defendant will act on the decision of the court … he may ask that the court simply declare the legal position without the sanction of an order or an award of damages.

MERRY, *supra* note 59, at 141.

The *BLIS Glossary*, *supra* note 7, translates "injunction" as 禁制令 or 強制令; and, "declaration" as 宣告.

131. For additional information on the topic of subleases/underleases, *see* 17(1) HALSBURY'S, *supra* note 57, at paras. 235.075–235.077. *See generally* GOO & LEE, *supra* note 24, Chapter 7 at section 6 ("Assignment of Leases and Reversion").

132. For instances where a lease may confer upon the tenant an option to purchase the landlord's interest in the demised premises, *see* 17(1) HALSBURY'S, *supra* note 57, at para. 235.101; SIHOMBING, STUDENT'S GUIDE, *supra* note 106, at 1378–1384.

133. In *Fujitsu Hong Kong Ltd v Kwan Sit-cham* [1991] HKDCLR 23 the judge implied a term that the landlord must pay interest for the deposit.

If there is a sale of the premises and thus a change of landlord, the practice of transferring the deposit money to the new landlord should be avoided. Repayment of the deposit is a personal obligation of the original landlord who remains liable to the tenant, and the tenant cannot recover the deposit from the new landlord. An agreement between the three parties involved that the deposit will be repaid by the purchaser to the tenant following termination of the tenancy would solve the matter.

M. Determination of a Lease

A lease may terminate either by its own terms or prematurely through a breach of a particular covenant. The methods of determination discussed below are the most commonly recognized ways, albeit not necessarily all the ways by which a lease may be terminated.[134]

i. *Lapse of Time*

One way in which a lease will determine is by the passage of time. A tenancy for a fixed term ends automatically upon expiry of the last day of the term. This rule does not apply to periodic tenancies. If a fixed term tenancy terminates and the landlord continues to accept rent, a new periodic tenancy will be created by conduct.[135]

ii. *Notice*

A lease may also be terminated by notice. The lease itself may state the period of notice required for determination. If there is no provision in the lease, the notice period for periodic tenancies is generally one full period for short-term periodic tenancies and six months for tenancies from year to year.[136] Where a periodic tenancy is determinable by notice of a specified length, the notice must be given to expire at end of the year[137] unless the lease otherwise provides in a break clause.[138]

---

134. For discussion of the option to purchase the premises by the tenant, *see* 17(1) HALSBURY'S, *supra* note 57, at paras. 235.101–235.104. For the option to renew a lease, *see id.* at paras. 235.106–235.107.
See generally GOO & LEE, *supra* note 24, Chapter 7 at section 7 ("Determining a Lease").
135. *See, e.g.*, MERRY, *supra* note 59, at 160–165.
136. *See id.* at 245–254 for detailed information concerning commercial tenancies in Hong Kong.
137. Alternatively at the end of the quarter, or, as the case may be.
138. *See also* 17(1) HALSBURY'S, *supra* note 57, at paras. 235.108–235.110 for a discussion of an option to determine a lease before the expiration of the lease term.

The notice must comply with any requirements set out in the lease. Where no requirements are specified, the notice must be in writing.[139] A notice to terminate a tenancy pursuant to the *Landlord and Tenant (Consolidation) Ordinance* must be in the prescribed form, but otherwise the only requirement is that the notice must be reasonably clear and certain. The notice must describe the premises so that the property can be ascertained with certainty. A notice to quit a part of the premises is ineffective because a landlord cannot be forced to take back only part of the leased property. The notice must also give a clear date when the tenancy will cease.

iii. Surrender

A third manner of terminating a lease is by surrender.[140] Upon the tenant's surrender of the lease, the lease will merge with the landlord's reversion, and be extinguished.[141] A surrender does not affect any rights to sue accrued prior to the surrender, and has no impact upon any sub-lease; the surrender will only affect the lease being surrendered.

A surrender must be made by agreement of both parties, either by a term in the lease itself or by a special agreement.[142] The *Conveyancing and Property Ordinance* requires that a surrender be made by deed and that the surrender must be registered at the Land Registry unless the lease falls within section 4(2)(d) of the Ordinance, *i.e.*, one which takes effect in possession at best rent for a term not exceeding three years. If the lease is an equitable lease, the surrender may be made in writing under section 5 of the *Conveyancing and Property Ordinance*.[143] A surrender requires the payment of stamp duty.

---

139. *See Conveyancing and Property Ordinance*, *supra* note 43, at section 62(1).

140. Concerning this procedure, *see* 17(1) HALSBURY'S, *supra* note 57, at para. 235.448. The *BLIS Glossary*, *supra* note 7, translates the term "surrender" as 退回.

141. "Reversion" is defined by BLACK'S LAW DICTIONARY, *supra* note 20, at 1345, as the:

> interest that is left after subtracting what the transferor has parted with from what the transferor originally had; specif., a future interest in land arising by operation of law whenever an estate owner grants to another a particular estate, such as a life estate or a term of years, but does not dispose of the entire interest.

The *BLIS Glossary*, *supra* note 7, translates the term "reversion" as 復歸權益.

142. *See*, *e.g.*, 17(1) HALSBURY'S, *supra* note 57, at paras. 235.448–235.456; MERRY, *supra* note 59, at 187–190.

143. CURZON, *supra* note 4, at 221 defines the phrase "equitable lease" as "A lease which does not satisfy the necessary requirements for a legal lease but is, nevertheless, valid in equity." The definitions of "equitable interest" and "legal estate" are set out in section 2 of the *Conveyancing and Property Ordinance*, *supra* note 43.

Surrender can be implied or inferred by the conduct of the parties. Any action which is incompatible with the continued landlord-tenant relationship results in an implied surrender of the lease. For example:

- a new grant to the tenant, with the tenant's consent, of a new lease, results in the old lease being surrendered;[144]
- the tenant delivers actual possession to the landlord during continuance of the lease with the landlord's consent and acceptance;[145]
- change of the tenant's capacity inconsistent with the tenancy;[146] and,
- the landlord grants a new lease to a third person with the tenant's consent.[147]

iv. *Merger*

Merger is another method by which a lease may be determined. A merger takes place where the different interests merge into one interest. A merger occurs when the landlord's reversion and the lease becomes vested in either the tenant or a third person.[148]

> Merger is similar [in effect] to surrender. In both cases the reversion and lease become vested in one person so as to extinguish the lease. In a surrender, that person is the landlord—in a merger, it is the tenant or a third party. …
>
> A merger at law is automatic, but in equity it is dependent on intention and will not occur unless intended by the person acquiring the lease and reversion.[149]

144. This matter is discussed in further detail in 17(1) HALSBURY'S, *supra* note 57, at para. 235.451.
145. *Id.* at para. 235.450.
146. *See id.* at para. 235.453.
147. *Id.* at para. 235.454 explains in greater detail:

> The grant by the landlord of a new lease to a third person, with the tenant's consent, operates as a surrender of the old lease, provided the old tenant gives up possession to the new tenant at or about the time of the grant of the new lease. The same effect is produced where the landlord, with the tenant's consent, accepts another person as tenant, and that other person takes possession …

148. *Id.* at para. 235.448 n. 1 comments that:

> A merger occurs where the tenant acquires the landlord's reversion or a third person acquires both the lease and the reversion with the result that the two interests merge, being in the ownership of the same person. The principle underlying surrender and merger is the same, namely that the lease and the reversion become vested in the same person …

See, e.g., MERRY, *supra* note 59, at 190.
149. NIELD, *supra* note 27, at 299–300.

v. *Forfeiture*

Another method of determining a lease is by forfeiture.[150] A lease can be forfeited for breach of covenant where the lease contains an express provision for such action. A lease can also be forfeited for breach of condition. In a lease subject to Part IV or Part V of the *Landlord and Tenant (Consolidation) Ordinance* (Cap 7), failure by a tenant to pay rent may result in forfeiture of the lease.[151] As such, a breach of a covenant does not automatically give a landlord the right to re-enter and to take possession unless this right is stated in the lease. Should there be a breach of a contractual condition, the common law would grant a right to repossess. A breach makes the lease voidable; there is no automatic termination of the lease. In the event of non-payment of rent, a formal demand must be made by the landlord before re-entry, unless either the right of re-entry expressly excludes a need to do so, or the rent is at least six months in arrears and the value of the goods on the premises that may be subject to distress would not cover the cost of the arrears.[152] Forfeiture does not negate any rights to sue which accrued prior to the forfeiture.

Before a landlord can re-enter, a notice must be given as required under the *Conveyancing and Property Ordinance*.[153] When the forfeiture is for non-payment of rent, the landlord must first demand the rent due unless:

- the terms of the lease have waived this requirement;
- rent is in arrears for at least six months; or,

---

150. *See, e.g.*, MERRY, *supra* note 59, at 171–181.
The *BLIS Glossary*, *supra* note 7, translates the term "forfeiture" as 沒收租賃權.

151. *See Landlord and Tenant (Consolidation) Ordinance*, *supra* note 86, at sections 117, 126.

152. The *BLIS Glossary*, *supra* note 7, translates the term "distress" as 扣押. This topic is explored in more detail in section III.M.*vii*.

153. *Conveyancing and Property Ordinance*, *supra* note 43, at section 58(5) provides that:

For the purposes of this section—

(a) "lease" (租契) includes an original or derivative under-lease; also an agreement for a lease where the lessee has become entitled to have his lease granted;
(b) "lessee" (承租人) includes an original or derivative under-lessee, and the persons deriving title under a lessee;
(c) "lessor" (批租人) includes an original or derivative under-lessor, and the persons deriving title under a lessor;
(d) "under-lease" (分租租契) includes an agreement for an under-lease where the under-lessee has become entitled to have his under-lease granted;
(e) "under-lessee" (分租人) includes any person deriving title under an under-lessee.

- in the event of a distress action, there are insufficient goods on the premises to cover the arrears.

Where the forfeiture is for breach of either a covenant or a condition other than for non-payment of rent, section 58 of the *Conveyancing and Property Ordinance* obligates the landlord to serve notice on the tenant. Section 58(1) provides:

> A right of re-entry or forfeiture under any proviso or stipulation in a lease for a breach of any covenant or condition in the lease shall not be enforceable, by action or otherwise, unless and until the lessor serves on the lessee a notice—
>
> (a) specifying the particular breach complained of; and
>
> (b) if the breach is capable of remedy, requiring the lessee to remedy the breach; and
>
> (c) specifying the compensation, if any, which the lessor requires in respect of the breach,
>
> and the lessee fails, within a reasonable time thereafter, to remedy the breach, if it is capable of remedy, and to make reasonable compensation in money, to the satisfaction of the lessor, for the breach.

If the tenant fails to remedy the breach, the landlord may re-enter by self-help or through court proceedings. The landlord will usually start court proceedings for possession of the premises as forcible entry poses certain risks. If the tenant fails to comply with the notice, forfeiture of the lease may proceed. Positive covenants, *e.g.*, the tenant's covenants to make certain repairs or to pay management fees, usually can be corrected. Negative covenants, *e.g.*, a covenant not to assign, appear to require a court to determine whether late compliance and/or compensation could make good the injury to the landlord arising from the breach. Some covenants are incapable of remedy, such as covenants against assignments, sublets and immoral use.

a. Relief against Forfeiture

A tenant may challenge forfeiture proceedings if waiver or estoppel exists, and may also ask for court relief. Hong Kong courts have equitable powers to grant relief against forfeiture where the action is based upon the tenant's failure to pay rent. This equitable power has largely been replaced by statutory powers.[154] Section 58(2) of the *Conveyancing and Property Ordinance*

154. *See, e.g., High Court Ordinance* (Cap 4) sections 21F–21H, which provide that relief will be granted to the defaulting tenant if the rental arrears and costs are paid in full before the time for acknowledging service of the writ or before a possession order is executed. Similar provisions can be found in the *District Court Ordinance* (Cap 336) section 69.

also provides a tenant with the right to apply for relief from forfeiture for breach of covenant. A court has broad powers to grant relief. The right, however, cannot be exercised until the landlord starts proceedings, and this right may still be exercised after the landlord has taken possession without an order. If relief is granted, conditions may be imposed. Note that the grant of relief from forfeiture revives the lease. However, once the landlord has re-entered, the court's statutory power to grant relief ends.

Forfeiture of a head lease terminates a sub-lease. A sub-tenant can apply for relief against the head landlord under the *Conveyancing and Property Ordinance*. If the relief is granted to a sub-tenant, a new lease is granted to the sub-tenant but not for a term longer than the sub-tenant's original sub-lease.[155]

The lease is considered terminated from the date the court proceedings are started or when the landlord writes to the tenant forfeiting the lease. The tenant is to pay *mesne* profits, *i.e.*, market rent, to the date on which the tenant actually vacates the premises.[156]

b. Waiver

For a breach of covenant other than non-payment of rent, the landlord may waive the breach and continue with the lease.

> A landlord will be unable to enforce a right of re-entry if he has waived the breach that gave rise to the right. …
>
> A waiver will not prevent a landlord from forfeiting the lease where the tenant again breaches the same covenant. Thus, where the breach is continuing the landlord may rely on a future breach despite an earlier waiver of the same breach, unless his act of waiver was such that it condoned the future as well as the past breaches, or was so soon after waiver that the landlord must have known that the breach would still be continuing.[157]

To establish the defence of waiver, a tenant has to prove that the landlord has knowledge of the breach and that the landlord acknowledged the continued existence of the lease.[158] A waiver usually arises where the landlord

The *BLIS Glossary*, *supra* note 7, translates the term "waiver" as 放棄; and, "estoppel" as 不容反悔法.

155. *Conveyancing and Property Ordinance*, *supra* note 43, at section 58(4).

156. *See, e.g.*, Goo & Lee, *supra* note 24, Chapter 8 at section 9 ("Mesne Profits"); Merry, *supra* note 59, at 199–201; 17(1) Halsbury's, *supra* note 57, at para. 235.478 for a detailed explanation of *mesne* profits.

157. Nield, *supra* note 27, at 294–295 (citation omitted).

158. *See, e.g.*, Merry, *supra* note 59, at 176–179.

accepts or demands rent from the tenant with the knowledge of a breach of covenant. Some breaches, such as a breach of the covenant against assignment, are once-and-for-all breaches. Other breaches are continuing breaches so there can be no waiver of a continuing breach. In the case of *Chinachem Investment Co Ltd v Chung Wah Weaving and Dyeing Factory Ltd* [1978] HKLR 83, the tenant covenanted not to use the car park for purposes other than parking, and, loading and unloading vehicles. Later, with advice from the landlord, the tenant installed machinery in the car park. The landlord sued for possession alleging forfeiture for breach of covenant. The court held that the landlord had waived the tenant's breach for the duration of the lease.

vi. Estoppel

Estoppel is an equitable remedy which courts use to do justice and prevent unfairness. Estoppel has undergone changes in recent times, with the traditional categories of estoppel having merged to some degree. Nonetheless, the essential purpose of estoppel has remained unchanged: to prevent unfairness. As applied in this section, estoppel would prevent, for example, a landlord from supposedly waiving a breach of the tenancy agreement by the tenant and then to claim that the tenant had breached the agreement. Such a course of action by the landlord would be unfair to a tenant who had relied upon the landlord's waiver.[159]

vii. Distress

In the event of non-payment of rent, the landlord may forfeit the lease, if legally possible, or may recover the rent in arrears by action for non-payment and distraint. Also known as "distress for rent", the term "distraint" is defined as taking the tenant's personal property in order to pay the arrears of rent under a current lease. Distress involves the seizure, detention and sale of the tenant's goods. Distress for rent is a common law remedy, which is now only available to landlords and only while they remain as landlords.[160] Further, distress is only available for unpaid rent; not for other outstanding

159. For an in-depth discussion of estoppel in the context of Hong Kong property and conveyancing, *see* GOO & LEE, *supra* note 24, Chapter 3 ("Proprietary Estoppel"); SIHOMBING, STUDENT GUIDE, *supra* note 106, at 839–847.
160. *See* 17(1) HALSBURY'S, *supra* note 57, at para. 235.227.

obligations such as management charges. A landlord cannot distrain for more than 12 months' rent. A landlord loses the right to distrain upon the sale of the landlord's reversion. At the time of any sale of reversion, the purchaser cannot distrain for rent in arrears as the purchaser is not entitled to them as landlord.

Distress for arrears of rent can only be levied under Part III of the *Landlord and Tenant (Consolidation) Ordinance*.[161] The landlord makes an *ex parte* application to the District Court for a distress warrant.[162] An affidavit is attached to this application setting out details of the landlord, premises, rent due, and the period for which rent is due. There is no duty of full disclosure as in other *ex parte* applications, *e.g.*, the landlord need not disclose any dispute with the tenant.

The court issues a warrant directing the bailiff or other court officer to execute distress within six days. Prior to performing the distraint, the landlord is obligated to pay the fees for the warrant. In carrying out the distraint, subject to some exceptions, the bailiff may seize goods in the tenant's apparent possession, such as:

- movable goods;
- property in the house or on the premises; and,
- property in the apparent possession of the debtor, except for:
  - things in actual use;
  - tools and implements not in use, if there are other movable property;
  - property of another;
  - clothing; or
  - goods delivered to custody of law or person in public trade.

The bailiff impounds the property and prepares an inventory for the purpose of selling the property by public auction. During this process, there is no opportunity for the tenant to be heard prior to seizure.

The levied items will be subject to sale unless the debtor tenant arranges to pay the debt owed to the landlord. Generally, when confronted with this situation, the defaulting tenant makes arrangements to pay the arrears. The tenant may apply to the court for an extension of time in which to pay the arrears.[163] Alternatively, the tenant may challenge either the distraint action

161. *Landlord and Tenant (Consolidation) Ordinance*, *supra* note 86, at sections 75–114.

162. The *BLIS Glossary*, *supra* note 7, translates the term "*ex parte* application" as 單方面的申請.

163. For a more detailed explanation of this procedure, *see*, *e.g.*, 17(1) HALSBURY'S, *supra* note 57, at paras. 235.236–235.254; MERRY, *supra* note 59, at 100–117.

itself or the right to seize an article under the distraint warrant.[164] If these acts are not taken or the tenant is unsuccessful, the failure to pay will result in a sale of the seized items with the proceeds of the sale generally being distributed in the following order:

- the costs of the distress for rent action in the court;
- payment of the debt owed to the landlord; and,
- the remaining funds, if any, to the debtor.

Further, a distraint seizure of third-party goods in the tenant's apparent possession may be challenged by the rightful owners under sections 93 and 95 of the *Landlord and Tenant (Consolidation) Ordinance*. Challenges under section 93 must be brought within five days of the seizure. Such proceedings are known as "interpleader" proceedings.[165]

N. Domestic Leases

i. General

Part IV of the *Landlord and Tenant (Consolidation) Ordinance* pertains to domestic tenancies.[166] A "domestic tenancy" is defined as "a tenancy of premises let as a dwelling."[167] "Tenancy" is defined to include an oral or written tenancy and includes a sub-tenancy and agreement for tenancy,[168] but is not defined to include a licence or tenancy at sufferance.[169]

---

164. *See Landlord and Tenant (Consolidation) Ordinance*, *supra* note 86, at section 93.

165. The *BLIS Glossary*, *supra* note 7, translates "interpleader" as 互爭權利訴訟.

166. Section 2 provides:

> "domestic premises" (住宅處所) means premises the subject of a separate letting (including any bed-space, cubicle, room, floor or portion of a floor or building) which are used wholly or primarily for human habitation:
>
> > Provided that the following shall not be deemed to be domestic premises within the meaning of this definition
> > (a) any building or portion of a building which is used for habitation only by caretakers or watchmen not exceeding 2 in number;
> > (b) any building or portion of a building which is used for habitation only by office attendants or their families;
> > (c) any particular portion of an hotel or boarding-house which is let by the keeper of such hotel or boarding-house to a guest of such hotel or boarding-house …

Part IV provides: "'domestic tenancy' (住宅租賃) means a tenancy of premises let as a dwelling". *Landlord and Tenant (Consolidation) Ordinance*, *supra* note 86, at section 115(1).

167. *Id.* at section 115(1).

168. *Id.*

169. 17(1) HALSBURY'S, *supra* note 57, at para. 235.483 explains:

The *Landlord and Tenant (Consolidation) (Amendment) Ordinance 2004* revised the existing *Landlord and Tenant (Consolidation) Ordinance* with effect on 9 July 2004. The amendments removed the security of tenure provisions for domestic tenancies. As of that commencement date, there will no longer be any statutory control for domestic tenancies in regards to rent or security of tenure. For domestic tenancies in existence before 9 July 2004, and where the Part IV tenancy renewal procedure had commenced before this date, the Part IV procedure, which allowed a tenant the right to renew the tenancy, continues to apply.

ii. Post-Amendment Law

As a result of the amendments imposed by the *Landlord and Tenant (Consolidation) (Amendment) Ordinance 2004*, there can arise three scenarios:

(1) Post-amendment domestic tenancies, *i.e.*, those tenancies created on or after the commence date of 9 July 2004.
(2) Transitional domestic tenancies, *i.e.*, those tenancies in existence prior to the commencement date and where the Part IV tenancy renewal procedures have not commenced.[170]
(3) Pre-amendment tenancies, *i.e.*, those tenancies in existence prior to the commencement date and where the Part IV tenancy renewal procedures have commenced.[171]

Due to the passage of time, it is increasingly unlikely that situations falling within scenarios 2 and 3 would now arise. Therefore, only the first scenario is presented.[172]

Under the amended Ordinance, a domestic tenancy created on or after 9 July 2004 will determine upon expiry of the tenancy agreement. Domestic

---

> A tenancy means a tenancy entered into orally or into writing and includes an agreement for a tenancy and a sub-tenancy. ... a tenancy arises when exclusive possession of premises are given for a term at a rent ... A tenancy is to be distinguished from a licence to occupy premises. A tenancy at sufferance, which is not based on consensus and creates no interest in land, is not truly a tenancy.

See, e.g., Street v Mountford [1985] AC 809, HL. For more detailed discussion of the lease/licence distinction, *see* section III.E.

170. *Landlord and Tenant (Consolidation) (Amendment) Ordinance*, *supra* note 86, at section 5(2).
171. *Id.* at section 5(1).
172. For a discussion of the application of the second and third scenarios, *see* the first edition of this publication.

tenancies will terminate according to the terms of the lease agreement or as the parties may mutually agree. Without a contractual notice period or mutual agreement, a fixed term tenancy will end upon expiry while a periodic tenancy will be terminated by a notice to quit in accordance with the common law.

The *Landlord and Tenant (Consolidation) (Amendment) Ordinance 2004* repealed a substantial portion of the provisions of Part IV of the *Landlord and Tenant (Consolidation) Ordinance*.[173] However, certain Part IV provisions remains in force: the requirement of filing Form CR109 with the Commissioner of Rating and Valuation,[174] the implied covenants and forfeiture clauses,[175] and, the prohibition of harassment of a tenant. Note that consequential amendments to the *Landlord and Tenant (Consolidation) Ordinance* and other ordinances affecting the landlord-tenant relationship have been made.[176]

O. Commercial Leases

Part V of the *Landlord and Tenant (Consolidation) Ordinance* applies to non-domestic tenancies,[177] with certain exceptions.[178] Non-domestic leases pertain to premises used primarily for commercial activity, *e.g.*, offices, shops, restaurants, etc. The previous sections of this chapter concentrated on domestic tenancies. This section reviews briefly commercial leases and tenancies, although in many respects the same law governs both types of tenancies. Therefore, this section addresses the matters peculiar to commercial leases: rent increases and determination.[179]

---

173. For example, the following sections of the *Landlord and Tenant (Consolidation) Ordinance*, *supra* note 86, have been repealed: 116(3), 116(4), 116(4A), 117(1), 117(2), 118, 119K, and, 119M–119Q.
174. *Id.* at section 119L.
175. *Id.* at section 117(3).
176. *Landlord and Tenant (Consolidation) (Amendment) Ordinance*, *supra* note 86, at Part IV.
177. *See*, *e.g.*, *id.* at section 2 which also states: "'business premises' (商用處所) means premises which are not domestic premises". Part V states in part:

    > … this Part shall apply to every tenancy … whether the same be effected orally or in writing and notwithstanding any provision in such tenancy, including any provision purporting specifically to exclude the provisions of this Part.

    Landlord and Tenant (Consolidation) Ordinance, *supra* note 86, at section 121(1).
178. *E.g.* tenancies for a fixed term of three years or more which contain no provisions for early termination other than for breach of condition of the tenancy.
179. For in-depth analysis of this topic, *see* 17(1) HALSBURY'S, *supra* note 57, at paras. 235.505–235.510. *See* MERRY, *supra* note 59 at 245–254 for detailed information concerning commercial tenancies in Hong Kong.

Commercial premises' rents tend to be higher than that of similar residential premises and be of longer duration. To protect a landlord's interests, there frequently are provisions for rent adjustments at regular intervals throughout the duration of the commercial lease. The revised rent nonetheless must be capable of being calculated with certainty.[180] Several methods are available to a landlord to implement an increase with the rental amount capable of being calculated with certainty. One method employed by landlords to implement a rent increase is the "rent escalation" clause which may permit rent increases linked, for example, to increases in the Consumer Price Index. Another method available to landlords is the "turnover rent" clause which permits rent increases to be directly proportional to the success of a tenant's business. Rent review clauses may also be accompanied by "break clauses" which allow commercial tenants to determine the lease without breach if the tenants are dissatisfied with the rent increase. Finally, absent a provision in the tenancy agreement to the contrary, the tenancy may be subject to forfeiture if the rent is not paid within 15 days after it has become due.[181]

The *Landlord and Tenant (Consolidation) (Amendment) Ordinance 2004* removed from Part V the six-month written notice requirement for the termination of non-domestic tenancies as of 9 July 2004.

If the commercial lease has not expired and thus no Part V notice has been served by 9 July 2004, the tenancy may be terminated in accordance with the terms of the lease agreement or as mutually agreed between the parties.[182] Absent any agreement to the contrary, a fixed-term tenancy will

180. Merry, *supra* note 59, at 81.

181. *Landlord and Tenant (Consolidation) Ordinance*, *supra* note 86, at section 126.

182. *See Landlord and Tennant (Consolidation) (Amendment) Ordinance*, *supra* note 86, at section 9:

> (1) Notwithstanding the repeal of section 122 of the principal Ordinance on the commencement date—
> (a) a notice of termination served under section 122(1) of that Ordinance before that date shall have effect in relation to which it applies; and
> (b) the definition of "notice of termination" in section 120A of that Ordinance shall continue to apply in relation to that tenancy.
>
> (2) On and after the commencement date, a tenancy to which Part V applies and which is in existence on the day before the commencement date, but in respect of which no notice of termination has been served before the commencement date under section 122(1) of the principal Ordinance —
> (a) may be terminated in accordance with its terms or as otherwise agreed between the parties; or
> (b) if it is a tenancy which was continued by virtue of section 122(4) of that Ordinance, may be terminated either as a month to month tenancy or as agreed between the parties.

end upon the expiry of the term and a periodic tenancy may be terminated by a notice to quit at the length of a full notice period in accordance with the common law.[183]

A tenant in possession of commercial premises may also give notice of termination. If the lease is for a periodic tenancy, the tenant must give notice of at least one month before determination can lawfully occur.[184] If the lease term is for a fixed period, then the notice should be given at least one month before the tenancy's expiry. If the tenancy agreement so provides, the notice by the tenant may be more than one month in advance of the termination date.[185]

IV. FIXTURES

At common law, the ownership of realty includes ownership of everything above the land and everything beneath the land. The maxim *quicquid plantatur solo, solo cedit* represents the principle that whatever is attached to the soil becomes part of the land. Thus, land includes any buildings that are erected on the land. This maxim also embodies the law relating to fixtures.

The concept of fixtures applies to both freehold estates and leasehold estates. "Fixture" is a term given to items that becomes so attached to the land or a building as to form, in law, a part of the land. Such items are therefore considered to be realty. The distinction between fixtures and "fittings", *i.e.*, chattels that are not attached to land, is crucial whenever there is a transfer of a freehold or leasehold estate. For example, purchasers ought to know the chattels they are entitled to use as their own and sellers ought to know which fittings are removable.[186]

---

(3) Proceedings relating to Part V which are pending in the Tribunal on the commencement date, and decisions of the Tribunal relating to that Part which have not been given effect to on that date, may respectively continue and be given effect to on and after the commencement date notwithstanding the repeal of certain provisions of that Part by section 8 of this Ordinance.

(4) Proceedings relating to provisions of Part V saved by this section may be commenced in the Tribunal on or after the commencement date.

183. MERRY, *supra* note 59, at 41–43.

184. *Id.*

185. *Id.*

186. *See generally* SIHOMBING, STUDENT'S GUIDE, *supra* note 106, at 71–73, 1359.
The *BLIS Glossary*, *supra* note 7, translates the term "fixture" as 固體附着物; and, "fitting" as 裝置.

Whether an object is a fixture is not always easily determined. Frequently, the determination is a question of fact for a court to decide on a case-by-case basis. Whether a chattel has become a fixture depends on the degree of annexation and the purpose of annexation.[187] If these guidelines are applied correctly, the purpose of annexation should be evidenced by the degree of annexation.

A chattel is not considered a fixture unless it is actually fastened to, annexed to, or, connected with the land or a building.[188] A chattel attached to land, however slightly, is *prima facie* deemed to be a fixture. For example, in *Buckland v Butterfield* (1820) 2 Brod & Bing 54, a veranda connected to a house was considered a fixture because it was attached to land. The burden of proof that a chattel is not a fixture rests upon the party claiming the contrary.

The "purpose of annexation" test helps determine whether a chattel has been fixed for its more convenient use as chattel or for the more convenient use of the land or building. In *Australian Provincial Assurance Co Ltd v Coroneo* (1938) 38 SR (NSW) 700, the court held that the test would be whether an object is affixed with the intention that the object remains in position permanently or for an indefinite or substantial period, or, whether the chattel has been fixed with the intent that the object shall remain in position only for some temporary purpose.

For example, in the case of *Holland v Hodgson* (1872) LR 7 CP 328 the court held that blocks of stone placed one on top of another without any mortar or cement for the purpose of forming a dry stone wall would become part of the land. Those same stones, if deposited in a builder's yard and for convenience were similarly stacked on top of each other in the form of a wall, would remain as chattels.

A greenhouse attached to the external wall of a house is a fixture because it cannot be moved.[189] A movable greenhouse might be considered a chattel.[190] An air conditioner which fits into a window is presumed to be a fixture as it could not be enjoyed separately from a room and its purpose is to improve the premises.[191] One court determined that air conditioning machines placed or resting by their own weight on the floor of a garage

187. *See also Elitestone Ltd v Morris* [1997] 2 All ER 513; 17(1) HALSBURY'S, *supra* note 57, at paras. 235.126–235.127; MERRY, *supra* note 59, at 204–208.

188. *See also* 17(1) HALSBURY'S, *supra* note 57, at para. 235.128.

189. *Goldful Way Development Ltd v Wellstable Development Ltd* [1998] 4 HKC 679.

190. *Deen v Andrews* [1986] 1 EGLR 262.

191. *Loong, Irene and Pun Tsun Hang* [1959] HKDCLR 192. Yet, in the case of *Yu Yiu Kong Samuel v Kobylanski Stephen Andre* (2001) DCCJ No 15371/2000, the court stated:

adjoining a restaurant were not to be considered fixtures.[192] Another court found an air conditioning system to be a fixture because the air conditioning system was either affixed to the building or affixed to an item which is already a fixture.[193]

If a chattel becomes a fixture, its ownership will belong to the landowner and will pass with the ownership of the land. A vendor is not entitled to remove fixtures upon any sale of land without having agreed specifically with the purchaser to do so. The right to remove fixtures also arises in the following situations:

- Mortgagor and mortgagee: fixtures, whether annexed to the land before or during the life of the mortgage, will become subject to the mortgage and can only be removed with the consent of the mortgagee. Thus, the fixtures will pass with the land to the mortgagee even though they are not mentioned in the mortgage document. This rule applies to both legal and equitable mortgages. If the fixtures are affixed or annexed by a third party, and both the mortgagor and the third party agree that the mortgagor will allow removal, the third party's rights are superior to the mortgagee's.
- Vendor and purchaser: fixtures pass to the purchaser. Subject to any express reservation, a conveyance would pass the title of the fixtures to the purchaser. Fixtures are considered to be part of the purchase price. If a vendor wishes to remove fixtures, the vendor must make specific arrangements with the purchaser.
- Landlord and tenant: all fixtures attached by a tenant *prima facie* form part of the reversion to the landlord. Because of the injustice this rule might cause, the law has developed to allow a tenant the right to remove trade fixtures or ornamental and domestic fixtures during its tenancy, provided removal will be without substantial or irreparable damage to the land.

> If the item is intended to be permanent and to afford a lasting improvement to the land or building, it will be a fixture. If the attachment is intended to be temporary and no more necessary for the use and enjoyment of the item, it remains a chattel ... Applying these tests... the air-conditioning unit ... a window-type air-conditioner, was not a fixture. Its attachment to the wall was only temporary. It could have been removed without much damage to the wall. Such an air-conditioner was no different in nature from a ceiling fan or wall lamp. All of these items are ... chattels rather than fixtures.

192. *Penta Continental Land Investment Co Ltd v Chung Kwok Restaurant Ltd* [1967] HKDCLR 22, 26.
193. *Orient Leasing (Hong Kong) Ltd v NP Etches* [1985] HKLR 292, 298.

- Trade fixtures are considered to be fixtures used for the purpose of conducting a trade or a business and thus can be removed by the tenant, *e.g.*, pipes and vats used by a tenant for a brewery, or petrol pumps and car lifts at a garage/repair shop are considered to be trade fixtures.[194]
- Ornamental and domestic fixtures are chattels affixed for ornament of the land or the building, or, for convenience.

> Objects which have been fixed to the land by way of ornament or for domestic convenience and utility have from the earliest times been removable by the tenant provided that the lease does not provide to the contrary and that they are capable of being severed without irreparable injury to the land.
>
> Articles which form an essential part of a house at the time of its construction may not be removed; and it is doubtful whether such articles may properly be called fixtures of any description. Skylights are not fixture but form part of the roof.[195]

These fixtures may be removed, provided that the removal does no substantial damage to the land or the building.

So long as a chattel can be removed without doing irreparable damage to the demised premises, neither the method nor the degree of annexation, nor the quantum of damage that would be done either to the chattel itself or to the demised premises by the removal, have any bearing upon the tenant's right to remove it, except in so far as they indicate the intention with which the tenant affixed the chattel to the premises. Where trade fixtures have to be taken to pieces in the removal, in general it is essential that they are capable of being put together in the same form in some other place. Buildings of a permanent nature are not removable, but a temporary corrugated iron shed used for trade is removable. Glasshouses are removable when erected for the purpose of business by a market gardener but, when erected for ornament or convenience, are not removable. Slight buildings, erected for the purpose of trade, and buildings which are accessory to removable

---

194. For comments concerning lease provisions to leave fixtures, *see* 17(1) HALSBURY'S, *supra* note 57, at para. 235.137. Concerning a landlord's remedies for the wrongful removal of fixtures, *see id.* at para. 235.138. Commenting further on trade fixtures, *id.* at para. 235.131 states:

> A tenant may remove fixtures if they have been affixed for the purposes of trade or manufacture, so long as the lease does not provide to the contrary, and so long as they are capable of being severed from the land without irreparable injury to it. …

See also MERRY, *supra* note 59, at 206–207.

195. 17(1) HALSBURY'S, *supra* note 57, at para. 235.132 (citations omitted). *See also* MERRY, *supra* note 59, at 207.

machinery are removable.[196] If a tenant removes fixtures, the tenant must repair any damage to the property caused by the fixtures' removal.

In summary, although the concept of fixture is relatively easy to understand, the application of this concept may be difficult. An example of this difficulty is provided by several court cases previously discussed concerning whether window-type air conditioners are fixtures or personalty. Items considered to be fixtures become part of the land and ownership of the items or fixtures will be transferred with the title to the land. Whether an item is to be considered as a fixture will depend upon the reason for attaching that item to the land and the extent of that attachment.

V. ADVERSE POSSESSION

A landowner has the right to keep unwanted or uninvited people off the land and the right to sue in court for an order for possession against any trespasser.[197] Adverse possession denotes the occupation of land in a manner inconsistent with the rights of the true owner. However, if the person has adversely possessed the land for such a period of time as specified by law, the actual owner may not enforce its rights against the occupier.[198]

---

196. 17(1) HALSBURY'S, *supra* note 57, at para. 235.133.

197. *See* KEVIN GRAY & SUSAN GRAY, ELEMENTS OF LAND LAW paras. 9.1, 10.1 (5th ed. 2009).

198. For a discussion of the policy behind adverse possession, *see* HILARY LIM & KATE GREEN, CASES & MATERIALS IN LAND LAW 60–64 (2nd ed. 1995) [hereinafter LIM & GREEN].
16 HALSBURY'S, *supra* note 29, at para. 230.132 states:

> Most acquisition of land by the operation of limitations occurs in the New Territories, although the legislation applies to any land in Hong Kong, whether unleased Government land or land subject to a Government lease. Apart from claims to New Territories land, adverse possession claims are rare. The acquisition of possessory title involves evidence of the operation of the Limitation Ordinance, and of possession by the adverse possessor for a sufficient period of continuous possession adverse to that of the true owner. …
>
> …
>
> One problem which resulted in contradictory decisions was the effect of the New Territories (Renewable Crown Leases) Ordinance, which facilitated the renewal of those Crown leases which had been granted for 75 years only in the New Territories but which gave an option to renew for a term of 24 years less three days from 1 July 1973 by automatically exercising the option. The Ordinance provided that the new lease was to be subject to existing rights, easements, tenancies or other burdens or incumbrances of whatsoever kind or nature. In many cases of adverse possession the limitation period of 20 years had not been perfected prior to 1973. In some cases, courts held that the Ordinance preserved the accruing rights to enable pre-1973 and post-1973 periods to be added together; other courts said that the Ordinance did not extend the original lease but granted a new lease and so the pre-1973 accruing rights were lost from 1973. The Privy Council has now decided that accruing rights were preserved.

P. J. Dalton explains the policy behind this principle as being a:

> statute has placed a limit on the time after which a claimant to an interest in land may bring an action to establish it in the face of the possession of another person holding under a later title … [Title] is extinguished or "barred" because the claim it gives to land has been allowed to remain unpressed for a long time in face of a rival title … [199]

The following points should be considered in cases of adverse possession:

- The length of the period: Section 7 of the *Limitation Ordinance* (Cap 347) provides that the limitation period for actions brought for the recovery of land by the government is sixty years, and by any other person the period is twelve years.[200]
- The running of time: section 8 of the *Limitation Ordinance* provides that time will begin to run against an actual owner of land only where:
  - the owner had been dispossessed or discontinued possession; and,
  - adverse possession of the land has been taken by some other person. An owner is presumed to be in possession of the land, even without any physical possession, unless the contrary is proved.

In *Boosey v Davis* (1988) 55 P & CR 83, 85, CA, the judge referred to the case of *Wallis's Cayton Bay Holiday Camp Ltd v Shell-Mex and BP Ltd* in his decision concerning adverse possession. The judge determined that possession by itself is not enough to give a title. It must be *adverse* possession. The true owner must have discontinued possession or have been dispossessed and another must have taken it adversely from the true owner.[201]

Possession with a licence, that is permissive use, does not constitute adverse possession unless the licence is revoked and the licensee continues in possession.

Two recent cases have arisen concerning adverse possession in highly developed areas of Hong Kong. The first concerns land in Causeway Bay. A

See also SIHOMBING, STUDENT'S GUIDE, *supra* note 106, at 52–68. *See generally* GOO & LEE, *supra* note 24, Chapter 5 ("Limitation Ordinance and Adverse Possession").

The *New Territories (Renewable Crown Leases) Ordinance* is now known as the *New Territories (Renewable Government Leases) Ordinance* (Cap 152).

Note, too, the time period for adverse possession has been reduced to 12 years from 20 years. *Limitation Ordinance*, *supra* note 18, at section 7.

199. P.J. DALTON, LAND LAW 153–154 (4th ed. 1996).

In the context of Hong Kong, *see Limitation Ordinance*, *supra* note 18, in particular sections 7–8.

200. The *BLIS Glossary*, *supra* note 7, translates the term "limitation period" as 時效期限.

201. *Wallis's Cayton Bay Holiday Camp Ltd v Shell-Mex & BP Ltd* [1975] QB 94, 103, CA.

family occupying land near the Lee Theatre claims to have been in possession of the property for approximately 50 years. The developer is attempting to remove the occupiers in order to develop the property, estimated to be worth up to HK$60 million. In the case of *Lee Theatre Realty Ltd v Tong Wah Jor*, unreported, CFI HCA 1251/2003, the court determined that the family squatting on the land did not have exclusive possession and did not have the requisite intent to exclude the owner from possession of the land. The court's decision in 2009 was that the calculation of the then required 20 year period did not begin until the 1990s.[202]

The second case is *Lam Che v Foung Sheu Kwun*, unreported, CFI HCA 486/2010, [2010] HKEC 1252. This case involved a flat in Ma Tau Kok Road in To Kwa Wan. In this instance, the tenant lived in the flat since 1973. After 1984, however, the owner seemed to have disappeared. For more than 25 years, the tenant paid the rates and other related expenses. By 2010, despite the wide publicity engendered by this case in the media, the owner or her heirs could not be located. The court determined that the tenant had met the prescribed time requirement, exclusive possession and the intent to exclude the owner. Accordingly, pursuant to the *Limitation Ordinance*, the court determined that the owner's title had been extinguished and awarded title of the flat to the tenant.

In summation, adverse possession allows another person to claim title of the property from the owner. Therefore, if an owner ignores or allows another person to use or claim ownership of land without any challenge or assertion of ownership for the statutory time period, the owner risks the property being claimed by the adverse possessor.

VI. ENCUMBRANCES

Section II of this chapter provided the statutory definition of "encumbrance". An encumbrance may also be defined as a:

> claim or liability that is attached to property or some other right and that may lessen its value, such as a lien or mortgage; any property right that is not an ownership interest.[203]

202. The defendant's unsuccessful appeal is found at CACV 279/2009, [2010] HKEC 302, CA.
203. BLACK'S LAW DICTIONARY, *supra* note 20, at 607.
See generally GOO & LEE, *supra* note 24, at Chapters 13 ("Land Covenants"), 14 ("Easements").

An encumbrance may thus be considered as a legal obligation or duty imposed upon the real property rather than upon an individual.

"Servitude" is a term derived from Roman law meaning an encumbrance consisting of a right to the restricted use of land without the possession or ownership of that parcel of land.[204] Because of the physical proximity of land and the potential flexibility of land use, the law has developed such that some rights allow use of a neighbour's land for occasional purposes. Thus, it is possible to create either rights over or interests in a neighbour's land, known as the "servient tenement", without the right to occupy or to possess that neighbour's land. These servitudes thus can restrict or impinge upon a landowner's rights to use the land in some manner. The three main types of servitudes are:

- easements;
- *profit à prendre*; and,
- restrictive covenants.

As both easements and *profit à prendre* are similar, they are presented first. Review of restrictive covenants follows. Next is a survey of a different type of encumbrance, known as mortgages.

A. Easements

An "easement" is the right annexed to land to use, or to restrict the use of, the land of another person in some way. As noted in the case of *Metropolitan Railway v Fowler* [1892] 1 QB 165, 171, CA an easement is "some right which a person has over land which is not his own." An easement is thus a right enjoyed by an owner of one parcel of land, known as the "dominant tenement", over another owner's parcel of land, known as the "servient tenement". Examples of easements include: right of way, right of light and right of support.

Easements are generally positive, as illustrated by a right of way, a right of support for a building or a right to draw or discharge water. Easements may also be negative, for example a right to prevent another from using the land in a particular way: the right to light and air, which a neighbour may not obstruct by erecting a building.

"Incidents of a novel kind cannot be devised and attached to property at the fancy or caprice of any owner."[205] In other words, the creation of an

204. LexisNexis, *supra* note 123, at 1747 translates "servitude" as 地役.
205. Lim & Green, *supra* note 198, at 170.

easement requires certain conditions, the same conditions as the creation of a profit.[206] In *Re Ellenborough Park* [1956] 1 Ch 131, the owners of nearby houses claimed the right of compensation for loss of their right to walk in and enjoy the neighbouring park. The court held that damages would only be awarded if the right amounted to an easement. The judge stated that in order to find the existence of this right:

> (1) there must be a dominant and a servient tenement; (2) an easement must 'accommodate' the dominant tenement, that is, be connected with its enjoyment and for its benefit; (3) the dominant and servient owners must be different persons; and (4) the right claimed must be capable of forming the subject-matter of a grant.[207]

Easements thus have four characteristics. First, there must be a dominant and servient tenement.[208] An easement is a right over one piece of land, the servient tenement, enjoyed by another piece of land, the dominant tenement. An easement must be attached to, and benefit, a dominant tenement. Without a dominant tenement, the right would be only a licence.

The second characteristic is that the easement must accommodate the dominant tenement. An easement "must have some natural connection with the estate as being for its benefit."[209] This right must also be connected with the usual and normal enjoyment of the dominant tenement so that it benefits the dominant land and is not merely a personal benefit to the current owner.[210]

---

206. *See* J. Gaunt & P. Morgan, Gale on Easements (18th ed. 2008); Cheshire and Burn's Modern Law of Real Property (E.H. Burn & J. Cartwright, eds., 17th ed. 2006).
207. [1956] 1 Ch 131 at 140.
See generally Goo & Lee, *supra* note 24, Chapter 14 at section 2 ("Acquisition of Easements").
208. MacKenzie & Phillips, *supra* note 27, at 502–503 states:

> It is not sufficient for the right to confer a merely personal advantage on the current owner. Such a personal right is said to be an interest "in gross" and it is not possible to have an easement in gross. All easements must be "appurtenant", that is, they must benefit identifiable land.

Chan Sik Cheung v Director of Lands [1995] 3 HKC 199, 208 states that easements in gross are "unknown and do not exist in Hong Kong".
209. *Bailey v Stephens* (1862) 12 CB (NS) 99, 115.
210. Nield, *supra* note 27, at 320.
The court in *Hill v Tupper* (1863) 2 H & C 121 stated: "It is not competent to create rights unconnected with the use and enjoyment of land and annex them to it so as to constitute a property in the grantee." In this case, the owner of the land on a bank of a canal leased the land to Hill with the exclusive right to place pleasure boats on the canal. Subsequently, Tupper placed competing pleasure boats on the same stretch of water. The issue concerned whether Hill had an easement or a personal licence. The court held that the right was only a licence as the right Hill acquired was to exploit an independent

The third characteristic is that the right must lie in grant.[211] A right over land cannot amount to an easement unless it is capable of forming the subject matter of a grant.[212] A right will not be considered an easement if the right requires the servient land's owner to incur any expenditure or take any positive action. The servient owner's role in an easement is passive: allowing the dominant owner to use the easement and not interfere with the easement or its use. A servient owner cannot generally be required to repair the subject matter of the grant. A right will not be classified as an easement if it excludes the servient owner's occupation of the servient land or if it constitutes joint occupation of the servient land.

The fourth characteristic is that the dominant and servient owners must be different persons because identical ownership of the dominant tenement and the servient tenement would eliminate the need for any easement. Two tenements may, however be owned by the same person in different capacities. For instance, a person may own the dominant tenement beneficially and own the servient tenement as a trustee.

B. *Profit à Prendre*

The court in *Duke of Sutherland v Heathcote* [1892] 1 Ch 475 defined *profit à prendre* (also known as a "profit") as "a right to take something off another person's land."[213] A profit differs from an easement in that a profit is the right to take some part of the servient tenement, *e.g.*, its natural products, including any wild animals, soil or minerals. By comparison, an easement merely confers a right to use the servient tenement in some way.

The right to remove product from another individual's land generally requires this product to be an article of value taken off the soil, *e.g.*, sand, gravel or topsoil, or the produce of the land, *e.g.*, firewood, fodder for stock, or fish. A profit may also be a right to "hawk, hunt, fish and fowl," that is the right to take creatures living on the soil. The creature(s) taken must be capable of ownership. The right to take water from a river, spring, and the

---

business enterprise and was not to accommodate the riparian land. The court noted that the grant operated as a licence or a covenant on the part of the grantors and is binding upon them and the grantee Hill, but gives the grantee no cause of action for any infringement of the supposed exclusive right.

211. Black's Law Dictionary, *supra* note 20, at 1006, defines "lie in grant" as "to be passable by deed or charter without the ceremony of livery of seisin".

212. *Id.* at 1561 defines "subject matter" as "the thing in which a right or duty has been asserted; the thing in which a right or duty has been asserted; the thing in dispute".

213. [1892] 1 Ch at 484.

like is an easement rather than a profit because water is not considered to be part of the soil nor is it owned by anyone.

A profit can be enjoyed by one person to the exclusion of all others, in which case it would be considered a "several profit". Alternatively, a profit can be enjoyed by one person in common with others, that is, it would be considered a "profit in common".

A "profit appurtenant" is a type of *profit à prendre* where the benefit is attached to a dominant tenement by act of the parties.[214] Four conditions, the same as those for the existence of an easement, are required for a profit appurtenant:[215]

- there must be a dominant and a servient tenement;
- the benefit must add to the amenities of the dominant tenement and not just confer a personal benefit;
- the right or the benefit must be capable of being granted by deed; and,
- there must be separate ownership of the dominant and the servient tenements.

A "profit in gross" gives the benefit to the grantee personally regardless of occupation or ownership of land. A profit in gross thus requires no dominant tenement. For example, a right to take fish from a canal without stint[216] can be a profit in gross.[217]

A "profit pur cause de vicinage" only exists in the form of a common of pasture. It is a right enjoyed by commoners of adjoining commons, for example where the cattle on one common are allowed to stray on the other common.[218]

A "profit appendant" is one which is attached to land by operation of law.[219]

214. The *BLIS Glossary*, *supra* note 7, translates the term "appurtenant" as 從屬 and 附屬於.

215. *See*, *e.g.*, *id.*; 16 HALSBURY'S, *supra* note 29, at paras. 230.616–230.635.

216. *I.e.*, without any limitations.

217. MEGARRY'S MANUAL, *supra* note 35, at 422–423; MEGARRY & WADE, *supra* note 35, at para. 27–058.

218. As this is rare in Hong Kong, no further comments are made. For additional information, *see*, *e.g.*, MEGARRY & WADE, *supra* note 35, at para. 27–057; MEGARRY'S MANUAL, *supra* note 35, at 422.

219. *See Bettison v Langton* [2001] UKHL 24.

C. Creation of Servitudes

Servitudes may be created by several methods. These methods are discussed below in brief detail.

i. *By Statute*

Through legislation, the Hong Kong government may acquire certain rights over private property for public works. The right to carry electric power, gas and telephone lines over or under land will often be negotiated if this right affects private property. This right of way is sometimes referred to as a "wayleave" or as a "statutory easement".[220]

ii. *By Express Grant*

In law, the grant of a *profit à prendre* or an easement must be for an interest equivalent to an estate for a term of years absolute, and it must be granted by deed and registered. An unregistered grant will be null and void against any purchaser for value without notice.[221] A legal easement in Hong Kong must be created for a term of years.

> The term of the easement must not exceed the period of the lease of either the dominant or servient land. ... An easement for another period than a term of years, for instance for life, cannot exist at law but only in equity.[222]

iii. *By Express Reservation*

On occasion, a legal easement may be created when a vendor sells part of the land and reserves a profit or an easement over a portion of the land sold. This profit or easement is termed a "reservation" because the owner has not granted any rights to the grantee but rather has reserved a right for the

---

220. *Cross-Harbour Tunnel Co Ltd v Commissioner of Rating and Valuation* [1977–1979] 1 HKC 81 uses the term "wayleave" while the *Electricity Networks (Statutory Easements) Ordinance* (Cap 357) refers to "statutory easements".

221. Notice that in equity an agreement for the grant of a profit may be enforced in the absence of a deed. "Equity looks on that as done which ought to be done"; hence, an oral agreement for valuable consideration to grant an easement will be considered in equity as a grant of an easement.

222. Nield, *supra* note 27, at 327.

benefit of the retained dominant land from the remainder of the land to be sold, which is destined to become the servient land.

iv. *By Implied Grant*

The law, generally, is reluctant to imply a grant of a servitude in favour of a grantor when the grantor parts with a portion of the land. To imply such a grant is contrary to the general principle that a grantor cannot derogate from its grant. Therefore, a grantor is required to make the reservation expressly in order to create a servitude. The law will only imply a grant of a servitude if such a grant was obviously intended or is of necessity. An implied grant of servitudes is:

> based upon the presumed common intention of the parties. In order to give effect to the transaction contemplated by the parties, it may be necessary to imply an easement where the parties have failed to mention the right expressly.[223]

For example,

> where an owner has been accustomed to using one part of his land in a particular way, which is of benefit to the rest of his land, his use is commonly termed a quasi-easement. All the elements of an easement are present except the diversity of occupation of the dominant and servient tenements. On the sale of part of the land, there is diversity of occupation and the right may develop into an easement displaying all the characteristics we have examined.[224]

Following are some instances where a grant of a servitude may be implied upon the sale of the quasi-dominant tenement:

a. Under the Rule in the Case of *Wheeldon v Burrows*[225]

The court in this case identified the rule as being one of intention, based upon the principle that a person cannot derogate from the grant made to the other party:

---

223. *Id.* at 331.

224. *Id.*

225. (1879) 12 Ch D 31.

As noted by NIELD, *supra* note 27, at 333–334, the similarity between the *Conveyancing and Property Ordinance*, *supra* note 43, at section 16 and the rule in *Wheeldon v Burrows* is striking, but there are a number of distinctions:

> on the grant by the owner of a tenement of part of that tenement ... there will pass to the grantee all those continuous and apparent easements (by which... I mean quasi-easements), or, in other words, all those easements which are *necessary to the reasonable enjoyment of the property granted*, and which have been and are at the time of the grant used by the owner ... for the benefit of the part granted.[226]

Three requirements must be satisfied before a quasi-easement can develop by implication into an easement:

- the quasi-easement must be continuous and apparent;
- the quasi-easement must be reasonably necessary for the enjoyment of the property sold; and,
- the quasi-easement must be in use at the time of the sale.

b. Arising by Necessity

"An easement of necessity is a right that is so essential to the enjoyment of the land that the land would be useless without it."[227] For instance in *Wong v Beaumont Property Trust Ltd* [1965] 1 QB 173 the court determined that "[i]n order to use this place as a restaurant, there must be implied an easement, by the necessity of the case, to carry a duct up the wall."[228] In this case, the:

> basement premises had been let upon the express understanding that the property was to be used as a restaurant. Later, after assignment by

---

-s 16 operates where there is diversity of occupation before the sale. It therefore does not apply to quasi-easements. *Wheeldon v. Burrows*, by contrast, operates in just this situation.

-s 16 operates only where there is a formal assignment or lease of the property but *Wheeldon v. Burrows* will apply where there is an agreement to assign or lease. [citation omitted]

-s 16 will pass rights that are not continuous or apparent or reasonably necessary for the enjoyment of the property. [citation omitted] In both cases, however, the right must be enjoyed at the time of the lease or assignment.

-s 16 and the rule in *Wheeldon v. Burrows* both give way to a contrary intention expressed by the parties. However, whereas *Wheeldon v. Burrows* is based upon the presumed intention of the parties so that a right cannot arise unless it is within the implied contractual rights of the grantee, s 16 may operate to create an easement to which the grantee had no right under the contract by which he acquired his interest in the land.

226. (1879) 12 Ch D at 49 (emphasis added).

227. NIELD, *supra* note 27, at 334.

228. [1965] 1 QB at 181.

> the original tenant, the assignee was required to improve ventilation if the restaurant business were to continue.[229]

In *Nickerson v Barraclough* [1981] 2 WLR 773, the court held that a way of necessity could exist only with a grant of land and depended on the intention of the parties; an implication from the circumstances that unless some way was implied, the land in question would be inaccessible.

An easement of necessity can only be implied if the needs of the dominant tenement are the same as they were at the date of the grant.

c. Servitudes of Common Intention

The *Wong* case discussed above might have been decided by implying that "the parties *intended* all rights which permitted the use of the premises as a restaurant."[230] The law will imply either the grant or the reservation of easements as necessary to give effect to the intention of the parties to a grant of real property, with reference to the purposes for which the granted land is to be used.[231]

> That intention may arise because the right is necessary for the use of the land ... or because surrounding circumstances are such that the parties must have contemplated such a right.[232]

In the case of *Stafford v Lee* (1993) 65 P & CR 172, 175 the court stated the law would imply the grant or reservation of such easements as are necessary to give effect to the parties' intention in a grant of real property, with reference to the manner or purposes for which the land is to be used. It is essential for this purpose that the parties should intend that the land should be used in some definite and particular manner. In this case, the claimant was the owner of woodland fronting on to a drive which ran to a public road. The claimant sought to erect a house on the land but was opposed by the respondent, the owner of the drive, who claimed that the claimant's right of way over the drive was for the purposes of using this land as woodland. No express right of way had been reserved on conveyance of the land in 1955. The claimant successfully obtained a declaration that it was entitled to use the drive for the purposes of building and using a house on its land. The Court of Appeal dismissed the respondent's appeal.

229. MacKenzie & Phillips, *supra* note 27, at 519.
230. *Id.* (emphasis in original).
231. *Pwllbach Colliery Co Ltd v Woodman* [1915] AC 634, 646–647.
232. Nield, *supra* note 27, at 334.

This category of implied easements may include a claim of a profit or an easement, even though not necessary to the enjoyment of the property, provided it can be shown that both parties intended to make such a grant.[233] An example is found in the case of *Cory v Davies* [1923] 2 Ch 95, where a row of terraced houses had been built with a drive in front and an exit to the road at each end:

> One of the owners barred the exit at his end of the terrace, requiring all traffic to go the other way. There was no express grant of an easement in favour of all the house owners over all parts of the drive, but the court found that the original parties had a common intention that the drive should be used in this way, and thus an intended easement was implied.[234]

d. Implied Reservation

Courts are reluctant to uphold the implication of a reservation in favour of the grantor where the quasi-servient tenement is sold, because a grantor should not be allowed to derogate from its grant unless the intention to derogate is clearly known to the grantee.[235]

> An easement may be implied, reserved in favour of the grantor on the basis of necessity, or due to the common intention of the parties; but the courts will adopt a stricter test than in the case of the implication of a grant in favour of the quasi-dominant tenement.[236]

e. Presumed Grant (Prescription)

The word "prescription" derives from the Roman legal concept of *praescriptio* and refers to the method by which those who retain land or some types of movable property for an uninterrupted period, usually of ten or twenty years, acquired ownership of that property. The basis of prescription in common law is the presumption that where a person is in undisturbed enjoyment of a right, that person is deemed to be in possession as of right. The following Latin maxim applies: *omnia praesumuntur rite er solemniter esse acta*—all acts are presumed to have been done rightly and regularly. Where a right is enjoyed for a sufficiently long time, the courts will presume

233. MacKenzie & Phillips, *supra* note 27, at 519–520.
234. *Id.* at 519.
235. Nield, *supra* note 27, at 335.
236. *Id.*

that the right is by virtue of an original grant of a *profit à prendre* or of an easement by prescription. In other words, a prescriptive easement is an acquisition of an easement by adverse possession. The user must have been as of right: that the right was acquired without force, without secrecy, and without permission. The use as of right means that "the use has been exercised as if a right had been properly granted to" the user.[237]

There are three ways in which a *profit à prendre* or an easement may be acquired by prescription:

(i) Prescription at Common Law—User Since Time Immemorial

The common law presumes a *profit à prendre* or an easement if it is proven that the right has been used since time immemorial.[238] Hence, a claimant had to show that the right had been enjoyed after 1189. The presumption may be rebutted by proof that this right did not or could not have existed at some time after 1189. Prescription has little, if any, application in Hong Kong.

> It is an established feature of prescription at common law that the right must be acquired by a fee simple owner of the dominant land against the fee simple owner of the servient land. The leasehold nature of land in Hong Kong thus excludes prescription at common law.[239]

(ii) Doctrine of Lost Modern Grant

The difficulties of evincing use since time immemorial resulted in the courts creating the legal fiction of a lost grant. This fiction provides the assumption that the grant has been lost, so that it cannot be produced. The legal fiction further provides that courts may presume a formal grant to the user had been made if the user can establish use for at least twenty years. This legal fiction "is so well established that it cannot be rebutted by evidence that no such grant was made."[240]

Courts will accept proof of a continuous use for at least 20 years as evidence that the right has been used or enjoyed since 1189. Thus, it is necessary to prove the continuous use as of right for a minimum period of 20 years.[241] Once this is done, the courts will presume that there was a grant.

---

237. *Id.* at 337.
238. *The Statute of Westminster I* 1275 later fixed the time as 1189.
239. Nield, *supra* note 27, at 337.
240. *Id.*
See Bridle v Ruby [1988] 3 WLR 191; *Tang Tim-fat v Chan Fok-kei* [1993] 2 HKLR 373; MacKenzie & Phillips, *supra* note 27, at 535.
241. *See Neaverson v Peterborough RDC* [1902] 1 Ch 557 where a claim was defeated by proof that during the period of time when it was possible to have made the grant there was no person who could lawfully have made the grant.

(iii) Prescription Act 1832

This statute was notorious for its poor drafting in that it did not simplify the requirements for demonstrating use by prescription under the common law or under the fiction of the lost modern grant. Instead, the statute further complicates the situation. Nonetheless, Parliament made no attempts to rectify this Act. The *Application of English Law Ordinance* (Cap 88) applied the *Prescription Act* 1832 to Hong Kong law. Note that this Ordinance has not been adopted as a part of the Laws of the Hong Kong SAR. As the *Prescription Act* no longer applies to the Hong Kong Special Administrative Region and as a detailed review and analysis of the Act is outside the scope of this work, no further mention of this Act will be made.

D. Extinguishment of Servitudes

Rights under both *profits à prendre* and easements may be terminated in several ways as discussed below.

i. *Legislation*

As statutes might create *profits à prendre* or easements, a *profit à prendre* or an easement may also be terminated by legislative action.

ii. *Express Release*

An express release, either by deed or court order, may extinguish a servitude. To be effective, the express release must be by deed, although equity may recognize a release effected by less formal means.[242] With the release, the easement or profit reverts to the servient owner, at which time the servitude merges with the servient owner's estate and ceases to be a servitude.

iii. *Implied Release*

An implied release may occur when the dominant owner has demonstrated the intention to abandon the easement or profit. The failure to use an easement or profit does not by itself prove abandonment. "Non-use will

242. Nield, *supra* note 27, at 341. An informal release will be effective provided it would be inequitable for the dominant tenant to claim that the right still exists.

only constitute abandonment if it is explicable only on the assumption that the dominant owner intended to give up the right."[243] There needs to be evidence of an intention to abandon the right because one need not exercise one's rights. For example, in the case of *Cook v Mayor & Corp of Bath* (1868) LR 6 Eq 177, a door had been bricked over for more than thirty years; this was held not be constitute an abandonment of a right of way. A prolonged non-use may demonstrate that the dominant owner has impliedly abandoned the right. The claimant in *Moore v Rawson* (1824) 3 B & C 332, who had demolished a wall containing windows and built a window-less wall in its place, was held to have shown an intention to abandon a right to light.

> If … the dominant tenement has been altered in such a way that the right claimed becomes unnecessary or impossible to exercise, then the alteration may be regarded as evidence of an intention to abandon the right. This presumption may be rebutted by evidence that the original character of the land may be restored in the future and that the need for the easement or profit would revive.[244]

The case of *Re Yateley Common* [1977] 1 All ER 505 suggested that to establish abandonment of a right of common, it must be established that the owner of the right has ceased to use it and never intends to use it again. If the dominant owner is able to justify the non-use, the owner is likely to be regarded as not having surrendered that right.

iv. *Unity of Possession and Ownership*

When the same person becomes owner and possessor of both the dominant and the servient tenements, the requirement of diversity of ownership is destroyed. Thus, a profit appurtenant to land or an easement will be extinguished when the tenements come into common ownership. The exception is where that individual owns the dominant and servient tenements in different capacities.

v. *Effluction of Time*

Easements in Hong Kong must be granted for a term of years, which generally will be for the shorter of the terms created by the Government leases of the dominant and servient lands. At the end of the term for which the easement is granted, the easement will simply expire by the effluction of time. Where

243. *Id.*
244. MacKenzie & Phillips, *supra* note 27, at 547.

there is a statutory renewal or extension of the Government lease term of the servient land, the grant may be deemed to continue.[245]

vi. *Alteration in the Dominant Tenement*

Where the dominant tenement is altered so that use or enjoyment of a profit appurtenant is no longer possible, the servitude is extinguished. For example, in *National Guaranteed Manure Co v Donald* (1859) 4 H & N 8, a canal, the dominant tenement, was converted to a railway. The conversion extinguished an easement of water for the canal.

E. Restrictive Covenants[246]

The development of covenants may be attributed to the need for land use control.

> The major function of the rules about restrictive covenants, is the control of land use. When the rules were initially developed in the nineteenth century, there was no public planning law ... A person selling land for building might extract a promise that only homes would be built (no shops or factories), and initially this was only enforceable in contract law, that is only against the person who made the promise (the covenantor) and not against his successors on the land.[247]

Restrictive covenants were first recognized in the case of *Tulk v Moxhay* (1848) 41 ER 1143, which is discussed below.

There are similarities between easements and restrictive covenants, including the requirements for dominant and servient tenements, proximity, and accommodation or benefit. Recall that easements may be positive or negative. A negative easement is one which "is enjoyed without any action by the dominant owner".[248] In other words, a negative easement restricts the servient tenement's owner use of its property.

245. Nield, *supra* note 27, at 340 (citing *Crown Leases Ordinance* (Cap 40) section 15; *New Territories Leases (Extension) Ordinance* (Cap 150) section 7).
246. This is a complicated area and is regulated in part by statute. A comprehensive discussion of covenants is outside the scope of this introductory work. The reader is referred to Goo & Lee, *supra* note 24, at Chapter 13 ("Land Covenants"); Nield, *supra* note 27, at Chapters 14 ("Leasehold Covenants"), 15 ("Land Covenants"). *See also* Clement Shum, General Principles of Hong Kong Law 254 (3rd ed. 1998) [hereinafter Shum]; 16 Halsbury's, *supra* note 29, at paras. 230.407, 230.463–230.482.
247. Lim & Green, *supra* note 198, at 192.
248. MacKenzie & Phillips, *supra* note 27, at 512.
See also Sihombing, Student's Guide, *supra* note 106, at 330–332.

A "covenant" is a formal deed between at least two parties and which creates obligations. One party, the "covenantor", agrees with the other party, the "covenantee", to perform or refrain from performing some act. The covenantor is bound by the obligation and the covenantee may enforce the benefit of the obligation.[249] A positive covenant requires the performance of some act, whereas a negative covenant forbids the commission of some act.

> In *Phipps v Pears* [1965] 1 QB 76 … courts would not readily accept the creation of new *negative* easements, because they have a tendency to restrict the servient tenement owner and hamper development of his property.[250]

If the agreement is a personal covenant with a landlord and lessee or with another landlord, the covenant only affects the concerned parties. Their successors cannot enforce the covenants, as there is no privity of contract.[251] The exception to this general rule is an equitable easement, where an agreement is not to perform some act but to restrict the use of the land for the benefit of another. These equitable easements are known also as "restrictive covenants". Thus, some covenants may run with the land, *i.e.*, they can be enforced by and against assignees of a lease and the purchasers of a leasehold estate when there is privity of contract between the parties.

The essential characteristic of restrictive covenants is that they must be negative in nature. Equity will allow covenants that "touch and concern" the land to run with the land. This is because of the unfairness to allow a person, who might have paid a lower price for the land due to restriction placed on its use, to disregard these restrictions with impunity. For example, in the case of *Tulk v Moxhay* (1848) 41 ER 1143, Tulk sold part of Leicester Square to Elms who covenanted on behalf of himself, his heirs and assigns not to build on the land. Elms sold to Moxhay who, knowing of the covenant, proceeded to build on the land. The court held that it would be inequitable that Elms, who paid a lower price for the land on account of restrictions, be able to sell it for a much higher price free from restrictions. The court found that Moxhay was bound by the restrictive covenant.

A restrictive covenant may be enforced by an injunction brought by the original covenantee or its assignee against the original covenantor or its assignee who has notice of the covenant.

249. NIELD, *supra* note 27, at 365.
250. MACKENZIE & PHILLIPS, *supra* note 27, at 512 (emphasis in original).
251. Privity of contract means that only parties to a contract can sue and be sued based on that contract.

The following are the major points to note about restrictive covenants:

- The common law requires the covenant to be negative in form; *i.e.*, a covenant to build only a one-storey house will not be enforceable, whereas a covenant to build house of not more than one storey will be enforceable. This common law principle has been modified by the Conveyancing and Property Ordinance, sections 41 and 42, allowing the enforcement of both positive and negative covenants.
- The covenant must touch and concern the land, *i.e.*, the covenant must confer a benefit on the land by protecting its value or amenities, and, not bestow a personal benefit. Section 39 of the Conveyancing and Property Ordinance assumes that all land-related covenants intend that the covenant's benefits should run with the land unless otherwise stated.[252]
- The person seeking to enforce the covenant must be the landowner—a lesser interest in the property is insufficient to support a claim. As the law only acknowledges legal estates, the covenantee and assignee must hold the same legal estate. Section 39 of the Conveyancing and Property Ordinance permits an assignee who takes a legal estate to claim the benefit of a covenant by an assignment at law. A legal lessee or a legal mortgagee can thus claim the benefit upon satisfying the stipulations.[253]
- If the claimant of a covenant's benefit is not the original covenantee, the claimant must demonstrate that the equitable benefit of the covenant has been expressly assigned to the claimant, that this benefit was originally annexed to the land, or, that this benefit relates to land subject to a building scheme or development.
- When a claim is made against the assignee of the original covenantor, it must be proved that the assignee has knowledge, also known as "notice", of the covenant which burdens the land. Notice can be actual or constructive. Constructive notice is when there has been no exercise of proper diligence in searching documents of title and records in the Land Registry. Sub-lessees are deemed to have notice of covenants contained in the head lease and are therefore bound in equity.
- The right or benefit conferred is enforceable only by injunction rather than by damages.

252. Nield, *supra* note 27, at 378.
253. *Id.*

F. Mortgages

The definition of a "mortgage" is: the transfer, or the creation, of an interest in land for securing the repayment of a debt or for the performance of an obligation. The mortgage is a security interest in real property. The manner in which such an interest can arise in Hong Kong is discussed in this section. The "mortgagor" is the borrower/debtor in this transaction, and the "mortgagee" is the lender/creditor. The amount of money borrowed is referred to as the "principal". The mortgage is a personal covenant to repay the principal of the loan and the interest owed thereon by a certain date, together with a formal conveyancing of the land to the mortgagee as collateral, with a proviso for redemption. The mortgagor's possession of the land, however, remains undisturbed. The mortgagor has the right to redemption of the mortgage, and on payment of the debt or discharge of the obligation, the mortgagor can exercise this right to re-convey the land back to itself.

"Tacking", also known as the "right to tack", is a feature of mortgages. Tacking is the right to add a further advance, *i.e.*, a later loan, to the earlier debt which is secured by the mortgage, so that the additional loan shares the priority of the earlier debt and thus takes priority over any intervening mortgages securing other debts or loans.

A mortgage may be given over a freehold estate or over a leasehold estate. There are two types of mortgage: legal and equitable.[254] These are discussed immediately below.

i. Legal Mortgage

Prior to the *Conveyancing and Property Ordinance*, a mortgage was made by an assignment or sub-demise of the interest in land to the mortgagee. This assignment would be subject to re-assignment of the property to the mortgagor upon the repayment of the loan. At law, the mortgagor had to repay strictly in accordance with the mortgage terms. Failure to do so would result in the mortgagee retaining the property assigned as security, and the mortgagor's right to redemption is thus terminated. For example, if a mortgagor was one day late in repaying the loan, the prospect of recovering the mortgaged property could be forfeited.

254. *See generally* GOO & LEE, *supra* note 24, Chapter 15 at sections 2 ("Creation of Legal Mortgages or Charges"), 3 ("Creation of Equitable Mortgages"); SIHOMBING, STUDENT GUIDE, *supra* note 106, at 1263–1308; NIELD, *supra* note 27, at Chapter 17 ("Mortgages").

Equity remedied this situation by recognising that a mortgagee was intended only to hold the premises as security for the loan, and conferring an equitable right of redemption to the mortgagor. Under this equitable right, the mortgagee is compelled to return the realty to the mortgagor upon repayment of the loan, even if payment was made after the date for payment. Equity thus allows the mortgagor a reasonable extension of time to repay and fulfil the obligations. Equity would not assist the mortgagor where the loan repayment was delayed too long or if the limitation period for bringing a redemption action had expired.

In the past, the mortgagor's right in equity to claim redemption represented the mortgagor's equitable interest in the property. This interest is known as the mortgagor's "equity of redemption". Under the common law, the mortgagee held the legal estate in the land; the mortgagee was thus the legal owner holding the legal title. Equity, however, recognized the mortgagor as the actual or effective owner of the land which was subject to a mortgage. The mortgagor's equity of redemption could be transferred to the mortgagee. Prior to the implementation of the *Conveyancing and Property Ordinance*, all subsequent mortgages took effect by an assignment of the mortgagor's equity of redemption; in other words, by equitable mortgages.

Presently, all legal mortgages are created by a charge, which is in the form of a deed expressed to be a legal charge. A "charge" is a hypothecation that allows the property, *i.e.*, the subject of the charge, to be taken when the chargor, *i.e.*, the debtor, defaults on the repayment of a debt.[255] Pursuant to section 44 (1) of the *Conveyancing and Property Ordinance*:

> a mortgage of a legal estate, including any second or subsequent mortgage of that legal estate, may be effected at law only by a charge by deed expressed to be a legal charge.

The same remedies are available to a chargee for a charge created under this section as to a mortgagee holding a mortgage obtained by assignment. According to section 44(2) of the *Conveyancing and Property Ordinance*, a charge is in substance a mortgage:

> Under a mortgage effected by a legal charge, the mortgagor and the mortgagee shall have the same protection, powers and remedies

255. BLACK'S LAW DICTIONARY, *supra* note 20, at 811, defines "hypothecation" as "[t]he pledging of something as security without delivery of title or possession". The *BLIS Glossary*, *supra* note 7, translates this term as 押貨預支.
For further discussion of a "charge", *see generally* GOO & LEE, *supra* note 24, Chapter 15 at section 4 ("Fixed and Floating Charges").

> (including but not limited to those relating to foreclosure[256] and the equity of redemption but excluding the power of the mortgagee to enter into possession before any default by the mortgagor) as if the mortgage had been effected by way of assignment of the legal estate before the commencement of this section.

If a document is in substance a mortgage, it will be treated as a mortgage by the courts regardless of its title or its form. In *Ng Shou Chun v Hung Chun San* [1994] 1 HKC 155,158–159 the parties entered into a main contract for the purported sale of the property with a collateral contract for its repurchase and the court stated that:

> equity looks at the substance of the transaction, not the form. ... a sale, with a collateral agreement for repurchase by the vendor within a stipulated time, has been held by the courts to be ... a transaction by way of mortgage. The undervalue, and the highly unusual provisions of the agreement here, suggest that this was just such a transaction. ... but the circumstances seem to me ... to be consistent more with a transaction by way of charge to secure the repayment of [the loan] than with a genuine transaction of sale and purchase.

There is an essential difference between a mortgage and a charge. With a charge, there is no conveyance of property subject to a debtor's right of redemption. Rather, the legal estate remains with the mortgagor, who is capable now of creating subsequent legal mortgages. The charge grants the chargee, *i.e.*, the lender, certain rights over the property as security for the repayment of a loan or the performance of an obligation. A mortgage, on the other hand, involves the conveyance of property to secure repayment of a debt or the performance of an obligation.

The change created by the *Conveyancing and Property Ordinance* is that a mortgagee is no longer the sole legal owner of the mortgaged property and a mortgagor's rights over the property are no longer limited to the equitable right of redemption. Under the legal charge created by the Ordinance, a mortgagor retains ownership in the property, subject to a mortgagee's rights to use the property as security for repayment of the loan. A mortgagee can now no longer claim to be a holder of a leasehold estate. Today,

---

256. The term "foreclosure" is defined in BLACK'S LAW DICTIONARY, *supra* note 20, at 719, as a "legal proceeding to terminate a mortgagor's interest in property, instituted by the lender (the mortgagee) either to gain title or to force a sale in order to satisfy the unpaid debt secured by the property". The *BLIS Glossary*, *supra* note 7, translates "foreclosure" as 取消回贖; and, "foreclosure action" as 止贖訴訟. The *Stamp Duty Ordinance*, *supra* note 95, at section 2 translates "foreclosure order" as 止贖令.

a mortgagee's interest is an encumbrance upon the land, which gives the mortgagee certain rights over that property which may be exercised should the mortgagor fail to repay the loan.

ii. *Equitable Mortgage*

An equitable mortgage is created by the transfer of the entire equitable interest to the mortgagee, subject to an agreement to return this interest to the mortgagor upon repayment of the loan.[257] The mortgagor's right in equity to redeem the property represents the mortgagor's equitable interest in the property. Under the common law, the mortgagee held the legal estate in the land; the mortgagee was the legal owner, holding the legal title. Equity, however, recognized the mortgagor as the real or effective owner of the land subject to a mortgage. The mortgagor's equity of redemption could be transferred to the mortgagee. Prior to the 1984 implementation of the *Conveyancing and Property Ordinance*, all subsequent mortgages took effect by an assignment of the mortgagor's equity of redemption, *i.e.*, equitable mortgages. An equitable mortgage can also be created by a charge.[258]

---

257. 16 HALSBURY'S, *supra* note 29, at para. 230.640 defines "equitable mortgage":

> An equitable mortgage is a contract which creates a charge on the property but does not convey any legal estate or interest to the creditor; such a charge amounts to an equitable interest. Its operation is that of an executory assurance which, as between the parties, and so far as equitable rights and remedies are concerned, is equivalent to an actual assurance, and is enforceable under the court's equitable jurisdiction.
>
> As a general rule all property, whether real or personal, which may be the subject of a legal mortgage can equally be charged in equity.
>
> An equitable mortgage may be made either (1) by an agreement to create a legal mortgage; (2) by a mortgage of an equitable interest; (3) by a deposit of title deeds; or (4) by an equitable charge.

See also SIHOMBING, STUDENT'S GUIDE, *supra* note 106, at 1261–1265; JUDITH SIHOMBING & MICHAEL WILKINSON, HONG KONG CONVEYANCING, vol. 1(B), Chapter XIII, paras. 1001–1004 (2010) [hereinafter SIHOMBING, HK CONVEYANCING].

The *BLIS Glossary*, *supra* note 7, translates "equitable mortgage" as 衡平法按揭.

258. 16 HALSBURY'S, *supra* note 29, at para. 230.641 defines equitable charge as follows:

> An equitable charge on land is a security which does not create a legal estate, but only confers upon the creditor an equitable interest in the land. It entitles the holder to have the property comprised in it sold by an order of the court to raise the money charged on it, but, in the absence of any express provision to that effect, or unless it is a mortgage by deposit of title deeds, it does not amount to an agreement to give a legal mortgage, although, it may, if registered, take priority over subsequent transactions. Even if the security provides for a legal mortgage to be granted, it is still an equitable charge …

See also SIHOMBING, STUDENT'S GUIDE, *supra* note 106, at 1261–1265; SIHOMBING, HK CONVEYANCING, *supra* note 257, vol. 1(B), Chapter XIII, at paras. 754–801.

An equitable mortgage arises where the mortgagee only receives an equitable interest in the land.[259] The equitable mortgagor has the equity of redemption.[260] Examples of equitable mortgages include a beneficiary under a trust of land or a purchaser under an agreement to buy land.[261] There are several reasons for a mortgagee acquiring only an equitable interest in land. First, the mortgagor's interest in the land may only be an equitable interest. Second, the mortgage may have been executed in an informal manner and thus does not meet the formal requirements of a legal mortgage.[262] Because equity regards "as done that which ought to be done", equity will still consider the mortgage agreement to be enforceable.

---

259. SHUM, *supra* note 246, at 258.
260. BLACK'S LAW DICTIONARY, *supra* note 20, at 620, defines "equity of redemption" as being:

> The right of a mortgagor in default to recover property before a foreclosure sale by paying the principal, interest, and other costs that are due. • A defaulting mortgagor with an equity of redemption has the right, until the foreclosure sale, to reimburse the mortgagee and cure the default.

16 HALSBURY'S, *supra* note 29, at para. 230.642 defines this right as follows:

> Incident to every mortgage is the right of the mortgagor to redeem, a right which is called his equity of redemption, and which continues notwithstanding that he fails to pay the debt in accordance with the proviso for redemption a legal obligation for which time of the essence. This right arises from the transaction being considered as a mere loan of money secured by a pledge of the estate. Any provision inserted in the mortgage to prevent redemption on payment of the debt or performance of the obligation for which the security was given or which allows the mortgagee to return the property encumbered is termed a clog or fetter on the equity of redemption, and generally is considered to be void against a consumer whereas as against a commercial party it will be void only if unreasonable. It is thought that the right to redeem is so inseparable an incident of a mortgage that it cannot be taken away by an express agreement of the parties, to the effect that the mortgage is not to be redeemable or that the right is to be confined to a particular time or to a particular description of persons. The right continues unless and until, by judgement for foreclosure or, in the case of a mortgage of land where the mortgagee is in possession, by the running of time, the mortgagor's title is extinguished or his interest is destroyed by sale either under the process of the court or under a power in the mortgage incident to the security.

See also SIHOMBING, STUDENT'S GUIDE, *supra* note 106, at 1259–1261; SIHOMBING, HK CONVEYANCING, *supra* note 257, vol. 1(B), Chapter XIII, at paras. 1–2, 5–50.
The *BLIS Glossary*, *supra* note 7, translates "equity of redemption" as 衡平法贖回權.

261. NIELD, *supra* note 27, at 445.
262. *E.g.*, there is no mortgage deed, but the debtor/mortgagor deposits the title deed as security. The deposit is treated as evidence of an agreement to create a mortgage and as partial performance of that agreement.

Equitable mortgages may be created by:

- a written agreement which is not accompanied by the deposit of the title deeds;
- the deposit of only title deeds without the agreement, if such deposit amounts to part performance of the agreement to give security;
- the written agreement and the deposit of documents of title; or,
- a conveyance to a second mortgagee of the mortgagor's interest in the land. As the holder of the first mortgage has the legal interest, any subsequent mortgagees can only acquire an equitable interest.

The two common ways in which an equitable mortgage may arise are, first, by the mortgaging of an equitable interest owned by the mortgagor, and second, by an informal or a defective mortgage of a legal estate.

Equitable mortgages can be registered in the Land Registry. Under section 3 of the *Land Registration Ordinance* (Cap 128), a registered equitable interest in land is effective over prior unregistered interests in this land and interests which are subsequently registered.

The most common type of equitable mortgage found in Hong Kong occurs where a mortgage is given on land held under a Government lease granted with a set of Conditions of Sale, which are conditions or requirements not yet fully satisfied. Until the conditions have been satisfied, the grantee does not enjoy any legal estate under the Government lease - the grantee only enjoys an equitable interest in an agreement to grant a lease. Section 46 of the *Conveyancing and Property Ordinance* provides that an equitable mortgage under these circumstances will be converted to a legal charge upon compliance with the conditions and the mortgagor's legal estate is deemed granted.[263]

Following implementation of the *Conveyancing and Property Ordinance*, the mortgagee of an equitable mortgage by deed is granted the same powers as a legal mortgagee.[264] An equitable mortgagee cannot deal with the legal estate unless authorized by a power of attorney under seal contained in the mortgage. Where an equitable mortgage is not made by deed, the mortgagee has no power:

- to take possession without a court order;
- to sell; or,
- to appoint a receiver.

263. NIELD, *supra* note 27, at 445. *See also* SIHOMBING, STUDENT'S GUIDE, *supra* note 106, at Chapter 13 ("Security Transactions Over Land").

264. *See, e.g.*, *Conveyancing and Property Ordinance*, *supra* note 43, at section 50(1).

Further, no covenants for title are implied in an equitable mortgage under section 35 of the Ordinance. An equitable mortgagee may apply to an appropriate court for foreclosure upon default.

iii. *Landholding in Hong Kong: Leasehold Mortgage*

As title to land in Hong Kong is by leasehold, focus now turns to the creation of such mortgages. There are three ways to create a leasehold mortgage. The first method is by assignment. Assignment traditionally meant the mortgagor transferred or assigned the interest in the land to the mortgagee, vesting ownership in the mortgagee. Thus, by an assignment, the leaseholder transfers the entire remainder of the lease term to the mortgagee with the provision for re-conveying upon repayment of the loan by the mortgagor. In an assignment, the mortgagee is effectively substituted for the mortgagor in the landlord-tenant relationship and becomes personally liable to the landlord for the covenants contained in the lease.

The second method of creating a mortgage over a leasehold interest is by sub-demise. The term "sub-demise" refers to the situation where a mortgagor grants a sub-lease to a mortgagee for a term of years which must be at least one day less than the mortgagor's lease. However, in practice, the term is approximately ten days less than the term remaining in the main lease in order to allow time to the mortgagor to grant a subsequent mortgage if desired. Additionally, the sub-lease will cease in accordance with its terms or upon the repayment of principal and interest by the mortgagor. Finally, the mortgagee is not personally liable to the landlord for the covenants of the lease because there is no privity of contract and no privity of estate between the lessor and the mortgagee.

The third manner in which a leasehold mortgage may be created is by a charge. The expression "charge" refers to the security for payment of a debt where the creditor has a right to receive payment out of some specific fund or out of the proceeds of the sale of realty. A charge is preferred over the above two methods as a charge does not require the landlord's consent.

iv. *Mortgagee's Rights and Remedies*

In a mortgage relationship, the parties have certain rights and certain remedies in the event of default. A "right" is a privilege to which a person has a lawful claim. This privilege or interest is recognized and protected by law. A "remedy" is the means provided by law to recover rights, or, to obtain compensation.

A mortgagee's general rights and remedies include several alternatives in the event of a mortgagor's default.

a. Damages

One alternative is to sue for the debt owed under the loan. Suing on the debt is a common law right based on contract as the mortgagor promised to repay the loan. If the mortgagor fails to repay the loan, the mortgagee may sue for the breach of a personal covenant. This remedy is appropriate where the value of land has dramatically increased.

b. Entry into Possession

Another alternative is for the mortgagee, or a receiver, as explained below, to take possession of the defaulting debtor's premises:

> At common law, if the legal mortgage is by assignment, the ownership of the legal estate is vested in the lender, who is thus entitled to take possession as soon as the mortgage is executed, even if the mortgagor is not in default. In practice, the mortgage usually states that the mortgagor has quiet possession until default. In fact, this remedy of taking possession is seldom resorted to because the mortgagee is strictly accountable to the mortgagor for any loss occasioned by his own default. He is accountable not only for such rents and other incomes from the property which he receives, but also for those rents and incomes which he ought to have received had he exercised due diligence and proper management. Under the statutory legal mortgage, the mortgagee does not have possession before default.[265]

Usually, however, the mortgagee would first secure a court order in accordance with Order 88, Rules of the High Court. Courts have restricted the mortgagee's exercise of this right to instances of breach by the mortgagor and in order to protect the security. Section 44(2) of the *Conveyancing and Property Ordinance* has preserved this right.[266] An equitable mortgagee has no right to possession.

---

265. SHUM, *supra* note 246, at 260.

266. Section 44(2) of the *Conveyancing and Property Ordinance*, *supra* note 43, provides:

> Under a mortgage effected by a legal charge, the mortgagor and the mortgagee shall, subject to this Ordinance, have the same protection, powers and remedies (including but not limited to those relating to foreclosure and the equity of redemption but excluding the power of the mortgagee to enter into possession before any default by the mortgagor) as if the mortgage had been effected by way of assignment of the legal estate before commencement of this section.

Where a tenant is in lawful occupation of the property, the mortgagee takes possession by notifying the tenant to pay rent directly to the mortgagee. The priority of a mortgagee's and a tenant's interests determine whether the mortgagee is able to secure a possession order against the tenant.

A mortgagee in possession of the property becomes liable to the mortgagor under lease covenants and is liable to the mortgagor for defaults. The mortgagee is accountable to the mortgagor for the income which would have been received from the property but for the neglect of the mortgagee. The mortgagee must take care to maximize the return from the property.[267]

The mortgagee may escape liability by appointing a receiver to take possession of the defaulting mortgagor's premises. Under section 50(2) of the *Conveyancing and Property Ordinance*, the receiver is "deemed to be the agent of the mortgagor and the mortgagor is solely responsible for the receiver's acts and defaults." Where the mortgagor is a company, section 87 of the *Companies Ordinance* requires a notice of possession be filed in the Companies Registry.

c. Foreclosure

A third option is foreclosure, which is an equitable right allowing a mortgagee to obtain a court order ending the mortgagor's right to redeem the property and vesting the legal estate in the mortgagee.[268] This right is preserved by in the *Conveyancing and Property Ordinance*.[269] This right arises as soon as the contractual date for redemption has passed, but usually is not exercised unless the mortgagor fails to repay for an unreasonable time. The right to foreclosure is available to all legal and equitable mortgagees. The foreclosing mortgagee's rights are subject to any prior mortgagee's rights.[270] The procedure for

---

267. *Palk v Mortgage Services Funding PLC* [1993] 2 WLR 415. *See also* 16 HALSBURY'S, *supra* note 29, at para. 230.773; SIHOMBING, STUDENT'S GUIDE, *supra* note 106, at 1302–1308; SIHOMBING, HK CONVEYANCING, *supra* note 257, vol. 1(B), Chapter XIII, at paras. 1552–1604.

268. "Foreclosure" as defined in BLACK'S LAW DICTIONARY, *supra* note 20, at 719, is "[t]o terminate a mortgagor's interest in property, instituted by the lender (the mortgagee) either to gain title or to force a sale in order to satisfy the unpaid debt secured by the property".

269. The *Conveyancing and Property Ordinance*, *supra* note 43, at section 53(2) provides:

> (2) Where a mortgagee obtains an order of foreclosure absolute, that order shall (unless it otherwise provides) operate—
>
> (a) to assign to the mortgagee the mortgagor's estate in the mortgaged land, subject to any other mortgage having priority to the mortgage under which the foreclosure order was obtained; and
>
> (b) to discharge that land from the mortgage under which the foreclosure order was obtained and any subsequent mortgage.

270. SHUM, *supra* note 246, at 260–261.

foreclosure is set out under Order 88, Rules of the High Court. This Order provides for issuing an order *nisi* to account for the money owed and for its payment within a fixed period, failing which the order *nisi* becomes final.[271] Unlike other jurisdictions, foreclosures are infrequent in Hong Kong. Generally, a Hong Kong mortgagee prefers to exercise its power of possession and sale; or, a mortgagee will exercise its right to appoint a receiver.[272]

d. Exercise of the Power of Sale

Another option available to a mortgagee is a sale. In theory, a mortgagee:

> has no implied power to sell the mortgagor's property free from the equity of redemption. In practice, the mortgage deed may contain an express power of sale enabling the mortgagee to sell the property out of court and free from the equity of redemption.[273]

Under the *Conveyancing and Property Ordinance*, a mortgagee can sell the defaulting mortgagor's mortgaged property subject to prior interests, but free from the mortgagor's right to redeem and free from subsequent mortgages and all other estates, interests and rights to which the mortgage has priority.[274]

---

271. An order *nisi* is a temporary order which will become final unless opposed by the other party. *See infra* note 447.
272. *See generally* 16 HALSBURY'S, *supra* note 29, at paras. 230.790–230.792; SIHOMBING, STUDENT'S GUIDE, *supra* note 106, at 1295–1308; SIHOMBING, HK CONVEYANCING, *supra* note 257, vol. 1(B), Chapter XIII, at paras. 1451B, 1552–1600; vol. 2(F), Chapter XIII, at paras. 81–115.
273. SHUM, *supra* note 246, at 259.
Section 51 of the *Conveyancing and Property Ordinance*, *supra* note 43 provides, in part, that:
    (1) Unless the contrary intention is expressed, there shall be implied in any legal charge or equitable mortgage by deed, the powers, exercisable by the mortgagee, a receiver (acting personally or through their agents) and any person entitled to give a receipt for the mortgage money on its repayment, mentioned in the Fourth Schedule.
    (2) Any power exercisable under a mortgage shall be subject to any prior estates, interests and rights to which the mortgaged land is subject.
    (3) No power of sale shall empower a mortgagee or a receiver under an equitable mortgage, by virtue of that mortgage only, to assign the legal estate in the mortgaged land.
    (4) The powers implied by subsection (1), and the provisions of the Fourth Schedule relating to the exercise of those powers may be varied or extended by the mortgage deed and, as so varied or extended, shall have effect as if contained in this Ordinance.
    (5) This section shall not apply to any mortgage executed before the commencement of this section.
274. 16 HALSBURY'S, *supra* note 29, at para. 230.777. *See generally id.* at paras. 230.776–230.787. *See also* SIHOMBING, STUDENT'S GUIDE, *supra* note 106, at 1302–1303; SIHOMBING, HK CONVEYANCING, *supra* note 257, vol. 1(B), Chapter XIII, at paras. 1554–1705.

Section 51 of the *Conveyancing and Property Ordinance* and paragraph 8 of the Fourth Schedule give the mortgagee the power to conduct a sale. Powers of the mortgagee are provided in section 11 of the Fourth Schedule.[275] Section 51(4) permits the alteration of these powers:

> The powers implied by subsection (1), and the provisions of the Fourth Schedule relating to the exercise of those powers may be varied or extended by the mortgage deed and, as so varied or extended, shall have effect as if contained in this Ordinance.

A mortgagee may be appointed as the attorney of the mortgagor to sell the realty. However, the general practice is for the mortgagee or its appointed receiver to repossess the premises and sell the same under the statutory power of sale. A mortgagee exercising the power of sale must use due care to secure a proper price for the premises.[276] Should the sale price be less than market price, the mortgagee is responsible for the difference to the mortgagor or a second mortgagee. A guarantor is also owed this obligation.

Section 52 of the *Conveyancing and Property Ordinance* is intended to protect the purchaser at a foreclosure sale:

> Where a sale is made under a mortgage, the title of the purchaser shall not be affected by the fact that no case had arisen to authorize the sale or that due notice was not given or that the power was otherwise improperly or irregularly exercised; but any person who suffers loss through an unauthorized, improper or irregular exercise of the power of sale shall have a remedy in damages against the person exercising the power.

---

275. *Conveyancing and Property Ordinance*, *supra* note 43, Fourth Schedule, at para. 11 provides:

> The powers mentioned in paragraphs 2 to 9 shall not be exercisable unless—
> (a) notice requiring payment of the mortgagee money has been served on the mortgagor; or on one of the several mortgagors, and default has been made in payment of the mortgage money or part thereof for one month after such service; or
> (b) interest under the mortgage is in arrear and unpaid for one month after becoming due; or
> (c) there has been a breach of a provision, express or under this Ordinance, of the mortgage other than a covenant for payment of the mortgage money and interest.

276. In *Tse Kwong Lam v Wong Chit Sen* [1983] 3 All ER 54 the court held that the mortgagee had failed to take reasonable care to obtain market price where notice of the foreclosure auction was advertised only shortly before the auction; the reserve price was determined arbitrarily without any advice from a qualified valuer; and only one bid was received, which came from a related company.
A receiver in similar circumstances has the same duty to act in good faith.

Section 54 of the *Conveyancing and Property Ordinance* regulates the distribution of the sale proceeds. This section provides:

> Any money received by a mortgagee or a receiver from the sale ... shall be applied according to the following priority-
> (a) in discharge of all rent, taxes, rates and other outgoings due and affecting the mortgaged land;
> (b) unless the mortgaged land is sold subject to a prior encumbrance, in discharge of that prior encumbrance;
> (c) in payment of the receiver's lawful remuneration, costs, charges and expenses and all lawful costs and expenses properly incurred in the sale or other dealing;
> (d) in payment of the mortgage money, interest and costs due under the mortgage,
>
> and any residue shall be paid to the person who, immediately before any sale or other dealing, was entitled to the mortgaged land or authorized to give a receipt for the proceeds of the sale of that land.

Under section 55(1) of the *Conveyancing and Property Ordinance*, a mortgagee's receipt is a good discharge:

> A receipt in writing of a mortgagee or a receiver shall be a sufficient discharge for any money arising under a power of sale or for any money or security comprised in the mortgage or arising under it; and a person paying that money or transferring that security shall not be concerned to inquire whether any money remains due under the mortgage.

e. Receivers

A fifth alternative is to appoint a receiver. The term "receiver" denotes an individual appointed either by a court or privately to take possession of the property. A receiver is to hold the realty for the purpose of paying the creditors. Pursuant to section 50 of the *Conveyancing and Property Ordinance*, a mortgagee may appoint a receiver when the mortgage money has become due.[277] "Due" refers to the time after the legal date for repayment or when

277. Section 50 of the *Conveyancing and Property Ordinance*, *supra* note 43, provides:

> (1) There shall be implied in any legal charge or equitable mortgage by deed, where the mortgage money has become due, a power exercisable in writing by the mortgagee and any person entitled to give a receipt for the mortgage money on its repayment to appoint a receiver or receivers of the mortgaged land and the income thereof, to remove any receiver appointed and appoint another in his place.

an instalment is overdue. If payment is on demand, the authority to appoint a receiver arises at the mortgage's creation. This authority is to be in writing. The receiver appointed is the mortgagor's agent. The provisions concerning the appointment may be varied or extended by the express terms of the mortgage.

The authority to appoint a receiver is implied in all mortgages by deed, unless expressly contradicted, according to section 51(1) of the *Conveyancing and Property Ordinance*. In practice, the mortgage deed usually provides for the mortgagee to appoint a receiver who has extensive management powers.[278]

> A mortgagee under a mortgage by deed, whether it is legal or equitable, has a statutory power to appoint a receiver provided the mortgage was entered into after 1 November 1984. A mortgage created prior to that date, or an equitable mortgage created otherwise than by deed, must contain an express power to appoint a receiver if the mortgagee is to avoid having to apply to court for the appointment of a receiver under the court's general equitable jurisdiction.[279]

In short, the appointment of a receiver gives a mortgagee all the advantages of possession without any of the liabilities.

Generally, the first mortgagee has both a common law and statutory right to hold the title deeds of the property until redemption. The mortgagee has the right to transfer the mortgage, *e.g.*, the mortgagee can sell its rights under the mortgage to another party without the consent of the mortgagor. The transfer must be by deed and registered. Another privilege which the mortgagee or its appointed receiver may exercise is lease and surrender, *i.e.*, to grant leases, surrender leases and/or accept the surrender of leases. Insurance may be required by the mortgagee from the mortgagor at its expense in order to insure against loss of the security, i.e., the property.

---

(2) Any receiver so appointed will be deemed the agent of the mortgagor and the mortgagor will be solely responsible for the receiver's acts and defaults.

...

(8) The provisions of this section are subject to contrary intention expressed in the mortgage deed and may be varied or extended by the mortgage deed, and, as so varied or extended, shall have effect as if contained in this Ordinance.

278. *See also* Shum, *supra* note 246, at 260.

279. Nield, *supra* note 27, at 477.

v. *Mortgagor's Rights and Remedies*

The mortgagor, like the creditor mortgagee, possesses certain rights and remedies. Foremost of these rights is the right of redemption. Under the right of redemption, the mortgagor can redeem or take back the estate by repaying the loan along with any interest. This right of redemption may be legal or equitable. Legal redemption is provided in the mortgage deed with a set date.

An equitable redemption must be exercised according to the rules of equity. A mortgagor must give prior notice to the mortgagee of the intent to redeem, usually six months' notice or six months' interest in lieu of notice. The mortgage deed may state a shorter notice period. There can be no agreement that disallows redemption as this would be inequitable and therefore would be void.

The mortgagor may take action in order to protect its possessory rights. Under both legal mortgages and equitable mortgages, the mortgagee has no legal right to possession of the property under the *Conveyancing and Property Ordinance*; otherwise, the mortgagor has the right to bring an action for trespass. If the mortgagee takes possession without giving notice to the mortgagor, the latter can sue for possession. Under a legal charge, the mortgagor retains the legal estate and the right to possession until default. The mortgagor is entitled to sue for the recovery of possession of the land, trespass, or other wrong done to the land. The mortgagor may also retain any rental or other profits that may accrue from the use of the land and may sue for the recovery of such rent or profits.[280]

The mortgagor has the right to lease the land or dispose of the property, but subject to the mortgagee's interests. Thus, the mortgagor has a right to grant a sub-lease, accept surrender of a lease, convey the property to a third party, or, grant a subsequent mortgage unless a contrary agreement is contained in the mortgage deed.

The mortgagor may commit waste so long as the waste does not render the security interest deficient:

> A mortgagor is not under a duty to refrain from committing waste unless the act of waste is so serious as to endanger the security itself. It is common practice, however, for the mortgage to contain both an express covenant from the mortgagor that they will keep the property

280. *Id.* at 462.

in good repair, and a right for the mortgagee to enter the property to inspect the state of repair.[281]

Another right available to the mortgagor is to inspect the title deeds. A mortgagee has a right to hold the title deeds to the mortgaged realty in order to protect its security; however, section 47 of the *Conveyancing and Property Ordinance* provides a mortgagor with a right to inspect the title deeds.[282]

VII. LEASEHOLD OWNERSHIP IN HONG KONG

In the following sections of this book, matters relating to Hong Kong conveyancing is presented in the general order in which the typical conveyancing process proceeds: sale and purchase agreement, nature of title, proof of title, remedies in the event of breach, assignment, completion and post-completion.[283]

However, before proceeding to conveyancing matters, two related subjects, Government leases and the use of deeds of mutual covenants for multi-storey building management, will be reviewed to provide some background information to the material presented in the subsequent sections.

In Hong Kong, the government disposes of land by granting long leases. These were known as "Crown leases" prior to 1997 and as "Government

281. *Id.* at 464.

282. *Id.* at 463.

283. As noted in 16 HALSBURY'S, *supra* note 29, at para. 230.133:

> The types of contract for the sale of land in Hong Kong include:
>
> (1) sales by Conditions of Sale; most alienation of land by the Government is effected by a public auction, and the contract is called Conditions of Sale under which the purchaser receives a leasehold estate; Other [*sic*] forms of alienation include Conditions of Exchange, and Conditions of Regrant.
>
> (2) secondary sales where the Government lessee sells his land, or more correctly assigns his leasehold, to a purchaser where no estate agent is involved, in most cases the parties will instruct a solicitor to act prior to being bound;
>
> (3) secondary sales where the Government lessee sells his land, or more correctly assigns his leasehold, to a purchaser where neither party instructs a solicitor initially, but both sign a contract, referred to as a Preliminary or Provisional Agreement, drafted by an estate agent who is agent for both vendor and purchaser, and who also signs the contract. Invariably this contract will be a binding agreement;
>
> (4) sales of uncompleted units in multi-storey developments, which are regulated by the Lands Department under the Consent Scheme; and
>
> (5) sales by mortgagees on the mortgagor's default.

See id. at para. 230.004, where the main ordinances relating to land are presented. *See generally* GOO & LEE, *supra* note 24, at Chapter 2 ("Sale of Land").

leases" after 1997. With one exception, all lands held by private persons in Hong Kong in essence are leasehold.[284] Under a Crown or Government lease, the Hong Kong government is the landlord. For the purposes of this chapter, leasehold estates are treated as realty.[285]

Although a tender system is used occasionally,[286] government land is usually sold by auction, in which the highest bidder becomes the lessee. The agreement between the government and the lessee sets out the provisions of the lease.[287] This agreement is known as the "Conditions of Sale".[288] The amount of the premium payable is the auction bid price.

---

284. The only freehold land in Hong Kong is St John's Cathedral which was granted in perpetuity but subject to the condition that the land continues to be used as a church. For a detailed history, *see* SIHOMBING, HK CONVEYANCING, *supra* note 257, vol. 1, at Chapters I ("Land Tenure in Hong Kong"), II ("System of Land Holding in Hong Kong").

285. This work will follow Hong Kong local practice:

> In accordance with local practice the Government lessee is referred to ... as the 'owner' of the land, despite the fact that he merely holds a leasehold estate. Then when that "owner" grants a sub-lease, the sub-lessee's interest is referred to as that of a "lessee".

16 HALSBURY'S, *supra* note 29, at para. 230.002.

See also SIHOMBING, HK CONVEYANCING, *supra* note 257, vol. 2(A), Chapter II, at para. 52; SIHOMBING, STUDENT'S GUIDE, *supra* note 106, at Chapters 8 ("Formation of Contract for Sale of Land"), 9 ("Contract – Vitiating Factors"), 10 ("Contract – Capacity, Status and Disabilities").

286. NIELD, *supra* note 27, at 303–304:

> Occasionally Government leases are granted otherwise than by auction. Privately negotiated Conditions of Grant may be made for public purposes, for instance, for a school. Where land is exchanged for other land, which is quite common where an old site is being redeveloped, it may be convenient for the lessee to surrender his old Government lease and obtain a new grant where, for instance, he wishes to change slightly the boundaries of the site or where evidence of his title is rather fragmented. In this case, Conditions of Exchange are issued. ... The Conditions of Extension may be issued where an additional area of land is granted as an extension to, and on the same terms as, an existing site. These other types of agreement for a Government lease are also governed by the *Conveyancing and Property Ordinance* (Cap 219) section 14.

287. A tenant's rights and obligations are usually set out in the Government lease or by implication of law, for example:

- quiet enjoyment;
- exclusive possession;
- assignment or sub-lease; and,
- offensive trade

288. There are five kinds of conditions:

- Conditions of Sale, under which land is sold;
- Conditions of Exchange, under which the granted land is exchanged for other land;

A certificate of compliance is issued by the government if it is satisfied that the obligations under the Conditions of Sale are fulfilled.[289] To encourage performance of these obligations, the government usually does not allow the lessee to dispose of the property until compliance with the conditions occurs.

Signing a Conditions of Sale, rather than the Government lease itself, provides the Government with a method to regulate land development and to avoid unnecessary expense and delay. In fact, despite the terms of the Conditions, which require the lessee to enter into the lease, it is the government's policy not to issue a lease unless specifically requested.[290] Section 14 of the *Conveyancing and Property Ordinance* (Cap 219) deems the registration of the Conditions of Sale with the Certificate of Compliance to be the equivalent of a formal Government lease.[291]

Most Crown or Government leases in Kowloon and in Hong Kong Island are granted for seventy-five years, with a right of renewal for a further

---

- Conditions of Grant, under which land is granted for a particular purpose;
- Conditions of Regrant, under which a grantee applies for a new grant upon the expiration of the lease; and,
- Conditions of Extension, under which additional land is granted by the government.

For a review of these conditions, *see* 16 HALSBURY'S, *supra* note 29, at paras. 230.108–230.114. *See also* SIHOMBING, STUDENT'S GUIDE, *supra* note 106, at 122–131; SIHOMBING, HK CONVEYANCING, *supra* note 257, vol. 2(A), Chapter II, at paras. 151–196, 251–311.

289. Various government authorities may issue the certificate, including: the Director of Public Works, the Registrar of Titles or the Director of Lands. A certificate of exemption is issued in the New Territories for buildings which do not need to comply with the *Buildings Ordinance* (Cap 123). A certificate of exemption has the same effect as a certificate of compliance. *See* 16 HALSBURY'S, *supra* note 29, at para. 230.108 n. 3 (citing *Chung Mui Teck v Hang Tak Buddhist Hall Association Ltd* [2001] 2 HKLRD 471, CA).

290. 16 HALSBURY'S, *supra* note 29, at para. 230.420 n. 7 comments:

> No Government lease has issued, since prior to 1970, on the completion of the building covenant in the conditions of sale, and consequently only the conditions of sale now represent the Government lease. The equitable interest of the purchaser becomes legal on the issue of a certificate of compliance from the Government indicating that the purchaser has observed the covenants in the conditions; there are usually two such covenants, namely the payment of the premium ... and the building covenant ...

291. *Conveyancing and Property Ordinance*, *supra* note 43, at section 14 states:

> (1) Where a person has a right to a Government lease of any land upon compliance with any conditions precedent, then, upon compliance with those conditions—
>
> (a) the equitable interest under that right shall become a legal estate in that land as if held under a Government lease issued in accordance with that right ...

seventy-five years, except for the early 999-year leases granted between 1849 and 1898. The Crown lease with an option to renew can be renewed at a rent which is fixed by reference to the land's rental value without payment of a further premium. Sections 3–5 of the *Government Leases Ordinance* (Cap 40) automatically extend all renewable seventy-five year or ninety-nine year Crown or Government leases in Hong Kong. Articles 121–122 of the *Basic Law* now provides for the grant of leases for fifty-year terms.[292]

---

(2) Where, under an agreement for a Government lease entered into before 1 January 1970, a person has a right to a Government lease upon compliance with any conditions precedent he shall be deemed, for the purposes of this section, to have complied with those conditions on the commencement of this section.

(3) Where under an agreement for a Government lease entered into on or after 1 January 1970, a person has a right to a Government lease upon compliance with any conditions precedent, he shall be deemed, for the purposes of this section, to have complied with those conditions—
   (a) upon the issue by the Government of a certificate that those conditions have been complied with and the registration of that certificate in the Land Registry under the Land Registration Ordinance (Cap 128); or
   (b) upon the endorsement by the Government on the Government lease of a note to the effect that those conditions have been complied with and the registration of a copy of that endorsement in the Land Registry under the Land Registration Ordinance (Cap 128); or
   (c) upon the entry on the register kept in the Land Registry under the Land Registration Ordinance (Cap 128) relating to the land of a note to the effect that those conditions have been complied with.

(4) Where a person has a right to a Government lease of any land and that right is not subject to any conditions precedent—
   (a) the equitable interest under that right shall become a legal estate in that land as if held under a Government lease issued in accordance with that right; and
   (b) for the purposes of section 42 and any other law, such a Government lease shall be deemed to have been issued on the commencement of the Conveyancing and Property (Amendment) Ordinance 1988 … or on the date of the grant of that right, whichever is the later.

(5) Where a person has a right to a Government lease of any land and that land is partitioned by assignment or otherwise by deed, this section shall apply to each part of that land constituted by that partition, as it applies to the whole of that land, as if there were a right to a Government lease of each such part.

(6) Where a person has a Government lease, or a right to a Government lease, of any land and additional land is granted to that person with the intent that he should hold it as part of the land leased, this section shall apply to that additional land as if that additional land were part of the land originally leased and held subject to any further conditions precedent imposed when that additional land was granted.

Leases in the New Territories were formerly granted for a seventy-five year term from 1 July 1898, renewable for another term of twenty-four years, less three days. From 1959, New Territories leases ran for ninety-nine years from 1 July 1898, meaning that they expired on 1 July 1997. Section 6 of the *New Territories Leases (Extension) Ordinance* (Cap 150)[293] extended all the leases in the New Territories to 30 June 2047, unless the lessee opted otherwise under section 5 of this Ordinance.[294]

Some Crown leases do not include an option to renew. Upon expiry of these leases, one of the following may occur:

- the land reverts back to the Crown, now the HKSAR government;
- the government resells the land by auction to the highest bidder;
- the government resells the land to the last lessee at market price; or,
- the government grants a new lease or the lessee renews the lease.[295]

---

292. Article 121 and Article 122 of the *Basic Law* provide respectively:

> As regards all leases of land granted or renewed where the original leases contain no right of renewal, during the period from 27 May 1985 to 30 June 1997, which extend beyond 30 June 1997 and expire not later than 30 June 2047, the lessee is not required to pay an additional premium as from 1 July 1997, but an annual rent equivalent to 3 per cent of the rateable value of the property at that date, adjusted in step with any changes in the rateable value thereafter, shall be charged.
>
> In the case of old schedule lots, village lots, small houses and similar rural holdings, where the property was on 30 June 1984 held by, or, in the case of small houses granted after that date, where the property is granted to, a lessee descended through the male line from a person who was in 1898 a resident of an established village in Hong Kong, the previous rent shall remain unchanged so long as the property is held by that lessee or by one of his lawful successors in the male line.

293. *New Territories Leases (Extension) Ordinance*, *supra* note 245, at section 6 states:

> The term of a lease to which this Ordinance applies is extended, from the date on which it would, apart from this Ordinance, expire, until the expiry of 30 June 2047, without payment of any additional premium.

294. *Id.* at section 5(1) provides:

> A lessee may exclude from the application of this Ordinance his interest under a lease, other than an undivided share in the land to which the lease relates, by registering in the Land Office register, before the appointed day, a memorandum in a form specified by the Land Officer.

295. This is the most common situation. For a further discussion of this subject, *see*, *e.g.*, 16 HALSBURY'S, *supra* note 29, at paras. 230.102–230.104, 230.116; SIHOMBING, STUDENT'S GUIDE, *supra* note 106, at 84–94. *See generally* SIHOMBING, HK CONVEYANCING, *supra* note 257, vol. 2(A), Chapter II, at paras. 52–264, 355–530.

Non-renewable Crown leases due to expire before 1997 may be extended without the payment of any premiums until 30 June 2047 at an annual rental of 3 percent of the land's rateable value.[296]

As previously stated, pursuant to either section 4 or section 5 of the *Government Leases Ordinance*, the right of renewal contained in the lease shall be deemed to have been exercised for renewable Government leases, and under section 9 at an annual rate of 3 percent of the rateable value of the land.[297] The government of the Hong Kong Special Administrative Region has stated that it will grant new leases for a term of fifty years without any premium, but at the annual rental of 3 percent of the rateable value of the land.

---

296. As summarized by one authority:

> All leases of land granted, decided upon or renewed before the establishment of the Hong Kong Special Administrative Region which extend beyond 30 June 1997 and all rights in relation to such leases are recognised and protected under the law of the Hong Kong Special Administrative Region.
>
> As to the leases of land granted or renewed where the original leases contain no right of renewal, during the period from 27 May 1985 to 30 June 1997, which extend beyond 30 June 1997 and expire not later than 30 June 2047, the lessee is not required to pay an additional premium as from 1 July 1997, but an annual rent equivalent to 3 per cent of the rateable value of the property at that date, adjusted in step with an changes in the rateable value after that date, is to be charged.

17(1) HALSBURY'S, *supra* note 57, at para. 235.019.

The *BLIS Glossary*, *supra* note 7, translates "rateable value" as 應課差餉租值.

297. Section 9 of the *Government Leases Ordinance* (Cap 40) states:

> (1) Subject to subsection (9) the new Government rent payable under a new Government lease shall be an amount equal to 3 per cent of the rateable value of the lot or section held under new Government lease.
>
> (2) Subject to the provisions of this section, the rateable value for the purposes of this section of a lot or section held under a new Government lease is the rateable value or interim valuation as set out on the relevant day in the list declared under section 13 of the Rating Ordinance (Cap 116), of the tenement, or, if there is more than one tenement, the aggregate of the rateable values and interim valuations as so set out of all the tenements comprised wholly or partly in the lot or section held under the new Government lease.
>
> ...
>
> (9) Where the person or all of the persons, if more than one, entitled to exercise the right of renewal contained in a renewable Government lease paid or agreed in writing with the Director to pay the new Government rent of a lot or section in an amount exceeding that which is specified in subsection (1) the new Government rent of the lot or section shall be-
>
> (a) for the period from the expiration of the renewable Government lease to the 30 June 1973 the amount so paid or agreed to be paid; and
>
> (b) for the period from the 1 July 1973 to the expiration of the term of the new Government lease the amount specified in subsection (1).

A Government lease is different from the usual landlord-tenant leases in that the former:

- is longer in duration;
- has lower rent but a large premium;
- contains terms giving the government greater control over the development and/or use of the land;
- allows the government to "resume", *i.e.*, to take back, land if required for public purposes.[298]

---

298. 16 HALSBURY'S, *supra* note 29, at para. 230.969 notes: "The Government lease invariably has a clause entitling the Government to resume land for public purposes." For detailed analysis of the topic of government resumption of land, *see id.* at paras. 230.038, 230.969–230.1014. Paragraph 230.038 provides an overview of this topic, stating in part:

> there is no compulsory acquisition of land in Hong Kong in the sense of the Government buying land from the owner under a compulsory order of sale. Instead the form of acquisition, by the Government of the land held under a Government lease prior to the termination of that lease, is that of resumption except where the land being compulsorily acquired or purchased under the Land Acquisition (Possessory Title) Ordinance. This entitles the Government as lessor to take back the land under the terms of the Lands Resumption Ordinance. Compensation is payable on resumption similar to that payable for compulsory acquisition.
>
> By contrast to resumption, the Government as lessor does have a right to re-enter as lessor and forfeit the lease where the lessee has breached the covenants in the Government lease, or has failed to pay rent or premium due. Re-entry can be physically taking back the land or merely re-entry in principle. … No compensation is payable in such cases, in respect of the interest in the land or for improvements.
>
> The right to resume land is given to the Government where that land is needed for public purposes. Resumption and acquisition result in the early determination of the lease without fault on either party. Fair compensation must be paid …

Note, however:

> A statutory power to resume land is usually a power to resume compulsorily and to resume the whole land or interests in it; however, the statute under which the statutory power arises may specifically authorise the taking of an easement or statutory right. In some cases there is no resumption or the taking of interests or rights, but merely the imposition of restrictions on the use of alienated land, for which compensation can be payable.

Id. at para. 230.971.

See also SIHOMBING, STUDENT'S GUIDE, *supra* note 106, at 147–171 ("Resumption of land"). *See generally* SIHOMBING, HK CONVEYANCING, *supra* note 257, vol. 1, Chapter II, at paras. 286–348 ("Statutory procedure for resumption and challenges thereto"); vol. 2(A), Chapter II, at paras. 401–430 ("Resumption of land and its procedures"), 431–530 ("Compensation").

Government leases usually contain provisions regulating assignments and sub-letting. If a lessee enters into an agreement to sub-let or under-lease all of the remaining interest in the lease, the transaction is effectuated by a type of deed known as an "assignment". In an assignment of a lease, only the parties to the lease have changed. There remains only one lease on the whole estate. In effect, the party receiving the assignment, the "assignee", from the original tenant, the "assignor", is substituted for the original tenant.[299] A lessee who makes an assignment transfers the remainder of the term to the purchaser, the assignee. Land sold in Hong Kong is actually the residue or balance of the term of the Government lease that is being assigned by the lessee to the purchaser. For instance, an owner who holds a Government lease of land for seventy-five years, of which there are sixty-five years still to run, sells that land by assigning the sixty-five year residue of this lease to the purchaser. The owner then has no further interest in the land. The assignment of short-term leases is less common. Such leases usually contain a covenant prohibiting the tenant from assigning its interest without the landlord's consent which shall not be unreasonably refused. An assignor remains liable for the performance of the covenants in the lease.[300]

Sub-letting differs from assignment in that the original lessee maintains the original landlord-tenant relationship. The original lessee also creates a new landlord-tenant relationship with the original lessee as the landlord and with the new lessee as the sub-tenant. Note that in many cases, the original lease contains a covenant against sub-letting without the original landlord's written consent.

A disposal for a period shorter than the residue of the term of the lease creates a new lease that is a separate interest or estate from the lease out of which it is created. The rental, term and covenants are distinct and need not be the same as the terms of the head lease. For instance, if a lessee holding a lease of seventy-five years wishes to allow another to have possession of the land for only five years of the seventy-five year term, the lessee will create a sub-lease giving the right to exclusive possession of the land for five years. At the end of the five-year term, possession of the land will revert to the lessee who may take up possession or grant another sub-lease.

299. The *BLIS Glossary*, *supra* note 7, translates "assignment" as 轉讓; and, "assignee" as 承讓人.

300. *See, e.g.*, 17(1) HALSBURY'S, *supra* note 57, at paras. 235.077, 235.337–235.339, 235.395.

VIII. MULTI-STOREY BUILDINGS IN HONG KONG

Multi-storey buildings are the most common type of building in Hong Kong. Multi-storey buildings are constructed on land held from a Government lease, and can be used for residential, commercial, or industrial purposes, or a combination thereof.[301] In relation to multi-storey buildings, Professor Judith Sihombing has observed:

> There were three main problems with early high-rise developments. First, the regulation of the management of the building had to be provided for. Usually this was done in the form of a deed of mutual covenant (DMC) which was not executed by all purchasers; under the DMC there were difficulties in ensuring that the benefit and the burden of covenants, especially positive covenants, affected all present and future owners of units. The rights of the owners were often subsidiary to the rights of the manager under the DMC; one way to avoid this was to incorporate. Secondly, the developer often wished to retain an interest in the land despite selling all units in the building, thereby disposing of all his rights; this was obtained by reserving rights for himself but without having any obligation to contribute to the upkeep of the building. The terms of the Building Management Ordinance now require the developer to contribute to the various charges associated with ownership of units in the building, or to have retained shares in the development to which an obligation to pay appropriate fees and charges has attached. The third problem concerned the sale of the units prior to completion of the building; this was not lawful by reference to the building covenant. Consequently purchasers could not protect their interests by registration.[302]

This section discusses the management of multi-storey buildings in Hong Kong by presenting a review of: the schemes of ownership in multi-storey buildings, management of a multi-storey building through incorporated owners, and, management of a multi-storey building through a deed of mutual covenant.

---

301. 16 HALSBURY'S, *supra* note 29, at paras. 230.419, 230.004, 230.107–230.114. *See also* GOO & LEE, *supra* note 24, Chapter 10 at section 9 ("Co-ownership and Multi-storey Building"); PAUL KENT, MALCOLM MERRY & MEGAN WALTERS, BUILDING MANAGEMENT IN HONG KONG (2nd ed. 2008) ; SIHOMBING, STUDENT'S GUIDE, *supra* note 106, at 274–291; SIHOMBING, HK CONVEYANCING, *supra* note 257, vol. 1, Chapter IV ("Co-ownership of Multi-Storey Buildings"); vol. 2(B), Chapter IV, at paras. 1–52.
302. 16 HALSBURY'S, *supra* note 29, at para. 230.422.

A. Ownership Schemes

Ownership schemes seek to address the sale of units prior to completion of a multi-storey building so that purchasers may protect their interests by registration of a memorial at the Land Registry. Registration normally would not be possible due to a covenant in the Government lease prohibiting the sale of units prior to completion.

Two schemes exist to achieve this purpose of protection of a buyer's title by registration: the Consent Scheme and the Non-consent Scheme.[303]

i. *Consent Scheme*

Under the Consent Scheme, a developer may sell units in an uncompleted residential, commercial or industrial development with the consent of the Director of Lands. Once consent is obtained, the sale and purchase agreement between the developer and the purchaser can be registered, thus giving the buyer some protection.[304] Certain criteria must be met before the Director of Lands will give consent. Only a brief summary of the points which seem relevant to potential owners of units in a multi-storey building are set out below.

- Consent to sell will be given no more than 12 months prior to the estimated completion date.
- The right to buy a unit will be by ballot.
- The preliminary agreement shall not be a binding contract.
- The formal sale and purchase agreement must be a standard form contract and must be signed by the purchaser within three days and by the developer within seven days.
- Only those signing the preliminary agreement are allowed to sign the formal sale and purchase agreement.
- A purchaser may not resell, or otherwise deal with the benefit of the sale and purchase agreement, prior to completion and assignment.

---

303. A detailed analysis of the consent and non-consent schemes is beyond the scope of this work. Further information may be found at *id.* at paras. 230.424–230.427; SIHOMBING, STUDENT'S GUIDE, *supra* note 106, at 291–296.
See generally SIHOMBING, HK CONVEYANCING, *supra* note 257, vol. 1, Chapter IV, at paras. 35–50 ("Consent scheme"); *id.* at paras. 61; 65–75 ("Non-consent scheme").
304. An unregistered or unregistrable sale and purchase agreement might result in a developer's mortgagee(s) having priority interest over the purchaser(s) in the development. This would be particularly relevant in the event of a liquidation of the developer.

- The preliminary deposit will be between 8 percent and 12 percent and a further payment up to 20 percent of the purchase price must be paid within fourteen days of executing the sale and purchase agreement.
- The sales brochure used to advertise the development must be approved by the Land Office and must contain certain information in a particular form. This information includes details of fittings, finishes, terms of the Government lease, typical floor plan, etc.[305]

ii. Non-consent Scheme

The Non-consent Scheme affords protection for purchasers of residential units in uncompleted buildings to which the Consent Scheme does not apply, but where the same solicitor represents both the developer and the purchaser. This scheme is regulated by the Solicitors' Practice Rules, Rule 5C.[306]

B. Incorporated Owners

Owners' meetings to discuss a building's management under a deed of mutual covenant did not lead to efficient management due generally to a lack of co-operation between the owners. As a result, the owners' committee could not function as a legal entity acting on behalf of all owners. Under the former *Multi-Storey Building (Owners Incorporation) Ordinance*, owners of a building could incorporate, giving the owners' corporation the authority to act on behalf of all owners in matters of common interest, particularly the management of the building.[307]

Incorporation transfers the owners' powers, rights, duties and privileges in the common property to the corporation.[308] The building's management is controlled by the incorporated owners acting through a management committee.[309] The management committee is responsible for the maintenance

305. *See, e.g.*, *http://www.hkclic.org/en/topics/saleAndPurchaseOfProperty/sale_and_purchase_of_property_under_construction/q1.shtml* (last visited 26 Feb. 2011); *http://www.hkclic.org/en/topics/saleAndPurchaseOfProperty/sale_and_purchase_of_property_under_construction/index.shtml* (last visited 26 Feb. 2011).
306. *See infra* section IX.C where this is discussed. The rule is set out *infra* note 362.
307. 16 HALSBURY'S, *supra* note 29, at para. 230.453. *See generally* GOO & LEE, *supra* note 24, at Chapter 16 ("Multi-storey Building Management"); SIHOMBING, STUDENT'S GUIDE, *supra* note 106, at 372–397.
308. 16 HALSBURY'S, *supra* note 29, at para. 230.456.
309. *Id.* at para. 230.430.

of the common parts and the corporation's property, the employment of tradesmen and professionals, insurance of the property and other similar matters.[310]

Owners may incorporate ownership of the building by registering a memorandum of incorporation with the Land Registry. Section 8 of the *Building Management Ordinance* (Cap 344),[311] sets out the procedures for incorporation and regulation of the incorporated owners' conduct.[312] This Ordinance also provides for the dissolution or winding up of the owners' corporation.[313]

---

310. *Id.* at para. 230.456.

311. Section 8 of the *Building Management Ordinance* (Cap 344) provides:

> (1) The Land Registrar shall, if satisfied that the provisions of section 3, 3A, 4 or 40C and section 7(2) and (3) have been complied with, issue a certificate of registration in such form as may be specified by the Authority from time to time.
>
> (1A) The Land Registrar shall not issue a certificate of registration to more than one corporation for a building in respect of which a deed of mutual covenant is in force.
>
> (2) With effect from the date of issue of the certificate of registration under subsection (1)—
>
> (a) the owners for the time being shall be a body corporate with perpetual succession and shall in the name of the corporation specified in the certificate of registration be capable of suing and being sued and, subject to this Ordinance, of doing and suffering all such other acts and things as bodies corporate may lawfully do and suffer;
>
> (aa) the corporation shall have, and be deemed always to have had, the power to hold an undivided share in the building, together with the right to the exclusive possession of any part of the building other than the common parts thereof; and
>
> (b) the management committee appointed under section 3, 3A, 4 or 40C shall be deemed to be the first management committee of the corporation.
>
> (3) A corporation shall have a common seal, the affixing of which shall be authenticated by the signature of the chairman and secretary of the management committee.
>
> (4) A corporation shall have a registered office in Hong Kong.
>
> (5) Schedule 3 shall have effect with respect to the meetings and procedure of a corporation.

312. 16 HALSBURY'S, *supra* note 29, at para. 230.430.

313. *See id.* at para. 230.462. The *Building Management Ordinance*, *supra* note 311, at section 33(1) states:

> A corporation may be wound up under the provisions of Part X of the Companies Ordinance (Cap 32) as if it were an unregistered company within the meaning of that Ordinance and the provisions of that Ordinance relating to the winding up of an unregistered company shall, in so far as they are applicable, apply to the winding up of a corporation.

C. Deed of Mutual Covenant

A deed of mutual covenant provides for the maintenance and management of the common parts of a multi-storey building. A deed of mutual covenant ensures that the benefit and burdens of the rights and obligations are annexed to all parts of the land and buildings and run with the ownership so that subsequent owners will be equally bound.[314]

A multi-storey building is divided into undivided shares by a document usually known as a deed of mutual covenant.[315] No separate leaseholds are issued to each individual owner. A purchaser acquires the undivided shares of and in the building but not in the flat. This purchaser does, however, acquire the right of exclusive possession of the flat, and perhaps car parking space(s), through the assignment. Each assignee becomes a co-owner, a tenant in common, with the other owners. As tenants in common, they enjoy unity of possession of the land and the building.

On a new development, the first purchaser of a unit in the building of undivided shares will, usually at the same time as the execution of the assignment, enter into the deed of mutual covenant with the developer—the owner of the rest of the whole building and, perhaps, the management company.[316] Subsequent purchasers of units within the building do not need

---

314. Hartley Bramwell, Conveyancing in Hong Kong 270–71 (1981). For an extensive review of DMCs, *see* Sihombing, HK Conveyancing, *supra* note 257, vol. 1, Chapter IV, at paras. 76–260.

315. 16 Halsbury's, *supra* note 29, at para. 230.438 n. 2 describes an undivided share as:

> an undivided share in the legal estate of the whole property. Without a Deed of Mutual Covenant (DMC), each co-owner of the property would be entitled to the full use and enjoyment of the whole property. The DMC governs the right of the co-owners amongst themselves and regulates, amongst other things, the portions of the property in respect of which each owner would have the exclusive right of enjoyment. That exclusive right of enjoyment cannot be assigned on its own, but has to be assigned by a vendor who was assigning that right of exclusive enjoyment together with an assignment of his right of exclusive enjoyment to some other part of the building with undivided shares …

See also id. at para. 230.432, where it is stated:

> In general, the deed of mutual covenant will provide that the owner will not be able to deal separately with the elements which make up his rights as tenant in common; thus his right of exclusive use to his particular unit cannot be dealt with separately from any rights he may have over other parts of the building such as a parking space. One owner may be treated as having exclusive rights over part of the common property due to his occupation of that common property; with this right comes the obligation to maintain that part of the common property.

316. Under the definition provided in the *Conveyancing and Property Ordinance, supra* note 43, at section 2.

to enter into the deed of mutual covenant themselves. The assignments by the developer to the subsequent purchasers will incorporate provisions giving those purchasers both the burdens and benefits of the deed of mutual covenant.[317] Subsequent purchasers are bound by the deed of mutual covenant by their assignments which incorporate the now registered deed and several sections of the *Conveyancing and Property Ordinance*.[318]

"assignment" (轉讓、轉讓契) includes—
(a) the transfer of the whole of the interest in land held under a government lease;
(b) a legal charge;
(c) a lease (other than a Government lease);
(d) a surrender;
(e) an assent; and
(f) every other assurance or conveyance of land by any instrument.

317. Unless the contrary intention is expressed in the assignment, Part I of the First Schedule of the *Conveyancing and Property Ordinance*, *supra* note 43, entitled "Implied Covenants in any Assignment of Land", is implied into every assignment by virtue of section 35(1)(a). Part I(B) contains the provision relating to deeds of mutual covenant.

318. As 16 HALSBURY'S, *supra* note 29, at para. 230.447 explains:

> The Conveyancing and Property Ordinance makes provision for the enforcement of the benefit and the burden of the covenants in the deed of mutual covenant (DMC) ... on registration of the DMC in the Land Registry. Registration operates to bind successors in title to the three original contracting parties. The DMC operates against morttgagees [*sic*] or tenants or occupiers claiming through the owner although there are certain exemptions in relation to positive covenants. The provisions of the Ordinance:
>
> (1) enable a person to take rights and liabilities under a deed, although not a party to it, subject to certain limitations; these limitations are that the party, or his successor in title, must have been in existence at the time the covenant was entered into, that the person was clearly intended to benefit directly by the covenant, and is capable of enforcing it; [CPO section 26]
> (2) provide that certain implied covenants of due performance are included in assignments without express mention; these must be expressly excluded if they are not to be inserted; [CPO section 35(1) and Schedule 1]
> (3) provide that, unless a contrary intention is expressed, covenants are deemed to be made with successors in title of the covenantee and similarly in respect of the covenantor; [CPO sections 39(1) and 40(1)]
> (4) provide that covenants are enforceable against successors in title if there is an intention that such persons should benefit; this intention is implied unless the contrary is shown; [CPO sections 41(2)(c) and 39]
> (5) enable a covenant to be enforceable despite the fact that the covenantor and covenantee own the same land; without this, the enforcement of the covenants in the DMC would be difficult as the parties are co-owners of the Government lease; [CPO section 41(7)]
> (6) provide for termination of liability in respect of the covenant when the covenantor no longer owns the subject land; [CPO section 41(8)]
> (7) provide that positive covenants will be enforceable against successors in title subject to certain restrictions in respect of non-owners; [CPO sections 41(2) and 41(5)]

The most effective way to make the proprietary covenants in the deed of mutual covenants (DMC) enforceable against successors in title to

---

(8) reserve the operation of covenants in a DMC entered into at a time when conditions of sale affected the land, but which were later replaced by the Government lease on the issuance of the certificate of compliance; similar provision is made in respect of a DMC registered prior to the conversion of the conditions of sale into the Government lease; [CPO sections 42(1) and 42(2)]

(9) provide that where the Government lease, having expired, has been renewed the pre-existing covenants are to continue in force under the new lease. [CPO section 42(3)]

See also id. at para. 230.436, and n. 2 thereto which states:

> To overcome problems with the enforcement of the covenants in the DMC against owners who were not parties to the DMC, the Law of Property (Enforcement of Covenants) Ordinance 1956 was enacted, the relevant provisions of which have now been subsumed into the Conveyancing and Property Ordinance (Cap 219) sections 39, 41 …

E.g., section 41 of the *Conveyancing and Property Ordinance*, *supra* note 43, provides in part:

(1) This section applies to an express covenant and a covenant implied by or under this Ordinance or any other law.

(2) This section applies to any covenant, whether positive or restrictive in effect—
 (a) which relates to the land of the covenantor;
 (b) the burden of which is expressed or intended to run with the land of the covenantor; and
 (c) which is expressed and intended to benefit the land of the covenantee and his successors in title or persons deriving title to that land under or through him or them.

(3) Notwithstanding any rule of law or equity but subject to subsection (5), a covenant shall run with the land and, in addition to being enforceable between the parties, shall be enforceable against the occupiers of the land and the covenantor and his successors in title and persons deriving title under or through him or them by the covenantee and his successors in title and persons deriving title under or through him or them.

(4) (a) For the purposes of the enforcement of a covenant, the following remedies shall be available—
  (i) proceedings for an injunction (including a mandatory injunction) or other equitable relief;
  (ii) an action for money due under the covenant;
  (iii) an action for damages (whether in respect of pecuniary or non-pecuniary kinds of damage).
 (b) For the purposes of ascertaining the existence, nature and effect of a covenant, a court of competent jurisdiction may make a declaration relating to those matters.

…

(9) A covenant in an instrument registered in the Land Registry under the Land Registration Ordinance (Cap 128) against the land affected by the covenant shall bind the successors in title of the covenantor and the persons deriving title under or through him or them whether or not they had notice of the covenant.

> the original parties to the deed, is by registration of the DMC in the Land Registry ...[319]

Thus, the rights and obligations of the developer and owners of undivided shares of property are regulated by the deed of mutual covenant. It should address: the owners' shareholding, covenants, personal rights and other matters pertaining to the management of land owned by many parties, and the covenants in the Government lease to which all owners are subject.[320] A deed of mutual covenant is thus a substantial document, typically referring to:[321]

- Regulation of ownership rights

  The allocation of shares and exclusive-use areas are set out. Each owner is given the exclusive right to hold, use, occupy and enjoy the unit and the enjoyment of the common parts. This right is assigned to subsequent purchasers. The allocation of shares reflects each owner's share in the proceeds of sale of the land if, for example, the building is demolished and the land is sold. The number of shares allocated to a purchaser may also determine the responsibility for payment of a proportion of the management and maintenance expenses of the building, but there may be a different division based on management shares.[322] Each owner's voting rights may also be related to the allocated undivided shares.

  A developer may retain certain rights under a deed of mutual covenant if some units remain unsold. It is very common for a developer

319. 16 HALSBURY'S, *supra* note 29, at para. 230.448. *See also* SIHOMBING, STUDENT'S GUIDE, *supra* note 106, at 340–341.
320. 16 HALSBURY'S, *supra* note 29, at para. 230.437.
321. *See also* the list of provisions typically addressed in a deed of mutual covenant presented in *id.* at para. 230.438.
322. As explained in *id.* at para. 230.431:

> The land is notionally divided into a number of equal undivided shares, and each owner is allocated a number of these shares proportionate to his interest as set out in the deed of mutual covenant (DMC). In general, unless the owners agree these assigned values cannot be altered by the management. For the purpose of deciding the quantum of each owner's share in the land and his liability for various obligations, the undivided shares are given a value by the developer. These "valued" shares are usually referred to as management shares. They are expressed to be a reflection of the purchase price paid, the size of the unit, the purchase of its use, and so on.
>
> In some DMC's, the term "management shares" is used in a different way to refer to either undivided shares in the common parts held by the manager as trustee for all owners, or undivided shares giving the manger the right to use parts of the common property for its commercial gain.

to retain the exclusive right to use some common areas, the right to name the building, the right to advertise on outside walls, and the right to designate common areas.

Other than the parties to a deed of mutual covenant, who have privity of contract, not every right reserved in a deed of mutual covenant is enforceable against the owners of undivided shares. Only those rights running with the land are enforceable.[323] For example, in the case of *The Incorporated Owners of Viking Garden v Golden Brains Ltd*, [1991] 1 HKC 353 the developer had reserved in the deed of mutual covenant the right to use the roof space of the building and to erect illuminated advertising signs. The Incorporated Owners contended that it had the right to the control, management and administration of the common parts, including the roof structure. The court held in favour of the Incorporated Owners that the developer had no right to affix the advertising sign to the roof structure except with the Incorporated Owners' consent.

In *Supreme Honour Development Ltd v Lamaya Ltd* [1991] 1 HKC 198 the court denied the respondent's right to name the building, a right reserved in the deed of mutual covenant, on the basis that such a right could not be enforceable because the right was a personal covenant rather than a land right.

- Management and maintenance
  The deed of mutual covenant will also provide for a manager or management company to be appointed and specify any powers and duties, which are usually quite broad. The management agreement, which is a personal agreement, does not confer any rights in the land. In practice, most management agreements are incorporated into the deeds of mutual covenant. Thus the deed binds all co-owners, the developer, and the property manager.

- Owners' representation
  A deed of mutual covenant may contain provisions for an owners' meeting to elect an owners' committee to liaise with management on policy decisions. In the absence of such provisions, the Eighth Schedule of the *Building Management Ordinance*,[324] formerly the *Multi-Storey*

323. *See Conveyancing and Property Ordinance*, *supra* note 43, at section 41(2).
324. The Eighth Schedule to the *Building Management Ordinance*, *supra* note 311, regulates the procedures for such matters as the meetings of owners and of the owner's committee.

Buildings (Owners Incorporation) Ordinance, provides for the collective representation of owners.[325] As explained by Prof. Judith Sihombing:

> The provisions of the Eighth Schedule ... unless inconsistent with the terms of the deed of mutual covenant (DMC), are implied into all DMC's and bind the owners and manager. The implied clauses may then be amended, deleted, or re-incorporated into the DMC by a resolution of the owners. The terms in the Eighth Schedule deal mainly with the calling and conduct of meetings of the owners' committee and owners.[326]

In accordance with section 34E of the *Building Management Ordinance*, the Ordinance's Seventh Schedule has mandatory application in all deeds of mutual covenant, regardless of commencement date.[327] The Seventh Schedule seeks the rectification of unfair terms in

---

325. As amended by the *Multi-Storey Buildings (Owners Incorporation) (Amendment) Ordinance* (No. 27 of 1993) which is derived from the results of the government's consultative paper: "Proposals to Remedy Unfair Provisions in Existing DMCs."

326. 16 HALSBURY'S, *supra* note 29, at para. 230.459.

327. For a summary of the mandatory provisions of the Seventh Schedule, *see* 16 HALSBURY'S, *supra* note 29, at para. 230.458.

Section 34E of the *Building Management Ordinance*, *supra* note 311, provides in part:

> (1) Subject to subsection (4), the provisions in the Seventh Schedule shall be impliedly incorporated-
> (a) into every deed of mutual covenant made on or after the material date; and
> (b) as from the material date, into every deed of mutual covenant made before that date.
>
> (2) The provisions incorporated into a deed of mutual covenant by virtue of this section shall-
> (a) bind the owners and manager of the building; and
> (b) prevail over any other provision in the deed that is inconsistent with them.
>
> ...

The Ordinance's Seventh Schedule provides for regulation of such matters as contained in the following headings:

1. Determination of total amount of management expenses
2. Keeping of accounts
3. Manager to maintain bank account
4. Special fund
5. Contracts entered into by manager
6. Resignation of manger
7. Termination of manager's appointment by owners' corporation
8. Obligations after manager's appointment ends
9. Communication among owners.

existing deeds of mutual covenant through the regulation of the assessment of management expenses and the procedure for removal of the manager.

Prior to the commencement of the *Building Management Ordinance*, if any provisions of a deed of mutual covenant were inconsistent with the *Multi-Storey Buildings (Owners Incorporation) Ordinance*, the former prevailed, subject to any express statutory exceptions. The *Building Management Ordinance* now expressly provides that the Seventh Schedule prevails over any inconsistent provisions in the deed of mutual covenant.[328]

Lastly, one should note that a deed of mutual covenant is a contract and as such may be varied or discharged under certain circumstances.[329]

IX. SALE AND PURCHASE AGREEMENTS

A sale and purchase agreement is a written agreement concerning the transfer of an interest in realty, *i.e.*, sale of land. A valid sale and purchase agreement is a legally binding agreement between the parties. In Hong Kong, there are several types of sale and purchase agreements:

- a preliminary agreement;
- a formal sale and purchase agreement; or,
- an oral contract, provided there is a note or memorandum of its terms sufficient to comply with section 3 of the *Conveyancing and Property Ordinance*.

A formal sale and purchase agreement may be in a standard form, in order to comply with the Consent and Non-Consent Scheme requirements, or the formal sale and purchase agreement may be in the form suggested in Part A of the Second Schedule to the *Conveyancing and Property Ordinance*.[330]

---

328. 16 HALSBURY'S, *supra* note 29, at para. 230.455.
See Building Management Ordinance, *supra* note 311, at section 34E(2). Section 34E is set out in *supra* note 327.

329. As it is unlikely that most readers of this work will experience the alteration or termination of a deed of mutual covenant, no further comment is provided here. For further information, *see* 16 HALSBURY'S, *supra* note 29, at para. 230.445; SIHOMBING, STUDENT'S GUIDE, *supra* note 106, at 376–382; SIHOMBING, HK CONVEYANCING, *supra* note 257, vol. 2(B), Chapter IV, at paras. 2151–2204.

330. *See infra* section IX.C.

A. General Legal Considerations

As a contract, a sale and purchase agreement requires the elements of a legally binding agreement to be present: agreement or consent, capacity, consideration, certainty of terms and the intent to be legally bound. Disputes arising from the transfer of realty generally involve a party's intention to be legally bound in a formal contractual relationship.

The transfer of an interest in real estate is required to be in writing. Section 3(1) of the *Conveyancing and Property Ordinance* provides that:

> Subject to section 6(2), no action shall be brought upon any contract for the sale or the disposition of land unless the agreement upon which such action is brought, or some memorandum or note thereof, is in writing and signed by the party to be charged or by some other person lawfully authorised by him for that purpose.

Similarly, section 5(1)(a) of this Ordinance provides that:

> Subject to section 6-
>
> (a) no equitable interest in land can be created or disposed of except by writing signed by the person creating or disposing of the same, or by his agent thereunto lawfully authorized in writing, or by will, or by operation of law.

In Hong Kong, the transfer of realty generally involves a preliminary agreement, followed by a formal sale and purchase agreement. As the *Conveyancing and Property Ordinance* applies to both agreements, these agreements ought to be in writing. An oral contract may be enforced if there is a subsequent note or memorandum sufficient to comply with the requirements of section 3(1).[331] Without a written note or memorandum, an oral contract for the transfer of realty would not be enforceable in the courts, although the contract may not be illegal or void.

In order to fulfil the requirements of section 3(1), this note or memorandum must contain details of the parties, the property, the price and the

331. An exception to the requirement for writing is contained in section 6 of the *Conveyancing and Property Ordinance*, *supra* note 43, which provides that a lease for a term of less than three years, which takes effect in possession at the best rent available, does not need to be in writing so as to comply with section 3(1).
The failure to comply with section 3(1) of the *Conveyancing and Property Ordinance*, *supra* note 37, will render the contract unenforceable, but not void. Thus, if the parties choose to honour the agreement by an assignment, the purchaser's title is not defective.

completion date.[332] Further, any particular terms which the parties intend to include must be inserted in the note or memorandum. The note or memorandum must come into existence after the parties make the agreement,[333] and must contain the parties' names or provide an adequate description. A description referring merely to "vendor" would be insufficient, but a description using terms such as "owner", "proprietor" or "mortgagee" would be sufficiently specific to identify the party.[334] Likewise, the note or memorandum must sufficiently describe and identify the property, *e.g.*, the address of a flat or the lot number of the parcel of land.

The note or memorandum must provide the selling price, the consideration, or a method for determining the price. A court has enforced a sale and purchase agreement as being sufficiently clear where the consideration was to be established according to the following clause:

> at such price not being less than £12,000 as may be agreed upon by two valuers one to be nominated by the lessor and the other by the lessees or in default of such agreement by an umpire appointed by the said valuers.[335]

In contrast, another court held that there was no methodology for determining the price where an option to renew a lease provided the consideration to be "at such rental as may be agreed upon between the parties."[336] Similarly, a court found that a sale and purchase agreement providing for an "agreement to negotiate a fair and reasonable" price was too vague to be enforced and thus was void for uncertainty.[337]

The writing must reasonably reflect the terms of the oral agreement. If any significant agreed oral terms are excluded from the note or memorandum, the agreement will be unenforceable. A court held that a document did not qualify as a note or memorandum where the parties orally agreed upon instalment payments of the purchase price but the document omitted this particular term.[338] Another court reached a similar result where an oral

---

332. *See* 16 HALSBURY'S, *supra* note 29, at paras. 230.162–230.164. No particular form or format is required for the writing. *See, e.g.*, *id.* at para. 230.158.
333. *See id.* at para. 230.157. The exception is where a written offer which is accepted verbally may be enforced against the offeror, with the written offer serving as the note or memorandum. *Id.* at para. 230.158.
334. For other examples, *see id.* at para. 230.162.
335. *Sudbrook Trading Estate Ltd v Eggleton* [1983] 1 AC 444, 474–475.
336. *King's Motors (Oxford) Ltd v Lax* [1970] 1 WLR 426, 427.
337. *Courtney and Fairbairn v Tolaini Bros (Hotels) Ltd* [1975] 1 All ER 716.
338. *Tweddell v Henderson* [1975] 2 All ER 1096.

agreement pertained to the sale of both land and chattels but the note or memorandum made no reference to the chattels.[339]

Courts will imply terms into an agreement in order to give effect to the contract.[340] However, courts will not re-write an agreement for the parties. Courts will not imply certain terms into an agreement; thus, these terms must be expressly included in the note or memorandum if they are to be enforceable. In *Kwan Siu Man Joshua v Yaacov Ozer* [1999] 1 HKC 150, CFA the agreement contained nothing more than the parties involved, the price and the property. The Court of Final Appeal held that, due to the volatile property market in Hong Kong at the relevant time, the date of completion should be an essential term of any contract. In the absence of such an essential term, there could be no binding agreement. Thus, this open contract was void.

The note or memorandum must be signed. If only one party signs the note or memorandum, it may only be enforced against that party. A note signed by an authorized agent may be sufficient to bind the principal. A solicitor, however, has no general authority to enter into contracts on behalf of the client. When expressly authorized, an estate agent can execute an agreement which binds the agent's principal.

The note or memorandum comes into being in order to memorialize an agreement. The note or memorandum must thus be subsequent to the agreement. If the term "subject to contract" appears on the note or memorandum, this term would prevent a binding agreement coming into effect because the term would show that the note or memorandum was merely a record of negotiations which could be altered, *i.e.*, "subject to" a later agreement. Thus, the document would not constitute a note or memorandum for the purposes of section 3(1) of the *Conveyancing and Property Ordinance*.

Generally, the parol evidence rule provides that oral evidence will not be considered where it contradicts the terms of a written agreement.[341] An exception is found in collateral contracts where one party makes a promise in exchange for the other party entering into the main agreement. In the case of *De Lassalle v Guildford* [1901] 2 KB 215 the purchaser refused to complete the contract until he secured an oral assurance that the property's drains were in order. In *Otto v Bolton* [1936] 2 KB 46 the purchaser refused

339. *Ram Narayan v Rishad Hussain Shah* [1979] 1 WLR 1349, PC.

340. On the topic of open contracts and implied terms, *see*, *e.g.*, 16 HALSBURY'S, *supra* note 29, at paras. 230.193–230.195. *See also* SIHOMBING, STUDENT'S GUIDE, *supra* note 106, at 812–813 and 1039–1046 for more details on implied terms and open contract. *See generally* SIHOMBING, HK CONVEYANCING, *supra* note 257, vol. 1(B), Chapter XI, at paras. 1–3.

341. *See* SIHOMBING, STUDENT'S GUIDE, *supra* note 106, at 831–832.

to complete the transaction until he received an assurance that the subject house was well built.

Section 3(2) of the *Conveyancing and Property Ordinance* states that nothing in subsection (1) shall affect the law relating to part performance. The courts will enforce an oral agreement for the sale of land by ordering specific performance—but no order for damages—where one party has partially performed the contract. There must be sufficient acts of part performance which evidence the existence of the contract. The acts of part performance must, therefore, be unequivocally referable to the contract.

Part performance may be found by the payment of money, provided the performance is clearly related to the contract. A husband's payment of money in return for a promise by his wife to transfer the house to him as part of their divorce settlement constitutes part performance. Partial performance of an oral contract may also be found by a purchaser's entry into possession with the consent of the vendor or by a commercial tenant of leased premises installing machinery on the property.

B. Preliminary Agreements/Provisional Agreements

Preliminary agreements, also referred to as provisional agreements, are very common in Hong Kong and are usually prepared by an estate agent and executed by the vendor, purchaser and estate agent. The estate agent executes the agreement to enable recovery of the agent's fee as part of the contract.

i. *Role of the Estate Agent*

An estate agent can serve as the agent for both the vendor and purchaser in a sale, receiving a commission from both parties. An agent acting for two principals with potentially conflicting interests can only do so with the express consent of the two parties with full knowledge of the situation.[342] Whether an estate agent will be the vendor's agent for the purposes of making representations will be dependent upon the facts of each case.[343]

A court found an estate agent liable in damages to a purchaser where the agent had, whilst acting for the vendor, failed to convey a purchase offer

342. *Richard Ellis Ltd v Van Hong Tuon* [1988] 1 HKLR 169, CA; *Chesterton Petty Ltd v Groeneveld*, unreported, CACV No. 69 of 2000, paras. 18–24.

343. *See, e.g.*, *Cheng Kwok Fai v Mok Yiu Wah Peter* [1990] 2 HKLR 440.

from a prospective buyer.[344] In another case, the estate agent's employee informed the purchaser that certain illegal structures could be ignored because the management committee would take no enforcement action. The court found that: the estate agent acted as agent for the vendor; the vendor failed to give good title as the estate agent did not notify the purchaser that the Building Authority had issued a removal order relating to the illegal structures; and, the vendor was liable to the purchaser but could be indemnified by the estate agent.[345]

In most cases, an estate agent will use its own preliminary agreement which will be signed by all the parties: the vendor, purchaser and estate agent. The terms of this preliminary agreement are generally unfavourable to a purchaser. For example, there will often be a clause permitting the vendor to withdraw from the agreement upon the payment of twice the preliminary deposit as damages to the purchaser.

ii. Contents of Preliminary Agreements

A typical preliminary agreement would include the following items:

- the parties' details;
- a description of the property;
- the sale price;
- payment of the initial deposit, normally one percent of the purchase price;
- payment of the main deposit, usually nine percent of the purchase price which, when combined with the initial deposit, will equal 10 percent of the purchase price;
- payment of the residue of the purchase price and completion date;
- the date for signing the formal sale and purchase agreement;
- payment of incidental expenses of the conveyance and stamp duty;
- the purchaser's liability on failure to perform the agreement;
- the vendor's right to withdraw upon payment of a liquidated sum to the purchaser;[346] and,
- payment of the estate agent's commission.

At times, a provisional agreement's contents, *i.e.*, the terms or words used, raise the issue of whether the parties intend to be legally bound by the document.

344. *Chan Yiu-ming v L & D Associates* [1992] HKDCLR 1.
345. *But Chung Yin v Billion Extension Development Ltd* [1997] 1 HKC 531.
346. The *BLIS Glossary*, *supra* note 7, translates "liquidated sum" as 經算定款項.

iii. Enforceability of Preliminary Agreements

An important issue concerning preliminary agreements is their legality. The status of the preliminary agreement as a legally enforceable contract is disputed where market conditions might cause one of the parties to wish to withdraw from the agreement. As an illustration, if the property market rises, the vendor might wish to resile from the agreement in order to obtain a higher price for the property. If the property market falls, the purchaser might wish to withdraw from the agreement as the property would be worth less than the purchase price. Most preliminary agreements are drafted allowing the vendor to withdraw from the agreement upon payment of a sum as liquidated damages. In most standard form preliminary agreements, there will be no such provision in favour of the purchaser.

Whether a preliminary agreement constitutes a legally binding agreement is dependent upon the parties' intention as evinced by the agreement's terms. The issue is whether the execution of a formal agreement is a precondition before the parties become legally bound; or, whether execution of the formal agreement is the method by which the preliminary agreement, which already binds the parties, will be performed.

> The question whether parties have entered into contractual relationships with each other essentially depends upon the proper understanding of the expressions they have employed in communicating with each other, considered against the background of the circumstances in which they have been negotiating ... Where they have expressed themselves in writing, the proper construction of the writing against that background will answer the question. The purpose of the consideration is to determine whether the parties intend presently to be bound to each other or whether ... they do not so intend until the occurrence of some further event, including the signature of some further document or the making of some further arrangement. The question is one as to expressed intention and is not to be answered by the presence or absence of any particular form of words.[347]

If the signed preliminary agreement states that "the vendor agrees to sell and the purchaser agrees to buy," the agreement is likely to be binding. In the case of *Yeung Siu Hong v Chan Siu Mee Sandie* [1992] 2 HKC 559

347. *Daiman Development Sdn Bhd v Mathew Chin Teck* [1981] 1 MLJ 56, 58; cited with approval in *Lam Tam Yi v Chak Wai Man* [1993] 1 HKC 537, 541.
See also the case of *Kwan Lai Kit Eddie v Leung Muk Lan*, unreported, (2000) HCA 2179/1998; Goo & Lee, *supra* note 24, Chapter 2 at section 1 ("Stage One: Pre-formal Contract").

the court interpreted a preliminary agreement omitting this phrase to be an "agreement to agree" rather than as a binding agreement.

Branca v Cobarro [1947] 2 All ER 101 is a case where the language in the agreement provided that "this is a provisional agreement until a fully legalized agreement drawn up by a solicitor and embodying all the conditions herein stated is signed." There was a provision requiring payment of a deposit. The court determined the agreement to be legally binding, noting that the required payment indicated the intent to be legally bound.

The case of *Chan Yock Kwong v Wong Hee Mao* [1962] HKLR 480 involved a Chinese language agreement providing that the formal agreement was to be executed within one week and that the purchaser was to pay a deposit upon signing this document. The agreement also provided that if the purchaser defaulted, the deposit would be forfeited. Should the vendor default, twice the amount of the deposit is to be paid as compensation to the purchaser. The court stated:

> both the parties were clearly determined to hold themselves … bound, but realized the desirability of a formal document … it was a provisional agreement to last until superseded by the formal agreement … [The clauses] contained provision for the manner in which the transaction, already agreed was to go through, and they do not … suggest that the fully legalized agreement is in any sense to be a condition to be fulfilled before the parties are bound. … the full terms of the transaction were agreed … which agreed terms were to be reduced into a more formal shape, and it is to be noted that the parties themselves admitted that the agreement accurately set out what they agreed … as the formal agreement, which was to supersede the present agreement, has never been signed, the present agreement remains operative … it is a binding contract.[348]

Chinese-language agreements, often headed *lum see hip yee* or *lum see* (臨時協議或臨時), have also raised similar difficulties in interpretation. The courts have applied the same criteria—determining the parties' intentions—to these agreements as to preliminary agreements. In *Lam Wa Leung v So Chung Shek* [1983] 2 HKC 630 the court interpreted the term *lum see* as meaning temporary or provisional; yet the court held that entitling or naming an agreement as *lum see* would not automatically preclude a legally binding agreement. In another case, *Lam Mean-soon v Luk Fuk Enterprises Ltd* [1980] HKLR 741, the court found a *lum see* agreement to be binding,

348. [1962] HKLR at 492.

where the translation stated, "This order is only of a temporary nature. Both parties must attend and sign a separate formal Sale and Purchase Agreement." The judge stated that the court:

> should not rivet its attention on one word and determine the nature of the document on that word alone, but that no matter how unambiguous that word may be when used in isolation, it should regard the whole document so as to see the context in which the word was used and thence to perceive the intention of the parties.[349]

Thus, the same test of intention will apply to *lum see* agreements as to other preliminary agreements.

If the preliminary agreement is not binding, the purchaser will be entitled to the return of the deposit. If the preliminary agreement is binding, the general principle is that the initial deposit will be returned to the purchaser if the agreement is not completed, unless there is a contrary provision in the preliminary agreement. A vendor should ensure a provision in the preliminary agreement for forfeiture of the deposit in the event of breach by the purchaser. The deposit may not be forfeited if the forfeiture is a penalty rather than a genuine pre-estimate of loss.

A conditional agreement expressly states that it is "subject to" or "conditional upon" a particular event, *e.g.*, subject to contract or subject to the securing of a mortgage. If the condition is a condition precedent, there will be no binding agreement until the condition is fulfilled, *e.g.*, the contract is signed or the mortgage secured.[350] If the condition precedent is too vague, the agreement might be void for uncertainty. This would be the case where the contract's validity is premised upon the condition precedent. Thus if the condition precedent is void, the contract does not come into effect.[351]

Additionally, a general principle holds that a conditional contract is not binding until the condition precedent is fulfilled. In *Lung Yuk-lun v Gratefulfit Industrial Ltd* [1992] 1 HKLR 1 the mortgagee's consent to the

349. [1980] HKLR at 746.

350. In *Regal Success Venture Ltd v Jonlin Ltd* [2000] 2 HKC 199, CA; on appeal [2000] 4 HKC 143, CFA a clause in the sale and purchase agreement stipulated that the vendors must show good title to the satisfaction of specified solicitors, failing which the purchasers could terminate the agreement. The court held that the agreement was a conditional contract.

351. In *Lee-Parker v Izzet* [1972] 1 WLR 775 the agreement was "subject to the purchaser obtaining a satisfactory mortgage." The court determined the phrase to be a condition. However, the condition was void because it was too vague to be enforceable. As the phrase was considered to be a condition precedent, the uncertainty destroyed not only this clause but the whole contract which was premised upon this clause. *Id.* at 779–780.

sale of the realty was a condition precedent. The vendor failed to obtain the mortgagee's consent. Consequently, the court held the agreement to be unenforceable by the purchaser, even though the purchaser was prepared to redeem the equitable mortgage and such preparedness would have ensured that the lender would have given its consent.[352]

Another general principle is that the phrase "subject to contract" in a preliminary agreement constitutes a condition precedent. The parties will not be bound until the formal agreement has been signed. However, there are two exceptions to this general rule.

The first exception is where the words are determined to be meaningless in the context of the agreement or in the factual situation. For example, where the parties are already bound by a preliminary agreement and the term "subject to contract" is used in subsequent correspondence, the words will have no meaning or effect in the context of the agreement.[353] The term might also be ineffective in the factual circumstances. For example, in a case involving a tender, the letter of acceptance incorporated the term "subject to contract". The court determined these words to be meaningless as all the agreement's terms were already contained in the documents.[354]

The second exception to the general rule is where the parties to the agreement have subsequently waived the effect of the term "subject to contract". The Court of Appeal held in *Law v Jones* [1973] 2 All ER 437 that the parties could subsequently agree to waive the "subject to contract" provision and thereby create a binding contract. The court in *Cohen v Nessdale Ltd* [1981] 3 All ER 118 recognized that this exception could apply in a limited number of cases and that the waiver could be either expressed or implied from the parties' conduct.

Occasionally, parties fail to agree upon the terms of the formal sale and purchase agreement after entering into a binding preliminary agreement or an "open contract", which is a contract containing only the essential terms: parties, property and price. The parties therefore proceed upon the basis

352. [1992] 1 HKLR 1, 3.

353. *Au Wing Cheung v Roseric Ltd* [1992] 1 HKC 149, CA involved a concluded preliminary agreement. Subsequent correspondence concerning the anticipated formal sale and purchase agreement contained the heading "Subject to contract." The court held that the letter had no legal effect upon the already binding preliminary agreement.

354. *Michael Richards Properties Ltd v Corporation of Wardens of St Saviour's Parish, Southwark* [1975] 3 All ER 416. *Hong Kong Housing Authority v Hung Pui* [1987] 3 HKC 495 (rent was already agreed upon and the lease was already binding before the "subject to contract" letter was sent).

of either the preliminary agreement or the open contract. The courts will imply all the necessary terms in order to implement the agreement.[355]

For example, courts have implied the following terms:

- that the vendor will assign its full interest in the property;
- that the vendor will show and give good title to the property;
- that the subject property will be free from encumbrances except for those specifically set out in the contract;
- that time is of the essence for the completion of the contract;
- that completion will be effected within a reasonable time of the vendor showing good title in instances where no date for completion of the contract is specified;
- that the purchaser has the right to inspect the property prior to completion;
- that the purchaser may raise requisitions on title within a reasonable time after the receipt of the title documents;[356]
- that the vendor will give a good title in the assignment;[357]
- that the vendor will give vacant possession upon completion; and,
- that the vendor will deliver all relevant title deeds relating exclusively to the property to be assigned to the purchaser upon completion.

Because the parties are legally bound by the preliminary agreement, insertion of clauses in the formal sale and purchase agreement which are

355. The courts have approved this principle. *See Link Brain Ltd v Fujian Finance Co Ltd* [1990] 2 HKLR 353; *Yiu Yau-ping v Fong Yee-lan* [1992] 2 HKLR 167; *Liverpool City Council v Irwin* [1977] AC 239. *See also* 16 HALSBURY'S, *supra* note 29, at para. 230.195.

356. LEXISNEXIS, *supra* note 123, at 1632 translates "requisition on title" as 業權要求.

357. For a discussion of the covenants for title, *see* 16 HALSBURY'S, *supra* note 29, at paras. 230.361–230.369. For example, *id.* at para. 230.367 notes that:

> The implied covenant for quiet enjoyment is that the land may be quietly entered into and during the residue of the term of years created by the Government lease, and any renewal of it, be held and enjoyed by the purchaser and any person deriving title under him without any lawful interruption or disturbance. Such a covenant for quiet enjoyment limited to lawful disturbance by the covenantor or any other person for whose acts or omissions he is responsible is not broken by claims under title paramount to that of the covenantor, or by tortious acts other than those of the covenantor himself. Since the covenant is a future covenant, the damages seem to be measured by the loss to the covenantee when the disturbance takes place.

See also SIHOMBING, STUDENT'S GUIDE, *supra* note 106, at 530–533 ("Duty to Show Title"), 758–759 ("Breach"); SIHOMBING, HK CONVEYANCING, *supra* note 257, vol. 1(A), Chapter V, at paras. 4–16. As Romer LJ stated in *Timmins v Moreland Street Property Co Ltd* [1958] 1 Ch 110, 132: "If no interest is mentioned [in the memorandum of agreement], then prima facie an unencumbered freehold interest will be implied."

inconsistent with the terms of the preliminary agreement requires the other party's consent. A court stated this principle thus:

> Where a party presses for a term which does not properly ... reflect a provision as agreed as part of the provisional agreement ... [and] where the other party rejects inclusion of that term, then it is clear that the original party is able to fall back upon the provisional agreement and enforce it as an open contract ... The intended subsequent agreement was to make formal and express what had been informal and perhaps only implied. Failure to achieve the desired formality does not affect the contractual rights and obligations already in place by virtue of the underlying provisional agreement.[358]

Another court reached the same conclusion where the vendor sought to impose restrictions in the formal sale and purchase agreement upon the purchaser's right to raise requisitions on title.[359] The same principle applies to the inclusion of new terms by the purchaser.[360] The courts will allow those terms or conditions which would be implied into an open contract to be included in the formal agreement.

C. The Formal Sale and Purchase Agreement

The formal sale and purchase agreement supplants the preliminary agreement. The formal sale and purchase agreement contains the detailed

358. *Chu Wing Nin v Ngan Hing Cheung*, unreported, (1992) HCA 9409/1991.
See also the case of *Walford v Miles* [1992] 2 AC 128. The Miles owned a photograph processing business which they wished to sell along with the business premises. The Miles and Walford entered into negotiations for the purchase of the property. The main terms of the sale and purchase agreement had been agreed. There was an alleged collateral "lock-out" agreement concluded 18 March between the parties that the Miles would terminate negotiations with any other potential purchasers, even if they had received a satisfactory proposal from any third party before the deadline, they would not deal with that party or give further consideration to any alternative.
The trial court found in favour of Walford's claims of repudiation of the contract and misrepresentation, concluding that the March 18th agreement was an enforceable collateral agreement to the main contract for the sale of the business and business realty. On appeal, a majority of the court held that the March 18th agreement was no more than an agreement to negotiate and thus unenforceable. A further appeal to the House of Lords re-affirmed the principle that a contract to negotiate is unenforceable because, like an agreement to agree, it lacks the necessary certainty: the March 18th agreement did not specify the time period the vendor was to abstain from negotiations with other parties so the agreement was also uncertain in that respect.

359. *Keung Shiu Tang v DH Shuttlecocks Ltd* [1994] 1 HKC 286, CA. *See generally* Goo & Lee, *supra* note 24, Chapter 2 at section 2 ("Stage Two: Contract").

360. *Mak Lai Man v Lam Siu Yiu Peter* [1993] 1 HKC 452.

provisions governing the sale. Only provisions consistent with the terms of the binding preliminary agreement may be inserted in the formal sale and purchase agreement unless the other party consents to the inclusion of other provisions.

i. *Generally*

In cases where the parties have separate legal representation, the agreement is drafted by the solicitor for the vendor and approved by the solicitor for the purchaser. Joint representation of parties to a conveyancing transaction by a solicitor is generally prohibited because of the potential conflict of interest. However, there are exceptions to this general prohibition. Rule 5C of the Solicitors' Practice Rules provides that a solicitor may not represent more than one party to a conveyancing transaction except:

- where the Consent Scheme applies and its regulations are followed, *e.g.*, use of the prescribed sale and purchase agreement;
- where the Non-Consent Scheme applies and its regulations are followed, *e.g.*, inclusion of the prescribed mandatory terms in the sale and purchase agreement;
- where there is a first sale of a completed development, provided the mandatory agreement is used;
- where there is a sub-sale in any of the above three situations. *i.e.*, a confirmatory sale;
- where the parties are associated parties;
- where the consideration is less than $1 million;
- where mortgages are involved; and,
- where leases are involved.[361]

The form of the formal sale and purchase agreement may be:

- in the standard form required for agreements made concerning sales of realty governed by the Consent Scheme;
- in the standard form and containing the mandatory clauses prescribed for agreements made in relation to sales of realty governed by the Non-Consent Scheme;

361. The Law of Society of Hong Kong, *The Hong Kong Solicitors' Guide to Professional Conduct*, Vol. 2 *Solicitors' Practice Rules*. Rule 5C may be found at: *http://www.hklawsoc.org.hk/pub_e/professionalguide/volume2/default.asp?cap=18#5C* (last visited 26 Feb. 2011).

- in the approved form and containing the prescribed clauses required for first sales of property where the parties are jointly represented;
- in the approved form and containing the mandatory clauses in respect of a sub-sale of property in the above three cases where there is joint representation of the parties;
- in compliance with Form 2 of the Third Schedule of the *Conveyancing and Property Ordinance*; the parties may choose to incorporate by reference the clauses set out in Part A of the Second Schedule to the Ordinance[362] (This form and the incorporated clauses may be varied or amended by agreement of the parties.); or,
- in the form and with the contents decided upon by the parties and their solicitors.

ii. The Contents of the Sale and Purchase Agreement

This section reviews the terms and conditions of a sale and purchase agreement. The sale and purchase agreement selected for this discussion is Form 2, set out in the Third Schedule to the *Conveyancing and Property Ordinance*. This document is titled "Agreement for Sale of a Residential, Commercial, Industrial or Other Unit in a Completed Building" (hereinafter referred to as the "Form"). This agreement is in two parts: the terms or the conditions of the agreement and a Schedule containing the property description. Identified below and briefly discussed are some of the more common clauses found in the Form.

Also noted and reviewed below is the document titled "Covenants and Conditions Which May Be Incorporated by Reference", which is set out in Part A of the Second Schedule of the *Conveyancing and Property Ordinance* (hereinafter referred to as "Part A"). Section 36 of the Ordinance provides that the terms in Part A may be incorporated into the parties' agreement. Consequently, the conditions will not apply to the parties unless they have expressly incorporated the terms in full or in part.

Clause 1 of the Form is the agreement by the vendor to sell and the purchaser to buy the property described in the Schedule and the interest therein to be sold. Clause 1 states:

---

362. *Conveyancing and Property Ordinance*, *supra* note 43, at section 36 provides: "The covenants and conditions mentioned in the Second Schedule, or any of them, may be incorporated into any instrument by reference."

> The Vendor sells and the Purchaser purchases the land described in the Schedule hereto ("the Property") for the residue of the term of years created by the Government lease referred to in the Schedule.

This language is appropriately used where the vendor holds the legal estate and is conveying the same to the purchaser. If the vendor holds an equitable estate, the vendor can only sell what it has: the equitable interest.[363] In this instance, the wording should be:

> The Vendor sells and the Purchaser purchases all the former's estate, right and interest in the land described in the Schedule hereto ("the Property").

Clauses 2 and 3 of the Form pertain to the sales price, the deposit and its disposition. The purchase price, stated in Clause 2, is usually payable in three stages. The first stage is the initial deposit, usually one percent of the purchase price payable upon signing the preliminary agreement. The second stage is the main deposit, normally 10 percent of the purchase price payable on signing the formal sale and purchase agreement. This amount is reduced to nine percent if the initial one percent deposit has already been paid at the signing of the preliminary agreement. The third stage involves payment of the remainder of the purchase price on completion.

Pursuant to Clause 3 of the Form, the main deposit is to be paid to the vendor's solicitor, not as agent for the vendor, but as stakeholder. The purpose is to safeguard the deposit money. Should the vendor's solicitor receive the purchaser's deposit, as agent for the vendor, the vendor can require its agent, *i.e.*, the vendor's solicitor, to pay the deposit over to the vendor:

> The task of a stakeholder, when paid a deposit by the parties to a contract for the sale of property ... is to hold the stake upon the happening of the events that are specified in the contract. Thus, if in due course the sale of the property is completed or for any reason the deposit is forfeited, it would be his duty to pay over that money to the vendor. Alternatively, if for any other reason the sale is not proceeded with, he must pay the money to the original depositor, that is to say the purchaser.[364]

363. For a discussion of equitable estates, *see, e.g.*, SIHOMBING, STUDENT'S GUIDE, *supra* note 106, at 127–131.

364. *Rockeagle Ltd v Alsop Wilkinson* [1991] 3 WLR 573, 577–578.
Clause 13 of Part A of the Second Schedule provides, in relation to payment of the remainder of the purchase price:

Failure by the purchaser to pay the deposit will entitle the vendor to cancel the contract and sue for damages.

Clause 4 of the Form provides for completion and payment of the remainder of the purchase price. Matters relating to completion, *e.g.*, apportionment of expenses, rents and outgoings, are found in Part A. Clause 4 of the Form provides for completion in person, known as "formal completion". Completion in person occurs where the vendor, purchaser and their solicitors, and in appropriate situations, the solicitor of the parties' mortgagees, meet together in the vendor's solicitor's office. There, the vendor executes the assignment in the presence of the purchaser and receives the remainder of the purchase price. Instances of formal completion are rare in Hong Kong. More commonly, completion is accomplished by "undertaking". The parties' agreement to completion by undertaking must be expressed in the sale and purchase agreement, as the right to complete by undertaking will not be implied by the courts.

Clause 1 of Part A provides:

> The rents and profits shall be received and all outgoings shall be discharged by the vendor up to and inclusive of the actual day of completion, and as from but exclusive of that day all outgoings shall be discharged by the purchaser. All such rents, profits and outgoings shall, if necessary, be apportioned between the vendor and the purchaser and paid on completion.

This provision stipulates that outgoing items, *e.g.*, Government rent, rates, management fees, electricity, water and telephone rental charges, will be paid by the vendor up to and including the day of completion and all subsequent charges shall be the purchaser's responsibility. The vendor, as a rule, sends the purchaser a completion statement identifying these charges and their apportionment. The purchaser typically pays what is owed to the vendor at the date of completion.

> (1) The vendor's solicitors are the vendor's agents for the purposes of the receipt of any money due under this agreement and any payment made under the agreement to the vendor's solicitors shall be a full and sufficient discharge of the purchaser's obligation in respect of that payment.

Under this condition, the vendor's solicitor receives the remainder of the purchase price as the vendor's agent, rather than as a stakeholder. Again, this is intended to protect the purchaser. If the purchase money is paid to a solicitor who absconds with the funds, the money must be paid again by the purchaser if the solicitor were acting either as the purchaser's agent or as a stakeholder. If the solicitor acts as the vendor's agent, the funds are deemed to have been received by the vendor, and the purchaser will not have to pay the purchase money again. *Edward Wong Finance Co Ltd v Johnson, Stokes and Master* [1984] AC 296.

The parties should agree and stipulate the method of payment of the remainder of the purchase price, *e.g.*, by cashier order or bank certified cheque. Absent an express agreement to the contrary, payment by personal cheque is unacceptable.

Clause 5 of Part A governs conveyances subject to tenants. A vendor generally will give vacant possession of the subject realty. If the premises are sold subject to a tenant, reference should be made to Part A's Clause 5. Vacant possession is interpreted to mean that there are no occupants of the property from whom the purchaser has to recover possession; and, that there is no physical impediment left in or on the premises which might interfere with the purchaser's enjoyment of the property.[365] The purchaser should also seek an express provision by the vendor that no third party interests exist in the property, *e.g.*, tenant's or other occupier's interests.

Clause 6 of the Form provides that: "Time shall in every respect be of the essence of this Agreement." Should a party desire time to be of the essence, this provision should be inserted into the agreement. Inclusion of this

---

365. In *Prime Win Enterprises Ltd v Nova Management Consultants* [2004] 2 HKC 587 the parties agreed to a break lease and the landlord had inspected the empty premises. However, the tenant failed to surrender the keys to the premises to the landlord after the inspection; rather, the tenant gave the keys to the management office which did not return the keys to the landlord for approximately six months. The court found the tenant liable for the rent for this six-month period as the landlord did not have control or vacant possession of the premises without the keys thereto. In *Wealthy China Trading Ltd v Huie Man Kit* [1999] 3 HKC 832 the court found that a shop attached to an outside wall would affect the purchaser's use of the exterior wall; therefore, the vendor had failed to deliver vacant possession. However, a small amount of chattels left behind would come within the *de minimis* rule according to the court in *Grandwide Ltd v Bonaventure Textiles Ltd* [1990] 2 HKC 154.

See also 16 HALSBURY'S, *supra* note 29, at para. 230.225, which states that:

> … the property is sold with vacant possession. If no tenancies are disclosed and no statement is made as to possession, the implication is that the purchaser is to have vacant possession except in the case of the completion of a sub-sale in a confirmation transaction.

A confirmation transaction:

> occurs where the vendor sells to a purchaser under a Sale and Purchase Agreement (SPA), and prior to completion the purchaser sells on to a sub-purchaser under a Sub-Sale and Purchase Agreement (SSPA). The SSPA is usually completed prior to the SPA, with the result that the purchaser is unable to give vacant possession until he receives it from the head vendor on completion of the SPA …

Id. at n. 2.

Confirmation sales are discussed in further detail *infra* Section X.B.

provision in a formal sale and purchase agreement is important in relation to the purchaser's obligation to complete in a timely manner. The vendor can consider any delay by the purchaser as repudiation of the agreement and the deposit can be forfeited.[366]

If the parties agree that completion shall take place on or by a certain date, the midnight rule will apply—the parties have until midnight on the specified date to accomplish completion. No latitude will be afforded, however, where the parties have specified in the agreement the precise time by which completion must take place.

> When the parties appoint a specific time by which acts are to be performed, they have said by implication that those acts cannot be performed beyond that time, in accordance with the contract.[367]

Clause 8 of Part A provides:

> Such of the documents of title as relate exclusively to the property the subject of the agreement shall be delivered to the purchaser. All other documents of title in the possession of the vendor shall be retained by the vendor who shall, if so required on completion of the sale, give to the purchaser a covenant for safe custody thereof and for production and delivery of copies thereof, such covenant to be prepared by the purchaser.

If this condition is not included in the sale and purchase agreement, the courts will require the vendor to deliver to the purchaser at completion all the title documents relating exclusively to the property assigned.[368]

Clause 7 of Part A, concerning requisitions on titles,[369] states:

---

366. The *de minimis* rule only applies where time is not made of the essence: *World Ford Development Ltd v Ip Ming Wai* [1993] 1 HKC 98, CA. Note, however, that in the case of *Chong Kai Tai v Lee Gee Kee* [1996] 1 HKC 105, CA; [1997] 1 HKC 359, PC the court held that it will be implied that time of completion is of the essence in Hong Kong conveyancing transactions.
367. *World Ford Development Ltd*, *supra* note 366, at 108.
368. In *Yiu Ping Fong v Lam Lai Hing Lana* [1998] 4 HKC 476 the court held that vendor must explain the reason the original document is unavailable. *See also* the case of *Donpower Trading Ltd v Apexcom Ltd* [2010] 1 HKLRD 915, CA (interpreting the application of sections 13(1) and 13A of the *Conveyancing and Property Ordinance* upon a vendor's obligation to produce title documents and the giving of good title).
369. It is common to include a provision giving the purchaser an express right to raise requisitions. This right will be implied by the courts unless the parties have expressly reserved this right. *Active Keen Industries v Fok Chi Keong* [1994] 2 HKC 67, CA. The term "requisitions" is defined below.

(1) Any requisition or objection in respect of the title shall be delivered in writing to the vendor's solicitors as soon as practicable after delivery of the title deeds and, in any event, not later than 14 days prior to the date of completion.

(2) If the purchaser shall make and insist upon any objection or requisition either as to title or any matter appearing on the title deeds or otherwise which the vendor shall be unable or (on the grounds of difficulty, delay or expense or on any other reasonable grounds) unwilling to remove or comply with, or if the title of the vendor shall be defective, the vendor shall notwithstanding any previous negotiation or litigation be at liberty to annul the sale in which case the purchaser shall be entitled to the return of his deposit but without costs or compensation and, if that return is made within 7 days, without interest.

The first section of this clause provides for the raising of requisitions on title.[370] The time limitation will not prevent the purchaser from raising requisitions as to matters of title of which it was unaware from the title deeds supplied, even after the agreed period has expired if the requisitions go to the root of the vendor's title.[371] Where the purchaser should have known of a title defect from the documents provided, the requisition must be made within the agreed time limit. The purchaser may not, simply because the

---

370. 16 HALSBURY'S, *supra* note 29, at para. 230.209 explains:

> Requisitions are demands or requests made by the purchaser in respect of those matters of concern arising from the title evidenced in the documents produced to the purchaser by the vendor.

See also SIHOMBING, STUDENT'S GUIDE, *supra* note 106, at 531, 699–723; SIHOMBING, HK CONVEYANCING, *supra* note 257, vol. 1(A), Chapter VI, at paras. 319–334; vol. 1(B), Chapter XI, at paras. 3, 109–109.3; vol. 2(D), Chapter VI, at paras. 546–561.

Absent agreement to the contrary as to title, a contract for the sale of land implies an agreement on the part of the vendor to make a good title to the property being sold. Good title is defined as marketable title, a title which at all times and under all circumstances can be forced on an unwilling purchaser. It is generally sufficient good title is proved by the time fixed for completion. 16 HALSBURY'S, *supra* note 29, at para. 230.233.

See also SIHOMBING, STUDENT'S GUIDE, *supra* note 106, Chapters 5 ("Nature of the Title to be Made or Given"), 6 ("Proof of Title"); SIHOMBING, HK CONVEYANCING, *supra* note 257, vol. 1(A), Chapter V, at paras 170–175; 16 HALSBURY'S, *supra* note 29, at paras. 230.237–230.244.

See generally GOO & LEE, *supra* note 24, Chapter 2 at section 3 ("Stage Three: Between Contract and Completion").

371. *See, e.g.*, *Gold Check Investments Ltd v Star Investment Ltd*, unreported, (1992) HCMP 592/1992, a case involving the requisition as to a missing Crown lease; 16 HALSBURY'S, *supra* note 29, at paras. 230.209, 230.243.

16 HALSBURY'S, *supra* note 29, at para. 230.209 states that:

requisition goes to the root of title, raise the requisition later where the defect could have been uncovered within time through due diligence.[372]

The second section allows a vendor to annul the agreement when unable or unwilling on certain specified grounds to give a good title. Four elements are required:

- the purchaser's objection or requisition;
- the vendor's reasonable inability or unwillingness to remove the objection;
- the vendor's communication to the purchaser of this inability or unwillingness; and,
- despite this communication, the purchaser insists upon the objection.[373]

The second section of Clause 7 of Part A cannot be relied upon where a vendor has bad title, or, has acted in bad faith or recklessly in entering the contract. This exception will apply if the vendor knew of the defect when entering the contract.

> The sale and purchase agreement usually provides that any requisition or objection arising on the title is to be made as soon as practicable after delivery [of] the title deeds, and not later than 14 days prior to the date of completion. ... The purchaser is not precluded from making any requisition as to matters subsequently discovered which were not disclosed from the title deeds even if the time has expired. There is no time limit for the making of requisitions on title ... The conditions may also specify a time within which the vendor must reply to the requisitions, and within which the purchaser must make observations on that reply.

16 HALSBURY'S, *supra* note 29, at para. 230.209 n. 5 states in part:

> If a purchaser is not negligent in failing to spot a potential defect in the vendor's title, the requisition is not out of time ... Even if a requisition goes to the root of title, if a purchaser, having used due diligence, is unaware of a potential defect in the vendor's title, the time limit imposed in the agreement does not run ... Requisitions which go to the root of the title can be raised out of time. However, where a purchaser, having used due diligence, should have been aware of a potential title defect, he cannot ... by virtue of the fact that the alleged defect goes to the root of the title, raise the requisition out of time ...

372. *See also* SIHOMBING, STUDENT'S GUIDE, *supra* note 106, at 700–715 (citing *Tread East Ltd v Hillier Development Ltd* [1993] 1 HKC 285, CA); SIHOMBING, HK CONVEYANCING, *supra* note 257, vol. 2(D), Chapter VI, at para. 550.

373. As explained in 16 HALSBURY'S, *supra* note 29, at para. 230.211:

> If the purchaser insists on any requisition or objection as to title which the vendor is unable or on some reasonable ground unwilling to remove or comply with, then, notwithstanding any intermediate negotiation or litigation, or any attempt to remove or comply with the same, the vendor may by notice in writing annul the sale upon returning the deposit, and the purchaser will have to return the title deeds, or certified copies of them, and any other documents furnished to him.

Clause 3 of Part A reinforces the common law principle concerning the condition of the property: "The purchaser purchases with full knowledge of the physical condition of the property and takes it as it stands." Thus, the purchaser bears the risk of the property being defective and requiring repair. The vendor has no obligation to notify the purchaser of known defects.[374]

However, liability might attach where a vendor or its agent misrepresents facts or warrants the condition of the property, in which case the purchaser may recover damages but cannot rescind the contract. Clause 6 of Part A provides, in part, that:

- No error, omission or misstatement herein or in any plan furnished or any statement made in the course of the negotiation leading to the contract shall annul the sale or entitle the purchaser to be discharged from the purchase.
- Any such error, omission or misstatement shown to be material shall entitle the purchaser to proper compensation, provided that the purchaser shall not in any event be entitled to compensation for matters falling within clause 3 or 5(3) hereof.
- No immaterial error, omission or misstatement (including a mistake in any plan furnished for identification only) shall entitle the other party to compensation.
- The *Misrepresentation Ordinance* (Cap 284) applies to this agreement.

A note of caution is provided in *id.* at para. 230.244:

> Some conditions of sale give the vendor the right to rescind the contract in the event of any requisition ... being made which he is unable or unwilling to comply with, and it is ... for the purchaser to take care that he does not, by making a requisition not really essential, run the risk of losing the purchase. More usually the right of rescission is made to arise only when a requisition is persisted in, and the purchaser runs no such risk in making the requisition in the first instance. Requisitions should, however, never be frivolous or unnecessary. They should either call attention to a real or apprehended defect in the title, or ask for relevant information. The vendor cannot rely on the clause if he has no title, or if he acts in bad faith or recklessly.

374. *Id.* at para. 230.227 states:

> The vendor has no obligation to disclose any defect in the habitability or physical condition of the property, whether these defects are patent or, in some cases, latent, and he is not liable for physical defects nor is he obliged to abate the purchase price for any such defects.

Contrast this with the vendor's obligation to disclose all latent title defects. If a vendor:

> wishes to prevent a purchaser from objecting to a defect he must do so in plain terms, stating clearly the exact nature of the defect to which the purchaser is not to make objection.

Id. at para. 230.185.

Clause 11 of the Form provides that the "stamp duty and land registration fees payable on the assignment made pursuant to this Agreement shall be borne by ..." In order to avoid doubt, the parties should unambiguously state in the sale and purchase agreement in what proportions or which party will be responsible for the legal costs, the stamp duty and the registration fees. Responsibility for payment of these fees is subject to negotiation. This is discussed in more detail below.

Legal fees incurred for the drafting and for the approval of a sale and purchase agreement are usually borne by the party incurring the fees, *i.e.*, the vendor pays its own solicitor's fees for drafting the agreement and the purchaser pays its own solicitor's charges for approving the agreement. Legal fees incurred by the purchaser's solicitor for drafting and by the vendor's solicitor for approving the assignment are the responsibility of the purchaser according to the agreement. However, section 34A of the *Conveyancing and Property Ordinance* stipulates that where the parties are separately represented, any term in the sale and purchase agreement requiring the purchaser to pay the vendor's legal costs will be void where:[375]

375. Section 34A of *Conveyancing and Property Ordinance*, *supra* note 43, states in part:

(1) This section applies to an agreement for the sale and purchase of undivided shares in land, together with a right to exclusive occupation of a unit or other interest—
  (a) in an uncompleted development of the land; or
  (b) in a completed development of the land where-
    (i) the vendor is the developer of the whole development; and
    (ii) no assignment of the unit or interest has been executed since the date on which the relevant occupation permit or certificate of compliance was issued in respect of the development.

(2) This section also applies to an agreement for the sub-sale and sub-purchase of undivided shares in land, together with a right to exclusive occupation of a unit or other interest in an uncompleted or completed development referred to in subsection (1), but only where a solicitor or solicitor corporation, or 2 or more solicitors practising in partnership or association, is or are authorized, by or under the Legal Practitioners Ordinance (Cap 159), to act for both the sub-vendor and the sub-purchaser of those undivided shares.

(3) Any provision of an agreement to which this section applies is void in so far as it would, but for this section, have the effect of requiring the purchaser or sub-purchaser of the undivided shares in the relevant land to pay the costs of the vendor or sub-vendor in or in relation to-
  (a) preparing, completing, stamping and registering the agreement; or
  (b) preparing, obtaining approval for and executing any instrument that gives effect to the agreement; or
  (c) preparing and executing any relevant preliminary agreement.

(4) Subsection (3) has effect only where the vendor and purchaser, or the sub-vendor and sub-purchaser, under the agreement have separate legal representation.

...

- the sale of a flat is in an uncompleted development;
- the first sale of a flat is in a completed development by the developer; or,
- there is a sub-sale of the flat in either of the above situations.

A purchaser might consider including the following terms in the sale and purchase agreement concerning the property's condition and the enjoyment thereof:

- there are no illegal structures on the premises and that any structure in or on the premises has been erected in accordance with the *Buildings Ordinance* (Cap 123) and regulations made thereunder;[376]
- the vendor has received no notice requiring the demolition, repair or reinstatement of the premises or the surrounding slopes;
- the vendor has received no notice from the co-owners or manager of the building to carry out repairs or improvements of a substantial nature to the common parts of the building; and,
- the vendor has received no notice under the *Lands Resumption Ordinance* (Cap 124) or any similar notice relating to the resumption of the property.

If the purchaser wishes to gain access to the premises before the completion date for purposes such as renovation or decoration, the parties should make express provision in the agreement and the purchaser should be permitted to enter as a licensee. The agreement should provide for:

- the purchaser to observe the covenants and conditions in the Government lease and in the deed of mutual covenant;
- the purchaser to pay the outgoings for this period; and,
- the purchaser to indemnify the vendor in respect of any liability the vendor might suffer as a result of this early occupation.

The purchaser should also consider including a related clause that early entry or use of the premises does not imply acceptance of the title.

A vendor is entitled to recover the management deposit paid pursuant to the deed of mutual covenant. The parties might agree that the purchaser repays the management deposit to the vendor and the vendor agrees to ensure that the manager will repay the deposit to the purchaser when the

376. Some cases have decided that illegal structures made the vendor incapable of giving good title. *See Giant River Ltd v Asie Marketing Ltd* [1990] 1 HKLR 297; *Homyip Investment Ltd v Chu Kang Ming Trade Development Co Ltd* [1995] 2 HKC 458. *See also Chi Kit Co Ltd v Lucky Health International Enterprise Ltd* [2000] 3 HKC 143, CFA, where the property was encumbered by the obligation of the Owners' Incorporation to pay a portion of the damages in a negligence action.

purchaser sells the property. In such an agreement, a purchaser is at risk as the covenant to repay the management fees is a personal one. If the vendor or the mortgagee conveys the premises to a third party, the purchaser will be unable compel that third party, as the successor in title to the covenantor, to refund the management fees.[377]

A sale and purchase agreement should address the matter of fixtures and fittings. Fixtures and fittings to be conveyed as part of the property should be specified in a separate schedule to the agreement. As fixtures pass with the land, theoretically fixtures need not be listed separately. However, in order to avoid a dispute as to whether an item is a fixture, the parties should make provision for the item to be included as part of the sale. As fittings are not considered to be part of the land, they are thus not subject to stamp duty. Therefore, the sale of fittings would best be included in a separate clause or schedule in the sale and purchase agreement which would include a separate consideration for the fittings. The vendor should warrant that the fittings are not subject to claims by other parties.

To ensure a seamless transaction, a purchaser should include in the sale and purchase agreement the right to inspect the property prior to completion. Although this is an implied contractual right, an expressed provision to this effect should be considered for inclusion in the agreement.

Stamp duty is paid on the sale and purchase agreement for residential property. The *Stamp Duty Ordinance* (Cap 117), section 29B(5) provides, in part, that the following information be provided in all sale and purchase agreements:[378]

---

377. *Crocodile Garments Ltd v Prudential Enterprise Ltd* [1989] 1 HKC 474 (assignee from covenantor not liable to repay deposit); *Hua Chiao Commercial Bank Ltd v Chiaphua Industries Ltd* [1987] All ER 1110, PC (mortgagee not liable to repay deposit).

378. Section 29B(5) of the *Stamp Duty Ordinance*, *supra* note 95, states in part:

> (5) The following matters are specified for the purposes of subsection (1)—
> (a) the name and address of the vendor and of the purchaser of the immovable property;
> (b) if the vendor or purchaser is an individual, his identification number;
> (c) if the vendor or purchaser is not an individual but is registered under the Business Registration Ordinance (Cap 310), the business registration number of the vendor or purchaser;
> (d) the description and location of the immovable property;
> (e) a statement as to whether the immovable property is residential property or non-residential property, within the meanings of section 29A(1);
> (f) the date on which the agreement for sale was made;
> (g) if the agreement for sale was preceded by an unwritten sale agreement, or an agreement for sale, made between the same parties and on the same terms, the date on which the first such agreement was made;

- whether the property is residential or non-residential;
- that the agreed consideration is set out in the agreement;
- that the completion date, if available, be stated in the agreement; and
- that any other payments made in respect of the sale are set out in the agreement, *e.g.*, commissions to estate agents.

The parties should agree expressly as to the available remedies in the event of a breach of the sale and purchase agreement. Clause 10 of Part A pertains to a purchaser's default and provides in part:

> If the purchaser shall fail to comply with any of the terms and conditions of the agreement the deposit money shall be absolutely forfeited as and for liquidated damages (and not as a penalty) to the vendor who may (without being obliged to tender an assignment to the purchaser) rescind the agreement and either retain the property the subject of the agreement ... or resell the same ... Any deficiency arising from such resale and all expenses attending the same ... shall be made good and paid by the purchaser ...

This clause provides that breach by the purchaser would result in forfeiture of the deposit to the vendor and possible liability for any difference, *i.e.*, any loss in the subsequent re-sale of the property to another party. Unless justified as a genuine pre-estimate of loss, the forfeiture of a deposit would be considered as an unlawful penalty.[379] The conventional deposit of 10 percent of the purchase price, however, will be subject to forfeiture upon

---

> (h) a statement as to whether or not a date has been agreed for a conveyance on sale pursuant to the agreement for sale and, if so, that date;
> (i) a statement as to whether or not there is an agreed consideration for the conveyance on sale that is to, or may, take place pursuant to the agreement for sale and, if so, the amount or value of the consideration;
> (j) the amount or value of any other consideration which each person executing the document knows has been paid or given, or has been agreed to be paid or given, to any person for or in connection with the agreement for sale or any conveyance on sale pursuant to that agreement (excluding legal expenses), together with the name, address, and the identification number or business registration number of each person receiving or to receive such consideration, and a description of the benefit to which the consideration relates;
>
> ...

379. *Workers Trust and Merchant Bank Ltd v Dojap Investments Ltd* [1993] 2 WLR 702, PC. Hong Kong courts approved this decision in *Wan Moon Ling Wandy v Sino Gain Investment Ltd* [1997] 2 HKC 592; *Silverpole Ltd v China Pride Investments Ltd* [1994] 2 HKC 341; *Luen Wai Crane Engineering Co v Ajax Pong Construction Equipment Ltd*, unreported, (1994) HCA 5972/1992; *Dawson Enterprises Ltd v Talisteam Ltd* [1994] 2 HKC 327.

rescission even if there is no evidence that it is a genuine pre-estimate of loss since the deposit serves the purpose of an earnest intention of performance, which was liable to forfeiture on rescission. "There is no principle of law to the effect that a genuine deposit may not be effected by more than one payment."[380] If the amount of the deposit is a conventional sum, its forfeiture has been held by the courts to be justified in the event of the purchaser's breach. Courts:

> will uphold provisions for the forfeiture of a deposit, *inter alia*, where it is shown that the deposit did not exceed a conventional percentage of the purchase price even if it in no way represents a genuine pre-estimate of the vendor's loss.[381]

Clause 11 of Part A pertains to a vendor's default, providing in part:

> In the event of the vendor failing to complete the sale in accordance with the terms of the agreement it shall not be necessary for the purchaser to tender an assignment to the vendor for execution before taking proceedings to enforce specific performance of the agreement or for damages for breach of the agreement.

Clause 12 of Part A provides that the vendor and any other necessary parties will execute a proper assurance to the purchaser, that is, the vendor will convey its interest in the property by the proper and effective means, *i.e.*, an assignment.

D. Remedies

The contractual remedies available to a vendor and purchaser in the event of a breach of contract by the other party include:

- specific performance of the agreement by the breaching party;
- the innocent party may accept the other party's repudiatory breach as discharging the innocent party from future obligations;
- rescission by the innocent party;
- an action for damages; or,
- any remedies expressly provided in the sale and purchase agreement.[382]

---

380. *Wan Moon Ling Wandy v Sino Gain Investment Ltd*, *supra* note 379.
381. *Id.*
382. Only remedies available under contract law are discussed here. Other remedies available for a breach of the sale and purchase agreement may be found in tort law, *e.g.*, misrepresentation or fraud.

i. *Specific Performance*

A contract for the sale of land is specifically enforceable, as land is considered to be unique. Specific performance is available where one party fails to complete by the agreed date regardless whether time is of the essence. Specific performance may also be granted in favour of a sub-purchaser against the vendor even where the original purchaser is uncooperative. Specific performance is a desirable remedy for a vendor where the market is falling or for a purchaser where the market is rising.[383] Note that this remedy is available only where the innocent party is able and willing to fulfil its own obligations under the agreement.[384]

Specific performance is an equitable remedy, thus it is made available to the injured party at the court's discretion. The court may refuse the remedy where:

- the party seeking specific performance has been guilty of delay, *i.e.*, *laches*;
- the contract is void or voidable, *e.g.*, misrepresentation or mis-description is involved;[385]
- specific performance is impossible, *e.g.*, the property has already been assigned to another person who is an innocent third party entering into the contractual relationship;
- prejudice or hardship to third persons are of such a nature as would result in an unjust outcome if specific performance is granted;[386] or,

383. *Wellfit Investments Ltd v Poly Commence Ltd* [1995] 3 HKC 56 (holding that specific performance is an appropriate remedy as, *inter alia*, the property market had risen substantially).

384. An exception to this rule is found in Clause 11 in Part A of the Second Schedule to the *Conveyancing and Property Ordinance*, *supra* note 43, which provides:

> In the event of the vendor failing to complete the sale in accordance with the terms of the agreement it shall not be necessary for the purchaser to tender an assignment to the vendor for execution before taking proceedings to enforce specific performance of the agreement …

385. *See*, *e.g.*, *Charles Hunt, Ltd v Palmer* [1931] All ER Rep 815, where the court refused to grant specific performance in favour of the vendor who had represented the premises as "valuable business premises" when, in fact, there were restrictive covenants that severely restricted the land's use and value. In the case of *Re Puckett and Smith's Contract* [1902] 2 Ch 258, the court refused specific performance on the grounds that the vendor had described the land as suitable for building when there was an underground culvert preventing building on part of the land.

386. In *Chu Kit Yuk v Country Wide Industrial Ltd* [1995] 1 HKC 363, the prospective purchaser sought specific performance but the court determined that the property's subsequent purchaser, had committed considerable sums of money towards the purchase such that specific performance in favour of the prospective purchaser would be unjust to the subsequent purchaser.

- there has been inequitable conduct on the part of the party seeking specific performance, *e.g.*, fraud or undue influence.

The remedy of specific performance can be expressly excluded in the sale and purchase agreement.

ii. Repudiation and Rescission

Where one party commits a repudiatory breach of the contract, the innocent party may consider the repudiation as discharging its contractual obligations. If the innocent party chooses to accept the repudiation, there is no requirement that this acceptance be made within a reasonable time, provided the innocent party shows no signs of continuing with the contract in the interim. In *Cox v Crook* [1981] ICR 823 the court held:

> If one party ... commits a repudiatory breach of contract, the other party ... can choose one of two courses: he can affirm the contract and insist on its further performance or he can accept the repudiation, in which case the contract is at an end. The innocent party must at some stage elect between these two possible courses ... But he is not bound to elect within a reasonable or any other time. Mere delay by itself (unaccompanied by any express or implied affirmation of the contract) does not constitute affirmation of the contract; but if it is prolonged it may be evidence of an implied affirmation ...[387]

In Hong Kong, *Ford Joint Ltd v Keen Lloyd (Holdings) Ltd*, unreported, (1999) HCA 21393/1998 applied this statement of law.

A party accepting the repudiation is discharged from all obligations of further performance under the contract. The injured party may also seek damages. By expressly or impliedly waiving the right to rescind the agreement and thus affirming the contract, the innocent party loses the right to be discharged. For example, in the case of *Hillier Development Ltd v Tread East Ltd* [1993] 1 HKC 285, CA a waiver occurred when the purchaser, despite a defective title, forwarded a draft assignment and inquired of the vendor as to the disposition of the remainder of the purchase price.[388]

The innocent party may rescind the agreement. That party may rescind where the circumstances surrounding the making of the contract would

387. [1981] ICR at 828.

388. *See also Chan Kam Hung v Light Ltd*, unreported, (1993) DCCI 16919/1992 where the purchaser's submission of the engrossed assignment constituted waiver; *Chan Kin Leung v Lok Kar Cheong*, unreported, (1998) HCMP 3993/1997 where waiver was implied from the construction of the text of correspondence between the parties' solicitors.

entitle the innocent party to treat the contract as terminated *ab initio*.[389] For example, where mistake, undue influence or fraud affected at least one party during negotiations leading to the formation of a contract, rescission is possible. To effect rescission, it is essential that the parties can be placed in the same position they were in prior to the making of the contract, in other words *restitutio in integrum* must be possible. Because the parties are returned to the position they were in before the contract came into being, there is no damage and thus there will be no award of damages.

iii. Action to Recover Damages

Damages may be awarded for breach of contract:

- independently of any other remedy;
- in place of or in addition to an order for specific performance; or,
- upon acceptance of the repudiation of the contract by the innocent party.

Damages are not available as a remedy where the innocent party has rescinded the contract.

A purchaser may seek damages for a breach of the sale and purchase agreement while electing to complete the contract. This situation might arise where the property's value is less than the contract price, *e.g.*, as a result of the vendor's misdescription of the realty. In *Watson v Burton* [1957] 1 WLR 19 the court awarded damages because of the vendor's misdescription as to the land's saleable area. In *Citilite Properties Ltd v Innovative Development Co Ltd* [1997] 2 HKC 74 the vendor warranted the property's saleable area to be approximately 1,000 square feet more than it actually was. The court concluded that the claimant did not receive the benefit of its bargain and awarded damages for the diminution in value of the premises.

Section 17 of the *High Court Ordinance* (Cap 4) provides that the court may award damages in addition to or in substitution for the remedies of an injunction or specific performance.[390] Monetary damages, in addition to specific performance, may be awarded where the innocent party has suffered losses which the remedy of specific performance could not compensate, *e.g.*, the purchaser lost rental income for the period completion was delayed.

389. The *BLIS Glossary*, *supra* note 7, translates the term "*ab initio*" as 從一開始.

390. Section 17 of the *High Court Ordinance*, *supra* note 154, states:

> Where the Court of Appeal or the Court of First Instance has jurisdiction to entertain an application for an injunction or specific performance, it may award damages in addition to, or in substitution for, an injunction or specific performance.

Upon the wrongful repudiation by one party, the innocent party may choose to accept the repudiation, rescind the contract and sue for damages. This might be the only remedy available for the injured party if, for whatever reason, specific performance is unavailable.

The innocent party may recover damages in respect of loss that flows from the breach or which was within the knowledge or contemplation of the parties. This principle is stated in the case of *Hadley v Baxendale* (1854) 9 Ex 341:

> [such damages may be recovered] as may fairly and reasonably be considered arising naturally, i.e., according to the usual course of things, from such breach of the contract itself, or such as may reasonably be supposed to have been in the contemplation of both parties, at the time they made the contract as, the probable result of the breach of it.[391]

Victoria Laundry (Windsor) Ltd v Newman Industries Ltd [1949] 2 KB 528 clarified this test: reasonable foreseeability or predictability depends upon the parties' knowledge at the time they enter into the contract. For example, in *Haw Hong International Ltd v Kei Oi Wah Linia* [1990] HKLRD 502, the respondent tenants of the subject property repudiated the agreement. The claimant landlord accepted the repudiation and relet the premises at approximately 30 percent lower rent as a result of the intervening Tiananmen massacre on 4 June 1989 which created uncertain social and economic conditions. In assessing damages to be awarded to the landlord, the court found that the events in Beijing were not totally unpredictable to the public in Hong Kong; and hence, the damages arising therefrom were not too remote.

Should a purchaser fail to complete, the vendor will be able to obtain damages calculated as the difference between the contract price and the market price at the time of the property's resale less any forfeited deposit. Hence, if property market values fall in the interim, damages may be considerable; if the market rises, damages, if any, would be nominal.

The actual sale price is often the best evidence of the market price. As noted in *Hee Tak Lee Co Ltd v Keen Lloyd (Holdings) Ltd*, unreported, HCA 20799/98:

> The price at which the seller has resold is strictly not to be taken in preference to the market price, but it has been taken in most cases on the ground that the resale price affords good evidence of the market [price].

391. (1854) 9 Ex at 354.

The vendor can also recover any costs of the resale. Repair expenses or reinstatement expenses may be recoverable where the purchaser was allowed early occupation and damaged the property. The vendor cannot recover legal costs paid in respect of the aborted transaction or the estate agent's fees paid.[392]

A purchaser may rescind the agreement and seek damages where a vendor commits a breach of the contract, other than by failing to give good title. A purchaser's damages would be the difference between the contract's purchase price and the costs of purchasing a similar property on the open market, *i.e.*, the market value.[393] The court will admit the sale and/or purchase prices of comparable property in order to assist in ascertaining market value. The purchaser may also recover as damages any deposit paid and costs involved in the new purchase.

Certain expenditures will not be recoverable by a purchaser as damages where a vendor breaches the contract other than by failing to provide good title. These unrecoverable expenditures include any stamp duty paid on the sale and purchase agreement,[394] estate agent's fees and legal costs incurred in the failed transaction.

Damages are usually determined or assessed as of the date of the breach. For a vendor, this application will determine the vendor's damages by ascertaining the property's market price at the date of the purchaser's breach. For a purchaser, this application will determine the purchaser's cost of acquiring a similar property in the open market at the time of the vendor's breach.

The exception is where, at the court's discretion, justice requires the amount of damages to be assessed at another time. The date of assessment is important where the property market is experiencing wide fluctuations. Where a vendor is in breach and the market is rising, the purchaser may

---

392. HARVEY MCGREGOR, MCGREGOR ON DAMAGES para. 22–037 (18th ed. 2009):

> These expenses would have been incurred even had the buyer not defaulted: putting the seller into the position he would have been in had the contract been performed still entails his having incurred these expenses.

393. In *Cheng Wai Keung Daniel v Chui Ka Yuen Danny* [1987], unreported, (1987) HCA 3766/1985 the purchaser suffered substantial damages as the contract was on particularly favourable terms, such that the difference between the purchaser's bargain price and market value was greater.

394. The court did not permit the recovery of conveyancing costs or stamp duty.

> [The claimant] cannot not claim the benefit of the bargain, or, rather, the damages awarded to him for the loss of it, and also at the same time claim a refund of the money which he had to pay out by way of stamp duty to achieve the bargain in the first place.

Kwok Chung Hon v Lo On Wa [1996] 4 HKC 191, 196.

be awarded damages assessed at a later date than the date of the breach.[395] Where a purchaser is in breach and the market is falling, damages may be awarded in favour of the vendor as at the date of the actual resale of the property, provided the vendor does not unreasonably delay the sale.[396] Where a vendor fails to mitigate its loss, the courts may decline to award the difference between the contract price and the actual sale price eventually obtained.[397] The courts will also look to a later date than the date of the breach for the assessment of damages where the innocent party attempts, although unsuccessfully, to obtain specific performance of the contract.[398]

Where a vendor is in breach of contract by failing to give good title, the purchaser's damages are limited[399] to recovery of the deposit with interest, conveyancing costs, *e.g.*, fees for approving the sale and purchase agreement, fees for drafting the assignment, and, stamp duty.[400] There are three

395. *See, e.g.*, *Lee Hon Kai v Wellsburg Industrial Ltd*, unreported, (1995) HCA A1485/94 where the court held that the respondent must pay damages to compensate for the increased market value of the property, with the date of valuation based on the time claimant was notified that the sale would not be completed, when the respondent has knowledge that the market is rising and fails to complete a sale.

396. In *Wing Wong Co Ltd v Chui Yuk Ming*, unreported, (1988) HCA 10099/1983 the purchaser defaulted. The court found that the vendor attempted to mitigate the loss by selling the property immediately but was unable to do so for three years. The court assessed damages on the difference between the contract price and the eventual price obtained on sale.

397. The court in *Wing Wong Co Ltd v Chui Yuk Ming*, *supra* note 396, adopted this approach. In *Harmony Fit Co Ltd v Jade Fit Co Ltd*, unreported, (1998) HCA 13040/1997 the purchaser defaulted on the contract and subsequently made a lower offer to be paid three months later. The vendor rejected this offer; however, at the eventual resale, the property realized a lower price than purchaser had offered. The court held that the vendor did not fail to mitigate his losses as he had acted reasonably, not expecting a sudden downturn in the market. Contrast this decision with that of *Kwok Wai Kong v Luk Ping Hung* [1999] HKCU 1273, (1999) HCA 4447/98 where the court assessed damages at the time of the breach rather than at another date because the vendor did not act reasonably, *i.e.*, attempting to sell within a reasonable time.

398. This was the state of affairs in *Yuen Kong Ling Cana v Lai Kam Hon* [1993] 2 HKC 728.

399. *See Bain v Fothergill* (1874) 7 LR 158 which set out this rule. Some judges have stated that this rule does not apply in Hong Kong. *See, e.g.*, *Roseric Ltd v West River Development* [1993] 2 HKC 404; *Lee Siu Wai Florence v Priway Investments Ltd* [1998] 1 HKC 228. Yet, in *Ma Hon Ming v Lee Tsan Sum*, unreported, (2000) HCA 1620/1998 the court applied the *Bain v Fothergill* rule.

> Previously it was thought that the rule in *Bain v Fothergill* ... applied in Hong Kong. However it is now clear that the rule no longer applies, if it ever did. See *Grand Trade Development Ltd v Bonance International Ltd* [2001] 3 HKC 1'37 [*sic*], CA ..."

16 HALSBURY'S, *supra* note 29, at para. 230.312 n. 1.

400. In *Ma Hon Ming v Lee Tsan Sum*, *supra* note 399, the court allowed recovery of the stamp duty but not the real estate agent's commission.

exceptions to the rule. The first exception involves a fraudulent vendor.[401] The second exception involves a defect in title which arose after the execution of the sale and purchase agreement but prior to completion.[402] The third exception is where the vendor has failed to take reasonable steps to remove the defect in title.[403]

iv. *Other Remedies*

The parties may agree the remedies available either in the preliminary agreement or in the formal sale and purchase agreement. If properly worded, these remedies in the event of breach may be exclusive in that other remedies or damages available to the innocent party are excluded. The following terms are commonly found in such agreements.

a. Forfeiture of Deposit

Clause 10 of Part A provides:

> If the purchaser shall fail to comply with any of the terms and conditions of the agreement the deposit money shall be absolutely forfeited as and for liquidated damages (and not as a penalty) to the vendor who may ... rescind the agreement ...

Thus this statutory provision provides for the forfeiture of the deposit to the vendor upon the purchaser's breach.[404] A deposit of 10 percent or less of the agreed purchase price will usually be treated as a genuine pre-estimate of loss. In *Sung Wai Kiu v Wong Mei Yin* [1997] 1 HKC 288 the court found that the forfeiture of a 35 percent deposit to be a penalty. An exception can, however, be found in *Polyset Ltd v Panhandat Ltd* [2000] 4 HKC 203 where

---

401. *Flureau v Thornhill* (1776) Win BI 1078 (purchaser of real estate not entitled to damages for loss of bargain when title is defective and vendor cannot eliminate the defect).
402. *Wroth v Tyler* [1974] Ch 30 (specific performance was an unreasonable remedy when vendor's wife opposed sale, but claimant could recover damages for increased real estate value as a substitute for specific performance).
403. *Malhotra v Choudhury* [1980] Ch 52 (claimant entitled to damages for the value of realty at the time of judgment when respondent does not use best efforts to carry out a contractual promise).
404. The Privy Council in *Workers Trust and Merchant Bank Ltd v Dojap Investments Ltd, supra* note 379, held that forfeiture of a deposit constitutes a penalty unless the forfeiture could be justified as a genuine pre-estimate of loss. This decision has been approved by Hong Kong courts in *Silverpole Ltd v China Pride Investments Ltd, supra* note 379; *Luen Wai Crane Engineering Co v Ajax Pong Construction Equipment Ltd, supra* note 379; *Dawson Enterprises v Talisteam Ltd, supra* note 379.

the court allowed forfeiture of a 35 percent of the purchase price deposit, finding it to be a genuine pre-estimate of loss considering the lengthy period between contract formation and completion as well as the property market's volatile fluctuations.

Another exception concerns confirmors where a sum exceeding 10 percent is considered to be a proper deposit.[405] Generally, forfeiture will depend on the terms in the contract. In *Wan Moon Ling Wandy v Sino Gain Investment Ltd* [1997] 2 HKC 592 the purchaser gave two deposits which together amounted to ten percent of the total price. Upon default, the purchaser claimed that the second payment should not have been forfeited because the second payment was part of the purchase price. The court determined that "both payments were intended to constitute a deposit to secure or guarantee performance of the contract" given the fact that the parties' agreement referred to the first payment as an initial deposit with the second payment described as a "further deposit and part-payment of purchase money."[406]

In the event of the purchaser's breach, the vendor can retain any part payments and the deposit by the purchaser only if the sale and purchase agreement expressly so provides. In the case of *Goldspeed Investment Ltd v Easy Success Enterprises Ltd* [2000] 2 HKC 183 the purchaser paid a HK$2,520,000 deposit along with two instalment payments of HK$2,520,000 each towards the purchase price of HK$25.2 million for a floor of a commercial building under construction. The purchaser failed to complete, resulting in the vendor retaining the monies paid. The purchaser sued for the return of the two instalment payments. The vendor eventually sold the subject premises, its value having fallen to HK$10,200,000 along with another floor for a total of HK$35.3 million. The court held, in relation to the vendor's right to retention of the instalment payments, that:

> payments in the event of determination of the agreement could only have arisen from the terms of the agreement. … [Absent] such term, the defendant [vendor] would not be entitled, on the termination of

405. A confirmation situation arises:

> When the purchaser has disposed of the land before the completion of the contract, it is usual to make the assignment direct to the second purchaser. The original purchaser usually executes the assignment as confirmor. The vendor may assign to the sub-purchaser directly if the purchaser causes the sub-purchaser to repudiate the Sub-Sale and Purchase Agreement, and the sub-purchaser wishes to obtain the land.

16 HALSBURY'S, *supra* note 29, at para. 230.321. Confirmors and confirmations are discussed *infra* note 422 and accompanying main text.

406. [1997] 2 HKC at 599–600.

> the agreement, to retain the part payments as security for any loss it might sustain on a resale.[407]

The court concluded that the subject clause did not entitle the vendor to deduct the unliquidated damages from the part payments; however, the vendor's counterclaim:

> is sufficient to extinguish the plaintiff's [purchaser] claim for return of the part payments ... As against a claim arising out of a transaction between the parties, there could be set-off in equity a cross claim arising under the same transaction whether sounding in debt or unliquidated damages ...[408]

b. Liquidated Damages: Payable by Vendor

Commonly in preliminary agreements, there is a clause allowing the vendor to pay the purchaser twice the initial deposit as liquidated damages should the vendor fail to complete. This clause would also specify that the purchaser shall have no other remedy, either for specific performance or for damages. The courts have held that this clause, if clearly drafted, is enforceable and would thus limit the purchaser to an award of liquidated damages.[409]

The clause will be construed *contra proferentem*.[410] Should a vendor fail to make prompt repayment of the deposit together with an equal sum as stipulated in the agreement, specific performance would remain available to the purchaser. The clause is required expressly to exclude specific performance. The court granted the remedy of specific performance in *Cheung Bing Sum*

---

407. [2000] 2 HKC at 188.

408. *Id.* at 192.

409. *Kentex Investment Ltd v Hui Lap Ping Sam*, unreported, MP 3447/91. In *Wong Lai-fan v Lee Ha* [1992] 1 HKLR 125, 127, CA the term provided:

> Should the Vendor after receiving the initial deposit paid hereunder fail to complete the sale in the manner herein contained the Vendor shall immediately compensate the purchaser with a sum equivalent to the amount of the initial deposit as liquidated damages together with the refund of the initial deposit and the Purchaser shall not take any further action to claim for damages or to enforce specific performance.

The Court of Appeal ruled that the intention of the clause was clear and the purchaser could not enforce the agreement through an action for specific performance. Other courts reached the same conclusion in *Lee Tat Kwong v Choi Pui Kei Stephen* [1991] 2 HKC 109 and in *Cheerup Ltd v Wong Sau Fong* [1996] 4 HKC 92.

410. BLACK'S LAW DICTIONARY, *supra* note 20, at 377, defines this term as "[t]he doctrine that, in interpreting documents, ambiguities are to be construed unfavorably to the drafter." KRISHNAN ARJUNAN & ABDUL MAJID BIN NABI BAKSH, BUSINESS LAW IN HONG KONG (2nd ed. 2009) translates "*contra proferentem*" as 不利於提出合約的一方.

Juana v Lee Leo [1994] 3 HKC 132 where the provision stated, "in the event of breach [the vendor], apart from compensating the deposit in double, shall also be liable for the losses incurred by the purchaser, Mr. Leo Lee."[411] Likewise, in *The Thompsett Mind Ltd v Triumph Field Ltd*, unreported, (1993) HCA 1826/1992 the court allowed specific performance where the clause stated that upon the vendor's failure to complete, the "vendor shall immediately compensate the purchaser with a sum equivalent to the amount of the initial deposit as liquidated damages together with a refund of the initial deposit." The clause did not exclude specific performance.

c. Liquidated Damages: Payable by Purchaser

The parties may agree to the inclusion of a provision in the sale and purchase agreement whereby the purchaser, upon breach, agrees to pay the vendor liquidated damages of the difference between the contract sum and the sum obtained by the vendor upon eventual sale. The Court of Appeal enforced such a clause in *Bestech Development Ltd v Fu Wai Loi*, unreported, (1992) CACV 121/1992 where the court provided that a calculation for damages did not include the expenses arising from the letting of the property prior to resale to another purchaser after the original purchaser's default or the interest paid by the second purchaser for the delay in completion. The court stated:

> On those facts the question for decision on the appeal is this: Is the purchaser entitled to be credited against his liability to the vendor for the deficiency on the resale with the sums received by the vendor which, but for the purchaser's breach of contract in failing to complete the original sale, the vendor would not have received? The answer is that the purchaser is not so entitled. It is clear law that the intention of the parties in the case of liquidated damages is to be implemented by holding the plaintiff entitled to recover the stipulated sum on breach without requiring proof of the actual damage and irrespective of the amount of the actual damage ...[412]

A sale and purchase agreement may contain an agreed stipulation that the purchaser may cancel the agreement by paying double the preliminary deposit. The Court of Appeal upheld such a clause in *Cheong Pik Shan v Lee Bun*, unreported, (1994) HCA 3113/1992.

---

411. [1994] 3 HKC at 139. Affirmed on appeal by the Privy Council on other grounds at [1996] 4 HKC 130.
412. (1992) CACV 121/1992 at 8.

d. Exclusion of Common Law Remedies

Similar to the rules governing exclusion of the remedy of specific performance, common law remedies, *e.g.*, damages, can be excluded by the insertion of an express and clear provision in the sale and purchase agreement. In *Goldspeed Investment Ltd v Easy Success Enterprises Ltd* [2000] 2 HKC 183 the parties had a contractual provision that the purchaser in default should pay any deficiency in the resale price if the premises were resold within six months. The realty was not resold within that time period. The court found that the contractual provision did not displace the common law right to damages.

X. ASSIGNMENT

The function of an assignment is to transfer title from a transferor, *i.e.*, the vendor, to a transferee, *i.e.*, the purchaser. An assignment is given effect by a legal document known as a "deed". The required form of the assignment is determined by whether the transferor possesses a legal or equitable interest in the estate.

A. Formal Requirements and Practices

Section 4(1) of the *Conveyancing and Property Ordinance* provides that a legal estate in land can be created, extinguished or disposed of only by deed.[413] Section 4(2) of the Ordinance provides the exceptions to the general rule found in section 4(1).[414] These exceptions involve the:

- assent by the personal representative(s) of a deceased;
- surrender, *e.g.*, of a lease;

413. In *Wu Koon Tai v Wu Yau Loi* [1995] 2 HKC 732, CA (overruled by the Privy Council on another issue; *see* [1996] 3 WLR 778) the judge found that a purported conveyance written in Chinese and which failed to comply with section 4(1) to be void.

414. Section 4 of the *Conveyancing and Property Ordinance*, *supra* note 43, states in full:

> (1) A legal estate in land may be created, extinguished or disposed of only by deed.
> (2) This section does not apply to—
> (a) an assent in writing by a personal representative;
> (b) a disclaimer made in accordance with section 59 of the Bankruptcy Ordinance (Cap 6) or section 268 of the Companies Ordinance (Cap 32);
> (c) a surrender by operation of law, including a surrender which may, by law, be effected without writing;

- grant, disposal or surrender of lease taking effect in possession for a term not greater than three years at the best rent which can be reasonably obtained; or,
- creation or disposal of a legal estate by operation of law; *e.g.*, a deceased's property vesting in the Official Administrator by operation of law (*Probate and Administration Ordinance* (Cap 10)).

Where an assignment is in writing but does not amount to a deed, the courts may exercise equitable jurisdiction by construing the assignment as a contract to assign.[415] Provided that the contract can be specifically enforced and provided that no discretionary bars preclude such action the assignee could enforce the contract of assignment.[416] Before specific enforcement of the contract, the assignee is regarded as having equitable title to the property.[417]

Section 5(1)(a) of the *Conveyancing and Property Ordinance* states in part, "no equitable interests in land may be created or disposed of except by writing signed by the person ..."[418] The exceptions to this general rule include the following situations:

(d) the grant, disposal or surrender of a lease taking effect in possession for a term not exceeding 3 years (whether or not the lessee is given power to extend the term) at the best rent which can be reasonably obtained without a premium;
(e) other assurances not required by law to be made in writing;
(f) a receipt not required by law to be under seal;
(g) a vesting order or vesting declaration by a court or other competent authority;
(h) a creation, extinguishment or disposal of a legal estate in land by operation of law.

415. The *BLIS Glossary*, *supra* note 7, translates "equitable jurisdiction" as 衡平法司法管轄權.

416. *E.g.*, if the assignee commits a breach or is not willing to perform its obligations. *See* the case of *Parker v Taswell* (1858) 2 De G & J 559. In *Wu Koon Tai v Wu Yau Loi*, *supra* note 413, the parties did not sign the document.

417. *Walsh v Lonsdale* (1882) 21 Ch D 9. This is an operation of the maxim that "equity regards as done that which ought to be done." Thus it is regarded in equity as if a decree of specific performance has already been granted.

418. *See Town Bright Industries Ltd v Bermuda Trust (Hong Kong) Ltd* unreported, (1999) CACV 137/1998 where the court found that:

> It is apparent from these cases that for the purposes of 53(1)(c) of the Law of Property Act, 1925 (on which section 5 of the local Ordinance is based) a [written] direction given to a trustee by a person entitled in equity directing it to hold the trust property in trust for another is a disposition of his equitable interest …

Thus, property held by trustees may be assigned through a written document to the trustees.

- leases for less than three years can be created orally pursuant to section 6(2) of the *Conveyancing and Property Ordinance*;
- possessory titles acquired without any written document;
- the doctrine of part performance might render an oral agreement to sell land enforceable; or,
- proprietary estoppel.

An assignment is usually prepared by the purchaser's solicitor. An exception involves the assignment of a flat in a large development, where all the assignments are usually drafted by the vendor's solicitor to ensure uniformity.[419] A sample form, entitled "Assignment of a Lot or Section of a Lot or of a Residential, Commercial, Industrial or Other Unit in a Completed Building", is provided in Form 1 of the Third Schedule to the *Conveyancing and Property Ordinance*. The use of this form is not mandatory.

The date to be inserted in the assignment should be the deed's delivery date, *i.e.*, the date on which the assignment takes effect as the duty to stamp and register the document runs from the date of the deed.

It is professional misconduct for a solicitor to backdate a deed in order, for example, to avoid the consequences of a subsequent encumbrance such as a charging order. Likewise, it is professional misconduct for a solicitor to postdate the deed in order, for example, to extend the period for stamping and registration.

All the required parties to the transaction must join in the assignment. It is no longer necessary to make successors in title parties to an assignment as section 39(1) of the *Conveyancing and Property Ordinance* states:

> A covenant relating to any land of the covenantee shall be deemed, unless the contrary intention is expressed, to be made with the covenantee and his successors in title and persons deriving title under or through him or them.

Section 40(1) provides the same for the covenantor:

> A covenant relating to any land of a covenantor or capable of being bound by him, shall be deemed, unless the contrary intention is expressed, to be made by the covenantor on behalf of himself, his successors in title and persons deriving title under or through him or them.

---

419. As noted in 16 HALSBURY'S, *supra* note 29, at para. 230.317:

> In general in the absence of agreement to the contrary, the purchaser prepares the draft assignment and submits it to the vendor for approval; however, where the property is contained in a large development it is usual for the vendor-developer's solicitor to prepare a standard form assignment.

A purchaser's failure to execute an assignment pertaining to the sale of realty does not invalidate the document. In *Choi Hung Investment Co Ltd v Chinco Investment Ltd* [1995] 1 HKC 203 the court found that:

> the absence of a valid execution of an assignment by the assignee does not affect title to the property. It might affect the enforceability of the covenants ... but not his title ...[420]

A mortgagor or chargor is a required party to a mortgage or charge. Therefore, this party should execute the documents in order to validate the same. The mortgagee or chargee is a necessary party to the reassignment or to the discharge. Likewise, this party needs to sign in order to have a valid document.

For deeds of gift, the only necessary or required party is the donor, who must execute the deed.

The full names of the parties, both English and Chinese, executing the document should be given together with their Hong Kong identity card numbers and addresses. Depending upon the facts of each case, difficulties might arise over the use of names. In *Tsang Bing Kwan Andes v Korea Marvel Co* [1997] 3 HKC 565 the court noted:

> Amongst those deeds was a confirmation dated 12 October 1996 stating that Korea Marvel Co Ltd had changed its name to Hansol Electronics Inc as of 31 October 1995. ... the confirmation was executed almost a year after the change of name and that notwithstanding the change of name, the provisional agreement was entered into by the vendor under its old name. A requisition was raised, *inter alia*, relating to this change of name. ... The vendor does not only have to make good title at completion but is also under an obligation to show good title by properly answering the requisitions raised by the purchaser at a reasonable time before completion is due to take place.
>
> In the present case, by supplying documents in a foreign language after the close of business on 23 December, the date for completion, the respondent had clearly not discharged its obligations.[421]

The court held that the purchaser could rescind the contract. On the other hand, in *Sunluck International Development Ltd v Hing King Development Ltd*

420. [1995] 1 HKC at 206–207. The principles of the case are limited to its facts as the identification of the purchaser was in issue: this case was distinguished in *Liu Moon Ping v Wong Kwok Tung & OD* DDCJ 1912/2003 (2005).
421. [1997] 3 HKC at 566–567.

[1997] 4 HKC 134 the court held that two errors in the Chinese characters of the vendor's name presented no real risk, on the facts, to the purchaser.

B. Confirmations

A confirmation occurs where the vendor agrees to sell property to $Purchaser_1$ but, before completion, $Purchaser_1$ agrees to sell the same realty to $Purchaser_2$. In this scenario, assignment of the legal estate will be directly from the vendor to $Purchaser_2$. Because $Purchaser_1$ has an equitable interest in the subject property under the sale and purchase agreement, $Purchaser_1$ joins in the assignment in order to confirm conveyance of its equitable interest in the property to $Purchaser_2$. Therefore, the necessary parties are: vendor, confirmor ($Purchaser_1$) and, where covenants are given, the ultimate buyer, $Purchaser_2$.[422]

Note that in order to be an effective confirmation, a corporate confirmor must execute the deed in accordance with its articles of association. In *Qualihold Investments Ltd v Bylax Investments Ltd* [1991] 2 HKC 589 the claimant declined to accept as valid an earlier conveyance of the property

422. Note that the Hong Kong government recently banned the use of certain confirmation sales in an attempt to prevent the formation of a bubble in the property market:

> The Lands Department will disallow confirmor transactions of first-hand uncompleted flats which are granted pre-sale consent by the department on or after today. In other words, purchasers of those flats will not be allowed to re-sell, sub-sell or transfer the benefits of the agreements for sale and purchase before completion of the transaction.

Communication release by Financial Secretary John Tsang on the Hong Kong government's website: *http://www.info.gov.hk/gia/general/201008/13/P201008130227.htm* (last visited 26 Feb. 2011).

For a definition of marketable title, *see* 16 HALSBURY'S, *supra* note 29, at para. 230.233 n. 3. *Id.* at para. 230.262 explains:

> Upon the making of an enforceable contract for sale the purchaser becomes the owner of the land in equity, and can dispose of his beneficial (from the bare trust which comes into existence on the entry into the valid contract for the sale of land) or equitable interest (the interest arising traditionally under a valid contract for the sale of land) to a third person.
>
> It has been common for the purchaser to sub-sell the property prior to completion, and to provide that the sub-sale is to be completed immediately prior to the head sale. In most cases the assignment will be from the vendor to the final purchaser (the sub-purchaser) with the head purchaser (the sub-vendor) executing it as confirmor.

Concerning confirmations *see also* SIHOMBING, STUDENT'S GUIDE, *supra* note 106, at 1118–1120; SIHOMBING, HK CONVEYANCING, *supra* note 257, vol. 1(B), Chapter X, at paras. 64, 67–77; vol. 2(E), Chapter X, at para. 504.

executed by Fullway as a corporate confirmor. The claimant declined to complete the sale on the basis of a defective title. Fullway's corporate memorandum and articles of association provided that every document required to be sealed should be deemed to be properly executed if sealed with the company seal and signed by any two directors or the managing director. Only one director had executed the document on behalf of Fullway and this individual was not the managing director at the time and was not otherwise authorized by a vote of the board of directors to sign the document.[423] The court decided the claimant need not proceed with the purchase of the property as:

- Fullway failed to assign such interest as it had in the property by a duly executed assignment;
- Fullway's purported request and direction to the vendor to assign the property to $Purchaser_2$ was ineffective; and,
- Fullway's purported covenant that it had not created a defect or encumbrance affecting $Purchaser_2$'s title to the property was also ineffective.

C. Nominations

A similar procedure occurs with nominations.[424] A sale and purchase agreement may contain a provision that the vendor agrees to sell to the purchaser

423. The principles of *Qualihold* are very limited today unless the company's articles of association completely exclude the operation of the *Conveyancing and Property Ordinance*, *supra* note 43.

424. Sihombing, HK Conveyancing, *supra* note 257, vol. 2(E), Chapter X, at para. 504 explains:

> Sometimes a purchaser does not intend to become the owner of the land, and, although not purchasing as agent for the intended owner, he will enter into the sale and purchase agreement with the intention that a third party will take the benefit of the assignment. This process is usually referred to as nomination and involves the purchaser nominating a third party as the ultimate party who is to be the assignee ... In general the identity of the purchaser will not be a matter of concern to the vendor, and he will not be able to avoid the contract on the ground that the nominee was not a party to the contract ... The right to nominate does not need to be included as a term of the contract, although there is no reason why such a term should not be included, either to allow a general nomination to any third party, or a specific nomination in favour of a third party named in the sale and purchase agreement. Nomination is sometimes used where the purchaser wishes to retain the beneficial interest in the land for himself but makes use of the trust to distance himself from the legal ownership.

See also 16 Halsbury's, *supra* note 29, at para. 230.320; Sihombing, Student's Guide, *supra* note 106, at 1120–1124; Sihombing, *HK Conveyancing*, *supra* note 257, vol. 1(B), Chapter X, at paras. 64–77.

or to its nominee. The purchaser may then in writing nominate $Purchaser_2$ to take the assignment. The necessary parties to the assignment will thus be the vendor and $Purchaser_2$ if giving any covenants. $Purchaser_1$ should relinquish any interest it may have in the property to ensure that $Purchaser_2$ receives an unencumbered title.

D. Covenants and Obligations

The covenants for title are regulated by section 35(1) of the *Conveyancing and Property Ordinance*.[425] The provisions of the sale and purchase agreement will determine which covenants of title should be incorporated into the assignment. Covenants for title are important because the doctrine of merger provides that the terms of the sale and purchase agreement merge into the conveyance upon execution of the assignment. Under this doctrine,

---

425. Section 35 of the *Conveyancing and Property Ordinance*, *supra* note 43, provides in part:

(1) There shall be implied—
  (a) in any assignment of the whole of the interest in land held under a Government lease, the covenant by a person who assigns, and the covenant by a person to whom an assignment is made, mentioned in Part I of the First Schedule;
  (b) in an assignment to a purchaser for valuable consideration, the covenants, by a person who is expressed to assign as beneficial owner, mentioned in Part II of the First Schedule;
  (c) in an assignment by way of voluntary disposition, the covenant, by a person who is expressed to assign as donor, mentioned in Part III of the First Schedule;
  (d) in any assignment, the covenant, by a person who is expressed to assign as trustee, confirmor, mortgagee, legal chargee, personal representative of a deceased person or under an order of court, mentioned in Part IV of the First Schedule; and
  (e) in a legal charge, the covenants, by a person who is expressed to charge as beneficial owner, mentioned in Part V of the First Schedule.

(1A) The covenants implied under subsection (1)(a) shall be covenants to which section 41 applies.

(1B) The benefit of the covenants implied under this section shall run with the land and shall be enforceable by the covenantee and his successors in title and persons deriving title under or through him or them.

(1C) In paragraphs (a) to (d) of subsection (1), "assignment" (轉讓) does not include a legal charge.

(1D) Unless the contrary intention is expressed, the liability of joint parties to any assignment or legal charge in respect of the covenants mentioned in subsection (1) shall be joint and several.

(2) The covenants implied under this section may be excluded, varied or extended in the assignment or legal charge.

...

in order to survive execution of the assignment, the terms contained in the sale and purchase agreement must be expressly stated in order to provide further protection for the purchaser.

Where a vendor assigns as beneficial owner, the following covenants are incorporated:

(a) that the Government lease is good, valid and subsisting;
(b) that so far as the same relates to the land assigned:
  1. the premium and Government rent have been paid
  2. the covenants, terms and conditions contained in the Government lease and any deed of mutual covenant have been observed and performed up to the date of the assignment;
(c) that the covenantor has good right and title to assign the land free from encumbrances except as specified in the assignment. This covenant replaces the sale and purchase agreement's provision that the vendor will give good title;
(d) that the land may be quietly entered into and enjoyed by the assignee without any lawful interruption or disturbance. This is the covenant for quiet enjoyment of the property in that the vendor must give the purchaser possession of the assigned land, which possession must be free from physical disturbance by the assignor, agents or servants;[426]
(e) a covenant for further assurance at the purchaser's cost. The covenant for further assurance provides that, at the purchaser's expense, the vendor will correct any defect(s) in title which he can remedy after completion.[427]

---

426. *See, e.g.*, *Yeung Wah James v Alfa Sea Ltd* [1993] 1 HKC 440 (demolition of bedroom wall and replacement with glass window); *Owen v Gadd* [1956] 2 QB 99 (prevention of access); *Perera v Vandiyar* [1953] 1 WLR 672 (cutting off electricity).

427. This subject is discussed in 16 HALSBURY'S, *supra* note 29, at para. 230.368, as follows:

> Under the covenant for further assurance the vendor is bound to do such further acts for the purpose of perfecting the purchaser's title as the purchaser may reasonably require and the vendor can properly do. The purchaser should tender a draft of the further assignment to which he considers that he is entitled, and should tender or offer to pay the vendor's costs. The vendor is entitled to a reasonable time to procure professional assistance. If the assignment is proper and he declines to execute it or to do any act which the purchaser can properly require, this constitutes a breach of the covenant. The purchaser cannot, by means of the covenant for further assurance, obtain a greater estate than that which was the subject of the original assignment, although if the vendor's title was defective the vendor may be required to assure an estate which he has got in since whether by devise or by purchase.

The liability of a vendor who assigns as beneficial owner does not amount to absolute legal responsibility. The vendor's accountability extends only to a breach committed by:

- the vendor;
- any person through whom the vendor has derived title other than by purchase, *e.g.*, liability for the acts of anyone who gifted the property to the vendor;
- any person assigning by the direction of the vendor; or,
- any person claiming by or through the vendor otherwise than by purchase for value, *e.g.*, mortgagees, lessees and licensees who derive title from the vendor.

On the part of the assignor assigning as a donor, there is only an implied covenant on the part of the donor for further assurance under section 35(1)(c) of the *Conveyancing and Property Ordinance*. Under section 35(1)(d), involving situations where the assignor assigns as a trustee, confirmor, mortgagee under power of sale, legal chargee under power of sale, or personal representative, the only covenant for title is that the person assigning has not encumbered the title.

E. Mortgages

Where a mortgagor/chargor charges the property as beneficial owner, the covenants implied in the legal charge are the same as for a vendor who assigns as beneficial owner, except that:

- the covenant for quiet enjoyment applies only where the mortgagee takes possession of the premises;
- the covenant for further assurance is at the borrower's cost; and,
- the chargor also covenants that it will continue to pay Government rent and perform the covenants in the Government lease during the currency of the charge.

See, *e.g.*, *Goldsteady Investment Ltd v Fatima Estates Ltd* (1995) MP 2943/95 where the vendor's assignment by way of power of attorney was defective because it had not been signed according to the company's memorandum and articles of association. A confirmatory assignment was ordered to cure the defect. *See also* SIHOMBING, STUDENT'S GUIDE, *supra* note 106, at 790; SIHOMBING, HK CONVEYANCING, *supra* note 257, vol. 2(F), Chapter XII, at para. 65.

F. Co-ownerships and Multi-storey Buildings

Land held by tenants in common requires a vendor to assign its right to exclusive occupation along with simultaneously assigning some of its undivided shares.[428]

A property developer may assign a fixed number of shares to a purchaser and retain the remainder. The developer may allocate the remaining shares as it desires, provided the total number of shares is not increased. Unless prohibited in the deed of mutual covenant, a subsequent owner of undivided shares may divide those shares and sell them to different purchasers. A vendor is not required to show the share allocation to the other flats. The vendor is only required to show the number of shares allocated to the flat to be assigned.

In order to sell shares in a multi-storey building, the number of shares allocated to the vendor needs to be accurately set out. The case of *Lee Tak Chun v East Weal International Ltd* [1994] 1 HKC 722 involved the allocation of 227 shares to a building's 35th floor which the owner then divided into twelve separate units. The court held that the vendor could not pass good title as there was no clear allocation of the shares to each of the units by the sub-deed of mutual covenant. The case of *Marking Ltd v Cheerifat Investment Ltd*, unreported, (1995) HCMP 2727/1995 had the opposite outcome. In this case, there were 138 shares in the building allocated to the whole ninth floor where the owner partitioned the space into separate units. The shares were then allocated to each unit in a control card and the share apportionment instrument was registered. The court held that the vendor had good title as there was a clear allocation of shares to the units, even though there was no sub-deed of mutual covenant. In *Goldjet International*

428. Several cases have examined this issue, *e.g.*, *Lai Wing Ho v Chan Siu Fong* [1993] 1 HKLR 319 (vendor attempted to sell exclusive right to roof without assigning the shares); *Modern Sino Ltd v Art Fair Co Ltd* [1999] 3 HKLRD 847 (vendor assigned shares to purchaser together with the right to exclusive possession of the house and subsequently assigned the right to exclusive possession of certain car parks "to the intent and purpose that the car parks shall attach to the house" held that when assigning the car parks, no shares were assigned; therefore, the assignee could only acquire a licence to the car parks); *Jumbo King Ltd v Faithful Properties Ltd* [1999] 4 HKC 707, CFA (vendor assigned shares to the purchaser together with right to the exclusive use of certain roofs and utility rooms; held since the vendor had the right to exclusive possession of the roofs and utility rooms, it could properly assign them to the purchaser provided the vendor simultaneously assigned some shares in the building; the fact that no shares were allocated to the roofs and utility rooms was immaterial).

Investment Ltd v Ling Ki Wai [1997] 3 HKC 503 the subdivision registers had been opened based upon assignments of flats and the control card showed the allocation of shares. Thus, good title had been shown.

XI. COMPLETION

Completion involves the payment of the purchase price by the purchaser in return for the execution of the property's assignment by the vendor. Post-completion involves the stamping and registration of the assignment. Completion is frequently made more complicated by the involvement of a purchaser's mortgagee. The vendor's mortgagee may also be involved in this process where the vendor intends to pay off the outstanding mortgage from the funds received from either the purchaser or the purchaser's mortgagee.

A. Completion Practices

Completion may either take place in person, known as "formal completion", or by way of "solicitors' undertakings". With formal completion, which is infrequent in Hong Kong, all the involved parties' solicitors attend, usually at the office of the vendor's solicitor. The purchase money is given to the vendor and, where appropriate, to its mortgagee. Any outstanding mortgage(s) is discharged, following which the vendor executes the assignment.

Completion is more commonly accomplished in Hong Kong through solicitors' undertakings.[429] Completion by way of mutual undertakings consists of the cheque for the purchase money being sent to the vendor's solicitor in return for an undertaking by the vendor's solicitor to return the requisite documents within a specified time. If the property is subject to a mortgage which will be discharged before completion, there ought to be separate cheques: the amount of money required to discharge the mortgage

429. The subject of completion was introduced in Section IX.C.*ii*, *supra*.
If the parties desire completion by way of mutual undertakings, an express provision should be included in the sale and purchase agreement as the courts will not imply this term into the agreement. *Chong Kai Tai v Lee Gee Kee*, *supra* note 366.
See THE LAW SOCIETY OF HONG KONG, *The Hong Kong Solicitors' Guide to Professional Conduct*, *supra* note 361, at vol. 1. Available at: *http://www.hklawsoc.org.hk/pub_e/professionalguide/volume1/default.asp* (last visited 26 Feb. 2011).
See generally GOO & LEE, *supra* note 24, Chapter 2 at section 4 ("Stage Four: Completion").

will be paid in one cheque made payable to the mortgagee, and the residue in another cheque made payable to the vendor's solicitor.[430]

Each method of completion has advantages and disadvantages. The advantages of formal completion include:

- safe procedure for vendors and purchasers;
- relatively expeditious procedure; and,
- safety for the purchaser's mortgagee and the purchaser in that the assignment and mortgage can be registered almost immediately and certainly in time to comply with the backdating provisions of the *Land Registration Ordinance* (Cap 128).

A disadvantage of formal completion is the logistical arrangements required to enable all the parties and/or their solicitors to be present. Also multiple sales of high-rise buildings make formal completion impracticable.

The advantage of completion by undertaking is that it is convenient for solicitors and banks/mortgagees. This is particularly applicable in the sales of multiple units in high-rise buildings. There are several disadvantages to completion by undertaking:

- time delay; particularly by a vendor's mortgagee in executing documents. This delay adversely affects the stamping and registration for priority purposes, as documents should be registered within one month of execution. Penalties for late stamping may also be incurred. It is improper to misdate intentionally a document for the purposes of gaining priority in registration.
- The solicitor provides the undertaking whereas the client executes the documents. The solicitor cannot require the client to honour the undertaking.

B. Stamp Duty

Stamp duty[431] is payable upon every conveyance on sale,[432] including the sale of property but not gifts of property or mortgages of property. If the

430. In *Tse Chun Hung Herby v Chang Chung Paul* [1999] HKCU 375, (1999) HCA 9293/91, the purchaser's solicitors requested instructions from the vendor's solicitors concerning the allocation of the outstanding purchase price, as the property was subject to a mortgage. The vendor's solicitors did not respond and the sale fell through. The court held that there was an implied term in the sale and purchase agreement that the balance of the purchase price would be paid by split cheques. The vendor breached the agreement by failing to do so.

431. As noted at 16 HALSBURY'S, *supra* note 29, at para. 230.349:

sale of property is below market value, the Stamp Office will assess the true value of the property and charge duty on the true value.[433]

Residential property sales require the sale and purchase agreement, rather than the assignment, to be stamped.[434] The stamp duty on the sale and purchase agreement is assessed on an *ad valorem* basis. Where the full stamp duty has been paid on the sale and purchase agreement, the assignment is only stamped with a nominal $100 stamp. This would not apply where a nominee of the purchaser is involved, because the assignment is made to a person other than the purchaser named in the sale and purchase agreement. In this circumstance, the *ad valorem* stamp duty must be paid again.[435]

The stamp duty normally is due within 30 days of the signing of the sale and purchase agreement or the assignment. If a preliminary agreement is superseded by a formal agreement between the same parties on the same terms within the first 14 days allowed for stamping, the time for stamping

---

> A document requiring a stamp cannot be admitted in evidence in legal proceedings unless it is duly stamped or payment of the duty and certain further sums is made or an undertaking to pay is given. The proper stamping of title deeds is an important matter of title because, if the owner of the property is called upon to defend his right or to attack a wrongdoer with regard to the property, he must produce his title deeds in evidence and thus he cannot do so as long as the requirements for the admission of any deed have not been complied with.

See also SIHOMBING, STUDENT'S GUIDE, *supra* note 106, at 1202–1204, 1309–1316; SIHOMBING, HK CONVEYANCING, *supra* note 257, vol. 1(A), Chapter VI, at para. 152.5; vol. 2(F), Chapter XIV, at paras. 2–4.4.

432. The *Stamp Duty Ordinance*, *supra* note 95, at section 2 defines "conveyance on sale" to reference:

> every conveyance whereby any immovable property, upon the sale thereof, is transferred to or vested in a purchaser or any other person on his behalf or by his direction, and includes a foreclosure order.

433. *See, e.g.*, the First Schedule to the *Stamp Duty Ordinance, supra* note 95, which sets out the fee schedule for a conveyance on sale, and, an agreement for sale.

434. This does not apply to commercial and industrial property. The intention is to reduce speculation and dampen rising property prices by having the parties pay the stamp duty on each sale and purchase agreement rather than on the assignment. Prior to the changes in the Ordinance, it was possible for a series of sale and purchase agreements to be entered into prior to completion, with each sale and purchase agreement being a transaction for a higher sales price of the property. There would thus be no stamp duty costs imposed upon these purchasers turned vendors in the rising property market. *See* SIHOMBING, HK CONVEYANCING, *supra* note 257, vol. 1(B), Chapter XIV, at para. 4; SIHOMBING, STUDENT'S GUIDE, *supra* note 106, at 1202–1204, 1309–1316.

435. The *BLIS Glossary*, *supra* note 7, translates the term "*ad valorem*" as 從價費.

the subsequent agreement is 30 days from the date of its execution. Stamp duty should be paid promptly so that the stamped document can be registered.[436] Finally, the stamp duty may be refunded if there is a failure to complete.[437]

C. Land Registration

The *Land Registration Ordinance* creates a system of public record for the registration of deeds, conveyances, judgments and other instruments affecting realty. This type of land registration system is called a deeds registration system. In order to obtain protection of one's property interests, the holder of that registrable interest in land must register an instrument which shows that interest. Priority is given to registered instruments either in accordance with the date of registration or as otherwise provided by law.[438] Registration also facilitates the tracing of title and determining whether there are any defects in that title.

Under this registration system, the doctrine of notice has been modified. As explained by one authority:

> The terms of the Land Registration Ordinance operate to preclude a registering party being affected by notice of a prior unregistered, registrable interest except perhaps in cases where the conduct of the registering party has amounted to actual fraud. This is contradictory to the terms of section 4 of the Ordinance. So it would require the court to accept that the element of "bona fide" cannot allow protection to a purchaser who is "mala fide". The consequence is that although notice is irrelevant—the conduct of purchaser has been such that the court cannot overlook the deceit or "moral turpitude" of his actions. The ability to ignore the prior interest even extends to those prior interests under which the interest holder is in occupation of the land at the time the registering party enters into its contract. However, if the occupier's interest is not in writing, then section 4 is inoperable, and the incoming

---

436. 16 HALSBURY'S, *supra* note 29, at para. 230.386 states that registration is:

> to protect priority of registration and to give notice of the registered interest to subsequent purchasers and mortgagees. A complementary result is that the register acts as a record of transactions so that these can be relied upon in establishing the details of the title to the land.

437. *Stamp Duty Ordinance*, *supra* note 95, at sections 29C(5A), 29C(5B).

438. 16 HALSBURY'S, *supra* note 29, at paras. 230.382–230.383.
See also SIHOMBING, STUDENT'S GUIDE, *supra* note 106, at 1362–1363; SIHOMBING, HK CONVEYANCING, *supra* note 257, vol. 1(B), Chapter XIV, at para. 121; vol. 2(F), Chapter XIV, at para. 72.

> purchaser may find he takes subject to the prior interest of which he had notice. Further, the Ordinance provides that an unregistered interest in writing is null and void against the registering party even if he had constructive notice of it, prior to registration.[439]

Section 2 of the *Land Registration Ordinance* provides:

> The Land Registry shall be a public office for the registration of deeds, conveyances, and other instruments in writing and all deeds etc. … by which any parcel of ground or premises may be affected, may be entered and registered in the said office …

The following documents, also referred to as "instruments", should be registered: sale and purchase agreements; assignments; deeds of mutual covenants; mortgages and charges; discharges of mortgages; certificates of compliance; occupation permits; *lites pendentes*;[440] charging orders; covenants; powers of attorney affecting land; and, long term leases.[441] The exceptions to this rule include:

- short-term leases, *i.e.*, those of less than three years' duration, do not have to be registered;[442]
- floating charges are not registrable until crystallization but should be registered upon crystallization;[443]
- licences do not affect land and therefore may not be registered; and,
- wills cannot be registered.

---

439. 16 HALSBURY'S, *supra* note 29, at para. 230.383.
See also SIHOMBING, STUDENT'S GUIDE, *supra* note 106, at 1362–1363, 1366–1370; SIHOMBING, HK CONVEYANCING, *supra* note 257, vol. 1(B), Chapter XIV, at para. 123.

440. As defined in section 1A of the *Land Registration Ordinance*, *supra* note 96:

> "lis pendens" (待決案件) means—any action or proceeding pending in a court or tribunal that relates to land or any interest in or charge on land; and a bankruptcy petition.

Black's Law Dictionary, supra note 20, at 1015, defines *lis pendens* as a "pending lawsuit".

441. A court has stated that an option to purchase should be registered as it affects land or premises, even if the option to purchase is contained in a short term lease which itself need not be registered. *Markfaith Investment Ltd v Chiap Hua Flashlights Ltd* [1990] WLR 76.

442. *Land Registration Ordinance*, *supra* note 96, at section 3(2) provides:

> All such deeds, conveyances, and other instruments in writing, and judgments … which are not registered shall, as against any subsequent bona fide purchaser or mortgagee for valuable consideration of the same parcels of ground, tenements, or premises, be absolutely null and void to all intents and purposes: Provided that nothing herein contained shall extend to bona fide leases at rack rent for any term not exceeding 3 years.

443. *Id.* at section 2A stipulates:

Regulation 5 of the Land Registration Regulations (Cap 128A) states that registration is made by delivering the instrument together with a memorial of the instrument in the prescribed form to the Land Registry.[444] The present procedure for the District Land Registries requires the memorial to be presented for registration together with a photocopy of the instrument, whereupon both are registered. In the Urban Land Registry, the memorial and a

---

(1) A document effecting a floating charge, whether or not it specifically identifies any land charged, is not, for the purposes of section 2, a deed, conveyance or other instrument in writing by which any parcel of ground, tenement or premises in Hong Kong may be affected.
(2) A document effecting a floating charge created before, on or after 1 November 1984-
(a) becomes a fixed charge on the land intended to be affected;
(b) and for the purposes of section 2, is a deed, conveyance or other instrument in writing by which any parcel of ground, tenement or premises in Hong Kong may be affected, upon crystallization of that charge … as evidenced by a certificate signed by or on behalf of the chargee.
(3) For the purposes of section 5, the time of execution of a charge mentioned in subsection (2) is the time of signature of the certificate mentioned in that subsection.

444. Land Registration Regulations (Cap 128A) regulation 5 provides:
(1) Registration of an instrument under the Ordinance shall be effected by delivering into the Land Registry such instrument together with a memorial thereof in the form specified by the Land Registrar and by compliance with the Ordinance and these regulations.
(2) A memorial shall, unless the Land Registrar otherwise permits, be on paper of A4 size.
(3) Delivery of an instrument and memorial into the Land Registry may be effected by—
(a) personal delivery; or
(b) sending the instrument and memorial by post.
(4) Subject to paragraph (5), the delivery of an instrument or memorial into the Land Registry by post shall be regarded as having been effected when the instrument or memorial is received by the Land Registrar.
(5) For the purposes of these regulations, the date of receipt of an instrument or memorial sent to the Land Registrar by post shall—
(a) where the instrument or memorial is received by the Land Registrar before 1:30 p.m. on any day on which the Land Registry is open to the public, be that day;
(b) where the instrument or memorial is received by the Land Registrar
(i) after 1.30 p.m. on any day on which the Land Registry is open to the public; or
(ii) on any day on which the Land Registry is not open to the public, be deemed to be the next following day on which the Land Registry is open to the public.

For further information, *see www.landreg.gov.hk* (last visited 26 Feb. 2011).

copy of the instrument are presented and a microfilm copy is retained for the purposes of registration. Under Regulation 7 of the Land Registration Regulations, the memorial must be prepared and verified by a solicitor. As the microfilm is in black and white, rather than in colour, any plan mentioned in or attached to an instrument delivered for registration must be colour coded so that the colour can be identified, *e.g.*, R (red), Y (yellow), etc.

Registration of property instruments does not confer ownership rights but does affect priority of the instruments. Under section 3(1) of the *Land Registration Ordinance*, all instruments shall have priority according to their respective registration dates. Section 3(2) of the *Land Registration Ordinance* stipulates that all documents relating to land, which are not registered shall be absolutely void as against a subsequent *bona fide* purchaser or mortgagee for valuable consideration. This does not apply to interests exempt from registration, such as short-term tenancies.

These exceptions are found in section 5 of the Ordinance. One exception provides that all instruments registered within one month of the date of execution shall have priority according to their execution dates. Another exception, also found within section 5, pertains to charging orders and *lites pendentes*.[445] A duly registered charging order or *lis pendens* will have priority from the commencement of the day following the date of registration of the order *nisi*.[446] The case of *Wong Kam Wing v Cyril Murkin (HK) Ltd* [1989] 2 HKC 603 states that the priority of charging orders depends on the order of registration of the orders *nisi* rather than dates of the orders absolute.

Example I

An assignment is executed on 1 July and not registered until 10 August. A charging order *nisi* was registered on 2 August. *Prima facie* the effective date of the assignment is 10 August. The provision in section 5 relating

445. Section 5 of the *Land Registration Ordinance*, *supra* note 96, states:

> All deeds, conveyances, and other instruments in writing, and judgments, which are duly registered within the respective times next mentioned, that is to say, all deeds, conveyances, and other instruments in writing which are registered within one month after the time of execution thereof respectively, and all judgments which are registered within one month after the entering up or recording thereof, shall severally be in like manner entitled to priority, and shall take effect respectively by relation to the date thereof only in the same manner as if this Ordinance had not been passed.

446. As defined by BLACK'S LAW DICTIONARY, *supra* note 20, at 1144, *nisi* is an order or such "having validity unless the adversely affected party appears and shows cause why it should be withdrawn ..." *See supra* note 272.

back to date of execution provision does not apply as the assignment was not registered within 30 days of its execution. The charging order takes effect the day after the registration of the order *nisi*, *i.e.*, that is 3 August. Therefore, the charging order should take priority over the assignment and the assignee is bound by the charging order. However in *Yau Siu Yeung v Wing Sum Lo* [1988] HKC 693 and *Ng Kam Ha v Vincent Sina Traders* [1987] HKLR 1193 the court held that the vendor had conveyed all its interest in the land at the date of the assignment's execution, regardless whether the assignment was registered. As the assignment predated the charging order, the property is not affected by the charging order.

Example II

A sale and purchase agreement is executed on 1 July and registered on 20 July. A charging order *nisi* is registered on 10 July. The assignment is executed on 15 July and registered on 20 July. The charging order binds the land as, at the time of its registration, the vendor still holds the bare legal estate, as the equitable interest in the property has passed to the purchaser. The charging order binds the property and the purchaser must pay the purchase money to the chargee to the extent that is necessary to discharge the order. Coming to a similar conclusion, the court in *Tse Fook Choy, Joey Callan v Kwong On Bank Ltd* [1999] 3 HKC 126, 131 held that "no charging order created after the date of the contract could gain priority to the interest of the purchaser or his successors in title".[447]

XII. HONG KONG TITLES REGISTRATION: AN OVERVIEW[448]

The *Land Titles Ordinance* (Cap 585) establishes a new form of land registration in Hong Kong called the "titles registration" system, which replaces the deeds registration system that had existed for more than 160 years.[449] The Ordinance, enacted in 2004, has been undergoing subsequent review for legislative amendment.[450] The review will culminate in the Land Titles

447. These two examples were provided in Prof. Michael Wilkinson's lecture notes for the Overseas Lawyers Qualification Examination (June 2002).

448. This section is adapted from SEBASTIAN KO, "Indemnity, Title Risks And The Land Titles Ordinance Of Hong Kong: A Balancing Act" (LLB(Hons) Thesis, Monash University, 2006) and is first published in STEPHEN D. MAU, *Property Law in Hong Kong: An Introductory Guide*, Chapter 12 (2010). The content is republished here with the necessary permission.

449. PETER WILLOUGHBY & MICHAEL WILKINSON, REGISTRATION OF TITLES IN HONG KONG v (1995).

450. BILLS COMMITTEE, *Summary of the proposed amendments mentioned in the papers provided by the Administration from April 2003 to early April 2004* (2004), at 27–28.

(Amendment) Bill (hereinafter LTAB), which aims to improve the drafting and provide substantive changes to the Ordinance.[451] At the time of writing, the Ordinance was expected to commence in 2013.[452]

A. Objectives of Titles Registration

Improvement of title security is the primary objective in developing the Hong Kong titles registration system.[453] In the common law tradition, land registration is established to enhance both the security of existing property rights (hereinafter static security) and the security of transfer and acquisition (hereinafter dynamic security).[454] Static security provides an incentive to improve and utilize land. Dynamic security increases commercial certainty and reduces transaction costs, which contribute to efficient transactions and benefit the land and capital markets by improving their access to land resources.[455] Improving both types of security is necessary for achieving the aspiration of land registration to facilitate transfer and make conveyancing "cheap, quick and safe".[456]

A titles registration system improves dynamic security by creating risks to static security through a statutory warranty of title (hereinafter referred to as "statutory warranty"),[457] which is based on a set of registration rules that operates alongside the general law rules of conveyancing.[458] Titles registration upholds "the reasonable expectations of purchasers that they will gain an indefeasible [or statutory warranted] title if they register an instrument in good faith".[459]

451. At the time of writing, the government was proposing amendments to the *Land Titles Ordinance* (Cap 585).

452. HONG KONG LAND REGISTRY, *Progress Report on Land Title Ordinance Review and Timetable for Amendment Bill*, May 2007. *See http://www.landreg.gov.hk/en/pdf/progress.pdf* (last visited 26 Feb. 2011).

453. HOUSING, PLANNING AND LANDS BUREAU, *2006–07 policy agenda: Ongoing initiatives: http://www.devb-plb.gov.hk/eng/policy/agenda2006–07_p2.htm* (last visited 26 Feb. 2011).

454. PAMELA O'CONNOR, "Registration of invalid dispositions: Who gets the property" in MODERN STUDIES IN PROPERTY LAW vol. 3, at 50 (E. Cooke, ed., 2005) [hereinafter O'CONNOR, REGISTRATION].

455. *See* S. ROWTON SIMPSON, LAND LAW AND REGISTRATION 17–18 (1976) [hereinafter SIMPSON].

456. *Id.* at 19–21.

457. *I.e.*, the government "guarantees" title.

458. DOUGLAS WHALAN, THE TORRENS SYSTEM IN AUSTRALIA (1982), at 345–346.

459. O'CONNOR, REGISTRATION, *supra* note 454, at 64.

An entry of the register may be correct under the registration rules, but incorrect under the general law.[460] As such, registration rules and the general law may conflict where registration of a void disposition confers title. The general law doctrine of *nemo dat quod non habet* (hereinafter *nemo dat*) protects an owner against the loss of ownership by fraud.[461] The *nemo dat* rule states that a vendor without good title cannot convey or give good title. Thus, a fraudster acquires no title by fraud and has no title to pass.[462] Essentially, a titles registration system abrogates the doctrine of *nemo dat*, and permits registration of titles as a result of fraud in some cases.

B. Deeds vs. Titles Registration

The fundamental principle of the pre-existing deeds registration system is that registration of the instrument will usually give the purchaser priority over unregistered but registrable instruments, or instruments registered subsequently.[463] The *Land Registration Ordinance* (hereinafter LRO) does not, however, confer registered interests priority over interests that have not been created by registrable instrument, *e.g.*, interests arising informally under adverse possession, constructive trusts, and estoppels.[464] A deed, registered or not, is mere evidence of a transaction affecting land, and does not prove title. Nor does it prove the validity of the underlying transaction, and "may not be consistent with a previously registered transaction or even with actual fact".[465]

Conveyancing under the deeds registration system required careful and time-consuming title investigation by conveyancers to mitigate risks of title defects. As Simpson noted, strict conveyancing rules, registration practices and operational improvements in the Hong Kong Land Registry enabled the

460. If the discrepancy cannot be rectified under the statute, then the registered interest is *indefeasible* in Torrens jurisprudence. Although *indefeasibility* is sometimes used loosely to describe the effect of registration in creating title, the paper refers to such an effect as *statutory warranty* to avoid confusion, and because the *Land Titles Ordinance* permits rectification. *See* ADRIAN J. BRADBROOK, SUSAN MACCALLUM & ANTHONY MOORE, AUSTRALIAN PROPERTY LAW: CASES AND MATERIALS (3rd ed. 2007), at [3.7], [3.8].

461. *See generally* MEGARRY'S MANUAL, *supra* note 35, at 138–145.

462. *See* JUDE WALLACE, "A methodology to review Torrens systems and their relevance to changing societies from a legal perspective" (Paper presented at the UN-FIG Conference on Land Tenure and Cadastral Infrastructures for Sustainable Development, Melbourne, 25–27 October 1999), at 5–6.

463. *Land Registration Ordinance*, *supra* note 96, at section 3(1). The general law doctrine of notice applies. *See Wong Chim Ying v Cheng Kam Wing* [1991] 2 HKLR 253.

464. *Land Registration Ordinance*, *supra* note 96, at section 3(2).

465. SIMPSON, *supra* note 455, at 15.

local deeds registration system to function successfully for a long time.[466] The existing conveyancing system governed by the *Conveyancing and Property Ordinance* continues to apply to uphold conveyancing standards and prevent improper conduct in the new titles registration system, albeit with some amendments.

The quality of title in the deeds registration system is ultimately a matter of opinion, even if conveyancers could obtain all available evidence. The present title may still be vulnerable where documents are missing or improperly executed, or where unregistrable interests exist.[467] By contrast, investigation of the dealings leading to registration of the present registered owner is unnecessary in the titles registration system, as the register is supposedly conclusive record of title.[468] Rather than inferred from a deed, title is vested by registration.[469] Simpson stated that "[t]he register records not merely evidence but what in effect is a judgment, final, complete and always up to date ...".[470] A person will acquire a statutory warranted title if the person purchases *bona fide* and, in most jurisdictions,[471] for value, from a registered proprietor, and registers his or her deed of transfer or mortgage.

The registered title cannot be set aside, notwithstanding any defect in the vendor's title or invalidity of conveyance, except in circumstances where the statute allows an entry in the register to be rectified or set aside.[472] Under the *Land Titles Ordinance*, rectification may be granted in cases of fraud, mistake or omission, and reverses the registration or discharge of interests.

C. Transitional Arrangements

When the *Land Titles Ordinance* commences, a "daylight conversion" regime will bring land into the titles registration system in two periods. Land granted under a Government lease on or after the *Land Titles Ordinance* commencement date will be registered in the titles registration system.[473] Land already registered under the deeds registration system will

---

466. *Id.* at 108–109.
467. *Id.* at 19.
468. *Id.* at 16.
469. *Id.* at 15–20.
470. *Id.* at 19.
471. Pamela O'Connor, "Double indemnity: Title insurance and the Torrens system" (2003) 3(1) Queensland University of Technology Law and Justice Journal 141, at 148 [hereinafter O'Connor, Double Indemnity].
472. Simpson, *supra* note 455, at 15–20.
473. *Land Titles Ordinance*, *supra* note 451, at section 20.

be automatically converted into titles registration system land 12 years after the date of commencement of the *Land Titles Ordinance*.[474] Consequently, when the *Land Titles Ordinance* commences, land in the primary property market will be registered, but land in the secondary market will not be registered until the 12-year transition period ends. In the interim, however, a caution against conversion may be registered under the LRO to delay conversion, for example, until a dispute is settled. Also, registration of caveats for interests unregistrable under the LRO would ensure their priority survives conversion. Otherwise, any unregistered interest or right is liable to be extinguished by title registration. Where instruments await registration under the LRO, conversion will be delayed until registration under the LRO is completed.

D. Hong Kong Titles Registration: Features

In the *Land Titles Ordinance*, the statutory warranty rule consists of the provisions that concern the vesting of statutory warranted title, which is qualified by the rectification provisions and other exceptions to statutory warranty.[475] Sections 25 and 26 of the *Land Titles Ordinance* operate to vest statutory warranted title in transfer of land and long-term lease, respectively, by: (i) the positive affirmation of title vested upon registration; and (ii) the negative warranty that the registered owner or lessee takes free of all interests and claims other than the statutory exceptions.[476]

The titles registration system generally permits exceptions to statutory warranty for practical reasons. The *Land Titles Ordinance* provides five major exceptions.[477] Firstly, registered interests are held subject to the terms of the Government lease granting use of the relevant land. The Government lease evidences the root of title in Hong Kong,[478] as practically all land is held by the government.[479] Secondly, the *Land Titles Ordinance* recognizes the priority of particular unregistered interests known as "overriding

474. *Id.* at sections 20, 24; Schedule 1.

475. As such, the nature of the statutory warranty and its exceptions in the Hong Kong titles registration system determine the level and type of risks to dynamic and static security.

476. James Hogg, Registration of Title to Land Throughout the Empire (1920), at 96.

477. *Land Titles Ordinance*, *supra* note 451, at sections 25(1), 26(1). *See* Goo & Lee, *supra* note 24, at 309–312.

478. Goo & Lee, *supra* note 24, at 5–10.

479. *Basic Law*, *supra* note 292, article 7. But one plot of land is freehold for historical reasons.

interests",[480] although some may be registrable.[481] Overriding interests include rights acquired by adverse possession (including inchoate rights), short-term leases, certain easements and covenants, Chinese customary rights and public rights.[482] These interests substantially qualify the conclusiveness of registered title, but are maintained for various policy reasons, such as the alleviation of administrative burden of registering interests. Thirdly, the provisions preserve the operation of other registered interests, and trustee duties where the registered person holds the relevant interest on trust.[483] Fourthly, the Hong Kong Land Register (hereinafter Register) may be rectified in cases of fraud, mistake or omission. Fifthly, unregistered interests and certain statutory obligations bind successors in title, whose registered interests resulted from voluntary transfers.[484]

Generally, the *Land Titles Ordinance* does not recognize unregistered interests, unless they are capable of registration. However, the *Land Titles Ordinance* expressly recognizes that registrable interests and interests protected by an entry in the Register may be effective in equity without being registered yet.[485] Between settlement and registration, a purchaser has only an equitable interest, which is subject to equitable priority rules.[486] This represents a "registration gap" in static security, as the statutory warranty in many registration systems "does not guarantee the validity or the priority of interests in registered land until they are registered".[487] Uncertainty arises as titles registration system modifies the operation of the general law rules

480. *Land Titles Ordinance*, *supra* note 451, at sections 25(2)(c), 26(2)(c).
481. *Id.* at section 28(2)–(6). *N.b.* LTAB (working draft, June 2006) does not add any new overriding interest, but proposes to omit first charges under the *Estate Duty Ordinance* (Cap 111). Under the draft Bill, *Land Titles Ordinance*, *supra* note 451, at section 28(6) would be deleted and replaced by a new provision that *inter alia* redefines the scope of the Registrar's power to register and remove overriding interests.
482. *Id.* at section 28. *N.b.* substantial changes to *Land Titles Ordinance*, Schedule 3 will likely be proposed in future drafts of the LTAB, which would require registration of burdens created by other legislation to be binding on the Register (HONG KONG LAND REGISTRY, BRIEFING NOTE TO THE WORKING DRAFT OF THE AMENDMENT BILL, June 2006).
483. *See Land Titles Ordinance*, *supra* note 451, at sections 25(2)(b), (3), 26(2)(b), 26(3).
484. *Id.* at section 27.
485. *Id.* at section 32(2).
486. *Wong Chim Ying v Cheng Kam Wing* [1991] 2 HKLR 253, at 277. *But see* BILLS COMMITTEE, REPORT TO THE HOUSE COMMITTEE MEETING ON 25 JUNE 2004: LAND TITLES BILL (2004), at 28.
487. O'CONNOR, DOUBLE INDEMNITY, *supra* note 471, at 149–150. *N.b.* the quote refers to the New Zealand system, and applies to Hong Kong, but is not true of all titles registration system. *See Land Titles Ordinance*, *supra* note 451, at section 35. *C.f. Brown & Root Technology v Sun Alliance* [2000] 2 WLR 566.

of conveyancing, but does not completely override them.[488] Certainly, the *Land Titles Ordinance* provides measures for protecting interests by special entries in the Register, which restrain dealings by delaying or preventing the registration of interests until a dispute is settled, or an investigation is made. These measures include cautions, inhibitions and restrictions,[489] and may be used in respect of trusts and unregistered interests.[490]

Purchasers are,[491] however, expected to make enquiries beyond the Register for certain unregistered interests, including overriding interests and equitable interests.[492] In particular, registered proprietors hold their title subject to the rights of a person in adverse possession of the land. This creates the risk that a purchaser may acquire an interest from a registered proprietor whose title has been extinguished by adverse possession under the *Limitations Ordinance* (Cap 347). Despite the establishment of the titles registration system, purchasers must still physically inspect boundaries to mitigate the risks of encroachments and discover adverse possessors. By contrast, statutory rights, such as public rights, require the inspection of relevant government registers.[493]

---

488. *See* Simon Cooper, "Equity and unregistered land rights in Commonwealth registration systems" (2003) 3(2) *Oxford Journal of Legal Studies* 201, at 207.
489. *See* Bills Committee, Inhibitions, Restrictions and Injunctions: A Comparison (2003), at 2–5.
490. These "aggressive" protections may be inappropriate in most familial dealings. *See First American Title Insurance Company, Submission to the Bills Committee* (2003), at 3.
491. "Mortgagees" are included in references to "purchasers" in this section.
492. The effects of overriding interests are the same regardless of registration. LTAB (working draft, June 2006) proposes to expressly capture this exception to the general rule (*i.e.* a registered interest holder generally are not subject to an interest that is registered later).
493. Due to the numerous exceptions to statutory warranty, the new system in Hong Kong hardly resembles a titles registration system, at least in the typical forms adopted in countries such as Australia, England and New Zealand. If the Hong Kong system is in fact a titles registration system, then the exceptions and the lack of protection for equitable interests in the registration gap seriously weaken its security of title.

Index